ALSO BY STEPHEN R. PLATT

Provincial Patriots: The Hunanese and Modern China

AUTUMN IN THE HEAVENLY KINGDOM

AUTUMN IN THE
HEAVENLY KINGDOM

CHINA, THE WEST, AND
THE EPIC STORY OF THE TAIPING CIVIL WAR

Stephen R. Platt

ALFRED A. KNOPF   NEW YORK   2012

THIS IS A BORZOI BOOK
PUBLISHED BY ALFRED A. KNOPF

Grateful acknowledgement is made to the University of Washington Press for permission
to reprint excerpts from *The Taiping Rebellion: History and Documents,* volumes two and
three, by Franz Michael with Chung-li Chang, copyright © 1966–1971 by Franz Michael.

Library of Congress Cataloging-in-Publication Data
Platt, Stephen R.
Autumn in the Heavenly Kingdom : China, the West, and the epic story of the
Taiping Civil War / by Stephen R. Platt.—1st ed.
p. cm.
"This is a Borzoi book"—T.p. verso.
Includes bibliographical references.
ISBN 978-0-307-27173-0
1. China—History—Taiping Rebellion, 1850–1864. 2. China—Relations—Western
countries. 3. Western countries—Relations—China. 4. China—History—Taiping
Rebellion, 1850–1864—Participation, Foreign. 5. Visitors, Foreign—China—History—
19th century. 6. Europeans—China—History—19th century. 7. Americans—China—
History—19th century. 8. Manchus—History—19th century. 9. Ethnic conflict—China—
History—19th century. 10. China—Ethnic relations—History—19th century. I. Title.
DS759.P57 2012
951'.034—dc23   2011035137

Maps by Stephen R. Platt and David Merrill

Jacket image courtesy of the National Palace Museum, Taiwan, Republic of China
Jacket design by Brian Barth
Manufactured in the United States of America
First Edition

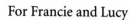
For Francie and Lucy

Blessed are the peacemakers:
for they shall be called the children of God.

—Matthew 5:9

CONTENTS

DRAMATIS PERSONAE

IMPERIAL GOVERNMENT

XIANFENG, *emperor of the Qing dynasty*

PRINCE GONG, *Xianfeng's half brother*

SUSHUN

ZAIYUAN

MUYIN — *Manchu advisers to the emperor*

DUANHUA

YEHONALA, *a concubine of Xianfeng, later Empress Dowager Cixi*

WENXIANG, *a grand councillor*

SENGGELINQIN, *a Mongol bannerman and general*

GUO SONGTAO, *a Chinese official*

ZHANG GUOLIANG, *a former bandit, general of the Green Standard*

HE CHUN, *a general of the Green Standard*

WU XU, *the* daotai *of Shanghai*

XUE HUAN, *governor of Jiangsu province*

TAIPING REBELS

HONG XIUQUAN, *the Heavenly King*

HONG RENGAN, *Hong Xiuquan's cousin, the Shield King and prime minister*

LI XIUCHENG, *the Loyal King*

LI SHIXIAN, *Li Xiucheng's cousin, the Attending King*

CHEN YUCHENG, *the Brave King*

TAN SHAOGUANG, *the Esteemed King*

SHI DAKAI, *the Wing King*

GAO YONGKUAN, *the Receiving King*

THE PROVINCIAL ARMIES

ZENG GUOFAN, *commander in chief of the Hunan Army*

ZENG GUOQUAN
ZENG GUOHUA   *Zeng Guofan's younger brothers, commanders*
ZENG GUOBAO   *in the Hunan Army*

ZUO ZONGTANG, *a general in the Hunan Army*

BAO CHAO, *a Sichuanese commander in the Hunan Army*

DUOLONGA, *a Manchu cavalry commander in the Hunan Army*

LI HONGZHANG, *Zeng Guofan's student, commanding general of the*
    Anhui Army

CHENG XUEQI, *a turncoat from the rebels, commander in the*
    Anhui Army

OTHER CHINESE

YUNG WING, *a graduate of Yale University in the class of 1854*

YANG FANG, *a Shanghai banker, patron of the Ever-Victorious Army*

YANG CHANGMEI, *Yang Fang's daughter, married in 1862 to Frederick*
    Townsend Ward

BRITISH

In Government

LORD PALMERSTON, *prime minister*

LORD RUSSELL, *foreign secretary*

WILLIAM GLADSTONE, *chancellor of the Exchequer*

COLONEL WILLIAM H. SYKES, *member of Parliament for Aberdeen,*
    Scotland

Diplomats and Consular Officials

JAMES BRUCE, *eighth Earl of Elgin, British plenipotentiary*

FREDERICK BRUCE, *James Bruce's brother, British minister to China,*
    1860–1864

THOMAS F. WADE, *an interpreter, later professor of Chinese at Cambridge*

Harry Parkes, *an interpreter and consular officer*
Frederick Harvey
Thomas Taylor Meadows ⎯ *consuls*
Robert Forrest

Military

Rear Admiral James Hope, *Royal Navy commander in chief of East Indies and China Station, 1859–1862*
Captain Roderick Dew, *captain of HMS* Encounter
Charles Gordon, *commander of the Ever-Victorious Army, 1863–1864*
Sherard Osborn, *commodore of the Anglo-Chinese Flotilla*

Other

James Legge, *a Scottish missionary, later professor of Chinese at Oxford*
Joseph Edkins, *an English missionary*
Jane Edkins, *Joseph Edkins's wife*
Griffith John, *a Welsh missionary*
Thomas Bowlby, *a reporter for* The Times *of London*
John Scarth, *a businessman*
Horatio Nelson Lay, *inspector general of Imperial Maritime Customs*

AMERICAN

Frederick Townsend Ward, *soldier of fortune and founder of the Ever-Victorious Army*
Henry Andrea Burgevine
Edward Forester ⎯ *Ward's lieutenants*
Issachar Jacox Roberts, *a missionary from Tennessee*
Anson Burlingame, *U.S. minister to China, 1861–1867*
Josiah Tattnall, *commodore of the East India Squadron, 1858–1859*

FRENCH

BARON GROS, *French plenipotentiary*

REAR ADMIRAL AUGUSTE LÉOPOLD PROTET, *commander in chief of French forces in China*

RUSSIAN

NIKOLAI PAVLOVICH IGNATIEV, *a diplomat*

SWEDISH

THEODORE HAMBERG, *a missionary*

CHRONOLOGY

1837

Hong Xiuquan has first visions.

1839–1842

Opium War between Great Britain and the Qing dynasty.

Hong Kong ceded to Great Britain.

Shanghai opened as treaty port.

1843

Hong Xiuquan begins preaching among the Hakkas.

1850

MARCH 9 The Xianfeng emperor accedes to the throne.

SUMMER First uprisings of the Society of God Worshippers in Guangxi.

1851

JANUARY 11 Hong Xiuquan announces founding of Taiping Heavenly Kingdom.

Taiping Rebellion begins.

1852

Hong Rengan meets Theodore Hamberg.

1853–1854

Hong Rengan studies with Hamberg in Hong Kong.

1853-1856
Crimean War.

1853

JANUARY 8 Zeng Guofan receives instructions to organize militia in Hunan.

JANUARY 12 Taiping conquer Wuchang.

MARCH 19 Taiping conquer Nanjing, massacre Manchu population.

APRIL 27 British ship *Hermes* visits Nanjing.

1854

FEBRUARY Zeng Guofan's Hunan Army begins fighting Taiping in Hunan.

MAY Hong Rengan travels to Shanghai, trying to get to Nanjing.

JULY 27 Yung Wing graduates from Yale University.

OCTOBER 14 Zeng Guofan's militia forces take back Wuchang.

OCTOBER 25 Battle of Balaclava, Crimean War.

1855-1858
Hong Rengan in Hong Kong, employed by London Missionary Society.

1855

JANUARY-FEBRUARY Disastrous defeat for Hunan Army at Jiujiang.

FEBRUARY 11 Zeng Guofan attempts suicide.

APRIL 3 Taiping reoccupy Wuchang.

SEPTEMBER Muslim rebellion breaks out in southwest China.

1856-1860
Arrow War (Second Opium War) between Great Britain and the Qing dynasty.

1856

SEPTEMBER 2 The Eastern King and his followers killed in coup in Nanjing.

OCTOBER 8 Smuggling ship *Arrow* boarded by Qing authorities at Canton.

DECEMBER 19 Hunan Army recaptures Wuchang.

1857–1858
Sepoy Mutiny in India.

1857
APRIL 20 Lord Elgin appointed plenipotentiary to China.

DECEMBER 28 Allied forces bombard, occupy Canton
(take possession January 1).

1858
MAY Hong Rengan leaves Hong Kong for Nanjing.

MAY 20 British and French fleet attacks Taku forts,
goes on to invade Tianjin.

JUNE 27 Treaty of Tianjin signed between Britain and China.

NOVEMBER–DECEMBER Elgin's fleet sails up Yangtze River past
Nanjing to Hankow.

NOVEMBER 1 Great Britain institutes direct rule of India; East India
Company dissolved.

NOVEMBER 15 Major Taiping victory against Hunan Army at
Three Rivers, Anhui.

Zeng Guofan's brother Guohua killed.

1859
APRIL 22 Hong Rengan arrives in Nanjing, is promoted to
Shield King on May 11.

JUNE 25 Repulse at Peiho River: British fleet devastated at the Taku forts.

1860
MAY Taiping armies rout imperial siege troops at Nanjing.

JUNE Zeng Guoquan lays siege to Anqing (will last until September 1861).

Frederick Townsend Ward enlists foreigners for rifle corps in Shanghai.

JUNE 2 The Loyal King occupies Suzhou.

JUNE 10 Zeng Guofan appointed acting governor-general of Jiangxi, Anhui, and Jiangsu; receives full appointment on August 10.

JULY 15 The Loyal King sends letter stating that the Taiping won't harm foreigners at Shanghai.

JULY 16 Frederick Townsend Ward's militia captures Songjiang.

JULY 28 Zeng Guofan sets up headquarters in Qimen.

JULY 30 Frederick Townsend Ward attacks Qingpu, is defeated.

AUGUST 1 Allied fleet lands at Beitang.

AUGUST 2 Joseph Edkins and Griffith John arrive in Suzhou to meet Hong Rengan.

AUGUST 19 British and French forces attack Taiping rebels at Shanghai.

AUGUST 22 British and French forces capture Taku forts in north China.

SEPTEMBER 22 The Xianfeng emperor abandons the capital.

OCTOBER 13 British and French troops occupy Beijing. Issachar Roberts arrives in Nanjing.

OCTOBER 18 British troops burn the Summer Palace.

OCTOBER 24 Sino-British Treaty of Beijing signed.

1861

FEBRUARY 9 Confederate States of America founded in Montgomery, Alabama.

FEBRUARY 20 Admiral Hope makes first visit to Nanjing.

MARCH 4 Abraham Lincoln sworn in as U.S. president.

MARCH 22 Harry Parkes meets with the Brave King at Huangzhou.

APRIL 17 Lincoln gives order to blockade Confederate ports.

MAY 13 Great Britain grants belligerent status to the Confederacy.

MAY 19 Frederick Townsend Ward arrested in Shanghai.

MAY 31 U.K. Parliament debates belligerent status of Taiping.

JUNE 7 U.K. Parliament debates recognition of the Confederacy.

JULY 21 First Battle of Bull Run.

AUGUST 22 The Xianfeng emperor dies.

SEPTEMBER 5 Hunan Army forces conquer Anqing, slaughter 16,000 survivors.

NOVEMBER 8 *Trent* Affair (U.S. Civil War).

Coup d'état in Beijing; Sushun and other regents executed.

DECEMBER 9 Taiping take Ningbo.

DECEMBER 15 Zeng Guofan given military control of four provinces.

DECEMBER 29 The Loyal King Li Xiucheng conquers Hangzhou.

1862

JANUARY 20 Taiping forces attack Wusong, begin siege of Shanghai.

JANUARY 22 Issachar Roberts flees Nanjing, writes denunciation of Taiping.

FEBRUARY 10 Taiping forces defeated by Ward's Ever-Victorious Army at Songjiang.

FEBRUARY 22 Admiral Hope submits plan for clearing rebels from area of Shanghai.

Beginning of alliance among British, French, and Ward.

APRIL Li Hongzhang's Anhui Army transported to Shanghai by steamship.

APRIL 25 Li Hongzhang becomes acting governor of Jiangsu.

MAY 10 British and French forces retake Ningbo from Taiping.

Beginning of Allied campaign in Zhejiang.

MAY 12 Allied forces and Ward capture Qingpu.

MAY 13 Duolonga captures Luzhou from the Brave King.

MAY 15 Brave King captured in Shouzhou, executed on June 4.

MAY 17 French Admiral Protet killed by Taiping bullet; French troops rampage.

MAY 30 Zeng Guoquan pitches camp at base of Yuhuatai.

Beginning of the siege of Nanjing (will last until July 1864).

SUMMER Major cholera epidemic in Shanghai.

Massacre of Taiping prisoners makes world newspapers.

JULY 20 U.S. Minister Anson Burlingame arrives in Beijing.

SEPTEMBER 17 Battle of Antietam in U.S. Civil War.

SEPTEMBER 21 Frederick Townsend Ward dies of bullet wound
in Ningbo.

OCTOBER 13 Li Xiucheng launches assault on Zeng Guoquan's forces at
Yuhuatai (will continue for forty-five days, until November 26).

DECEMBER 13 Major Union defeat at Fredericksburg, Virginia.

1863

JANUARY 1 Abraham Lincoln issues Emancipation Proclamation.

JANUARY 7 Zeng Guofan's brother Zeng Guobao dies of
typhoid at Nanjing.

FEBRUARY 13 Anglo-Chinese Fleet begins departing from
England for China.

MARCH 25 Charles Gordon takes charge of the Ever-Victorious Army.

JUNE 13 Zeng Guoquan's forces take control of Yuhuatai.

Shi Dakai surrenders in Sichuan, executed on June 25.

JULY 1–3 Battle of Gettysburg; tide of U.S. Civil War turns against
the Confederacy.

AUGUST 2 Henry Burgevine defects to the Taiping.

SEPTEMBER Yung Wing meets with Zeng Guofan at Anqing.

Sherard Osborn arrives in China to take command of the
Anglo-Chinese Fleet.

OCTOBER 15 Burgevine surrenders.

NOVEMBER 19 Lincoln delivers Gettysburg Address.

NOVEMBER 20 Lord Elgin dies in India.

DECEMBER 4 Esteemed King Tan Shaoguang assassinated by other Taiping generals who surrender Suzhou to imperial forces under Gordon and Cheng Xueqi.

DECEMBER 6 Li Hongzhang takes control of Suzhou, executes generals who surrendered.

End of Military cooperation between Britain and Qing imperial government.

1864

MARCH 19 Ulysses S. Grant put in charge of all Union Armies.

MAY 31 Ever-Victorious Army disbanded.

JUNE 1 Hong Xiuquan dies.

JULY 19 Zeng Guoquan conquers Nanjing.

JULY 22 Li Xiucheng captured in outskirts of Nanjing.

JULY 28 Zeng Guofan arrives from Anqing to take possession of Nanjing.

AUGUST 7 Li Xiucheng executed at Nanjing.

OCTOBER 9 Hong Rengan captured in Jiangxi province.

OCTOBER 25 The Young Monarch captured, executed on November 18.

NOVEMBER 23 Hong Rengan executed and cut to pieces at Nanchang, Jiangxi province.

1865

APRIL 9 Robert E. Lee surrenders at Appomattox Court House, Virginia.

PREFACE

The war that engulfed China from 1851 to 1864 was not only the most destructive war of the nineteenth century, but likely the bloodiest civil war of all time. Known in English as the Taiping Rebellion, it pitted the Chinese rebels of the Taiping Heavenly Kingdom against the waning authority of the two-hundred-year-old Qing dynasty of the Manchus, and in its brutal fourteen-year course at least twenty million people lost their lives to warfare and its attendant horrors of famine and pestilence. In terms of the U.S. Civil War, with which it coincided in its final years, the death toll of the Chinese civil war was at least thirty times as high.

Like most Americans, I did not learn about the Taiping Rebellion as part of my standard education. I managed to get through twelve years of public schooling, four years of college, and the better part of a year in China before reading about it for the first time, and I do not think my experience was uncommon. This war remains little known in the United States not just because our own civil war naturally occupies the center of our histories of the period but also because of a long-standing misconception that China in the nineteenth century was an essentially closed system and therefore that a civil war in China—no matter its scale—was something with relevance only to the country in which it was waged.

Part of my purpose in writing this book is to help restore China to its proper place in the nineteenth-century world. China was not a closed system, and globalism is hardly the recent phenomenon we sometimes imagine it to be. The Qing Empire was deeply integrated into the world's economy through trade, and there were thousands of foreigners living in Hong Kong and Shanghai. By consequence, the war in China was tangled up in threads leading around the globe to Europe and America, and it was watched from outside with a sense of immediacy. Furthermore, to compound the miseries of China's dynastic rulers, Britain and France mounted an entirely separate war against them in the late 1850s over trading rights and the stationing of ambassadors, which overlapped with the ongoing

Taiping Rebellion and helped push the empire to the brink of total collapse.

Americans should know about the Taiping Rebellion not just for the sake of understanding China's history, or because their own countrymen were involved in it, but also because it helps to illuminate the wider effects of the U.S. Civil War far beyond America's borders. The simultaneity of the Chinese and American civil wars was no trivial matter, and one of my underlying arguments in this book is that the launching of hostilities in the United States in 1861 helped shape the final outcome of events in China, by forcing Britain's hand. The United States and China were Britain's two largest economic markets, and to understand Britain's role in either war we need to remember that it was faced with the prospect of losing both of them at the same time. Order had to be restored on one side or the other, and while Britain could have intervened in the United States to reopen the cotton trade, for reasons that will be explained in the course of this book, it chose to launch itself into the civil war in China instead. In hindsight, the British prime minister would point to his country's intervention in China as being the reason why Britain could survive economic ruin while it allowed the U.S. Civil War to run its full and natural course unmolested. Or in other words, Britain's neutrality in the U.S. Civil War came at the expense of abandoning it in China.

This book is not a comprehensive history of the Chinese civil war, which, given its enormous scale, would too easily devolve into a numbing listing of dates, battles, and casualties. It is, however, an attempt to show the war from all sides, and to recapture a sense of what it was like to be alive at the time—both for the Chinese who were caught up in the conflict and for the foreigners who stood at the sidelines, traveled through it, and launched their own wars on top of it. I have tried to thread my way through the events of this chaotic time by holding closely to the experiences of a handful of individuals on each side who, to my mind, best embodied the choices, terrors, and opportunities of the era. To such extent as any individuals can be said to have shaped a war encompassing millions, the central figures in this book were the ones I felt were most directly responsible for steering it to its final outcome.

These characters range from a Taiping prime minister who spoke English, preached Christianity, and dreamed of a China with free trade and railroads and newspapers; to the American mercenaries lured to Shanghai by the rewards of fighting in the Chinese war; to the Western diplomats and missionaries whose attempts to make sense of the strange foreign world around them wound up shaping that world in permanent ways. On the dynasty's side, the character for whom the reader will need to be most patient—for he does not appear until chapter 6 when his role finally becomes central—is Zeng Guofan, the general who rose from a poor farming background to command a personal army every bit as vast, loyal, and ruthless as the army commanded by his counterpart, Ulysses S. Grant, in the United States, and whose power by the end of the war made even Grant look like a lieutenant in comparison. General Zeng's legacy has followed a rocky course in modern China: reviled for generations as a traitor to his race for supporting the Manchu ruling house, he has lately been resurrected as a model of what it means to be Chinese—or, more specifically, what it means to be moral and strong and disciplined in a truly native and Confucian way, uninfluenced by the West. He is one of the most popular historical figures in China today, with dozens of books on his life and letters readily available at any airport bookstore. The book at hand is the first in more than eighty years to try to bring him to life in English.

The story of this war is necessarily an international one, because the two sides in China were so intractably balanced that the final outcome was to a large degree determined by the diplomatic and military interventions of outsiders in the early 1860s. American and British historians have written a great deal of hagiography about the two most prominent foreigners who trained and led Chinese troops in this conflict, Frederick Townsend Ward and Charles Gordon. I have taken a fresh look at their records—and find that they appear quite differently when one approaches them with appropriate sympathy for the internal circumstances of the hideous war into which they inserted themselves. Ward and Gordon have traditionally been depicted as heroes, the foreigners ("gods," as more than one biography calls Ward) who swept in and put China right. Against the dismal succession of nineteenth-century Opium Wars and treaties at gunpoint, they have stood for rare moments of positive cooperation between China and the foreign powers. But that is a view based largely on ignorance of the circumstances of the larger war, and if there was any single spark that inspired me to go back into this period, it was an interview I happened upon from 1909, quoted in this book's epilogue, in which the eminent Japanese statesman Ito Hirobumi told a reporter that Great Britain's intervention in the Chi-

nese civil war was not, in fact, a heroic example of Sino-foreign cooperation. Rather, he said, it was the single greatest mistake the British ever made
in China.

Nevertheless, when I first started the research for this project, I half
expected to find that the foreign intervention had not actually mattered at
all. Western historians have long tended to exaggerate the role of foreigners
in Chinese history, and the British in Shanghai at the time unquestionably
had an inflated sense of their own importance to the country—even as
their understanding of what was actually happening in the interior was
extremely limited. In contrast, the histories of the war written in Chinese tend to focus instead on the provincial militaries and other domestic
forces, giving little weight to the likes of Ward and Gordon. The foreigners on the coast in Shanghai were but a pinprick at the edge of a much
larger war in China's interior—which is why I was surprised to find that
their role was, in fact, absolutely indispensable. Not only was the foreign
intervention crucial, it was also (and this was the most surprising to me of
all) largely informal, often halfhearted, morally fraught, and in many ways
effective purely by accident. Nevertheless, remarkably, the actions of the
foreigners coordinated neatly with those of the provincial militias from the
interior, almost completely in spite of themselves. In reconciling the Chinese and foreign records of this war, what emerges is a peculiar instance of
two forces fighting essentially the same war, independently of each other,
each imagining itself to be the only force that mattered. There are therefore
two interwoven narrative paths in this book: the one from outside that
leads to the foreign intervention, and the one from within that leads to
the rise of the Hunan Army. Together they tell the full military story of the
war's endgame.

As regards the participation of foreigners beyond just military personnel, the events of this period are a reminder of just how fine the line
is that separates humanitarian intervention from imperialism—and how
the trace and curvature of that line are often decided simply by who it is
from the one country who succeeds in claiming expertise on the other.
Much of the international side of my story concerns the efforts of outside observers to come to terms with what was happening inside the Qing
Empire—whether it was a rebellion, a civil war, a national revolution, or
simply a descent into anarchy—and how, on the basis of their conclusions,
they tried to convince their governments to take an active role on one side
or the other. At the heart of this process was an amalgam of individuals in
the consular service, in business, in the Protestant missions, in journalism,

and in government, who often disagreed fiercely with one another. Many of these individuals were conscientious and well-meaning. Some were not. But as is so often the case, even the monsters among them believed, at some level, that they acted only in the interests of humanity.

The reader who is already familiar with the events of the Taiping Rebellion will find certain differences in my telling of it. There are already excellent books in English on the origins of the rebellion and on the Taiping religion, so I have directed my energies elsewhere. This book focuses less on the origins of the war than on its conclusions, and less on the religious ideology of the rebels than on their attempts to craft a strong appeal on ethnic grounds. For a long time, Western historians of China believed that the ethnic differences between the ruling Manchus and the subject Chinese in this period were negligible or, at the very least, invisible. Conventional wisdom held that outsiders like the Manchus who invaded China simply became Chinese over time, and for that reason the racial—even genocidal—aspects of the Taiping were downplayed in relation to their religious appeal, which was assumed to be the more important.

In recent years, however, scholars who study the Manchus have found that in their own language, in their own documents, the Manchus were in fact fiercely aware of their ethnic differences from the Chinese. Judging from the propaganda circulated by the Taiping rebels in the later years of the war, it would appear that such feelings were mutual. In such a light, the more nationalistic appeals of the rebels—namely, that they were overthrowing alien rulers in order to restore the Chinese to power—need to be taken more seriously than they have been in the past. Religious conversion alone, even supplemented by conscription, can hardly explain the massive armies numbering in the hundreds of thousands that the Taiping were able to conjure in the later years of the war. The ethnic appeals of the rebels were certainly taken seriously abroad, where the strongest arguments for Taiping support in the Western world hinged not just on their alleged Christianity but on their perceived role as the liberators of the Chinese people from their Manchu overlords.

The reader may also notice that I generally prefer to describe this conflict as a civil war (a term used commonly for it at the time) rather than as the more familiar Taiping Rebellion. In writing about this conflict, Western historians have long taken the side of the dynasty, at least in their choice of terminology. The Taiping were indeed rebels, but to call the entire war the Taiping Rebellion is to cast the rebels forever in the wrong, and to lay all blame on them for defying their legitimate rulers and destroying what one might surmise was otherwise a peaceful and stable empire. In going back to the time, however, it is very difficult to distinguish which side was the more destructive and violent, especially in the war's final years. Historians in the People's Republic of China have typically held the opposite bias, treating the Taiping as proto-Communist peasant rebels and referring to the war as "the Taiping Revolution" or "the Taiping Uprising." I hope it will become clear to the reader of this book that just as it is unfair to suggest that the Taiping were solely responsible for the devastation of the war, it is likewise an exaggeration to claim they were building some kind of peasant utopia.

The most neutral Chinese term for this period, and the most alluring, is simply to call it "the Taiping Heavenly Kingdom." It is a term with no taint of war or destruction, which recognizes that, whatever one's opinion of its quality of government, this power, which held a significant portion of China's most wealthy and populous territory for more than a decade, was nevertheless best described as a country. It is in that spirit that I have approached it, and it was in that spirit that many outsiders saw it at the time: as a competing government, a competing state, a competing vision of what China should be.

In closing, I would add that while this book is intended as a window into the tumult of a particular corner of the nineteenth-century world, and a means of giving insight into a turning point in China's modern history, it can also be read simply as a moral tale, of conscience and fate, set against the backdrop of a falling empire. The Chinese characters at its center did not have the luxury the foreigners did, of escaping. This was *their* world, to make or destroy. As it pertains to them, this is the story of a handful of individuals torn from the fabric of their familiar lives and thrust into roles of historical consequence beyond anything they had ever dreamed. It is about the deliberate choices from which one can never turn back, the acts that, once committed, can never be undone, and the relentless erosion of options in a time of crisis—until nothing else remains but to push forward into the cataclysm, in hopes of somehow finding peace on the other side.

A NOTE ON ROMANIZATION

In rendering Chinese words, personal names, and names of places I have used the pinyin system of romanization, with the exception of the following, which are better known in English by their old spellings: the Yangtze River, Canton, the Taku forts, the Peiho, and Hankow.

Variant romanization in the quotations has been left intact as much as possible, since it conveys a certain flavor of the time that would be lost with standardization. Thus, Beijing may appear in quotations as Peking or Pekin, Nanjing may appear as Nanking or Nankin, and Taiping may appear as Taeping or Tai-ping. When standardization was necessary for the sake of clarity, it has been indicated in the notes.

0   500 Miles

RUSSIAN EMPIRE

Current China Border

Qing
Empire
(c. 1860)

Tibet

Sichuan

BENGAL

Yunnan

INDIA

BURMA

ANNA

SIAM

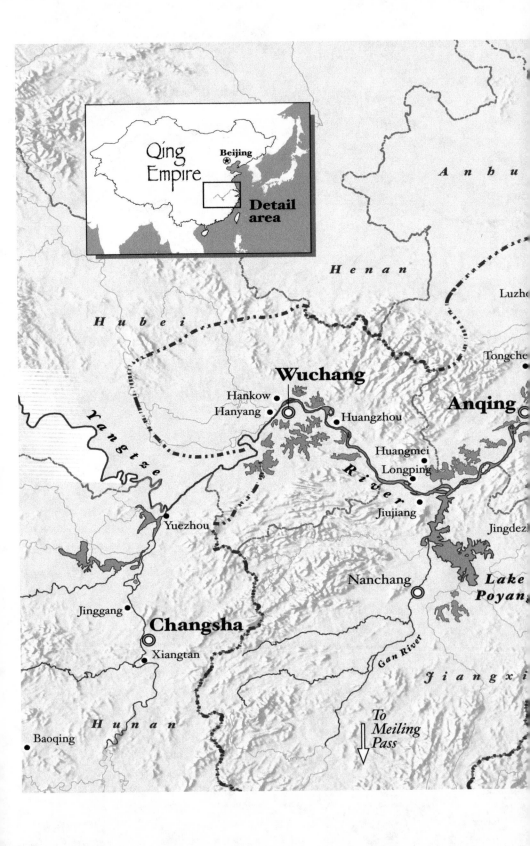

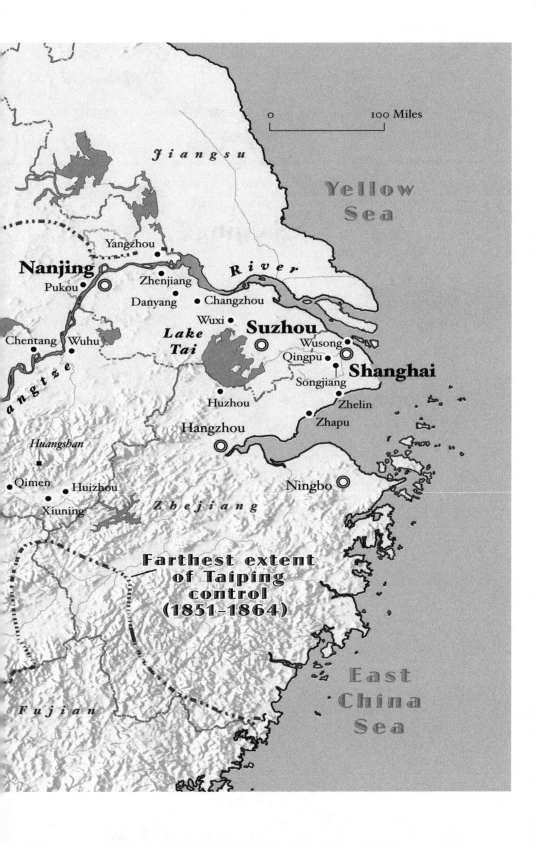

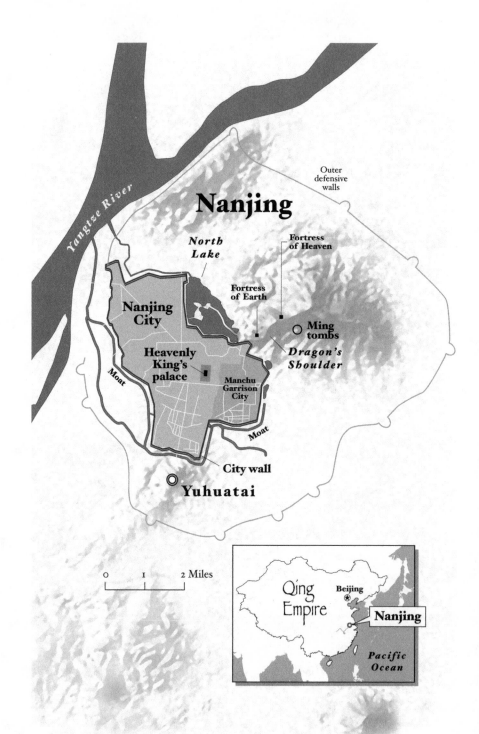

Nanjing

Yangtze River

Outer defensive walls

North Lake

Fortress of Heaven

Fortress of Earth

Nanjing City

Ming tombs

Heavenly King's palace

Dragon's Shoulder

Moat

Manchu Garrison City

Moat

City wall

Yuhuatai

0   1   2 Miles

Qing Empire

Beijing

Nanjing

Pacific Ocean

AUTUMN IN THE HEAVENLY KINGDOM

HEAVEN'S CHILDREN

On an early spring morning in 1853 just northwest of Beijing, the sun rises quietly over the Summer Palace of Xianfeng, the seventh emperor of the Qing dynasty. The palace sprawls luxuriantly over eight hundred acres of gardens and ornately constructed buildings, a world within the world of China, from which Xianfeng—like his royal ancestors—rarely needs to go out. There are wooded riding trails, lakes, and opera houses. The grandest landscapes of the empire have been lovingly re-created within the palace compound, in miniature, for the emperor's pleasure. At twenty-one, Xianfeng has been on the throne for only three years, but he was born here in this palace, and all he has ever known in his life has been his preparation to become the Son of Heaven and to rule China.

Xianfeng is a Manchu, not Chinese, descended from nomadic outdoorsmen and hunters originally from north of the Great Wall, which the earlier dynasties built to keep out his kind ("barbarians," the Chinese once called them). But his family has ruled China for more than two centuries now, since the collapse of the Ming dynasty under its own weight in 1644, and they govern through a certain indulgence, acting as stewards of Chinese tradition to maintain the loyalty of the Chinese scholars who do the real work of management and bureaucracy. As did the dynasties before them, they hold Confucian examinations to choose officials, recruiting loyal Chinese to administer the empire in their stead. And by now, after so many generations, few question that the Manchus rule by Heaven's mandate and that the Manchu emperor is indeed the divinely chosen ruler of the Chinese.

Xianfeng's life is a singularity—as emperor there is a color of fabric he alone can wear, ink he alone can use, a pronoun whose sole existence in the Chinese language is for him to refer to himself. And such, in a sense, is the condition of the Manchus more widely in the empire. They are a small elite (three men to a thousand Chinese at the time of conquest) with their own language and their own customs, intermarrying among their own people. Like Xianfeng in his palace, his world within a world, most of them live in a handful of cities of their own, the so-called Manchu garrison cities, gated cities within larger gated cities, separated by their own walls from the masses of Chinese outside.

There was a time when these Manchus were fierce, and the men would return to their northern homeland in the summer to practice the muscular arts of horsemanship and archery that made them proudly superior to the sedentary Chinese. But things changed as they grew accustomed to their comforts. The emperors are no longer as attentive as they once were, the Manchu men no longer so concerned with physical discipline, with sharpening their martial skills. And so on this spring morning in 1853, in the walled city of Nanjing a little over seven hundred miles to the south of Xianfeng's palace, as the rebels—chosen by a different heaven—smash through the outer walls of the city and shout to the civilians to show them the way to the devils, as they push through to the inner Manchu city, climbing over one another to scale the wall that encircles the isolated population within—as they do this, the men who count among the twenty thousand or so Manchus living inside the garrison do not take up their weapons but instead only throw themselves to the ground and beg for pity. The rebels slaughter them like animals, and then their wives, and all of their daughters and sons.[1]

PART ONE

Twilight

CHAPTER 1

THE PREACHER'S ASSISTANT

Hong Kong in 1852 was a diseased and watery place, a rocky island off the southern shore of the Qing Empire where the inhabitants lived in dread of what one described as "the miasma set free from the ground which was everywhere being turned up." A small British settlement sat between the mountains and the bay, but the emerald and sapphire glory of the scene belied the darkness below the surface. Leaving the concentration of godowns, military barracks, and trading firms along the colony's nostalgically named central streets (The Queen's Road, Wellington Street, Hollywood Road), one could find the grandest vistas in the gravel paths that led up the coast into the hills, but the European settlement soon gave way to scattered Chinese houses among fields growing rice and sweet potatoes unchanged in the decade since the British took the island as their prize in the Opium War. Some of the wealthier merchants had built opulent mansions in those hills, with terraced gardens commanding a view of the harbor and town. But as though their builders had strayed too far from the protection of the settlement, the inhabitants of those houses sickened and died. Marked as "homes of fever or death," the ghostly manors sat silent and abandoned, their empty gaze passing judgment on the settlers below.[1]

One of those settlers was Theodore Hamberg, a young Swedish missionary with a thin chinstrap beard that set off his delicate, nearly effeminate features. He was blessed with a lovely voice, and in his youth in Stockholm he had sung together with Jenny Lind, the "Swedish Nightingale." But while Lind went on to conquer the opera halls of Europe and America, bringing suitors such as Frédéric Chopin and Hans Christian Andersen to their knees along the way, Hamberg's life took an entirely different path. His strong tenor found its destined outlet in preaching, and in 1847 he left his native Sweden to sail to the opposite end of the world, to this malarial colony of Hong Kong, with the sole purpose of bringing the Chinese to their knees after a different fashion.

Theodore Hamberg might well have lived his life in obscurity, for his proudest accomplishments meant little to anyone beyond a small circle of Protestant missionaries. He was one of the first Europeans in his generation to brave the Chinese countryside, leaving the relative safety of Hong Kong to preach in a village outside the Chinese trading port of Canton a hundred miles up the Pearl River (though for health reasons he finally returned to the colony). He was also the first to learn to speak the dialect of the Hakka, or "guest people"—a gypsy minority thickly populous in south China. All of that might have meant little to anyone in the world outside except that one day in the late spring of 1852, one of his converts from the countryside brought a guest to meet him, a short, round-faced Hakka named Hong Rengan who had a remarkable story to tell.

The strangest thing about this Hakka, Hamberg recalled from their first meeting, was how much he already seemed to know about God and Jesus despite the fact that he hailed from well beyond the narrow reach of the Hong Kong missionaries. Hamberg listened with curiosity as Hong Rengan gave a baffling account of the events leading to his arrival in Hong Kong. He spoke of visions and battles, armies and congregations of believers, a heavenly prophet from among the Hakkas. He had, or at least so he claimed, been hunted by the agents of the Qing dynasty and had lived in disguise under an assumed name. He had been kidnapped, had escaped, and had lived for four days in the forest, six days in a cave. None of it made much sense, though, and Hamberg confessed, "I could form no clear conception of the whole matter."[2] Not knowing what to make of the story, he asked Hong Rengan to write it down, which he did, and then—though Hamberg had expected him to stay for baptism—he left without explanation. Hamberg put the sheets of paper with Hong Rengan's story into his desk and turned his mind to other matters. He would think little of them again for nearly a year, until the spring of 1853 when the news came that Nanjing had fallen in a torrent of blood, and Hamberg realized that the strange events sketched out in Hong Rengan's tale meant more than he had ever imagined.

News of the mounting upheaval in China reached Hamberg and the other settlers in Hong Kong and up the coast in Shanghai only in scattered and vague accounts. From Chinese government reports there seemed no pattern to the rising disorder of the early 1850s, no principle or cohesion. Local uprisings and small-scale banditry in China's countryside were a perennial thorn in the side of the imperial authorities, hardly anything new or noteworthy, though they certainly did seem to have increased in the years following the Opium War. Chinese travelers and clandestine Catholic missionaries deep in the interior forwarded rumors of some larger movement led by a man known as "Tian De," or "Heavenly Virtue," but just as many accounts reported that the man was dead, killed by imperial forces, or that he had never existed in the first place. In the absence of any clear news, the foreigners in their coastal ports paid little attention, concerned only that bandits might disrupt the production of tea and silk.

But the fall of the southern capital of Nanjing in 1853 brought a massive civil war right to the doorstep of the foreign settlement in Shanghai, which was just two hundred miles downriver where the Yangtze met the sea. Half a million rebels calling themselves the Taiping Tianguo ("Heavenly Kingdom of Great Peace") flooded down from central China on a grand flotilla of commandeered ships to Nanjing, leaving a swath of emptied cities and shattered imperial defenses behind them, and the debate was settled; this was no mere bandit uprising. Fear gripped the city of Shanghai. There was no direct communication with Nanjing, no concrete information (the American steamer *Susquehanna* tried to sail upriver to Nanjing to investigate but ran aground). Rumors spread that the insurgents would next march on Shanghai to attack the foreigners, and the city's Chinese population boarded up their houses, packed up their furniture, and took to riverboats or fled into the countryside for safety. The foreign settlers called up their unready defenses, rallying a haphazard volunteer defense corps to man the city walls and bringing up the few ships in ready reach—two British steamers and a brig-of-war, and one steamer each for the French and Americans.[3]

But there it ended, at least for the time being. The Taiping did not march on Shanghai, and the city's vigilance eased off. Instead, the rebels set their targets northward toward Beijing, the capital of the Manchu rulers, and dug in for a long and bloody campaign with Nanjing as their base of operations. Their "Heavenly Capital," as Nanjing was now renamed, lay tantalizingly just out of reach of Shanghai. One British ship did manage to visit in late April 1853 but brought back conflicting impressions of what was happening there, the clearest opinion being that of the British plenipotentiary, who declared the Taiping to have an ideology of "superstition and nonsense."[4] The visitors learned nothing about the rebels' origins.[5]

Despite the scarcity of clear information, raw accounts of the civil war in China radiated outward from Shanghai and Hong Kong to capture the imagination of the Western world. Europe had been through its own upheavals just five years earlier with the revolutions of 1848, and the events in China seemed a remarkable parallel: the downtrodden people of China, oppressed by their Manchu overlords, had, it seemed, risen up to demand satisfaction. *The Economist* called it "a social change or convulsion such as have of late afflicted Europe" and mused that "it is singular to find similar commotions at the same time in Asia and Europe."[6] Here was evidence that the empire at the other end of the world was now connected to the economic and political systems of the West.

Karl Marx, in 1853 a London correspondent for the *New-York Daily Tribune* struggling to give shape to his ideas on capitalism, likewise considered the rebellion in China to be a sign of China's integration into the global economy, describing it as the end result of Britain's forcing China open to foreign trade in the recent Opium War. In Marx's terminology, what was happening in China was not merely a rebellion or a hodgepodge of uprisings but "one formidable revolution," one that demonstrated the interconnectedness of the industrial world. Indeed, it was in China, he argued, that one could see the future of the West: "the next uprising of the people of Europe, and their next movement for republican freedom and economy of Government," he wrote, "may depend more probably on what is now passing in the Celestial Empire—the very opposite of Europe—than on any other political cause that now exists."[7]

As he explained it, the disorder in China had its roots in the opium trade; a decade earlier, Britain had cracked China's markets open with its warships, and in doing so it had undermined the "superstitious faith" of the

Chinese in their ruling dynasty. Exposure to the world meant the destruction of the old order, he believed, for "dissolution must follow as surely as that of any mummy carefully preserved in a hermetically sealed coffin, whenever it is brought into contact with the open air." But the effects of the Qing dynasty's dissolution would not be limited to China itself. The whole of the Taiping Revolution was, in his mind, Britain's fault, and now the effects of her actions overseas were going to be felt back home: "the question," he wrote, "is how that revolution will in time react on England, and through England on Europe."[8]

Marx predicted that the loss of China's markets to the Taiping Revolution would undermine British exports of cotton and wool. Merchants in a chaotic China would accept only bullion in exchange for their goods, sapping Britain's stores of precious metals. Worse, the revolution would cut off England's source of tea imports, and the price of tea (to which most of the British were addicted) would spike in England at the same time that a poor harvest in Western Europe looked likely to send food prices through the roof, reducing still further the demand for manufactured goods and undermining the whole manufacturing industry on which Britain's economy depended. "It may be safely augured," Marx concluded, "that the Chinese revolution will throw the spark into the overloaded mine of the present industrial system and cause the explosion of the long-prepared general crisis, which, spreading abroad, will be closely followed by political revolutions on the Continent."

If Marx was keen to convince the readers of the *New-York Daily Tribune* that the Chinese civil war was one of class struggle and economic revolution analogous to the movements in Europe, the editors of the *Daily Picayune* in the southern slave port of New Orleans saw it in rather different terms, after their own particular vision of the world. It was, as they saw it, a racial war, and China was a slave state in upheaval. The Taiping had emerged, the editors explained, from the southern provinces of Guangxi and Guangdong, whose inhabitants were "principally of the primitive Chinese race." The northern Manchus, in contrast, were "the ruling race in China" who had taken the throne two hundred years earlier, since which time "China has been accordingly ruled as a conquered country by its masters." The two races never mixed, they explained, and in accordance with their southern vision of a harmonious slave-based society, the *Picayune* offered that in China "The quiet, patient, laboring millions have submitted to their masters mostly with exemplary gentleness." The sole threat to the stability of this Manchu-Chinese country of peacefully coexisting masters and slaves was these "primitive" people of south China who refused to submit to the yoke. The Taiping Rebellion, then, was a dark analogy to an uprising of African slaves in the United States.[9]

The London *Times*, for its part, was the most prescient of observers, honing in immediately on the question of whether Britain should send its navy into the Chinese conflict and, if so, on which side. In an editorial on May 17, 1853, just after the news of Nanjing's fall reached London, *The Times* noted that the Taiping seemed unstoppable and that "according to all computable chances, they will succeed thus far in subverting the Government of China." *The Times* also ran a report from a Shanghai paper asking whether "a change of masters" was something desired by the Chinese nation at large, offering that the Taiping—though hardly beloved in northern China—represented a force of change that was indeed welcome to the Chinese, and "throughout the country the feeling seems to be growing deeper that the exactions and oppressions of the mandarins are no longer to be borne."[10] By the end of the summer, *The Times* declared flatly that the rebellion in China was "in all respects the greatest revolution the world has yet seen."[11]

But the rebels themselves were a cipher. The reader of *The Times* would easily conclude that the Taiping enjoyed the support, grudging at least, of the Chinese people and were poised to overthrow the Manchus and usher in a new era of government. But the editors also sounded a note of caution about Britain's ignorance. "We are without any substantial information as to the origin or objects of the rebellion," they wrote. "We know that the existing Government of China is likely to be subverted in a civil war, but nothing more." Britain, they worried, simply didn't know enough about the nature or ideology of the rebels to decide whether it should support or encourage them: "We cannot tell in the case before us on which side our interest or our duties may lie—whether the insurrection is justifiable or unjustifiable, promising or unpromising; whether the feelings of the people are involved in it or not, or whether its success would bring a change for the better or worse, or any change at all, in our own relations with the Chinese." As it turned out, however, answers to the most pressing of these questions—of the origins of the rebellion, of who the Taiping really were and what they believed in—were to be found in Hong Kong, scribbled on a few stray sheets of paper stuffed into a drawer in Theodore Hamberg's desk.

The following autumn Hong Rengan sought out Hamberg again, now in his village station outside Canton, and this time the missionary knew him for who he was: the cousin and lifelong companion of the Heavenly King of the Taiping, severed from the movement and blown to Hong Kong by the vagaries of chance. He was the only person in contact with a foreigner who had firsthand knowledge of the forces that had risen up in the interior of China—forces that now, as the world finally took notice and watched from afar, threatened to destroy the ruling dynasty from within. Hamberg and Hong Rengan formed a close friendship, the thirty-four-year-old missionary and the thirty-one-year-old refugee, and Hamberg finally got to baptize his friend in September 1853 before taking him back to Hong Kong.[12] Hamberg instructed Hong Rengan carefully in Lutheran doctrine, preparing him to serve as an assistant to the foreign preachers and eventually to take their brand of Christianity to the Taiping in Nanjing (though Hong Rengan later claimed that it was he who had spent those months teaching the foreigners, not the other way around).[13] As they worked together, Hamberg, with his halting command of Hakka dialect, managed to tease out the details hinted at in Hong Rengan's written account and to pull together the full story of who this man was and where he had come from.[14]

As Hong Rengan told the story, it was his cousin Hong Xiuquan, nine years older, who had always been the brilliant one. They lived in neighboring villages about thirty miles from the provincial capital of Canton, close enough to see the White Cloud Mountains northeast of the city on a clear day. The villagers were mostly relatives from their clan, which had once been a grand one—back in the days of the Song dynasty many of them had served as high officials and imperial advisers, but that was a very long time ago and now they were poor farmers. They did, however, have a small schoolhouse where Hong Xiuquan began studying the Confucian classics at the age of seven. He distinguished himself immediately and in a few years had memorized the Four Books, the Five Classics, and the other texts required for the civil service examinations. By his early teens, he had also read widely in Chinese history and literature and was so bright, his family believed, that he could understand the ancient texts at first reading without assistance. They dreamed that he would restore their long-lost family glory, and several of his teachers worked without pay in hopes that their reward would come when he passed the exams and became an official. As his need for more specialized training took him to schools farther from the village, his family pooled their resources to support him, though by age sixteen he was already supporting himself as a schoolteacher, with a small salary paid primarily in rice, lard, salt, and lamp oil.

Passing the Confucian civil service examinations was the key to gaining an official appointment in the Qing dynasty government, and that was the goal to which both cousins aspired. But the examinations were fabulously difficult, and failure at the provincial level usually meant years of waiting for the next chance to compete. The actual process of taking the provincial exam consisted of three days in a dank, musty cubicle in Canton, proving one's mastery of the Confucian classics. And though Hong Rengan himself never had much success, when Hong Xiuquan traveled to Canton to compete for the first time in 1827, he placed high in the rankings on the first day. As the examination wore on through its full span, however, his name slipped in the rankings, and by the end of the third and final day he had fallen out of the circle of winners. It was nine more years before he finally qualified to take the exam again, in 1836, and on that occasion he failed for a second time. Hong Rengan also never managed to pass, but it was Hong Xiuquan who had their entire extended family's hopes riding on him. So that may be why he was the one who finally suffered a breakdown.

Hong Xiuquan had his first visions in 1837, just after failing the examination for a third time. Weakened by the ordeal, he had to be carried home afterward. When he got there, he collapsed into bed and called his family, who crowded around him. He apologized to them that his life was over and he had let them down; then he closed his eyes and lost all strength. They thought he was dead. But eventually he woke up and began telling them about strange things he had seen while he was asleep. In his dream, a dragon, a tiger, and a cock had entered the room, followed by musicians with a sedan chair. They carried him away to a "beautiful and luminous place" full of men and women who rejoiced when they saw him and an old woman who washed him to remove the defilements from his body. A group of old men also appeared, and he recognized some of them as the sages of ancient China. They slit open his body with a knife, removed his organs, and replaced them with new ones, red in color. Then they closed him up, though later he could never find any trace of the incision. He was escorted into a grand hall, where in the highest position sat an old man in a black robe with a flowing beard of gold. The old man wept that the people of the world did not venerate him. "They take of my gifts," he told Hong

Xiuquan, "and therewith worship demons; they purposely rebel against me, and arouse my anger. Do not thou imitate them." He then gave Hong Xiuquan a sword for killing demons (but admonished him not to use it on his brothers and sisters), as well as a seal and a piece of yellow fruit, which he ate. It was sweet. The old man in black led him to look down at the people on the earth, where everywhere he could see defilement and perversion. Then he woke up.

Hong Xiuquan's visions continued off and on for forty days, and Hong Rengan stayed by his cousin's side listening in his waking moments to hear stories of what he had seen. There were other recurrent characters, one a middle-aged man he called "elder brother" who traveled with him to the "uttermost regions" of the world to slay demons with his sword. In another dream-vision, the old man in black was berating Confucius for failing to teach proper doctrine to the Chinese people, and Confucius humbly confessed his guilt and shame while Hong Xiuquan looked on. His brothers kept the doors to the house locked during those weeks, and they would sometimes catch Hong Xiuquan leaping about his room, shouting "Kill the demons!" and slashing wildly at the air. His insanity drew the curiosity and amusement of neighbors, who came to look at him as he slept, to see the famous madman close up. At one point he woke up claiming to be the emperor of China. His family was shamed and worried. As Hong Rengan explained to Theodore Hamberg, "His friends and relatives only replied, that the whole was strange indeed, without thinking at the time that there was any reality in the matter." What Hong Rengan did not believe at the time—but did believe by the time he recounted his story to Hamberg—was that his cousin's visions were, in fact, divine revelations.

Hong Xiuquan finally recovered, and Hong Rengan saw that he was literally a different person after his ordeal—taller, stronger, and vastly more intelligent. He was now more handsome, with fair skin and high nose. His gaze had become "piercing and difficult to endure." His voice boomed, and when he laughed, "the whole house resounded." Healthier and sharper of mind than ever before, he returned to his teaching and his preparation for the civil service exams. But he was no more successful than before. In 1843 he sat for the examination in Canton for the fourth time, and failed yet again. That was the year another cousin found a forgotten book in Hong's cabinet. It was a Christian tract in Chinese, which a missionary had pressed into his hands some years before in Canton but which he had never read. The cousin looked it over and thought it interesting, so Hong Xiuquan took the time to read it carefully. And thus came his epiphany.

That book, he told Hong Rengan, unlocked the secret of his dream-visions from six years before. After reading the basic tenets of Christianity, he suddenly understood it all: the old man in black with the golden beard who had commanded him was God, and the elder brother who had helped him slay demons was Jesus Christ. The demons were the idols worshipped by the Chinese in their Confucian and Buddhist temples, and his brothers and sisters were the Chinese people. Hong Xiuquan baptized himself, then threw away the Confucian tablets in his schoolroom.

Hong Rengan was Hong Xiuquan's first convert, along with a neighbor named Feng Yunshan. They baptized themselves in a river and took down the "idols" in their classrooms—the tablets and likenesses of Confucius that were icons of the state religion of Confucianism, which lay at the heart of the examination system. The three began studying together, gathering translated Christian texts where they could find them. Hong Xiuquan preached to them and soon to others drawn in by his message, using the Gospel tracts and his visions as complements—each, he claimed, proving the truth of the other. The Bible, he believed, had been written explicitly for himself.

The three believers—Hong Xiuquan, Hong Rengan, and Feng Yunshan—now began to convert their parents, their brothers and sisters, their wives and their children to the God for whom Hong Xiuquan was prophet. It didn't always go easily; Hong Rengan's older brother beat him with a stick for taking down the Confucian tablets, which caused his students to abandon the school and left him with no income. Hong Rengan, indignant, replied, "Am I not the teacher? How is Confucius able to teach, after being dead so long? Why do you force me to worship him?" Hong Xiuquan and Feng Yunshan left in 1844 to spread their word to other villages and far-flung family members throughout the province, and though Hong Rengan desperately wanted to join them, his relatives forced him to stay as a schoolteacher because he was only twenty-two years old. He had to put the Confucian tablets back up to get his students to return. But even staying put, he managed to baptize at least fifty or sixty converts, which was a good deal more than Hamberg would ever manage in his own career.

As Feng Yunshan preached from village to village in the mountainous regions of the neighboring province of Guangxi, the movement grew and spread. Autonomous congregations sprang up, numbering in the hundreds of followers who referred to themselves as part of a "Society of God Worshippers." They took Hong Xiuquan—whom many had never met—as their spiritual leader. When Hong Xiuquan came back home in 1845, Hong

Rengan noted a shift in his ideology; he was no longer solely concerned with Confucianism, with replacing it with the worship of God. There was a new tone to his preaching that disparaged the ethnically Manchu rulers of the Qing dynasty as the wrongful usurpers of China. "God has divided the kingdoms of the world, and made the Ocean to be a boundary for them, just as a father divides his estates among his sons," Hong Xiuquan explained to his cousin. "Why should these Manchus forcibly enter China and rob their brothers of their estate?" His religious movement was becoming a political one.

By 1847, there were about two thousand followers of the Society, primarily from the Hakka population. Emboldened by their faith and their numbers, they began smashing Buddhist idols and temples, raising the suspicions of the authorities. By 1849, the independent congregations were having fits, speaking in tongues. They looked to Hong Xiuquan to tell them which of their channeled words came from God and which came from the Devil. A pestilence ravaged the province in 1850, and when word spread that sick people could be healed by praying to Hong Xiuquan's God, the numbers exploded. Multitudes joined the Society, and after the disease had passed they gave credit for their survival to Hong Xiuquan's religion.

But none of that was enough to call an army into being. What tipped the scales was an outburst of violence between Hakka and "native" settlers in Guangxi province. The Hakkas, as latecomers, had to scrabble for land and water rights, and the more long-standing local families scorned them as interlopers. A small-scale war broke out between a handful of Hakka and native villages in the autumn of 1850; the natives burned down the homes of the Hakkas, and the Hakkas turned to the Society of God Worshippers for protection and support. Local authorities, already suspicious of the religious sect, now began to view it as a harbor for troublemakers. But according to Hong Rengan, Hong Xiuquan had foreseen all this and waited patiently to make his move.

As the Hakka-native violence spread, Qing officials—who blamed the trouble on the Hakkas—sent a body of soldiers to round up Hong Xiuquan and Feng Yunshan. Getting wind of the plan, a nearby congregation of God Worshippers armed themselves with swords and spears and marched overland to save their leader. They easily routed the outnumbered imperial soldiers, and Hong Xiuquan sent out word calling for all of the God Worshippers from across the districts to gather in one place for the first time and prepare for the next stage of their movement. Many had already sold their houses and land in preparation. Over the following days they assembled and found that they now numbered in the tens of thousands. With little effort they took possession of a small town, their first military victory. Imperial soldiers laid siege, firing on the God Worshippers from outside, but they managed to slip out in the middle of the night and in the morning the imperials fell on a nearly empty town. Troops dispatched to pursue them were cut down in the woods, and the imperial soldiers wreaked their frustrated revenge on the unfortunate townspeople who had stayed behind.

On January 11, 1851, Hong Xiuquan declared the founding of the Taiping Heavenly Kingdom, with himself as the new emperor, or Heavenly King, of China. Feng Yunshan and three other lieutenants were appointed kings of the four directions. Through 1851 and 1852, the Taiping army fought its way north, absorbing the poor and disenfranchised, the criminals, all those who feared or hated the reigning Qing dynasty authorities, all who would convert to their brand of Christianity and commit themselves to the destruction of Confucianism and, above all, the Manchu overlords. By the time they reached the Yangtze River cutting through central China in January 1853, there were half a million of them, though Feng Yunshan and untold numbers of others had died along the way. But Hong Rengan knew of this only through hearsay. He had been too late to the first assembly point and arrived at the town after the God Worshippers had already slipped out in the night. Trying to follow them, he had found only imperial patrols hunting for stragglers. And thus had begun his flight and his disguises, pursued by Qing agents who burned his home village to the ground, his kidnapping at the hands of a man who wanted the bounty on his head, his escape, and finally his asylum in Hong Kong with the Swedish missionary Hamberg.

The one thing Theodore Hamberg would do in his life to capture the attention of the world beyond his small circle of missionaries was to translate Hong Rengan's account into English and publish it. He did so because it had convinced him of what was, to him, the most marvelous, the most improbable and amazing fact of the rebellion: namely, that the rebels who had risen up from the heart of China to overthrow the Manchus were Christians. His book came out first in Hong Kong and Shanghai as *The Visions of Hung-Siu-Tshuen*, then in London as *The Chinese Rebel Chief*. It was nothing less than propaganda, seeking to convince the readers of the English-speaking world that the Taiping rebels worshipped the same God they did. It was, furthermore, an attempt to draw foreign support toward the rebels by awakening, in Hamberg's words, "a more lively and permanent sympathy . . . on behalf of the millions of China"—by which he did not, of course, mean the people of China who remained loyal to the Manchus. Finally, Hamberg published the book to raise money for the cause, of which he had, through his friendship with Hong Rengan, become a clear partisan. "It may add to the satisfaction of the readers," he wrote at the end of the volume, "to know, that while they are promoting the sale of the book, they are also relieving the distress of many who form the subjects of its pages."[15]

In May 1854, as he finished work on the book, Hamberg gave Hong Rengan and two friends money to travel to Shanghai in the hope that they could make their way up the Yangtze River across the Qing cordons to rejoin the Taiping movement in Nanjing. He loaded Hong Rengan down with gifts. There was a range of Chinese books: authorized Bible translations compiled by the foreign missionaries, along with translated works of history and several maps showing the world, China, and the Holy Land. Hamberg also gave him the standard tokens of the European trying to impress a Chinese audience—a telescope, a thermometer, a compass (though the Chinese had invented that one). He hoped that Hong Rengan would be the European missionaries' conduit to the Taiping.[16] And that would just be the start; Hamberg's real hope was that once they got to Nanjing he himself could follow them and join the movement as a religious teacher. Hong Rengan had mentioned on occasion how much he would like to have Hamberg with him in the Heavenly Capital, but Hamberg didn't want to be presumptuous and insisted that he wouldn't try to join the Taiping unless they gave him a formal invitation.[17]

The journey, however, was a failure. Hong Rengan had a falling-out with his missionary hosts in Shanghai (they found an opium pipe in his room, though he claimed that a visiting friend had left it there), and at any rate they didn't have the means to help him get to Nanjing. The Chinese portion of the city was in rebellion, controlled by a secret society sympathetic to the Taiping that didn't believe he was related to the Heavenly King and refused to help him. Hong spent a few months in Shanghai casting about and studying astronomy and mathematics at a missionary school before giving up on rejoining the Taiping. He took a steamer back to Hong Kong, sailing through the waters off the Chinese coast at a breathtaking speed, and wrote a poem comparing the choppy sea to a battleground, the sound of the ship cutting through the waves to "a host of ten thousand men in battle," suggesting a longing for the war in which he couldn't take part.[18] His Swedish friend wasn't there to greet him when he got back to Hong Kong, however; a few days after Hong Rengan's departure for Shanghai, the "miasma" of the colony caught up with Theodore Hamberg, and he died of dysentery at the age of thirty-five.[19]

————————

Hong Rengan's return to Hong Kong in 1855 promised to be a permanent one, and he found long-term employment as a catechist and assistant to the preachers of the London Missionary Society. He was well trusted, a baptized Christian known for his friendship with the late Theodore Hamberg, and his amiable personality won him the favor of the broader missionary community. His supervisor and closest collaborator for the following years was the stodgy muttonchopped Scottish missionary James Legge, who was embarking on a project to make English translations of the whole of the Confucian canon (the same texts on which the infernal civil service exams were based). Legge and Hong worked closely together and often preached in tandem—first Legge in his newly acquired Cantonese, then Hong Rengan in Hakka dialect. In contrast to his past practice, Hong Rengan's sermons in Hong Kong reflected James Legge's doctrine, not his cousin's.

Legge, who did not lightly praise anyone who was Chinese, held an unbounded affection for Hong Rengan and described him as "the most genial and versatile Chinese I have ever known."[20] Legge's daughter seconded this, testifying that her curmudgeonly father felt for Hong Rengan a "special affection and a warmth of admiration such as he gave to hardly any other Chinaman."[21] Indeed, there was something in Hong Rengan's personality—a quality of humility, of intelligence—that caught the attention of many of the missionaries he worked with. Another described him as "a man of exceptional ability and fine character," who possessed a "clear and intelligent acquaintance with Christian truth."[22] One of Legge's counterparts in the London Missionary Society quipped that whenever you saw a Chinese person having frequent conversations with Hong Rengan, "you may be sure there is something good going on in him."[23] And it wasn't just the foreigners who admired him; a Chinese doctor educated in Edinburgh likewise described him as "a man of great intelligence and considerable fluency of speech."[24] In light of later events, however, others would look back years later and wonder whether it had all been a ruse, whether Hong Rengan's "amiable disposition and Christian sweetness" that so endeared him to the foreigners had been nothing more than the clothing of a sheep, hiding a wolf within.[25]

The population of Hong Kong began to shift in those years after the fall of Nanjing. The Manchu government set into motion a broad campaign to hunt down and execute all of the followers of the Taiping they could capture, sending refugees fleeing to the safety and stability of the British colony. Qing officers couldn't touch the Taiping-controlled regions around Nanjing, but in other parts of China still nominally under the control of the central government, the purge of sympathizers was merciless. The government's targets included not just the partisans themselves but also the relatives—however innocent—of every known member of the Taiping movement out to the furthest branches of their family tree. The Qing governor-general in Canton, just a hundred miles up the Pearl River from Hong Kong, led an especially brutal regional effort to crush the sympathizers. In response to a secret society uprising that he determined (most likely erroneously) was in support of the insurgents in Nanjing, his agents cast a dragnet across the province in 1854 that ensnared an estimated 75,000 accused Taiping supporters. And for those who weren't immediately captured, the government set up suicide stations: pavilions with tools for killing oneself (daggers, ropes), emblazoned with placards calling for supporters of the insurrection to choose a quick self-imposed death over the eventual capture and dismemberment that would bring greater shame to their families.[26]

Through 1854 and into 1855, the governor-general in Canton oversaw what the British consul described as "a series of executions, among the most horrible for extent and manner, of which the world has any authentic records."[27] According to one British eyewitness, tens of thousands of accused Taiping supporters were slaughtered in the Canton execution ground, a narrow alleyway crammed with pottery (it being a marketplace in less troubled times) that stank with congealed blood. "Thousands were put to the sword, hundreds cast into the river, tied together in batches of a dozen," he testified, and he watched in horror as the accused were butchered—one executioner to grip the topknot of the bound, kneeling prisoner, and another to chop off his head with the sword. Despite the cramped quarters, the teams worked with revolting efficiency, and this witness counted sixty-three men decapitated in the space of four minutes before he had to stop watching. "I have seen the horrid sight," he wrote, "and the limbless, headless corpse, merely a mass of flayed flesh among headless trunks, that lay in scores covering the whole execution-ground." There were chests for sending the severed heads of the prisoners up to the governor-general as proof of effective punishment, but so many were executed that their heads wouldn't fit, and the executioners eventually packed only the ears (the right ears, specifically), which alone filled the boxes to overflowing.[28]

Another witness to the violence was a Chinese man named Yung Wing, who had just returned from the United States after graduating from Yale University in 1854. Thoroughly Americanized, he hoped to work for the Qing government and promote education reform on an American model. He traveled first to Canton to refresh his nearly forgotten Chinese but found a scene in the execution grounds that made him rethink his support for a government that could condone such barbaric acts. As he described it: "But oh what a sight! The ground was perfectly drenched with human blood. On both sides of the driveway were to be seen headless human trunks piled up in heaps waiting to be taken away for burial." So many were killed that "no provision had been made to find a place large enough to bury all the bodies. There they were left exposed to a burning sun. The temperature stood from morning to night in midsummer steadily at 90 Fahrenheit and sometimes higher. The atmosphere within a radius of two thousand yards of the execution ground was heavily charged with the poisonous and pestilential vapor that was reeking from the ground already over saturated with blood and from the heaps of corpses which had been left behind for at least two days."[29]

The executions in Canton were a major turning point in the fortunes of Hong Kong. Refugees flooded into the colony, not just the fugitives threatened by the governor-general's men but also wealthy merchants from south China seeking a more stable base from which to run their businesses. Hong Kong boomed as the new arrivals built houses, drove up the rents on existing structures, founded new trading companies, and generally infused a vibrant new life into the city.[30] The missionaries rejoiced; it may have been difficult for foreign preachers to travel to Canton, but in time, it seemed, all of Canton might eventually come to them. The brutal and bloody crackdown in Canton also cast the Qing government in a cold new light, and even those outside who questioned the motives of the Taiping couldn't defend the barbarism and horror of the existing regime's reaction to it.

Legge knew well that his thirty-three-year-old assistant, Hong Rengan, was the cousin of the Taiping Heavenly King, but he wasn't nearly as enamored of the rebels as Hamberg had been. He maintained that the Taiping weren't true Christians, insofar as their doctrines stemmed from their so-called Heavenly King rather than any accepted denomination. There was also the thorny issue of Hong Xiuquan's believing himself to be the younger brother of Jesus Christ. For all his affection for Hong Rengan, Legge was largely unconcerned about the doings of Hong's extended family and advised him constantly to put thoughts of Nanjing behind him, to devote his life instead to preaching and studying in Hong Kong—for if events in the wider sphere continued as they were going, he believed, surely all of China would be thrown open to the missionaries in time.

Hong Rengan, for his part, seemed to take Legge's advice to heart, and the years marched past. He took on a range of duties—visiting prisoners in the jail and preaching in the hospital, as well as traveling with Legge. There was an Anglo-Chinese College founded by missionaries, where Hong Rengan taught Chinese history and literature to Chinese Christian students, and he also helped Legge with his Confucian translations, leading Legge through the interpretations of the classics he had mastered for his now-abandoned dream of becoming a civil servant in the Qing Empire.[31] As the civil war in north China ground to a stalemate and the south of the country convulsed with reprisals, Hong Rengan worked safely, quietly, and efficiently as Legge's assistant in Hong Kong, far out of reach both of his brethren in the Taiping and of the Qing authorities, who would execute him on the spot if they could catch him.

Even more significantly for later events, Hong Rengan also gained an enormous amount of knowledge about life outside China during those years in Hong Kong. Not, perhaps, as much as Yung Wing, with his Yale education and years of residence in the United States, but certainly worlds more than any other supporter of the Taiping movement. Though still technically in China, Hong Kong was a node linked to the wider world of the British Empire. In the schools run by the missionaries and in the books they translated to promote the strengths and discoveries of their own civilization, he learned about European and American ideas of political economy, science, medicine, government administration, and even military science.[32] He saw the workings of the British colony—the ways in which life was ordered, the place of trade in its economy, the place of the church in its moral life. These were glimpses of a society far removed from the one he had known, and they left impressions he would long carry with him. Above all, though, it was an idyllic life in those years, and he and Legge interspersed their studies and preaching with hikes in the hills above the city. Through four years of warfare on the mainland, they enjoyed a life dominated by books, sermons, and picnics.[33]

But Hong Rengan's popularity cut both ways. For he was popular—

indeed, enormously popular—not just with the missionaries but also with the crowds of Chinese that gathered around him whenever he ventured out, the crowds of refugees driven to Hong Kong by the specter of the execution grounds in Canton. James Legge knew full well that those who pressed against Hong Rengan as he stepped off at the dock weren't asking him about religion, at least not in Legge's sense. They were asking about his cousin and the rebellion, and whether he would lead them to Nanjing and the Heavenly Kingdom. Other missionaries whispered that if Hong Rengan could just get to Nanjing, he could be the one to correct their doctrines after everything he had learned in Hong Kong. He could, single-handedly, be the man to bring true Christianity to China at last. And it was those missionaries who, behind Legge's back, had their way in the end.

Hong Rengan disappeared while Legge was away for home leave in the late spring of 1858. Other missionaries gave him money for the trip and promised a stipend for the family members he left behind, but with regard to Legge—who steadfastly told him to stay away from the Taiping—it was a secret. He left one record of his state of mind when he gave up the safety of Hong Kong. It was an optimistic poem of departure, the voice of a solitary traveler finally awakened, preparing to rejoin his family and his congregation:

> The southern flight of wild geese awakens me from my bed, and
> I arise to confront the wind-blown sails and the shining banks of the river.
> There are no musicians to honor my departure, so
> I'll write my own lines to fly on a banner from the mast.
>
> My thoughts are as deep as the spring grass, waving green;
> Though mountains divide them, the geese throng with excitement.
> Roll up your sleeves and steer your boat, pay no mind to me.
> From this point onward, the hero's powers will know no boundary.[34]

This time he didn't take a load of Bibles or a telescope, nor did he have the convenience of a steamship. He didn't take the crowds who had thronged him in Hong Kong or even the few family members who had managed to join him there. He left his older brother behind as head servant in Legge's household, where he would be safe. Then he set off alone, in disguise, to attempt the journey overland across seven hundred miles of war-torn Chinese countryside to Nanjing.

CHAPTER 2

NEUTRALITY

In early May 1858, eighteen hundred miles up the coast from where Hong Rengan was preparing for his departure, the 1,287-ton paddle steamer HMS *Furious* bobbed and creaked in the cold, muddy waters nine miles off China's northeastern shore. Pacing the deck was James Bruce, the eighth Earl of Elgin, stout of body, ruddy of complexion, and disarmingly gentle of demeanor. The *Furious* was his flagship, the linchpin in a fleet of twenty-one ships assembled by the governments of Britain and France that sat, ominously, waiting for orders from its joint commanders. They would have been within sight of shore if it hadn't been for the weather, a thick fog that boiled in spite of the howling winds, made painful by sandlike grit blowing down from the plains of Manchuria. Roughly once a week it cleared enough for the sailors to spot the defenses along the flat strip of shore marking the entrance of the waterway that led, eventually, to the imperial capital, Beijing. This was the mouth of the Peiho, the White River, which spread wide over six miles of shoreline in a bar only a couple of feet deep at low tide, and the defenses were the forts at Taku—five of them arranged along the two banks of the river's mouth. The Taku forts were the maritime gateway to the capital and the single most strategically important naval fortification on the entire Chinese coast.[1]

The French-British alliance was a new and tentative one, dating from the recently ended Crimean War, and France had sent Baron Gros to join Lord Elgin as joint commander of the expedition. A diplomatic party from the United States tagged along in a neutral capacity, as did the old enemy from the Crimea, Russia. The Americans sailed on the *Mississippi* and the Russians, confusingly enough, on the *Amerika*. To make the point that this was indeed a joint expedition, the French flagship *Audacieuse* served as the meeting space for the four countries' agents as they waited for the weather to clear.

Lord Elgin knew that his home government wanted him to take pains to show that Britain wasn't after a monopoly on the China trade, so it was vital that the French participate in this expedition as belligerents. For the same reason, he wished the Americans and Russians would abandon their neutral stance as well. The so-called treaty ports in Shanghai and down the coast were open to all, even though it was British guns that had opened them in the Opium War. Hong Kong alone was a true British colony, and that was a source of some small embarrassment. In any case, if this fleet should succeed in its mission, he knew that the neutral Americans and Russians would gain every concession and trading right the British and French sailors planned to risk their lives for, but without lifting a finger. That was a minor annoyance, though it at least helped support Britain's pretense that her goals in China were unselfish. As long as at least the French also manned their guns, Elgin could honorably claim that any fight with China's imperial government that might ensue was for the higher principles of trade and international relations, not for the expansion of the British Empire.

The fleet's presence had nothing to do with the war between the Qing dynasty and the Taiping, at least not that its commanders intended. Foreign governments had uniformly avoided taking sides in the Chinese civil war, preferring a principled stand of neutrality that cloaked a more calculating desire to wait and see which side would emerge victorious. Not that the same could be said for their individual citizens, a number of whom found gainful if short-lived careers as mercenaries for the imperial government, which paid "skipper's wages" in comparison to the paltry salaries of their own countries' services.[2] In 1855, the British governor of Hong Kong tried to stop the flow of opportunists from Hong Kong and Shanghai into the war zones by issuing a formal order that all British subjects in China must maintain "strict neutrality . . . between the different parties at present contending for dominion in that empire" and promising prison time or a hefty fine for any Crown subjects who violated neutrality.[3] The order, which carried the force of law, managed well enough to restrict intervention from the regular military, but it hardly mattered to the "deserters from ships, and unlucky gold-diggers from California" who formed the bulk of the mercenaries, and who avoided the governor's order by simply renouncing their British citizenship and becoming Americans. "Englishmen as such," noted one observer to the process, "disappeared from the stage altogether."[4]

Neutrality, however, could take many forms, and several foreigners with diplomatic clout—especially missionaries who cited Hamberg's evidence that the rebels were Christian—had gone so far as to advocate recognition of the Taiping as an independent government. Peter Parker, an American missionary who served as the U.S. commissioner in 1856, sent back dispatches to Washington claiming that public opinion in the Qing Empire had shifted decisively in favor of the rebels,[5] while another American missionary, William Alexander Parsons Martin, published an open letter to the U.S. government in 1857 declaring that the Taiping regime had "achieved its own independence" and that there now were, de facto, two Chinas. The new Christian Chinese state based in Nanjing would rule the rich tea- and silk-producing regions of the Yangtze Valley and to the south, he predicted, while the older China of the Manchus would continue to govern the extreme north from Beijing. He believed that the Manchu government was "too far gone in senility to afford any encouraging prospect of reformation" and therefore suggested that the foreign powers "consider the expediency of recognizing its youthful rival which, catching the spirit of the age, may be prevailed upon to unlock the treasures of the interior and throw open its portals to unrestricted intercourse."[6] The latter missionary now served as secretary and interpreter to the U.S. representative in Elgin's fleet.

Regardless of whether it formally recognized the Taiping, Britain's neutrality in the civil war did not inhibit it from picking its own separate fight with the Manchus at precisely the same time. Indeed, the fact that the Taiping had already brought the dynasty to its knees made for quite a nice window of opportunity. The rebels were draining off the dynasty's best resources and disrupting traffic on the Grand Canal, the centuries-old inland waterway that carried grain from the south to supply Beijing. Without grain shipments, Beijing would starve, and the capital's residents lived a precarious and fearful existence. Into this fragile state of affairs entered Britain with a new war on China—if it really deserved to be called a war—a haphazard and undirected one, entirely one-sided, that had grown from its increasingly forceful attempts to revise the 1842 treaty from the Opium War to give British merchants even greater access to Chinese markets. On the slimmest of pretexts (the 1856 arrest by Qing authorities in Canton of a Chinese smuggling ship named the *Arrow,* which happened to fly the British flag and whose boarding was thus taken as an insult to the British Crown), the Hong Kong governor demanded action, and back in London Lord Palmerston, the prime minister, dispatched Elgin on a mission to China in 1857, charging him to gain reparations and a new treaty at almost any cost. That meant negotiating with the emperor himself, or at least a commissioner stationed close enough to Beijing to speak on his behalf, which meant Elgin had to take his forces right to the emperor's doorstep at the Peiho.

There had been several delays along the way. Elgin left England with a respectable force of 1,700 troops in 1857, but as they passed through Ceylon on their way to China, the Sepoy Mutiny broke out in India. The desperate British governor in Calcutta begged Elgin to loan him the men, which he did. Elgin's troops proved indispensable during the bloody siege of Delhi that summer, and some said they turned the tide of the mutiny in Britain's favor.[7] But it derailed his own mission, and he had to stay for a time in India as a guest in the governor-general's opulent Calcutta mansion. There, in the very quintessence of colonial decadence, Elgin began to confront a certain discomfort that had been growing inside him since he had left on his mission: namely, that he found the conduct of his countrymen in Asia morally repulsive. As he wrote in Calcutta, "It is a terrible business, . . . this living among inferior races"—terrible, he meant, not because of the treatment of the natives per se but because the ostensibly civilized British degraded themselves when they assumed the position of racial superiors. Under such circumstances, he believed, all notions of Christian benevolence were forgotten, and with British men and women alike, all that remained in their minds was "detestation, contempt, ferocity, vengeance, whether Chinamen or Indians be the object."[8]

Nevertheless, he found himself drawn partly into their world and acknowledged with a measure of sarcasm that the awkward feeling of being surrounded by native servants "soon wears off, and one moves among them with perfect indifference, treating them, not as dogs, because in that case one would whistle to them and pat them, but as machines with which one can have no communion or sympathy."[9] Elgin's misgivings about Britain's colonial project in India helped compound his already ambivalent feelings about his country's past conduct in China, which he had studied on the voyage over. "It is impossible to read the blue-books," he wrote, "without feeling that we have often acted toward the Chinese in a manner which it is very difficult to justify." Though as with his musings on India, his line of thinking in this case did not lead to any particular sympathy for the oppressed; "and yet their treachery and cruelty," he concluded about the Chinese, "come out so strongly at times as to make almost anything appear justifiable."[10]

Leaving India with little more than a borrowed ship and a troubled conscience, Elgin had to wait several months in Hong Kong before new reinforcements arrived to replace the troops he had left behind in Calcutta. By then it was too late in the season to sail up the Peiho, which had frozen over with winter ice; Beijing would be landlocked until the spring. Anxious for some kind of productive action, he rallied with the French to bomb and then occupy the balmier southern city of Canton instead. It wasn't a perfect substitute for direct contact with the emperor in Beijing, but they hoped their display of firepower in the south would at least get the sovereign's attention. They didn't, however, realize the role they had begun to play in the civil war. For when they invaded and took possession of Canton, they also quite unintentionally put an end to the gruesome program of anti-Taiping executions under its governor-general—who happened to be the same official who had ordered the capture of the *Arrow*. British troops hunted him down for alleged crimes against the British Crown, and captured him as he tried to escape out the back of a colleague's home. They tied him up and shipped him off to India, where he would die in British captivity.

Now, after the spring thaw, here they finally were at the mouth of the Peiho, waiting patiently for an imperial commissioner to come and give them their new treaty. The weeks passed with a boredom numbing even to those who made their lives on ships. The vessels rocked sickeningly in the muddy swells, the bay so shallow that at nine miles out they sat at anchor in just twenty-five feet of water. By day there were the fog and sometimes the distant thread of shore; by night the black water glowed with a brilliant phosphorescence that served as the only reminder that there was supposed to be some kind of magic in this "celestial kingdom," as those who had never been there liked to imagine it.[11] Stores were running low. Some of the sailors sketched or read to pass the time; others took potshots at seagulls. The marines practiced drills in preparation for a land invasion.

Occasionally a junk-rigged ship with ribbed sails ventured out from shore carrying a handful of Qing officials under a flag of truce. The diplomatic discussions were empty, but the visits at least broke the monotony of the day, and all could sit down to a meal together. The French ambassador, Baron Gros, couldn't quite read the imperial officials or their motives, and the typical exchange found the Europeans asking to be allowed upriver to negotiate their treaty peacefully, while the Manchus made excuses to put them off. At one point an imperial official mentioned offhand that they weren't really all that concerned if the Allied fleet should decide to shell the forts, because the soldiers manning them were "merely Chinese." It was a bluff, perhaps (yet perhaps not), but in any case it was a clear reminder that this was an empire of two races—the ruling Manchus and the subject Chinese—which made the Europeans uncomfortable.[12]

As the weather cleared, the smaller boats made reconnaissance trips near the shore, close enough to see through a spyglass that the giant brass guns were being pushed on wheels to track them and the matches were kept lit and ready to fire the fuses. A boom had been laid across the main channel to block ships from passing. The French interpreter was disappointed by the landscape. "A country more parched, desolate, and miserable, it is impossible to imagine," he wrote. "Nothing is to be seen but mud, slime, salt-pans and a few sand-hills. Not a trace of vegetation meets the eye."[13] Proper intelligence was hard to come by, and they had to rely on the cagey Russians, whose shared border with the Qing Empire meant closer relations. A teacher who had just returned from a Russian college in Beijing reported that the emperor was livid at the demands of the foreigners, and few of his ministers dared to speak to him about anything having to do with diplomatic affairs. As the empire crumbled around him, the rumors said that Xianfeng was spending most of his time on horseback, trotting idly about the wooded parts of the Summer Palace grounds with his concubines.

A commissioner never materialized, and so on May 20, 1858, at eight minutes past ten in the morning, the fleet attacked. A signal flag went up, and the HMS *Cormorant*, its crew lying flat and hugging the deck, built up to full speed and smashed, shuddering, through the boom blocking the river, opening the route for the rest of the fleet. A trio of gunboats, one British and two French, took up position to attack the two forts on the north bank while three others attacked the south.[14] Pulling up the rear, six of the light gunboats towed launches with a landing party totaling 1,800 British and French marines. The initial response from the forts was more spirited than they expected, and it was hardly a textbook advance. One of the French ships got its screw caught in a fishing net and bobbed, helpless, for fifteen minutes in a hail of shot that killed eleven of her crew. But the Taku gunners had set their aim high, not expecting an attack at low tide, and most of their salvoes whistled harmlessly through the ships' rigging (Chinese cannons were lashed into place with ropes, so it was no simple matter to adjust their angle of elevation on the fly).[15] It was the erroneous shots, falling short of their mark, that proved most deadly. One French ensign's head was ripped off by a cannonball. Another shot cut a midshipman on the *Dragonne* neatly in two, the halves of his body flipping overboard as his sword fell clattering to the deck.[16]

As the Allied gunships took up positions, they laid in with broadsides of canister and grapeshot. Congreve rockets guided by long stabilizers hissed in fiery arcs to explode against the walls. The forts had been designed to withstand small-caliber fire from coastal pirates and Chinese rebels, and the gunners inside were largely unprotected from the shells of the British and French cannons. The northern forts, though sturdily built, were arranged obliquely to the channel and open behind, leaving them completely exposed from the flank to the long-range guns of the *Cormorant* as it steamed upstream beyond them to get a good angle. As the dead piled up behind the fortifications, the landing party hit the muddy flat and slogged forward to the wall of the first fort, muskets in hand. The Qing commanders hadn't encountered this tactic before, so their gunners all but ignored the landing party, keeping the concentration of their fire on the ships.[17] As the marines and blue-jackets stormed the defenses, shrieking and whooping and firing their muskets, the defenders turned and ran. There were few casualties in the landing party, save a handful of French troops caught near a powder magazine when it exploded. From a safe distance, the American observers watched through their glasses as bodies of Frenchmen were lofted through the air and fell back to earth at a distance from the fort.[18]

In the end, the invaders counted five hundred Chinese troops dead while the rest of the roughly three thousand who defended the forts had apparently scattered. It was nothing less than the fleet's commanders expected. (A *New York Times* correspondent who sailed on the American ship went so far as to brag that "The Allies must always be victorious where they can bring their floating batteries to bear.")[19] Elgin was certainly not surprised. Notwithstanding the Royal Navy's wisdom that "a ship's a fool to fight a fort," he had never imagined that the native Chinese defenses would hold out for long against his battle-hardened Crimean War veterans. He was, however, somewhat sniffy toward the French, who in his words had "blundered a good deal with their gunboats, and then contrived to get blown up by setting fire to a powder magazine."[20] The joint forces looted the forts, filling their ships with money, food, and especially the heavy brass cannons that were the real prize, worth hundreds of thousands of dollars apiece for the metal they contained. The inscriptions showed them to be new, cast during Xianfeng's reign. They also took note that despite the easy victory, the defenders' weapons weren't nearly as primitive as they had expected. Some of the guns were even British, salvaged from shipwrecks or purchased secretly in Shanghai, and the sandbag fortifications were professionally laid out. The victory was more one of training than of matériel. Nearby camps held glimpses of Qing military discipline: a soldier's body, beheaded for running away from his station; and, more disconcerting to European eyes, the body of one fort's commander, throat slit by his own hand in defeat.[21]

Bidding farewell to the larger ships, which drew too much water to cross the bar, the ambassadors and their entourages crowded onto the boats with shallower draft and entered the channel. The peasants watching from shore seemed terrified, and at one of the first villages they passed, the men all prostrated themselves on the ground by the side of the river, shouting something that Elgin's interpreter translated (awkwardly) as "Hail, great king! Oh pray be pleased to disembark and reign over us!"[22] As Elgin's secretary saw it, "The villagers were clearly under the impression that we were on our way to upset the dynasty."[23] It was not an unreasonable assumption. These were the first foreign ships to sail up the Peiho in anyone's memory, a fact of which captains and crew alike were proudly aware. Not that there hadn't been British ambassadors here before—Lord Amherst had come in 1816 and Lord Macartney before him in 1793. But those missions had been forced by Xianfeng's imperial ancestors to fly the distinguishing flag of a tribute mission come to honor the Qing throne. So now, as Elgin's fleet advanced up the river under their own national colors, they imagined themselves avenging the humiliations of the past—and, more even than that, finally teaching a lesson to an empire whose officials thought of them as barbarians.[24]

Beneath the pride, however, Elgin mused darkly on the other kind of uncharted territory into which they were embarking. "Whose work are we engaged in," he asked in a letter home, "when we burst thus with hideous violence and brutal energy into these darkest and most mysterious recesses of the traditions of the past?" But as with his earlier broodings, he did not find the necessary element of romance in his heart that would defend China on its own grounds, and he concluded almost nihilistically, "At the same time, there is certainly not much to regret in the old civilisation which we are thus scattering to the winds."[25]

They anchored that first night about twenty miles upriver from the forts. Bonfires blazed on the shore, conjuring demons in the murky shadows and setting the spans of the ships aglow in flickering outline against the blackened sky.[26]

The slow navigation up the Peiho toward Tianjin continued the next morning. The river meandered so lazily that the distance by water was at least twice that on land, but this was the only way to get the big guns to a place where they could unnerve the emperor. The riverbed was shallow and thick with sediment, so even the light gunships ran aground constantly; one of the French vessels grounded thirty-two times, another forty-two. Yet slowly they made their way, and slowly the river unraveled its mysteries; at one turn a human corpse edged into view, half buried in the mud of the riverbank. If it seemed abandoned by the world of men, not so for the two snarling bulldogs who fought over it, twisting to find an angle on each other's throat, forepaws pressed against the rotting carcass to stake their claim.[27]

The hours passed patiently, and the men on the ships saw neither imperial soldiers nor any kind of overt hostility from the crowds of peasants that traced their progression from shore, walking along beside them as the ships puffed their white smoke and pushed upstream against the current. These were not the howling masses of Chinese made famous by missionaries under attack. Nor did they appear as the incensed citizens of a nation invaded. The men on board the ships could find nothing to indicate whether they cared one way or the other about the fate of their emperor. (Indeed, for the mass of Chinese peasants the existence of the emperor was a distant abstraction, a choice made by Heaven in which they had no part.) As the fleet climbed the river without incident, the initial fear of the crowds gave way to a wary curiosity, even an odd sense of cooperation at times. When a ship ran aground in the mud, its crew would throw a rope to the crowd and the men on the shore would pull them free. This happened repeatedly. Some were paid for their efforts in ship's biscuits ("a great delicacy for them," the French attaché imagined), while others were paid in looped strings of copper cash looted from the Taku forts. There was more money, in exceedingly small denominations, than the crews knew what to do with; sometimes they simply flung handfuls of it at the crowd on the shore to watch the scramble.[28]

Upstream, mud gave way to intense cultivation—New World corn, millet, lettuce, radishes.[29] Piles of salt mined from the saline flats broke the monotony of the landscape, standing like cairns marking an uncertain path. A distant pagoda broke free from its shroud of mist. As the aggressors slid along into the reach of the walled city of Tianjin, the mud houses that flanked the river give way to denser wooden structures. Here was the junction of the Grand Canal, and mountains of rice and other grains lay along one bank—the tax revenues of the central government, what it had managed to collect from the territories that weren't cut off by the rebellion. Here the throngs of watchers became denser as well, crowding the rooftops to view the fleet, "an oblique plane of upturned faces and bare heads" that "extended almost from the surface of the water to the eaves of the houses."[30] As the boats in the river parted to give the fleet passage and the dynasty's soldiers failed to materialize, the European crews finally shattered the tense silence with a loud cheer. "We felt Tianjin was ours," recalled the captain of the *Furious*, "and that in it we held . . . the throat of China!"[31]

They anchored in Tianjin and gave up on the final overland leg to Beijing seventy miles away. The summer heat topped a hundred degrees in the sun, and European soldiers accustomed to cooler climates could barely move, let alone haul their weapons and equipment for miles through the brutal heat to the capital city. But their invasion this far was enough; the emperor capitulated and sent commissioners to negotiate a treaty that would keep them from moving beyond Tianjin. So they took up quarters for the month, Lord Elgin and Baron Gros claiming one of the grandest homes in the city as their headquarters, the British living in one half and the French in the other. The Americans and Russians rented a house across the river, though its owner offered to pay them money to stay away from it (wisely, it would turn out, when imperial officials punished anyone who held willing commerce with the invaders). The imperial commissioners soon arrived and began the negotiations for new treaties—four of them, one for each of the powers that sent a representative. Not that it was in any way an equal exchange, with the gunships bristling with ordnance moored expectantly in the river.

Britain's resulting Treaty of Peace, Friendship and Commerce, titled without a whit of intended irony, was one to delight the foreign merchants. According to its terms, British ships would now have the right to sail up the Yangtze, China's main artery reaching from Shanghai deep into central and western China. Beyond the five coastal treaty ports already open to foreign trade, ten others would be opened in the north, on Taiwan, and inland along the great Yangtze. To please the missionaries, who held such sway with the Americans, there were stipulations that foreigners could travel wherever they wanted in the empire and that native Christians would be protected (this was not, of course, understood to apply to the Taiping). Also, Qing officials weren't to be allowed to call the British "barbarians" anymore, not even in their private communications. The French, Russian, and American ministers all signed their own separate treaties in kind.

But beyond any of those terms, the clause of the treaty that troubled the Xianfeng emperor the most was the one that granted Britain the right to station an ambassador in Beijing, who would be allowed to come and go whenever he pleased. It had not been approved in advance, and as the dynasty depended above all on prestige to sustain its rule, it was potentially the most devastating. The emperor's stature had already been brought low by the ongoing war with the Taiping, but at least the influence of the rebels was in check and the north of China remained nominally in imperial hands. Nominally, that is, because in the vacuum of power as the Qing concentrated its best forces against Nanjing, bandit rebellions under a group loosely known as the Nian had broken out in the north and ravaged the countryside through which the fleet had just come.

On top of all this, to have foreign ships sailing up and down the main ceremonial waterway to the capital, carrying their ambassadors to and fro with no sign of tribute, no acknowledgment of the emperor's prestige—in full view of the river-dwelling public—meant that rumors would spread through the empire that the dynasty was not only incapable of keeping order within the country but also unable to command the respect of foreigners anymore. It would sever what slim threads of legitimacy the emperor still enjoyed. As a small reassurance, the commissioner who agreed to the clause suggested to Xianfeng that the treaties were nothing more than slips of paper to make the barbarians leave Tianjin, and the emperor could easily cancel them if he wished.[32] And so the foreign envoys were bid farewell to return to their home countries, with an appointment to return in one year with ratified copies of the treaties for exchange in Beijing. Xianfeng hoped very much that that would never happen.

Despite having just established himself for posterity as the figurehead of British gunboat diplomacy in China, Lord Elgin regretted his invasion of Tianjin—and indeed was ashamed of the whole sequence of events that had led up to it. The affair of the smuggling ship *Arrow* that had sparked Britain's new China war was, in his words, "a scandal to us."[33] But he knew that his misgivings put him in a minority. The massive weight of British public opinion came down firmly on the side of war with China (that is to say, war with its imperial masters, the Qing) for rejecting trade and insulting the British Crown. Against this popular sentiment, the majority Liberals in Parliament had in 1857 mounted a conscientious attempt to block Prime Minister Palmerston's call for war, with the young William Gladstone giving a fully two-hour-long speech ("the finest delivered in the memory of man in the House of Commons," according to one excited partisan) in which he charged that "the whole might of England" was about to be unleashed "against the lives of a defenceless people" in China.[34] When the vote in the Commons went Gladstone's way, Lord Palmerston simply dissolved the government and held new elections—dubbed the "Chinese elections" by the British press—which returned Palmerston's prowar faction to power in a popular landslide. Whatever Elgin's private misgivings might be, he knew exactly what his countrymen desired. And as he noted in his journal in November, a few months after the invasion of Tianjin, if the tone of the British papers was any indication, the public back home would have preferred that he had used far *more* force and "plundered the wretched Chinese to a greater extent than is the case."[35]

The craving for war with China's imperial government was abundant even in the United States, where news of the treaty arrived in record time, leading the first substantive news dispatch over the just-completed transatlantic cable.[36] A joyful response greeted the news of trade concessions, but the joy was tempered by grumblings of frustration—not because the youthful, righteous United States had been tainted by association with the predatory gunships of Britain and France but because it hadn't led the way. In an implicit attack on President James Buchanan's own policy of neutrality, a *New York Times* editorial declared that "the French and English, in commencing a war which must sooner or later bring the Chinese Government to terms, adopted the wiser and more politic course."[37] The new treaty held unprecedented value, the editors maintained, and constituted the "entire abandonment of that seclusive policy which has ruled in China from periods beyond the reach of history." It ensured that "one-third of the population of the globe . . . is opened to evangelical enterprise." Such grand results, they declared, proved beyond doubt "the necessity of maintaining a large military and naval force within striking distance of the capital."[38] In a separate editorial entitled (shortsightedly) "End of the China War," they even went so far as to declare that this treaty at gunpoint had been necessary because "force was the only argument which the Chinese could be made to recognize." American neutrality, far from being a point of moral pride, was for them instead a badge of weakness and passivity, for "in a matter of such great interest to us as our trade with China, we have allowed others to do the work and reap the honour, while we are content enough to pocket the profits."[39]

As a contrast to the model of aggressive diplomacy in China that so disturbed his conscience, Elgin was relieved to depart from Tianjin at the end of July and sail to China's smaller neighbor Japan, under instructions to sign a similar trade agreement with the government there. The conditions could hardly have been more different. The ruling Tokugawa Shogunate in Japan held every bit as much disdain for British trade and proselytizing as its counterpart government in China did, but it benefited from Japan's secondary status in East Asia—which proved an advantage when the vastness of Chinese markets ensured that the British guns aimed there first. Influential samurai in Japan had watched from the sidelines as Britain's ships broke China open in the Opium War of 1839 to 1842, so when the American commodore Matthew Perry first arrived on Japan's shore with a fleet of steamships in 1853, they sidestepped China's fate by willingly signing a trade agreement with him. By the time Elgin arrived in 1858 to open Great Britain's relations with Japan, the Japanese not only had a precedent in their treaty relations with the United States but also knew exactly what had happened so recently at the Taku forts when the Manchus had tried to block his advance.

With more than sufficient warning, the Japanese government swallowed its pride and welcomed Elgin and his ships without resistance. It agreed to a set of treaties parallel to the Chinese ones, with no exercise of violence.[40] In contrast to the mounting belligerence between Britain and the Qing dynasty, the Japanese fired a salute in Elgin's honor. The shogun's friendly diplomacy had its desired effect, and Elgin remembered the Japanese as "the nicest people possible. None of the stiffness and bigotry of the

Chinese."[41] That same lack of belligerence helped soothe Elgin's guilt over his country's broader conduct in Asia. On leaving Japan he wrote that it was "the only place which I have left with any feeling of regret since I reached this abominable East—abominable not so much in itself, as because it is strewed all over with the records of our violence and fraud."[42] The return to China, however, filled him with "a sort of terror."[43]

By the late autumn of 1858, Elgin's mission in Asia was complete, but before returning to England he took three weeks to make a voyage with a small fleet of five ships up the Yangtze River—through the Taiping-held territories—to the new treaty port of Hankow. Of all the ports opened by the treaty, Hankow was the one farthest up the river, and it was currently in imperial hands. On record, Elgin wanted to test whether Chinese officials on the river respected the status of the British flag under the new treaty, but it was also a chance to see the realm of the rebels. He had heard vague rumors about the Taiping while in Shanghai but wanted to gauge them for himself firsthand. Though the Tianjin treaty gave British ships the right to sail freely on the Yangtze, it was signed with only one of the two powers that controlled stretches of the river, and Elgin found the situation artificial. "As we have seen fit to affect neutrality between the Emperor of China and the rebels," he wrote to the foreign secretary, "we could not, of course, without absurdity, require him to give us rights and protection in places actually occupied by a Power which we treat with the same respect as his own."[44] In this case the neutrality of Britain in China's internecine war was, he recognized, an affectation, for no course of action involving the one party in China could be undertaken without benefit or disadvantage to the other.

From what little Elgin could see from the bridge of the *Furious* and a few short excursions inland, the impact of the civil war was more devastating than anyone in Shanghai had led him to believe. "I never before saw such a scene of desolation," he reported of the city of Zhenjiang, which stood at the strategic junction where the Grand Canal, which ran north toward the capital, met the Yangtze. Imperial forces had recovered Zhenjiang from the Taiping less than a year earlier, and nothing was left after the fighting but "heaps of ruins, intersected by a few straggling streets."[45] As another in his party described it, "[We] might have imagined ourselves in Pompeii. We walked along deserted streets, between roofless houses, and walls overgrown with rank, tangled weeds; heaps of rubbish blocked up the thoroughfares, but they obstructed nobody."[46] No more than a few hundred residents remained, scratching out a ghostly existence in a city that had held more than three hundred thousand before the war. The desolation of Zhenjiang was hardly isolated. As Elgin noted grimly in his account, "In order to save repetition I may here observe, once for all, that with certain differences of degree, this was the condition of every city which I visited on my voyage up and down the Yang-tze."[47]

Elgin's first direct contact with the rebels came in the form of a cannonball that sailed over the deck of his ship as the fleet worked its way upriver past Nanjing. He hadn't expected any hostilities, planning somewhat obtusely to slip past the main Taiping shore batteries on his way up to Hankow, sending a gunship ahead with a white flag of truce—which, however, had no particular meaning to the rebels. The defenders took Elgin's ships for imperial forces (which in fact clustered eagerly to Elgin's rear, hoping to use his fleet as a wedge to attack the rebel capital) and fired steadily on them as they steamed past, killing one British sailor and wounding two others. Elgin, oddly and perhaps undeservedly charmed, escaped injury, though one ball went right through his cabin and several others cut the rigging just above his head. "I hope the Rebels will make some communication, and enable us to explain that we mean them no harm," he wrote afterward, "but it is impossible to anticipate what these stupid Chinamen will do." In response, he sent his gunships back downriver the next morning to hammer on the rebel forts until, as he put it, "we had done enough for our honour."[48]

Once the Taiping commanders figured out what Elgin's small fleet represented, they began sending communications—first to apologize for firing on his ships and then to recruit him to help in their war against the Qing dynasty. Shortly after the cannonade at Nanjing, Elgin received a communiqué from a Taiping commander who asked Elgin and the other British captains "with all your heart and might, to assist [me] in annihilating the rebel vessels" (the rebels being, in this case, the imperialists who stood against the Taiping). He promised that they would be rewarded with honorific titles from the Heavenly King.[49] Elgin demurred. Later that day, a party of Taiping rebels came down to the water and gave him a gift of twelve fowls and some red cloth. A month later, on Christmas Day 1858, as his fleet passed the walled city of Anqing on its way back down to Shanghai, he received a letter from the Heavenly King himself, Hong Xiuquan, inviting him to join the Taiping in their divine mission of destroying the Manchus.

"The Father and the Elder Brother led me to rule the Heavenly Kingdom, to sweep away and exterminate the devilish spirits, bestowing on me great honor," wrote the Heavenly King to Lord Elgin. "Foreign younger brothers of the western ocean, listen to my words. Join us in doing service to the Father and Elder Brother and extinguishing the stinking reptiles."[50] As different as it may have been in language and origin, the intent of the message wasn't so far removed from the wish of Elgin's home public in England that he make war on the Manchus.

Some of the communications went to individual commanders, and on the same day Elgin received his letter from Hong Xiuquan, the captain of HMS *Retribution* received an exceedingly polite note from a local Taiping official, expressing hope for a gift of some foreign rifles and cannons. The British captain replied with equal politeness that the guns were for their own use and that "our country's law prohibits us from giving aid to either party in a conflict." Two days later, the Taiping commander wrote again to say that he hadn't meant to imply that he wanted the large cannons on board the gunship but only "one or two small cannons, some packs of gunpowder, and ten or more gun barrels." He understood that Great Britain had legal strictures against sharing artillery and other weapons but appealed to their shared Christianity. You and I, he wrote, "are both sons of the Heavenly Father, God, and are both younger brothers of the Heavenly Elder Brother, Jesus. Our feelings towards each other are like those of brothers, and our friendship is as intimate as that of two brothers of the same parentage."[51]

That shared Christianity was the most difficult quandary of the British presence in China. For Britain believed itself to be a Christian country, and the appeals of the Taiping scarcely fell on deaf ears. Furthermore, coming as they did at a time when Britain and France had just concluded (they thought) a new war against the Qing dynasty—at a time when the Taiping's hopes for an alliance with the foreigners contrasted so sharply with the long-standing Manchu efforts to keep them out—it seemed clear that in many ways what the British wanted in China was something they were far more likely to get from the rebels than from the imperial authorities. Certainly no one in the Qing government had ever referred to a Briton as his "brother."

There were, however, two major obstacles standing in the way. The first was the principle of neutrality—the idea being that to enter into friendly relations with the Taiping might cause further damage to the Qing, damage Elgin already regretted having caused, and that Britain would thus be taking a side in the civil war against its own declared principles. In other words, neutrality effectively dictated that if Great Britain were at war with the Manchus it shouldn't at the same time be friendly to the Taiping. The other issue was whether the Taiping were really Christian in the same sense as England, and that was something the missionaries were still trying to figure out.

Elgin's inclination to keep the rebels at arm's length was reinforced by the advice of his interpreter, Thomas F. Wade. Wade was reputed by some people—by no means all—to have the best language skills of any Englishman in China (in a later career, he would be the first professor of Chinese at Cambridge), and, in an important departure from the missionaries who translated for the Americans, his background was military. He had come to China as a lieutenant in the 98th Regiment and learned the language by brute force: fifteen hours a day of study with teachers in Hong Kong. His teachers had been government employees and, to a lesser extent, military officers, with the result that he possessed a strong command of the language of bureaucratic communications and most of his information and opinion came from government publications. His circle of acquaintances included high-ranking Chinese officials, the elite of Chinese society, in contrast to the poor and downtrodden souls among whom the Protestant missionaries spent most of their time. If the missionaries had gone to China in hopes of empowering the lowest classes, Wade's respects came to lie instead with the elites. As the rebels were from the poorest classes of Chinese and from the "uncivilized" south near Canton, none of them exhibited the level of culture and refinement he had come to admire in his imperial counterparts. And so he, in contrast to most of the missionaries, was utterly contemptuous of them.[52]

Wade's contempt came through clearly in the language of his written reports. One of his first Taiping visits during the Yangtze voyage was to a fort "which was in general very ill-armed and filthy," where the commander was "a dirty, but not ill-looking man, in a yellow robe, with a handkerchief wrapped around his head." Wade noted that his guide and the commander were both Cantonese and that "the hall was soon filled with a number of men, speaking the dialect of Canton." They crowded in, a "dense mob" with "not a semblance of order." A man who obligingly took down their order for supplies was "a particularly dirty Fujian man" who "wrote an execrable hand, and was evidently of no higher caste than his fellows," the whole lot of whom appeared to Wade "a gang of opium-smoking pirates."[53] The Taiping at Anqing, which he visited a few days later, likewise spoke Cantonese (he noted six times in a two-page report), and though they were "more healthy-looking, and better dressed" than the previous group, one who dared approach Wade at his boat "looked, what I have no doubt he was, an opium-smoking coolie."[54] As for the letter of apology from the Taiping for firing on Elgin's ships, Wade's flat judgment was that "As a specimen of Chinese composition the whole thing is much below par."[55]

As much as Elgin's combativeness toward the Qing government had delighted his countrymen, his disdain for the Taiping rebels exasperated them.[56] For the rebels controlled access to some of the richest tea- and silk-producing regions in China, and the British traders in Shanghai were desperate for access to them. The few ships that did manage to sneak upriver to trade with the rebels came back flush with rich cargo, and in the eyes of the foreigners in Shanghai, Elgin had squandered his chance to enter into a trade agreement with them. Rather than opening relations with the rebels, they complained, he preferred to stick to his insufferable principles and look to the day when the Qing would regain control of the river's full range—a day few desired to wait for, if they even believed it would ever come.

Elgin's reports had little to tell a curious public about the prospects of the Taiping for winning the war. On the one hand, he suggested that "there is little or nothing of popular sympathy with the rebel movement" in the areas he visited—though he admitted that most of the places he had actually visited were under imperial control. On the other hand, the Chinese he spoke with through Wade seemed to have no particular loyalty to the Manchu government either, and he gained the impression that "the general attitude of the population does not argue much enthusiasm on either side of the dynastic controversy," viewing as they did the ongoing civil war "with feelings akin to those with which they would have regarded earthquake, or pestilence, or any other providential scourge."[57]

Even as Elgin's and Wade's accounts described the utter ruin of the cities, however, they made clear that there was no way to know which side had caused the devastation. And though they painted the Taiping themselves as despicable and unpopular characters, they also brought evocative news that perhaps life in the Taiping-controlled regions wasn't as awful as the imperial rumors suggested. The cities may have been empty, but the rural areas held, by Elgin's observation, an "industrious, frugal, and sober population" that was, "generally speaking, well-doing and contented."[58]

Ultimately, Elgin came away from his voyage on the Yangtze even more disturbed about the moral implications of Britain's involvement in China than when he had arrived. He was desperate to return home and put Asia behind him for good, and when in January 1859 a group of British traders at Shanghai wrote a letter to thank him for the new treaties with China and Japan and "the valuable results which have been obtained,"[59] his response to them was scathing. "Uninvited, and by methods not always of the gentlest," he shot back, "we have broken down the barriers behind which these ancient nations sought to conceal from the world without the mysteries, perhaps also, in the case of China at least, the rags and rottenness of their waning civilizations." He admonished the merchants to consider the moral underpinnings of their desire for an open China. "Neither our own consciences nor the judgment of mankind will acquit us," he concluded, "if, when we are asked to what use we have turned our opportunities, we can only say that we have filled our pockets from among the ruins which we have found or made."[60]

In the early summer of 1859, exactly one year after the invasion of Tianjin, a new Allied fleet appeared at the mouth of the Peiho. This time Lord Elgin's role was played by his younger brother, Frederick Bruce, who had come along on the previous mission as a secretary to his older brother. When Elgin stayed on in China to explore the Yangtze, it was Frederick who had taken the treaty back to England to be ratified, and Prime Minister Palmerston had given him the honor of making him the British plenipotentiary and putting him in charge of the voyage back to China to make the exchange with the emperor. Once the ratified copies were exchanged, Frederick Bruce would take up residence in Beijing as Britain's first minister to China. Bruce was a shy man, still a bachelor at age forty-five, and he had a problem with blushing. He wore long whiskers to cover his face, though the bald top of his head would still turn red when he was embarrassed.[61]

Ratified treaty in hand, Frederick Bruce planned this time to sail up to Tianjin and then continue overland all the way to Beijing. There had been rumors that the emperor would try to put them off, but all involved knew from the Allied success at the forts the previous year that there was really nothing the imperial armies could do to stop them. So when a Qing emissary told Frederick Bruce that the emperor would not permit him to come to Beijing by way of the Peiho—but only by a secondary route used for tribute missions, which the British took as an insult—Bruce refused the change of course and insisted on sticking with the original plan. Thus in June 1859 the fleet took up its position once again in the muddy swells off the Taku shore, ready if necessary to force its way up the Peiho a second time.

This fleet was somewhat more fractious than the previous one. The French, having grown uneasy in their short-lived alliance with Britain, had momentarily lost their taste for battle in China and sent even fewer men than the Americans, only 60 Frenchmen out of a total Allied force of more than 1,300.[62] The commander of the American flagship USS *Powhatan*, Commodore Josiah Tattnall, was a veteran of the War of 1812 whose dislike of the British was exceeded only by that of his men—who were fresh from a knock-down rumble in the streets of Hong Kong with a crew of British sailors, after which "it got to be the proper thing to thrash an English sailor on sight."[63] When they arrived at the Peiho, they discovered, sure enough, that the crew of the British flagship was the same gang of sailors they had just brawled with in Hong Kong.

In the year since Elgin's attack on the Taku forts, the emperor had transferred his most trusted and capable general, a Mongol of rich lineage named Senggelinqin, to take charge of coastal defense. Senggelinqin was a relentless and proud commander with rank nearly equivalent to a blooded prince, who had won honor and fame by turning back the Taiping's northern campaign in 1853. In that campaign, a Taiping expeditionary force had fought its way northward from Nanjing all the way to within eighty miles of Beijing before Senggelinqin's troops—aided by a bitter winter that had ravaged the southerners, who had never in their lives seen snow—turned them back and forced them to fall inward into a village fortification for an intractable stalemate. When the weather broke that spring, Senggelinqin, in the grand feat that cemented his reputation, ordered his troops to build a dirt-and-stone wall to encircle the entire Taiping army camp from a distance, while a crew of one thousand laborers spent a month digging a series of trenches to connect it, via a dry riverbed, to the Grand Canal, forty miles away. When they opened the breach, the waters of the canal rushed in to fill the containing wall, flooding the Taiping camp to its rooftops and drowning the army of rebels into submission.

Senggelinqin had little but contempt for the foreign military and was reluctant to be called back from the internal wars to deal with coastal defense. A hard-bitten Mongolian cavalryman who preferred the bow and arrow to the musket, he had never encountered European gunships and put little stock in the tales of their invincibility.[64] Nor did he particularly understand the attention given to confronting a foreign army numbering in the hundreds while Taiping legions in the tens and hundreds of thousands roamed at will elsewhere in the empire. But after the Taku forts fell to Elgin in the summer of 1858, the emperor charged Senggelinqin with rebuilding them to ensure that they couldn't be stormed so easily again, and he took to the task with ardor.

Xianfeng's advisers disagreed bitterly about how to handle the scheduled return of the foreign fleet. Some advised accepting it, if not welcoming it. One adviser, a Chinese official named Guo Songtao, argued that it would be in the dynasty's best interests to grant the foreign powers the trade relations they sought and focus instead on fighting the rebels. Rebellion was internal, he said, a "danger of the stomach and heart," but the foreigners were external and wanted only trade, so the solution to the foreign problem lay with solving trade issues, not resorting to the military.[65]

Indeed, in the longer span of China's history, closure to the outside world was typically a sign of a dynasty's weakness, not its strength. The greatest dynasties of the past had overseen vast trading empires spanning half the globe, and they had commanded tribute from multitudes of vassal states. But the Xianfeng emperor ruled at a very weak time indeed, and he preferred the advice of counselors who promised him strength through closed borders. A small handful of close Manchu advisers fell on this side, as did Senggelinqin. To Senggelinqin's face, the moderate Guo Songtao argued for a peaceful approach. "We've never had any success to speak of with our coastal defenses," he said. "They are not effective, and we simply must not rely on them."[66] But Senggelinqin thought he could teach the Europeans a lesson when they came back, and that was just what the emperor wanted to hear. In spite of Guo Songtao's opposition, Senggelinqin went ahead with his preparations for war.[67]

To British scouts, the defenses appeared on sight to be somewhat improved—two visible booms across the river rather than one, and a certain amount of new construction on the forts. But there didn't appear to be many defenders, certainly none of the flags and gongs of an impending battle, and the portholes for the guns were covered with matting. Informers told them that there was just a skeleton crew, enough to keep Taiping junks from gaining access to the Peiho. So as an experiment they cut through the first boom, which appeared somewhat less substantial than the second. They encountered no resistance. On June 25, 1859, a fine, clear morning, the gunboats assembled about eight hundred yards from the forts. The signal flag was run up, and, in a direct repeat of the last round, the British admiral's ship, *Plover*, built up a full head of steam and charged forward to break through the second boom and smash open the waterway to the Peiho.[68]

That was when everything went wrong.

The Qing engineers had learned several lessons from the humiliation of 1858, and the new boom—made of full-sized tree trunks slung together lengthwise with heavy chains—stopped the *Plover*, shuddering, in its course. As the other gunships circled in the river, unable to advance, the mats covering the portholes were cast aside to reveal a full complement of defenders, and a thunderous cavalcade of shot and shell began to pour down from the forts. The first salvo took the head off the *Plover*'s bow gunner, and three other sailors fell to the deck wounded. For three hours the *Plover* foundered under heavy fire, until finally the hull burst and the ship sank into the mud; only one of her crew survived the day. The ships that brought up the rear fared no better, as Senggelinqin's men proved far more capable gunners than their poorly trained counterparts a year earlier. Two of the British gunships ran aground, useless, while two others were cut to splinters and sank outright. Others foundered, taking on water, trying to retreat as the smaller guns of the fort picked off their crews and officers man by man.

Yet the landing party surged ahead as planned, and that was when defeat turned into disaster. When the fort guns went silent in the early evening, the British officers took it to mean that the forces manning them had fled, as they had the previous year. Instead, it turned out to be a ruse to entice the landing party to storm the beach; this time, the defenders were prepared for the kind of attack that had surprised them the last time.[69] There were now two trenches in front of the walls filled with water and mud, wide and deep, with a vicious abatis of iron spikes immediately behind them.[70] But those mattered only if the marines could even get to the trenches; the landing had been delayed for so long that by the time their barges approached shore the tide was all the way out, and the thick mud of the exposed banks seized the feet of the attackers or caused them to fall, slipping in their thin-soled shoes, helplessly shot to pieces by the gunners on the fort. Cannons loaded with shreds of iron sprayed their loads over the infantry, mowing down whole rows of them in a blast, while those who made it to the trenches found a mixture of mud and water too thin to stand in and too thick for swimming. Those who avoided drowning in the muck of the trenches or being cut down attempting to remove the abatis huddled at the base of the fort wall with soaked and useless ammunition, praying for rescue as darkness fell and the defenders dangled sizzling fireworks on long poles over the edge of the wall to illuminate their cowering forms to archers above. One boat managed to gather a handful of the wounded, but as it tried to steam its way out of range a well-aimed shot broke it in half and it sank, drowning all on board.[71]

In the thick of the fighting, upon hearing news that the British admiral James Hope had been shot, Commodore Josiah Tattnall of the *Powhatan* decided to cast American neutrality to the wind and enter the battle. Tattnall was from Georgia, a loyal southerner with a strong sense of racial pride (the passing of two years would find him a senior officer in the Confederate Navy), and whatever his complaint against the British, they were fellow white men while the Chinese were not. "Blood is thicker than water!" he shouted (as his lieutenant Stephen Trenchard recorded it for posterity), and "he'd be damned if he'd stand by and see white men butchered before his eyes. . . . Old Tattnall isn't that kind, sir. This is the cause of humanity."[72] Tattnall's intervention hardly turned the tide of battle; the primary contribution of the Americans was to tow more British marine reserves forward to their deaths in the disastrous landing. Some of his men operated the British guns, firing at the fort while Tattnall tended to the British admiral. One American died. But what little effect Tattnall's breach of neutrality had on the course of the catastrophe that day, it gave Americans a taste of blood in China and set a new tone for British-American friendship; as the London *Times* commented afterward, "Whatever may be the result of the fight, England will never forget the day when the deeds and words of kindly Americans sustained and comforted her stricken warriors on the waters of the Peiho."[73]

By sunrise the next morning, more than four hundred British were dead or wounded, a shocking twenty-nine of them officers, and the survivors limped sodden and muddy back to their ships. These veterans of the Crimean War had never known such defeat. It brought to their minds the disastrous charge of the Light Brigade five years earlier at the Battle of Balaclava in the Crimea; indeed, one of the marines declared he would rather relive that battle three times over than what they'd just suffered at the Taku forts.[74] But whereas Alfred, Lord Tennyson himself had enshrined that earlier defeat in an immortal poem on the blind nobility of war, when the gallant British horsemen had charged heedlessly "Into the jaws of Death/ Into the mouth of Hell," the disaster at the Peiho found its enduring lesson in a somewhat less noble vein, handled by decidedly lesser poets. Tattnall's words were rewritten into poetry and song as a paean to white unity:

"Old Man" Tattnall, he who dared at Vera Cruz,—
Saw here, crippled by the cannon; saw there, throttled by the
    tide,
Men of English blood and speech—could he refuse?
I'll be damned, says he to Trenchard, *if old Tattnall's standing by*
Seeing white men butchered by such a foe.
Where's my barge? No side-arms, mind you! See those English
    fight and die—
Blood is thicker, sir, than water. Let us go.[75]

Senggelinqin rejoiced in his well-earned victory. Writing to the emperor shortly after the repulse, he acknowledged that the British and French might return with more ships but asserted confidently that with one or two more similar thrashings "the pride and vainglory of the barbarians, already under severe trial, will immediately disappear." Should that happen, "China can then enjoy some decades of peace." The emperor might not even need to fight them again, he added, for the victory at the Taku forts had been so decisive that "the barbarians, already somewhat disillusioned and repentant, may lend themselves to persuasion and be brought under control. If they of their own accord should wholeheartedly become obedient, then peace would be secure and permanent."[76] The emperor's response was guarded: he admonished his military officials to watch the coast carefully, as the foreigners "may harbor secret designs and hide themselves around nearby islands, waiting for the arrival of more soldiers and ships for a surprise attack in the night or in a storm." But ultimately he shared Senggelinqin's sense of relief and expressed hope that the need of the foreigners for Chinese goods would mean that the Chinese and foreign merchants in Shanghai could sort out their problems between themselves with no need for an ambassador and certainly no need for a new treaty. "The key to the situation," he concluded, "is now at Shanghai, not Tianjin."[77]

As the British left, licking their wounds, the American interpreter and missionary Samuel Wells Williams wrote to his brother from on board the *Powhatan* that it was possibly the worst defeat the British had suffered since the 1842 massacre of Major General William Elphinstone's army in

Afghanistan—though in this case he thought the humiliation was even greater, for in Kabul, "the elements killed ten times more than man," while at the Peiho it was entirely a failure of arms and tactics. And worst of all, this was China. "It was a new and strange narrative," wrote Williams, "for English soldiers who had always been victorious over the Chinese."[78] The shock of the Taku repulse to the British psyche was deeper than anything Xianfeng's advisers could know or imagine. Something important had shifted in the course of that day, and the high-spirited swagger of Britain's previous wars in China—the sense among her military that Asia was little more than a playground for their invincible ships—was broken. Replacing it were the bloody taste of humiliation and a hunger for revenge against the "inferior race" that had beaten them. It was, Williams brooded, "a defeat likely to prove more disastrous to the Chinese than any beating they ever had."[79]

CHAPTER 3

THE SHIELD KING

As Elgin's fleet made its successful entrance into Tianjin in the summer of 1858 and then tested the realm of the rebels along the Yangtze, Hong Rengan was making his way by a far more circuitous route across southern China toward Nanjing to rejoin his cousin. Leaving James Legge's home in Hong Kong in May, he traveled first to Canton, safe (for him, at least) under British and French occupation, and then set out northeast through Guangdong province along the riverways leading into an ever-thickening succession of mountain ranges. The dense settlements that crowded under the commanding walls of Canton soon gave way to a landscape of scattered houses, villages nestled in the valleys, and terraced fields chipped into the sides of mountains. Inns and restaurants dotted the main thoroughfares, alive with the currents of rumor from wayfarers come down from the north. The best-traveled of those roads had signposts showing distance and direction, some paved by the grace of earlier dynasties that had mustered armies of laborers to mine boulders from the mountainsides and hammer them into cobbles.

For the most part, travelers through those parts were porters carrying wares to sell, and Qing soldiers patrolled the routes in search of bandits who lay in wait by night. Hong Rengan traveled as far as the trading junction of Nanxiong county and then turned north on an ancient stone road that led up into a wilderness of cliffs and craggy pines. Steps carved into granite climbed through switchbacks like spiral staircases up the sides of the mountains leading to the Meiling Pass, the gateway dividing the southern part of the empire from the Yangtze Valley. Beyond lay Jiangxi province and, beyond that, the Taiping capital of Nanjing. He entered the current of porters crossing the pass—they worked in pairs, fore and aft with a quick step, loads slung on a length of bamboo across their shoulders, singing to keep their rhythm—a nearly unbroken flow of humanity moving along the road like water in a river, one line coursing north and the other south. At the peak, the road squeezed through a twenty-foot-wide passage carved into the rock of the mountain, framed with a limestone archway where Qing sentries watched the traffic with a wary eye for rebel couriers. Hong Rengan, dressed as a peddler, was unremarkable to them, and he passed without incident.[1]

In Jiangxi he continued northeast along the Gan River but soon came to the edge of the active war zone, just outside the realm of Taiping control, where a cordon of imperial armies was encamped. The armies were effective only by virtue of their massive size; there was scant overarching command, and unskilled officers had gained their posts through patronage rather than talent. Morale among the underpaid troops—many of them addicted to opium—was abysmal.[2] Easily enough, Hong Rengan managed to attach himself to one of the outlying units in order to join its march eastward toward the porcelain-producing city of Jingdezhen. But when Taiping forces attacked, the imperial unit dissolved in panic and Hong Rengan had to flee in the chaos and butchery of defeat, escaping with only the clothes on his back.[3]

He worked his way westward this time, away from the active fighting and up toward the Yangtze River where it coursed through Hubei province. The territory along the Yangtze had been fought over for more than five years now by the imperial and rebel sides, conquered and reconquered in turn, and for long stretches it was hard to tell that there had ever been a normal pattern of human life. Cities were emptied; houses had been stripped of wood to their window frames to make cooking fires for the passing armies.[4] Even in the more prosperous stretches of the river valley there was a quietness, a stirring of ghosts where a dense rural society had once lived, and the underpopulated farms were unable to muster enough hands to bring in what little harvest they could coax from the soil. On his route Hong Rengan met a soldier, whose name he later forgot, who had a plan to buy goods in the imperially controlled river town of Longping and then sell them to the rebels downriver in Nanjing. The soldier had no capital, but he did have contacts, extensive enough to be confident he could get through the siege lines with his wares. His plan seemed plausible enough that Hong Rengan gave him a piece of gold leaf he had kept sewn safely into the fabric of his jacket, and became his partner.[5]

While the soldier went to Longping to buy the goods for their trading scheme, Hong Rengan waited for him in the city of Huangmei, about fifteen miles to the northeast. The soldier had a contact there, a magistrate named Tan from his home village, and there were rumors that a Taiping detachment had been spotted nearby. Hong arrived too late to see the rebels—they had already vanished—but he spent a pleasant afternoon talking with Magistrate Tan, who found Hong's intelligence and education so impressive that he offered him a job on the spot as his secretary. It was a coveted job for an unemployed scholar, especially in such times of uncertainty, but it was also a long-term position and Hong could only think of Nanjing, so he gave an ambiguous reply. In the end, he wound up offering his services as a doctor to Tan's nephew, who had blistering headaches, and thereby made himself useful in the family's home. At loose ends waiting for his partner and unable to travel to Nanjing without him, Hong Rengan stayed with Magistrate Tan's family as the weeks, and then the months, passed.

New rumors came, murmurings that the Qing encirclement was tightening around Nanjing and the rebel capital would soon fall. Hong Rengan became anxious again and decided to leave Huangmei. Magistrate Tan, grateful for Hong's treatment of his nephew, gave him a letter of introduction and enough money to resume his pilgrimage, and Hong put on his peddler disguise once again to make his way down to Longping alone.[6] Movement was difficult, and imperial troops—of wildly varying degrees of discipline—were everywhere. A Qing patrol captured him in October, though they had no idea what a valuable bounty he was (they didn't think to open the seams of his coat, where along with the gold leaf he had hidden an outline of his family history). They found nothing on him more incriminating than some medical texts but still kept him prisoner for several days—perhaps as a conscript, perhaps hoping for ransom—until he managed to escape.[7] Some disaffected imperial soldiers then helped him get the rest of the way to Longping, where he stayed hidden in a house that served as a secret way station for Taiping refugees. The house's owners, like many, had grown weary of the depravities of the imperial forces and gave their tacit support to the rebels. There is no record of whether he ever found his nameless soldier friend again or recovered his gold leaf.

In December 1858, he crossed paths with Lord Elgin. From his place of hiding, Hong Rengan heard that foreign steamships had been spotted on the Yangtze and that they were on their way back down to Shanghai. He ventured down to the waterfront in time to see Elgin's fleet at anchor. He was acquainted with Thomas Wade, Elgin's interpreter, from their days in Hong Kong, and tried to get on board one of the vessels to find him, in hopes that the British fleet might give him passage as far as Nanjing. He didn't manage an audience with Wade, nor would the men he spoke to let him ride with them, but he did at least convince one of the British sailors to take back a letter addressed to James Legge and his other missionary friends in Hong Kong.[8] It informed them that he was still alive and still trying to get to Nanjing.[9] A few months later he surfaced again, finally making contact with a Taiping patrol in Anhui province in the spring of 1859. When he told them his story, they took him for a Qing spy and sent him under armed escort to the garrison in nearby Chentanghe. There, under interrogation from the garrison commander, he opened the seam of his jacket and removed the hidden scrap of paper that described his family history. It was enough to convince his questioner that he was, indeed, from the same village as the Heavenly King. The commander escorted him personally down the river on a Taiping boat, and he arrived at last at the Heavenly Capital on April 22, 1859, after nearly a year of travel.[10]

Nanjing was the grandest of China's cities in its heyday, the original capital of the Ming dynasty, rich with temples, government offices, and trading houses laid out along wide avenues roughly following the four directions of the compass. A twenty-three-mile-long wall wrapped around the metropolis with towers and parapets reaching seventy feet high, now densely fortified with cannons at the point where the city's northwest corner met the Yangtze River (and where imperial fleets huddled just out of range). As the Jerusalem of the Taiping, it had taken on a new character. Following their invasion in 1853, the rebels had torn down and burned most of the elaborate Daoist and Buddhist monasteries and forced the city's residents into a short-lived segregation, with men and women living in separate communal residences, organized into collective work brigades with shared property and shared worship in Protestant churches. By the time of Hong Rengan's arrival, marriage was again permitted, and though the Sabbath (on Saturday) was still fiercely kept, in other ways the puritanical ideals of the original movement had eroded. Opium had returned in force. Compared to its grandest days under the Ming, when the population had counted a million souls (more than all the capitals of Europe combined), the vast city now seemed nearly empty. After the bodies of the slaughtered Manchu population had been dumped into the Yangtze to float away downstream, the civilian residents of the city were allowed to come and go, and much of the population had drifted off to the countryside. For reasons of security, the city's thronging markets had long been shut down—as Hong Rengan well knew, pretending to be a peddler was the easiest way for a spy to move around undetected. The resultant capital of the Taiping was lovely and overgrown, with grand palaces for the kings and ruins where the old temples had stood, the broad avenues even more coldly beautiful in their liberation from the press of life.

The Heavenly King's palace was as magnificent as anything he had dreamed in his fevered visions before the war. Passing the drummers that flanked the main gate, visitors entered a cavernous reception hall in lacquered wood carved with dragons that wound their way up the pillars to the distant ceiling. The walls were inlaid with gold, and nearly everything that touched the king's fingers—chopsticks, bowls, brushes—was fashioned from gold as well. His chamber pot was made of silver. Behind the main hall lay the vast inner sanctum where Hong Xiuquan lived, attended by a host of palace women, as distant from the daily workings of the capital as was his imperial counterpart in the Summer Palace outside Beijing.[11]

By the time Hong Rengan arrived, his cousin had retreated from public life and was spending his days behind the palace walls reading scripture. Almost nobody was allowed to visit him save the women of the inner palace. His scrawled writings, in imperial vermilion ink, were posted on the walls outside to be promulgated throughout the city, and they showed that his visions had only intensified in the years since the first uprising. Some gave force and encouragement to the rebellion. "Those who are against us will be killed," read one. "Those who obey us will be saved. No one will escape from the three of us, the Father and the sons." (The sons were himself and Jesus.) Another read, "First, I strike at the edge of Heaven. Second, I strike at Hell. Third, I strike for the survival of the human beings. Fourth, I strike for annihilation of the devils." Others brooded on the concept of sacrifice. "Be not afraid that the people of the world know not the truth.

One day you may have to starve to death. One day you may have no road on which to travel."[12]

Hong Rengan's reunion with his cousin was, by his own account, bittersweet. It was eight years since they had last seen each other, and much had happened. The rumors that had reached Hong Rengan's ears during his travels had not been hopeful. Despite the encouraging weakness of the Manchu government in the face of the foreign powers, Nanjing was surrounded. The mass of Taiping troops had left the city, marching in three separate armies on far-ranging foraging expeditions, while the imperials had concentrated all of their power on trying to sever the lines of communication that brought food and grain back to Nanjing. The Heavenly King's removal from active leadership of the Taiping government had allowed a secondary king, the Eastern King, to take charge of the capital and the command of the armies with a harsh program of discipline (beheading for fornication or drunkenness)[13] and to experiment with a utopian vision of communal land reform that he planned to implement over all the regions under Taiping rule. By 1856, the Eastern King ran the capital as if it were his own domain, and rumors in Shanghai reported that the Heavenly King was dead or had been usurped. He hadn't, though; a bloody coup that year under murky circumstances ended with the severed head of the Eastern King being hung for public display on a wall across from the Heavenly King's palace, while Taiping troops massacred six thousand of the fallen king's followers and every member of his family.

Since the suppression of the Eastern King, Hong Xiuquan had needed an adviser he could trust, and now he found that adviser in Hong Rengan. The Heavenly King showered his beloved cousin with titles, promoting him swiftly through the ranks. Little more than two weeks after Hong Rengan's arrival, he even went so far as to break a previous promise never to appoint another king and gave that rank to Hong Rengan.[14] In full, Hong Rengan's new grandiose title was "Founder of the Dynasty and Loyal Military Adviser, the Upholder of Heaven and Keeper of Order in the Court: The Shield King." As "loyal military adviser" he joined the top echelon of Taiping military officers, and as "keeper of order in the court" his cousin put him in charge of the entire civil government of Nanjing, with rank equal to that of the deceased Eastern King. In spite of Hong Rengan's long absence from the movement, assisting James Legge and Theodore Hamberg safely in Hong Kong while the rebel armies clawed and bludgeoned their way through central China, he was now being offered a position in the Taiping command that was second in power only to the Heavenly King himself.

Hong Rengan's unexpected arrival may have seemed to his cousin a sign from God, but it sparked a dark resentment in others who had served the movement since the beginning of the war. Such was the case with a young but ambitious military officer named Li Xiucheng, who commanded the defense of Nanjing. Li, a poor and nearly illiterate farmer, had joined the Taiping not for religious reasons but simply out of the mixture of poverty and fear that abounded in southern China and gave the anti-imperial rebellion its astounding force. Li had grown up in mountainous Guangxi province, where the first uprisings had taken place. He wasn't a God Worshipper, though everyone where he lived knew about the mysterious "Master Hong" who would later become the Heavenly King. Li's family were dirt poor, scrabbling out a bare existence with hillside farming and a bit of hired labor and making charcoal, but even so "it was difficult to make ends meet each day," he recounted, "and to get enough each month was even more difficult."[15]

A branch of the Taiping army on the move from imperial pursuers camped in Li Xiucheng's mountain village for five days in 1851, eating everything they could find, even what the villagers had hidden. But instead of resenting them as bandits, the nearly starving Li found something attractive in their communal provisions—the commander announced that anyone who became a God Worshipper could eat with them for free, so Li and his family joined them for a meal. When the army decamped from the village, Li and his family left with them. Like others who renounced their village lives to join the millenarian Taiping, the last thing Li did before leaving with the Taiping army was to follow the commander's orders and burn down his own family's house. There would be no homecoming until Jerusalem. And after just a few days of marching, he found himself in a predicament shared by all of the other farmers and villagers who joined the sinuous march of the Heavenly Army—they passed farther beyond their homes than they had ever been in their lives. They no longer knew the roads. The imperial forces were following behind. There was no turning back, even if they had wanted to.[16]

Uprooted from his life as a charcoal maker, Li proved a natural leader of men and a tactical genius in the raw. After the founding of the Heavenly Capital in 1853, he moved steadily up through the ranks of the army, from battalion commander to general. In the chaos that followed the Eastern King's death in the coup of 1856, he was promoted into the top leadership of the Taiping armies, and by the time Hong Rengan arrived he was one of Hong Xiuquan's most trusted generals. He was not, however, a king. And when the cousin arrived from his sojourn among the foreigners in Hong Kong and was suddenly promoted above Li Xiucheng after all his years of service, it planted a burning seed of jealousy. Li himself gained the rank of king a few months later, anointed as the Loyal King, but the lateness of the appointment and the Heavenly King's clear preference for his cousin only nourished that jealousy, which continued to grow.

Hong Xiuquan was aware of the disaffection of his officers, so he called for the full congregation of Taiping leaders to assemble in the main reception hall to honor the appointment of the Shield King. Amid a clamor of drums and gongs he announced to his ministers that henceforth all matters in need of decision within the capital should be referred to the sole authority of the Shield King. As the crowd murmured its disapproval, he stood Hong Rengan on a platform to receive his seal of authority. Sensing the undercurrent of anger in the audience, Hong Rengan tried to turn down the appointment, but his cousin whispered to him that all would be well. "The wave that crashes with great force," he said softly, "soon spends itself and leaves peace." So Hong Rengan accepted the seal, and from his position on the platform he spoke to the crowd. With the self-possessed rhetorical power that had so impressed the missionaries in Hong Kong, he preached now to the congregation of Taiping leaders. He expounded on the policies of the Eastern King, criticizing them point by point and offering improvements. The crowd went silent. "They saw that I could stand in front of a multitude and hold forth flawlessly on doctrinal issues," he later recounted, "and so they accepted me as their model of wisdom."[17]

The rebel movement had flagged since its occupation of Nanjing in 1853, when the revolutionary momentum of the march gave way to a sedentary government with a bureaucracy, taxation, and all the other civil policies that fell so far beyond the purview of its leader's apocalyptic visions.[18] The Eastern King had built a promising, if harsh, civil government, but now it was in tatters. And though religion was the basis of Taiping ideology, it wasn't enough on its own. The original core of the Taiping had been God Worshippers, but legions of followers who had joined later (such as Li Xiucheng) had been drawn by the promise of an escape from grinding poverty and, more abstractly, from the oppression of the Manchu imperial government. They participated in religious rituals because such participation was required and enforced; many surely came to believe deeply in the doctrines they were taught, but it is difficult to distinguish between dutiful observance and authentic piety.[19] It was clear to Hong Rengan that commanding the loyalty of the movement's followers meant giving them more than just the hope of spiritual salvation; they also needed earthly rewards, the promise of a better life in a new state.

It was on this foundation that Hong Rengan began to imagine a lasting structure for the future Taiping government and society, one that would weave together threads of Chinese tradition with his knowledge of the industrial societies of the West. He infused it with a prototype of ethnic nationalism that had simmered in China since the Manchus first conquered the empire. Indeed, Hong Rengan's very first major proclamation as Shield King served to fan the flames of that ethnic resentment, calling on his people to "rejuvenate China and resist the northern barbarians"—meaning the Manchus—"in order to wipe out the humiliations of two hundred years." Since the fall of the Ming dynasty in 1644, he declared, "We mouth their language . . . we live together with their members, and our people suffer from the vileness of the Manchu dogs."[20]

The cause of Chinese liberation from the Manchus resonated not just with the followers of the Taiping but also with those who watched from outside. For the unusual Taiping religion might raise eyebrows among the more dogmatic missionary authorities, but there was little doubt abroad that the Taiping Rebellion was a genuine attempt to liberate the Chinese people—universally accepted as the natural and rightful rulers of the territory of China—from their alien overlords. Though some observers (such as the editors of the New Orleans *Daily Picayune*) might see the racial uprising as a threat,[21] most in the United States and Europe sympathized with the will to freedom they saw in the Chinese insurgency. As one Shanghai resident put it, "Americans are too firmly attached to the principles on which their government was founded and has flourished, to refuse sympathy for a heroic people battling against foreign thraldom."[22] Western papers commonly described the Qing rulers as "tartars" from Manchuria, as the overlord class, as China's imperial masters, as the conquerors. Or as one American missionary described the cause of the war, "A portion of the Chinese have risen to deliver their country from the domination of an alien race."[23]

Hong Rengan hashed out his vision for the future Taiping state in a document titled "A New Work for the Aid of Government," which was the first truly global proposal for reform in China's history. In the traditional dynastic vision, as carried on through the reign of the Qing dynasty, China's rulers imagined their empire to be the center of world civilization, to which outsiders (barbarians) were welcome to come and trade, provided they acknowledged the cultural superiority of the Chinese throne. This was the worldview with which England had come into repeated conflict. In contrast, Hong Rengan knew from experience that the British were both militarily powerful and fiercely proud, so he suggested that in communicating with them the Chinese should stop using terms like "barbarian" and instead start expressing ideas such as "equality, friendship, harmony and affection."[24]

Similarly, he thought the traditional tribute model of diplomacy, in which foreigners were encouraged to come to Beijing to pay homage to the emperor as vassals, should be abandoned as a relic from the past with no use to the contemporary world. "Human beings are not willing to be considered inferior," he noted with a degree of cultural relativism often thought to be absent from imperial China. If in the past others had pretended to treat the Chinese as superiors, he argued, it was only because they had been forced to, "not out of wholehearted submission." There should be a new diplomacy of equals, so "friendly relations can be established with foreign countries." The only lasting way to gain the respect of other nations, he wrote, was "by the perfection of government within and the demonstration of faith without." That is, only by looking inward to reform and establishing itself as a model of government in the new era could China once again command the respect it had enjoyed in the past.[25]

From his experience living in Hong Kong, Hong Rengan had come to view China as merely one state among many, with much to gain from studying the other powers of the nineteenth-century world. Foremost was the Christian religion, of the kind he had learned from Theodore Hamberg and James Legge in Hong Kong, which he believed was the key to the strength of Western countries. Without exception, he argued in his treatise on government, it was the Protestant Christian nations—England, the United States, Germany, the Scandinavian countries—that were the strongest and most prosperous in the modern world, followed by the slightly weaker French Catholics and Orthodox Russians, who still believed in "miracles and mysticism." By his account, the states that hewed to Old Testament Islam or, worse, Buddhism, were uniformly weak, and many had become colonies of the stronger nations. He equated China under the Manchus to Persia, where the people accepted their slavelike status without complaint.

The "most powerful nation" in Hong Rengan's eyes was Great Britain, whose ruling house he believed to have lasted a thousand years (making it more enduring than any dynasty in China). He explained that its strength derived from the intelligence of its people and its system of laws, which China should emulate. But his greatest admiration was for the United States (called the "Flowery-Flag Country" in Chinese by reason of its stars and stripes), which he termed "the most righteous and wealthy country of all." The heart of America's greatness was, he believed, in its magnanimity and sense of equality. Despite the United States' military strength, he wrote, "she does not encroach upon her neighboring countries," and when gold was discovered in California all comers were welcome. The acceptance of foreigners in the United States was so extensive that some even had become officials there. Hong Rengan also glowed about American democracy, especially the notion that all people (at least all "people of virtue") should have a say in choosing their leaders and setting policies of the government. "Those elected by the majority," he wrote, "are considered worthy and capable, and decisions reached by the majority are considered just."[26]

In his treatise on government, Hong Rengan also took the time to describe the breadth of his own foreign contacts. He listed his many missionary friends from the "strong" countries, including British missionaries such as James Legge and a handful of Americans he had met in Shanghai. He reserved a special place for the late Theodore Hamberg, who, he said, "was extremely fond of me."[27] The catalogue of his foreign friends served two purposes—to Hong Xiuquan and the Taiping leadership, for whom the document was written, it carried the implicit promise that they would have foreign cooperation in their project of building a Christian state in China. And to the foreigners to whom it was eventually leaked (a writer in *The London Review* described it as "one of the most curious documents ever issued"),[28] it suggested that the new prime minister of the Taiping viewed them as brothers and that his future state would be the one to finally open wide the dusty gates of China.

But religion and international diplomacy were just a beginning. With remarkable prescience, Hong Rengan proposed that China must tap into the emergent global industrial economy if it wanted to be strong. Though he described the Holy Trinity (the traditional one, not the one including the Heavenly King) as the "greatest treasure" of a state, it was followed closely by a long list of "middle treasures" more material in nature, including steamships, trains, clocks and watches, telescopes, sextants, and revolving guns. Siam, he suggested, had learned how to build steamships and thereby made itself into "a country of wealth and civilization."[29] The Japanese, unlike the Qing rulers of China, had opened willingly to foreign trade and "will certainly become skillful in the future." And that, he believed, was exactly the path that a Taiping-ruled China should follow.

Hong Rengan's treatise presented, for the very first time in a Chinese context, a vision of the country as a modern industrial power. He offered a litany of proposals that in one form or another would become catchphrases for later Chinese reformers into the twentieth century and beyond. The new China, he argued, would have to begin with a strong legal system, one based firmly on the rule of law. There had to be patent rights so that "imitators will be convicted and punished," and Chinese entrepreneurs would then have the encouragement they needed to invent machines that could match those of the Westerners. He called for a revolution of transportation: steamships, which at the time were possessed solely by foreigners; railroads, for a country that had none (Chinese workers might have built the United States' railroads in the 1860s, but when Hong Rengan wrote his tract there wasn't so much as a mile of track in his own country). A hierarchical system of highways could link the provincial capitals to one another with major roads, while narrower ones would branch out to the townships and villages. If the government dredged the major rivers, boats powered by fire and steam could ship cargo and passengers to and from the deepest parts of the empire. Mines could be opened for a range of precious materials—"gold, silver, copper, iron, tin, coal, salt, amber, oyster shells, jade and precious stones"—with profits shared by the prospectors and the state (for all under the ground was God's gift to mankind equally, but individuals needed personal incentive to do the work of finding it). Private merchants could apply for permission to establish banks and issue paper currency, which could be carried more easily than the Qing dynasty's silver ingots and copper cash and would further fuel the development of the economy. He even called for the founding of Western-style insurance companies that could offer policies to protect people's homes, property, and livelihoods.

The recommendations continued. He argued that developing China's transportation infrastructure was necessary not just for the sake of creating economic wealth but also to allow for the free movement of information within the empire. His proposal called for newspapers of every imaginable description, from local dailies to provincial monthlies that would report major news events as well as the prices of commodities in China's various regions, with harsh punishments for false reporting. A government office would collect all of the newspapers and forward them to the sovereign in the capital—not so he could censure their writers but so he could learn the true circumstances of his kingdom.

Politically, however, Hong Rengan's imagined state would be an unequivocal theocracy, and a fundamentalist one at that. There were benevolent aspects to this: inspired by the work of the missionaries he had known in Hong Kong and Shanghai, he called for the Chinese to develop Christian social institutions to provide for orphans and widows, the disabled and the destitute. They would be taught music and literature, and, when they died, they would be buried with kindness. "These poor people make their plans cautiously and they calculate deeply," wrote Hong, "many of them are often persons of ability."[30] The drowning of infants would be prohibited, as would the selling of children.

At the same time, it would be a harshly puritanical society, where the power of the government would be used to prevent sinful practices. Alcohol, tobacco, and opium would be strictly forbidden, along with dramatic plays and colorful Daoist rituals and Buddhist ceremonies that distracted the people from their work. Feng shui—the geomantic study of wind and water—was a superstition that stood in the way of mining and moving the land, and it should be eradicated. Lazy people would be turned in by their families and sent into exile, so their laziness wouldn't infect anyone else. A range of punishments would keep offenders in line, though he believed the myriad methods of execution developed over the years in China should be abandoned. For the worst offenders, China's many gradations and creative varieties of capital punishment should, he wrote, should be replaced by the single, decidedly Western, method of hanging—from a gallows, with proper advertisement beforehand so a crowd could watch.

But first a true state would have to be founded. And before that state could be founded, the war had to be won. In their younger years Hong Rengan and his cousin had talked about a plan for building a kingdom, and it hadn't included the north. Their original strategy had been to set a foundation in Nanjing, expand their reach down the Yangtze River to Zhenjiang to seize control of the Grand Canal, and claim Anqing upstream to control the upper reaches of the Yangtze. Then they would consolidate the seven southern provinces, campaign westward to take Sichuan and Shaanxi, and thus would the kingdom be established—a southern empire stretching from the Yangtze River to the ocean. Its borders would match closely with the emotionally laden Chinese heartland, roughly the old boundaries of the ethnically Chinese Ming Empire. It would abandon the much larger expanse of the Qing dynasty, which had conquered vast territories in the north and west inhabited mostly by Manchus, Mongols, and Central Asian Muslims.[31]

That strategy had not been followed, however. After the fall of Nanjing, the Taiping forces got only as far as consolidating Zhenjiang and Anqing before abandoning the southern strategy and instead turning north toward Beijing in their failed attempt to cut the head off the existing imperial state. By the time Hong Rengan arrived, the Taiping capital was in desperate straits. The rebels had lost much of the southern territory they had conquered in the initial campaign. They still held the strategic Yangtze city of Anqing upstream, but imperial forces had retaken Zhenjiang (the ruined city where Elgin's party had imagined themselves in Pompeii). More pressing, imperial forces had set up massive encampments of soldiers numbering in the tens of thousands at strategic points to the north and south of Nanjing and kept it under effective siege, with only a single supply line left open to bring grain and salt to the capital city.

These imperial troops were divided into two main camps, one north of the Yangtze River near Yangzhou and one to the south just beyond Nanjing. They were the leading forces of the central empire, the counterparts of Senggelinqin's army in the north, and their commanders had been chasing the Taiping from the beginning. The southern camp had dug in just ten days after the fall of Nanjing, when the pursuing forces had finally caught up, and it had stood its ground almost continually ever since. Whereas a Manchu general named He Chun commanded the northern encampment, the southern one was in the hands of the far more capable Chinese general Zhang Guoliang, one of the emperor's most valuable assets. In the 1840s, Zhang had been a bandit leader in the same region of Guangdong where the Taiping had originated (some sources have him born in the same county as Hong Xiuquan).[32] A Robin Hood figure, his 10,000-strong army ravaged the province under the mantras "take from the rich to save the poor" and "kill the officials but spare the people." But when imperial forces finally captured him in the early 1850s, he went over to the emperor's side and took his men with him. He Chun was a talented commander, but it was Zhang Guoliang who really struck fear into the hearts of the Taiping generals.[33]

Zhang Guoliang's siege troops in the southern camp stayed safely out of range of the cannons on the city walls, and their numbers were too great to be easily scattered by Taiping sorties from the city that swept out in the dark of night on horseback. At the same time, Nanjing was too well fortified for the besiegers to have any effect against its massive walls and bricked-up gates, so for six years the two sides had been at a stalemate, an advance on one side matched eventually with retribution by the other. The pattern repeated on scales both small and large; a brilliant series of Taiping victories in 1856 smashed the imperial lines, but then came the Eastern King's coup and the internal collapse of the Taiping leadership. In the three years since then, the imperials had rebuilt their ranks and commenced digging a containing trench below Nanjing that by 1859 stretched forty-five miles with more than a hundred guard camps along its length blocking access to the capital from the south and east.[34] He Chun and Zhang Guoliang, in their twin camps, were preparing for what they hoped would be a final assault to crush the rebel capital.

In the face of resentment from the more experienced Taiping military leaders, Hong Rengan was surprisingly forthright in his new position as commander in chief. They grumbled that he just wanted power and fame, but he replied angrily, "When I was in Guangdong and heard news that the Heavenly Capital was surrounded on all sides, I didn't hide from difficulty but risked my life to come to your aid. How can I be the kind of person who covets salary and prestige? Look—the capital is surrounded on four sides with only a single supply line open. . . . How can we contend with the enemy?"[35]

Hong Rengan presented a bold plan to relieve the capital. The rebels would send a small expeditionary force in a wide, sweeping arc beyond the rear guard of the imperial armies down into Zhejiang province, to attack its weakly defended capital, Hangzhou. A hundred and fifty miles southeast of Nanjing, Hangzhou anchored the supply line that supported the southern camp. Because He Chun and Zhang Guoliang had concentrated all of their forces around Nanjing, they would have no reserves to save Hangzhou, so they would have to transfer forces from the great camps at the Nanjing siege to stave off the Taiping rearguard action. As Hong Rengan planned it, he would recall the roving armies under two of the Taiping's most talented field commanders—Chen Yucheng, known as the Brave King, and a younger cousin of Li Xiucheng known as the Attending King—and have them return to the capital from their distant foraging campaigns. As soon as the imperial forces around Nanjing had thinned sufficiently, the expeditionary force at Hangzhou could secretly retreat as the combined armies of the Brave King, the Attending King, and the Loyal King swept in from three sides to crush the weakened imperial camps between them and raise the siege.

The Loyal King agreed that the plan might work to break the siege but wondered what lasting good it would accomplish. It would, he said, reconcentrate the Taiping forces in Nanjing where they had few supplies. So Hong Rengan laid out the full scope of his revised strategy for winning the war. The rice-growing southern provinces, Sichuan in the west, and the Great Wall to the north were all at least a thousand miles from Nanjing, he noted, but the east—with the grand and wealthy cities of Suzhou and Hangzhou and access to the ocean—was far closer. "The land there is vast," he noted, "and the treasuries are flush." So that was the direction in which they must attack. Seizing on their momentum from routing the imperial siege camps (if the first part of the strategy worked), they could make an immediate turn east and conquer the cities between Nanjing and Suzhou in one swift campaign that would ensure them supplies, arms, measureless wealth, and new recruits.[36]

But that would be just the beginning, and here Hong Rengan began to play upon his relations with the foreigners. With the wealth they gained from occupying Suzhou and Hangzhou, he explained, they could arrange to rent or purchase twenty steam-powered ships from the foreigners in Shanghai. Such a fleet would enable them not only to patrol the Yangtze River unopposed but also to lay claim to the southern coast along Fujian and Guangdong down to Hong Kong. The next step would be to send one column of soldiers from Jiangxi province along the south of the Yangtze River to invade Hunan, and another on the Yangtze's northern bank to invade Hubei and seize Hankow, thus solidifying the Taiping's command of the entire Yangtze River Valley and cutting the Qing Empire in two. The consolidation of the south would follow easily, and with troops and horses from the south they could finally capture Sichuan and Shaanxi and complete Hong Xiuquan's original vision of a southern empire reuniting the heartland provinces of the Ming. Beijing and the northern provinces would be cut off from all grain tribute. As the new Taiping state took form in the south, the Qing dynasty would starve and wither away.[37]

The success of his plan depended on a measure of support from the foreigners in Shanghai, in particular their willingness to supply steamships, but that was precisely why Hong Rengan was such a remarkable gift dropped into the lap of the Taiping leadership. He had better contacts among the foreigners, and a better knowledge of their customs and beliefs, than any other official in China, be he Taiping or imperial. The Heavenly King immediately seized on the opportunity Hong Rengan's experience offered. It wasn't just that Hong Rengan understood the foreigners after spending several years living and working with them; even more important was the fact that *the foreigners knew* that Hong Rengan understood them, that he was the only man in China who properly understood their religious practices, their science, and their culture. They would therefore look to him as someone who could be trusted to give them the open trade relations and missionary access they wanted. The Heavenly King put Hong Rengan in charge of foreign relations and encouraged him to invite their representatives for meetings once the siege was lifted.[38]

On February 10, 1860, Li Xiucheng the Loyal King left Nanjing via the lone open route, through Pukou across the river to the north, with six thousand handpicked soldiers disguised in imperial uniforms stolen from the slain enemy in earlier battles. So weak was the coordination among the concatenation of forces on the dynasty's side—local militias, organized militias, Green Standard forces—that Li's men were able to seize and garrison several towns along their route before looping around to the southeast and finally arriving at Hangzhou without warning on March 11. The attack would have been a complete surprise if Li's goal had been simply to invade the city, but he intended instead to terrorize it. His men first took the time to plant hundreds of Taiping banners in the hills outside the city walls to deceive the defenders into thinking their total forces were massive. Then his main force attacked the front gate of Hangzhou head-on while his sappers tunneled under the city walls and planted explosives, blasting open a breach on March 19.

Hell unleashed itself in the besieged city as its untrained militia defenders broke ranks and desperately looted the homes of their neighbors before running from the Loyal King's onslaught. The leaders of the civil government abandoned their offices, some leading their bodyguard detachments in ransacking the city's richest homes before making their escape as well, leaving no command in place whatsoever. As Li Xiucheng's small force fought its way through the breach in the city wall, local citizens did battle in the streets with the looters who were supposed to be defending them, compounding the war dead with the lynched, the mangled, and the burned.[39] Fires raged. The city's women, following generations of moral instruction on how to behave in times of chaos, began putting themselves to death—tens of thousands of them by the end. Like other Confucian governments before it, the Qing dynasty had celebrated female suicide as the pinnacle of virtue, and it ramped up its honors for women's suicide in the course of the civil war.[40] Female suicide became a kind of perverse defensive measure against the rebels. Fearing rape and murder when the Taiping entered the city, the women of Hangzhou acted as they had been taught: they hanged themselves, poisoned themselves, stabbed themselves with knives, and threw themselves into wells to drown.

The Manchu commander in Hangzhou retreated with his troops back into the inner garrison city, which held this time against the fierce but lightly manned attack by the Loyal King's troops. Unable to break into the Manchu garrison after six days, Li finally had to abandon the attack and retreat overland back to Nanjing. But he had accomplished his objective, and the plan had worked perfectly. Zhang Guoliang heard the reports that Hangzhou was being stormed by a multitude of Taiping troops. He had no clear intelligence about the size of the attacking army, so he shifted nearly a quarter of his total siege force to relieve Hangzhou. Moving swiftly along back roads, again in disguise, the Loyal King and his troops rode on commandeered horses back to Nanjing, leaving smoking chaos in the city behind them. When Zhang Guoliang's relief troops finally arrived at Hangzhou after their forced march, they found no Taiping presence there. Nor, for that matter, could they find any semblance of a civil government. So, like the others before them, they just looted whatever was left.[41]

By April, the main Taiping armies of the Brave King and Attending King had returned to the outskirts of Nanjing, and with Li Xiucheng leading the garrison forces who poured out from the city, they threw their full combined weight on the weakened imperial ranks.[42] The southern camp dissolved in a panicked retreat as Taiping forces totaling more that a hundred thousand men overran them from three directions. Li Xiucheng's cavalry smashed into the rear lines of the southern encampment from behind, crushing them into their own defensive works where thousands of imperial soldiers were cut down, their bodies left to choke the trenches they had dug with their own hands. The waterways overflowed their banks with the dead.[43] Dropping their weapons and flags in the rout, the remnants of the imperial army fled on foot. As the pursuers became the pursued, weeks of desperate retreat followed until the Taiping finally overran them in the city of Danyang, forty-five miles to the east. The Manchu general He Chun committed suicide by eating raw opium, and Zhang Guoliang, the Robin Hood who had taken the emperor's side, drowned while trying to escape from Danyang.[44] In the central theater of the war, there were no more capable commanders left.

CHAPTER 4

SOUNDINGS

In the spring of 1860, the end of imperial civilization rolled toward Shanghai like a tidal wave. "The glow of the fires illuminates the sky," wrote a Chinese observer near Shanghai, "and the cries of the people shake the earth."[1] Throwing off their imperial cordon, the rebel armies reared up from the Heavenly Capital and coursed eastward, meeting no resistance from the dynasty's shattered forces. Local militia defenses scattered in fright as Li Xiucheng's men swarmed through Jiangsu province, conquering cities dense with refugees from the years of fighting up the Yangtze River. After driving the imperials to Danyang, which they captured on May 19, they moved swiftly down the path of the Yangtze to capture Changzhou a week later and Wuxi three days after that. But it was Suzhou, the legendary city of gardens along the Grand Canal, that was the greatest prize, with its wartime population of two million providing a vast source of new recruits and its merchant homes flush with treasure. The Taiping army's momentum was irresistible; when Li Xiucheng's forces marched on Suzhou from Wuxi, arriving before the city's walls on June 2, 1860, sympathizers inside the city simply opened the gates to welcome their new masters, and the Loyal King captured the city of gardens without a fight.

The Chinese who lived in the path of the rebel march faced the same choices as the millions already drawn into the war: they could fight if they were especially brave, joining neighbors in a militia to try to protect their village or town, though their ranks inevitably broke in the face of over-whelming rebel numbers; or they could show allegiance to the rebels by changing their hairstyle. The Qing required all males to shave the tops of their heads and grow a single long braid down the back known as the queue. The Taiping rebels, by way of defiance, refused to shave their heads and allowed their hair to grow long and wild on the top, often woven with ribbons of colored silk. Many peasants simply tried to appease both sides, growing their hair long on top when the Taiping took over but keeping their long braid wound up underneath to hide it, so that if the imperial troops should drive the rebels back, they could unfurl their queue and shave the top of their head again to avoid execution by the imperial side as "longhairs."

Those of a certain station, however, had different choices. Their wealth and status depended on the survival of the dynasty, and with a rebel victory, they feared, everything would be lost. They were the ones most likely to commit suicide—which they did in droves as Suzhou and other cities fell. If they owned land elsewhere, they could try to move their families to safety (the elderly mothers, with their bound feet, were the most difficult to transport). But as the rebellion spread through Jiangsu province and down into Zhejiang, there were few places left for refuge. Those who could, pushed into the international city of Shanghai for protection under the small population of foreigners. But even there a sense of safety was tenuous, and apocalyptic rumors spread through the local population that a million Taiping soldiers under Li Xiucheng were on the move toward Shanghai, with a flotilla of ten thousand boats so large it took three full days to pass on the river.[2]

By the spring of 1860, the treaty port of Shanghai had more than half a million Chinese inhabitants, a figure that was rising quickly as new waves of refugees crowded the foreign settlements and created massive problems of sanitation and shelter. The city was divided into four sections, arranged along the Huangpu River at the easternmost reach of Jiangsu province, which emptied ten miles to the north into the mouth of the Yangtze and thence into the ocean. At the southern end was the old Chinese city, which had been Shanghai's full extent before the coming of foreign settlements after the Opium War. It was enclosed by a roughly circular defensive wall twenty-five feet high and filled with narrow, twisting streets. It continued to be governed by the Qing civil authorities and was home to most of Shanghai's population.

Moving northward along the Huangpu, one entered into the French concession, crowded with Chinese houses, and then the much larger British concession, which was home to the stretch of developed waterfront known as the Bund, bristling with piers, warehouses, and offices, where at any given time two or three hundred ships might be moored along the riverside. The British concession was laid out on a linear grid—with a racetrack, Protestant church, and customshouse—and covered a parcel of land comparable in size to the entire Chinese city. It nestled in the junction of the Huangpu to its east and the narrow Suzhou Creek (a tributary of the Huangpu) to the north. Finally, crossing the Suzhou Creek one found an amorphous and sparsely settled American concession, consisting mostly of swampland.[3]

The foreign population typically numbered about two thousand settled persons, with a transient population of ships' crews adding another two thousand to the total, depending on the time of year and the state of trade. The British dominated the community, seconded by the French, while the mere handful of Americans had little to do (in calmer times, at least) but complain about being outnumbered by "arrogant stiff-necked Englishmen, full of Cockneyism and conceit."[4] Densely packed settlements called suburbs crowded just outside the protective walls of the Chinese city, especially on the riverward side, containing among them Shanghai's wealthiest merchant homes, while the land to the west of the walls, away from the Huangpu River and toward the interior, soon gave way to small villages among cotton fields and orchards, and finally to what one resident described as a "queer flat lonely country" of muddy rice paddies intersected by narrow irrigation creeks.[5]

It was not, by any stretch of the imagination, a beautiful city. Newcomers arriving from England with grand visions of "an El Dorado of wealth of hope and fortune"[6] found Shanghai instead to be a dirty, overcrowded settlement of "ill built houses reeking with impurities and fevers and vile stenches."[7] One newly arrived missionary declared the city to be "one of the filthiest in this world. I have seen nothing to be compared to it in dirt and filth, it surpasses everything."[8] Another warned anyone who wanted to walk in the surrounding countryside that they would be overwhelmed by the "dung boats, dung tanks, dung buckets, dung carriers" that fertilized the rice paddies with human feces.[9] But as unappetizing as it may have been to its foreign residents, it was the most advantageous port in China for seagoing trade. With ready access to both the ocean and the Yangtze River, it was an ideal point for exchange between the riverborne trade of tea and silk from China's interior and the seagoing commerce in cotton textiles and opium, which were brought in mostly by British ships (the opium via India). Indeed, so immensely profitable was the traffic in tea and silk that the fastest merchant ships in the world had been built specifically for the purpose of dominating the China trade. But now, as the Taiping swept down the river, the British authorities in Shanghai issued an injunction against trading with the rebels, and fear set into the foreign community that their immensely profitable commerce was about to grind to a halt.

The ranking British official in Shanghai in 1860 was Frederick Bruce, Lord Elgin's younger brother. He had retreated there after the Taku repulse in 1859, and insofar as he had failed to exchange the ratified treaty he could not properly be called an ambassador, but he was still plenipotentiary, and he now acted as the chief supervisor of British trade in China. He was deeply embarrassed by the British defeat at Taku, which was partly attributable to his own stubbornness in refusing to take the alternate route to Beijing that had been offered (which the American ambassador had done, with successful results). Bruce was therefore determined to walk a fine and careful line in his position of authority in Shanghai. With regard to the ongoing Chinese civil war, he was pedantic in his determination to act with perfect neutrality and have nothing to do with the conflict. To that end, he had issued the injunction against trading with the rebels, for he believed that such trade would constitute British support for the rebellion.

At the same time, he also tried studiously to avoid giving aid to the imperial side—which was somewhat easier to justify, since it was the imperials who had attacked his fleet. But the British had interests and investments in Shanghai, and the local Chinese officials were adept at playing upon them. The ranking Qing official in Shanghai was Wu Xu, a fat mandarin of about fifty years old who served as the *daotai* (the highest imperial rank at the city level, something like a mayor appointed by the provincial governor). Despairing of the imperial military's incompetence against the Taiping rebels, Wu Xu had begun to hound Bruce for British support in defending Shanghai against their advance. If the Taiping captured Shanghai, he warned, they would shut down all foreign trade and drive out the British settlers. Bruce wanted to keep his distance from the imperial authorities to avoid any appearance of breaching neutrality, but he had heard the shocking accounts of anarchy in the streets of Hangzhou when

Li Xiucheng had attacked it, and he began to worry that something similar might unfold in Shanghai.

There were already problems. The most imminent threats weren't the rebels themselves so much as the legions of renegade imperial troops who had taken up quarters in Shanghai's Chinese city and its suburbs after fleeing from Suzhou and Hangzhou. Bruce reported in June 1860 that the defeated imperialists "have revenged themselves for their defeat by pillaging the defenceless villages on their line of retreat," and he worried that they would destroy Shanghai from within.[10] In a repeated pattern, thieves—be they imperial soldiers, rebel sympathizers, or simply everyday bad elements—would raise the false alarm that the Taiping were attacking and then, in the bedlam that ensued, set about ransacking the homes of the rich.[11] "The beaten troops, the victorious insurgents, and the vagabonds of the city itself," wrote Bruce, "all join in plundering the wealthy and respectable inhabitants."[12]

Weighing the fearful possibility of chaos breaking out in the foreign settlements under his watch, Bruce decided that it was Britain's moral duty to protect Shanghai—not just the foreign settlements but also the Chinese city they abutted. That part of Shanghai was officially the jurisdiction of the Qing civil government and not under foreign control, but he feared a humanitarian disaster if chaos in the imperial city should spread into the neighboring foreign settlement—and he thought a limited intervention by the British forces in place might stop this from happening. So he sent off to London for permission to set up defenses of the walled Chinese city "to prevent, if possible, the scenes of bloodshed and pillage being enacted here, which took place at Hangzhou, when that city was lately assaulted by the insurgents."[13]

At the same time, he also made it quite clear that if the British *did* set up a defense of Shanghai, it would be strictly limited to the city itself. In writing to the foreign secretary back in London, Bruce mentioned that Wu Xu had tried to get him to send a preemptive British force out to Suzhou to check the rebel advance, and he had flatly refused. (Not so the French, who took a more cavalier attitude toward intervention; after hearing a report that the Protestant rebels had murdered a French Catholic missionary, they eagerly got up a force of 3,000 troops to march on Suzhou. Only Bruce's refusal to lend British support scuttled the mission.)

Bruce was in a bind. To defend Shanghai, even only to protect British citizens and property, would effectively strengthen the hand of the very power that had sprung such an atrocious surprise attack on his fleet at Taku a year earlier. "No course could be so well calculated to lower our national reputation," he worried, "as to lend our material support to a Government the corruption of whose authorities is only checked by its weakness."[14] But as the rumors of an impending rebel attack on the international city swelled and intensified, the British merchants clamored that something had to be done to protect them. It would be months before Bruce could hear back from London whether he might be authorized to defend the city, and so, on his own initiative, he began to call up volunteers. It seemed a nearly hopeless endeavor, though; there were only a handful of British cannons to be dragged together, along with a few hundred inexperienced volunteers to man the walls. And if the rumors were true, legions of rebels were on their way.

Though some hoped the Shanghai foreign settlement might serve as a model of European order planted in China, the complicated division of jurisdictions in the international city (each nation with its own military force, each foreign citizen liable only to his own country's authorities) proved attractive to somewhat less orderly elements from abroad as well. As the trading ships sailed in and out, exchanging not only their cargoes but sometimes their crews, ne'er-do-wells from around the earth collected in Shanghai to dwell in the spaces between its laws. As one young American described it to his mother in dismay after a few years in the city, "The place swarms with Californians, Negro minstrels, gamblers, horse jockeys and the worst of both sexes fill the streets . . . the place promises in a short time to become a second San Francisco in its early days."[15]

Some foreigners, however, were too sinister even for Shanghai. Such were the members of an irregular military force that had begun to drill in a muddy village twelve miles to the west of Shanghai in the spring of 1860, entirely unwelcome in the city itself. There were about two hundred Europeans and Americans in the unit, wearing a hodgepodge of uniforms that betrayed their motley origins. Some wore the sharp-cut red coats and dark pants of the British marines, others the blue jackets and white bell-bottoms of the French sailors, still others the gray, tattered fabrics of the merchant crews.[16] For arms, they had Colt revolvers and Sharp's repeating carbines, and their objective was the Taiping-held town of Songjiang, about ten miles farther from Shanghai, which—along with Qingpu to its northwest—was one of two strategic walled towns that were necessary stepping-stones for any invasion of Shanghai from Hangzhou or Suzhou, respectively. Their patrons were a group of Chinese merchants in Shanghai led by a banker named Yang Fang who bankrolled the mercenaries' salaries at a ridiculously high rate of a hundred dollars a month per man, more than enough to lure professional soldiers to jump ship and join the alcoholic dregs of the merchant crews who made up the bulk of the force. On top of the salary, the sponsors promised a reward of more than a hundred thousand dollars if the foreign contingent could defeat the Taiping garrison at Songjiang and drive it from the town—along with anything they could loot from the city.

The commander and organizer of the force was an American a few months shy of his twenty-ninth birthday named Frederick Townsend Ward. He hailed from the stormy gloom of Salem, Massachusetts, the shipping town that had once ruled the old China trade. By the time of Ward's youth it had long been in decline, steeped in the fading and salt-eroded memories of its lost grandeur. Ward grew up in a decaying mansion just a few doors down from the House of the Seven Gables, where Nathaniel Hawthorne's sister lived, the home Hawthorne brought to life in 1851 as a gothic embodiment of not just Salem but New England itself at mid-century. With impenetrably deep black eyes and an unruly thatch of raven hair worn long over his ears, Ward carried with him the melancholy darkness of his northern home.

The models for Ward's army were the so-called filibusters, American soldiers of fortune who operated in Central America in the mid–nineteenth century and who—unlike the purely mercenary kind of soldier for hire—fought not just for the salaries they were paid but with the hope of establishing their own governments and ruling their own states. Ward had been frustrated in his early attempts to follow a traditional military career. He failed to gain admission to West Point in 1846 and spent a year at Norwich University, the private military college in Vermont, without graduating.[17] His real military training came from a more informal route. Making his way to Central America in 1852, he enlisted under the notorious William Walker, who in the early 1850s raised a small army of Americans to foment a civil war in Nicaragua in order to overthrow its government and build a "Yankee state" there.[18] Ward fought under Walker and served as his training officer in 1853, leaving after a year to launch his own career—too soon to see his patron finally succeed in conquering Nicaragua and install himself as its president in 1856. But because such forces operated outside the national militaries of the great powers, their successes were typically short-lived. By the time Ward started training his own filibuster troops outside Shanghai in the spring of 1860, British forces had captured Walker and put him under detention for violating the neutrality laws. Soon after Ward launched into his first battles against the Taiping in China, his mentor was executed by firing squad in Honduras, on the other side of the world.

The civil war in China was a fantastic opportunity for a would-be filibuster, and the port of Shanghai was, in a very real sense, the other end of a thread connecting through history back to the land of Ward's birth. He had been to China once as a restless youth and made his way back in 1859 to get in on the war. Based on what he had heard about the situation from outside, his plan was to join the rebels in overthrowing the Manchu government.[19] But from Shanghai it turned out to be difficult to make contact with the Taiping, so he found work on a French steamer named the *Confucius*, which some wealthy Chinese merchants in Shanghai had hired to protect their business interests against pirates on the Yangtze. It was but a short step from fighting river pirates to raising a land force to protect the outlying towns, and both Ward and the captain of the *Confucius* were brought in under the local military authorities as an adjunct fighting force, taking their orders from Bruce's imperial counterpart the Shanghai *daotai*, Wu Xu.

In this manner, Ward wound up taking the dynasty's side (if indirectly) and he began to recruit a mélange of Europeans, Americans, and Filipinos to fight in the region just outside Shanghai. He self-consciously styled himself an adventurer, dressing in a tight-fitting black uniform to match his long black locks, wearing no insignia, and carrying a swagger stick in lieu of a sidearm. His army was strictly illegal, a bald violation of the neutrality ordinance, and he enlisted so many deserters that his wounded soldiers couldn't even go to Shanghai for medical help lest they be locked up and court-martialed.[20] But as long as he, and they, didn't mind killing a few Chinese rebels in open combat, there would be a lot of money in it for all of them.

From the standpoint of Ward's Chinese backers, the value of this foreign militia—despite its very small numbers in comparison to the enemy—was an almost mythical belief in the superior weapons and skills of foreign soldiers that dated back to the British victories in the Opium War. Most important, they hoped that the other side held such a belief strongly enough that they would simply retreat or surrender if faced with

Caucasian opponents. Ward's army was meant to be a spearhead, and an imperial army 10,000 strong would follow just behind it, to invade and garrison each city after the foreign troops stormed its gates. It wasn't an entirely new tactic; as early as 1853 an American soldier reported meeting a Chinese commander near Canton who had dressed up his officers as Europeans to fool the rebels. The commander himself had been a servant to an Englishman and had traveled with him to England, where he had picked up a bit of the language as well as the dress. As he told his visitor, "Rebel man think me English—Merican, all same. On that wall, I number one man."[21] Such was the case with Ward's militia: be they polished professionals or tottering drunkards, the important point was that they had white skin, foreign dress, and repeating arms.

Ward's men made their first attack on Songjiang in April 1860 and did not prove their worth. With no artillery to blast open the gates, Ward planned for his soldiers to sneak up to the city under cover of darkness, throw up scaling ladders, and climb the walls to take the sentries by surprise. But the men got thoroughly drunk in preparation for their adventure, and as they approached Songjiang they made so much noise singing and swearing and arguing among themselves that they woke up the Taiping sentries, who cut them to pieces when they tried to climb the ladders.[22] After a hasty bout of recruiting to replace the dead from that first debacle, and with the purchase in Shanghai of a pair of half-ton Napoleon field guns (the same smooth-bore cannons used widely by both sides in the U.S. Civil War), Ward went in again in July with about 500 troops, this time containing a greater number of Filipino "Manilamen" from the merchant sailing vessels. Under cover of a drifting fog, his artillerymen sighted their Napoleons on the eastern gate of Songjiang, and when night fell they blasted it open with 12-pound shells as the rest of the troops rushed into the breach through the darkness.

It threatened to be an even worse disaster than their first attack, though, for when they got through the outer gate they found that the inner one had been built at a right angle to the first and was untouched by the artillery barrage. They were stuck in the wall: couldn't get through the inner gate, couldn't retreat, couldn't bring their Napoleons across the moat. They were open above to Taiping defenders who—though they couldn't get a direct shot—dropped stinkpots filled with burning sulfur on them all night long.[23] Ward's men managed to budge the inner gate a couple of feet by igniting some bags of gunpowder they'd dragged along, and as they pushed one by one through the gap into a hail of fire (one Englishman's head was split in two at that point), their repeating arms proved effective enough at close quarters to clear a way up the inner wall to a safe corner at the top of the gate, which they held through the night against the city's defenders. Their imperial backup finally arrived after dawn, whereupon the Taiping garrison fled. Most of the 500 foreign mercenaries by that point were dead and all but 27 of the survivors seriously wounded.[24]

It wasn't a spectacular victory, but the city, after a fashion, was theirs, and Ward set up headquarters in the Confucian temple. With Songjiang as a base (and a hospital) he and his lieutenants regrouped and wooed new recruits from Shanghai, and on August 1, 1860, they set out to attack the other strategic city, Qingpu, ten miles to the northwest. This time it was back to failure again, for it turned out the Taiping in Qingpu had managed to assemble their own foreign force, under an English coastal pilot named Savage who brought several of his comrades with him to the Taiping side to man the big guns.[25] Ward's imperial backup army never showed up, and in the fighting Ward took a bullet that punched through both cheeks and disfigured him for the rest of his life.

Under the incapacitated Ward's lieutenant (and with fresh recruits from Shanghai, mostly Greek and Italian) the force threw itself on Qingpu again two weeks later, this time with the imperials behind them, but succeeded only in stirring up a reinforced Taiping garrison that now numbered nearly 50,000 men and drawing Li Xiucheng himself into the battle. Li led a surprise flanking maneuver that routed the mercenaries; even with imperial backup in tow, Ward's men not only failed to take Qingpu but nearly managed to lose Songjiang as well when Li Xiucheng chased them back across the province, decimating the imperial troops along the way and harassing them from outside their own gates for nearly two weeks. The lone silver lining for Ward was that his counterpart, Savage, who had joined in the chase back to Songjiang, was shot in the fighting and died soon afterward in Nanjing.

Not all the foreigners were so hostile to the coming of the rebels. In early July 1860, as Ward was preparing to attack Songjiang, a small boat left Shanghai for the interior, carrying five British and American missionaries. Their goal was to make contact with the Taiping authorities in Suzhou, eighty miles distant along a hazardous water route by river and canal. Barely ten miles out from Shanghai, they skirted the last of the rapidly disappearing imperial guard posts and entered into the arena of the war. Refugees shuffled toward the safety of Shanghai amid the crackle of distant gunfire, while untethered village defense groups patrolled the riverbanks, threatening violence on anyone who dared land on their muddy shores. "Here and there a solitary old man or woman may be seen," reported one of the travelers, "moving slowly and tremblingly among the ruins, musing and weeping over the terrible desolation that reigns around."[26]

The leader of the group was Joseph Edkins, a senior member of the London Missionary Society with a broad white sweep of a beard. His first posting had been in Hong Kong in 1848, and he kept up a close friendship with James Legge, with whom he liked to play a game of reciting entire books of the New Testament from memory (Legge usually won). Legge had recently written to Edkins that there had been no news from Hong Rengan since the letter from Elgin's ship several months earlier and asked him to find out what he could about the fate of their mutual friend.[27] So when the party happened upon a detachment of Taiping cavalry riding alongside the river, Edkins's first question to them was if they knew the name of Hong Rengan. Their answer—that he was now their prime minister in Nanjing, second only to the Heavenly King—was utterly astounding to Edkins and the others. A connection was now established, and the travelers followed the Taiping horsemen back to their camp, where they were delighted by the unexpected friendliness they encountered. Another member of the traveling party, a Welsh Congregationalist named Griffith John, described the rebels as "strong in muscle, free and bold in manner, and open in countenance," terms never commonly used by the British to describe the Chinese. Excited and emboldened, the travelers left their hosts and pressed onward toward Suzhou with newly issued Taiping passports in hand.

These missionaries had long welcomed the destruction of the civil war, because they saw God's hand at work in the Taiping armies. "Prophecy has said, 'I will shake the nations,'" wrote Edkins a few months before his trip to Suzhou, "and in China there has commenced an era of change, when multitudes are suffering present calamities for the ultimate good of the whole nation."[28] But it was one thing to reflect on such calamities from the relative safety of Shanghai, another to enter their midst. As the boat edged deeper into the war zone, the heady optimism of the missionaries ran up against countercurrents of horror. It was their fourth night, finally approaching the conquered city of Suzhou, that they would have forgotten if they could. For that was the night that their little boat slowed in its progress, the putrid smell of rot grew and thickened, and finally they came to a stop. Peering out into the twilight by the soft glow of their lanterns, all they could make out on the still surface of the dark water, for hundreds of yards in front of them, were the bodies of the dead—cold, nameless, and uncountable—that jammed the canal like so many logs. But there was no turning back. The missionaries pushed their boat forward into the grim mass, oars thudding dully in the blackness, until exhaustion finally overcame them and they had to sleep, there, in the unforgiving embrace of the multitudes.[29]

The shaken travelers arrived the next morning at Suzhou, where they learned that the savagery of war was consuming not only the mortal but also the divine. The rebels had reserved a special kind of violence for the icons of China's traditional religions, and Griffith John described temples where "It is common to see the nose, chin, and hands cut off" of the wooden deities. "The floors of these buildings are bestrewn with relics of helpless gods," he wrote, "Buddhist and Daoist, male and female. Some are cast into the canals, and are found floating down the stream mingled with the debris of rifled houses and the remains of the dead."[30] Other statues were removed from the city and set up on hillsides with rebel flags as decoys to lure the imperial troops into battle.[31] But Griffith John's unease at witnessing such violence was tempered by the joyful realization that here was proof that the Taiping opposed idolatry. The very zeal of their desecration of the Buddhist and Daoist temples was evidence of the rebels' intent to instill China with Protestant Christianity. Such news would be anathema to the Catholics of France (as one analyst in London observed, "The French have reasons for fearing Tae Ping ascendancy; for an image is to them an image, whether baptized or unbaptized, and an image-worshipper is an image-worshipper").[32] But to the Protestants of England and the United States it was, as it were, a godsend.

Hong Rengan was still in Nanjing when they arrived, but Li Xiucheng held court in Suzhou, and he invited the missionaries for an audience. They found themselves welcomed with a six-gun salute and ushered along an aisle flanked by servants and officers standing at attention into a red-carpeted reception hall amid the celebratory clash of drums and gongs. To their eyes, the Loyal King seemed a gentle, almost intellectual presence, with "small keen features," wearing spectacles and wrapped in an imperial yellow silk robe. Edkins pronounced him to have "the character of a good man," who kept his troops well disciplined for the sake of "protecting the suffering people, who are the victims of this civil war, from injury and insult."[33] (Others, in other contexts, found him to be animated with twitching wiriness and a restless, searching energy.)[34] The audience did not last long, but it was enough for the missionaries and the rebel general to find themselves in agreement on the basic tenets of their religions, and on the calendrical dates of their Sabbath. Satisfied, and knowing that their mercantile brethren in Shanghai cared less about doctrine than profit, they also asked Li Xiucheng if he would allow the silk trade to continue under Taiping rule, and Li replied that such trade was exactly what his regime desired. They left the Loyal King with a gift of Chinese-language Bibles and departed, in excitement, to return home and share the remarkable news.

Edkins and his companions returned straightaway to Shanghai, where Edkins breathlessly wrote up his experiences for publication. His report in the Shanghai English-language newspaper, *The North-China Herald,* was a forceful defense of the rebels against the imperial propaganda that had been circulating about them in the city. "A great deal has been said about the cruelty of the 'long-haired rebels,'" wrote Edkins, "but in this there has been much exaggeration and misrepresentation."[35] If they committed any crimes of war—murder, loot, pillage—he argued, it was only for the sake of survival, and besides, those crimes were the work of only the newest recruits, who hadn't yet received proper religious instruction from their superiors; whenever a senior Taiping leader arrived, the criminals were promptly executed. He maintained that most of the deaths in the captured city of Suzhou (including those from the canal that haunted his nightmares) were victims of suicide, not murder. And the imperial forces were by far the worse offenders. Given time, a Taiping victory—which one of his informants predicted in two years' time—would bring an end to bloodshed and disorder in China and usher in a new era of peace and morality. Edkins declared, "They are revolutionists in the strictest sense of the term; both the work of slaughter and of plunder are carried on so far as is necessary to secure the end. These are evils which necessarily accompany such a movement, and are justifiable or otherwise in so far as the movement itself is so."[36] There was no question in his mind that the movement *was* justified, and therefore so were the unfortunate, but temporary, disturbances it caused.

Edkins spoke glowingly of the promise a Taiping China would hold for the Protestant countries of the West, dismissing concerns over their doctrinal oddities. It wasn't that the Taiping were so blasphemous as to believe Hong Xiuquan was the divine son of God, he explained, only that they thought he served a similar mission to Jesus Christ, whom the Old

Testament–influenced rebels didn't quite understand had achieved apo-theosis. They could be educated. Edkins admired the immanence of their religion. "The Deity is with them," he wrote, "not an abstract notion, nor a stern implacable sovereign, but a loving father, who watches tenderly over their affairs, and leads them by the hand."[37] If the Qing were to fall and the Taiping succeed, the Christian rebels could be counted on to "set on foot a more rigid and vigorous morality than that to which the Chinese have long been accustomed."[38] It would be a moral state—and a Christian state.

Above all, in language calculated to appeal far beyond the circle of the missionaries and their supporters, he declared that it would be a state friendly to the West. The Taiping always referred to foreigners as "our for-eign brethren," he emphasized, and it "would be most pleasing to them" to open the entire empire to foreign trade. Furthermore, Edkins recounted, the Taiping "say that foreigners will be respected whenever they pass through their territory." The coming of that future state was all but assured, he concluded, for "They seem now to be taking a hold of this empire with an iron grasp, and treading it like conquerors." Not only was a Taiping vic-tory inevitable, then, but the goal of the rebels to promote friendly diplo-macy and welcome trade was exactly what the foreign powers had been demanding, in vain, from the Manchus for so many years.[39]

Edkins's most smitten convert was his young wife, Jane, who wept in sadness when he first left Shanghai and again with joy when she heard his account of Suzhou under the rebels. She was just twenty-one years old, and they had been married for only a year (she was so frail that her family had worried about her traveling with him all the way to China, but such was the lot of a missionary's bride). "Is not this insurgent movement truly wonderful?" she wrote to her mother-in-law from Shanghai in July 1860. "These rebels keep sabbath as we do, they pray to God daily, they read the Scriptures, they break the idols, and they long for the time when, instead of those heathen temples, they shall have Christian chapels, and worship together with us . . . is it not a remarkable era in China?"[40] Later, as rumors intensified that the Taiping were advancing toward Shanghai and as the foreign commanders called up their volunteers to defend the walls, she went further: "I profess to be a rebel at heart somehow," she wrote to her father, "and have a secret wish to welcome them."[41]

A few weeks later, toward the end of July, Joseph Edkins and Griffith John returned to Suzhou for a second visit after receiving two personal letters of invitation, one from Li Xiucheng and the other from Hong Ren-gan. Hong Rengan's invitation was "the most cheering, delightful news that ever rang in the ears of missionaries," wrote Jane Edkins, and she wished she could join their new expedition but conceded that "the scenes through which they must pass are too trying for a lady."[42] Griffith John wrote that the letters from Hong Rengan and Li Xiucheng "breathe a manliness and a kindliness of spirit . . . such as could never have been written by an unchristian Chinaman. I see in them a new element—an element which Christianity alone could infuse."[43]

In their return to Suzhou at the beginning of August, Edkins and John found an even warmer welcome than they had enjoyed on their first visit. Hong Rengan, draped in silk robes and wearing an embroidered gold crown, seemed almost embarrassed by his position. He insisted on greeting them after their own fashion—no kowtowing or kneeling, but instead a hearty handshake, and he dismissed his host of attendants and removed his crown to talk informally with them. They talked of old times, of old friends and the progress of the missions. They prayed together. They sang hymns that Hong Rengan remembered fondly from his days with the London Missionary Society, and he confided that he had never been so happy as when he was a preacher's assistant in Hong Kong. They talked of China's future, and he suggested that the rebellion was secondary in importance to the work the missionaries were doing—that China had to be Christianized no matter what happened to the dynasty. For his own part, he said that all he wanted was to lead the Taiping toward a correct understanding of religion. Yes, his cousin had made him a king, but it wasn't an office he could refuse. He prayed, recounted Griffith John, "that all the idols might perish, that the temples should be converted into chapels, and that pure Christianity should speedily become the religion of China." It was, to the visiting missionaries, "a spectacle never to be forgotten."[44]

The prospect of one of their native preachers ascending into the future government of China thrilled the international missionary community. The London Missionary Society's *Missionary Magazine* gave notice of Hong Rengan's rise in October 1860. "We feel assured," wrote the editors, "that our readers will unite in fervent supplication to the God of all grace, that this individual . . . may be preserved amidst the perils of his high position."[45] The *Missionary Magazine and Chronicle* laid out a brief biography of "this now distinguished Chinaman," promising that the facts of Hong Rengan's life would be sure to "awaken a lively and prayerful solicitude on behalf of a man so singularly raised by the providence of God to the highest post of honour and influence in the councils of the victorious leader of the Chinese insurgents."[46]

James Legge himself wrote that with his old and dear friend Hong Rengan in Nanjing, "There is, then, one individual at least among the insurgent hosts who is fully acquainted with the truth."[47] Legge claimed that Hong Rengan had had only two goals when he left for Nanjing: "the correction of religious errors" among the rebels and "to commend a line of policy conciliatory to foreigners . . . to secure, if not their co-operation in the objects of the rebellion, at least their sympathy." Here was the sum total of Western hopes for a new China: that it should be properly Christian and that it should be friendly to the West. By November, representatives from nearly all of the major missionary organizations in England joined together in sending a letter to the foreign minister calling for Britain to continue its policy of strict neutrality in the Chinese civil war, citing as justification the rebel movement's "decided attachment to Christianity."[48]

The public press in Britain reverberated with celebrations of Hong Rengan to the reading public. An article titled "The Chinese Revolution" in *Tait's Edinburgh Magazine* announced that "We have now . . . an influential leader of the revolution, whose acquaintance with Christianity, and also with European habits . . . were acquired at Shanghai and Hong Kong from our own missionaries and those of the States." Due to this "humble and poor missionary," it read, the "glad tidings of salvation" were now "embodied in the state documents of the Taiping movement."[49] Joseph Edkins had translated Hong Rengan's treatise on government into English, and the article's author went through a summary of Hong Rengan's plans for the Taiping kingdom—the railroads and factories, the end of opium, the introduction of science—and concluded that, given the great hostilities between Britain and the Qing government, the time was ripe for "seeking peace with the new power" of the Taiping.

A separate article in *The London Review* announced, "This seems almost incredible, so total is the change from all that Europeans have been accustomed to expect and receive at the hands of men in power in China; but its correctness admits of no question."[50] Describing the visit between Joseph Edkins and the Shield King, its unnamed author declared, "Had any romance-writer, twenty years ago, pictured a scene in China, in which native and Englishman played the respective parts here described, what would have been thought of the probability of his conception? . . . had a missionary orator sketched it in anticipation for the year 1860, would not even zealous and confident Christians have regarded it as wild?"[51] Only now, it seemed, could the British see the Taiping rebels clearly, for what they really were: "the Tae Pings are not a myth," this writer proclaimed,

but a power. After ten years' of changeful fortune, sometimes seeming, to the eye of Europe, at the threshold of empire, sometimes
almost forgotten, they now stand up before us, counting their subjects by tens of millions; lords of the finest territories of China,—
of those from which we cheer our tables with tea and enrich our
toilets with silk; holding the Grand Canal and the Yangtze as Tae
Ping waters; sitting royally in the traditional capital of the empire,
and thence shaking a menacing hand against the foreign dynasty
at Pekin. They are without doubt at present the most formidable
native power in China, and, so far as we know, in eastern maritime
Asia.[52]

The veil, as it were, had been lifted.

CHAPTER 5

AN APPOINTMENT IN THE NORTH

While Hong Rengan and Li Xiucheng were in Nanjing plotting to break the imperial siege of their capital in the winter of 1860, an entirely separate campaign against the Manchus was taking shape at the other extreme of the continent. On January 24, 1860, Earl Grey stood up in Britain's House of Lords to announce his shock at having just discovered that for three months already, "our ports and arsenals have resounded with the din of preparation" for a war of revenge against the Qing dynasty.[1] The mission had been in secret preparation almost since the first news of the repulse at Taku reached England in 1859; Prime Minister Lord Palmerston wanted blood, and Emperor Napoleon III readily agreed to a new joint expedition to send Lord Elgin and Baron Gros back to China to finish what they had started.

The new mission did not, however, come with the blessing of Britain's Parliament—which was supposed to control the government's purse strings. In this case, however, it had been completely ignored. Earl Grey claimed that the government was readying artillery, gunboats, and stores for an expeditionary force numbering what he feared would be as many as 10,000 soldiers for an invasion of northern China. He condemned the secret preparations and challenged the wisdom of renewing Britain's war against the Qing dynasty. "We must consider," he admonished the lords, "whether our great trade with China—a trade which, directly and indirectly, contributes more to our prosperity than that which we carry on with any other nation of the world, with the single exception of the United States . . . is likely to be promoted by burning the cities and slaughtering the inhabitants of that vast empire." And if the country did launch this war, he warned them, "there may be no retreat, save by pulling down the ancient and already tottering fabric of the Chinese Empire."²

Despite Grey's objections and the lack of any approval from Parliament, the war went ahead. The armada the two countries assembled from Britain, India, and France to escort Lord Elgin and Baron Gros back to the Peiho in 1860 was on a nearly unprecedented scale. There were 41 men-of-war in total, trailing 143 transports. Those transports carried a huge arsenal of field artillery, along with more than a thousand cavalry horses in cramped stalls. Commissariat officers fanned out in advance to Singapore, Japan, Shanghai, and Manila to purchase draft animals—2,500 mules, bullocks, and ponies, with drivers—to pull the artillery and supply wagons overland once the army got to its destination. In its fullest form, the invasion force would comprise some 24,000 British, French, and Indian troops, attended by thousands of support personnel.³

It was, in short, an army more than twice as powerful as even Earl Grey had feared, and in the minds of those who knew of its creation, it was strong enough to bring down the Qing dynasty if its commanders so chose. Elgin himself reflected on such a possibility in a letter to Lord Russell that July. "We might annex the Empire if we were in the humour to take a second India into hand," he wrote in bleak amusement, "or we might change the Dynasty if we knew where to find a better."⁴ According to a Russian diplomat, Elgin later wondered privately whether Britain should "recognize as Chinese Emperor one of the leaders of the rebel movement assuming he would agree to the favorable conditions of the Tianjin treaty." Not only would that give Britain its desired trade concessions and thereby end the conflict, but also it would prevent further repetitions of the resistance the Qing had exhibited because "if the capital of China were moved nearer to our military presence like Nanking . . . England could control the Chinese Empire with four gunboats." The easier route to satisfying Britain's desires, it seemed, would be through the Taiping rather than the Manchus. As for the future of the Manchus in that case, Elgin allegedly told his Russian counterpart, "Let the north disappear or form a separate government, we don't have any trade interests there."⁵

Britain's quarrel with the Manchus in Beijing and Frederick Bruce's fears of a rebel invasion of Shanghai were, in the minds of those caught in the middle of the looming events, entirely separate things. So even as he worried about protecting Shanghai from the Taiping, and even as he mulled the fine (that is, nearly invisible) distinction between defending Shanghai and supporting the Qing dynasty, Frederick Bruce was urging Britain to bring new force to bear in north China. He believed that no concessions could be gained from the Qing government without it. "It may be very difficult to justify in England the course adopted," he had written to Russell back when the new war against the Manchus was first taking shape, but still he thought that the "true policy of China" was to allow foreigners in only after they knew they couldn't keep them out by force.[6] According to Bruce's informers, the "war-party" in the Qing government (others called them China's Tories), which included Senggelinqin and the emperor's senior Manchu advisers, had achieved ascendance after Elgin's invasion of Tianjin in 1858. Bruce was fully convinced that "nothing short of the complete defeat of this hostile party, and a lesson which will teach the Chinese that perfidy and bad faith lead necessarily to signal punishment, will enable us to place our relations for the future on a secure basis." That is, the only way for Britain to achieve amicable relations with the Qing government (and, incidentally, to finally get Frederick Bruce into his embassy) was to strike at them with even greater force than they had before.

But the two events *were* simultaneous, and the Allied forces began to arrive in China just as the foreign residents of Shanghai were cowering in fear of an imminent attack by the rebels. The Chinese population of Shanghai emptied as families shut their homes and shops and moved onto rented boats that floated ten deep in the river, crowded with people and possessions, ready to cast off the moment the enemy army appeared.[7] Then, right in the midst of the panic, Lord Elgin arrived on June 29, 1860, with a fleet of French and British gunboats. Here, it seemed, was the *deus ex machina* to save Shanghai from a Taiping invasion. While the bulk of the British forces camped in the south of China on Kowloon peninsula across from Hong Kong, the French troops and the gunships joined Baron Gros and Lord Elgin in Shanghai, and the merchants in the foreign settlement thrilled because now they were saved—for after all, Lord Elgin was Frederick Bruce's brother, and surely he would look out for their interests.

It very soon became apparent, however, that the Allied commanders had no intention of helping Frederick Bruce defend Shanghai. They proved unswerving in their plan to force a treaty ratification in the north and therefore departed from Shanghai almost as soon as they arrived, leaving the city with only a scant defensive force of a couple of gunboats and some stray divisions of Sikh troops. The merchants cried that they had been abandoned by their own countrymen in their greatest hour of need. Furious at the departure of Elgin's fleet, they turned a wary eye back toward the western horizon, beyond which the rebels loomed. They tried not to think too hard about the dire prophecies of the imperials in their midst, and prepared for the worst.

Left to his own devices in Shanghai after his brother departed for the north, Frederick Bruce refused to countenance the possibility raised by Joseph Edkins and the other missionaries that the rebels under Hong Rengan were actually friendly, not hostile, to foreigners. Bruce had little experience in China (beyond his most recent experiences, there was just a short stint in Hong Kong in the 1840s). He did not speak the language, he had few contacts, and he had barely traveled anywhere in the country. But he was a man of strong convictions. He had read a few books—enough to let him think he knew much more than he did—and the horrible embarrassment at the Taku forts had left him with the unshakable certainty that all Chinese, no matter what stripe, were duplicitous. And so, although he had no power to prevent Edkins and John from visiting the rebels, he turned a deaf ear to the news they brought back from Suzhou because he was positive that they were being duped.

Bruce warned Edkins against encouraging British support for the Taiping, writing to him on July 28 that "Similarity of belief and sympathy are not grounds sufficient to justify a foreign nation in taking part in a civil contest."[8] Specifically, he judged that what he termed the Taiping's "novel anxiety for foreign intercourse" must either be a ruse to gain foreign support or—in a wondrous tautology—something that, if it were true, would alienate their countrymen and make it impossible for them to rule China. In spite of his disgust with the Manchu rulers in Beijing, Bruce saw the Taiping as "merely a body of men in arms against their legitimate Government," and in such terms, they were but rebels. Following the views of Thomas Wade, Bruce believed that the force of stability and tradition in China lay with the "legitimate" Manchus in the capital, no matter how corrupt and xenophobic they might be.

Bruce did, however, dutifully forward the gleanings of Edkins and other missionaries to the Foreign Office in London. He reported that Hong Rengan, among other things, advocated "intercourse with foreigners on a footing of equality, the introduction of steam-vessels, railways, and other western inventions," and that his tract on government contained "sounder and more enlightened views of Christianity" than the British were used to seeing from the Chinese.[9] Nevertheless, Bruce dismissed any prospects such an attitude might afford for relations between Britain and the Taiping. He said there was no way to know whether Hong Rengan was sincere or deceptive, and suggested that he had probably "written this work in the hopes of enlisting the sympathies of Christendom in his favour." Having little regard for the honesty of any Chinese, Bruce was inclined toward the latter interpretation. And as he had told Edkins, he believed that the Chinese people—not just the officials and scholars but even the peasants—were so wedded to the sages of Confucian tradition that even *if* Hong Rengan's tract were genuine and the Taiping wanted equal diplomacy and a Christian society, that very fact would make it impossible for them ever to succeed in winning the support of the great mass of Chinese people. In Bruce's mind the hatred of foreigners and the hatred of foreign religions were such immutable and unchanging aspects of Chinese culture that it was impossible even to conceive of a rebel victory. So he held fast in his determination to defend the Chinese city of Shanghai from the Taiping hordes. On principle, he at least tried to notify the rebels of his intent, sending a boat up the river with a letter for them. But the crew of the boat returned without finding anyone they could give it to.

Others tried to sway Frederick Bruce from his convictions, notably a British consul named Thomas Taylor Meadows who thought Bruce was dead wrong in his judgment of the rebellion. Meadows, who at that time was serving in Shanghai, had a much longer experience in China than did Bruce, and unlike his superior he both spoke Chinese and had traveled to the interior. He maintained what appears to have been the most effective network of Chinese informants of any foreign official then resident in China, and for a long time he had believed the success of the Taiping to be inevitable.[10]

Meadows had worked out a theory of political change in China, which he published in a book titled *The Chinese and Their Rebellions* while on home leave a few years earlier. In that widely read book he argued that rebellion was a natural cycle in Chinese politics. In the long span of Chinese history, he wrote, "periodical dynastic rebellions are absolutely necessary to the continued well being of the nation . . . only they are the storms that can clear the political atmosphere when it has become sultry and oppressive." That is, rebellions like the one Bruce imagined to be hopeless were in fact one of the elemental forces that had ensured the longevity of the Chinese state through such a long succession of empires. China, wrote Meadows, "respects successful rebellions, as executions of the Will of Heaven, operating for its preservation in peace, order, security, and prosperity."[11]

As it pertained to British policy during the Chinese civil war, Meadows maintained that the worst thing the Western powers could possibly do would be to interfere in any capacity at all. For even if they were to interfere for purely humanitarian reasons—say, to put an end to the horrific suffering and bloodshed in the ongoing conflict—such interference in the natural course of rebellion "could, if unsuccessful, only produce a prolongation of the state of anarchy, or of civil war." Yet such an *unsuccessful* interference, he went on, would actually be the mildest possible outcome; far worse would be a *successful* interference, the "certain result" of which would be "an internally weak government; and an internally weak government is identical with a cowardly government, a vicious government, and a cruel government."[12] That is to say, if Britain did not allow the rebellion in China to follow its natural course, it would at best contribute to an even more intractable state of anarchy and at worst condemn the Chinese people to rule by a corrupt and cruel government that should rightly have fallen.

Meadows would turn out to be the most prescient of the foreign observers of his time. But his rank of consul was such that he had to take his orders from Bruce, and so Bruce's conception of the Taiping prevailed. In late July 1860, Meadows presented Bruce with a sealed letter that had been brought by a courier to Shanghai, addressed to the representatives of the United States, France, and England. It was from Li Xiucheng. Bruce declined to open it, saying he didn't want to involve himself with the rebels. A few days later, Meadows took another letter to Bruce, this one from Hong Rengan and similarly addressed to the foreign representatives. Meadows tried to make it clear to his superior that Hong Rengan was "well known to the Protestant missionaries of Hong Kong and Shanghai, among whom he lived as a Christian convert."[13] But once again Bruce refused to open the letter. He told Meadows that it was "both inexpedient and objectionable on principle that Her Majesty's Consuls should hold any communication with the insurgents at Suzhou," so he directed Meadows, quite bluntly, to "take no notice of it."[14] Both letters were returned unopened.

The letters were fatally important. In his unread letter, Li Xiucheng the

Loyal King notified the foreign authorities that the Taiping were on their way to Shanghai and intended to take possession of the Chinese section of the city—and only the Chinese section of the city—from the Manchu government. He stated that the rebels had no quarrel whatsoever with their foreign brethren and pledged not to harm any of them or their property. To that end, he explained, he had issued orders that any Taiping soldier who harmed a foreigner should be put to death. He hoped that the ministers in Shanghai would call their people together and ask them to stay indoors during the Taiping approach, hoisting yellow flags above their doors to signify that there were foreigners in the house. Were they to do so, he could ensure that none of their citizens or property would be touched when the Taiping drove the imperials from their Shanghai base. Li Xiucheng closed his letter to the foreign ministers on a friendly note, saying that he looked forward to holding discussions with them once he arrived at Shanghai, and he wished them good health.[15]

On the afternoon of August 17, 1860, the sky to the west of Shanghai grew dark with the smoke of distant burning. The next morning came the broken ranks of imperial soldiers, running for the gates of the city, hounded close behind by rebel horsemen. The British let a few of the imperials through the gate into the safety of the Chinese city, and then, fearing the rebels would storm the gates when the retreating troops tried to escape inside, they destroyed the bridge leading across the moat. As the Taiping advance guard rushed forward, the spotters in their wooden towers atop the wall gave a shout, and the British and French artillery let loose with a deafening barrage of canister and grapeshot that lit up the ground in the rebels' path. The improvised British and French defenses—mountain howitzers, Chinese guns rigged up by British marines, Sikh sharpshooters wielding Brown Bess muskets—proved deadly. The handful of imperial troops who made it safely through the gate climbed to the top of the wall, where they sat, lit their pipes, and dangled their legs off the side to enjoy the show that began unfolding below.[16]

The rumored Taiping invasion turned out to be an absurdly small force, a few thousand men at most and only lightly armed (there were also a handful of foreigners among them, as the British forces would discover later when they sifted through the dead bodies). While the British and French gunners watched from above, Taiping soldiers ducked into and out of cover near the walls—hiding behind burial tombs, stands of brush, buildings—their bafflement apparent even from a distance. They didn't shoot back. Yet whenever one showed his face, down came the rain of fire from the wall. One Taiping detachment tried to march forward waving imperial flags captured from the outlying battery—it was shot up, and when it dropped the false colors and raised its own yellow flags, the punishment was even worse. Another detachment rushed in with banners flying, impelled by a man waving an enormous black flag that the Taiping used to drive forward reluctant troops. A well-aimed shell from half a mile away arced lazily through the air and dropped, exploding right in the middle of the pack and flattening the flag bearer to the ground.

In baffled disarray, the rebel soldiers mustered in one of the suburban houses, but the spotters in their towers on the city wall could see the bright yellow flags they carried and tracked them easily. An expert shot from a gunship in the river screamed through the air, cleared the British settlement, and dropped to earth right on top of the house. Then came another shell and another and another at ten-minute intervals—missiles shrieking through the darkness as night fell and sending up thunderous explosions that shook the ground and thrilled the hearts of the population safe inside the wall.[17] As night gave way to morning, a report came that the *daotai*'s forces were mutilating captured rebels (one was first disemboweled and then beheaded), so the British commanders asserted their nonalliance with the Qing authorities by ordering that no Taiping prisoners be turned over to them. But that would be the full extent of their moral high ground, for with the dawn of the following day the French took over and made the imperials look like dilettantes. In order to prevent the rebels from using the houses in the suburbs as cover to approach the city walls, the French commanders decided to destroy the suburbs themselves.[18]

Early on the morning of August 19, French troops moved through the crowded Chinese settlements under the city walls, firing their muskets at will and setting fire to the houses and shops in an orgy of conflagration. These were the wealthy mercantile districts of Shanghai, and entire warehouses of sugar and soy went up in colorful explosions.[19] An eyewitness report published a few days later in *The North-China Herald* and relayed from there back to the papers in London described a panicked scene, with French soldiers rushing "frantically among the peaceful inhabitants of the place, murdering men, women, and children, without the least discrimination." The French atrocities were at least as awful as those of the imperial-ists. "One man," the correspondent wrote, "was stabbed right through as he was enjoying his opium-pipe. A woman, who had just given birth to a child, was bayoneted without the faintest provocation. Women were ravished and houses plundered by these ruthless marauders without restraint."[20] Another witness estimated that the French left tens of thousands of Chi-nese homeless in the course of defending against a lightly armed Taiping force that numbered, by his estimate, 3,000 at most.[21]

The irony that the British should attack the rebels even as Elgin's armies were sailing north to make war against the imperial government was not lost on the editors of *The New York Times*. An editorial on Octo-ber 1 entitled "The Chinese Rebellion and the Allies" ridiculed the British for turning the rebels back at a time when they themselves were planning a full-scale war on the Manchus in Beijing. "It is quite possible, and even highly probable," it read, "that were the rebels moving toward Peking by an inland route, the wisdom of encouraging rather than obstructing their march would be recognized." It seemed a fact lost on the British that their goals and those of the rebels were identical and would lead *together* to the inevitable end of the dynasty: "the success of the European enterprise [Elgin's advance], aided as it is by the warfare of the Tai Ping, must involve the overthrow of the Tartar supremacy, and the eventual elevation of a dif-ferent race to imperial influence."[22]

But unlike Frederick Bruce, the editors of *The New York Times* had absorbed the reports of the missionaries and believed that the Taiping would bring precisely the kind of China the British forces were fighting for. "The interests of unrestricted trade, of religion, and of civilization gener-ally," the editorial continued, "strengthen the hope of the present rebellion becoming the successor of the expiring dynasty; thus enthroning a rule distinguished by its friendly temper toward foreigners, and anxious to pro-mote all those means of intercourse, of which the reigning Princes are so incurably jealous." It seemed obvious to them that China's future lay with the Taiping, and the editorial warned that "Any unfriendly action toward this rising power is therefore a serious misfortune."[23]

The Taiping retreated, but the suburbs of Shanghai burned for days. Watchers from outside were aghast at the so-called victory the Allies had secured. As a writer in the *London Quarterly Review* put it, "we slaughtered men whom we had never notified of our hostility, and who avowed and showed themselves our friends."[24] *The New York Times* followed its previous warnings with a front-page condemnation of the French and British actions, headlined "The Visit of the Rebel Forces to Shanghai: No Attack Made by Them," in which the paper's China correspondent summed up the atrocities committed by French troops in Shanghai and pronounced that "for such barbarity there is no excuse." The correspondent argued that "the rebels seem to have come with no other object than to get possession of the Chinese city" and pointed out that the Taiping—who always treated foreigners with "marked politeness," even when they were being shot at—not only hadn't fired back, they also hadn't touched the foreign concessions, which, unlike the Chinese city, were unwalled and therefore easily overrun. Their restraint under fire was all the more remarkable, observed the *Times* correspondent, given that "the notorious Col. Ward, so called" and his mercenary army of "runaway sailors, Manilamen, and foreign vagabonds" had been harassing them unprovoked outside Shanghai for months. The proper action of the foreign powers all along, he concluded, would have been to let the Taiping have the city. Trade could have gone on as usual, the rebels would have held the Chinese city as their right, neutrality would have been properly observed, and there would be peace.[25]

In all, this attack on the Taiping at Shanghai would do more to build sympathy for their cause abroad than anything that had gone before, for it brought them to the front pages. Once a cipher, now they were held up as a Christian, pro-Western alternative to the universally reviled Manchu rulers in Beijing. In the eyes of many in Britain and America, the clash at Shanghai was at best a regrettable misunderstanding, at worst a despicable act of aggression against innocent victims, a trespass on the wrong side of the civil war. "We are proud of our political creed and our sacrifices for political liberty," wrote one man in England to decry the injustice at Shanghai, "but is it the wind or the sky that changes in a voyage over the Indian Ocean, that all our professions here should there be turned into a burning and mean lie against freedom and men struggling to be free?"[26]

All of which is to say that in spite of the repulse, the Taiping were still in the ascendant. And although they suffered losses at the hands of the British at Shanghai, those losses were nothing compared to what was about to befall their enemies in Beijing. For no sooner did the Taiping retreat from Shanghai, and no sooner did a sense of calm reinfuse the city, than the eyes of the world turned instead toward the north, drawn by reports just beginning to arrive from Taku, detailing the heavy fighting under way as Elgin's army lumbered down the path of its own dark logic.

The military force that escorted Lord Elgin and Baron Gros back to China was nothing if not colorful. There were the Europeans: British artillerymen in dark blue uniforms; French infantry with light blue jackets, white pants, and large square backpacks; British infantry with pith helmets and khaki tunics or red coats (depending on the temperature); and the mounted King's Dragoon Guards with their scarlet jackets, high white helmets, and razor-sharp sabers. Then there were the colonial troops, including fifty Algerian cavalry in "Arab costume" who formed the bodyguard of the French general.[27] The largest number of colonial troops was from India, more than 4,000 of them, including two large forces of Sikh cavalrymen with flowing black beards—Probyn's Horse in blue-black serge tunics with gray turbans, Fane's Horse in light blue coats with turbans of red. The British commissariat provided rations not just of biscuit, salted beef, and sherry for the expedition but also of mutton, turmeric, chilies, and ghee.

This time, the British also raised a "native" force to support their invasion army: about 3,000 Chinese men from Canton, primarily Hakkas, hired to carry supplies for the military train. They were salaried at the rate of nine dollars a month and given daily rations of rice and salted meat. Each wore a dark Chinese jacket and loose pants with no shoes, and on the front of each jacket was a circle containing the wearer's number and the company to which he belonged. Thanks to a rumor that the members of the force would be used as cannon fodder in the front lines, recruitment had been difficult and the enlistees were thought to be "the scum only of the population of Canton."[28] Some in the British entourage found their presence unsettling. "[H]owever valuable their services," wrote one medical officer, "it is difficult to lose sight of the fact that they are Chinese subjects, allured by the all-powerful attractions of the dollar to act against their government."[29] And yet, there they were. The quartermaster general recorded that "they are industrious and good-tempered, and appear to have no sympathy with the Northern Chinese."[30] They all wore pointed bamboo hats, emblazoned on the front with the letters "CCC": Canton Coolie Corps.

The invasion force also included a number of noncombatants of various descriptions. There was an amateur French zoologist who hoped to use the expedition as a chance to investigate Chinese fauna (during the campaign Elgin himself was reading Charles Darwin's recently published *Origin of Species*, which he thought "audacious").[31] Another French scholar went along at his government's behest to study political economy, in the guise of an official *mission scientifique* that was in fact devoid of actual scientists.[32] Then there were the journalists. Thomas Bowlby of *The Times,* one of the world's first embedded reporters, was already famous for his vivid accounts from the Crimea, and he now joined Elgin's retinue with the plan of keeping the British public supplied with a blow-by-blow account of the events unfolding in north China. Afterward, he hoped to go to Suzhou to report on the rebels.[33] The editors of the English-language *North-China Herald* and *China Mail* also came along; one of them looked so much like Lord Elgin that people kept confusing them.[34] *The Illustrated London News* sent a sketch artist to make firsthand drawings of the campaign. And finally there was an Italian photographer named Felice Beato, with all of his equipment, who went into raptures over scenes of violence and would in some cases re-create them after the fact by rearranging the corpses of dead imperial soldiers into aesthetically pleasing configurations.[35]

Felice Beato was hardly the first to see a certain beauty in the carnage of the Chinese civil war. As Lord Elgin's secretary had described a running battle he witnessed along the Yangtze in 1858, "The hurrying of bodies of men to and fro over the fields—the waving of flags and firing of gingalls—the thunder of our own heavy guns—the groups of country people hastening across the drawbridge into the city for refuge, staggering under heavy loads, and driving cattle before them—the smoke of their burning homes rising up to the cloudless sky—all combined to form a scene to gaze upon which, as it lay mapped out beneath, must have stirred the heart and sent the blood tingling through the veins of the most unimpassioned nature." He reflected happily at the time that "It is so seldom that we experience emotions which unite in themselves at one and the same moment the highest amount of aesthetic and animal excitement."[36] Likewise, an air of festivity attended the invasion forces.

Elgin's orders were simple: to sail once more up the Peiho to Tianjin, ratify the treaty, and force the emperor to apologize for the attack on the British fleet at the Taku forts the previous year. He was also to secure an indemnity from the Qing government to reimburse Britain for the costs of the war. The imperial forces under Senggelinqin knew well in advance that the Allies were coming and what they were coming for, so the Taku forts were heavily manned in preparation for showing the foreigners another repulse at the site of their previous humiliation.

This time, however, the Allies simply avoided Taku and landed a few miles to the north. At half past three on the afternoon of August 1, 1860,

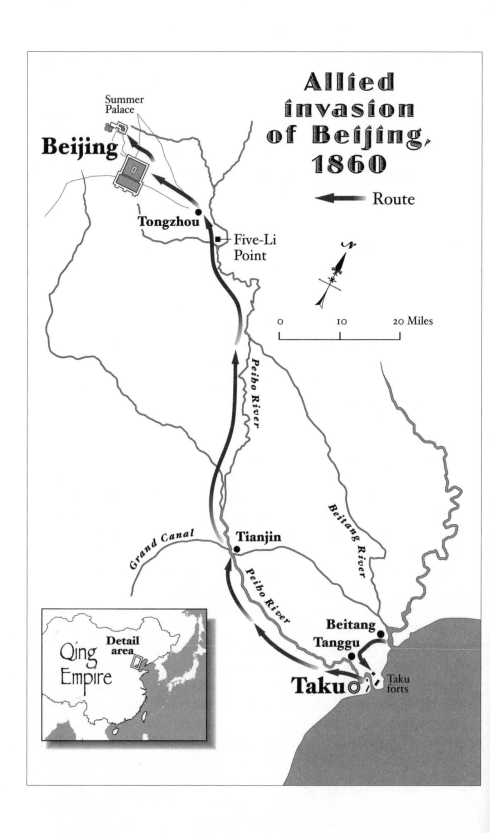

Allied
invasion
of Beijing,
1860

Route

Summer
Palace

Beijing

Tongzhou

Five-Li
Point

Peiho River

Grand Canal

Tianjin

Peiho River

Beitang River

Beitang
Tanggu

Taku

Taku
forts

Qing
Empire

Detail
area

0   10   20 Miles

with two hundred British and French ships hovering at anchor offshore, an advance force of 400 Allied troops landed just below the smaller Beitang River, seven miles up the coast from the Peiho.[37] Heavy rains that morning had worsened already muddy conditions, and they had to wade through brackish waist-deep water to get to shore; then, abandoning their pants in some cases, they slogged across three-quarters of a mile of thick, ankle-deep mud to get to a causeway that rose six feet above the tidal mudflats and led to the nearby walled town.[38]

Unlike the large forts at Taku to their south, the lesser defenses around Beitang appeared to be unprepared, and the advance party was able to take possession of the causeway without a shot being fired. As darkness fell, the Chinese defenders of the two forts that guarded the banks of the river abandoned their posts and disappeared. The men of the Allied advance party made camp as best they could that night and slept fitfully, exposed on the causeway under the lantern glow of a full moon, just a short distance from the gates of the town they planned to enter by force in the morning. Near midnight, eight Allied gunboats slid into reach up the river to take up their own positions for the morning's assault. And then—as if, thought one of the men on the ground, it couldn't bear to watch what was unfolding below—the moon went dark with an eclipse.[39]

At daybreak the soldiers occupied the town and started turning out its thirty thousand inhabitants from their homes of mud and straw. The main fleet pulled in close to shore and began to discharge the bulk of the Allied forces and support personnel. The town of Beitang was "dirty beyond expression," wrote one member of the advance force, "the smell unbearable." Of the pestilent causeway on which they had spent the night, he thought "no place can be conceived as more likely to produce fever or ague."[40] But the town gave them a secure foothold at a safe distance from the Taku forts, which they hoped this time to take from the landward side. As the transports off-loaded their cargoes of men, animals, and artillery and as the town's docks grew high with piles of ammunition and food supplies, the British and French troops began rifling the town's emptied houses in search of loot.[41] It surprised them what rich treasures were to be found in such outwardly humble dwellings.

Though the imperial forces were concentrated at Taku, Senggelinqin had, in fact, prepared Beitang for the chance that the foreigners might land there. His men had set several large traps in the forts—disguised ground surfaces that gave way to pits containing large mousetraplike devices connected to barrels of gunpowder that would explode if anyone fell on them.

He hadn't reinforced the garrison because he expected that the Allies would simply be blown up if they tried to enter the forts.[42] However, a local informant currying favor with the foreigners tipped them off to the locations of the pitfalls, and French sappers managed to dismantle the traps before anyone fell in.[43] The informant also gave them a gauge of the forces that were guarding the Taku forts down the coast to their south—at least 15,000 imperial troops under Senggelinqin's command, he thought, counting among their number a force of 6,000 Mongolian cavalry.[44]

Heavy rains kept the Allies in Beitang for several days, waiting restlessly for orders to advance inland along the narrow causeway that would take them overland to the town of Tanggu on the north bank of the Peiho, a few miles upriver from the Taku forts. Once the looting was done, a strange mood settled in. The British and French soldiers had divided the town between them, and each viewed trespassers from the other side warily. It was humid and hot, ninety degrees or more in the sun (when it shone), and the streets of the town were a morass of mud and garbage. The forts flooded from the rain, and horses stood in water up to their knees. On the morning of August 9, still waiting for orders to advance, a group of six bored French soldiers stripped naked and spent the morning running and slipping about gaily in the mud near their headquarters with long sticks, chasing down scavenger dogs and beating them to death.[45]

The centerpiece of the British field arsenal for this campaign was the brand-new Armstrong gun, which had never yet been used in war. Instead of being cast, the gun was built up of concentric tubes of wrought iron that gave it enormous resilience in a relatively small size. It was light, weighing less than seven hundred pounds, half the weight of other guns with similar caliber. And due to an innovative rifling system it was also stunningly accurate, with a tested range of up to five miles. It was expensive and therefore controversial (it would be short-lived in the British army), but Thomas Bowlby, the London *Times* journalist, became a smitten partisan in the course of the campaign and reported it to be without question "the best gun yet used in action."[46] Beyond lightness and accuracy, it was also uniquely destructive. It fired a proprietary 12-pound shell that burst into forty-nine angular fragments, which appeared to be the most brutal antipersonnel weapon in existence. "Their effect is frightful," Bowlby wrote of the shells, "and the range over which they spread death and destruction almost incredible."[47] The British chaplain reported "limbs blown away, bodies literally burst asunder."[48] The artillerymen were excited to test the guns in battle for the first time.

Late on August 11, the weather finally broke, and at four the next morning the Allied soldiers began filing out from Beitang to march overland in two divisions toward Tanggu. The first division followed the causeway, while the second swept widely through the muddy fields to its right, in order to turn the left flank of any imperial forces waiting ahead. The first two miles, before they reached harder ground, were the worst. Thick mud seized the wheels of the artillery carts, some of which sank up to their axles and had to be abandoned.[49] The cavalry horses went in knee-deep. At around eleven in the morning an entrenchment came into view with a mass of Mongolian cavalry behind it. The Armstrongs opened fire—their first use against human beings.[50] The Mongolian cavalry advanced against them nonetheless, swarming around the mud-encrusted second division. The Sikh and English cavalry charged into their ranks to drive them off, only to have them reappear from other directions.[51] But eventually the Mongols withdrew under fire from the Armstrongs and the infantry's muskets and left the army to continue its advance, scavenging and denuding the gardens of the towns it passed.[52]

On August 14, the Allies took Tanggu. The work of capturing the town was done by thirty-six guns and two rocket batteries, supported by infantry. It didn't take long with the new weapons. "The Armstrong gun," wrote a British lieutenant to his commander after this battle, "is *a great success.*"[53] With the upriver site in control, a reconnaissance party rode downriver to test the strength of the Taku forts and was driven off by heavy fire. It reported back that the forts at the mouth of the Peiho appeared to be as full as they could be of defenders.

After a six-day delay to bring the rest of their supplies and equipment along the causeway from Beitang, on August 20 (a day after the French down at Shanghai burned the suburbs to drive out the Taiping) the Allied forces set up six artillery batteries within half a mile of the northernmost of the Taku forts and called in eight gunboats to attack from the south. Just before sunrise the next morning, the northern fort opened fire on their position. The Allies responded with their own guns, gradually rolling forward to within five hundred yards of the fortress walls, with the infantry following close behind. At 6:30 A.M. a powder magazine blew inside the northern fort with a massive explosion—but, remarkably, the defenders kept to their guns. The Allied artillery pounded away with Armstrongs,

8-inch mortars, 24-pound howitzers, and French 12-inch *canons rayés* (all of which were smaller than the Chinese-made brass cannons firing back at them from the fort), and then, after two and a half hours, the infantry stormed the walls. By a few minutes past eight, the fort was theirs. Inside, they found utter carnage—more than a thousand of the defenders had been killed, including Senggelinqin's second in command. Thanks largely to the Armstrong shells, the inside was, as Thomas Bowlby described it, "a mass of brains and blood smelling most foully."[54] They also discovered why the defenders hadn't given up after the magazine explosion: the fort had been barricaded from the outside, so that no one inside could escape.[55]

Once the Allies took possession of the northernmost fort, the others were uselessly outflanked, as they had been built to withstand attacks only from the river and were open from behind. By evening all five had surrendered. The Taku forts were in hand, at a cost of just over 350 Allied casualties.[56] "Thus," wrote Thomas Bowlby for his *Times* readers, "in a ten days' campaign were the Peiho forts taken, the disaster of last year avenged, the Chinese war of 1860 brought almost to a close."[57] The engineers began tearing up the defenses at the mouth of the river, opening the Peiho fully to the British and French gunships. Felice Beato began arranging corpses to make a series of photographs imagining the storming of the forts as if they had been taken by water rather than by land. And Lord Elgin repeated his winding journey up the shallow river to Tianjin once again, departing on the morning of August 25 and finding no resistance from imperial forces along the way. The infantry sailed with him on the gunships, while the cavalry rode overland on the twin banks of the river. By August 27, the Allies were encamped just outside Tianjin, and the ambassadors had once again taken up quarters inside the city in preparation for ratifying the treaty at last.

The lead negotiator on the British side was a scrappy young interpreter named Harry Parkes, a short, hyperenergetic terrier of a man with brilliant blue eyes, muttonchop whiskers, and an unusually large head. He was a sharp-tempered concentration of energy and could not abide sitting still.[58] His career spanned the full range of Britain's hostile relations with China; at the tender age of fourteen he'd been present at the signing of the Treaty of Nanjing, which had ended the Opium War in 1842. In 1856, he had been Britain's consul in Canton when the *Arrow* was boarded, and he had been instrumental in the push for reparations.[59] Since the occupation of Canton by the Allies in 1858, Parkes had served as the city's de facto British governor. Now, at age thirty-two, he was already one of the seniormost British diplomats in China and easily the most headstrong of the lot.

With the apparent end of hostilities, the Allies rejoiced that finally the war was over. Lord Elgin told Thomas Bowlby that he was anxious to withdraw Britain's forces from north China as soon as possible and hoped they could vacate Canton as well.[60] "I do not now expect to hear another gun fired," wrote Harry Parkes to his wife.[61] But the negotiations proved inconclusive. Two Qing commissioners arrived in Tianjin on September 2, and Parkes, speaking for the Allies, demanded ratification of their treaties, the right to station ambassadors in the capital, and a war indemnity of 8 million taels of silver for each party (nearly 3 million pounds sterling apiece for England and France, though it was rumored to be costing Britain a million pounds a month just to maintain its expeditionary force).[62] The Qing commissioners signaled their acceptance of all terms. But when Parkes asked to see their credentials a few days later, it turned out they had misrepresented their status and actually had no authority to sign on behalf of the emperor.[63] And so, on September 7, reasoning that it would be impossible to ratify the treaties anywhere other than under the walls of the capital, Lord Elgin and Baron Gros made the fateful decision to push onward toward Beijing.

It was, in its way, a thrilling prospect. "I am at war again!" wrote Elgin in a letter home on September 8. "My idiotical Chinamen have taken to playing tricks, which give me an excellent excuse for carrying the army on to Pekin."[64] The army was thrilled, and its officers were thrilled. The journalists, especially, were thrilled. Bowlby looked forward to seeing the Allied armies "afford a lesson to the effete and faithless clique of Mandarins who direct the policy of this empire." The already hawkish articles he had been sending back to the London *Times* rose to a new level. "By arms alone can China be opened to trade," he declared in his dispatch of September 9. "An ambassador must negotiate with an army by his side, ready to act at a moment's notice."[65] By coincidence, the issue of *The Times* that reached Elgin's party in the mail delivery from London that week contained two strongly worded leaders, written the previous July, expressing the editors' hope that the Allies might find the means to drive all the way to Beijing.[66] And so, as Elgin and his army advanced, they did so with the faith that it was just what the public back home wanted them to do.

After Beitang and the Taku forts fell so easily, Senggelinqin was prepared to commit suicide. But orders came telling him to retreat northward to the city of Tongzhou, just outside Beijing. Tongzhou stood firmly on the road from Tianjin to Beijing, and there he would prepare for a last stand if the foreigners should dare to advance toward the capital.[67] He sent up 10,000 of his foot soldiers and 7,000 cavalry from Taku, and on September 8 they would be joined by 40,000 more Mongolian troops, putting the total size of his forces at nearly 60,000 men, a grand army to stand between the Allied forces and the emperor.[68] His instructions, however, were not to attack but only to ensure peace while protecting the capital behind him.

The emperor sent two new commissioners to forestall the Allied advance from Tianjin. Harry Parkes took charge of the resumed negotiations, riding out in advance of his army with a white flag, across the enemy's lines into Tongzhou to meet with the new commissioners. He traveled with a small entourage that included the *Times* reporter Bowlby, Lord Elgin's secretary Henry Loch, and a detachment of Sikh cavalry. When the new round of negotiations began on September 14, Lord Elgin was still about twenty-five miles distant on the road from Tianjin, accompanied by a force of only 2,500 infantry, 600 cavalry, and twenty guns.[69] The Allies were stretched thin by this point, having to keep the roads open and garrison supply depots all the way back via Tianjin to the coast.

This time, the new commissioners had real authority; they were two senior Manchu advisers to the emperor, Zaiyuan and Muyin, the first of whom had royal blood and was the emperor's cousin. On the very first day of negotiation at Tongzhou, after eight hours of discussion, they accepted all of Parkes's terms. They also agreed to a protocol for ratification: the Allied forces would be allowed to advance to a place known as Five-Li Point, which was still six miles from Tongzhou and twenty miles from Beijing. From there Lord Elgin would leave behind the rest of his forces and proceed to Tongzhou with an escort of a thousand men to sign the treaty with the commissioners. Then Elgin and his escort would continue to Beijing to meet with the emperor for the formal ceremony of ratification. Parkes made a quick trip back to Elgin's camp to report on the success of his negotiations, and on September 17 he returned to Tongzhou to finalize the details with the commissioners and prepare for Elgin's arrival.[70]

By the time he got back, however, the emperor had already given secret instructions to Senggelinqin to destroy Elgin's party when it arrived to sign the treaty. The imperial forces at Tongzhou were hard at work setting up hidden artillery batteries and sequestering forces under cover in the millet fields that lined the roadway, in preparation for launching a surprise attack on Elgin's entourage when it arrived at Five-Li Point.[71] When Parkes got back to Tongzhou, the negotiations suddenly faltered. In spite of the apparent desperation of Zaiyuan and Muyin to gain peace, the discussion got hung up on the issue of whether Lord Elgin would kowtow before the Xianfeng emperor. Harry Parkes said absolutely not, for Elgin was an emissary from the queen of England, who was an equal of the Qing emperor. It was on this exact same issue of protocol that Lord Macartney's embassy in 1793 and Lord Amherst's in 1816 had both foundered—though this time the British felt themselves in a position to force the issue.

The question of kneeling was, however, a concession that the commissioners could not make. The humiliation to the emperor would be too great to sustain, for the prestige of the dynasty rested on ceremonies that acknowledged the emperor's eminence over his Chinese subjects and foreigners alike. Indeed, the commissioners well knew that the Xianfeng emperor was bitterly angry and wanted no more compromises. Muyin had tried to have an audience with him at the Summer Palace just before he left for Tongzhou, and he had been turned down. When he asked why, the palace eunuch guarding the gate told him he should not disturb the emperor. "The power of the empire is lost," Muyin told him, "and yet you fear disturbing the emperor?" Muyin got his audience in the end, and one of the questions he asked the emperor was what should be done about imperial officials who fled from the path of the Allied advance. Xianfeng's answer was simple: "Behead them."[72]

Zaiyuan insisted to Parkes that all ministers of the government had to kneel before the emperor, no matter their rank. "We are not Chinese ministers," replied Parkes, "so why should we kneel?"[73] They proposed that Elgin stand at a distance and not actually face the emperor. Parkes would have none of it. It was on this issue of ceremony that the new round of negotiations broke down. Muyin secretly informed Senggelinqin that the peace talks had failed, and the Mongol general went into action. On the afternoon of September 18, Senggelinqin's forces took Harry Parkes hostage, along with twenty-five other foreigners who had crossed the lines to Tongzhou with him, including Elgin's secretary Henry Loch, the one-man French *mission scientifique,* the *Times* reporter Thomas Bowlby, three British officers, and nineteen Sikh cavalrymen. The prisoners were hauled into Beijing in wooden carts. Parkes and Loch were shackled and incarcerated in the Board of Punishments to await execution. The rest were taken to the Summer Palace for interrogation. Meanwhile, the imperial forces at Tongzhou readied for battle.

At five that afternoon, Baron Gros's secretary rode breathless into Elgin's camp to tell him that Senggelinqin's troops had just occupied Five-Li Point, the site to which Elgin was supposed to be proceeding with his escort. The sound of musketry was already audible in the distance ahead of them. It wasn't until late that night that Elgin learned that his chief negotiator, Harry Parkes, had been taken hostage.[74] The next morning, Elgin's commanders sent back to Tianjin for reinforcements and then, without waiting, prepared to march on Tongzhou with what they had.

The small Allied force fought its way forward, finally meeting head-on with the bulk of Senggelinqin's army just outside Tongzhou on September 21. Wildly superior in numbers, the swift Mongolian cavalry charged in a broad wave at the left flank of the approaching Allied force, which marched in three columns: cavalry on the left, artillery in the center, infantry on the right. The British and French cavalry quickly split and pulled aside as the artillery at the center wheeled their guns around to bring them to bear on the charging Mongol horsemen. Then the Armstrong guns did their work, pouring salvo after salvo deep into the ranks of the oncoming imperial cavalry, with shuddering effect.[75] The Mongol horsemen pulled up in confusion, at which point the British cavalry charged full force into their midsection, breaking through the imperial lines and scattering them into a chaotic retreat.

Then came the real slaughter. "Our artillery opened fire upon the retreating forces with good effect," wrote a phlegmatic British officer, "firing slowly, every Armstrong shell bursting amongst them and bringing down the enemy in clumps."[76] As one rueful Chinese account described the rout that day, "Our cavalry went out in front, but they were Mongolian horsemen who had never seen battle before. As soon as they heard the sounds of the foreign cannons, they turned back. The foot soldiers behind them scattered ranks, and then everyone trampled one another."[77] By the end of the day, the imperial army was broken and its remnants retreated to the vicinity of Beijing. The Allied soldiers occupied Tongzhou and settled in to wait patiently for the arrival of their reinforcements from Tianjin, along with the supplies, ammunition, and heavy siege guns they would need before advancing on the capital itself.

That evening, the Xianfeng emperor moved from the Summer Palace into the Forbidden City, the imperial district at the north end of Beijing, where he normally disliked spending his time. Once he was inside, the gates of the Forbidden City were shut, with no one allowed in or out. Then, when the courtiers of the city couldn't know what was happening inside, the emperor slipped out the back gate and abandoned the capital altogether, fleeing for the safety of the northern mountains with a large retinue of servants, palace women, and Manchu advisers accompanying him. Not a word was said publicly, and the performance at the imperial opera hall still went on as usual that evening as if nothing had happened.

The next day, word finally leaked out that the emperor was gone and the city's officials—both Manchu and Chinese—went into a panic, filling carts with their possessions and trying desperately to evacuate the capital. The price of renting a cart doubled and kept rising until there were none left. The government dissolved as officials abandoned their offices, and the civil defense bureau put up proclamations around the city announcing that any resident of Beijing who managed to catch a looter was authorized to beat him or her to death on sight.[78]

The city practically emptied of all its wealthiest inhabitants, as all those with the means to leave Beijing hired carriers to take them north, out of the range of the coming assault. The gates of the city were then shut and barred, and the price of food skyrocketed. Silver couldn't be had for any amount of copper cash. The sedan-chair market was empty. By October 4, facing the inevitable, the merchants who remained in Beijing assembled a thousand cows and goats and began preparations to welcome the coming invaders with a grand feast.[79]

The first line of the Allied columns crested a dike on October 5 and came into view of the long, low walls of Beijing across a wide plain of yellow earth. Senggelinqin was already on his way north with his Mongol cavalry, and the remaining imperial forces simply melted away before the Allied advance.[80] Tired from the march, they paused and made camp for the night just two miles from the city. The next morning, an advance detachment of British cavalry and French infantry set out for the Summer Palace, where they still expected to find the emperor in residence.[81] Entering through the outside gates, they found it empty and undefended. And then the looting began for real.

A British officer recalled arriving at the Summer Palace that first day, in the midst of the burgeoning free-for-all, to find "some men, quite off their heads with the excitement of looting a palace, and for no apparent reason tearing down grand embroideries. I saw one man send the butt of his rifle through a huge mirror." The officer made his way through the palace until he came to "a great hall with grand-looking vases, apparently gold, and some splendid bits of jade-carving." He felt like "a boy suddenly told to take what he likes in a pastry-cook's shop" and was "puzzled where to

begin." Having heard that jade was particularly valuable, he "made a collection that probably has rarely been seen," which he loaded onto his pony,
and then he took off for camp with both arms around his load of priceless
treasures. On the way he encountered some Sikh cavalry, whom he admonished in Hindustani, "Be quick or it will all be gone!" and they took off like
a shot.[82]

The breakdown of discipline as the fever for looting swept through the
ranks embarrassed and angered the British commanders, who tried to keep
their men in camp to prevent them from pillaging the palace—though the
French got free rein, which sparked the jealousy and resentment of their
British counterparts. The British commanders eventually ordered all of
their soldiers to hand over their loot to be sold collectively at auction in
Beijing, with the proceeds to be divided evenly by a "prize committee." (The
one who made off with the jade regretfully gave up his booty at that point,
at which a friend chided him, "Eh, ye big fule!")[83] Lord Elgin was revolted
by the heedless destruction left by the looters, especially the French, whom
he blamed for the worst excesses. "Plundering and devastating a place like
this is bad enough," he wrote, "but what is much worse is the waste and
breakage. . . . French soldiers were destroying in every way the most beautiful silks, breaking the jade ornaments and porcelain, etc. War is a hateful
business. The more one sees of it, the more one detests it."[84]

One of the emperor's brothers, Prince Gong, had been left behind in
Beijing to make peace with the Allies when they arrived, and one of the
first things he did was to release Harry Parkes and Henry Loch on October
8. Over the following days, several of the other hostages were returned as
well. All had horrific tales to tell of their incarceration. The most valuable
prisoners—Parkes the negotiator and Elgin's secretary Loch—had been
treated tolerably well after an initial series of beatings, though they had
suffered constant threats of execution.[85] But the others had been freely tortured and humiliated, denied food and water, and tied up by their wrists
in cords so tight their hands turned black and swelled until, in some cases,
they burst. Of the twenty-six prisoners taken on September 18, fifteen died
in the course of their short captivity: one Frenchman, four Britons, and ten
Sikhs. Their bodies were mutilated and packed in quicklime, so that after
they were given back to the Allied forces, they were recognizable only by
their clothing. Among the dead was Thomas Bowlby, the hawkish reporter
from the London *Times*. According to a Sikh who had been imprisoned
with him, "Mr. Bowlby died the second day after we arrived; he died from
maggots forming in his wrists; he was dressed in a kind of grey check. His

body remained there nearly three days, and the next day it was tied to a crossbeam and thrown over the wall to be eaten by dogs and pigs."[86]

As news of the torture and death of the hostages spread through the Allied ranks, a poisonous fury took root and swelled and grew. The soldiers demanded revenge. One general proposed sacking the capital. "Could we have had our way," said another, "every mandarin in Pekin would have been strung up."[87] As Elgin explained it later, he felt there was only one course of action his army could possibly take that would suitably punish the Qing government for having kidnapped Harry Parkes and his traveling party, and for murdering Thomas Bowlby and the others—one course of action, that is, that would ensure that Britain's punishment would fall entirely on the head of the Manchu sovereign himself, rather than on the already suffering residents of his capital. And so, against the protests of Baron Gros and in spite of his earlier expression of regret for the destructiveness of looting, Elgin instructed the British army to burn the Summer Palace to the ground.

With the emperor in flight and the city abandoned by its officials and its defenders, the capital of the once great Qing Empire was utterly helpless. But the Allies left the city itself untouched as on October 18, four miles to the northwest, British forces began the work of methodically destroying the eight-hundred-acre complex of buildings and gardens where the Xianfeng emperor had been born, where he had lived for most of his life—and indeed, which had been practically the only world he had ever known. There were so many ornate buildings on the grounds, covering more than a square mile, that it took them two full days of burning and breaking and smashing before the major structures were destroyed. The imperial treasures that had proven too heavy or unwieldy to loot and carry back to England and France (or sell at auction in Beijing) were smashed and burned as well.[88]

Most of the obvious valuables had been looted already, but there were still a few unexpected discoveries in the course of demolition. A company of Punjabi infantry happened upon several thousand pounds' worth of hidden gold, which they took back with them to India. A little Pekingese dog was discovered curled up in a wardrobe, and a British officer took him back to England as a present for Queen Victoria. She was a great lover of dogs, and "Looty," as he would be named, became one of her favorites.[89] The strangest find of all, however, was in a carriage house on the palace grounds, where the pillaging soldiers happened upon a large store of gifts left over from their countryman Lord Macartney's failed embassy in 1793. There were a full-sized British-made state coach, astronomical and scientific instruments, and two 12-pound English howitzers with crates of ammunition, all of which had been presented to the Xianfeng emperor's great-grandfather on behalf of King George III.[90] The gifts were still in pristine condition, the apparently untouched tokens of a friendship that never was.

As the first plumes of smoke rose into the sky from the spreading conflagration below, the unbridled joy of destruction and burning was tempered, for those who thought more deeply about it that day, with a strange mixture of awe and regret, a fear of the darkness released from their own inner natures, "glorying," as one put it, "in the destruction of what they could not replace."[91] The demons who danced among the red flames were themselves. But for the emperor, the Qing dynasty, China—it was an ominous moment indeed. Those who looked on, humbled in a way they couldn't quite describe, knew that they were witness to the end of a dynasty and perhaps to the end of a civilization as well. As the British interpreter Robert Swinhoe reflected, watching with a wistful eye as the grand edifices of the emperor's palace were put to the torch, "as roof after roof crashed in, smothering the fire that devoured its sustaining walls, . . . it betokened to our minds a sad portent of the fate of this antique empire, its very entrails being consumed by internecine war . . . beset on all sides, with nought to turn to for succour, it at last succumbs with a burst of vapour, lost in the ashes of its former self."[92]

PART TWO

Order Rising

CHAPTER 6

A RELUCTANT GENERAL

October 16, 1860, dawned cold in the sharp-cut mountain valley in Anhui province where General Zeng Guofan dragged himself from his bed, weakened from an extended bout of vomiting the night before. He was a sturdy man in his late forties, five foot eight with a broad chest and sad, deep-set eyes intensified by a long goatee beard that fell down over the front of his robes. Old age hadn't yet settled onto him, though the pressures of war were bringing it close. He blamed the vomiting on drinking too much tea before his dinner, but it was only one of a growing list of wretched disorders that wore him down, like his heart palpitations or the insomnia that kept him awake deep into the night and haunted him with exhaustion by day. On this particular morning he went through his normal routine: receiving visitors in his tent, catching up on correspondence, busier than usual so he had no time for his customary game of Go with a subordinate. It was only after lunch that the courier arrived, bearing an official message from Beijing informing him that the emperor and his entourage had left for the hunting grounds in Manchuria, and the British and French armies were only a few miles from the capital. There wasn't anything that could be done, he wrote in his diary with despair. At least not that he could do.

Coming to terms with the helplessness of the emperor's flight, he broke down into tears.[1]

Indeed, from where he sat in his headquarters in the town of Qimen, wrapped in the mountains of southern Anhui and fighting a protracted rear-action campaign against the farthest Taiping stronghold up the Yangtze, there *was* nothing he could do. In name at least, he was now the commander in chief of the dynasty's campaign against the Taiping rebels— a mantle he had inherited unexpectedly when the siege camps at Nanjing had collapsed that spring and the generals Zhang Guoliang and He Chun had both died. But he was four hundred miles on the other side of the Taiping domain from Suzhou, where the Loyal King's victorious armies roamed at will, and still farther from Beijing, where the British and French armies were nearing the imperial capital. It was too late for his forces to be of any use in either of those places. So he pulled himself back together and focused on the few things he actually could do something about. He sent a man up with a rope to measure the height of a steep mountain that faced his camp. He continued with his paperwork. He went to bed that night and once again braved the demons that haunted his sleep.

This wasn't where Zeng Guofan had expected his career to lead, nor could he have predicted that this remote valley in rural Anhui province would be, as now seemed to him likely, the place where he would die. He wasn't a fighting man but a scholar: a man of books and poetry and moral philosophy who had started his life under circumstances not so far removed from those of Hong Xiuquan and the millions of others who tried their hands at the imperial examinations. There had been nothing especially promising in his background, the eldest of five sons born to a farming family in rural Hunan province. It wasn't that the men of his family were unlettered, but none of them had ever made any headway on the exams. His father was the first in the family to try in earnest, and he had failed the lowest examination, the district-level *xiucai*, sixteen times before finally passing it in 1832, when he was already well into middle age. Zeng Guofan, however, showed far greater talent (at least of the kind the examiners were searching for), and he managed to pass that same examination the year right after his father did, while he was still just twenty-two years old with a full career ahead of him. It hadn't been effortless—he had failed six times before he passed—but with concerted effort and a willingness to punish himself, he managed to claw his way up the ranks. The following year, he passed the provincial exam that had forever eluded Hong Xiuquan and then went on for the top examination in the empire, administered by the emperor in Beijing. After failing it twice, he passed with brilliance in 1838, winning the coveted *jinshi* degree and an appointment to the Hanlin Academy.[2]

In an empire governed by Confucian scholars, the Hanlin Academy was the repository of the most elite of the elite, and Zeng Guofan's selection in 1838 saw him joining a group of a hundred or so students and faculty culled from an imperial population numbering roughly 400 million.[3] The senior Hanlin scholars were the custodians of interpretation of the Confucian texts; they chose the questions for the examinations and oversaw their administration. They tutored the emperor and the young princes who might someday be emperor themselves. Those men were the monarch's brain trust, the think tank that converted ancient and arcane philosophical texts handed down over millennia into meaningful policy and governance. For the junior members such as Zeng Guofan, it was an introduction to the halls of power—a stipended period of study with the most talented scholars in the empire and an entrée into the social world of court life in the capital. His appointment marked the beginning of what would be a graceful climb through the intricate architecture of the dynasty's bureaucracy. Whereas in Hong Xiuquan the confounding difficulty of the examinations bred madness and revolt, in this favored child, Zeng Guofan, it bred loyalty and gratitude.[4]

The rewards of success on the examinations entailed not just power and prestige but, more tangibly, wealth. Zeng's family had gone into great debt to fund his education, and even with the Hanlin stipend he had little money in Beijing. But that changed with his first appointment outside the capital, administering the provincial examination in the capital of Sichuan in 1843. Lower officials currying favor pressed him with gifts, as did the grateful families of the scholars who passed. He returned to Beijing with sixteen sedan chairs loaded down with furs, jade, and silver—more than enough to clear all of his outstanding debts.[5] At the same time, however, he was wary of the corruption and obsession with material pleasure that dominated life at court. He chafed at the insincere flattery and politics that formed the basis of so many friendships in the capital and wrote home to his brothers that he didn't want any friends who didn't improve him as a person.[6] His wariness of Beijing society only increased as he came under the influence of a coterie of distinguished teachers in Beijing who espoused a rigid school of moral philosophy known generally as Neo-Confucianism, deeply grounded in ideas of self-discipline and self-cultivation. Under their guidance, he began to examine himself with a keenly judgmental eye and to set strict lists of rules to govern his daily conduct: to rise early and spend an hour in quiet thought each morning. To stay indoors at night. To avoid starting a new book until he'd finished reading the last one. To keep a diary every day. To walk a thousand paces after each meal. The list went on and on.[7]

If his mother hadn't died in 1852, Zeng Guofan's career might have been a relatively predictable one—rarefied, to be sure, but unremarkable. As it happened, however, she passed away that summer just as the Taiping army was carving its original course northward from Guangxi, through Hunan and up to the city of Wuchang in Hubei province. Under normal circumstances, officeholders in the Qing dynasty were never assigned to posts in their home provinces; it was a hedge against localized power, ensuring that officials were more loyal to the emperor than to the people they governed. An official of Zeng's stature found himself back in his birthplace only if he retired, if he was cashiered for incompetence, or, as was the case here, if one of his parents died and he had to withdraw from public life for the customary three years of mourning. After receiving the news of his mother's death in the spring of 1852, he turned his back on the life of the capital and returned to Hunan. The provincial capital, Changsha, was under siege, so he took a roundabout route that steered wide of the burgeoning rebellion and arrived home in the late autumn.

Order was collapsing in his home province. As the imperial armies tried to concentrate on the fast-moving Taiping forces, they had left a vacuum in their wake that was irresistible to outlaws, and gangs of bandits ravaged villages and towns with near impunity. In response, the worried emperor issued orders for civil officials to start mustering local militia forces to protect their jurisdictions. But those militias were, by and large, small and ill equipped. Their hastily recruited soldiers had no experience in fighting, and weapons were hard to come by. With the exception of a unit of 2,000 men who successfully held the walls of Changsha against the rebels, most of the militia units were worse than ineffective. Their leaders were self-interested and reluctant to leave their immediate homes. It was difficult to coordinate them, and when they were enticed to fight elsewhere, many simply wound up looting the remains of what was left after the Taiping armies had passed.[8]

In early January 1853, as conditions in the central empire deteriorated, the emperor issued an order for Zeng Guofan to take charge of the haphazard militia units in Hunan and use them to restore order to his province. Similar orders went out to individuals in neighboring provinces as well, and all were rooted in desperation—essentially an admission that the imperial forces couldn't contain the rebellion. In Zeng Guofan's case the order broke with all precedent by granting him the power to take up broad-based military affairs in his home region. But the emperor knew him to be loyal and chose him not because he had shown any aptitude for military affairs (which most scholars disdained, martial bravado being an affectation of the ruling Manchus, not the subject Chinese)[9] but because he was convenient: he happened to be there on the ground already and was familiar with the region and its people. He hadn't come on especially strong recommendation; it was his teacher in Beijing, Tang Jian, who had suggested his name to the emperor, noting that although Zeng Guofan was quite learned, he actually wasn't all that talented. Zeng's latent skill, according to Tang Jian, and the reason he might be a good choice for the mission, was that he knew how to use men. "He is good at recognizing talents," Tang told the emperor, "and is capable of synthesizing people's good points. If he is willing to use the wisdom of others as his own . . . he might make a fine leader."[10]

Zeng Guofan didn't want the appointment. He had scarcely been home four months when the orders reached him, and he hadn't even finished the rituals for burying his mother, let alone observing the proper mourning period.[11] He had no practical military experience (nor did he care to gain any), and the shepherding of the militias struck him as an impossible task. So he decided to refuse the appointment, and drafted a memorial declining it on the grounds that he needed to continue mourning his mother. It was no small matter to refuse the emperor's orders, but one's parents were supposed to come first. His sentiments were genuine; he wrote to a friend in Beijing that day that he simply couldn't abide the guilt of leaving his mother unburied.[12] But his stance of propriety also masked a skepticism that the militias *could* ever be properly organized. He would have to travel throughout the districts raising money from gentry who had no interest in helping one another, and he didn't see how that would result in anything more than trouble.[13]

But then came the news that on January 12, 1853, the Taiping rebels had conquered Wuchang, the capital of neighboring Hubei province to the north of Hunan. They now controlled the middle reaches of the Yangtze River. The crisis was becoming larger than anyone had expected. Zeng Guofan's father and brothers, along with a close friend, pleaded with him to take up the appointment so he could help save their native place from destruction. In the end they convinced him, and he tore up the draft memorial and accepted the mission.[14]

———————

The Qing dynasty's standing military was divided into two vast and separate forces. The elite forces were the hereditary banner armies, composed of Manchus and Mongols, which operated in the north. These were the personal armies of the emperor and the Manchus more widely, and their forces were concentrated where the emperor lived, as well as in their traditional homeland of Manchuria and the handful of garrison cities scattered about the empire. They reached their peak in the days of the great eighteenth-century frontier wars, when they consolidated vast regions of Central Asia under Manchu rule. But they had been on the decline since then, and—with a few notable exceptions—the soldiers of the new generation were but shadows of the great warriors from whom they were descended. There were roughly 130,000 banner troops based in the region around Beijing but none at all in the province of Guangxi, where the Taiping had originated.

Below the banner forces, and responsible for maintaining control throughout the bulk of the empire, were the Green Standard armies, whose soldiers, and most of whose officers, were ethnically Chinese. Roughly speaking, while the Manchu bannermen guarded the emperor and his people, the Chinese soldiers of the Green Standard kept order in the far-flung expanses of the dynasty's territory, and their standing numbers were proportionally greater: 600,000 on the books in the early 1850s.[15] However, that high figure was illusory, as commanders typically inflated their personnel numbers in order to embezzle extra pay and supplies. And the soldiers were profoundly undertrained, as it had been more than a generation (fifty years, in fact) since they had been mobilized for large-scale warfare.

To make matters worse, although the Green Standard was far greater in number, the elite banner armies commanded the lion's share of the Qing military budget, leaving the larger Chinese force not just underprepared but underfunded as well. The campaigns of the eighteenth century had drained the Qing dynasty's military treasuries, which were far from being replenished by the 1850s. Widespread cost-saving measures meant little or no improvement in military technology and poor maintenance of the arms stores that did exist. By tradition, individual soldiers were responsible for purchasing and maintaining their own hand weapons (swords and knives, mostly), but in peacetime they preferred to use their meager salaries for other purposes, such as buying food for their families or purchasing opium. The state provided the firearms (matchlocks, effective in Central Asia but already obsolete in Europe by the time of the American Revolution), and those too were in poor repair due to cost-cutting efforts. An imperial statute of 1816 decreed that weapons should not be replaced until they had been used for thirty or forty years. Many in actual use were more than a century old.[16] The nineteenth-century Qing military thus suffered from a fatal combination of too much peace and too little prosperity.

By the time the Taiping broke out of Guangxi and headed north, the Green Standard functioned less as an army than as a vast network of police forces or constabularies spread out over the empire. Green Standard units kept local order and protected imperial grain shipments, as well as performing such mundane tasks as transporting prisoners and moving the mail. Commands were fragmented and distributed among local civil and military officials in jealous competition with one another—a deliberate measure to make sure a mutinous Chinese commander couldn't organize them against the dynasty. But the absence of any clear chain of command also made it nearly impossible to mobilize them against a large and swift-moving enemy such as the Taiping.[17]

Zeng Guofan was well aware of the Green Standard's deficiencies. As early as 1851, while still in the capital, he had advocated reducing its numbers. The provincial forces were bloated with superfluous soldiers who had nothing to do, he wrote to the emperor. Idle and bored, they took up with local bandit gangs. They smoked opium and set up gambling houses. They went AWOL and caused trouble, and when they were actually called upon to fight, they paid ne'er-do-wells to take their places and fill the ranks. "As soon as they spy the enemy, they run away," he wrote, "and when the enemy departs, they come back and murder the locals [to dress them up as rebels] and claim victory."[18] To a friend, he wrote that "even if Confucius himself came back to life, he could spend three years and still not manage to correct their evil ways."[19] When he accepted the emperor's mission in 1853, Zeng Guofan took his criticisms even further. The Green Standard forces were always chasing the rebels' tail, he wrote, and never attacked them head-on. They used cannons and muskets to attack from a distance, but he'd never heard of them fighting in close quarters with small arms. This, he wrote, showed that they were poorly trained, lacked courage, and had no martial skills to speak of.[20]

So he proposed to start from scratch with a new kind of force. Taking as his model a general of the Ming dynasty who had formed militias to fight Japanese pirates on the coast, Zeng proposed building a force that would be small and efficient. It would be carefully trained, and its soldiers would be courageous. In a broad sense, the army he began to assemble in 1853 was a military outgrowth of his Neo-Confucian sense of moral order; just as he had learned to discipline himself, so would he discipline his army. He pleaded for patience from the worried emperor. "We aim for excellence, not sheer numbers," he wrote. "And we want it to be truly effective, not just available quickly."[21]

He started with strict guidelines for recruitment. First, the soldiers should, like himself, be young men from rural, not urban backgrounds. "Those who want a strong army use soldiers from the mountain villages," he explained in an 1855 memorial, "and they avoid the men of the cities and waterways."[22] In his own version of the pastoral romantic, he believed that "Those who live their lives in the mountains and rural areas are tough, while the ones from the river villages are slippery. The cities are full of lazy and carefree wanderers, while the rural villages have men who are simple and sincere." Second, he insisted that recruitment should take place only through personal channels. He would choose his own commanding officers from among his brothers, friends, fellow scholars, and others brought in through careful interviews—and they, in turn, would select their own subordinates. The process would repeat itself down through the ranks all the way from the top to the bottom, where foot soldiers were recruited by officers from their own home districts, to fight alongside their neighbors.[23]

In terms of the relationship between officers and men, it was a Confucian scholar's vision of an army. Confucius taught that the relationship between father and son was the absolute moral foundation of a society, and Zeng encouraged an analogous bond of affection between his officers and soldiers. This was hardly to encourage indulgence (he was a famously strict father); rather, its purpose was to build an unbreakable sense of duty. In 1858, he instructed his commanders that they "should act towards their soldiers like a father acts toward his sons or an elder brother toward his younger brothers. When the elder is strict, the younger will be well disciplined, and the family will flourish. If he spoils them, they will be headstrong and arrogant, and the family will decay."[24] Likewise, in an essay on "Forgiveness" he insisted that punishment was the key to maintaining harmony within a group. Small kindnesses, he believed, were entropic; the father who pardons his son's faults eventually loses control of his family, and soldiers who aren't punished by their officers become rude and disobedient. "Forgiveness cannot govern the people," he concluded, "indulgence cannot order a family, and generosity cannot control an army."[25] The family analogy also worked from bottom to top, and from the foot soldiers on up to the generals; he encouraged each to "serve his superior in the same way a son serves his father."[26]

These personal ties were inviolable. No soldier or company officer was expected to answer to a commander with whom he lacked a personal relationship. And generals could not overleap their senior commanders to give direct orders to the lower ranks.[27] At its extremity, this meant that when a general transferred one of his commanders, the entire pyramid of command below that man was transferred along with him. The officer replacing him would, if new, have to begin the process of recruiting his own command from scratch.[28] And by the same logic, when a commander was killed in battle, the soldiers under him either had to be rerecruited into new units through personal channels or else discharged and sent home.[29] Were Zeng Guofan himself to perish, the army would dissolve.

Zeng also encouraged loyalty by paying his men extremely well. When funds were available (which they rarely would be, though the enlistees didn't know that), a foot soldier in Zeng Guofan's force received a salary of just over 4 taels of silver per month, nearly triple the wage of his Green Standard counterparts.[30] In addition, there were generous prizes to be won in battle: 10 taels of silver for killing a bandit, 15 for capturing one alive, and if they should capture a Taiping (a "longhair" bandit, as distinguished from an everyday one) it was worth 20 taels, or nearly five months' wages. Any soldier who captured a rebel horse could keep it as his prize; if he didn't want it, he could hand it over to his superior and get 10 taels of silver. Smaller prizes rewarded the capture of matériel: 5 taels for a barrel of gunpowder, 3 for a cask of lead bullets, and 10 for a large cannon or 5 for a small. They would get 3 taels each for a musket (or "bird gun") and 2 each for captured swords, spears, and banners.[31] These were fantastic incentives to poor farmers, though they also suggest that valor didn't come for free.

After recruitment came indoctrination. The farmers who enlisted in Zeng Guofan's army had, by and large, no military experience at all; they were a blank slate. So he gave them an imperial mandate when they first entered camp. "We have enlisted you to become militiamen and to exert your strength on behalf of the dynasty," went his instructions to new recruits. "The food and supplies with which we feed and nurture you every day all come from the coffers of the emperor."[32] This was the core, and nearly the fullest extent, of their ideological indoctrination: an admonition to serve the country and to feel gratitude toward the emperor. The rest of their psychological training broke down into extremely concrete and personal terms: learn to kill or be killed. "The reason we want you to learn martial arts is so that when you go forth to fight the bandits you will fight to the death," he told them. "If you do not hone your skills every morning, then when you encounter the bandits you will not be able to kill them, and they will kill you." He told them to take a personal stake in their own training. "You study martial arts to protect your own life: practice to the point of excellence, charge in with courage, and you might not be killed. But the second you turn back, your life is over. This principle is clear." The only way to be truly brave, Zeng believed, was to have no fear of death. And so he also appealed to their sense of fate. "If it is not your time to die," he explained to the new soldiers, "then even if ten million of the enemy surround you, they will not be able to kill you because you will have divine protection. But if it *is* your time to die, then even if you stay home and sit still, doing nothing at all, death will still find you."

For those to whom personal loyalties, generous pay, and a sense of fate weren't enough to ensure bravery, there was also a ruthless list of punishments—for, as Zeng had explained to his officers, without strict punishment there was no way to control an army. So faking an injury in order to get compensation meant forty strokes of the cane and an immediate discharge. Soldiers who ran from battle were, if caught, beheaded. And a soldier who gave a false report of meritorious deeds would not just be decapitated but also have his head hung on display as a warning to others.[33]

It was here that the specific nature of Zeng's original recruitment process became especially important. For in the vast, amorphous Green Standard army, a would-be soldier could simply show up and enlist. By the same token, he could also simply disappear. The personal nature of the Hunan militia's recruitment process, however, made desertion nearly impossible, and therein lay a great efficiency of Zeng's system. Every soldier was recruited at home, in person, in his own district. The soldiers in his unit would know exactly where he lived, and most likely had grown up with him. The officer who enlisted him would, by Zeng Guofan's strict instructions, have taken down not just the man's name but also his fingerprints and the names of everyone in his extended family—some of whom were required to provide personal guarantees for his service.[34] By such means, no soldier from this army could ever run from battle and expect to simply disappear into the countryside; justice could always be exacted on his family.

The first obstacle to actually building this force wasn't the enemy but the local officials with whom Zeng competed for funds, weapons, and supplies. They were protective of their own jurisdictions and generally refused to support him unless explicitly forced to. It didn't help that his unorthodox position carried a title as vague as "Imperially Dispatched Vice President of the Board of War, Former Vice President of the Board of Ritual,"[35] which had no obvious significance to the provincial officials and was easily ignored. Nor did it help that thanks to the hastily improvised nature of the mission, his seal—the physical manifestation of his authority—was carved not from jade but from wood, leading some to conclude that it was forged. He also had no compelling authority over the Green Standard commanders with whom he was supposed to coordinate, and at the outset they found Zeng Guofan so irritating that they sometimes attacked his militia forces instead of the enemy. Soldiers from his army were repeatedly detained and sometimes killed by Green Standard forces, and once, in 1853, they came after him directly and burned down his headquarters.[36]

The dynasty's central government traditionally supplied the armed forces with funds and equipment, but it was so bankrupt by the time of the Taiping Rebellion that there was nothing extra to give Zeng or the other new militias that cropped up across the country. The emperor therefore granted the leaders of those forces exceptional permission to raise their own funds by a variety of means, including collecting transport taxes on the rivers, selling degrees and honorary ranks to the wealthy, and straightforward fund-raising. Zeng therefore had to appeal directly to the wealthy landowners and merchants in Hunan for support, though they were not naturally inclined to support activities outside their own home spheres. So he needed a message. He was only vaguely aware of the apocalyptic Christian doctrines that had bonded the early Taiping armies together, but it was enough for him that they had destroyed Confucian temples in the cities they conquered. Those temples, with their rituals in honor of the sage and the state system they represented, were the very foundation of his life's career. Thus his appeal for support did not center on the threat that the Taiping rebels posed to the Qing dynasty, whose waning authority hadn't proven to be much of an inspiration (especially in Hunan, where hundreds of thousands from the general population had already joined the rebels). Instead, he reached further back beyond the rule of the Manchus to charge that the Taiping Rebellion imperiled Confucian civilization itself.

In a public proclamation of 1854, Zeng appealed for contributions to his militia by laying out the threat the rebels posed to China's known way of life. "Everywhere they pass through," he wrote, "every boat large or small is stolen, every person rich or poor is plundered and left with nothing, and not even an inch of grass remains."[37] In a particular appeal to the scholars, he warned that the Confucian texts were banned under the Taiping. "Scholars cannot read the classics of Confucius," he wrote, "but instead there are the so-called words of Jesus: the 'New Testament' book. They take thousands of years of Chinese manners, ethics, classics and laws, and in a single day sweep them away completely!" This was a far greater crime than a mere threat to the rule of the Manchus. "How could this be just a disturbance to our Qing dynasty?" he continued. "It is the most extreme threat to our Confucian teachings since the dawn of the world." There had long been rebellions in China, he said, but never before had they turned on Confucianism itself. Even the worst of them had left the ancestral temples untouched. Beneath his words lay the dark warning that the Taiping aimed not to become the next dynasty but to do away with dynastic rule altogether.

Zeng walked a fine line in that proclamation, for in such uncertain times even a formerly complacent subject of the emperor might throw his support to the rebels if he thought they were destined to win. The so-called Mandate of Heaven wasn't supposed to be permanent, and it was understood that every dynasty would eventually end. But the wealthy landowners to whom Zeng Guofan appealed most directly had prospered under this dynasty, and in rallying their support for his army Zeng had to convince them that it was not yet the natural time for the Manchus to fall. So he admitted that circumstances might look remarkably similar to what one expected at the end of a dynasty—widespread uprisings, near-total breakdown of government control—but he insisted that the emperor was better than that. Yes, he wrote, in the final days of the Han, Tang, Yuan, and Ming dynasties the government had lost its grasp on the countryside and "gangs of bandits were as thick as the hairs on your head." But the Xianfeng emperor, he argued, had not, like those past emperors, really lost control. Wishfully, perhaps, he wrote that Xianfeng "worries deeply and examines his conduct. He respects Heaven and feels pity for the people." The emperor hadn't raised taxes, he pointed out, nor had he conscripted soldiers to fight the rebels. This proved that he was still in control and that this would not be the end of the dynasty. In writing such an overt apology for the distant and removed emperor in the midst of untrammeled chaos, Zeng was addressing a concern that lay in every mind: namely, that the Manchus might be losing their mandate to rule.

Such an appeal might have resonated with educated gentry and scholars who owed their power and prestige to the reigning dynasty, but it is unclear what, ideologically, a farmer stood to gain from the continuance of Xianfeng's rule. Beyond basic security and reasonable taxation, there was little that the government in Beijing mattered to the people of the countryside—and this particular government was doing an especially poor job of ensuring security. But the peasants weren't providing the funds for his army, they were providing the manpower, and for that reason it was essential that Zeng Guofan should pay his farmer-soldiers well and teach them that their food and supplies were gifts from the emperor—even if in reality they were procured not from government stores but from local gentry. In the absence of unthinking loyalty to the sovereign, material enticements were necessary.

For weapons, Zeng Guofan's army used the same Chinese armaments that were found on both sides of the war. The primary weapons were the brutal implements for close combat: swords and spears of military origin, along with the tools of the farmer: hoes, long forks, and hatchets. Second to those were the firearms, especially the long matchlocks known as "bird guns" that were fired by lowering a lit fuse to a pan of gunpowder at the rear of the barrel. Matchlocks couldn't be fired in the rain, and the burning fuses were easily visible at night. They took about a minute to reload, but with careful training in repeated firing (which Zeng implemented in his camps) a team of experienced matchlock gunners firing in sequence could keep up a steady barrage. The heavier *taiqiang* or "carried gun," known in English as a gingal, was a large-bore matchlock about eight feet long that took three or four men to operate, either on a tripod or carried on two men's shoulders. It could throw a one-pound ball nearly a mile. And finally there were the wheeled brass cannons—large ones on the walls of cities, smaller ones pulled along on campaign—which were expensive and therefore relatively rare.

The Green Standard used weapons provided by the government, but Zeng Guofan got what he could from the provincial authorities and then set up armories of his own to make the rest. The rebel side, for its part, had had to be even more resourceful: the Taiping raided the arms stores of cities they captured, relied heavily on farming implements, and cast their own small cannons while on the original campaign north. When under siege, they even learned to boil down structural bricks to extract saltpeter for making gunpowder.[38] In time, both sides would try to equip themselves with repeating carbines from the foreigners in Shanghai. As an indication of just how stagnant the development of military technology was at that point in China's history (and of why those foreign guns would be so useful), when the Taiping captured the Hunanese city of Yuezhou in 1852, they unearthed a huge stash of rusty firearms left over from a war that had concluded in 1681. The guns might have been nearly two hundred years old, but the rebels were delighted to have them.[39]

In structure, the basic unit of organization for Zeng Guofan's army was the *ying*, or battalion, which he formalized at 505 men, including officers.[40] They could be grouped together to make forces of differing sizes but shared an internal structure that was inflexible. Each battalion was made up of four regular companies (*shao*)—designated fore, aft, right, and left—of 108 men each, plus a personal bodyguard of 72 men for the battalion commander and the battalion commander himself, to make 505. Each company was then broken down into eight squads (*dui*), of which two were gingal squads, two carried matchlock muskets, and four carried swords and spears. A normal squad had 10 soldiers, plus a squad officer and a cook. But since the gingals were so unwieldy, those squads had two extra, for 12 soldiers (three guns, with four men to operate each). Each company commander also had a seven-man entourage, including a lieutenant, five bodyguards, and a personal cook. The 72-man bodyguard of the battalion commander could be detached separately and operated as six squads, each with 10 soldiers, an officer, and a cook. Two of the squads manned the cannons, three carried swords and spears, and one carried muskets. Finally, there were the porters: 180 support personnel for each battalion, detailed to help carry the weapons, gunpowder, medicine, and clothing. Thus, cannons were few, and nearly half the soldiers didn't use firearms at all. These battalions were intended to be self-supporting and self-disciplining, to which end the battalion commander's 72-man bodyguard also functioned as a self-contained military police force to prevent the soldiers from committing crimes in nearby civilian towns when they were encamped.

To support the land troops, Zeng commissioned a freshwater navy to fight on the rivers and lakes. It was a completely novel plan; at the outset, neither he nor his generals had ever seen a gunboat, and there were no craftsmen in Hunan who knew how to build one. Nevertheless, he set up three shipyards and brought in outside experts to teach the locals how to build appropriate war craft. An adviser from Canton showed them how to make the large "fast crabs" that were the stock in trade of the southern opium smugglers, crowded with fourteen oars on either side and bearing a crew of forty-five. (Though they would prove so unwieldy that Zeng eventually abandoned them.) Two advisers from Guangxi province taught them how to make the more nimble "long dragons" and sampans that skimmed the southwestern riverways. The long dragons were ornate, colorful boats forty-five feet long and six across the beam, with sixteen oars and seven brass guns weighing about four hundred pounds apiece. They had a large sail mounted amidships and bristled with spears and swords and banners when they carried a full crew. The smaller sampans were open-decked with ten oars each, measuring thirty feet long and less than four wide, with a single brass gun pointing in each direction.[41] They were lovely vessels, and swift. As a young American described one he spotted on the Yangtze, "brightly varnished and bottom flat as boards can make it, she scarcely seems to touch the water."[42]

By February 1854, Zeng Guofan had thirteen battalions of land troops ready to fight, supported by ten naval battalions with a fleet of more than two hundred war boats, a hundred river junks bearing supplies, and one large, grand vessel for a flagship.[43] But it turned out that as a tactical commander, the bookish Zeng Guofan was an utter disaster. He was physically inept and could barely ride a horse. After some small initial success in pushing the rebels northward out of Hunan that spring, a brutal series of defeats sent his forces scurrying back through the province all the way to its capital, Changsha, as the rebels overran territory he had thought was secure. Following up on their victories against him, the Taiping pierced right through the heart of the province and conquered the major city of Xiangtan to the south of Changsha, which held one of his shipyards. They threw up defenses and commandeered a fleet of his boats. A separate Taiping force took the smaller city of Jinggang just to the north of the capital, and between them Changsha itself was now threatened. Zeng wrote a memorial to the throne taking full blame for his inexperience and asking to be punished.

In an attempt to break the potential siege of Changsha, Zeng divided his forces. He sent one column with naval support south toward Xiangtan and personally led a fleet of forty ships north to take back Jinggang. The river flowed from south to north, so Zeng was fighting with an upstream advantage. Nevertheless, the expected victory turned into a rout. Caught in a crosswind with a strong current, his inexperienced men lost control of their vessels. Those who didn't drown outright saw their boats captured and burned by rebels who waited on the banks, or who blocked them with a fleet several times larger than Zeng's. This time, he didn't write a memorial but instead took matters into his own hands; he rowed out of sight of his officers and tried to drown himself. A worried secretary who had followed in secret saw him fall into the water and managed to drag him out. His officers carried him back to Changsha to recover.[44]

Each defeat gave fodder to his provincial critics, and even as he lay recovering from his suicide attempt a group of imperial officials in Changsha were petitioning for him to be punished and his army disbanded. [45] But then came word of a decisive victory by the land forces he had sent south to Xiangtan. Four days of incessant attacks against the rebels' mudworks ended in a slaughter, with reports of ten thousand rebels killed and a thousand boats captured. The remainder of the Taiping force began to pull back in a wide retreat to the north, leaving Changsha safe for the time being. There was hope. Zeng soon learned to leave the battlefield command to others (as Tang Jian had told the emperor, his true talent was to use the talents of others). He had time to reconsolidate his forces and rebuild his navy, and through the summer and fall of 1854 they pushed the Taiping northward out of Hunan entirely and into Hubei province, where his forces reconquered its capital, the vital river city of Wuchang, in October.

The string of victories quieted his provincial critics for a time, but many in Hunan and Beijing remained leery of his unorthodox position. The Xianfeng emperor, at least, was delighted by the news that Zeng's force had recaptured Wuchang. "It is astonishing," he announced, "that Zeng Guofan, a mere scholar, could have accomplished such a wonderful deed!" But one of the emperor's counselors took a more jaundiced view, admonishing him that in the long run, the result of a provincial from Hunan raising an army of 10,000 men loyal mainly to himself "would not be a blessing to the empire."[46] The emperor had no reply to that.

As his army grew, Zeng Guofan collected the best commanders he could find. Most of them were Hunanese, beginning with his closest acquaintances and neighbors and fanning out through the local networks of scholars. Three of his four younger brothers would serve as commanders: Guohua, who was thirty-two years old in 1854, when Zeng Guofan was forty-three; Guoquan, thirty; and Guobao, twenty-six. But along with the Hunanese there were also several key commanders from other provinces, brought in by recommendation or poached from the upper ranks of the Green Standard. Some were even Manchus, the most valuable of whom was a cavalry officer named Duolonga, who was exceptionally talented but high-handed and proudly illiterate in Chinese. His disdain for the non-Manchu commanders was palpable, and they for their part mostly refused to work with him.[47] For specific skills Zeng Guofan also relied on outsiders—cavalrymen, for example, he recruited from northern provinces, where the flatter topography produced better horsemen than did mountainous Hunan. He set up a separate pay scale for non-Hunanese: the officers were paid considerably more, presumably because they lacked the regional loyalty that helped motivate his fellows, though at the lower levels it was the Hunanese soldiers and porters who were paid equal or higher wages, showing their value in his eyes. The great mass of lower officers and foot soldiers were always from Hunan, so Zeng's overall organization came to be known as the Hunan Army.

It was a counterinsurgency force, and his motto—repeated constantly in his letters and commands—was "Love the People." Without winning over the local populations, he believed, his army would have no hope of success. And given the well-known depredations of the regular imperial forces, he tried to ensure that the Hunan Army would carry itself with more restraint. This was partly for the sake of propaganda, spreading the moral vision of a benevolent imperial government that cared for its subjects. But it was also practical, as armies on campaign depended heavily on the surrounding population for their food. When there were reliable supply lines feeding back along the waterways to Hunan, his army could receive a steady stream of personnel, letters, gunpowder, and silver, as well as barges carrying the fundamental foodstuffs: rice, salt, cooking oil, and charcoal. But vegetables and meat had to be purchased by the soldiers from markets that sprang up near their camps. And laborers to build walls and dig ditches around those camps had to be hired from the local population.

Though the officers were scholars who lived in a world of books and philosophy, his men were unlettered. So Zeng instructed them with songs. At one point later in the war, disturbed by frequent reports of misconduct by his soldiers, he composed a song titled "Love the People" to try to teach them how to behave while on campaign. Among the rules in the song (which reflected just as well what the soldiers *were* doing as what Zeng wanted them not to do): Don't steal doors from people's houses (to make fires). Don't trample their crops or make lots of noise when they are sleeping. Don't take their cookware or snatch their ducks and chickens. Don't force them to dig ditches. If you have no money, don't pick vegetables by the side of the road. "For every man you impress into service as a porter," went the song, "a family is left weeping and living in fear." And "We don't steal, the rebels steal; if we plunder, then we're just like the rebels." The song ended with the essence of his counterinsurgent vision of unity between the army and the peasants (a sentiment deliberately echoed in the early Red Army of the twentieth century): "The soldiers and the people are like one family, and no matter what, we won't bully them. Sing 'Love the People' every day, and in Heaven there will be peace, on Earth there will be peace, and among men there will be peace."[48] He ordered his commanders to teach their men to sing it whenever they had free time.[49]

———

A fter taking Wuchang in October 1854, the Hunan Army began to claw its way down the Yangtze River to the east. Their home province was finally secure behind them, and between their position at Wuchang and the massive Green Standard siege camps at Nanjing lay a winding stretch of river about four hundred miles long (three hundred as the crow flew) along which the Taiping held all of the strategic walled cities. As long as the rebels held those cities, they would always have a pathway open to their capital and the imperial siege of Nanjing could never be completed. So it fell to Zeng Guofan, against terrible odds, to take them back.

The Taiping armies were larger and had greater momentum, so Zeng Guofan's successes depended mostly on the enemy's attentions being directed elsewhere—though in most cases, his army's initial victories were followed by such sharp and complete reversals that any self-confidence he managed to gain was repeatedly broken. After pushing down along the river as far as Jiujiang, the city that commanded the junction of the Yangtze River with the enormous Lake Poyang to its south, a horrifically ill-conceived division of his forces in the winter of 1855 ended in February with his flagship in flames and his best ships bottled up in the lake by Taiping forces, unable to connect to the river and therefore useless to the greater army. As the scale of the loss became obvious and his men reached the verge of mutiny, he attempted suicide a second time by riding a horse awkwardly into the thick of the battle. Once again his officers managed to pull him back before he could complete the deed.[50]

After the fiasco at Jiujiang in February 1855, Zeng wound up stranded for eighteen months in Jiangxi province just to the west of Hunan, with more than ten thousand men but no funds with which to pay their salaries. The officials of that province were as contemptuous of him as the ones in Hunan had been, and they not only refused to lend support but mocked him publicly, leaving him humiliated and helpless to act as the Taiping armies stormed right back up the Yangtze and took back Wuchang that April. Only the bloody suppression of the Eastern King's coup attempt in the rebel capital in 1856, and the lull in Taiping power that followed it, finally gave him a window of relief. Toward the end of 1857, his father died and he returned home again for mourning. Disheartened by his failures and frustrated by the intransigent officials who constantly blocked his efforts, he submitted his resignation and left the army in the hands of his senior officers. The emperor accepted his resignation, with the condition that he would have to come back out to fight again if called. The leave of absence lasted about a year.[51]

––––––––––

Though the regional nature of Zeng Guofan's army made for usually close-knit fighting ranks, it also meant that the morale of his soldiers depended heavily on the security of Hunan province itself. It was therefore an extremely delicate matter to lead the army out of the province and down the Yangtze River into someone else's home territory. After all, the initial formation of the militia had been to restore order to Hunan in the wake of the Taiping invasion, and even Zeng Guofan's own decision to accept the emperor's mission hinged on his father's conviction that it was necessary to protect their home district. But once the goal of putting down the bandits and Taiping remnants in Hunan province was accomplished, Zeng set his sights down the river through Hubei, Jiangxi, and Anhui toward Nanjing. If he ever felt any personal misgivings about moving his army out of their home province, he did not share them with his family. By the summer of 1860, he would write in a letter home that his life now belonged to the empire as a whole. "Now that I've heard the will of Heaven," he wrote, "whether it takes me to Anhui or Jiangnan, there's nowhere I will not go. Early on, I put thoughts of death out of my mind, and when the time comes to face my end, I will have no feelings of regret. This is a great blessing."[52]

His officers and men, however, were not so divinely inspired, and in leaving Hunan they were also leaving their homes—and their parents, children, and wives—undefended. His orders directing the Hunan Army's campaign into the neighboring provinces of Jiangxi and Anhui therefore took care to point out that by fighting in those provinces the army would be protecting Hunan at its rear. But in a war with multiple moving fronts, such a strategy was sometimes untenable. In the spring of 1859, with his army bogged down in Jiangxi province fighting for the pottery-producing city of Jingdezhen on the far side of Lake Poyang, a separate, massive Taiping army under Shi Dakai the Wing King numbering between 200,000 and 300,000 soldiers (according to Zeng's intelligence) swept across Jiangxi to their south, and then coursed northward across the border into Hunan behind them.

Shi Dakai's invasion of Hunan was a shocking blow to Zeng Guofan's men, who began begging for leave to go home. But he didn't see any possibility of pulling back from Jingdezhen, which would only open a separate route for Taiping forces to threaten the upstream territories. So he transferred only a handful of commanders back to Hunan, with orders to pull together all of the discharged, furloughed, and retired Hunan Army veterans they could lay their hands on. And he asked his other officers to reassure their troops. "Hunan needn't worry that it doesn't have soldiers or commanders," he wrote to them. "Its only worry is that we couldn't pull them together in time to stop the rebels at the border." He had faith that the forces mustering in Hunan could hold off the invasion and ordered his commanders at Jingdezhen to "tell your men to go on fighting with their hearts at ease and to let go of their worries about affairs back home."[53] It was a wishful reassurance, but the hastily assembled defense forces did ultimately succeed, with 40,000 of them holding out through that summer against Shi Dakai's army at the walled city of Baoqing deep within the province, only thirty miles from Zeng's own native home. Shi Dakai finally gave up the siege and took his army southward into Guangxi in August. Only after Jingdezhen fell that same month did Zeng Guofan begin to send more help back to Hunan.[54]

. . .

The more experience he gained, the more stubborn he became. It was a trait born of balancing his responsibility to his own people—his family, his soldiers, their families in Hunan—against his responsibility to the Xianfeng emperor and the wider Qing Empire. When he drove his men to continue fighting through their homesick agony that spring and summer of 1859 at Jingdezhen, he was putting the imperial campaign against the Taiping rebels first, asking his men to set aside their personal worries and trust him. But sometimes it worked the other way. After he captured Jingdezhen, the emperor ordered him to take his army up the Yangtze River all the way to Sichuan, to the northwest of Hunan, to guard against the possibility that Shi Dakai would ultimately make his way up there and threaten control of that enormous and wealthy province. Such a redeployment would take Zeng Guofan and his army out of the main theater of the war, away from the campaign that protected Hunan at its rear and that—if it did succeed in conquering Nanjing—would give them credit for helping to put down the rebellion. So in this case, Zeng put himself and his men first.

He rebuffed the imperial orders by pleading compassion for the misery of his soldiers. "The Hunan militiamen in Jiangxi have been worrying about their homes," he wrote to the emperor. "They are responsible for their families, and their feelings of homesickness are strong. Because the situation in Jingdezhen was so serious, I wouldn't allow them to take leave, but if we now pick up and start marching toward Sichuan, our route will pass through Hunan province and one after another they'll all ask for leave. I don't have the power to stop them."[55] This was the drawback to working with militias, he said, for "after a long time on the march, they often start to think of going home." Even if he could keep them from taking leave to care for their families, the journey to Sichuan was arduous, more than a thousand miles, passing through the Three Gorges and other dangers, and his army was exhausted by the fighting in Jiangxi. "Personally," he wrote, "I fear the men wouldn't follow me gladly." His appeal worked, and with the support of others who petitioned that he was needed in the east, he was relieved from marching his army to Sichuan and left to continue the campaign downriver from Hunan.

But even as he tried to balance his affection for his men against his duty to the emperor, the sacrifices sometimes caught up to him. For the intimacy of their local origins also meant that his army's losses were felt all the more bitterly. Zeng Guofan's brother Guohua had developed into a respected battlefield commander when, in November 1858, he led his forces into a slaughter at the hands of a Taiping army at the town of Three Rivers in Anhui province. Guohua died in the battle, and the senior commander committed suicide. Altogether, six thousand Hunanese soldiers were massacred at Three Rivers, many of them from Zeng Guofan's own home district. Soon afterward came the butchery at Jingdezhen, and the Hunanese casualties mounted further. As Zeng Guofan mourned the loss of his brother Guohua at camp, and as another of his brothers (who would himself die in the war) swore revenge for their family's loss, back in Hunan the rice-terraced hills of Zeng's childhood rang with the cries of his grieving neighbors, who everywhere shouted from their rooftops, calling to the faraway ghosts of their dead sons and begging them to come home.[56]

U p until 1860, Zeng Guofan's army on the Yangtze played only a supporting role in the overall imperial campaign, which centered on the Green Standard forces under Zhang Guoliang and He Chun that were laying their ever-tightening siege of Nanjing. But then, just as it seemed that victory was within their reach, came the great reversal in the spring of 1860, when Hong Rengan's plan to break the encirclement succeeded with such stunning effect. By the end of May, the imperial armies were destroyed and their commanders dead, and the Taiping were exploding out of Nanjing toward the east. In the leadership vacuum that ensued, Zeng Guofan's time came at last. In June 1860, the Xianfeng emperor appointed him to the powerful governor-generalship of Anhui, Jiangsu, and Jiangxi, the three provinces most heavily ravaged by the war. In late August, Xianfeng also named him imperial commissioner in charge of the military affairs in those same three provinces, establishing him as the new commander in chief of the dynasty's forces in the Yangtze River Valley.

The frustration of constantly having to fend for his own army began to fall away, thanks to the desperation of an emperor who had (as one of Zeng Guofan's assistants put it) nowhere else to turn.[57] After years of scrabbling with recalcitrant provincial officials and jealous Green Standard commanders, those two appointments put Zeng Guofan simultaneously in charge of both the civil and military administrations in the primary theater of war. As commander in chief of the military, he could direct the remnants of the imperial army and the local militias to act in support of his Hunan forces. And as governor-general of the three provinces, he could appoint his protégés to important civil posts where they could squeeze the resources of those provinces—at least the parts of them that were still intact and still under imperial control—to give his army the funding and supplies it needed.[58]

The serendipitous promotions made him, if anything, even more stubborn. There was a long tradition of independent-minded commanders in China's history ("When the general is outside the capital," went the saying, "the ruler's orders won't all be followed"). And as Zeng Guofan developed into an experienced leader and gained further control over his own part of the campaign, it appeared at times that for all his professed loyalty to the dynasty, he would take direction from no authority above himself. His years of service in the capital before the war had taught him how ineffective the bureaucrats of the central government could be, how inexperienced and self-gratifying, and he did not want their inexperience to affect his campaign. Trusting only his own developing sense of strategy and knowing his army's limitations, he all but ignored many of the orders that issued from Beijing. As in 1859, when he had refused the orders to chase Shi Dakai into Sichuan, now in 1860 a new set of orders arrived, commanding him to abandon his campaign in Anhui and take his troops immediately downriver to protect Suzhou and Shanghai. But on the formal excuse that his forces were insufficient to help at the moment, he stayed where he was.

The strategy he had decided to follow, and from which he did everything possible not to depart, was one of encirclement. It was more than a little reminiscent of his obsession with the game of Go. He laid out his strategic vision in a memorial to the throne on November 11, 1859, while he was still operating as a supplement to the Green Standard's siege of Nanjing.[59] The dynasty was fighting two kinds of rebels, Zeng explained, and a distinction should be made between the "roving bandits" with constantly moving armies and the "pretender bandits" who wanted a capital and a throne. Shi Dakai, who had just crisscrossed the empire, and the Nian rebels in the north, with their vagabond armies on horseback, were all roving bandits. The only way to fight them was to prepare for their arrival, hold your position, and try to blunt their momentum. But with the pretenders—the most important being the Heavenly King in his capital at Nanjing—you could fight them by "severing their branches and leaves" (cutting them off from the foraging armies that supplied them) and then crushing them in their nests. He pointed out that the Green Standard had failed to surround Nanjing completely (indeed, the one free path they had left open would prove their undoing), and he believed that to really cut the city off, the imperials would first need to conquer a string of fortified cities along the Yangtze to its west, one by one, beginning with the Brave King's base at Anqing, the capital of Anhui province. Anqing, held by the rebels since 1853, was their farthest major anchor of control up the Yangtze. It projected defensive power over both the river and land approaches to Nanjing from the west. It was the choke point, and as long as the Taiping held it there was no way for Zeng Guofan's forces to move beyond them and no way to complete a siege of Nanjing. But if he could cut Anqing off and crush it, he thought he might be able to open the way to the rebel capital.

On the ground it wasn't such a simple matter. The rebels had vast numerical superiority (by 1860, Zeng Guofan's militia still only had about 60,000 men total),[60] and they were all but impossible to contend with in open combat. Reports compiled by his intelligence officers showed the wild range of irregular formations the rebels had been known to use. There was the protean "crab formation"—with a cluster of troops in the middle (the body of the crab) and five lines reaching out on either side—that could rapidly reconfigure itself as two columns, four columns, or a crosslike configuration of five phalanxes, depending on what they encountered. There was the "hundred birds formation," in which a large division would disintegrate into small clusters of twenty-five soldiers, each roaming freely like birds in a flock or stars in a galaxy so that it was impossible to tell the size of their force or where to attack them. There was the "crouching tiger," used in hilly terrain, where 10,000 or more rebels would hide close to the ground in total silence and then, as the imperials passed through a valley, suddenly leap up together in ambush.[61] In an open fight, the imperials generally didn't stand a chance.

So winning was a matter of manipulating the battlefield to his own advantage. In every military engagement, Zeng wrote in an essay on strategy, one side would always be the host and the other would be the guest. The host always had the advantage. The defenders of a walled city were always the host, while those who attacked it were the guest. The same was true of a fortified camp. If two armies met in the open, the one to reach the site of battle first would be the host, while the latecomer would be the guest. With two armies facing each other in stalemate, it was a matter of patience: The guest was the army that first gave a shout and fired its guns. The host was the one that waited.[62] With an inherently weaker army, Zeng Guofan tried to ensure that the rebels would always be their guests: by luring them into attacking his own defensive works or, failing that, provoking them into making the first move. To that end, he settled on a practice of using tightly fortified camps, planted in close proximity to the rebel forces, in hopes of drawing them into making the first attack.

In June 1860, when the majority of Taiping forces were distracted by their walkover victories in the east, Zeng Guofan moved into Anhui from the west and sent his younger brother Zeng Guoquan to lay down a quiet siege at Anqing. Guoquan led 10,000 Hunanese troops up close to the city wall, pitched camp, and—with the help of laborers hired from the local population—began to build two high earthen walls underscored on each side by a twenty-foot-wide moat. The walls ran parallel to the wall of the city and sandwiched the Hunan Army camp between them. The inner wall, facing the city, was to protect them from the forces within, and the outer wall was to protect them from relief forces. In essence it was, on a smaller scale, their own walled city. To further protect against reinforcements from the north, 20,000 cavalry under the Manchu commander Duolonga set up a line of obstruction outside the rebel stronghold of Tongcheng, forty miles north of Anqing, while Zeng Guofan's naval forces set up blockades on the Yangtze River a few miles above and below the city.

In late July, Zeng Guofan took the rest of his forces, about 30,000 men total, into the mountains of southern Anhui below the river. He made his headquarters in the walled town of Qimen, in a valley about sixty miles to the southeast of Anqing, with six battalions of his own. It was a rugged country with few roads, and he stationed the rest of his men under their commanders at a radius to control the approach from the east and to maintain an overland supply line to the west, leading through Jingdezhen (which was now his) back into Jiangxi province.

At first sight, he knew Qimen was the perfect place to make his headquarters. It was enveloped on all sides by a sawtooth quilt of mountain ranges, utterly unapproachable from the north or south, and his own forces controlled the road that ran from east to west. He was delighted. "The peaks rise ever higher in layers, and the mountains are four times as numerous as the ones back home," he wrote when he first got there. "There are sweet springs and luxuriant forests. It is delightfully secluded and quiet, and the passes need no more than a company to hold them. *This* is a place we can defend, with no need for greater forces."[63] From there, Zeng could coordinate the overall campaign for Anqing from a point of safety.

But as the summer of 1860 gave way to fall and the new war with Britain and France erupted in the north, his sanctuary in Qimen began to feel more like a prison. On October 10, orders from Beijing came, instructing him to send his very best field commander, a man from Sichuan province named Bao Chao, along with his 3,000 veteran troops, to help Senggelin-qin's banner forces defend against the Allies in the north. Zeng Guofan didn't think his army could possibly hold its position at Anqing without Bao Chao's support, and he was certain that Senggelinqin's elite Mongol cavalry could defend the capital. So, despite the immediacy of the emperor's crisis, he extemporized. It would be January before Bao Chao's forces could arrive in Beijing, he reasoned, and by then it would be winter and surely they would no longer be needed. In the meantime, he had staked all of his forces on the siege of Anqing, with almost nothing to hold his rear upstream. Failure at Anqing would throw open the gates for the Taiping to take back the Yangtze up to Wuchang and even threaten Hunan again. So he held fast to his foothold in Anhui with an almost pathological focus. His unwillingness to budge was as much a product of fear as of stubbornness, though; in private letters home, he confessed that he was barely holding his own.[64]

He did not obey the order, at least not directly. Instead, when Zeng Guofan finally wrote back, he asked the emperor to choose which of his commanders (including Zeng himself) he would prefer to lead a detachment of Hunan Army soldiers north to help Senggelinqin fight the foreigners. But there was no reason for such a memorial, other than to delay the dismemberment of his forces in Anhui.[65] It took two full weeks for a letter to travel the nearly eight hundred miles between Qimen and Beijing, and Zeng well knew that by the time he got his answer back at least four weeks would have passed. He had just stolen another month to continue his siege of Anqing. "Everywhere in the entire empire the rebels have gained the upper hand," he wrote in frustration to his brothers, "but here in Anqing alone, in this one single city, they are on the wane. How can we lightly pull back?"[66] With the entire world falling apart around him, he held his ground, believing that if he gave up even the small advantage he had in his mountain valley in the heart of the kingdom, all would be lost.

October wore on with a cold and persistent rain that ground Zeng Guofan's spirits into a bleak depression. He paced restlessly in his quarters, brooding on the fate of the emperor and wondering what he should do. He played endless games of Go, and obsessed about the passage of time.[67] "My eyesight dims with each passing day," he wrote to his brothers, "and my energy fades. Day by day I feel older. I live in deep terror that I am not up to this great responsibility."[68]

The campaign on which he had staked everything was not going well. Anqing was shut up like a drum. The rebel garrison inside apparently had plentiful stores and could wait as long as it needed for reinforcements. One of his most beloved commanders hadn't been heard from in days, since his garrison in the nearby town of Huizhou—which was supposed to protect Zeng's eastern flank—had suddenly been overrun by Taiping raiders. Rebel forces pressed invisibly from all sides of Qimen, and the town itself was clogged with thousands of defeated soldiers, who looted the shops and left nothing to buy in the markets.[69] Still, no word came from Beijing. So he held his ground, worried, and wondered if he would have to abandon Anqing to the Taiping—and with it southern Anhui, Wuchang, and possibly even Hunan and the central empire.

Finally, on the afternoon of November 6, 1860, he opened a letter from a friend in the north and learned for the first time that the British and French armies had not only successfully invaded Beijing but had gone on to burn the emperor's palace to the ground. His numbness gave way to shock. "I have no words to describe the depths of this pain," he wrote in his diary.[70] The ranks of the bannermen were scattered in the north. The Green Standard was routed in the east. The dynasty's traditional forces had failed on both fronts, against both enemies. Zeng Guofan now faced the grim prospect that he, alone, in all of the empire, still commanded an unbroken army. His campaign in Anhui was the only one left.

CHAPTER 7

THE FORCE OF DOCTRINE

On August 21, 1860, two days after his men were driven back from Shanghai under a storm of grapeshot and canister, Loyal King Li Xiucheng wrote an aggrieved letter to the British and American consuls to complain. "I came to Shanghai to make a treaty in order to see us connected together by trade and commerce," he wrote to them bitterly. "I did not come for the purpose of fighting with you." He accused the French of setting a trap. As he told it, some French citizens (along with unspecified others) had come to Suzhou earlier that summer and invited him to come to Shanghai to discuss friendly relations between their countries. "It never occurred to my mind," he wrote, "that the French, allowing themselves to be deluded by the imperial demons, would break their word and turn their backs on the arrangement made."[1] He was told that the Qing government had given the French a large sum of money to defend Shanghai, and it seemed to him "without doubt" that the money had been "shared amongst the other nations," as evidenced by the fact that none of the British or American citizens came out to negotiate with him but instead all joined the French in firing cannons from the city walls.

"It is impossible that the affair should be forgotten," he warned. But he was willing to forgive the British and Americans, because they were his fellow Protestants. As for the treacherous (and idolatrous) French, they were another matter, and he noted that it was just a matter of time until the Taiping controlled all of China, after which a day of reckoning would come. "With human feelings, and in human affairs, all acts have their consequences," he wrote. "The French have violated their faith, and broken the peace between us." Out of "magnanimity" he pledged that he personally wouldn't prevent them from coming into Taiping territory, but he also said that he couldn't guarantee the complicity of the many officers and soldiers "who have been subjected to their deceit" and were now "filled with indignation, and desirous of revenge." In conclusion, he swallowed his pride and reiterated that what the Taiping wanted, above all, was a peaceful relationship with their Christian brethren from England and the United States. "You and we alike worship Jesus," he reminded them. "There exists between us the relationship of a common basis and common doctrines."

Though Li Xiucheng authored the letter, the sentiment behind it was Hong Rengan's. For it was Hong Rengan whose strategy for winning the war depended on support from the British and Americans in Shanghai, especially their willingness to sell or lease the rebels steamships to ensure their command of the Yangtze River. As chief of staff and prime minister, Hong Rengan had the approval of his cousin to set the policy that the other kings had to follow. Since he believed firmly that the best hope for the rebels was in building peaceful relations with the foreigners in Shanghai, Li Xiucheng had to toe the line as long as Hong Rengan was prime minister. But he did so only with reluctance. Within the Taiping inner circle, Li Xiucheng disputed Hong Rengan's trust in the foreigners and took a more aggressive view. "Foreigners like to fight," he told Hong Rengan. "They don't like peace."[2]

The unexpected outbreak of hostilities at Shanghai had helped make Li Xiucheng's case and widened the existing rift between him and Hong Rengan. But for his own part, Hong Rengan laid the blame on Li Xiucheng rather than the foreigners. He said that they must have gotten wind of Li's belligerent views toward them, which would naturally lead them to think he was coming to attack. As Hong Rengan told it, the Loyal King was flush with military strength after sweeping through Jiangsu province and conquering Suzhou, and he treated Shanghai as though it were already in the palm of his hand. The foreigners, playing on his confidence, lured him in with an "empty city strategy": they led the Loyal King to believe the city was completely undefended and then, when he approached, launched a surprise attack. After the defeat, Li Xiucheng "finally began to see things my way," Hong believed, "though he wouldn't admit he had made a mistake."[3] Despite their disagreement on tactics, however, there was no question to either of them that the rebels needed Shanghai: it was rich in financial stores, it was a base from which to acquire foreign weapons, and it was a hive of imperial resistance within a territory otherwise under their control. But it was as yet unattained, and now it was up to Hong Rengan's diplomacy to bring it under their influence.

In his capacity as head of foreign affairs, Hong Rengan began to hold court in Nanjing, receiving a succession of visitors from Shanghai who brought him news, gifts, and at one point even his family members who had remained in Hong Kong.[4] His was one of the larger palaces in the capital, and it served not just as his home but also as the center for his work. Directly across from its front gate, facing the entrance, stood a massive stone tablet, fifteen feet high and ten wide, with an enormous Chinese character for "blessing" carved into it and painted over in gold.[5] Above the giant character were inscribed Jesus Christ's nine beatitudes from the Sermon on the Mount, tempered in meaning by their strange new context (none more so than the seventh: "Blessed are the peacemakers, for they shall be called the children of God"). Within lay the main public hall with its throne, where the Shield King held audience, dressed in imperial yellow silk robes, his hair done up with gilted pasteboard in the ornamental style of the old Ming dynasty.[6]

Beyond the main hall, a warren of dim hallways and doors led into his private quarters deep within the palace, his own room furnished mainly with a large bed decorated in jade and facing out onto a bright courtyard with a garden. Here he surrounded himself with fragmentary talismans of the industrial world abroad, mostly souvenirs from his visitors. In varying degrees of functionality, his shelves held a collection of foreign clocks, a barometer, a telescope, several Colt revolvers, a secondhand harmonium, two solar lamps, a bar of British soap, an English naval sword, and, as one intrigued visitor noted, "a jar of Coward's mixed pickles." There were reference books and picture books, and books that showed he was studying British military methods (including *The Principles of Fortification*, from the Royal Military Academy at Woolwich). There were Chinese publications from the Shanghai missionaries—who translated scientific material in hopes of convincing the Chinese that their religion had mastered the natural world—as well as the requisite Bibles and Gospel tracts. Then there were the Chinese luxuries, in only slightly better state of repair: golden chopsticks, jade teacups, fans made of silver. Here he entertained his foreign guests with dinners of beefsteak and port, speaking in English and showing off his mastery of knife and fork.[7]

Among Hong Rengan's first visitors in Nanjing was a former Southern Baptist preacher named Issachar Roberts, a profoundly unstable missionary from Sumner County, Tennessee, who had been briefly a teacher of Hong Xiuquan (and even more briefly of Hong Rengan) in Canton before the war. Roberts had been the only one to sense the true import of Hong Rengan's account to Theodore Hamberg back in 1852, though nobody had paid any attention to him at the time. White-haired and angular, he was a singularity within the missionary community, remembered by historians even of his own order as a man of "erratic and peculiar character."[8] The Baptist Board for Foreign Missions in Boston had rejected Roberts's first application to become a China missionary in 1836 (even the best of his references described his preaching as "not above mediocrity"), and so he had sponsored his own mission to China by donating a piece of land, the income from which was intended to cover all of his expenses.[9] On that basis, he had convinced the Baptists to take him on as a missionary free of cost and sailed for China, arriving in 1837. The land later turned out to be nearly worthless, but the Baptists were stuck with him.[10] Despite some success in his mission work in southern China, he proved unable to make friends with other missionaries, and his home board was repeatedly alarmed by reports about his behavior: that he had publicly abused one of his Chinese servants, that he had falsified the mission's contribution books.[11] The Baptists finally severed their ties with him in 1852, after Roberts refused to come to the aid of another missionary who had slit his own throat with a razor.[12]

But then, in 1853, Hong Xiuquan himself had issued an invitation for Issachar Roberts to come to Nanjing, with a letter that indicated his respect for Roberts's teachings. The letter gave Roberts a public counterweight to the humiliation of being stripped of his Baptist credentials, though it proved impossible at that time to get through the imperial blockades to Nanjing. Even if he could have gotten through, the U.S. commissioner threatened him with execution if he broke neutrality by visiting the rebels. So he sailed back to the United States, where he traveled about the southern and western states giving speeches in favor of the Taiping cause and raising money to return to China as an independent missionary to the rebels.[13] He drummed up a measure of fame, and the papers touted him as "the religious preceptor of [the] Tae-ping King, the chief of the patriotic revolutionary party."[14] After returning to China in 1856 with the money he had raised by his speeches, for four years he still failed to get into rebel territory. But in 1860, with the Shield King announcing a welcome to foreign visitors in Nanjing, his chance came at last and he eagerly made his way to the Taiping capital to rejoin his former students. He arrived in Nanjing on October 13, 1860, just as the British and French troops in the north were invading Beijing, and took up residence in a suite of upstairs rooms in Hong Rengan's rambling palace.

The Shield King put Roberts to work as an interpreter, giving him responsibility for missionary affairs in the Heavenly Kingdom. However, such service hadn't been Roberts's purpose in coming to Nanjing. Roberts believed (or at least so said the Anglican bishop of Hong Kong) that an accident of history had made him the spiritual teacher of a future Chinese emperor.[15] He had traveled to Nanjing expecting that the rebels would revere him as the mentor of the Heavenly King. But his reception unraveled differently than he had wished, and it took some time before he could even have a face-to-face audience with Hong Xiuquan. The delay was for reasons of ceremony not so far removed from the kowtow issue behind the warfare then enveloping the Manchu capital; the bevy of secondary kings insisted that if Roberts were to have an audience with the Heavenly King, he would have to kneel before him like the others, to show his subservience. Roberts, the proud American Baptist, refused. They finally allowed him an audience with Hong Xiuquan anyhow, but as he stood uneasily behind the long rows of assembled Taiping officials in their ceremonial robes, Hong Rengan suddenly bellowed at him before the entire hall, "Mr. Roberts, Worship the Heavenly Father!" and down went the white-bearded Roberts, caught off guard and embarrassed, instinctively kneeling down in worship before the man who had once been his student.[16]

Issachar Roberts lived a ghostly existence in Nanjing, drifting about in the tattered hand-me-down silk robes of Hong Rengan and wearing on his head what one visitor described as "a ridiculous-looking, gilt cardboard tiara, cut into fantastic shapes, and ornamented sometimes with what struck me as badly executed artificial flowers, and sometimes with little figures of tigers."[17] Thinking he would be the teacher, he lived instead in Hong Rengan's palace as, effectively, an assistant. But for all of his oddities, he became the mouthpiece Hong Rengan needed in Shanghai. In the absence of any direct rebel influence in that city, the foreign residents of Shanghai got most of their information about inland China from the Qing officials and merchants among whom they lived. The officials were de facto loyalists, and the Chinese merchants of Shanghai, who were getting extremely rich due to their carefully cultivated relationships with those same officials, had no interest in a change of government.[18] Viewed through their eyes, the Taiping seemed a force of unmitigated destruction. Moreover, the business investments of the foreigners—their ships and docks, their offices, banks, warehouses, and homes—were now located within a sanctuary of imperial control at the edge of a large territory governed by a party with which their own governments wouldn't allow them to trade. As their business fortunes threatened to falter, they blamed the rebels. Their Qing-loyalist neighbors warned ominously that a Taiping victory would destroy the ports altogether, and there was little evidence to contradict them. Thus, for all who regretted the fighting that summer on moral grounds, there were plenty in the influential foreign merchant community who sided with Frederick Bruce in thinking that the resistance against the Taiping invaders had been both heroic and necessary.

Against that current, Issachar Roberts would spend more than a year in the rebel capital writing letters to the English newspapers in Shanghai and Hong Kong reporting on the true conditions in Nanjing (as he saw them) and giving an ongoing public testament to the revolutionary potential of the Taiping government. His letters glowed. "I can't help but love the man," he wrote of Li Xiucheng in one of the first letters, published in Hong Kong's *Overland Register* that November. "He is one of a thousand! He is not only a man of learning, affable and amiable, but a king, and a general of no ordinary abilities, commanding more than a hundred thousand troops." Roberts relayed a message from the Loyal King to the foreign merchants that the rebels (whom Roberts termed the "revolutionists") in fact *did* want commerce with them. And given that, why would foreigners trade with the imperials over their fellow Christians? The Taiping, wrote Roberts, "are willing to trade on at least as good if not better terms! They have the means of commerce, teas and silks, within their territory." The only reason the foreign merchants didn't already enjoy a flourishing trade with the rebels was that their governments hadn't yet made a treaty with the Taiping. "Echo responds in England and France," he wrote, "—Why not make a treaty? Reverberation answers in the United States—Why not make a treaty? . . . why not make a generous treaty with them at once, giving them their due advantages which they have so worthily won by their sword, and [giving] their people the Christian religion?"[19]

. . .

Following shortly on Roberts's heels, the Welsh missionary Griffith John made his way to the rebel capital in November 1860. His companion from the harrowing journey to Suzhou the previous summer, Joseph Edkins, stayed behind because he wasn't feeling well (his wife, Jane, thought it was distress brought on by the ghastly apparitions he had seen on the first visit).[20] Griffith John was wary of the resentments the rebels might harbor after the attack on them at Shanghai—an attack that personally appalled him. "They came entertaining the most friendly feeling imaginable towards all foreigners," he wrote in sympathy, "but they were treated by us, and our allies the French, in a way that reflects disgrace on our flag."[21] He nevertheless found himself warmly received in Nanjing when he arrived, and he thrilled at the possibility of setting up a new base of missionary operations right in the capital of the Taiping. He wrote to Edkins, bursting with hope. "He says order, health, peace, and happiness reigned in Nankin," wrote Jane Edkins, recounting the letter, "and he urges on Mr. Edkins to think again if he will not cast in his lot with the rebels."[22]

Unlike Issachar Roberts, Griffith John as yet had no plans to stay for good; his was a scouting mission on behalf of the seventy or so Protestant preachers in Shanghai. And when he returned to the treaty port in early December, he brought them a trophy: an edict from the Heavenly King, written in imperial vermilion ink on yellow satin, welcoming foreign missionaries to take up residence in the Heavenly Kingdom. Here was the missionary community's most desired concession—one that Britain had just wrung from the Beijing government by force of arms—and the rebels were offering it of their own free will. It seemed a further sign that a divine hand was guiding the Taiping. "I firmly believe," John wrote to his fellow missionaries, "that God is uprooting idolatry in the land through the insurgents, and that he will, by means of them in connection with the foreign missionary, plant Christianity in its stead."[23]

The crucial phrase here was "in connection with the foreign missionary," for he believed, as did others among the religiously motivated Taiping sympathizers, that the rebels were as yet only the raw material of a Christian China. Hong Rengan, the Shield King, was where the promise lay; not with his elder cousin the Heavenly King (who, Griffith John believed, "writes like a lunatic"). As long as the Taiping followers believed in the divinity of their Heavenly King and as long as they accepted his practice of polygamy (even Hong Rengan, Griffith John discovered, had by this time four wives, insisting that he had to follow his cousin's custom if he wanted to have influence in the Taiping court)—as long as they held to such beliefs and practices, they were in error and couldn't be accepted as more than a sort of promising blasphemy; far more promising than the overtly anti-Christian Manchu rulers and Confucian gentry, but still short of the mark.

Moreover, correcting the doctrine of the rebels was, Griffith John believed, more than just an opportunity for the foreign missionaries: it was their moral obligation. As he saw it, the missionaries had caused the rebellion in the first place. It was their Bible and their teachings that had inspired the Heavenly King, and therefore it was their responsibility to make sure that it all came to a good end. As he put it in a pamphlet published a few months later: "Protestant missionaries in China! This Insurrection is your offspring."[24] Griffith John yearned for the chance to be the first (other than the erratic Roberts) to help Hong Rengan shape the doctrines of the rebels from their center. But friends in Shanghai prevailed upon him to wait. There was no direct communication between Shanghai and Nanjing yet, they warned him, so his mission would be cut off from the larger community. He would be completely dependent on the rebels for sustenance, and no one yet knew what the state of commerce on the Yangtze River would be or where the course of the war might go. It was dangerous. As an alternative, Joseph Edkins steered him toward Shandong province up the eastern coast, newly opened by Elgin's treaty, with twenty-nine million souls in need of saving (and the birthplace of Confucius to boot).[25]

In the end, Griffith John decided to wait at least until spring before deciding whether to set up a permanent mission in Nanjing. But there was no question in his mind where the future of China lay. As he wrote in a letter to the secretary of the London Missionary Society that February, the rebel victories and the Allied invasion of Beijing "have thoroughly undermined Manchu power. It must fall. There is no power to uphold it." There was nothing but certainty in his voice. "The Manchus," he wrote, "might as well attempt to blow the sun out of heaven as to quench this flame which their folly and tyranny have kindled."[26]

When Joseph Edkins had stayed behind, Griffith John had brought along a different companion to Nanjing. He was Yung Wing, the Chinese graduate of Yale University who had spent most of his life among Westerners in Hong Kong and New England, the same who had reacted with such horror to the programmatic executions of accused rebels in Canton when he first came back to China after college in 1855. He had found work as a tea trader in the interim, but he had political ambitions, and he now traveled to Nanjing with Griffith John "to find out," in his words, "the character of the Taiping; whether or not they were the men fitted to set up a new government in the place of the Manchu dynasty."[27] Yung Wing's concerns had less to do with religion and more to do with the ability of the Taiping to rule China in a European or American style. The journey made a favorable impression on him. He noted that the group oddly encountered no challenges from either imperial or rebel forces on their way first to Suzhou (where they found a handful of European and American military personnel and doctors offering their services to the Taiping) and then on to Nanjing. He described the rebels they saw along the way as "generally very civil," with a "considerate and commendable" attitude toward the peasantry. He noted that it was easy to assign blame for the devastation of the countryside to the Taiping, when in fact the imperial forces were no kinder in their own fields of action. Reaching Nanjing, Yung Wing first met with Issachar Roberts (for whom he had little regard) and then, on November 19, with Hong Rengan, to whom he brought a different kind of message than the missionaries had.[28]

Yung Wing and Hong Rengan had known each other in Hong Kong back when Hong Rengan was preaching with James Legge, and they shared a certain affinity in that both had been born to poor families in the same part of south China and both had found their lives profoundly changed by the years they spent living in foreign communities in Hong Kong and abroad. Both, also, now sought to use their foreign experience for leverage within China. Hong Rengan received his old acquaintance gladly and expressed hope that Yung Wing might join him in the Taiping movement. Yung Wing initially demurred, saying he had only come to learn more about the rebels, but he did give the Shield King a list of suggestions that he considered to be "the secret of the strength and power of the British government and other European powers."[29] If the Taiping would implement those modernizations, Yung Wing promised, he would pledge himself to their cause. (He did not want for a sense of self-importance.) The suggestions were:

1. To organize an army on scientific principles.
2. To establish a military school for the training of competent military officers.
3. To establish a naval school for a navy.
4. To organize a civil government with able and experienced men to act as advisers in the different departments of administration.

5. To establish a banking system, and to determine on a standard of weights and measures.
6. To establish an educational system of graded schools for the people, making the Bible one of the text books.
7. To organize a system of industrial schools.[30]

That is: to establish a modern military, American-style (and Christian) schools, and an industrial economy. Hong Rengan readily agreed; indeed, he had already proposed much of this himself in his treatise on government. But as the other kings were occupied elsewhere, he could not immediately promise Yung Wing that the suggestions would be carried out. They had to have a vote, he explained, and the majority would have to agree. So until then the matter of the reforms would have to wait (and after that, presumably, until the Taiping had actually won—for they were policies for an established government, not a warring party contending for power, to put into place).

Nevertheless, Hong Rengan remained hopeful of winning over Yung Wing, who would surely prove useful in attracting American support for the Taiping government. A few days later he sent Yung Wing a Taiping seal and ceremonial robes. Yung Wing declined the robes and seal, insisting that he couldn't become a Taiping official until he was sure the Taiping would implement his modernizations. But he did prevail upon the Shield King for a passport to allow him to travel freely through Taiping territory, which Hong Rengan granted. Yung Wing didn't say as much to Hong Rengan, but the reason he wanted the passport was not so he could learn more about the Taiping. Rather, he thought he might be able to make a fortune by purchasing the untouched stocks of tea that lay deep behind the blockades in rebel territory and selling them to the ravenous foreign merchants in Shanghai.[31] Yung Wing left Nanjing with Griffith John at the end of November, clutching his passport and his dreams of pristine mountains of tea, and made his way back downriver to Shanghai. Hong Rengan would never see him again.

———————

On December 2, the day after Yung Wing and Griffith John got back from Nanjing, Lord Elgin returned to Shanghai in triumph from his invasion of the north. He was brimming with satisfaction that his mission had been a success; in late October, with the first snows of the long northern winter already settling into the hills west of Beijing, he and Prince Gong had finally ratified the new treaty between China and Great Britain. It included all of the articles Elgin had first negotiated in 1858 when he had broken through the Taku defenses and invaded Tianjin. Among them: the establishment of new treaty ports, opening the Yangtze to British ships, and freedom for missionaries. The treaty also set a high indemnity that China had to pay Britain as punishment for Senggelinqin's attack on Frederick Bruce's fleet at Taku in 1859 and for his kidnapping of Harry Parkes and the others in September 1860. The French secured similar concessions.

In the Xianfeng emperor's eyes, the crucial point of the negotiations all along had been to keep the foreigners out of the capital. "A treaty signed under the city wall was the shame of the ancients," he told his negotiators. "It doesn't matter that an indemnity of two million taels would exhaust our treasuries; even if we *could* pay it, the barbarians are still demanding to enter the capital with a thousand men. Even women and children can see the evil intentions behind their outrageous requests."[32] But the foreign powers now had their right to station ambassadors, and in fact it was the indemnities—which the emperor considered secondary, since they concerned only money—that were the more serious threat to the dynasty. The British had originally demanded 4 million taels of silver, a sum worth about 1.3 million pounds sterling. But after having to fight their way to the gates of Beijing, they doubled the figure to 8 million taels, and Prince Gong had no choice but to grant it. The French demanded the same.

The empire that Xianfeng ruled was already fiscally broken when he came to the throne in 1851. An indemnity left over from the treaty that ended the Opium War in 1842 was compounded by ongoing corruption that saw vast sums leaking invisibly from the imperial coffers (in 1843, 9 million taels simply vanished from the treasury without account). And under Xianfeng's own rule, the state of affairs had worsened. As rebellions cut off vast regions of the empire and severed the Grand Canal, the imperial government lost much of the land-tax revenues that normally made up four-fifths of its income. Insurrections among miners in the south cut off the capital's supply of precious metals. Bandit armies in the northern plains disrupted the production of salt, a valuable government monopoly. By the time Prince Gong agreed to pay the British and French their indemnities totaling 16 million taels, the sum amounted to roughly eighty times the amount of silver that actually remained in the imperial treasury.[33] Paradoxically, the only meaningful source of revenue with which to pay the indemnity was the customs duty from foreign trade at Shanghai and Canton, meaning that the state of British and French trade in China became inextricably tied to the Qing government's ability to pay its new debt (and therefore the ability of Britain and France to receive it).

In Shanghai, Elgin learned firsthand about his brother's defense of the city from the rebels during his absence in the north. The irony was hardly lost on the British (save, perhaps, for Frederick Bruce) that they had gone to war against China's imperial government in the north at exactly the same time they were opening hostilities against its enemies, the Taiping rebels, at Shanghai. Lord Russell, the foreign secretary in London, learned about the surrender of the Taku forts and the attack on the Taiping at Shanghai on exactly the same day.[34] A bemused editorial in the London *Times* chalked it up to the oddness of China. "Generally speaking," it read, "when the population of a country is split into two factions, an invading force would be disposed to coalesce with one of them; but the politics of China resemble the zoology of Australia, and exhibit an inversion of all ordinary rules."[35] By way of explanation, one rather game British officer in Shanghai told his American counterpart, "My dear fellow, we always *pitch into the swells*. At the north the Imperialists are the swells, but down here, by Jove! the Rebels are, don't you know?—so we pitch into them both."[36] However, what seemed like good sport to some was to others a grievous miscalculation. *The New York Times* saw the Taiping rebels as natural allies of the foreign powers, for "all labor to the same end—the revivification of China by the humiliation, and if practicable the displacement of the actual bigoted and exclusive *regime*."[37] The *Overland Register* in Hong Kong charged that "a gross and unmitigated error has been committed at Shanghai," and declared that Britain should support the rebels because "in the political creed of the insurgent leaders there appears, from beginning to end, a complete revolution of the Chinese ideas in every important particular, and there is not an item of it that should not be met with the warm sympathy of every man who cares for the welfare of any country besides his own."[38]

No one expected further conflict, however. Now that the treaty was signed, Britain appeared to be at peace with the Qing government, and it was obvious from the Loyal King's letter in August that the Taiping maintained no hostility toward Shanghai. So the invasion force that had at its peak accounted for more than twenty thousand British and French troops in China was disbanded and sent home. By the end of December, half of the British forces had already returned to India and England (sparking rumors in China that the British were leaving because back home someone was attacking their own country).[39] Of the remaining British forces, most were stationed in the colony of Hong Kong, while roughly four thousand garrisoned Tianjin and Taku in the north—within striking distance of Beijing—to guarantee steady payments on the indemnity. Even then, there were grumblings that the high cost of maintaining this force in north China used up whatever payments it secured from the Qing government. As for Shanghai, by the end of 1860 there were only 1,200 British soldiers left in the city, and Elgin thought even that many would be unneeded.[40]

Elgin spent a month in the British settlement before leaving China for good. His work in the north was completed, and his final goal before returning home was to gauge the possibility of British relations with the rebels, who controlled most of the riverway that was now, thanks to his treaty, officially open to British trade. He gave no sign of pleasure about his brother Frederick Bruce's "defense" of Shanghai from Taiping attackers the previous summer and expressed overt dismay at seeing the charred remnants of the city's suburbs. He also heard a rumor—which was current in both the foreign and Chinese communities—that when the French had burned those neighborhoods on the excuse of protecting the city from the rebels, they had done so mainly because they wanted the land for themselves, to build a church.[41] "The French have some method in their madness," Elgin quipped in his journal. "[T]hey insist on having it now at the cost of the land, 'as there are no houses upon it.'"[42]

Though Frederick Bruce held obstinately to his negative view of the rebels, Lord Elgin counseled him to keep an open mind. In a private letter to his brother (who by this time was the ambassador, wintering in Tianjin and awaiting the preparation of his quarters in Beijing), Elgin told Bruce that between the imperials and the Taiping, "bad as they both are," he believed the rebels to have the brighter future. From what he had seen of the regions under Taiping control—of which Bruce had seen none—Elgin felt that the rebels exhibited "honesty and power."[43] And in what may have been a rebuke for Bruce's refusal to read the Loyal King's letter prior to the Taiping arrival at Shanghai, Elgin warned his brother not to accede to any Qing requests for Britain to avoid contact with the rebels: "it will never do to come under any obligation not to communicate with them on the Yangtze," he wrote. "It would be wrong in principle . . . and impossible in practice."

Winter had arrived, and there wasn't time to make another trip up the Yangtze himself, but Elgin left orders with the commander in chief of British naval forces in China, Rear Admiral James Hope, to pay a visit to the

Taiping at their capital come spring and to find out if there might be a basis for a friendly relationship between Britain and the rebels. It was a delicate situation, Elgin admitted, for the British held treaty relations with the Taiping's enemy. But he hoped that strict neutrality would allow Britain to benefit from interaction with both sides even as the Chinese war ground on. "I rather think better of the rebel prospects since I came here," he wrote in a private letter to Hope, "at any rate it is clear that we must not become partisans in this civil war."[44]

Having settled the war with the Manchus and now having set the wheels into motion for Admiral Hope to open relations with the Taiping, Lord Elgin's mission was complete and he sailed home at last. It would be a long voyage, but that was just as well; for even as he stopped off at Hong Kong on his way out of China, he began to get wind that the conduct of his army in Beijing was not being met with approval back in England. When he finally got home, there would be much to answer for.

Meanwhile, the Taiping military consolidation of China's wealthy eastern province of Jiangsu continued apace. As early as September 1860, an imperial supporter in the region noted that the rebels controlled every county around Shanghai except for those under the direct protection of foreigners, which still held out ("for the time being," he fretted, "though who knows what's coming?"). Like many Qing loyalists, this observer was despondent. "How can we possibly encourage the hearts of the people?" he wrote in his diary. "How can we restore our territory? My generation lives through this crisis, but we have nowhere to set our foot [to take action], and our voices can do no more than sigh."[45] The Taiping capitalized on such despondence, spreading broadsides to shake the will of those who hoped for the return of Manchu control. "The emperor of the Qing is the emperor of a lost country," read one proclamation in the city of Wujiang near Suzhou, "and his ministers are all the ministers of a lost country."[46] When the news of the emperor's flight from Beijing came down through the channels of rumor, it shook even the staunch loyalists to their core and forced them to confront the likelihood of a Qing collapse. "A ruling house of two hundred years, endangered in an instant," wrote the observer in his diary. "I never imagined the end would come so soon."[47]

The Taiping extended their control through the prosperous lower reaches of the Yangtze River, the region known as Jiangnan (literally,

"South of the River") that encompassed the confluence of Jiangsu, Anhui, and Zhejiang provinces. In Jiangsu province, home to Shanghai, the Taiping held the capital, Suzhou, along with the major cities of Danyang and Wuxi. Zhenjiang, the river city of ghosts, held out but the countryside surrounding it was all under the control of the Taiping. In Anhui they held the capital city, Anqing, though Zeng Guofan had just established his presence nearby. South of Shanghai lay Zhejiang province, where the wealthy trading city of Ningbo and the capital, Hangzhou, were in imperial hands for the time being. Li Xiucheng had attacked Hangzhou as his feinting maneuver during the relief of the Nanjing siege and unleashed hell within it, but he had not broken through to the Manchu garrison city, nor had he left troops to hold the city after darting back to Nanjing.

Taiping armies arriving in Jiangnan were met with a mixture of fascination and fear. One witness in Changshu county, about sixty miles west of Shanghai, described the parade of a rebel army through his town in the autumn of 1860. Curious townsfolk peered out from behind their gates as the Taiping officers passed, resplendent in their bright, colorful silks. They wore jackets of fox fur and capes of squirrel hide and rode slowly past on a succession of several hundred horses, as men with banners and spears lined the road. He estimated that 10,000 Taiping soldiers passed through altogether, and noted that they caused no harm at all to the townspeople. But then, after the bulk of the army had passed, came the devils who followed in their wake: a few hundred longhairs trailing behind the procession who went freely back and forth between people's houses, knocking on the (now-locked) gates. They broke into houses to commit robbery, rape, and murder. They grabbed young men and tied them together by their long braids, dragging them off in the direction in which the army had gone. The terrified witness thought it fortunate they didn't burn down the town as well. As the proud army faded away on the road to the south and the cloud of devils drifted after it into the distance, many of the townspeople left their homes to follow them. Some went in search of relatives who had been hauled off. Others hurried along to catch up to the army, to sell food to the Taiping troops. Others just wandered listlessly along the road, picking their way through the piles of debris and garbage left behind by the passing march to see if there was anything worth keeping.[48]

It was the fringe parties that were the worst, and the terror caused by those who followed behind the armies on the march paled in comparison to the ones who went in advance of the victorious siege armies, those who first entered the cities broken after weeks or months of resistance and who then fanned through the undefended countryside like a nightmare. Ragged and unkempt, completely out of control of the generals who would follow a day or two later when the cities were secure, these men committed atrocities that nearly justified the thousands of suicides that preceded their arrival. One witness in Zhejiang province's Xiangshan county described the rape of a new bride by dozens of those men, who disemboweled her groom—their primary target, because he had a shaved forehead in the Qing style—and left both of them for dead.[49] Another in the same province reported, "There were those who would cut open the stomach and drink the blood, and others who chopped off the four limbs. Some would dig out the heart and eat it . . . my pen cannot bear to write this."[50] They carried off women. They carried off young boys as conscripts and trained them to kill. If the Qing officials had already fled the city, another person reported, the vanguard troops would just murder a few cowering citizens and dress their corpses up in the clothes left behind by the imperial ministers, to invigorate the army that followed behind them.[51]

The pattern, such as it was, was this: where the generals resided, there was relative order. Soldiers who violated the Heavenly Army's strict rules of discipline were punished swiftly and mercilessly; heads hung on stakes, with placards nailed to them warning would-be rapists and looters. But at the fringes, where smaller groups of Taiping soldiers moved among larger civilian populations, control became tenuous. At the cusp of conquest, depravity could be unleashed as cities fell and imperial defenses crumbled. The violence of the conquering Taiping and the defeated imperialists was often impossible to distinguish. But once control was established and there was no threat of imperial reinvasion, things became quiet. Taxes were collected. Crops were grown. New officials were appointed. Decrees were promulgated and sometimes rescinded. Hair grew long on top in the rebel fashion. Queues usually weren't cut off (a welcome convenience, should the imperials reappear). Life went on.

In such areas of quiet control, a detachment of two or three "longhairs" arriving unexpectedly in a rural village under remote Taiping rule might occasion dread in the local population, the locking of gates. But as often as not they paid for the food they ate. And those same rebels might themselves travel in fear of being waylaid in the darkness, even knowing that such attacks would bring reprisal from garrison forces stationed in a city just a day or two's march away. The rumor of an approaching imperial force could bring relief to gentry who wanted their old lives back, but it meant terror for the peasants, to whom it signaled the return of chaos.

For if there was anything consistent in the reports of foreigners and literate Chinese elites on the will of the peasantry of China through this war, it was that they didn't care at all who was in charge; they simply wanted the fighting to end. They wanted order. Rarely did anything good come of the fighting, no matter whose side you were on.

The rules for the general population under Taiping rule were usually clear, if at times impossibly strict. Early in the war, a decree went out forbidding women in Hubei, Anqing, Nanjing, and Yangzhou to practice foot binding. (Foot binding, the forcible constriction of girls' feet to keep them about six inches long through their adult life, was a Chinese fashion that the Hakkas who founded the Taiping didn't themselves practice; they also opposed it on religious grounds.) The stated punishment for a woman who kept her feet bound was to have them cut off.[52] Though such uncompromising laws may have kept discipline in the military ranks, they were useless against popular customs, where enforcement would mean maiming a significant percentage of the female population. (The Manchus, it is worth pointing out, had also tried and failed to prohibit foot binding when they came to power in China.) A scholar living under Taiping control in Zhejiang's Shaoxing county in 1861 wrote that a rebel general had just given orders mandating decapitation for any man caught shaving the top of his head in the style of a Qing subject, anyone who smoked opium, or anyone who worshipped "demon" idols, especially Buddhist ones. Of all the proscriptions, it was the ban on opium that really dumbfounded the scholar. "Everyone under my dynasty smokes opium, from the wealthiest gentry all the way down to the servants and vegetable sellers in the market," he wrote in amazement. "Even the rebels themselves are deeply addicted to it, so how can they go around talking about cutting off heads?"[53] To Chinese and foreigners alike, the suppression of opium was both the best-known and apparently least effective of the Taiping government's social improvement campaigns.

Faced with so much new territory and an enormous rural population, in some cases the Taiping simply established agreements with existing local strongmen or gentry who were willing to collaborate, giving them autonomy over their immediate area in exchange for tax collection and an implicit agreement not to abet imperial forces in retaking the territory.[54] More often, though, they appointed a *xiangguan,* or local official, to take charge of collecting taxes and rounding up necessary supplies (bricks, wood, labor for public works), as well as keeping track of the local population. The opportunity for service under the Taiping redistributed power to

The Brave King, depicted as a socialist superman on a contemporary frieze in Anqing, China. No authentic images of any of the Taiping leaders are known to have survived the war.

Zeng Guofan, commander in chief of the
Hunan Army

Zeng Guoquan, younger brother of Zeng Guofan, depicted in a garden
study with children and cranes

Duolonga, on a lookout with binoculars

Bao Chao, on horseback, accompanied by Hunan Army spear-carriers

Li Hongzhang, commander in chief of the Anhui Army, 1879

Lord Elgin and Prince Gong, portraits taken by Felice Beato during the signing of the Treaty of Beijing in 1860

Interior of the north fort at Taku, after capture by the Allies.
Photograph by Felice Beato, taken at the point of British entrance.

Interior of the north fort at Taku, after capture by the Allies.
Photograph by Felice Beato, taken at the point of French entrance.

Harry Parkes

Rear Admiral James Hope,
a.k.a. "Fighting Jimmy"

Frederick Bruce, Lord Elgin's brother,
British minister to China, 1860–1864

Anson Burlingame,
U.S. minister to China, 1861–1867

City wall of Beijing, northeast corner. Photograph by Felice Beato.

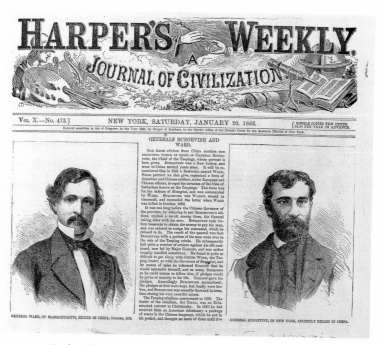

Frederick Townsend Ward and Henry Andrea Burgevine

Charles "Chinese" Gordon, in mandarin regalia

The Shanghai Bund, viewed from the north across Suzhou Creek, 1869

a certain degree in the countryside, insofar as the Qing had relied exclusively on wealthy landowners and successful scholars to keep local control. There were indeed plenty of former Qing officials and degree holders who made the transition to Taiping rule and became *xiangguan* in the new system. But at the same time, there were also many who would never have held such a position in the old society. The surviving rosters of the *xiangguan* list people with a range of backgrounds, including farmers and secretaries, tradesmen, and old men important only in their villages. There were silk weavers and monks, tofu sellers, and martial arts instructors. One county near Suzhou had a *xiangguan* whose profession was listed simply as "gambler."[55] Below these new officials, the Taiping also recruited talented locals to help staff the *xiangguan*'s offices, hunting especially for experts in geography, military tactics, medicine, mathematics, local customs, and astrological fortune-telling.[56]

Central as the Taiping religion was to Hong Rengan's appeal for foreign support, its attractiveness to the rebels' Chinese followers and subjects in the Jiangnan region of eastern China was questionable at best. Even their enemies distinguished between the "true longhairs" (the original faithful from Guangxi and Guangdong provinces in the south) and the multitudes who had entered the rebel movement later.[57] Though the Taiping visions of salvation and apocalypse may have motivated some, the rebels' appeal also rested heavily on more earthly issues of control, stability, and taxation (essential to the poorer classes) and, for those in more elite levels of society, the promise of an empire that would be ruled by Chinese rather than by Manchus.

Separately from his attempts to forge a religious bond with the international community in Shanghai, Hong Rengan also labored from within his palace to design a new government for the time when the Taiping would finally defeat the Manchus and rule China. In the 1850s, when Taiping leaders had tried to institute widespread land redistribution and enforce puritanical religious practices, they had failed; there was simply too much resistance from subjects who preferred to live their lives in an approximation of what they had been before. But with Hong Rengan's arrival, the policies became more accommodating as he sought compromises between the religious ideology of his visionary cousin and the institutions that had worked for so much of China's past. Which is to say that the government

Hong Rengan envisioned for China was not—at least in the small, preparatory scale that it took in his offices—a revolutionary one.

For one thing, Hong Rengan established a replica of the imperial government, with duties divided among the same six boards (finance, civil affairs, war, public works, rituals, and punishments) that formed the skeleton of the imperial bureaucracy in Beijing.[58] The Manchus, back in the 1600s prior to their conquest of China, had done the same thing, building a replica shadow government that matched the one in the Ming dynasty's capital, and it had proved an essential factor in their acceptance upon entering Beijing—for it contained the implicit promise that whatever they brought to their rule, they would not change the fundamental structures of the government bureaucracy. Hong Rengan's version of the six boards was as yet barely staffed and limited to a handful of rooms within his own palace in Nanjing (just downstairs from Issachar Roberts's quarters, in fact), but it nevertheless reflected a similar intent.

Then there was the examination system. The entire story of the Taiping Rebellion might be told, from one perspective, as the rage of a failed exam candidate writ large. But the rebel government in Nanjing nevertheless accepted that the existing examination system was an extremely effective mechanism for selecting loyal officials and that the educated of China looked forward to competing in it. And so, in the Taiping Heavenly Kingdom as under the Qing, talent was determined by examination—only now based on the Bible, not the Confucian classics. Loyalist scholars living under Taiping conquest tended to scoff at the Christian content of the Taiping examinations; one scholar near Suzhou who had to write on the topic "Paying tribute to the Heavenly Father" expressed bemusement that the Taiping meant something new by the Chinese character for "Heaven." Handing in his paper, he whispered to his examiner, "How can the Heaven I wrote about today somehow be different from the Heaven that used to be?" The examiner smiled silently and then ripped up the man's completed essay.[59] Others refused outright to take the exams at all and labeled those who took them as shameless (a response that echoed loyalists of the Ming who had scoffed when the Manchus began offering *their* examinations back in the 1640s). But avoidance of the Taiping examinations by Qing loyalists did create opportunities for others, and the new competitions turned out to be far less cutthroat than the old ones. On the district-level exams given near Suzhou in April 1861, for each group of one hundred youths who took the exam, forty or fifty passed. On the Qing exams, perhaps one of them would have. The delighted students received cash prizes along with their new degrees and the right to go on to the province-level exam in Suzhou and the national exam in Nanjing.[60]

Hong Rengan took charge of the Taiping examinations soon after his arrival in the capital, and he began to make changes to them. Some changes were minor (for example, he altered the names of the degrees ever so slightly). But some were far more significant. Because the original Taiping examinations covered only the Bible, many in China believed that the rebels had simply replaced Confucius with Jesus Christ. Zeng Guofan used precisely that claim in his appeal for support for his army in 1854, calling the war on the Taiping a war to save Confucian civilization. However, one remarkable sign of Hong Rengan's influence in Nanjing was that by early 1861 the Taiping examinations under his direction had begun to incorporate the Chinese classics as well. Under Hong Rengan, Confucius would have his place in the Heavenly Kingdom.

Thus, students sitting for the district exam in the spring of 1861 had to write essays not only on religious doctrine but also on the *Analects,* the book of Confucius's sayings. The full text of the examination is lost, but the essay prompt is recorded in various diaries; the allusion chosen was one with a particularly chilling resonance for the Taiping project of creating a new state from the ashes of war. In the passage selected, a disciple asked Confucius what the three most important pillars of a state were. Confucius replied that the state must have military power, it must provide food for its people to eat, and its people must have faith in their government. "But what if you can't have all three?" the disciple asked. "Then do away with the military," said Confucius. The disciple continued, asking what if the ruler had to give up one more thing. "In that case, do without food," Confucius told him. "There has always been death, but without faith there can be no state."[61]

Hong Rengan took the lead in writing and publishing Taiping political propaganda, which he printed in bulk on a Western lead-type press housed in his palace. Some of the publications echoed his belief in industrialization: the importance of railroads, mechanical weapons, steamships, and telegraphs, and the need for a national newspaper.[62] The press itself (originally built in Canton) was such an innovation, and his crew of printers readily mastered the foreign technology of movable type. The members of his staff were some of the most highly educated men in the rebel capital, men who, one visitor noted, were among the least religiously zealous in the city; one even confided to the visitor that he didn't believe in Hong

Xiuquan's visions.[63] Fittingly, the publications that emanated from that office contained not just the de rigueur religious propaganda based on the Heavenly King's visions but also a strong current of more secular appeals to sway those who had no interest in theology. In those documents, which were the dominant rebel propaganda of the war's final years, the civil war appeared less a struggle between religions than a war between races—a war of historical resentment and genocidal revenge pitting the Chinese against the Manchus.

One such publication, entitled *A Hero's Return to the Truth,* told the story of a high-ranking Chinese official of the Qing dynasty who had defected to the rebel side. It was written as a narrative, recounting the man's conversations with the Shield King, who corrected his misconceptions about Taiping belief. It was, above all, an ethnic appeal for support, directed at the elites who held power under the Qing dynasty. The protagonist was Chinese, but his family had long served in high-ranking positions under the Manchu dynasty. "In both flesh and blood I am a man of China proper," he declared. He had abandoned his service with the dynasty because it was crumbling and now went over to the Taiping because he was beginning to realize that although his family of officials had long considered themselves powerful under the Qing, in fact they were nothing more than slaves to the Manchus who controlled their country. Hong Rengan welcomed him and related a conversation with his cousin in which Hong Xiuquan had said, "For a land as extensive as the eighteen provinces to be under the yoke of the three provinces of the Manchu dogs, and for five hundred million Chinese to be subject to a few million Tartar devils is indeed sufficient cause for extreme shame and disgrace." The official realized that the Taiping were in fact the saviors of the Chinese people from the Manchus. Hong Rengan's words were "like a sudden thunderbolt breaking in my ear," he said, "awakening me for the first time from my idiotic dreams."[64]

According to this tract, the Taiping were not at all revolutionary. In fact, they were native traditionalists, continuing the legacy of all past Chinese resistance to outside conquest. Hong Rengan drew parallels between the Taiping and the loyal Chinese of the Ming dynasty, as well as the earlier Song dynasty, which had been conquered by northern ancestors of the Manchus. As so many Chinese had given their lives in the past to try to hold off the invasion of China by outsiders, so would the Taiping lead the Chinese to break though the illusion that the Manchus were their proper rulers. He even invoked the five great scholars of the Song dynasty—Zhu

Xi, Zhang Zai, Zhou Dunyi, and the brothers Cheng Hao and Cheng Yi—who had founded the school of Neo-Confucian philosophy that was so dear to Zeng Guofan. Their system of belief was at the very core of the civilization Zeng Guofan had staked his life on defending, but in Hong Rengan's hands, they became a reminder of why the Chinese must revolt against the Manchus. Great scholars like those, he pointed out, arose only during *Chinese* dynasties such as the Song and the Ming. Under conquest dynasties such as the Qing, when the Chinese were enslaved, their civilization weakened and festered. Again, the official said, he was shocked into awareness by Hong Rengan's words. "They are as cold water showering on the head," he told Hong Rengan, "and hot charcoal burning at the heart."[65]

Against the accusation that the Taiping wanted to destroy Confucian civilization, Hong Rengan explained patiently to the official in *Hero's Return* that it was only idolatry the Taiping wanted to get rid of. The books of Confucius were welcome, and his philosophy was still central to the Taiping vision of society; it was just that the Chinese had been corrupted into worshipping the sage as a false god in the Confucian temples, and *those* must be destroyed. Chinese scholars, he wrote, should "observe the benevolence, righteousness, and moral principles of Confucius and Mencius," but that did not mean they should "worship [them] with sacrifices." Wisdom, knowledge, and success were granted by Heaven, Hong Rengan explained, not by mortals. "How could the now-dead sages bestow fame or wisdom upon man?" Confucius and Mencius should be read and respected, but they should not be confused with God.

Hong Rengan thus put forward an appeal for support that rested not on religion alone but on harmony between the Taiping's religious beliefs and the longer history of China. It was another framework to compete with Zeng Guofan's—not Confucianism versus Christianity but Chinese versus Manchu. The central issue of the war, as Hong Rengan framed it, was the liberation of the Chinese people. It was a powerful appeal, and it targeted the exact same audience of wealthy gentry and educated scholars whom Zeng Guofan depended upon for his support. Along with his efforts to design a government that could inherit the existing bureaucracy and his attempt to widen the appeal of the Taiping examinations by including the Confucian texts on them, Hong Rengan's vision was one of stable transition, of endurance, of preservation. But despite the breadth of his efforts and the talents of his staff, Hong Rengan felt outnumbered at court. He had the faith of his cousin, which elevated him above all the others, but his fellow kings occasionally frustrated him. The ones who had been there from the beginning considered themselves "the heroic founders of the state," he complained. They were less concerned with the future, less concerned with how to win over the population or unify their government. "They only looked out for themselves," he wrote, "and didn't think about the big picture."[66]

———————

Real control still lay just outside the rebels' grasp. Weakened as the imperial government in Beijing was after the Allied invasion and the flight of the emperor, it still clung to the Mandate of Heaven by mere virtue of its existence, and as long as it did, its loyalists would fight for it to the end. The siege that Zeng Guofan had laid at Anqing up the river in Anhui province that fall, which he had managed to hold so steadily through the Taiping conquest of Jiangnan and the invasion of the capital by the Europeans, had by wintertime grown into a pressing source of concern to the Taiping downriver in their capital. For it was their choke point too. Their base in Anqing was the buffer that protected Nanjing from any advance from the north or west on the rebel capital, and failure to control the full length of the Yangtze would complicate the final stages of the strategy Hong Rengan and Li Xiucheng had agreed upon, namely, to consolidate the fertile southern provinces, rebuild the heartland of the old Ming Empire, and then starve the dry Manchu domains of the north into extinction.

By the late autumn of 1860, Li Xiucheng had to leave off his conquest of the eastern provinces to help relieve Anqing's garrison forces. The Heavenly King had actually ordered him to go north—most likely to strike at the weakened Manchu capital—but he refused, even as Zeng Guofan had refused his own emperor's direction when he thought he knew better. Instead, the Loyal King insisted that he had to take his men westward into Jiangxi and Hubei provinces, where a host of local leaders had pledged several hundred thousand followers to join the Taiping ranks.[67] Those expected recruits lay just on the other side of the Anqing siege. Leaving Nanjing in November, Li Xiucheng took his army on a roughly westward march down along the winding southern bank of the Yangtze, below which eventually lay Zeng Guofan's camp at Qimen.

Li Xiucheng's parting words to those who remained in the capital were stern instructions that they should begin stockpiling food. The Taiping now had control of the downward stretches of the Yangtze as far as Shanghai and so should fear no attacks from the east, he reassured them—but the next attack might come from upstream. "If Anqing can be held, there is no need to worry," he predicted, "but if it is not firm, the capital will not be secure."[68] Jade and silver would be useless if the war encroached further on Nanjing; they needed grain.

By early February 1861, even Hong Rengan had taken to the field at the Heavenly King's orders, leaving behind his palace and printing press and massing an army of his own to help in the coordinated relief of Anqing from the maddeningly entrenched Hunan forces. He had never commanded an army before—nor, for that matter, even fought in one (save for his brief enlistment in an imperial unit while trying to get to Nanjing). But he was the Shield King, and his followers, at least, had faith in him. A visitor from the London Missionary Society named William Muirhead was on hand to witness the pomp and circumstance of Hong Rengan's departure from Nanjing on the auspicious first day of the Chinese New Year.[69] It was the beginning of year 11 on the calendar of the Taiping Heavenly Kingdom. Hong Rengan sat calmly atop his throne, crowned in gold, his small person swallowed up in the luminous yellow silk robes that enfolded him. An assembled crowd of Taiping officers knelt down before his throne and sang in unison, "May the Shield King live a thousand years, a thousand years, a thousand times a thousand years!" Then Muirhead watched as the round-faced man who had once been his old friend James Legge's deferential assistant in Hong Kong stepped solemnly down from the throne and into a grand palanquin, borne by eight strong men, that carried him off to the war.

The words that rang in Muirhead's ears afterward were not the words of the song, however. They were the words Hong Rengan had spoken to him earlier, before the ceremony, when the two men had spoken privately about the dangers that lay ahead and Hong Rengan let slip a glint of the uncertainty (or was it fear?) that was lurking behind his placid demeanor. "Mr. Muirhead," he said then, "pray for me."[70]

CHAPTER 8

THE PERILS OF CIVILIZATION

The queen of England, at least, was pleased with the outcome of the war in China. In her speech opening Parliament on February 9, 1861, Victoria expressed her pleasure that Lord Elgin and Baron Gros "were enabled to obtain an honourable and satisfactory settlement of all the matters in dispute" in China and commended the British and French military commanders for having "acted with the most friendly concert."[1] But beyond the small circle of the queen, her prime minister, Lord Palmerston, and his foreign secretary, Lord Russell, Elgin was hard put to find supporters.

The *Times* editors had been the most sympathetic—their own correspondent Bowlby was the one who had been murdered, after all—and their editorial on Christmas Day 1860 suggested that perhaps Elgin had in fact been too gentle with the Chinese. Financially, at least, they thought he might have quadrupled the indemnity rather than just doubling it. The Chinese should realize they had gotten off cheaply, they said, for Britain had spent far more on the invasion force than it was to be reimbursed by the indemnity (later estimates would actually put Britain's cost of the war at several times the doubled indemnity). In the spirit of the season, though, they allowed that "peace is pleasant at any mere money sacrifice." As for the destruction in Beijing, they clearly felt that it was a just reprisal for the kidnapping of Parkes and the murder of Bowlby and the others in his party. "Their graves," said *The Times*, "may serve to record the crime of which the blackened ruins of the Summer Palace of the Emperor will long record the punishment."[2]

Other papers were less supportive. *The Illustrated News of the World*, for one, took a more contemplative view, tapping into the ambivalence of those in the British public for whom the news of Beijing's fall sparked not so much exultation as a kind of indeterminate anxiety. The Allied victory, it allowed, was "one of the most remarkable in the annals of the world," wherein "the capital city of a nation which numbers one-third of the human race has been captured by a handful of troops from the distant west." But it noted that the heady aura of triumph was "strangely blended with regret and misgivings . . . because we see not where it is to end." The war between China and Britain seemed almost unintentional, growing from a haphazard sequence of accidents, perceived insults, escalations, and petty retributions—yet it had reached the point where "nearly one-half the family of man is at deadly feud with the other." It agreed that the Chinese government had acted treacherously but also suggested Britain had been tainted by the violence she had brought to bear in return. "Enfield rifles will not teach them to tell the truth," the editors wrote, "nor soften the innate savagery of their passions." So instead of trying to ascribe blame, they instead expressed hope that this moment of history might simply pass. "It is now too late [to question] the origin of the war," they said, "we are in for it, and we must get out of it in the best way we can."[3]

Whatever one's opinion of the war or the treaty that ended it, it was the destruction of the Summer Palace that sent the real shock across the political spectrum. The French writer Victor Hugo, living in exile on an island in the English Channel as an opponent of Napoleon III's authoritarian rule, condemned the Allied destruction of the palace in a famous letter that cast France and Britain as a pair of bandits, plundering and burning their way through China.[4] There was now a legacy of rapacious Lords Elgin, he mused, for the Earl of Elgin who had just eviscerated the Summer Palace was none other than the son of the Lord Elgin who had looted the eponymous marbles from Greece a generation earlier; though if anything the son was worse than his father, said Hugo, because he had left nothing behind.[5] The Chinese emperor's Summer Palace had been one of the greatest wonders of world civilization, he wrote, ranking with the Parthenon in Greece, the pyramids of Egypt, the Colosseum in Rome, and Notre Dame in Paris. And now it was gone, thanks to the incendiary pillaging of those who equated Europe with civilization and China with barbarism. "This," he declared, "is what civilization has done to barbarism."

Criticism from a gadfly of the French regime was perhaps to be expected, but equally damning judgments came from the halls of Parliament itself. Debate erupted on February 14, 1861, as the two houses considered twin resolutions of thanks for the British commanders and troops who had successfully fought in the China campaign. In the House of Lords, the Marquess of Bath responded to Prime Minister Palmerston's defense of Elgin's conduct by stating for the record that "he could not . . . allow to pass unnoticed an act of vandalism, which, although it had been sanctioned by an English ambassador and defended by an English Minister, might, in his opinion, justly be ranked with such deeds as the burning of the library of Alexandria, or the sacking of Rome by the Constable de Bourbon."[6] Likewise, in the House of Commons, the Irish MP Vincent Scully referred to the burning of the Summer Palace as "that act which certainly in his (Mr. Vincent Scully's) opinion, and in that of a great many out of that House, was an act of barbarism and vandalism, for which it was difficult to find any precedent in ancient or modern history, and the nearest resemblance to which was the burning of Persepolis under somewhat similar circumstances by Alexander the Great."[7] What, Scully asked, if the Chinese upon conquering London had conducted themselves in a similar manner? "What was the object of burning the Summer Palace?" he demanded. "Was it to conciliate the Chinese, or was it to Christianize them?"

Elgin held fast in the face of his public shaming. In his mind, he had done it for the sake of the very people who now condemned him. Indeed, one of the most consistent threads running through his two voyages to China was the sense of an irresistible force—a collective, imagined will, projected from his country and his people—that guided his hand even against his own frequent and sometimes profound misgivings. In a speech at the Royal Academy soon after his return, he defended his decision to destroy the palace as being, in its context, Hobson's choice:

[I] assure you that no one regretted more sincerely than I did the destruction of that collection of summer-houses and kiosks, already, and previously to any act of mine, rifled of their contents, which was dignified by the title of Summer Palace of the Chinese Emperor. But when I had satisfied myself that in no other way, except, indeed, by inflicting on this country and on China the calamity of another year of war, could I mark the sense which I entertained, which the British army entertained . . . and which, moreover, I make bold in the presence of this company to say, the people of this country entertained—of an atrocious crime, which, if it had passed unpunished, would have placed in jeopardy the life of every European in China, I felt that the time had come when I must choose between the indulgence of a not unnatural sensibility and the performance of a painful duty. The alternative is not a pleasant one; but I trust that there is no man serving the Crown in a responsible position who would hesitate when it is presented to him as to the decision at which he should arrive.[8]

That is, it was a matter of putting his duty to Britain, to its army, and above all to its people above his own aesthetic sensibilities. Destroying the emperor's palace, he contended, had been the only way to assuage (preemptively) the anger of the British public over Senggelinqin's kidnapping of Parkes and murdering of the prisoners, without forcing upon them another war with China. It was a terrible loss, he admitted, but he believed that any responsible man would have done the same in his shoes, because it had been that or nothing.

But it was not the effect on China of the palace's destruction that he regretted; rather, what he regretted was that he had destroyed a beautiful thing. The same might be said of his critics as well, even Victor Hugo; it was not for China that they cried shame, but for art. Any genuine remorse in Elgin's speech was still colored by his underlying conviction that China was a country that somehow *demanded* British intervention. As regrettable as the loss of a palace full of imperial treasures might have been for the aesthetes of Europe, he had little sympathy for China itself. Its civilization, he believed, was lost to history. As he went on with his speech at the Royal Academy, he offered that although the Chinese had invented gunpowder, they had done little more with it than to make firecrackers. They had invented the compass but hadn't gone to sea. They had invented the printing press but had used it to produce nothing more than "stagnant editions of *Confucius*." It was Europe, he reckoned, that had made something useful of the Chinese inventions in the past, and in the future it would be no different. His summary judgment on the ancient kingdom he had just blasted open to foreign trade was that only Britain could bring Chinese civilization back to life. "I am disposed to believe," he concluded, "that under this mass of abortions and rubbish there lie hidden some sparks of a diviner fire, which the genius of my countrymen may gather and nurse into a flame."[9]

At the other end of the China war, the Xianfeng emperor's flight from Beijing in September 1860 ended in a leaking, run-down palace on the old imperial hunting grounds in the mountains a hundred and fifty miles northeast of the capital. In the dynasty's eighteenth-century heyday, this had been where the high-ranking Manchus went in the summertime to escape the heat and to hunt with the emperor, ranging on horseback through the forests and streams, practicing their archery, and celebrating the outdoorsmanship that they imagined made them so superior to the soft, bookish Chinese. But in more recent generations, the hunting grounds had fallen into disuse. After the fiscal crisis under Xianfeng's father, the site had been all but abandoned, and its maintenance funds had been diverted to help keep up the Summer Palace outside Beijing. Since then, the old hunting retreat had lapsed into an overgrown, derelict shell of its former glory.

Along with the retinue of servants and palace women who accompanied him, a handful of advisers came along as well. They represented the most adamantly militant of his Manchu cabinet, and most had been with him since he had first sat on the throne at the age of nineteen (he was now twenty-nine). There were Duanhua and Zaiyuan, who, along with the now-disgraced Senggelinqin, had been at the deathbed of the emperor's father, who had entrusted them to guide his son.[10] There was Sushun, the ruthless grand secretary and president of the Board of Revenue, who was Zeng Guofan's patron at court. These were the war hawks, the strongest voices of opposition to the foreign treaties, and they now effectively controlled who could visit from the capital and which messages would reach the emperor; it was far more power than they had exerted in the capital (though they had always exerted more than they should have). Edicts soon went out explaining that the emperor was on a "hunting voyage" and would remain there until further notice. The emperor's younger half brother Prince Gong, who had been left in charge of the capital when Xianfeng fled, was not one of the approved visitors; the advisers turned down his petitions to have an audience with his brother on the grounds that the emperor was too weakened by his traumatic escape to see him.

Prince Gong floated between two worlds, isolated from his brother's refugee court yet suddenly responsible for the capital and the vast kingdom it governed. A slight twenty-seven-year-old with heavy-lidded eyes, a shy manner, and a smooth, boyish face, it fell to him to pick up the pieces after the war with England and France. He had always been smarter than his older brother, though. The throne didn't automatically fall to the eldest son, and he'd actually been a rumored favorite to become emperor up until 1846, when he was thirteen. As the story went, that was the year when their ailing father, the Daoguang emperor, had called his two favorite sons for an audience and asked them what they would do if they should become emperor. The younger replied with a list of detailed policy initiatives, which he planned to enact as soon as he ascended to the throne. The elder simply threw himself to the ground and wept—for becoming emperor would mean that his father was dead. The father pronounced that the elder son was the filial one, while the younger was merely talented. He made the elder his imperial heir, and the younger became a lifelong prince.[11]

After the Allied armies withdrew, Prince Gong wrote a series of petitions to his brother, imploring him to come back to Beijing: the war was over, he pleaded, the foreign armies had retreated, and the sovereign was needed in the capital to reassure his people. In an ironic confirmation of Elgin's belief that the destruction of the Summer Palace would teach the Chinese government to deal honestly, Prince Gong assured Xianfeng that there would be no more fighting with the British and French as long as they followed the treaty. "If in the future we show the foreign barbarians faith and sincerity," he wrote, "when they return to the capital next spring they will not likely cause difficulties." To a certain measure, he implied, the court's duplicity had brought its own ruin, and he cautioned that "if we attempt to deal with them with false words and deceptive behavior, it is something that I . . . do not dare to risk."[12]

But Xianfeng refused to go back to Beijing. The armies may have withdrawn, he wrote in response to Prince Gong's petitions, but there were still foreigners in the capital. (He was livid that his brother had agreed to allow ambassadors into Beijing.) If he went back, who was to say that the foreign armies wouldn't come again, forcing him to flee yet again and creating even worse disorder than already existed?[13] So the emperor stayed at the hunting retreat with his empress and concubines and his close circle of militant Manchu advisers. And far from making any preparations to return to the capital, he ordered his staff to start making improvements to the long-neglected gardens and opera theater in his new home.[14]

As the autumn of 1860 gave way to the winter of 1861 and the northern rivers turned to ice, Prince Gong gained a respite. Couriers brought him dire reports from Zeng Guofan on the fighting around Anqing, but that was far away to the south and the imperial capital was safely landlocked for the season. Frederick Bruce was spending the winter at Tianjin and wouldn't come to Beijing until after the Peiho had thawed in the spring. And so, with no sign of the emperor's return, Prince Gong and a genial middle-aged grand councillor named Wenxiang who had also stayed behind turned their attention to figuring out a means to accommodate the European ambassadors when the time came, while avoiding the humiliation of granting them an audience with the (absent) emperor.

Their solution, outlined in a proposal in early January 1861, was to establish a separate office to manage foreign affairs. It would be outside the imperial city and thus safely distant from the emperor's inner sphere, but it would be staffed by top Manchu officials (Prince Gong and Wenxiang chief among them), who could deal directly with the ambassadors and also have access to the highest echelons of the dynastic government. It was designed to please both sides, giving the foreign ambassadors the access they demanded while keeping them at arm's length from the inner world of the emperor. The emperor approved the proposal from his exile; either he'd resigned himself to the inevitable presence of Europeans in his capital, or he hoped this would at least keep them at a bit of a distance until they could be gotten rid of altogether.

The proposal for this Office of Foreign Affairs was part of a larger plan for juggling the dynasty's many threats, which Prince Gong also now outlined for his brother. The Taiping rebels, he reasoned, were like a disease of the inner organs; they were the most urgent of the dynasty's problems. Foreigners like the British, meanwhile, were like afflictions of the limbs: threatening but external, and therefore secondary. He proposed that the dynasty's first order of business should be to do everything in its power to exterminate the Taiping rebels. Until the Taiping were suppressed, the Qing government should appease the foreign powers and avoid any conflict with them; later, once the rebellion was over, it could bring them under control as well.[15] (Chiang Kai-shek would use an almost identical metaphor in the 1930s to justify appeasing the invading Japanese while continuing to fight the Chinese Communists under Mao Zedong.)

In the same vein, Prince Gong also began to think seriously about whether the Manchus should avail themselves of outside help against the Taiping. In the wake of the new treaties, while the British in London were fretting over the moral implications of their China policy, Russia—free from the Anglo-American obsession with neutrality—had been angling for favor in Beijing by offering direct military aid to the Qing government. In addition, since the Taiping had cut off the Grand Canal, they offered shipping aid, suggesting that they could coordinate with the U.S. Consulate in Canton to bring southern rice to Tianjin by an ocean route that would steer widely clear of the rebels' area of control.

Of the four major foreign powers in China, the Russians were in many ways the odd ones out. They still bore a grudge against Britain and France from the Crimean War, for one thing. And whereas the British, French, and Americans all wanted above all to expand waterborne trade in the coastal and river ports (an interest shared by all maritime powers and therefore ripe grounds for cooperation), Russia alone shared a land border with the Qing Empire—one, moreover, that was thousands of miles long. Russian diplomats therefore saw in a compliantly weakened Manchu government the chance to expand their own territory and develop a cross-border trade with China to the exclusion of European and American merchants. The tsar's representatives had offered Xianfeng rifles as early as 1857, and during the negotiations at Tianjin in 1858 they volunteered military advisers as well—if, in exchange, the dynasty would give Russia control of the territory north of the Amur River in the Manchu homeland.[16]

Xianfeng rebuffed those overtures, and so in 1860 a talented young Russian diplomat named Nikolai Pavlovich Ignatiev followed Elgin's expedition to Beijing in hopes of gaining new leverage. After the Allies invaded Beijing, Ignatiev managed to negotiate a new Sino-Russian treaty with Prince Gong—in secret, after first playing the part of "impartial" mediator between the Europeans and the Manchus. Against the threat of allowing the Europeans to topple the Qing regime, he pressured Prince Gong into granting Russia control of a vast region north of the Amur that measured more than three hundred thousand square miles—several times larger than Korea, which it abutted to the north—as well as a significant tract of borderland along the north of Xinjiang in the Qing Empire's far west. To defend Russia's acquisition of this new territory (a land concession to make Hong Kong look like a pinprick) and in the hope of establishing preeminence over the other foreign powers in Beijing, Ignatiev reiterated his country's desire to help the Manchus put down their internal rebellion.[17] As he proposed it to Prince Gong, along with the gift of rifles promised earlier, three or four hundred Russians on steam-powered gunships could coordinate with Qing imperial troops on land and together conquer the rebel capital at Nanjing.

This time, Prince Gong took the offer seriously. With the emperor's permission, he referred the question to a small handful of high-ranking Chinese officials, a group that included Zeng Guofan. Some who read the proposal supported it. The Chinese superintendent of trade in Shanghai suggested paying the foreigners on the basis of loot: if the Russians captured a Taiping-held city, the spoils could be divided in two, with half going to the depleted imperial coffers and the other half to reward military merit. Of the portion allotted to merit, the Chinese fighters would get two-fifths and the foreigners would get the rest.[18] (Putting aside the issue that the "spoils" would be property stolen from his own countrymen, it is worth noting that it was in this official's jurisdiction that Frederick Townsend Ward had already been hired under somewhat better terms, without the knowledge of Beijing.) From the other side of the debate, the director general of grain transportation responded that it was preposterous for the Russians to pretend that a few hundred men on a handful of boats could defeat the Taiping rebels—and on the wild chance that they *did* succeed, they would surely blackmail the government with ever-increasing demands. The plan had no merit, he concluded, and could only endanger the dynasty further.[19]

From his base in Anhui province, Zeng Guofan struck a more ambivalent pose. Writing in December 1860, he advised against immediately accepting foreign military support but allowed that it might come in handy later. There was no enmity between China and Russia, he wrote, so this wasn't necessarily an insidious offer, and the dynasty did have a precedent for accepting such aid: the emperor's great-great-great-grandfather Kangxi had used Dutch ships against rebels on Taiwan in the seventeenth century. But Zeng Guofan's own naval forces were well in place on the Yangtze River, he wrote, and in Hunan he was having more ships built, so he didn't need Russian support on the water. The real problem was on land; his army had absolutely no route by which to advance on Nanjing, so it would be impossible to coordinate an attack per Ignatiev's plan. Zeng Guofan advised that the government defer Russia's offer of help until his land forces had recaptured enough Taiping territory to be able to threaten Nanjing properly.

As for moving grain, he reminded the emperor that there was a long pattern of self-interested foreigners offering China aid in times of crisis. "Since ancient times," he wrote, "whenever outsiders helped China, as soon as they were done they always came up with unforeseen demands." Everything had to be hashed out clearly in advance, he warned, and they had to understand the character of the foreigners they were dealing with. Not all of them were the same. He sketched out the differences between the ones at hand (none of whom, for the record, had he ever met). In his opinion, the British were the most cunning, followed by the French. The Russians were more powerful than either the British or French. The Russians often fought with the British, who were therefore afraid of them. Americans, by contrast, had a "pure and honest" nature, and they had always been respectful and submissive toward China. When the British and French had invaded Canton in 1858, Zeng noted, the Americans hadn't helped them in their treachery. They also hadn't taken part in the fighting at the mouth of the Peiho (he was unaware of Josiah Tattnall's supporting role in 1859). Therefore, he wrote, "we can see that the Americans are sincere and obedient in their dealings with China and aren't part of some unbreakable clique with the British and French." It was worth considering the aid of the Americans and Russians to move grain to the north. But whatever the outcome at the moment, he felt it was most important for China to improve its own technology so it wouldn't need outside help in the first place. "If we study how they make their cannons and ships," Zeng concluded, "it will be of great benefit to us in the long run."[20]

The emperor took the advice of caution. He accepted ten thousand rifles and eight cannons from the Russians (which would arrive in a year) but declined the offer of naval assistance.[21] For as Prince Gong had written to him on January 24, the real problem was that if he let the Russian gunships sail up to Nanjing without Zeng Guofan's forces there to meet them, the Russians might just decide to throw in their lot with the rebels.[22]

———————

By February 1861, reports had begun to surface in the British press that Admiral Hope was planning to lead a Royal Navy squadron up the Yangtze River to open relations with the Chinese rebels. Such had been the substance of Elgin's parting orders to him, but as with most China policy under Palmerston's government, the expedition had no prior approval from even the foreign secretary, let alone Parliament. In the House of Lords on February 19, Earl Grey demanded information on the government's plans to meet with the rebels and used Hope's planned voyage as an occasion to revisit the origins of Britain's war in China—a war he had opposed as unjust from the very beginning. In a sweeping speech on the history of British relations with China, he argued that the civil war in China was in fact the fault of his own country.

Earl Grey was as qualified as anyone in Parliament to judge Britain's foreign policy; he had served as undersecretary for war and the colonies in the early 1830s during the prime ministership of his late father (the previous Earl Grey, namesake of the tea), and he had later served terms as both secretary for war and colonial secretary. At its root, his speech on February 19, 1861, echoed Karl Marx's writings for the *New-York Daily Tribune* back in 1853: he argued that Britain's predatory trade policies dating back to the first Opium War had, by destabilizing the government of China, brought about the widespread outbreaks of rebellion against its rule that now culminated in the Taiping. Therefore, the misery of the Chinese people over the past two decades and the horrific warfare that now scourged their homeland were Britain's fault. And this was not, he declared, a new phenomenon. "My Lords," he intoned, "our experience of India ought to warn us upon this subject. It ought to teach us that it is easy to destroy an Asiatic Government, but not so easy to replace it."[23]

Whereas Marx had envisioned a Chinese revolution as a spark to light up the oppressed nations of Europe, Grey saw it instead as a prelude to a new chapter of British colonialism in Asia, one he did not welcome. He argued that Britain's military interventions in China had now driven the Qing dynasty to the very edge of collapse—and if that collapse should in fact take place, it would become Britain's humanitarian duty to step in and help the suffering people of the country (as, he offered, they had just done with the state of Oudh in northern India). Should Britain heed its moral obligations in China, warned Grey, "we may be irresistibly led on, until nothing remains for us, but to take its administration into our own hands." In other words, China would become the new India.

But nobody wanted another India. Since the Sepoy Mutiny in 1857, there had been little but exhaustion in Britain over the incredible political and military costs of the colonial enterprise. In the wake of those uprisings, the East India Company had been nationalized, and the government itself now bore direct responsibility for the colony. There were not the funds, the military resources, nor the public will to commit the sheer numbers of British humanity needed to take over the administration of yet another empire—one, moreover, with three times the population of India—just for the sake of keeping access to China's tea and silk and its markets for textiles and opium. So Grey reminded his fellow lords of the enormous sacrifices Britain had already made for the sake of its colony in India and then, building to the climax of his speech, warned them darkly that "the difficulties of India are nothing compared with those to be expected in China, if you should there also pull down the national institutions and Government. And this, my Lords, is what I fear you are doing."

Earl Grey saw nothing Britain could do to stave off the collapse of the

Qing, so he called for strict neutrality in the Chinese civil war. He commended Frederick Bruce for rebuffing the Qing officials who had asked him to send British troops to reclaim Suzhou from the Taiping the previous summer and for restraining the French in that instance. But he also criticized him for "most unadvisedly" attacking the Taiping when they had arrived at Shanghai in August. As the Manchu imperial government grew weaker, Grey predicted, and as the rebels increased their control over the silk-producing regions of China, there would be further calls for Britain to help the tottering dynasty. But in China, he argued (drawing from Thomas Taylor Meadows's influential book on Chinese rebellions), rebellion had long been the people's "only check on abuse and tyranny." To those in Britain who might call for intervention to stave off a Qing collapse and avoid the colonization that would follow, he had only the harshest of words: "If, after having so weakened the Chinese Government that it cannot protect itself against rebellion, you interfere . . . you will remove the only efficient check on that venality and corruption of the mandarins which is so much complained of, and thus bring on the people the evils of misgovernment." The choices he saw facing Britain were bleak: to abandon China to collapse; to intervene and force the Chinese to endure their enslavement by the discredited Manchu government; or to take control of the empire itself. None was welcome, and the vaunted Elgin treaty, Earl Grey concluded, contained in it little more than the seeds of future war.

In response to the liberal Earl Grey's speech, a Tory voice did him one better. The most stunning judgment of all that day came from Edward Law, the Earl of Ellenborough, a controversial former governor-general of India. He accepted Lord Grey's premise that the British were morally responsible for the misery of the Chinese but turned his colleague's conclusions on their head. "Opening trade," he argued bluntly, "means opening fire." He reminded the Lords what Elgin's first experience with the Taiping had been when he had steamed past Nanjing in the *Furious* in 1858—namely, that they had shot at him. Ellenborough reasoned that if Britain were now to send Admiral Hope up the Yangtze, it would surely provoke a new round of fighting with "these banditti—for banditti they are."[24]

But in fact, he thought a new round of fighting might be a good thing. For if Hope's expedition to Nanjing should result in a war with the Taiping rebels, Britain could then make good for the damage it had caused in its wars against the Manchus in China. Fighting the Taiping, Ellenborough offered, was "the only way in which we can . . . put an end to the horrid combinations of those miscreants, who to their bloodshed and massacre add the crime of blasphemy; who violate women, who destroy men and all men's works." He agreed with Lord Grey that Britain had a humanitarian duty thanks to its past actions in China—but rather than calling for an end to armed intervention, he instead proposed that the best way for Britain to fulfill that duty was to make war on the rebels as well. "It is only in using our arms and our strength in repressing those banditti," he concluded, "that we can in any manner atone for the great miseries we have brought on the Chinese Empire, and for the injuries we have done to humanity by our conduct in these wars."

Neither of those critics of Palmerston's war, it should be noted, imagined the Taiping to be a viable alternative to the Manchus. But there was little reason they would have. After all, it was difficult enough for British subjects in Shanghai to form a coherent impression of what the rebels were up to in Nanjing, just two hundred miles away—and as difficult as it was for them, it was all the more so for British statesmen who lived thousands of miles away, with a two-month lag in communications and with far more business to attend to than just the distant matter of China. Most members of Parliament relied for their knowledge of what was happening in China on the official reports culled and printed by the Foreign Office for their enlightenment: the so-called Blue Books. The Blue Books were, of course, dominated by the voice of Frederick Bruce, who, as the British minister in China, was the official whose opinion was most trusted by his government. Unlike his more open-minded brother Lord Elgin, Frederick Bruce had made up his mind early on—and firmly—that the Qing dynasty was the only power in China that was capable of governing. In consequence, most of the members of Parliament came to believe the same.

Furthermore, Lord Russell's office in London compiled and printed those Blue Books, and the publication of relevant documents could sometimes be substantially delayed. As a case in point, on the very day Grey and Ellenborough were standing before the House of Lords and lamenting the absence of any power other than Britain that could take the place of the Manchus in China, Thomas Taylor Meadows—Grey's authority on Chinese rebellions and the British consul who had tried in vain to get Frederick Bruce to read the letters from Li Xiucheng and Hong Rengan—was writing to Lord Russell from Shanghai to state his unequivocal belief that the Taiping were destined to rule China. The Qing government of the Manchus, he wrote, had "received its death-blows" from Elgin's invasion. As Britain was now searching for a new power, a new government, to replace the Manchus, Meadows reported that "We have such another power in the

Tae-pings, and such another Government in the Government which they have established at Nanking."[25]

Meadows's letter was a lengthy and forceful defense of the capacity of the Taiping to govern, but although he expressed his opinions on the same day the debate in London was taking place, his letter did not reach Lord Russell until the following April, and then Russell's office did not print it for the Blue Books until fully a year after *that,* in April 1862, when, as it turned out, it no longer mattered. Meadows himself was soon transferred from Shanghai to a remote port in the north. Some saw it as a punitive move, though the appointment had in fact been pending before he wrote his letter. Whichever the case, with his transfer from Shanghai he was effectively removed from the picture.[26]

Sympathy for the Chinese rebels was far greater outside the halls of government, where a range of voices in the British press begged the public to look beyond the negative images in the Blue Books. The Methodist-affiliated *London Review* accused Frederick Bruce of ignoring the positive reports of his own country's missionaries in favor of highlighting a single harshly negative account of Nanjing by an American named Holmes (who reported that he had discovered in the rebel capital "nothing of Christianity, but its name falsely applied—applied to a system of revolting idolatry").[27] The *Review* charged Holmes with being a completely unreliable source, "a young man, who has been a short time in the country, and who is said to have little or no knowledge of the dialect being spoken." Holmes, they argued, couldn't communicate properly with the rebel leaders, and his outrage stemmed mostly from a matter of politesse: he had been deeply offended that the Taiping had asked him to kneel during his visit. By the same reasoning, they suggested scornfully, "a New Zealand Chief at the White House ought to claim that the President should rub noses with him." The *Overland Register* in Hong Kong, for its part, contrasted Griffith John's positive account of Nanjing with Holmes's negative one by dividing them under two headers: "men of education," for Griffith John and, for Holmes, "illiterate and blundering bigots."[28]

Though much support for the Taiping came from the missionaries, they were hardly alone. A British businessman named John Scarth, who had just returned from more than a decade of merchant activity in China, published a series of pamphlets in London attacking Britain's apparent preference for the Manchus. In one entitled "Is Our War with the Tartars or the Chinese?" Scarth argued that the British had apparently aligned themselves with the Tartars (the Qing dynasty) against the Chinese people themselves (the Taiping). His own sympathies were clear enough from the epigraph on the front page of his pamphlet, a quotation from the *Athenaeum* reading in part, "it may be that, in spite of foreign opposition and the diabolical cruelties of the mandarins, the cause of freedom will triumph [in China], and the Tartars be driven from the land they have scourged for so long."[29]

Scarth argued that the Taiping were "not merely a rebellion against the Tartar dynasty, but a revolution in the most extended sense of that word." But it was difficult for the British public to see them clearly, he said, because the foreign reporters in Shanghai got too much of their information from the Qing sympathizers among whom they lived. They therefore diminished any positive news about the rebellion, he wrote, while regularly "[abusing] the insurgents in set terms." As for the overseas press, he maintained that the correspondents of the London *Times* simply parroted the deeply opinionated views of people such as Elgin's interpreter Thomas Wade (the one who had described the rebels he met as "a gang of opium-smoking pirates"). For comparison, Scarth declared that the Taiping were every bit as justified in their rebellion as the Italians, who were then fighting to unify their country. "Take all the tyranny that was ever perpetrated in Naples," he wrote, "and all the misgovernment of Rome, they would not show a tithe of the oppression to which the Chinese people have had to submit under their Tartar rulers. Why, then, should not the Chinese rebel? Is it only Italians that are to have our sympathy?"[30]

In the same nationalist vein, in the spring of 1861 the *Dublin University Magazine* ran an article on the Chinese rebels (which *The Economist* deemed "a fair case . . . in their favor")[31] calling for "an intelligent press, imbued with a strong love of national rights" to sift again through the reports from China. The author of the article followed John Scarth in comparing the Taiping Rebellion to the unification movement in Italy (a movement that Palmerston, by contrast, supported) and questioned the morality of any British policy that would stand in the way of "an imposing portion of China, entitled, as truly as Italy or France, to right its own wrongs." Echoing the critics in Parliament who sensed in Bruce's actions at Shanghai a nonchalance toward intervention, the author threw the British government's own words back at it. "Shall we hold up a Government which Lord Elgin admits is the worst in the world," he asked, "by putting down, if possible, men who proclaim to friends and foes their wish to make China a Christian nation?"[32]

The issue, as these writers framed it, was less a matter of religion than of national self-determination: the Taiping were a rebellion of the Chinese people against Manchu tyranny, and to stand in their way was to side with the tyrants. This argument was deeply interwoven with the religious one, but it could also stand alone, for the rebels' brand of Christianity might be imperfect or even unpalatable, but they nevertheless had the right to national freedom. And that was an exceedingly powerful argument in Britain because it was the Liberals who held elected power in the government. Palmerston, for all of his foreign aggressions, was a Liberal, and the members of his party tended to view foreign affairs through a moral lens. Lord Russell insisted repeatedly to Parliament that Britain was holding to a strictly neutral path in the Chinese civil war, and he had to do so precisely because the others in his party kept expressing their doubts that this was in fact the truth. But there was more than one moral lens through which to view China, and one man's national liberation was another man's humanitarian disaster. Palmerston and Russell, via Bruce, mistrusted the Taiping, and so their side of the argument would hold consistently to the message that the Taiping were a force of anarchy and rapine, and if Britain had any moral calling at all in China, it was to prevent them from brutalizing the Chinese within Britain's own small sphere of influence at Shanghai.

Though none in Parliament spoke in actual support of the reigning government of the Qing dynasty (whatever anyone's misgivings about the destruction of the Summer Palace, there wasn't a man there who didn't despise the Manchus for the events that had provoked it), the rebels did have an enthusiastic and extremely partisan supporter in the House of Commons—and he was in many respects the very last person one would expect to have played this role. He was a seventy-one-year-old former chairman of the East India Company named William Henry Sykes, a Scotsman who had begun his career at age thirteen as a cadet in the East India Company's military arm. Over the following five decades he had worked his way up to the rank of colonel, gained a seat on the company's board of trustees, and finally assumed its chairmanship. As chairman of the board, Colonel Sykes had seen the East India Company through its nationalization in 1858, when the British government took over control of India from the joint-stock trading company that had originally conquered and founded it.

In retirement, Colonel Sykes had been elected to Parliament in one of the seats for Aberdeen, Scotland. He was a formidable presence in the House of Commons, not just for his vast experience in India but also as a past president of the Royal Asiatic Society who had read everything he could get his hands on about China.[33] He had a passion for statistics and was one of the founders of the Statistical Society of London—later to be the Royal Society for Statistics—which put him in the company of Thomas Malthus and Florence Nightingale. He was also, despite (or perhaps because of) his life's service to the British Empire in India, intensely moralistic about his country's policies in Asia.

On March 12, Sykes demanded of Lord Russell what policy Britain intended to follow with the Taiping—whom he termed China's "national party" because he, like Scarth, believed them to represent the Chinese people against Manchu tyranny. Did Britain intend to keep its forces in China? If so, he charged, it might well find itself reprising the role played in 1644 by the Manchus, who had been called in to help the Ming dynasty against an internal rebellion, "and they had put down the rebellion and the Emperor also."[34] (He was almost accurate in that statement; the last Ming emperor was already dead when the Manchus entered China, though they had indeed been invited to help put down a domestic rebellion, and they did indeed take the throne for themselves.)

Sykes went on to describe how the Manchus had refused to assimilate to Chinese society and how even after two hundred years they still lived in their separate garrison cities, a ruling elite kept apart from the mass of the subject population. He described the course of the rebellion up to the fall of the siege camps the past spring and attributed that military victory to Hong Rengan finally joining them at Nanjing. Hong Rengan, he went on, was "the real cause of the renewed vigour of the rebels." He was "an able man who had been educated by missionaries at Hong Kong, and had become a convert and preacher of Christianity." Later in the speech he marveled at Hong's treatise on government and the future that it portended for China. "In one chapter," announced Sykes, "he advocates the introduction of railroads, steamers, life and fire insurances, newspapers, and other western inventions. . . . Who knows but that ere many decades shall have passed over our heads, this noble country—vast in its extent, and exhaustless in its resources, will be penetrated and intersected by railroads, and startled into life by the rattling of the fire-carriage, and the flashing of the electric stream?"

Sykes channeled the voices of the Shanghai missionaries but added the weight of his own military and commercial experience. He spoke of the rebels at Suzhou "courteously receiving visits from Europeans of all nations, mercantile men, missionaries, and others" and writing letters to state their intention to take Shanghai peacefully "for the national party."

He repeated the story from *The North-China Herald* about Frederick Bruce refusing to acknowledge the letter from Li Xiucheng and the violence that had ensued—how the rebels had been treated as target practice when they had arrived in peace at Shanghai and how they had never fired a single shot in return. This, charged Sykes, showed that Britain's representatives had all but ignored Lord Russell's instructions to remain neutral. British troops had acted as, in a word, "mercenaries." It was "a proceeding which left an almost indelible stain upon our honour."

Sykes suggested that the "strange anomaly of fighting for our enemies and killing our would-be friends" at Shanghai derived entirely from Bruce's bigotry toward the Taiping. To put all blame on one side in a civil war was to become a partisan, and in so many words he charged Bruce with partisanry. "Mr. Bruce states the rebels create a desert wherever they go," said Sykes, but he himself believed the truth to be quite different: he had collected statistics showing that the export of tea and silk through Shanghai had in fact *increased* in the years since the rebellion had conquered China's most productive provinces. It was now more than ten times as great as it had been before the Taiping existed. He quoted Griffith John's report that Nanjing was coming back to life and being rebuilt, and he described the edict of religious toleration that John had received from the Heavenly King. Foreign travelers, Sykes claimed, regularly reported being robbed by imperial forces but were usually treated kindly by the rebels. He quoted Issachar Roberts as saying that the Taiping wanted peaceful trade with Britain and that the Loyal King "wishes to maintain the greatest friendship and cordiality, both in commerce and religion."

The Taiping, he concluded, were nothing less than "an insurgent national party, holding one third of China, pledged to the expulsion of the Tartars, the extinction of idolatry, and the introduction of the Christian religion." Everything, that is, that Britain should champion. Against them stood "a feeble, foreign Tartar despotism, which has proved faithless to treaties with European nations, and is inimical to Christians." What was there to choose between? Yet Britain had, in its actions at Shanghai the previous summer, sided with the latter. How much longer, he asked Lord Russell, would this policy continue?

Russell, in a blustering response, charged Sykes with willful naiveté and declared that "there does not appear to be a word of truth" to the belief that the Taiping represented the Chinese people against the Manchus, nor that they were Christian. He repeated Frederick Bruce's reports that the rebels were rapacious criminals who made a mockery of the Christian religion and that they had come to Shanghai with only the most violent of intentions. Neutrality allowed for self-defense, Russell contended, and he swore that he would not "[allow] the towns where our merchants are congregated to be destroyed, simply because some persons in this country have a false notion that they are a national party and that we ought to support them."[35]

Sykes kept at him, though. On April 12, he got the floor again and brandished a sheaf of articles from Shanghai's *North-China Herald* that, he said, gave direct support to his previous arguments. He asked Lord Russell if any of them had been made available to the members of Parliament. Russell all but ignored him, veering instead into a lengthy discourse (nearly three thousand words in the official transcript) in response to a previous question about affairs in Germany and Denmark before finally concluding with a dismissive comment that "my honorable and gallant Friend the Member for Aberdeen (Colonel Sykes) is, I think, the only person in the House who takes an interest in the Taepings."[36] The printers at the Foreign Office, he stated, were too busy to make anything else available.

But even as the debates were gearing up in London, Admiral Hope was already on his way to Nanjing. In early February 1861, he left the foreign settlements at Shanghai and steamed up the Yangtze in his dispatch vessel *Coromandel,* pushing hard through a cold, muddy current swollen by several days of heavy rain.[37] Hope was a lanky, aristocratic-looking man with large ears, a clean-shaven face, and a plucky heedlessness that had earned him the nickname "Fighting Jimmy" from his adoring men.[38] His fifty-one-gun flagship was far too large to maneuver nimbly on the river, so he left it behind in Shanghai as he shepherded a small squadron of gunboats reclaimed from the British fleet that had so recently invaded the north. They sailed in three parallel lines through the rain, the smaller vessels going ahead to take soundings and signal the depth of the opaque river to the following ships with deeper draft. Still, despite Hope's care the ships ran aground with numbing regularity, and it took them more than two weeks to complete the voyage of two hundred miles. A jaunty delegation of officials, missionaries, and businessmen rode along in small luxury on a river steamer nicknamed the "floating hotel" (until it too ran aground, after which they called it the "shoregoing craft"). This made for the largest foreign party yet to visit Nanjing.

The lead negotiator of the expedition was none other than Harry

Parkes, fresh from escaping death at the hands of Senggelinqin in Beijing. Sailing separately, he reached Nanjing on February 24, and the rest of the expedition joined him four days later, after stopping at the ruined city of Zhenjiang along the way to drop off a lonely consul (who now waited patiently for business to commence, his Union Jack flapping forlornly on its pole). They found Issachar Roberts resident in Nanjing and also William Muirhead, who had stayed on for a couple of weeks after Hong Rengan's departure in early February. In contrast to Lord Ellenborough's predictions of cannon fire, the party was made to feel welcome and took up quarters in the palace of the absent Loyal King.

On March 1, Harry Parkes explained Britain's plans for trade on the Yangtze River to a pair of lesser Taiping kings who had been left in charge when the others departed for the campaign in Anqing. He told them that Britain's treaty with the Manchu government gave British ships the right to trade in the city of Hankow in Hubei province—part of a three-city nexus with Hanyang and the provincial capital, Wuchang—which lay upriver beyond Anqing and was for the moment under imperial control. As the rebels controlled most of the territory in between, Parkes informed them that regardless of who held power along the banks, Britain claimed the right for its ships to sail the full length of the river freely. Furthermore, he told them, Admiral Hope intended to leave the six-gun paddle frigate *Centaur* at Nanjing to protect any British subjects who might happen to stop there.

The kings relayed Parkes's message to Hong Xiuquan in his palace, seven miles away on the other end of the overgrown city from where the British fleet bobbed mischievously at anchor. Several hours later they brought back word that the Heavenly King had received a vision that warned him not to allow the foreigners to leave their gunboat, so they couldn't grant that request. But after some extremely heated negotiation (during which Parkes reportedly shouted at them, "He must have *another* vision!") they finally relented and conceded to Parkes's terms.[39] As regarded any plans the rebels might have to attack cities with British interests, Parkes warned them that if they should attack Zhenjiang (where they had just dropped off the consul) or Jiujiang (upriver beyond Anqing), both of which were still under imperial control and only just opened by the treaty, they had better not harm any British subjects or their property. In return, he promised that British forces would not oppose a Taiping attack on those cities as they had done at Shanghai.[40] Parkes himself didn't feel any particular affection for the rebels, who reminded him of "a pack of robbers who have just looted a city,"[41] but as long as British traders could go about their business unmolested by them, he thought that they would be perfectly acceptable. As he wrote in one report, "we found these 'princes,' of whom we saw two, reasonable enough, and if they will keep their hands off our ships as they pass up and down, our principal object will be attained."[42]

Parkes had unflagging faith in the positive effects of foreign trade on the Yangtze, which he thought of as "a warm stream of commerce passing through the main artery of this sickly country."[43] But his faith in this instance was tested by the fact that the two commodities the rebels seemed to want more than anything else were guns and opium. The latter might have sparked the interest of Shanghai's opium merchants (who worried, apparently in vain, that their trade would be shut down by the Taiping), but Parkes couldn't escape the literally explosive potential of unrestricted private British commerce through the heart of China's civil war zone. And the open-door welcome to arms dealers wasn't just on the side of the rebels, either. "It is the same . . . on the side of the Imperialists," he wrote; "opium and arms, opium and arms, is the one cry we hear from mandarins, soldiers, and people, at every place we have yet come to." Delighted as he was to see the major cities of the Yangtze River opening to foreign trade, he nevertheless worried that "much harm as well as good may result from the intercourse."[44]

Between the rebels and the imperials, Parkes saw little for the British to prefer. In spite of his harsh treatment at the hands of the Manchus, he remained disinterested in the civil contest, and his opinion on the relative merits of the two sides was shaped, he claimed, by the words of a peasant he had met along the river, who, "seeing that for a few moments he was out of the hearing of other people, told me a piteous tale of his own sufferings, and of the desolation of the country round." Parkes recounted the peasant's view, one that was echoed innumerable times in the course of the war: "He drew little distinction between Imperial troops and rebels—he had suffered alike at the hands of both."[45]

In contrast to Parkes's pragmatism, Admiral Hope followed Frederick Bruce in viewing the rebels as a force of destruction that should be kept at arm's length from British interests—though to a far greater degree than Bruce, he believed Britain should use force to achieve that end. Privately, Hope envisioned the future of the treaty ports as oases of stability, protected by British arms and providing security for native merchants through what he foresaw as "a period of anarchy, indefinite in duration" in

China, "in which the commercial towns of the empire will be destroyed, and its most productive provinces laid waste."[46] To that end, Hope believed, the British should establish a radius around Shanghai of two days' march (one hundred Chinese *li,* roughly thirty English miles) and prevent the Taiping from entering within it.

Such a radius would be a truly extreme interpretation of neutrality—a projected defense of British interests, as it were—and it fell directly afoul of Britain's stated policy, at least as Lord Russell was then defending it to Parliament. But the lanky James Hope was, in the words of one of his contemporaries, a man for whom "the exigencies of the situation were everything, the official balance very little, the fear of responsibility nothing."[47] Russell and Bruce might cling to their high-minded theories and their moral principles of neutrality, but the navy had its own responsibilities, and Hope considered himself a man of the moment, a man of action. By the time he returned down the Yangtze from Hankow a month later, stopping off at Nanjing again on his way back to Shanghai, he had already made up his mind that a rebel-free radius of thirty miles around the treaty port was exactly what Parkes should demand from the Taiping leaders.

And so, on Hope's instructions, at the end of March Parkes entered a new round of negotiations with the two lesser kings, from whom he requested, first, a promise from the rebels not to approach within two days' march of Shanghai and then—once they seemed likely to agree to the first—not to approach within two days' march of *any* of the treaty ports. This would be in the Taiping's own interest, he told them with no small measure of chutzpah, for it ensured that when they did finally conquer the empire, those important trading cities would be undamaged by the war. The negotiations, predictably, bogged down. Parkes began to grow suspicious that the kings didn't have any power (it was unfortunate for all concerned that Hong Rengan was gone from the capital at this point). So he left them and marched all the way across Nanjing to see the Heavenly King for himself. But when he got there, the guards wouldn't let him into the palace. Parkes's impatience grew as the hours passed and he sat, fuming, in an outer courtyard. There was little to do but stare angrily at the wall—where, much to his offense, hung a map of the Taiping Heavenly Kingdom in which Britain and France appeared merely as tiny islands huddled in the upper-left-hand corner. But finally, through a succession of messages carried in and out by the palace women (Parkes's on paper, Hong Xiuquan's on yellow silk), they came to an agreement: Hong Xiuquan would notify his commanders near

Shanghai to stay thirty miles from the city for the rest of the year.[48] The other cities he could not speak for; his armies in the field might need provisions from them. Parkes left Nanjing wondering just how much control the Heavenly King actually had over his agents in the field.

The same, of course, might be wondered of Lord Russell.

Admiral Hope did make a few concessions to his country's neutral policy. For one thing, he ordered the authorities at Shanghai to begin rounding up British subjects who had enlisted as mercenaries in the Chinese civil war—though this was as much to punish desertion from his own force as to uphold the long-standing neutrality ordinance. The foreign mercenaries on the rebel side were thought to be based in Nanjing, so a consular official named Robert Forrest left Shanghai in March 1861 to make a journey overland through Taiping territory to the rebel capital. His plan was to reconnoiter with Hope on his way back down from Hankow and to try to scout out renegade Englishmen along the way.

Forrest was the first British agent to explore anything of the rebel kingdom beyond the immediate edge of the waterways, and his account gave the readers of the Blue Books their first glimpse of the world on the other side of the Chinese war. It began predictably enough as he confirmed the utter desolation of the countryside for a mile or so on either side of the Yangtze and the Grand Canal, but then he went on to report that life under the rebels farther inland was actually far better than had been thought.[49] He discovered a vibrant underground trade between imperial Shanghai and rebel Suzhou, with constant traffic by a fleet of several thousand small boats whose owners had managed to buy into a scheme that got them past both imperial and rebel pickets. He spoke to a number of rebel soldiers along his journey, many of them conscripts (some, even, with the name of the Taiping Heavenly Kingdom tattooed onto their cheeks to keep them from escaping), but they nevertheless seemed to him happy and well fed. They got plenty of rice each day, they told him, and said they were unconcerned about the future. What pain their faces might have masked, however, is unknowable; the most outwardly joyful persons he encountered, full of "swagger and airs," were the boy soldiers, kidnapped from their families, who chased after him and called him a foreign devil.

Leaving the bone-whitened banks of the Grand Canal, Forrest set off inland and entered an entirely different world.[50] The people there "were not alarmed at the sight of strangers as were the few wretched people along the canal," he wrote. In comparison to the ghostly emptiness of the riverbanks, life inland seemed to exude "confidence and safety." People were back at work in the fields. He noted the many proclamations of laws, which gave order to daily life. The people he met told him of the miserable destruction when the rebels had first come, of the kidnappings and looting and flights of refugees, but he reported that the period of chaos appeared to be over and "they are now, I am glad to say, fast returning to their homes." The picture he painted of the world under the Taiping in the countryside matches a number of accounts left by Chinese gentry who lived through the period—that for the most part, after the conquest the people were left alone. In larger towns there was a Taiping *xiangguan* ("in whom the people seem to have confidence," Forrest believed), but in the more rural areas the only tangible presence of the rebel authorities, other than the lack of shaved heads, was that every month or so, someone would come to collect taxes in grain or cash. Which is to say, it wasn't much different from rural life under the Qing. Barring the return of warfare to the region, Forrest predicted, "the villages around will soon become peopled, and the land resume its wonted fertile appearance."[51]

Forrest saw only one man with blue eyes along his route but gathered what information he could of the foreigners in rebel service. In Nanjing he discovered more than a hundred of them, Europeans and Americans, fighting for the Taiping. Their full extent hadn't been known earlier, since whenever a foreign ship came to dock, they would all hide. Forrest prevailed on the rebel kings to hand over those who were British subjects, twenty-six of them as far as he could tell. Only a handful admitted to having joined the Taiping ranks voluntarily (for a salary of 60 taels per month, on par with that of a battalion commander in Zeng Guofan's army).[52] Others claimed, now that they were faced with arrest, that they had been crimped, or "Shanghaied," as later slang would put it: out drinking in a Shanghai watering hole, someone had slipped them a sedative, and they woke up on a boat halfway to Nanjing staring into the barrel of a gun. Or so they said. The men were in "a most miserable condition," he reported, "getting no pay, but plenty of rice and spirits. They were allowed to plunder wherever they went, but seem to have had little success." In that, they were in remarkably similar straits to their counterparts under Frederick Townsend Ward on the imperial side, against whom they had fought at Qingpu and Songjiang until their leader, Savage, was killed.

It was a rough life to be sure. One of the men was ridden with dysentery and died a few days after Forrest's arrival. Another told Forrest that an Italian in their number had recently murdered an Irishman and threw him into the moat, with no apparent consequences. Native troops had no monopoly on atrocity, Forrest learned, for his own countrymen "made no secret of such crimes as rape and robbery, and even hinted at darker deeds." By the time he got to Nanjing, they were on their way to attack Hangzhou in Zhejiang province and their former leader, Savage, had been replaced by an American known only as Peacock, of whom the men were in awe. "He is of high rank among the Taepings," they told Forrest, "and has the power of life and death." With no jurisdiction over the citizens of other countries, Forrest had to leave the bulk of the mercenary force behind as he escorted the twenty-six confirmed British subjects onto the *Centaur* under armed guard and transferred them down to Shanghai to be tried en masse for violating the neutrality ordinance.[53]

For consistency, Admiral Hope tried to shut down the foreign mercenaries on the imperial side as well. A British consul was pleased to report on May 2 that Her Majesty's forces had caught thirteen members of Frederick Townsend Ward's militia at Songjiang, one of whom testified that there were now only eighty-two foreigners left fighting on the imperial side (fewer than in the Taiping's foreign militia). Twenty-nine of them were deserters from the Royal Navy. The informer also painted Ward as something of a tyrant, who would rather lock a man up or let him disappear into the hands of imperial thugs than allow him to quit the force and return to Shanghai.[54]

They finally arrested Ward himself on May 19, as he was trying to recruit new blood for his militia in Shanghai. Since he was from Massachusetts, the only person in the international city who had jurisdiction over him was the U.S. consul, but things got complicated when Ward, his speech slurred by the scarred mass in his cheek left over from his bullet wound the previous fall, claimed that he was no longer a U.S. citizen and had become a subject of the Qing emperor. He was engaged to marry a Chinese woman (though the timing would suggest a hastily arranged union, insofar as a surviving letter of congratulations from the father of the would-be bride to Ward's father is dated ten days *after* his arrest).[55] To back him up, the provincial governor in Shanghai, who happened to be one of his patrons, produced papers proving Ward's Chinese citizenship. The papers were fake; the imperial government would, in fact, make him a citizen, but not until the following February.[56] Yet they were convincing enough that the U.S. consul refused to prosecute him.[57] The British didn't want to set Ward free to keep luring their men into China's imperial service, but there seemed to be no legal basis for a trial, so Admiral Hope simply locked him up in a room on his flagship while they tried to figure out how to dispose of him. Ward jumped ship through an open window late one night, a waiting sampan picked him up out of the harbor, and he disappeared back into his world of shadows.[58]

CHAPTER 9

ENDURANCE

The city of Anqing lay on the northern bank of the Yangtze, at a point where
the wide, meandering river flowed briefly in a direct line from west to east
before slipping around an island and then diverting northward to continue
on toward the ocean, nearly four hundred miles away. A high, crenellated
brick wall roughly a mile long on each side surrounded the city, its southern face running along the bank of the river, which here flattened out into
a sandy beach. Between the beach and the city wall lay a narrow buffer of
land that had held dense settlements and markets in the years before the
war, but by 1860 everything on it had been leveled and cleared save for a
single seven-story fluted pagoda to the east of the city, surrounded at its
base by its own protective stone wall. Otherwise the riverbank was a fea-
tureless waste, leaving no protection or shelter for enemies landing from
the river. Anqing was hardly the largest of China's provincial capitals, but it
was nevertheless a grand fortress more than a square mile in size, dominating the river and the surrounding countryside. From a military standpoint
its siting was perfect. It sat on a high piece of ground that fell away on all
sides, giving a clear view and a tactical advantage. And it was exceptionally difficult to approach by land: along with the Yangtze, which enclosed
it to the immediate south, there were broad lakes a few miles to the west

and close by to the east, which, along with the northerly bend of the river, enveloped the hinterland of the city with water on three sides. Six miles to the north, a steep chain of mountains rose into the mist and impeded most of the approach from that direction as well, save for one lone mountain pass—the Jixian Pass—which had its own stone fortifications.[1]

Strategically, Anqing operated as a fulcrum. It projected defensive power eastward over the approaches to Nanjing from the north of the Yangtze River, and was also the base for all of the Taiping's operations to the north and west, through Anhui and into Hubei. And of course, it controlled the river upon which it was founded. The Yangtze was half a mile wide here, but the channel for deeper boats ran up close to the northern bank—so close that the captain of a passing ship could see right into the black maw of a cannon pointing down at him from the city wall.[2] The masters of Anqing could thus play havoc with the waterborne supply line of any imperial army that managed to move beyond them into Taiping territory.[3] Zeng Guofan had to have it before he could push his army any closer to Nanjing. And the Taiping had to hold it if they wanted to recapture the northern bank of the Yangtze up to Wuchang and eventually link up with the wandering army of Shi Dakai in Sichuan.

With vigilant defense it was nearly impossible for an enemy force to approach Anqing, but when Zeng Guofan began his campaign for it in the summer of 1860, the defenders were not being vigilant. The city (which the Taiping had held for seven years) was the domain of Chen Yucheng, the Brave King, a precocious rebel general only twenty-five years old who had conquered Wuchang at the startlingly young age of eighteen and was known to his enemies as the "Four-Eyed Dog" due to a fearsome pair of black birthmarks under his eyes.[4] In the spring of 1860, he decamped with the bulk of his army eastward to help Li Xiucheng break the imperial siege of Nanjing, leaving behind a garrison force numbering roughly 20,000 soldiers to hold the city and protect Anqing's civilian population—among which were four or five thousand women and perhaps double that number of children, along with the Brave King's own family.[5] The garrison soldiers were unseasoned recruits from Hunan and Hubei provinces, and he left them with strict orders to defend the walls but not to sortie from the gates to engage the enemy. And so, when Zeng Guofan took advantage of the Brave King's absence to send his brother with 10,000 soldiers down through the northern approach to Anqing, through the Jixian Pass between the mountains, scaring off the defensive pickets into the rain, they managed to set up camp within gunshot of the city walls against little resistance.[6]

As with the other cities they held, the Taiping treated Anqing primarily as a military camp. The massive outer gates gave way inside to neatly kept neighborhoods with steep cobbled streets preserved for the garrison troops and civilian population, while beyond them were large uninhabited stretches of housing that would soon be torn down to provide wood for fuel, bricks for the construction of new redoubts along the wall, and open space to reclaim for gardening. The city's residents could grow vegetables in abundance. They were also well provisioned to start with, so there was no particular sense of concern as the garrison troops barricaded the gates to wait for the Brave King's return, and took turns watching out over the plain from a lookout on top of the wall while the tiny Hunan Army soldiers down below made themselves busy.[7]

―――――――

Zeng Guofan's siege of Anqing was not initially a pressing concern for the Taiping leaders. They knew the city to be well fortified, and the garrison, though inexperienced, had double the numbers of the force under its walls. A plan to relieve Anqing materialized in September 1860 as a secondary objective within the larger Taiping plan to reclaim control of the Yangtze River up through Wuchang. This was the second phase of Hong Rengan's strategy—in which, after consolidating the lower reaches of the Yangtze to the east of Nanjing, they would turn their attention upstream. But after the repulse at Shanghai in August it was clear that the foreigners would not sell them the steamships Hong Rengan had counted on to transport the Taiping armies up to Wuchang, so they had to go on foot. After the main work of consolidation around Suzhou in the east was done, Chen Yucheng the Brave King and Li Xiucheng the Loyal King embarked on a massive pincer operation westward on opposite banks of the river, planning to converge upstream from the Hunan Army forces at the scantily defended Hubei capital of Wuchang.

According to the plan, the Brave King would take a large army of 100,000 around to the north through Anhui, try to break the siege of Anqing in the early winter en route, and then continue on to seize the smaller city of Hankow on the northern bank across from Wuchang by spring. Li Xiucheng would mirror the Brave King's path with a smaller force on the southern side of the great river, plowing through Zeng Guofan's headquarters in Qimen at the same time the northern forces were breaking the siege of Anqing under his brother Guoquan, and then follow around from below to come up and rendezvous with the Brave King in April for a joint attack from both sides on Wuchang—which, because Zeng Guofan had staked almost his entire force on Anqing, had a defensive garrison numbering only about 3,000 troops.[8] Any of Zeng Guofan's forces that remained after the main operation would be trapped, their lines of supply and reinforcement cut off, and the joint Taiping armies under the Brave and Loyal kings could then march back down the twin banks of the Yangtze, with Wuchang as their base, and crush the Hunan Army where it lay.[9]

The Brave King set out from Nanjing in October 1860, crossing over to the northern bank of the Yangtze and then marching his men westward into Anhui province to test the strength of the imperial lines. This was some of the most bitterly fought territory in the country, where the ravages of the northern Nian bandit armies reached down to overlap with the fighting between the imperialists and the Taiping (fifty years after the war was over, travelers through the region would still lament that its scars hadn't healed). Relations between the Taiping and Nian leaders were tendentious, but they shared the common enemy of the imperial government and occasionally found common ground. In this case, the Brave King recruited a Nian general to join him with an army on horseback, which made a series of feinted side attacks to confuse the imperials and disguise the main route of his march. In late November, he made his move and turned sharply south to bear straight down on Anqing. But just beyond Taiping-held Tongcheng to the north of the siege, he stumbled onto the enormous force of 20,000 imperial cavalry under the Manchu general Duolonga, whom Zeng Guofan had stationed south of Tongcheng to protect Anqing from just such an approach.

Unable to break Duolonga's cavalry lines and finding his slower forces consistently outflanked by the swift northern horsemen, the Brave King pulled back to the protective walls of Tongcheng and abandoned the northern approach to Anqing. He held Tongcheng against imperial attacks through the winter and then decamped at the beginning of March, just after the start of the Chinese New Year (and just as Hong Rengan was leaving the capital to bring him more support). This time he led his forces in a grand sweep to the northwest beyond the range of the cavalry, and then turned sharply southwest in a beeline toward the three-city nexus of Wuchang, Hankow, and Hanyang on the Yangtze River. In a final, punish-

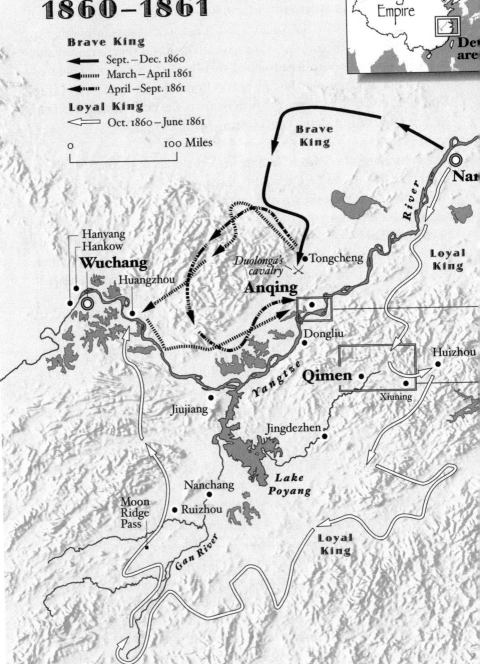

Siege of Anqing
1860–1861

Brave King
- ← Sept.–Dec. 1860
- ← March–April 1861
- ← April–Sept. 1861

Loyal King
- ⇐ Oct. 1860–June 1861

0   100 Miles

Qing Empire   Beijing

Det
are

Brave King

Na

Hanyang
Hankow
Wuchang
Huangzhou

Duolonga's cavalry

Tongcheng

Anqing

Loyal King

Dongliu

Huizhou

Qimen

Xiuning

Jiujiang

Jingdezhen

Yangtze

Nanchang

Lake Poyang

Moon Ridge Pass

Ruizhou

Gan River

Loyal King

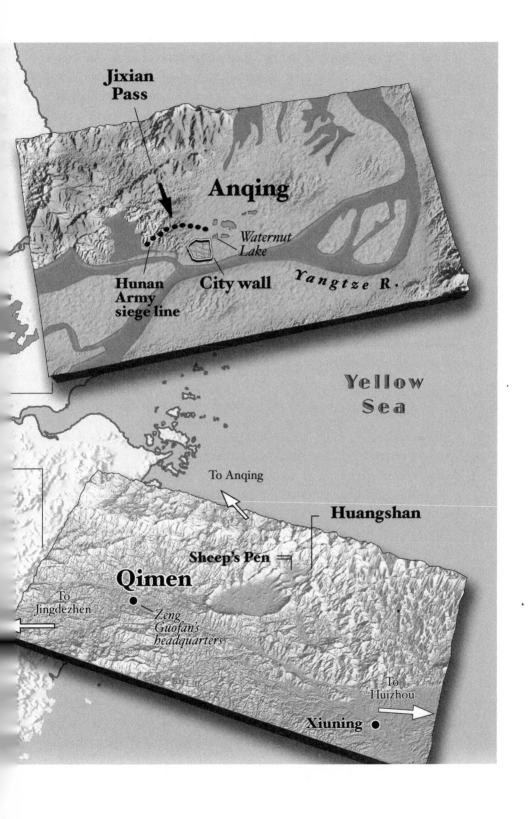

Jixian
Pass

Anqing

*Waternut
Lake*

Hunan
Army
siege line

City wall

Yangtze R.

Yellow
Sea

To Anqing

Huangshan

Sheep's Pen

Qimen

To
Jingdezhen

*Zeng
Guofan's
headquarters*

To
Huizhou

Xiuning

ing burst of speed they covered two hundred miles on foot in just eleven days, punching through several pockets of militia resistance along the way. A detachment of the Hunan Army's cavalry charged due west to try to cut them off, but it arrived too late, and on March 17, 1861, an advance party of the Brave King's forces arrived outside the river town of Huangzhou on the Yangtze's northern bank, just fifty miles downstream from Hankow and Wuchang.

Surprising the two thousand imperial soldiers and cavalry who garrisoned Huangzhou, the advance party slaughtered them all and commandeered their horses.[10] Then they began tearing down houses to throw up three lines of wood and stone defensive barricades around the town while the rest of the Brave King's army continued to stagger in, exhausted from the long march. Some were so depleted by the time they got past the blockades that they simply fell to the ground and went to sleep in the street, without even removing their loads.[11] With Huangzhou in hand, Chen Yucheng now had a perfect base from which to attack Hankow upstream and complete his side of the pincer maneuver.

———————

In his headquarters in Qimen, below the river and sixty miles southeast of Anqing through a heavy range of mountains, Zeng Guofan greeted the news of rebel movements with worry. Independently of the huge new operation afoot—of which he was as yet unaware—separate Taiping forces had been harassing his defensive outposts around Qimen since the early fall. By the late autumn a rebel army under Li Xiucheng's cousin the Attending King had captured the town of Xiuning, thirty miles to his immediate east, which commanded the only road in that direction. He dispatched his best field commander, Bao Chao, to try to take it back. Though his forces were well trained, they were outnumbered and had scant intelligence on the rebels' broader plans.

In the midst of this, the news about his brother across the river at Anqing wasn't entirely encouraging. Things were still quiet at the siege thanks to Duolonga's blockade, but Guoquan was an inexperienced leader and Zeng Guofan learned that his officers had been paying the mass of laborers—the ones who were digging their moats and building their defensive walls—with rotten, moldy grain that the starving peasants had no choice but to accept. Zeng Guofan wrote an angry letter to his brother demanding that he make sure they were paid with silver, because word was spreading that the Hunan forces were corrupt and cruel. "You must nurture the people for their own sake, and choose officials who will act on their behalf. What I hate is when officials don't show love for the people," he wrote.[12] The only good news, such as there was, was that in the late fall he learned that the foreign armies had left the capital after sacking the emperor's palace, and it seemed that they didn't intend to take over the empire for themselves, which was a lone source of relief.

On November 23, 1860, Zeng Guofan celebrated his fiftieth birthday by the Chinese calendar. It was not a festive occasion. "My years have passed as wasted time," he wrote in his diary. "Dejected, I now become an old man."[13] He was on an inspection tour at the time, making the rounds of the mountain peaks surrounding an oval-shaped valley about ten miles northeast of Qimen. The valley was flat and broad, about twelve miles by four, crammed with wealthy merchant villages and dense tea farms and ridged all around with brilliant razor-sharp peaks that reached up more than three thousand feet. It was like an oasis within the mountains that pressed so close all around, you could practically touch them. To the northeast lay the mile-high granite peaks of Huangshan, the Yellow Mountain, with its twisted pines and fingerlings of stone pressing into the sky. Due north, threading through a sea of overlapping ranges, lay the narrow path that was the most likely approach for an army from the north to enter the valley.

After an early breakfast and some paperwork, he left around seven in the morning to climb the arduous graveled path up to the Sheep's Pen, a strategic peak seven miles north of his camp that watched over the approach through the northern mountains. At 2,700 feet, on a fine day it gave a stunning view down the other side, through waving groves of bamboo to a tiny farming village on the valley floor, and for miles into the distance along the rippling channel of pine-forested valleys leading away to the north. But this wasn't a fine day, and a heavy blanket of clouds hung over the pass, so dense that he couldn't make out anything at all from the lookout at the top.[14]

The weather was getting cold in the higher elevations, and over the next two days his scouts confirmed that the other routes leading in through the mountains were blocked with snow. The valley was safe for the winter. So he finished his inspections and returned to Qimen on November 26.

Five days later, on the first of December, Li Xiucheng's entire army crossed over the Sheep's Pen from the north and entered the valley.

Zeng Guofan got the news that afternoon. He immediately dispatched his fastest couriers to ride for help, and stayed up all night in terror. The morning saw him grim with exhaustion and worry, with only 3,000 troops of his own at his headquarters to fend off the rebel army.[15] His nearest supporting forces were under Bao Chao, thirty miles away to the east at Xiuning,[16] and Li Xiucheng's army had materialized right between them. He had little hope. But he tried to put on a stoic face as he wrote to Guoquan at Anqing to explain the situation. He had done everything he could, he wrote to his brother, and for the enemy still to come like this, through the fog and the snow, could only be Heaven's will. Now the rebels were just fifteen miles from his undermanned headquarters. "It's just a stone's throw," he wrote, "and there are no obstacles to stop them. . . . All we can do now is study our defenses and, when they come, try to hold out until someone comes to help us."

He had thought many times over the years about how he would face his death when it came, and his voice in the letter was steady and accepting. "I look back on my fifty years," he wrote in its conclusion, "and though I regret that my scholarship is still incomplete, at least I am guilty of no great crimes." His final words were moral advice for his family: he asked Guoquan to "guide our younger brothers and sons and teach them to be diligent within, and modest without, to guard against arrogant habits. Beyond this, I have no other will."[17] There it ended and there he sat, composed, waiting for his fate to run its course.

But Li Xiucheng didn't attack him that day. He had no idea how weak Zeng Guofan's forces in Qimen were, nor did he know that the Hunan general's best troops were a day's march in the other direction. His own men were exhausted from their trek through the mountains and snow and needed rest. And he didn't want to risk a pitched battle against unknown odds when his real objective, the hundreds of thousands of new Taiping followers who awaited in Jiangxi and Hubei provinces, lay far beyond.[18] So, after capturing the county seat in the center of the valley, he paused. That pause was enough.

It was Bao Chao—who would just then have been arriving in Beijing if Zeng Guofan had followed the emperor's orders—who the next morning swept into the valley from the east with a full force of cavalry and drew up lines of battle. The first day, the two sides fought to a standstill. The second day was a bloodbath. Bao Chao's men were fewer but far better rested and equipped, and the Loyal King, with an eye on further objectives, finally called a retreat and pulled his weary men back into the mountains, disappearing once again into the fog and leaving four thousand dead and wounded behind him on the valley floor.[19]

For Zeng Guofan in his position south of the river, the winter was one of constant uncertainty and movement, of lines of supply and communication cut and reopened, strategic towns lost and regained. The Taiping armies outside Qimen—three of them altogether, not including Li Xiucheng's personal army, which had moved on toward Jiangxi—fanned out and began picking off the towns controlling the roads leading away from his headquarters one by one. On December 15, they took the town to his west and severed his communications with his brother at Anqing. Eight days later, they took another town to his south and cut off his overland supply route from Jiangxi province. He sent Bao Chao south and another commander west to take them back but knew those were desperate moves. He had lost the initiative and was reduced to putting out fires when they erupted. But it was all he could do, and he wrote to Guoquan that "if they don't succeed, my supply lines will be disrupted. Everything is falling apart . . . the forty or fifty thousand troops under my command will be defeated if they don't have supplies."[20]

On December 27, Zeng Guofan wrote to one of his naval commanders that everything was going wrong in southern Anhui,[21] and by early January, his men were fighting back renewed invasion attempts through the Sheep's Pen.[22] Qimen was being harassed on all sides, and he now began to suspect that the skirmishes on both sides of the river were distractions in the service of a master plan to relieve Anqing.[23] Still, it was all he could do to fend off the constant attacks. Fierce battles in February and March saw the fighting encroach to within twenty miles of his Qimen headquarters again. He owed his life to Bao Chao, who charged back and forth across the province to attack the raiding armies as they appeared. And he owed his army's sustenance to a Hunanese general, Zuo Zongtang, who defended the porcelain-producing city of Jingdezhen to the southwest, the walled city that controlled Zeng Guofan's sole remaining supply line from Jiangxi province. But when that city fell to Li Xiucheng's cousin on April 9, Zeng Guofan's supplies were finally cut off completely, along with all communications with the world outside.[24]

Fearing the starvation or slaughter of his troops trapped inside the rebel encirclement, he joined with one of his commanders to lead 9,000 of them eastward to break through the Taiping cordons. In that he saw the only hope of survival. "My mouth and tongue are dried up, and my heart is afire," he wrote in his diary in anticipation. "I almost don't know what joy there is to be found in life, nor what sorrow there is in death."[25] But at the walled town of Huizhou, at the edge of the cordon, they met with disaster. The rebel garrison managed to sneak out under cover of darkness and set fire to Zeng Guofan's camp, burning it to the ground and scattering his soldiers into the night.

Zeng Guofan fell back to Qimen with no food or supplies and no route for escape. On April 22, 1861, he wrote a somber letter to his sons back home in Hunan with the resigned certainty that the war, for him, was now over. In his diary, he described it as his will.[26] He told his sons that the situation he now faced was as bleak as in January 1855, when he had lost his naval fleet at Lake Poyang and tried to commit suicide. His forces were still intact this time, he wrote, but "we are surrounded on all sides. Our supplies are all cut off. On top of that, to meet with such defeats—the morale of our army is truly shaken."[27]

In the will, he told his sons not to become military men. This general, who had only ever wanted to be a scholar, looked back on his own career and saw it as a failure. "At its root, leading an army is not something I was good at," he told them. "Warfare calls for extremity, but I am too balanced. It calls for deception, and I am too direct. How could I possibly manage against these monstrous rebels?" He told them to avoid following any path like his own, save for the quiet Confucian scholarship that was his only true pride. "All you should do is pursue your studies with a single mind," he told them, in memory of happier times—before the war had swallowed him whole, before he had given his life to the imperial service. "You must not become soldiers," he told them. "And you need not become officials, either."[28]

After his capture of Huangzhou on March 17, 1861, Chen Yucheng the Brave King was positioned to go on and take Hankow fifty miles upstream, on the northern bank of the Yangtze across from Wuchang. From that base, he could prepare for the impending arrival of Li Xiucheng's army from the south in April. But Hankow was one of the ports opened to British trade by Elgin's treaty, and by the most capricious of coincidences, the Brave King's arrival at the edge of the Yangtze overlapped with Admiral

Hope's expedition—which had just made its initial visit to Nanjing at the end of February and was now upriver in Hankow, where Hope and Parkes were making arrangements to station a British consul before heading back down to Nanjing again for their second visit (the one during which Parkes would demand that the Taiping stay thirty miles from Shanghai).

And so it was that on March 22, 1861, just five days after the Brave King's army captured Huangzhou, Harry Parkes showed up to pay him a visit. The advance force of rebels in the city—about twenty to thirty thousand men at that point, with several tens of thousands still on their way—were hard at work building defensive barricades as the gunship *Bouncer* pulled up offshore, dropped anchor, and discharged Parkes (much to the amusement of many of the soldiers, who had never seen a European before). Striding purposefully into town, the diminutive Parkes took note of three proclamations: one inviting the townspeople to trade with the army, one forbidding the soldiers to loot, and the third, "appended to the heads of two rebels," warning what would happen to soldiers who violated the second proclamation. The rebel troops seemed to him haggard but friendly, with no signs of infighting or discontent, and he ascertained that they came from all over the empire, though primarily from Hubei and Hunan provinces, just like the garrison soldiers in Anqing. These were men from the Brave King's territory in central China. Parkes was ushered across town to the main government office, where he entered through a gauntlet of halberds and banners to find the Brave King himself seated for audience. He was "a young-looking man, robed in a yellow satin gown and hood embroidered with dragons," and Parkes found him to be pleasantly modest and highly intelligent.[29]

Chen Yucheng was remarkably open with Parkes—he, like the Heavenly King, carefully followed Hong Rengan's injunction that the rebels needed to cultivate the friendship and goodwill of foreigners. He told Parkes the story of his current campaign, leaving out the fighting with Duolonga's cavalry that had blocked his northern approach to Anqing back in November. But he did reveal quite candidly the strength of the various Taiping armies and their relative positions in the overall campaign, and explained their plan to converge on Hankow and Wuchang in April. He said that his immediate objective was to break the siege of Anqing, and to that end he had come north around the imperial forces and was now firmly planted at their rear. "So far he had been completely successful," reported the impressed Parkes, who noted that the Brave King's final breakneck march had turned the flank of the imperial forces and he was now poised either to attack them from the rear once the rest of his army arrived or to capture Hankow upstream and hold it as a base for the coming of the other Taiping armies in a few weeks. (As Parkes well knew, Wuchang was so poorly defended that the entire population of the three cities was at that moment fleeing into the countryside in abject panic at the news of a rebel approach.) Hankow could be the Brave King's easily, as soon as he wanted—but, he told Parkes, he was now uncertain about whether he should attack it, because the British were there.

Parkes's response would be more consequential than he could possibly know. "I commended his caution in this respect," reported Parkes, "and advised him not to think of moving on Hankow." He explained to the Brave King that the British now had important interests in that city and there was no way for the Taiping to occupy it "without seriously interfering with our commerce." Parkes didn't say as much in his report, but behind those words lay a threat that, while unstated, would nevertheless have been crystal clear to the Brave King. Chen Yucheng was not privy to Parkes's negotiations with the Heavenly King, nor was he aware of the British debates over their neutrality policy or even of the limited power that Parkes, a mere interpreter, was supposed to exercise. Given those limitations in his knowledge, he would clearly understand Parkes to mean that if he dared to approach Hankow with his army, the British guns would meet them in the same way they had met Li Xiucheng at Shanghai the previous summer. "It was necessary that their movements should be so ordered as not to clash with ours,"[30] Parkes reported to Bruce as justification for warning the Brave King away from Hankow.

The Brave King tried to negotiate. He said he understood Parkes's concerns but suggested that perhaps the British could go about their business in Wuchang and Hankow while he, and the army under Li Xiucheng that was soon to arrive, could take the third city in the nexus, Hanyang. Parkes said absolutely not, for they were all commercially linked (and though Elgin's treaty specified only that the British could trade in Hankow, Parkes liked to think of "Hankow" as encompassing all three of the cities). "The rebels could not take any one of these cities," he insisted, "without destroying the trade of the whole emporium." The Brave King reluctantly agreed, and told Parkes he would wait for the rest of his army to arrive "and then be guided by circumstances as to his next operations." But after Parkes departed he was left unsure whether to take on the Anqing siege forces from the rear with no support, or to stay with the original plan and strike at Hankow in defiance of Parkes's warning. As the latter option had now become a matter of foreign relations, he had to send a courier back to the capital in Nanjing to get instructions.[31] And so the initiative won by his sprint to Huangzhou began to leach away. The imperial cavalry that had chased him across Anhui had reached Wuchang and sounded the alarm. As his army dug itself in at Huangzhou, waiting for instructions that would take months to arrive, the imperial defenders of Wuchang and Hankow were calling up reinforcements and sharpening their swords to prepare for a rebel attack they now knew full well was coming.

Meanwhile, downriver in Anqing the garrison was holding on into its eighth month of siege. The pitched battles around Tongcheng to the north and Qimen to the south were so far away as to be invisible to them. Where they stood, everything was quiet. Zeng Guoquan's lines of vallation had grown to surround the entire city on its landward sides with a sequence of walls and moats about two miles from the city walls, forming what was effectively a new fortress on the outside, engulfing the fortress of Anqing within. The naval forces that patrolled the river just out of sight completed the encirclement.

The population within the city was on rations, but generous ones: a catty of rice (about a pound and a third, providing more than 2,000 calories) per day, and the residents had vegetables from the gardens they were growing, along with any small animals they could catch. Parkes stopped through on his way down to Nanjing just after visiting the Brave King and noted that although they looked a little "pinched," they were healthy and visibly content. They expressed no particular urgency about being rescued and asked him if the Brave King was planning to attack Hankow. ("I replied that I believed he would avoid that port," reported Parkes.) They also asked him, when he got to Nanjing, to please tell Hong Rengan to send them rice, cooking oil, and salt. And it was on that request that the anxiety behind their smiles began to show. For after Parkes reembarked on his steamship, they sent messengers after him to press him with a handful of gold bangles in hopes of ensuring his goodwill. Insulted that they should think he could be bought, Parkes refused the gifts with an angry burst of indignation, and nobody visited his ship again.[32] When the rebel kings down in Nanjing later asked him if a British ship might carry supplies up to Anqing for them, he told them it couldn't possibly be done and offered them a stern lecture on "the rights and duties of neutrality."[33]

But even without Parkes's help, the Anqing garrison had other avenues of supply. A steady traffic of foreign steamships was now beginning to navigate the river on their way up to Hankow, and some of those ships were perfectly happy to drop anchor outside Anqing's southern gate (facing the river, out of sight and range of the siege forces) to unload food and weapons at inflated prices for the soldiers who came out to trade with them. There was nothing Zeng Guofan's naval blockades could do to stop the vessels without violating the new treaty, and so, after firing a desultory shot or two across the bow, his patrols had to let the foreign-flagged ships go where they might, and the smugglers made good business of it at Anqing.

In addition to the foreign ships, which supplied them on a larger scale, on a more intimate level there was actually a market outside the walls. The siege had been at a deadlock for so long that this market had sprung up between the defenders and the besiegers, where the prisoners inside could buy some of their necessities from the very people who were imprisoning them.[34] This was partly due to financial problems on Zeng Guofan's side; the Hunan Army was nine months behind in meeting its payroll, which meant that its soldiers wanted money just as much as the people inside the city wanted food.[35] But it also reflected the reality that both sides of the siege were from the same homes and similar backgrounds; here at this city in Anhui province, there were as many men from Hunan inside fighting for the rebels as there were outside on the imperial side besieging it. It was simply a matter of where they had cast their loyalties in the early days of the war, on which side they had staked their futures. Otherwise they were as close to brethren as strangers in China could get. They spoke the same dialects, came from the same regions. In the absence of strict orders from their officers to attack—which would come in time, but not yet—the soldiers on each side held their ground and watched out for the others with wary eyes.

Li Xiucheng's army didn't show up in April as expected. After retreating from the valley abutting Qimen in December, he steered wide of Zeng Guofan's forces and relied on the other Taiping armies in southern Anhui to keep the Hunan Army's leader bottled up, in hopes that with enough harassment Zeng would call off the siege and pull the Anqing forces south for his own protection. With Zeng Guofan trapped, the Loyal King set his sights westward toward Jiangxi and Hubei, where the hundreds of thousands of promised recruits lay. His route meandered in a rough semicircle down through southern Anhui below Zeng Guofan, then west into Jiangxi below Lake Poyang, and finally up into the province of Hubei toward Wuchang, where the Brave King was waiting for him.

He was out of his natural domain. This part of the empire was the Brave King's territory; the Loyal King's place was in the east. And down below the river, where he was, most of the towns were under imperial control, even if weakly guarded. So his army had to fight its way through, siege after siege, darting from one town to the next, threading a needle back and forth along the network of fortified settlements to gather provisions and horses. Zeng Guofan had no forces to spare to chase after him, so the towns fell before Li Xiucheng's army one after the other, mostly with ease. But it was still a slow progress, and by April, when the Brave King expected him at Wuchang, his army was still down deep in Jiangxi province, more than two hundred miles to the south of where it was supposed to be.

It was a strange journey, and his own recollections of it were almost mystical. In early April, his army arrived at the Gan River, which cuts through Jiangxi province from south to north. The river was cold and swollen with snowmelt, and his army had no boats with which to cross, so they could move no farther to the west. There were enemy militias on the other bank, and scouts spotted imperial gunboats patrolling the river. So he marched his men south along the riverbank but still could find no crossing. Then one day, as if by an act of God, the waters suddenly dried up. His army crossed the river on foot.[36]

As he later explained the tardiness of his movements, he felt a certain duty to the people they encountered along the way. In early May his forces mustered in the city of Ruizhou, still more than a hundred and fifty miles from Wuchang. Though he wanted to move on, the people at Ruizhou asked him to stay. He found that his reputation as a leader was known even in this region deep in the center of the empire (the phenomenon was confirmed by several independent accounts of the era). In a time of lawlessness, his presence projected order and security. It was an attractive force, and the promised recruits came to him. As he waited at Ruizhou, some 300,000 new followers came to him as the weeks passed, and by the time he moved again northward toward Wuchang, his army had grown many times over.[37] But the new followers were untrained and had only the weapons they had brought with them from their farms. Also, as Zeng Guofan knew, the larger the army, the greater the challenge of feeding and training it.

The strangeness pervaded his dealings with the enemy as well. Some of his men captured an imperial commander on the way to Ruizhou, defending the Moon Ridge Pass, and they brought him along as a prisoner. At Ruizhou, they brought him before Li Xiucheng to be punished. But Li, after talking to the man, decided that he was too talented to waste by execution, and he invited him to join the Taiping. The officer refused, saying that as a prisoner "he was no longer master of his own wishes." Moved by the man's loyalty, Li let him go free and gave him 60 taels of traveling money to return to his own side. He refused to take the money. Departing from the Taiping camp, he made his way back across Jiangxi to rejoin the imperial forces under Zeng Guofan's general, Zuo Zongtang. But in a war with little forgiveness, this officer had already used up his allotment. When he returned to his own side, he was beheaded as a traitor.[38]

At the head of his multitudes, Li Xiucheng finally arrived outside Wuchang in June, two months late for his rendezvous. Communication across the river had proven nearly impossible, and Li Xiucheng still expected to find the Brave King ensconced in Hankow on the northern bank, ready to mount a joint attack on Wuchang and then head downriver toward Anqing. What he learned instead was that his counterpart had left without waiting for support, and—worse by far—he hadn't secured Hankow. By that time, the imperial-held cities around Wuchang had enjoyed three full months of warning to call up reserves, and they were heavily defended.

With vast numbers of untrained men, Li Xiucheng didn't dare to approach any closer than the outskirts of the county. The Brave King had left behind a garrison in Huangzhou to coordinate with Li Xiucheng when he arrived at Wuchang, but the river was so well controlled by Zeng Guofan's navy that it turned out to be impossible to get letters across. In desperation, Li Xiucheng had to ask the new British consul at Hankow to deliver a letter for him to the garrison at Huangzhou. In that letter, Li Xiucheng told them he had only the haziest of details of the Brave King's operations north of the river, and he asked for immediate information so he could plan his own army's movements accordingly. The British consul kept the letter as a souvenir and never delivered it.[39]

With no reply from the forces on the northern bank and no information about the movements of the Brave King in Anhui, Li Xiucheng was left with no role to play in the larger campaign. He couldn't remain where he was, because he didn't feel confident his untested army could take Wuchang, and word came from the east that Bao Chao's army was coming for him. He envisioned a disastrous slaughter if Bao Chao's crack veterans should catch up to his inexperienced, ill-equipped recruits. So at the end of June, he abandoned the western campaign and took his enormous army of new followers down out of Hubei and back toward the safety of his own territory in the east. Bao Chao's army followed in pursuit, but Li Xiucheng's God was still with him. The imperials nearly caught his army at a small tributary near the Gan, but a great wind came up just after the Loyal King's men swam across, blowing so strongly and fiercely that no boats could cross the river for four days, and by the time Bao Chao's men could resume their chase, the Loyal King's army was already far ahead of them and the pursuit was hopeless. Leaving behind garrisons to hold the string of cities he had conquered along the way, Li Xiucheng retraced his jagged route back through Jiangxi and across southern Anhui and finally divided his army into two columns to enter the eastern province of Zhejiang, taking advantage of the vulnerability of its capital city, Hangzhou, while Zeng Guofan's forces were tightening ever more closely around Anqing behind him.

When Li Xiucheng had failed to materialize in April, the Brave King had acted alone. There was no response yet from Nanjing to approve an attack on Hankow with its British presence, so he decided to leave a garrison at Huangzhou and take his best troops downriver to attack the Anqing siege forces himself, without the support of the Loyal King's army on which he had planned. On April 27, he arrived at the Jixian Pass at the head of 30,000 troops, to reclaim his city. Scaring the outnumbered Hunan Army troops into the cover of their dense ring of defensive works, his men began the process of building yet another set of fortifications outside Zeng Guoquan's encirclement, effectively containing the besiegers from the outside. A British naval officer from his ship's deck noted this "strange sight" unfolding as the rebel and imperial forces arrayed themselves in concentric rings—the Brave King's army in a wide perimeter, surrounding Zeng Guoquan's siege forces, which in turn surrounded the walled city of Anqing, with the rebel garrison and civilian population inside at its core. The Brave King's men built a series of heavy wooden stockade forts at the Jixian Pass and set up eighteen more stockades on either side of Waternut Lake, which bounded the city on its eastern side and marked the endpoint of Zeng Guoquan's encirclement. Taking nominal command of the lake, the rebels built a series of pontoons and makeshift rafts and began ferrying emergency supplies across to the city.[40]

After three days of hard attacks, however, the Brave King's men failed to break through Zeng Guoquan's main defensive works, with their high walls and deep moats. They could not advance inward to open the siege. But they couldn't move north either, for there was one more layer in the radiating system of encirclements—one far out of the view of anyone watching from the river. Even as he threatened dominance over Zeng Guoquan's siege forces inside the Jixian Pass, the Brave King was himself cut off from outside support by the continued presence of Duolonga's vicious imperial cavalry thirty miles to his north, the same force that had prevented his attempt to drive straight down on Anqing back in November. Duolonga's cavalry blocked the passage between his army at Anqing and the Taiping-held city of Tongcheng, which was the first step on the line of communication and reinforcement leading back toward the rebel capital at Nanjing. Unable to break the siege alone, and with no support from Li Xiucheng's army on the Yangtze's southern bank, the Brave King turned out to be less the savior of Anqing than the latest entrant in the grand game of envelopment and strangulation.

On May 1, hope arrived for the Brave King when an army of 20,000 Taiping reinforcements under Hong Rengan's command reached Tongcheng. This was the end of the journey that had begun back in February when William Muirhead had watched him leave the capital. The orders that had sent him into the field had come on the heels of the Brave King's first failure to break the cavalry lines at Tongcheng, and Hong Rengan's military role was clear—to support the Brave King in defeating those forces. But he had come with some reluctance, for he suspected that politics were at work behind him. In the orders sending him out of the capital, he sensed the jealousy of the other members of Hong Xiuquan's family (especially Hong Xiuquan's son), who resented his enormous influence over the Heavenly King. In them he also sensed the resentment of the other kings, who had endured the hardships of the winter campaign while he enjoyed a sedentary life in the capital with his family, writing treatises on government and receiving foreign visitors.[41]

He had first gone south from Nanjing into Taiping-held regions of Anhui and Zhejiang to find soldiers and officers. It wasn't difficult for him to raise an army, because the tide ran with such strength in the rebels' favor.

Even Zeng Guofan expressed amazement at the sheer numbers of Taiping troops at this time, who seemed to keep appearing without cease. After the fall of the siege camps and the capture of the major cities in Jiangsu the previous year, Zeng estimated that the Taiping armies had grown more than tenfold, and he complained that whenever the militias and imperial armies crumbled, the majority of their broken ranks chose to join the rebels.[42] For the Shield King (like the Loyal King in Jiangxi) it was less a matter of recruitment than of gathering. By the time he returned north of the river and marched westward to reinforce the Brave King's position at Tongcheng, he had under his command an army nearly half the size of Zeng Guofan's total Hunan force.

Hong Rengan was a different model of the scholar turned general. He did not have Zeng Guofan's strategic sense, nor his instinct for discipline and order. But he had faith in the power of ideas and composed a series of poems while on campaign to inspire his followers. "A brush stands erect like a weapon," he wrote upon receiving the Heavenly King's mandate. "It sweeps away the thousand armies, and what is left of their formations?"[43] Hong Rengan's campaign writings marked a sharp contrast with the image he projected to his foreign missionary friends. Gone was the genial, self-deprecating preacher. Replacing him was the voice of a man who would lead a nation. In one poem he wrote of the "vile stench of the Tartars" that darkened the sky and asked "Who will renew Heaven and Earth and set right the universe?" The poem's conclusion projected sheer power:

My will upheaves the rivers and mountains. My heart desires action.
In my bosom I embrace the whole of the cosmos, swallowing even my anger.
I condemn the guilty. I console the people.
And on the day I return,
The grass and the woods will sing together,
To proclaim the grace of the dew and rain.[44]

On May 1, Hong Rengan's army took up positions outside Tongcheng and sent scouts through the hills to make contact with the Brave King's encampment at the Jixian Pass.[45] On May 6, they divided into two columns and advanced south. Both columns were beaten back savagely by Duolonga's cavalry. It was at that point that the Brave King, hearing that his support forces were blocked at Tongcheng, made perhaps his worst mistake of the entire campaign. He left 12,000 men behind to hold the stockades at Jixian Pass and Waternut Lake and withdrew with the rest of his men northward to attack Duolonga's cavalry from below, in coordination with a new attack by Hong Rengan from above. He didn't expect to be gone long. At the dawn of May 24, their combined forces attacked Duolonga in three columns, two from the north and one from the south, but a spy had revealed the plan, and they fell into an ambush. Duolonga sent a detachment of cavalry around to the Brave King's rear to fall on his troops from behind, scrambling the attack and sending him north to Tongcheng in a chaotic retreat with heavy casualties. The rout severed the Brave King from his 12,000 men at Anqing and left them without reinforcement or the direct leadership of their general.

The defeat also marked the end of Hong Rengan's first foray into military command. He had been absent during Harry Parkes's visits to the capital, the second of which had been so high-handed and unnerving that the Heavenly King had decided he could no longer abide the Shield King's absence. And so Hong Rengan's military failure at Tongcheng happened to coincide with the arrival of orders from Nanjing recalling him to the capital to take charge again of the deteriorating state of Taiping diplomacy.[46]

After the Brave King's botched division of his forces, the 12,000 soldiers holding the stockades—4,000 men at Jixian Pass and 8,000 at Waternut Lake—were left with only the supplies they had carried in with them. They still outnumbered Zeng Guoquan's siege forces, but only slightly, and imperial reinforcements were on their way. When Zeng Guofan first learned that the "Four-Eyed Dog" had arrived at Anqing, he ordered Bao Chao to ferry his army across the Yangtze River from the south to help his brother hold out against the larger rebel force. After mustering on the Yangtze's northern bank at the end of May, Bao Chao's army had marched through the mountains from the west toward Anqing. The day after the Brave King withdrew to Tongcheng, they swept in and fell hard on the four orphaned rebel stockades at Jixian Pass. It took only a little over a week to break them. On June 7 (about the time Li Xiucheng finally showed up outside of Wuchang), the first three stockades at Jixian Pass surrendered, and Bao Chao's men killed all 3,000 men inside them.[47] The fourth stockade held out a few days longer before meeting the same fate. In all, Bao Chao had his troops keep only one prisoner alive from the stockades: the senior Taiping commander, a veteran officer who was beloved of his men and invaluable to the Brave King. Bao Chao spared him so he would still be alive when they dismembered him under the Anqing wall for the benefit of the garrison inside.[48]

While Bao Chao's forces were breaking the stockades at Jixian Pass, Zeng Guoquan's forces concentrated on the larger body of troops in the eighteen stockades guarding the water passage across Waternut Lake. Those stockades held out longer than the ones at the pass, but they finally ran out of food at the beginning of July and signaled their willingness to surrender.[49] Zeng Guoquan was never quite as hardened as his older brother, however, and he worried that their offer to surrender might be a ruse of some kind. To ease his concerns, one of his battalion commanders suggested getting the rebels to send out their weapons first. Guoquan agreed, anxiously telling the officer to arrange it quickly. The next day, July 7, the 8,000 rebel soldiers in the Waternut Lake stockades surrendered all of their weapons: six thousand foreign rifles, eight thousand long spears, a thousand gingals, eight hundred Ming dynasty matchlocks, and two thousand horses.

Zeng Guoquan had no idea what to do with the prisoners, who were almost as numerous as his entire siege force and (to him) frighteningly tough. The same battalion commander who had arranged the surrender said it would be best to kill them. "But even then we need some kind of plan," Guoquan told him. So the commander came up with one: to open the gates of the camp and bring the prisoners in ten at a time, so they could be beheaded in batches. "In half a day, we could be done," he thought. Zeng Guoquan couldn't stomach the plan, so he left it to the commander, who went back to his camp, made preparations, and then, by his own account, supervised the butchering of eight thousand prisoners in the course of a single day, starting at seven in the morning and finishing by the light of lanterns just after the sun went down that night.[50]

Zeng Guofan was delighted by his brother's success, which gave him hope that Anqing might fall at last. He wrote several letters to Guoquan over the following days—first more sanguine, suggesting his brother find a way to bury the thousands of corpses or else pile them onto old boats and send them down the river so the stink wouldn't bring disease into his camp.[51] But as he realized that the slaughter was weighing heavily on Guoquan's conscience, his letters became more reassuring. On July 12, he tried to put his brother's mind at ease by telling him that if Confucius were alive, he too would say that it was right to exterminate the rebels.[52] By July 19, he sounded almost exasperated with his brother's misgivings. "Since you lead an army, you should take the killing of rebels as your purpose," he wrote. "So why regret killing a lot of them?"[53]

But the siege still ground on. Even as Bao Chao and Zeng Guoquan fought off the Taiping relief armies (and shut down the markets outside), foreign ships were still bringing supplies to the rebel garrison at Anqing from the riverside. A British emissary (likely Parkes) was supposed to visit Zeng Guofan's camp in May, and Zeng planned to "treat him like a person, not treat him as a devil" in hopes of getting him to stop the deliveries. By early June, the emissary still hadn't come, and Zeng wrote in a letter home that there was now a daily traffic of foreign ships up and down the river. One had landed just the previous week to deliver salt and oil to the garrison. "Here we suffer through this siege," he wrote, "but the rebels are still being supplied without a break."[54] Two days later he wrote to Guoquan that if the foreign ships didn't stop bringing supplies to Anqing, there would be no way to master the city. Meanwhile, his own troops' food supplies on the south of the river were vulnerable, and he saw no good way to force his lines open again. "If the foreign ships can be stopped, we will see our day of conquest at Anqing," he wrote. "But if they can't be stopped, there is nothing we can do."[55]

By mid-June, his patience finally ran out after he heard a report from one of his brother's spies that the most recent ship had unloaded nearly two hundred tons of rice at Anqing, enough to feed its population for more than a week.[56] Despairing of the foreign emissary's arrival, Zeng wrote to the governor-general in Wuchang to complain, and the governor-general forwarded his complaint to Beijing. At the same time, Zeng Guofan ordered his gunboats to begin escorting all foreign ships that passed Anqing on the river. The problem was that his captains had no idea what to do if a ship under foreign flag should refuse their orders and drop anchor outside the rebel city.[57] Sinking a foreign merchant vessel could mean starting a new war with the British.

In this case, the nascent Office of Foreign Affairs in Beijing worked like a charm. Zeng Guofan's complaint made its way to Prince Gong in Beijing, who on July 18 wrote to Frederick Bruce to protest the landing of foreign ships at Anqing. Prince Gong claimed the right of imperial forces to board any foreign ships that tried to land in rebel territory and, if warranted, to seize their cargoes and arrest their crews. He asked Bruce to provide a certificate in Chinese and English from the British authorities in Shanghai authorizing the Qing government to search ships under foreign flag. Bruce didn't actually believe that foreign ships were supplying the rebels, but on the chance that they were, and given his existing feelings about the rebels, he didn't think that it was a proper business for the British to be involved in. He also worried that such smuggling might lead the imperial government to institute a full blockade of the river at the expense of regular trade. So he took action. Grumbling that "nothing is so difficult as restraining foreigners in a country where the Government is unable or unwilling to assert its own rights," on July 23, Bruce wrote to the British consul at Shanghai and told him to warn the foreign merchants that the imperials were planning to attack any ship that tried to run their blockade of Anqing, and if that should happen, the British navy would neither protect them nor demand any compensation for the damages.[58] The shipments stopped.

By late summer, Zeng Guofan knew from captured letters that the population inside Anqing was finally running out of food.[59] In the meantime, he himself was barely holding on. He had survived being cut off at Qimen back in April only because Zuo Zongtang had managed to reconquer Jingdezhen and reopen his supply lines. But for the sake of his own safety—and to maintain closer communications with his brother—he abandoned Qimen in early May. At the same time he sent Bao Chao across the river, he also moved his headquarters to a large boat on the southern bank of the Yangtze at Dongliu, just twenty-five miles up from Anqing. At Dongliu he was protected by his navy, he could keep up direct communications with his brother at Anqing, and he was free from dependence on the vulnerable overland routes that supplied Qimen.

Writing home in the early summer, he revealed just how personal the campaign had become. "The destiny of our family, and the security of the empire, both depend on whether or not we recapture Anqing," he wrote in a letter home.[60] More than ever, he had come to identify his entire life and career, as well as the future of his family, with the single goal of recovering the city of Anqing for the empire. If the empire survived, his family would prosper. If it fell, his family would be lost as well. There was no longer any distinction in his mind between the prestige of his brothers and sons and the survival of the Qing; their fates were one and the same, and without a victory at Anqing, all would be lost. As the southern Taiping forces began to peel off, unexpectedly disappearing overnight from towns they had been holding, it became clear that Li Xiucheng was planning something in Zhejiang province to the east, but Zeng held to his siege with a monomaniacal intensity. In midsummer, the emperor ordered him to send Zuo Zongtang from Jingdezhen to help defend Zhejiang's capital, but he refused. The emperor also ordered him to send one of his admirals to the southern province of Guangdong, and he refused that as well.[61] He could see the noose tightening around Anqing and didn't want to let go.

Meanwhile, in the heat of an extraordinarily brutal summer, the Brave King tried one last time to lift the siege. Unable to break the ranks of cavalry below Tongcheng, he took the remains of his army, along with the forces left to him by the now-departed Hong Rengan, on one last far-ranging march in a grand circle to the northwest, then down through the mountains along the border with Hubei and back inward along the northern bank of the river below Duolonga's line of defense, a circuit of well over two hundred miles that on August 24 let him back in again through the Jixian Pass, where his men reoccupied their stockades and prepared for an all-out attack on Zeng Guoquan's siege works from behind.

As the broiling summer came to a close, the fighting at Jixian Pass built to a frenzied crescendo. Calculation and patience gave way to desperation: the Brave King's to rescue his family from the city, the garrison's to get out before it starved to death. To prevent an escape by water, Zeng Guofan's naval forces portaged some of their gunboats from the river to Waternut Lake and now patrolled there, blasting away at anyone who tried to flee the eastern gate and get away by raft.[62] August ended with a cacophony of gunfire and thundering cannon, and rising above it all were the hair-raising cries of the rebels as they threw themselves against Zeng Guoquan's entrenchments, row upon row of them—the garrison pouring out from the city from one side, the relief forces raining down from the other—the living clambering over the dead even as terrified gunners blasted new openings through their ranks, through seven days and nights of bloodshed and confusion, of blind panic and guttering swords, until on the night of September 3 it all suddenly ended, and the deafening explosions and screams of the rebels gave way to a quiet glow of licking flames north of the city, which grew and rose and finally mounted into the night sky with a roar as the Brave King, giving up once and for all, set fire to his stockades at Jixian Pass and withdrew, leaving Anqing to its fate.[63]

M ost of the surviving garrison soldiers appear to have escaped the city that final night, through a tunnel they had been digging under the wall. The burning stockades to the north may have proved a helpful distraction, though at least one source claims that their escape was by prior arrangement with someone on the imperial side, in exchange for handing over the city without a fight. In any case, they left behind all of the civilians, along with a few cadaverous gunners on the wall, chained to their cannons. When the Hunan Army entered the city on September 5, it was no longer defended.[64]

The depths of misery inside were beyond anything even the hardened veterans had imagined. After the foreign ships had stopped coming in the early summer, and after the stockades at Waternut Lake had been broken in early July, there had been no more shipments of food into the city at all. By the end of the summer, the daily rice rations were long gone. The vegetables and weeds from the gardens had been eaten. All of the animals, even the rats, were gone, and there was nothing left to sustain the starving thousands inside. Or, almost nothing. The victors who entered the city on September 5 discovered, to their horror, that the markets of Anqing had never closed. The price for human meat had reached half a tael per catty by the end, or about thirty-eight cents a pound.[65]

Already back in the summer, Zeng Guofan had written to his brother about what they should do when Anqing finally surrendered. "When we conquer the city, the proper thing to do will be to kill a lot of people," he wrote to Guoquan. "We shouldn't let compassion lead us to err in the grand scheme of things. What do you think?"[66] Loving the people did not mean loving the ones who sided with the rebels. All told, about sixteen thousand people are thought to have survived the siege of Anqing, most if not all of them civilians. The reports of what happened to them afterward differ primarily as to whether or not Zeng Guofan's officers first separated out the women before they killed everyone who was left.[67]

CHAPTER 10

HEAVEN AND EARTH

It was a time of strange astrological portents. In July 1861, a giant comet with a brilliant tail appeared in the northwestern sky and struck fear into the residents of Beijing, who took it as an omen that the emperor would never come back to them.[1] Then, at the dawn of September 5, the sun and the moon rose together, and the five known planets stood in a line across the sky like a string of pearls.[2] Watchers across China rose early to try to see the rare alignment. Some said it was a sign that the dynasty would be restored to power, but at least one observer wondered what Heaven really meant by the display. "I look up with reverence to Heaven above," he wrote, "and don't know whether to feel encouragement or fear."[3] Zeng Guofan himself took the alignment of planets as an auspicious sign, and indeed Anqing would fall within the day.[4] But even as he mulled over the mystery of Heaven's will, the news of the emperor's death was already speeding on its way to him in the hands of a courier charging southward on horseback from Beijing.

Xianfeng died on August 22, 1861, barely a month past his thirtieth birthday. The proximate cause may have been tuberculosis, but in a more poetic sense he died of shame and disgrace, never having returned to the capital from which he had fled. "Heaven has collapsed," wrote Zeng Guofan when the news reached him on September 14, "the earth is split open."[5] It shattered his spirit completely. He lay awake that night, thinking about the fate of this unfortunate Son of Heaven. "My emperor, from the time he came to the throne until today, over the course of twelve years, never knew a day when he wasn't consumed by worry over our dangers," wrote Zeng in reflection. "Now Anqing is finally conquered, and the longhairs have begun to weaken. It looks as if the war has reached a turning point. But my emperor did not live long enough to hear the report of victory, so his dejection and melancholy will follow him into eternity. What a terrible agony that is for me, and for all of his ministers."[6]

The untimely death of Xianfeng bode ill for the dynasty as a whole, for a monarch's health and longevity were clear signs of Heaven's pleasure with his rule. The Manchu ruling house had rested its claim to legitimacy in large part on having produced two of the longest-reigning emperors in China's entire history, including Xianfeng's great-grandfather Qianlong, who had governed for an unprecedented sixty-three years in the eighteenth century. So it was deeply unsettling that Xianfeng should die of disease only eleven years into his reign, while he was still a very young man. Even more disturbing, however, was that the dynasty's continuance into the future depended on the throne being passed down from father to son, and as it happened, Xianfeng was nearly infertile.[7] In spite of the constant attentions of his eighteen concubines and wives through his years in the pleasure gardens of the Summer Palace, Xianfeng had managed to father just one son who could inherit his throne. That son was, in August 1861, only five years old.

The Taiping were overjoyed by the news of Xianfeng's death, which came to them by way of a foreign visitor from Shanghai. Hong Rengan, recently returned from the field, wasted no time issuing a proclamation attributing the emperor's untimely death to his moral depravity. "Xianfeng, the demonic imbecile, was a gambler and a drunkard," he wrote in one of his more venomous moments. "He exhausted the treasury, squandering it like dirt and sand. The Summer Palace was his resort of debauchery, in which he founded a male section for sexual perversion. Now the resort has become a pile of ashes and [Xianfeng] himself has fallen into Hell." As to the child heir, Hong Rengan wrote that Xianfeng "left behind a little demon who is several years old and will find it difficult to continue the demon rule." The iron was hot, and the end of the dynasty was at hand. "This is precisely the time for us to seize the opportunity to uphold Heaven," he declared, "and render ourselves not unworthy in our role as heroes of the world."[8]

Hong Rengan's charges against Xianfeng weren't entirely his own invention; he was partly channeling currents of rumor that had reached a flood crest over the preceding year, namely, that the many disasters which plagued the empire had been caused by the moral corruption of Xianfeng and his Manchu court, who clearly had angered Heaven and forfeited their divine mandate to rule. A doctor attached to the British Legation in Beijing reported several months prior to the emperor's death that the elites of the capital appeared to have already given up on the Qing dynasty. Those he spoke to weren't rebel sympathizers by any stretch, but they did tell him that "they profess no love for or confidence in the stability of the present dynasty." "They say that it was once a good one, that it has lasted two hundred years," he reported, "but that the virtues and military energy that once characterised it have become effete through luxury and debauchery."[9] Such "luxury and debauchery" typified a popular view of Xianfeng's life—that he whiled away his days carelessly, sequestered inside the Summer Palace with his concubines, as the empire outside crumbled. From that point of view, the British and French destruction of the Summer Palace was an act not of imperialism but of divine judgment.

But those Beijing elites did not (like Zeng Guofan) perceive the end of the dynasty to be necessarily a tragedy; it was simply the natural course of the world that dynasties should come to their ends and give way to others stronger. "They consider that its time has come," the doctor wrote, "and that by Divine fiat it must fall, its condition being now so prostrate as hardly to admit of permanent resuscitation. That prostration, they say, is simply the moral deterioration of the elements composing it."[10] Harry Parkes heard a similar refrain from the imperial officials he spoke with during his Yangtze voyage. Even the governor-general in Wuchang, Parkes reported, one of the most powerful men in the entire Qing civil administration, "seemed to see in its duration, which is above the average of former Dynasties, a sufficient reason for its decay." He told Parkes that "the fault of the Government lay . . . in the utter falseness of the system, and it was vain to look for reformation in the provinces until this had first been effected in Peking." That governor-general was only one of many officials in the Yangtze region who voiced similar views, and Parkes reflected that "it is one of the unfortunate signs of the period that so many of the authorities in high position are ready to admit a ruinous condition of affairs, but can suggest no remedy, nor account for the result in any other way than on fatalist principles."[11]

The Taiping, who were just coming to terms with their horrible loss at Anqing, weren't yet in a position to march on Beijing, but the death of the Manchu emperor gave them renewed energy as they recalibrated to account for the defeat. The Brave King was cut off with the remnants of his army in northern Anhui, but Li Xiucheng's forces now marched almost unopposed in the east. Before departing on the failed western campaign, Li had conquered most of Jiangsu province west and north of Shanghai; now, returning from his journeys through Jiangxi and Hubei, he turned his army's attention to Zhejiang province to its south. After Jiangsu and Anhui, Zhejiang was the third most densely populated province in the empire, holding twenty-six million people—almost the full contemporary population of the United States—in an area slightly smaller than Kentucky.

Li Xiucheng planned his conquest of Zhejiang province with increasing independence from Hong Rengan. As prime minister, Hong Rengan was supposed to coordinate between the kings and give approval to their movements. But Hong Rengan didn't want Zhejiang, at least not yet; he wanted Anqing, and even after the city's surrender he still believed Li Xiucheng and the Brave King could mount a new campaign to take it back from Zeng Guofan. Control of the Yangtze was still the key to his strategic vision of consolidating the southern empire, and he was loath to let it slip away from him. He wrote to Li Xiucheng from Nanjing that autumn, begging him to leave off his conquest of Zhejiang and take his army back up the river to continue the fight against Zeng Guofan. "From ancient times," Hong Rengan wrote to him, "the Yangtze has been described as a serpent, with its head at Hubei, its body in Anhui, and its tail in Jiangnan. We don't have Hubei, and if we let go of Anhui as well, the serpent will be sundered, and the tail won't survive for long on its own."[12] Li Xiucheng replied that the Anhui capital, Anqing, was now hopeless, and he declined to leave Zhejiang.[13] Hong Rengan was furious, but there was nothing more he could do.

Hong Rengan's description of the Yangtze as a living creature with its head near the Hubei capital of Wuchang and its tail near Shanghai was an ancient military tenet (one to which Zeng Guofan subscribed as well) that emphasized not just the upstream advantage of Wuchang and Anqing but also their control over vast areas of inland agricultural production that had been far more important to earlier dynasties than China's pirate-ridden coast.[14] That old tenet could not, however, account for the unprecedented economic development of Shanghai and the other coastal treaty ports in the nineteenth century, nor for the new importance of seagoing trade in procuring weapons and supplies. Li Xiucheng recognized that there were far greater financial and military resources to be won in the east now than there had ever been in ancient times, and so, despite Hong Rengan's efforts to steer him back to Anhui, he held to his plan to consolidate the wealthy and populous eastern provinces, and as a consequence the overall momentum of the Taiping strategy shifted to the east.

Hong Rengan had returned from the failed Anqing campaign a different man from the one who had left. Some combination of the heady taste of command, his experience of military defeat at Tongcheng, and the continued absence of any meaningful foreign support for his movement released a darker side of his personality. He became more bitter in his propaganda against the Manchu government, more contentious with the other kings. And in his absence from the capital, there had—as he had feared—been a subtle but important restructuring. By the time he got back to Nanjing, an edict had circulated stating that the Shield King's seal was no longer needed for memorials to be forwarded to the Heavenly King, so he was no longer the exclusive mediator between Hong Xiuquan and the world outside.[15] The Heavenly King's son was now listed next to his father on edicts, putting him into a position above Hong Rengan. Hong Rengan remained the prime minister in charge of foreign relations, and he still controlled the governmental administration of the capital (the other kings came to his offices for audience, never the other way around), but he was no longer the unquestioned second in command of the movement. The demotion, however slight, rankled him, and the Loyal King's willingness to disregard his orders, even if only from a distance, suggested that the Shield King's position in the overall chain of command was no longer quite as certain as it had been.[16]

To outsiders, at least, Hong Rengan was still as impressive as ever. Robert Forrest, the British consular official who had come to Nanjing to round up the British mercenaries, spent several months living in a boat anchored on the Yangtze and met with Hong Rengan after his return from the field. He described Hong Rengan as "the most enlightened Chinaman I ever saw,"[17] and at one point pronounced that "If all Taipingdom was composed of such men, China would be theirs in a short time."[18] A Royal Artillery captain named Thomas Blakiston took down Forrest's words and used them as the basis of an influential book he published in London the following year titled *Five Months on the Yang-tsze,* which helped reintroduce the British reading public to the Shield King, reminding them of the enlightenment he might bring to a China under Taiping rule. The book was hardly a defense of the Taiping per se, and Forrest found much to regret in Nanjing; but he also saw no hope for the dynasty, whose corruption he called "a national dysentery."[19]

Forrest's judgment was that the only thing Britain could do was to stand back and let the war play itself out. The British must look to the big picture—the "'Great Whole,' in the vortex of sublunary affairs"—in which questions of temporary injury to foreign trade, or the spread of Christianity were meaningless. China had to go through its own turmoil, he argued, so that a new order might finally emerge, and "Heaven forbid that England, or France, should ever make confusion worse confounded by interfering in the internal struggle now raging!" Although Forrest wasn't an overt partisan, he did admit that his affections lay with the rebels, who had treated him with "civility" and "actual courtesy" during his stay in Nanjing. "It is impossible to live among a set of people and not take an interest in them," he told Blakiston, "and in a certain way to like them."[20]

But there had been several diplomatic setbacks during Hong Rengan's absence from the capital. The most troubling were the insupportable demands of Hope and Parkes: that the Taiping must stay thirty miles from Shanghai, and perhaps the other ports as well, for the year. But even beyond those official contacts, some of the Taiping's strongest supporters in the missionary community had, while Hong Rengan was away on campaign, given up on their plans to live in Nanjing. Joseph Edkins came for his first visit to the capital in March, just after Hong Rengan's departure. Edkins's initial impressions of Nanjing were as positive as those of Griffith John had been the previous fall. He wrote back to his wife, Jane, that the rebel capital was "beautiful for situation" and the Heavenly King seemed to be "a persuadable man on religious points."[21]

For almost trivial reasons, however, Edkins's plan to move to Nanjing fell through. The Heavenly King granted him a house in Nanjing for his mission, but it was small—too small for two families—and Edkins and Jane couldn't find another missionary couple who were willing to live in such close quarters with them. With Hong Rengan away in the field, there was nobody in the capital to advocate for better accomodations on their behalf. Edkins couldn't bear to leave his young wife in Shanghai, but if they lived in Nanjing together without any other missionaries around, there would be nobody to keep her company or protect her when he was out preaching. "Nobody thinks it would be right," wrote Jane to her parents back home. "I could not at any time long be left alone." Also, her health was frail, and Joseph Edkins (unlike many of their missionary colleagues) was no doctor. For her part, she worried that her constant need for his company "would necessarily fetter him in his work."

So they put aside their plan to live in Nanjing with the rebels and decided instead to go to Tianjin. There, they could work with the British troops who still garrisoned the city, and, as it was now a treaty port, they could rent housing as they saw fit. Jane would have no shortage of English company, and eventually, they hoped, they might be allowed to set up a mission in nearby Beijing. But in the end those hopes would come to naught when Jane died of heat and diarrhea that summer at the age of twenty-two. Her husband dressed her in her wedding gown, and buried her in Tianjin.[22]

Griffith John also decided against living in Nanjing during those months. He made a second visit to the rebel capital in April 1861, while Hong Rengan and Li Xiucheng were both afield with their armies. He found the city to be quiet and ghostly, nearly empty of ordinary people. All the stores had been closed at the Heavenly King's orders, to satisfy his rising paranoia that imperial spies were stealing into the city disguised as merchants. To Griffith John the people seemed fearful of their ruler, who was ever more capricious and volatile; most recently, a handful of store owners who ignored his order to close up shop had been summarily executed. Nevertheless, the Taiping leaders Griffith John met with were still welcoming to him, and told him they hoped he would stay and preach. But along with his uneasiness about the state of Nanjing, he worried about the hostility toward the rebels he sensed from the Shanghai foreign community. One shipper, representing many who blamed the rebels for interfering with the silk and tea trades, had refused to convey John's colleague Edkins to Nanjing, saying "he would do nothing to assist him to go among these 'worthless fellows.'" In the face of such attitudes, Griffith John worried that he would be without support or communication if he lived among the Taiping.

In the end, he opted instead to set up his mission in Hankow, the treaty port across from Wuchang which Hope and Parkes had opened in March 1861. By the time he arrived there by steamer in August, the siege of Anqing downriver was grinding to its end and Hankow was securely in imperial hands. It had a British consul (the same who had pocketed Li Xiucheng's letter), and it had regular mail service, which made it a much safer prospect for him than Nanjing. He did not, however, find the same openness and hospitality as in Nanjing, where the Heavenly King himself had given him an edict welcoming foreign missionaries. Hankow and Wuchang were dominated by Zeng Guofan's followers, and they—in contrast to the rebels—didn't appear to care for the foreign missionaries at all. Zeng Guofan had cast the struggle between the Qing and the Taiping as a war between native Confucianism and foreign Christianity—and from that point of view, the missionaries were preaching the doctrine of the rebels. For that reason, hatred of Christians was becoming a point of pride for the Hunanese. Griffith John got a taste of what his fellow missionaries would face in the provinces under Zeng Guofan's influence when he attended a breakfast at Hankow with an unnamed general from the Hunan Army. After bragging about "the military glory of Hunan, and the martial courage of the Hunan men," the general explained to Griffith John that "there was no danger of their ever believing in Jesus, or of His religion ever taking a deep root in that celebrated province."[23]

At least Issachar Roberts stayed on in Nanjing, living in his upstairs suite through the entire time Hong Rengan and the others were gone. The white-haired Baptist had become more confused in his position, though, and visitors reported that he still nurtured a grudge for having been forced to kneel in front of Hong Xiuquan (during what turned out to be the only time he was ever permitted an audience with the Heavenly King). He also complained that the Taiping leaders were unreceptive to his religious instruction.[24] Nevertheless, he continued to defend the rebels in the English-language press. In March 1861, a couple of weeks after Hong Rengan left to begin raising his army, Roberts wrote to *The North-China Herald* in Shanghai to repudiate those who claimed that the Taiping weren't able to govern and could only make war. "This is not the time to talk about peace," Roberts wrote. "Talk about peace to them before 'the devilish imps' are exterminated,—you might as well have talked to Jehu about peace before the house of Ahaz was exterminated."[25]

Roberts's apologia for the Taiping's continued war against the Qing dynasty sparked ridicule from the editors of the English-language papers, though often followed by backlash from his supporters. *The North-China Herald* published an editorial condemning him in September 1861, but then almost immediately printed a retraction of it after receiving, in the editors' words, "communications, which, we must confess, are much more in his favor than we supposed could possibly be the case."[26] The *China Mail* charged that Roberts viewed the rebels in a light "neither wise nor warrantable" and that he claimed for them "the same right and duty to exterminate their opponents as was possessed by the Jews under their theocracy."[27] But nevertheless they printed his letters in their entirety, and those letters made their way out into the English-speaking world. In the United States, especially, his letters found a warm reception and sparked widespread sympathy for the Taiping, because Issachar Roberts was one of their own.[28]

Roberts's vision was one of Old Testament fire and brimstone, with the Taiping as the agents of God's wrath. "A revolution, and especially civil war," he wrote to the *China Mail* in July 1861, "is and must always be unpleasant to the common people."[29] But behind the violence in China he saw a "higher power" at work. "God had not been an idle spectator of the [Taiping] movement," he wrote. "He has said, 'the nation and kingdom that will not serve me shall perish.'" What the world now saw unfolding in China, Roberts claimed, was nothing less than God's punishing vengeance against the Qing Empire—indeed, against all of the dynasties of China's history—who would not serve Him. As when Joshua destroyed the Canaanites, so, Roberts believed, were the Taiping serving Jehovah's will in laying ruin to the empire of the Manchus. "And in fact," he concluded, in one of the coldest rationales ever given for the war, "would it not be better in the highest sense of the word for half the nation to be exterminated, than to go on as they have been doing, if the other half would thereby learn righteousness!"

The five-year-old heir to the Qing imperial throne was the son of one of Xianfeng's concubines, a pretty young Manchu woman named Yehonala who had been chosen by Xianfeng to be his consort when she was just fifteen. At twenty she had borne him a son, and by chance that boy was one of only two of Xianfeng's children to survive longer than a day (the other, a girl, was ineligible to rule).[30] When the boy became heir apparent, the young Yehonala's status at court rose from third-tier imperial consort to mother of the reigning emperor, a rank to compare with that of the late emperor's wife, and she would thereafter be known in China and abroad by her title in that capacity: the Empress Dowager Cixi.[31] Along with Queen Victoria, the empress dowager would in time become one of the two most powerful women in the nineteenth-century world; but at the moment, her position as mother of the new emperor was still mainly one of prestige.

As for the real transmission of power, just before Xianfeng died he issued an edict naming his eight closest Manchu advisers—Sushun, Zaiyuan, Muyin, Duanhua, and four others—to be the regents for his heir. Traditionally, when a new emperor was too young to rule, power was entrusted to one or more regents, usually brothers or cousins of the previous emperor, who would govern on the youthful sovereign's behalf until he reached the age of majority. Such had been the case with two young emperors early in the dynasty, though the experience of those years had taught that regents were not, generally speaking, eager to give up power when the time came. Dark struggles had followed the coming of age of those early emperors. But thanks to the remarkably young age of Xianfeng's successor, Sushun and the other new regents could look forward to ruling the empire for at least a decade before the boy might challenge them.

These were the same advisers who had traveled with the emperor into exile, the same Manchu war hawks who so deeply resented the presence of Europeans in the empire. They dreamed of abrogating the new treaties and were suspicious of Prince Gong's apparent softness toward the foreigners. With their ascent to power, his plan for the new Office of Foreign Affairs—namely, to do everything possible to appease the Europeans while focusing the dynasty's remaining strength on fighting the Taiping—was thrown into question. For Zeng Guofan, however, their assumption of the reins of government bode very well, since his chief patron in the imperial court, Sushun, was the new regency's *primus inter pares*. In fact, the very edict of transition naming the imperial heir had been written in Sushun's hand; the Xianfeng emperor had been so weak on his deathbed (or so said the official records) that he'd been unable to write the edict himself and had instead dictated it to his most trusted adviser.[32]

The only check to the power of the new regents was the pair of empresses dowager: Yehonala and Xianfeng's widow. Before his death, Xianfeng had given each of them an imperial seal, which had to be stamped upon any edict sent out in the name of the new emperor for it to be legitimate. All such edicts would be composed by the regents, but the empresses dowager held an effective veto power by their possession of the seals. The elder empress proved compliant, as expected, but it soon became apparent that Yehonala did not intend to follow the regents without question. As she asserted her independence and threatened to withhold approval for their policy decisions, tensions began to mount between the all-male regency and the mother of the new emperor.

The tensions came to a head in late October, when the Xianfeng emperor's mortal remains were finally brought back to Beijing. It was a grand procession, with the emperor's body on a bier carried by 124 bearers. As the head of the regency, Sushun escorted the body, while the others went ahead in order to be in place to meet the funeral procession when it arrived at the capital. The two empresses dowager traveled with the forward party, escorting the boy emperor in a closed palanquin, the child sitting firmly (and symbolically) on his mother's lap. The other regents accompanied them, just in front. They arrived on November 1 to the greeting of a host of officials and soldiers dressed in the white color of mourning and throngs of curious watchers. It was a brilliant day, cool and clear, without a cloud in the sky.[33]

The empresses had one day in the capital before Sushun would arrive, and they worked quickly. Prince Gong came out to meet them as soon as they arrived at Beijing. He was accompanied by a detachment of body-guard troops. The regents who traveled in front of the empresses tried to block him from approaching the boy emperor, just as they had prevented him from holding audience with his brother in exile. But the capital was now Prince Gong's territory; he was popular for having restored order to Beijing after the war with Britain and France, and the city's reorganized garrison forces were loyal to him.[34] When the regents tried to prevent him from approaching the boy emperor, he threatened violence by his body-guard and forced his way through.

The empresses had been holding secret meetings for weeks with Prince Gong's younger brother at the hunting retreat, and the two parties—the empresses with their imperial seals and the prince with his influence in the capital—now followed a previously agreed plan. Prince Gong accompanied them into Beijing and stayed close by in their company. That afternoon, while Sushun was still en route with the late emperor's body, Prince Gong held an audience and read aloud an edict in the name of the child emperor, authorized by the seals of the empresses dowager, charging Sushun and the others with treason. Shortly afterward, he produced another imperial edict calling for their arrest and punishment. A detachment of Manchu guards under the command of Prince Gong's younger brother rode out to Sushun's camp that night and arrested him in his tent. The other members of the regency were captured in their Beijing quarters, and Prince Gong publicized the edicts throughout the capital.

The accusations centered on the disastrous foreign war. Among their many crimes, the regents were charged with having caused the war with England and France by misleading Xianfeng with treacherous advice. They were blamed for having kidnapped Harry Parkes and the other envoys, thereby breaching faith with the Allies and provoking Elgin's invasion of the capital. Along with holding them accountable for the foreign invasion, the edict also accused them of preventing the emperor, against his own will, from returning to Beijing afterward.[35] To complete the list of accusations, the empress dowager personally charged them with faking the edict that had named them regents. She claimed to have been present at Xianfeng's bedside the entire day before his death and said that he had been too enfeebled to speak, let alone dictate his will.

Their trial was swift. Within a week, the Imperial Clan Court (the empire's highest tribunal) found the regents guilty of all charges as listed. Five were stripped of rank and banished to the western frontier. The three senior members—Zaiyuan, Duanhua, and Sushun—were sentenced to death. In an ostensible display of compassion, the empress dowager granted the elders Zaiyuan and Duanhua the privilege of strangling themselves with silk, though in truth that was only a symbolic allowance; they were really hanged in a dungeon of the Imperial Clan Court.[36] She showed even less indulgence to Sushun, her chief rival. At two in the afternoon on November 8, in front of a massive crowd of spectators, he was beheaded in the Beijing cabbage market.[37]

The same edict that had ordered the arrest of the regents also requested, in the voice of the child emperor, that his mother the Empress Dowager Cixi "should in person administer the government" and that she should be "assisted by a counselor or counselors, to be chosen from among the princes of the highest order, and immediately allied to the throne."[38] Thus did the empress dowager, with Prince Gong as her chief adviser, become the new ruler of the Qing dynasty.

———

After his return to Nanjing, Hong Rengan continued to meet with the missionaries who came to the capital, though he had begun to tire of trying to please them. Most weren't nearly as diplomatic or tactful as Griffith John and Joseph Edkins had been. The China mission was as liberating as it was dangerous, and it attracted more than its share of zealots and men of questionable character. In Shanghai's international community, many (if not most) looked askance on the missionaries who dwelled among them; a young American wrote home that missionaries "abound, but I regret to say are not in such good repute as they are at home."[39] A British customs official who attended a missionary service led by "an individual who had evidently forsaken a cobbler's stall for what seemed a more respectable vocation" commented afterward in his diary that "It is a sad pity that people at home should not be able to get a higher class of men for missionary work."[40]

It was one such missionary, unnamed in the sources, who got Hong Rengan into trouble with his cousin the Heavenly King. The foreigner had spent several weeks at Nanjing, living in a boat on the river by night and preaching in the city by day. As the official in charge of foreign relations, Hong Rengan was responsible for the missionary's conduct in the capital, but he couldn't follow the man around every day. Unsupervised, the missionary began to preach in the streets that Hong Xiuquan was not the true Heavenly King and the Taiping Heavenly Kingdom was not the true Heavenly Kingdom. Reports of his blasphemy made their way to Hong Xiuquan, who took note. Then, one night, the missionary, claiming he had urgent business with Hong Rengan inside the city, convinced two gatekeepers to open one of the Nanjing city gates against their orders, endangering the defense of the capital and playing directly into the Heavenly King's paranoia of secret infiltrators. The guards, according to Hong Rengan, "were beaten with one thousand blows, and very narrowly escaped decapitation."[41] Hong Rengan's cousin then relieved him of responsibility for the kingdom's foreign relations.

Soon after this incident an old friend from Hong Kong, Josiah Cox of the London Missionary Society, arrived in Nanjing. Cox had known Hong Rengan back when he had worked with James Legge, but he found it difficult to make out in the visage of the Shield King the preacher's assistant he had once known. Hong Rengan had put on a great deal of weight since then and seemed "more coarse" than in the days when he had been a "thin, hard-worn, active Native Helper."[42] At their first audience Hong Rengan held himself at a remove, cold and uncertain on his regal throne, seeming almost embarrassed by Cox's presence. When he spoke to the missionary, there was weariness in his voice. "Mr. Cox," he said, "you know I have been friendly to foreigners and the Missionaries; it has involved me in trouble, and led to my degradation." He was apologetic but frank. "I should have hastened to welcome an old friend," he continued, "but I am ashamed to see you." Cox tried to cheer him with good news: in England, he told

Hong Rengan, they now knew who the Shield King was and what he represented for the future of China. They had great hopes for him. "Many there
watch your career with solicitude," said Cox, "and the elders of our church
charged me to exhort you to adhere firmly to the holy Scriptures." "I am
obliged," Hong Rengan replied.[43]

Cox then asked about opening a mission in Nanjing, and Hong Rengan very nearly exploded. Standing up, red in the face, he shouted that it
was a missionary who had damaged his reputation so badly in the first
place. He told Cox about the foreigner who had preached the heresy of the
Heavenly King, how he had used Hong Rengan's name to open the gates at
night. I "was degraded two steps," he told Cox, "and had the administration
of foreign affairs taken out of my hands" thanks to the thoughtless behavior of that missionary. "I have nothing to do with foreign affairs now," he
told Cox angrily, "and you must not speak to me on business." Then he sat
down again in his throne, smoothed his yellow robes, and tried to regain
his composure.

Hong Rengan allowed Cox to stay in Nanjing for only one night and
part of the following day, but that was enough time for the missionary to
learn that Hong Rengan's family and friends in Nanjing were deeply worried about him. Issachar Roberts whispered that two of Hong Rengan's
printing staff had just been executed on the Heavenly King's orders for
failing to make a change to a text that the Heavenly King had demanded.
Hong Rengan's brother (the one he had left behind as a servant in James
Legge's home) had recently come with his son to live with Hong Rengan
in Nanjing, and he told Cox in private that "Missionaries ought not to
come, for the doctrines are different, and the Heavenly King will not allow
other doctrines than his own." For the sake of his brother, he begged Cox
not to preach in Nanjing, lest people say, "Another friend of the Shield
King is attacking our doctrine."[44] That doctrine, furthermore, was becoming increasingly hostile to the teachings of the Western missionaries. In a
series of recent edicts, the Heavenly King had made it clear that there was
no Holy Ghost; he himself formed the third part of the trinity with God
and Jesus Christ. With Hong Rengan's influence on the Heavenly King in
danger, Cox worried that relations between the foreign missionaries and
the Taiping leaders, and therefore the relations between their governments,
would only get worse.

But behind the wall of fear and uncertainty, the old Hong Rengan—the
round-faced Hakka who had turned up on Theodore Hamberg's doorstep
in the spring of 1852, the man for whom James Legge had felt such a "spe-

cial affection and a warmth of admiration"—still showed through at times. The moment of clarity for Josiah Cox came on the afternoon of the first day of his visit. They dined together, and afterward Hong Rengan finally relaxed into his old self, recovering "his old fond fluency of talk," as Cox affectionately put it. He told animated stories of his journey from Hong Kong to Nanjing and confided breathless hopes for the future of the Taiping kingdom. He complained about the difficulty of keeping discipline in an army on campaign. He gave Cox a tour of his palace rooms that day, full of books and foreign souvenirs, though it was the treasures in gold and silver that caught the missionary's reproachful eye. "Ah! you are changed and possess riches now," he said to his old friend, looking around disapprovingly at Hong Rengan's earthly treasures. "*I* remain what I was," said Cox, "and possess peace."[45]

A shadow came over Hong Rengan. "Many are Kings on earth," he replied, "who find no place in Heaven."

CHAPTER 11

CROSSINGS

When Karl Marx predicted in 1853 that the Taiping Rebellion would cripple British trade in China and thereby "throw the spark into the overloaded mine of the present industrial system," he was initially wrong. British trade with China in fact increased during the rebellion, limited only by Frederick Bruce's injunction against trading with the rebels. Chinese merchants in Shanghai, Canton, and the other treaty ports still purchased cotton textiles and Indian opium, and sold tea and silk, in generally increasing quantities. Defying all predictions and expectations, British trade increased even as the war enveloped the region surrounding Shanghai. For as it turned out, when local transport networks broke down, the only option left for Chinese merchants was to sell their stocks of tea and silk to the foreigners for export. And so, even after the Taiping swept across Jiangsu province in 1860—and even after the British opened fire on them from Shanghai—silk exports not only did not decline, they in fact rose 30 percent over the following year.[1] The civil war in China, it turned out, was not enough to throw the balance of Britain's global trade off its axis. At least, not when the Chinese war raged alone. But when the civil war in the United States broke out in the summer of 1861, the axis finally began to tremble.

As British policy makers had been confronting the likely collapse of the

Qing Empire in the spring and summer of 1861, on the opposite side of the world the United States was thundering down its own separate path into bloody disintegration. When Earl Grey stood before the House of Lords and warned that "it is easy to destroy an Asiatic Government, but not so easy to replace it," his speech came just ten days after the founding of the Confederate States of America in Montgomery, Alabama. While Admiral Hope was opening relations with the Chinese rebels that March, Abraham Lincoln was inaugurated president in Washington. By April, as the fighting between the Hunan Army and the Taiping intensified in Anhui, eleven U.S. states had seceded from the Union. And as Bao Chao and Zeng Guoquan were busy slaughtering rebel prisoners by the thousands outside Anqing in July 1861, the first major battle of the U.S. Civil War broke out at Bull Run near Manassas, Virginia.

Britain was trapped between the two wars. The United States and China were its two largest markets (China both directly and via India), and the textile factories in Lancashire that were the core of British industry depended for their livelihood on the stability of both countries. Those English factories got three-quarters of their raw cotton from the U.S. South, and nearly half of their finished products went on to be sold in the Far East.[2] The looming loss of the American cotton supply conjured a very real fear in political circles that England's domestic manufacturing economy would collapse—a fear that many in the Confederacy counted on to bring Britain into the American war on their behalf. And indeed, though England's warehouses entered the fateful year of 1861 filled to the rafters with raw cotton stocks, the fear of future disruptions soon drove prices so high that the industry lost its ability to make profits in Asia. The Chinese grew and processed cotton themselves, but the industrialized British had been able to undersell them—until the outbreak of the U.S. Civil War, after which their prices rose so high that the Chinese stopped buying from outside. British exports to China dropped off a cliff; the textile trade lost two-thirds of its value from 1861 to 1862 and kept falling.[3] English factories began shutting down one after another, and by November 1862 the unemployment rate in Lancashire stood at 60 percent.[4] The cotton famine had begun.

But cotton was only part of the picture. Traditionally, Americans consumed two-thirds of the green tea purchased by British merchants in China. But with the loss of demand on that front as well, British traders had to dump their stocks on their own domestic market, with predictable results.[5] (As one British merchant in Shanghai put it succinctly, "The tea market at home has gone to the devil.")[6] Had the China trade existed in isolation, the British might have weathered the outbreak of war in the United States with only passing concern—just as they had abided the chaos in China while the United States still remained at peace. But the two countries' markets were, for them, so deeply and intimately connected that by the late spring of 1861 the simultaneity of the two wars threatened ruin for the British economy.

There was, however, a potential hedge against the crisis. The Chinese ports that were newly opened by Elgin's treaty were as yet moribund, but they held promise. With such drastic losses in Britain's familiar markets (in both the United States and China) the search was on for new ones, and the best possibility appeared to be the expansion of trade in China—not just import-export but *between* the treaty ports themselves, especially on the mighty Yangtze, where foreign steam-powered ships could enjoy a dramatic advantage over their sail- and oar-powered native competition. Thanks to the outbreak of the U.S. Civil War, the Chinese treaty ports took on a renewed importance as the untapped reserves that might save Britain's trading economy from collapse. And they happened to lie right through the center of China's war zone. As the United States plunged ever deeper into chaos, the situation triggered a reappraisal of Britain's formerly patient policy in China. There was, in short, no more time to wait: Britain *had* to have profitable and expanding markets in China, and initially at least, the most direct route toward that expansion appeared to lie with the rebels, with whom Britain had until now avoided opening trade relations.

To most people in Britain, China was remote and alien; but America was, as Josiah Tattnall had so gamely pointed out at the Peiho, related by blood. And so, in contrast to the slow indecision that had marked Britain's approach to the now ten-year-old Chinese civil war, the pace of events relating to the United States unraveled in the blink of an eye. On April 17, 1861, Abraham Lincoln announced a blockade of all Confederate ports, an act of war that established the conflict in the eyes of international law as a civil war rather than a mere insurrection. In response, the British government on May 13 announced its recognition of the belligerent status of the Confederacy, meaning that Britain would treat the South as a separate government contending for power and not as a lawless rebellion. In the name of Queen Victoria, it called for neutrality on the part of British subjects between the two sides.

Belligerent status meant, among other things, that the Confederacy could borrow funds from British banks and purchase arms and supplies (though not gunships) from British manufacturers. The South hoped it would lead a step further, to the formal recognition of the Confederacy as an independent state fighting off an invasion by the North. Toward that end, southern diplomats were dispatched to England and France to argue their country's de facto sovereignty, for the principles of international law were based on what actually was, rather than what was hoped for or claimed—or, as Lord Russell put it, "The question of belligerent rights is one, not of principle, but of fact."[7] Palmerston and Russell privately sympathized with Southern independence and hoped a permanent division of the United States might reduce the threat it posed to British dominance of world trade.

The parallels were obvious to all watchers of China in Great Britain, and on the same day the Crown granted belligerent rights to the Confederacy, the London *Times* ran an editorial calling for similar rights to be extended to the Taiping. The combination of the opening of the Office of Foreign Affairs in Beijing under Prince Gong (which it saw as a happy result of Elgin's "loud knocking at the gates of the Capital"), along with the great potential for trade with the rebels that it hoped would result from Admiral Hope's visit to Nanjing, made it seem likely that Britain could develop productive and friendly trade relations with both powers in China at the same time—a state of affairs that *The Times* felt would be "the first step into a great future destiny" there.

The key to profitable trade relations with both sides, the *Times* editors argued, was for Britain to maintain neutrality, and the key to neutrality was to recognize formally that the Taiping were, like the Confederacy, not merely a rebellion but a contending government. "We hope that this *de facto* Sovereign who has now been for 10 years enthroned in the Southern capital, may be at least acknowledged in his belligerent rights," they wrote, referring to the Heavenly King in Nanjing. Separately from any moral issues, they saw such recognition as a practical necessity for the future of British trade in China. "He holds the great waterway of China in his power," they went on, "and we must either treat with him or fight him. The first seems easy, the alternative would be madness."[8]

Two weeks later, on May 31, a Scottish MP from Greenock, Alexander Dunlop, moved an address in the House of Commons calling for the government to recognize the sovereignty of the Taiping within their regions of control. The address described the Taiping as "de facto Rulers of Provinces" and one of "two contending parties" in China—key phrases identifying them as a belligerent power—and it asked the government to enjoin

Britain's subjects in China to adhere to strict neutrality between the two sides. It was a mirror image of the policy just announced for the United States and would mean, for example, that Frederick Bruce could not forbid British merchants to trade with the Taiping, nor could Admiral Hope interfere when the Taiping army attacked a city held by the Qing. It also meant—though its author said that this wasn't his intention—that British merchants would be free to sell rifles, supplies, and unarmed steamships to the Chinese rebels. Gunships were another matter, still prohibited by the Foreign Enlistment Act (but the Confederates in the United States were already figuring out loopholes in that policy). The thirty-mile radius around Shanghai that Parkes and Hope were demanding would be unenforceable. And recognition of the Taiping as belligerents was, as in the American case, a step toward recognizing them as an independent country.

The neutral policy Dunlop called for should, according to Lord Russell's many insistences over the preceding months, have been the code of British conduct all along. But its introduction to Parliament showed that an increasing number of MPs had grown suspicious that the stated policy and the reality on the ground in China might be two very different things. In his introductory speech, Dunlop charged that "there was enough to show that the professions of neutrality with respect to the rebels by our representatives in China were not maintained." In his view, the parallels between the Confederacy and the Taiping were as plain as day. "The Taepings had waged war successfully with the Emperor of China for a long time," he argued, "and were as much entitled to be recognized as belligerents as the Secession States of America."[9]

Dunlop cited a litany of British breaches with neutrality, all at the expense of good relations with the rebels: Elgin firing on Nanjing when he had sailed past in 1858; Frederick Bruce accepting funds from the Qing government in 1860 to defray the cost of defending Shanghai—which, Dunlop claimed (tactfully avoiding the use of the term "mercenary"), had allowed the emperor of China to "point to our Queen as one of his vassals, providing troops for the defence of China, and receiving pay from him as if she were a vassal sovereign." He cited Frederick Bruce's warning to British merchants that to trade with the Taiping would be a violation of international law. "The same principle," said Dunlop, "had certainly not been applied to the Secession States of America, and British subjects had not been warned against holding intercourse with South Carolina." All he wanted, Dunlop said, was to see Britain's professed policy of neutrality followed. "If he received from the noble Lord an assurance that a policy of nonintervention would be pursued in China," he said, "he should be happy to withdraw his Motion."[10]

Dunlop had strong support. Another Scottish MP, Walter Buchanan of Glasgow, concurred that Britain should "adopt the principle in China which we have announced in Europe and America, as the keystone of our policy, the principle of non-intervention." He questioned why the British minister in China should give such obvious preference to the government of the Qing dynasty. "We see the ancient empire falling to pieces, and new and vigorous powers and races rivaling each other in progress and civilization," he said, "and shall we attach ourselves to the weakest, the most corrupt, and the least enlightened of them all?" The Taiping (and here he was referring to the influence of Hong Rengan) had "acknowledged and accepted the influences of western civilization" and had proven that "that they are not beyond the reach of new ideas, nor have entrenched themselves in the indifference and contempt of other nations, which distinguished the Manchus." In other words, the Taiping were the progressive party within the country, and if anyone was to have Britain's sympathy it should be them.[11]

As to the question of Taiping sovereignty, a third Scottish MP, William Baxter from Montrose Burghs, railed against those in Britain who dismissed the Taiping rebels as "mere robbers and freebooters, who roamed about the country committing murders and outrages" and who "had no regular Government or settled position whatever." In reality, he argued—and here was a sign that Sykes, Scarth, and the other pro-Taiping propagandists in London were getting their messages across—"The real fact was that they occupied six of the richest and most productive provinces of China; and, as [Palmerston] had recognized the belligerent rights of the Southern States of America, which had existed as a separate power only a few weeks, he did not see how he could refuse to recognize those of the Taepings, who had held a large portion of China for no less than eight years."[12]

Neither, Baxter reminded his listeners, had the Taiping ever committed atrocities against foreigners as the Manchus had done at Beijing.

Russell and Palmerston were wary. After all, the hope that Britain could enjoy profitable trade with the rebels in China assumed that those rebels could indeed govern and keep order within their own territory, and that was an assumption that neither of them—influenced as they were by the opinions of Frederick Bruce—was prepared to accept. So they countered that the motion to recognize the Taiping was moot; neutrality, they argued, had never been breached in China and never would be. Russell shared the just-received news of Admiral Hope's successful first visit to Nanjing and quoted Hope's promise to the Taiping kings that the British military would not prevent them from approaching the other treaty ports as they had done at Shanghai. "Is not that neutrality?" Russell asked. (The second round of negotiations, in which Hope and Parkes demanded the thirty-mile radius around Shanghai and tried to extend it to the other ports as well, was not yet known in England.) Russell mocked Baxter's claim that the Taiping were more humane than the imperials, suggesting that his opponent might be a sympathizer. "Now, I am very much more neutral than the honorable Member," said Russell with a smirk. "I never much admired the civilization, and still less the humanity of the Chinese."[13]

In a more conciliatory tone, however, Russell said it was impossible Britain would ever abandon its neutral policy in China. "That is the course we have pursued in other countries," he said, acknowledging their comparisons to the United States, "and I do not see why we should not pursue it in China." He saw "no probability" that the imperials would ever suppress the Taiping, or that the Taiping would overthrow the Qing fully, but he admitted agreement with his opponents that "we should not take part either on one side or the other. . . . I can assure the honorable Gentleman that the views of Her Majesty's Government will always be in favour of neutrality."[14] Lord Palmerston steered the debate to its close by reiterating that "Our policy is to maintain a strict bonâ fide neutrality." The new agreement between Admiral Hope and the Taiping would, he promised, ensure "that our commerce with these parts of the country which are occupied by them will be duly protected, and not subjected to any interruption." Britain, he said, would benefit from a growing trade with both the imperial government and the rebels alike and therefore had nothing to gain from breaking faith with either power. The motion was therefore unneeded.[15]

Dunlop was satisfied and withdrew the motion as promised. *The Times* read the debate as a victory, achieving "universal agreement that, however clearly we all see our way to the regeneration of China, it is in every respect desirable that we should in no way meddle in the matter."[16]

Meanwhile, Li Xiucheng's rebel armies were coursing through Zhejiang province unopposed. Zhejiang's capital city, Hangzhou, fell at the end of December 1861 after eight weeks of siege—a siege that proved far swifter and more effective than Zeng Guofan's at Anqing, in part because there were 2.3 million people inside the city and starvation hit quickly.[17] By December 13, all the food was gone, and the defending troops ate their cavalry horses and draft animals while the civilians boiled roots and tree bark.[18] On December 29, the inhabitants gave up their gates under circumstances depressingly similar to those of Anqing, with thousands dead of starvation in the streets. But there the similarity ended. Prior to the fall, Li Xiucheng's men had fired arrows into the city wrapped in messages promising not to harm the people and giving them a choice of joining the Taiping or going free.[19] The tactic largely seems to have worked. A week after the city fell, an imperial loyalist near Hangzhou wrote with frustration that "Because the Loyal King issued orders not to harm the people, the people didn't help fight against him ... Thus, none of the people suffered at the hands of the longhairs, and they all turned around and blamed the Imperials for their afflictions."[20] The same observer reported that most of the violence at Hangzhou had been self-imposed, not the work of rebel hands; the Manchus in the garrison city had burned themselves alive, while many of the Chinese imperial officials had slit their own throats, but the ordinary people came to relatively little harm in the capture of the city.[21]

Li Xiucheng knew the popular ramifications of Zeng Guofan's atrocities at Anqing and tried to take a moral high ground for the Taiping forces at Hangzhou. In contrast to past genocidal massacres of Manchus by the Taiping, Li Xiucheng gave the Manchus and imperial officials in Hangzhou the option of going free, though many chose suicide instead. The imperial governor of Zhejiang province hanged himself in his Hangzhou mansion as the Taiping entered the city, but Li Xiucheng paid for the man's body to be carried to Shanghai for burial with full honors, taking care even to put the governor's imperial robes and hat into the coffin along with his remains.[22] He said it was because he admired the man's loyalty. At least one Qing official was shocked by this unexpected gesture of respect from the rebel general. "How can a savage wolf have such feeling?" he wondered.[23]

Hangzhou was the capital and therefore the linchpin of the entire province of Zhejiang, and its loss was a dismal blow to the dynasty's prospects in eastern China. But in some ways, the Taiping's simultaneous campaign for the smaller coastal city of Ningbo was even more significant, because Ningbo was a treaty port. For the first time since the negotiations with Parkes and Hope at Nanjing, the Taiping tested Hope's promise not to stand in their way. Ningbo was due south from Shanghai across Hangzhou Bay, only about a hundred miles by ship and roughly double that distance over land, by a route that traveled inland to Hangzhou and then back out again to Ningbo. Because Ningbo was so close to Shanghai, its imperial officials hoped the foreigners might defend them as well, and they had long been petitioning Frederick Bruce to send them British forces. But Bruce knew that his home government did not want a repeat of the controversial defense of Shanghai, so he wrote to his consul at Ningbo that if the civil war should ever reach that city, he should state clearly that "we take no part in this civil contest."[24] At the same time, however, he wrote to Admiral Hope that though "I do not think we can take upon ourselves the protection of Ningpo," he did think a display of British naval power at the city might frighten the rebels away, if it could be done "without compromising ourselves in this civil contest."[25]

Admiral Hope interpreted the orders (and his own promise to the Taiping leaders) as he saw fit. In May 1861, as it became clear that the Taiping were setting their sights on Ningbo along with the rest of Zhejiang province, he sent Captain Roderick Dew in the fourteen-gun *Encounter* to dissuade them. Dew was to make contact with the Taiping commanders nearest Shanghai and do exactly what Parkes had done so successfully in keeping the Brave King from attacking Hankow that March, namely, "point out to him that the capture and destruction of the town of Ningpo would be extremely injurious to British trade." Hope instructed Captain Dew to warn the Taiping general "to desist from all hostile proceedings against the town" until British diplomats could communicate with the Taiping leaders at Nanjing. More insidiously, despite his promise that the British would not oppose the rebels taking control of the treaty ports, he put into words the very threat Parkes had left unspoken. "Without committing yourself to the necessity of having recourse to force," he told Dew, "you will remind him of what took place last year at Shanghae."[26]

After warning the Taiping against approaching Ningbo, Dew was then to proceed to the port itself and start helping the imperial officials there to "place every obstruction in the way of the capture of the town by the rebels." In a lone concession to the spirit of the neutral policy, Hope reminded Dew that his threat of British violence against the rebels was a bluff and that Dew must not, if the Taiping should push things to that point, open "actual hostilities" against them. But Hope seemed to think that even that restriction might be temporary, for he did ask Dew to report from Ningbo on "the amount of auxiliary European force which you think sufficient for its defence."

Nevertheless, the arguments by Sykes, Grey, Dunlop, Baxter, and others in Parliament had their effect, and Lord Russell stuck to his promises. He formally approved Hope's orders to Dew in a letter of July 24 to Bruce, but only at their literal wording, meaning as a bluff and only a bluff. He expressed a strong (and unfounded) hope that if the Taiping could be convinced willingly to stay away from those treaty ports, the imperial side might likewise agree to refrain from using the ports as safe bases from which to attack the rebels, and conflict could be avoided without damage to British trade. But there was nothing in the correspondence from either Bruce or Hope to indicate that the imperial government would agree to any such treatment of the ports as neutral zones. In any case, although he approved the letter of Hope's orders, there was an edge to Russell's reply that reflected his awareness that Hope was itching for an excuse to open hostilities. He concluded his letter to Bruce with a stern admonition: "You will understand, however, that Her Majesty's Government do not wish force to be used against the rebels in any case except for the actual protection of the lives and property of British subjects." Two weeks later, he made the government's demand for neutrality even more explicit: short of actually rescuing British subjects from "torture or capital punishment," he wrote, Britain's forces in China were to "abstain from all interference in the civil war."[27]

But James Hope and Frederick Bruce were already planning for the chance that the policy might change. On June 16, Bruce wrote to Hope to tell him, "I quite concur in the advantage to be derived from preserving Ningbo," but admitted that "my instructions do not justify me in using force for that purpose."[28] He asked Hope for patience, wondering if the neutral policy itself might give way in time. The Taiping had promised to avoid Shanghai for the rest of the year, he noted, and by then, the government back in London might have reconsidered its policy of nonintervention in light of the reports he had been forwarding of the destruction under the rebels. The Manchu government was obviously too weak to put down the rebellion itself, he told Hope, but if the Taiping won, he feared they would be even worse for British interests because they were full of "extravagant pretensions" and would surely prove "more impracticable and unmanageable than the existing dynasty has ever been."

Bruce was now musing openly. Perhaps Britain didn't have to stand by and watch China fall to the Taiping, he thought. There was another course, the one Hope had envisioned when he first went up the Yangtze: the British could take all of the treaty ports under their own protection. By an impressive contortion of logic, Bruce reasoned that they could even do this without violating Parliament's desire for neutrality. Since the customs duties from the treaty ports were being used by the Qing dynasty to pay Britain its indemnity from the war, Britain therefore had a direct national interest in seeing them continue. If the rebels conquered the ports and cut off the Qing government's trade income, the Qing would not be able to pay back the indemnity (of which several million taels still remained outstanding) and the rebels would thus have effectively severed Britain's own source of revenue—practically an act of war against Britain itself. Under those circumstances, Bruce thought Britain might be able to defend the ports from the rebels while still remaining technically neutral.

Following that thread to its reckless conclusion, Bruce asked Hope whether it might be possible to send an entire fleet of British gunships up to Nanjing. Since Britain didn't have enough soldiers in China to defend all of the treaty ports (in fact, Shanghai by this time had fewer than 800 British troops, most of them Indian),[29] maybe Hope's naval forces could "threaten [the rebels] with chastisement at their capital" in order to keep them away from the ports.

Admiral Hope, to his credit, replied on July 11 that an assault on Nanjing would be "the most impolitic act which could be committed."[30] (Russell, when he read Bruce's letter two months later, agreed strenuously.) Hope's reasons were purely practical, however. He explained to Bruce that Nanjing's size made it impervious to naval assault, so Britain would need to send in a large landing force. Even then, such an attack would probably succeed only in driving the rebels farther into the interior, with no effect on the overall course of the rebellion. As long as the Taiping kings remained at Nanjing, thought Hope, the British could at least negotiate with them. And though he didn't say as much, there was another side to the issue as well, for Hope knew full well the limitations of naval power. There was no question that Britain's gunships were far superior to anything the Taiping possessed on water, but they guaranteed dominance only of the immediate vicinity of the waterways. Nobody had any idea what would happen if the massive Taiping armies should engage British forces on land.

On Admiral Hope's instructions, Captain Dew began a delicate ballet between the rebels and imperials. First he sailed down to Ningbo in June to inspect the city's defenses. He found them abysmal. There were only a thousand disorganized men in the garrison, and the old guns on the city wall had no ammunition. He left the imperial commander with a long list of recommendations for strengthening his defenses, and then steamed back up to Shanghai and inland along the rivers and canals to visit the Taiping garrison at Qingpu, twenty miles from Shanghai. (Their presence there was not taken to be a violation of the thirty-mile radius, as they had already held the city before Parkes went to Nanjing.) Frederick Townsend Ward's reconstituted mercenary force had attacked Qingpu just before Dew arrived, and when Dew approached the city he was, predictably, shot at. Taking note of the hostility, he went down to visit the encampment of another army, at Zhapu on the coast of the bay about fifty miles from Shanghai and across from Ningbo. Dew's interpreter described the rebel officers there as a vision of spectacular perversion, "dressed gorgeously in the brightest coloured silks and all dirty and diseased, their arms covered in gold bangles and scabs." The first Taiping officer Dew met with expounded on the friendship between the Taiping and foreigners and tried to get Dew to wear his yellow turban.[31] The next day he met the officer in charge, who told Dew he wasn't planning to attack Shanghai or Ningbo and asked him for guns and powder. There were many foreigners, he told Dew, who came to the Taiping cities to sell guns.

After leaving the Taiping commanders, Dew steamed back down to Ningbo with twelve large cannons from the British armory in Shanghai to help reinforce the city walls. (Hope felt that this would not violate neutrality unless British soldiers actually operated them.) Dew found that in his absence the local authorities had done nothing to prepare for the city's defense "beyond picking the weeds out of the face of the wall." They had ignored his entire list of recommendations, and even the existing guns on the wall were still without powder or shot. But then again, during his first visit Dew had confided to Ningbo's imperial commander that he expected to get orders allowing a British defense of the city, so he was at least partially to blame if the Qing forces didn't bother to protect the city themselves.[32] Admiral Hope, when he learned of the miserable state of affairs in Ningbo, concluded that there was no point in Britain trying to cooperate with the Qing government. He later wrote to the Admiralty that Captain Dew had done everything possible to help the imperials defend the city "except the use of force in their favour," but that his assistance was "utterly useless . . . in consequence of the cowardice and imbecility of the mandarins."[33]

Ningbo emptied as the rebels approached. Everyone with the means to leave did so. The ranking imperial official, a *daotai*, purchased a small steamship and anchored it just offshore with his family and possessions on board, though the commander in charge of the city's defense—who had not been invited to escape with his civil counterpart—retaliated by ordering his men to prevent the *daotai* from leaving, and the ship sailed for Shanghai with only his family aboard. "The city is like a desert," wrote the newly arrived British consul, Frederick Harvey, on November 12, "and the only activity shown is amongst the shipping, where foreign steamers are busily engaged in conveying to Shanghae, at enormous rates, the Chinese residents, who are fast leaving the port."[34] On November 20, the foreign authorities asked all missionaries in the city who weren't fluent in Chinese to come to the foreign settlement, across the river to the east of the walled Chinese city, for protection.[35]

On November 26, with the rebels about thirty miles off, Consul Harvey reported that "the local authorities appear to be quite demoralized and helpless." On December 2, the Taiping were just a day's march from the city, and a British party rode out to ask their commanders to wait one week before beginning their assault. Reluctantly, they agreed (it is unclear why the British asked for this, unless Dew was still hoping that permission would come through for the *Encounter* to open fire on the rebels when they got to the city). The *daotai,* now effectively imprisoned in the city, offered the French customs collector 50,000 taels if he would pull together a for-eign militia to go out and fight the Taiping, though the plan fell apart when he refused to pay them in advance. In someone's desperate attempt to keep the local forces from deserting, fraudulent notices in Chinese appeared around town to the effect that six British and French men-of-war were on their way from Shanghai to defend Ningbo and were bringing 600 for-eign troops (including two hundred Sikhs, described rather ungratefully as "black devils").[36]

When the week of delay expired on December 9, 60,000 Taiping troops in two columns appeared outside the city gates with a maelstrom of ban-ners and gongs and blowing horns. A storming party went first, swimming the Ningbo moat with ladders in tow. They threw the ladders up against the wall and scaled them "like wild cats."[37] The defenders scattered, tore off their uniforms, and tried to blend in with the fleeing civilians. The storm-ing party dropped down the other side and opened the southern and west-ern gates for the rest of their armies to enter the city. "Ning-po," reported Consul Harvey soon afterward, "is now in the full and unquestionable pos-session of the Tae-ping forces."[38]

It was a relatively peaceful conquest. Contrary to Consul Harvey's expectations, there was no widespread murder. There were also no fires, except those the imperials set before they fled the city.[39] Despite a certain amount of looting, he was surprised to be able to report that the rebels exercised "wonderful moderation." After helping the *daotai* escape to Shanghai on a British ship (which he debated for a moment and then decided wouldn't be a breach of neutrality) Harvey joined his American and French counterparts in sailing across the river from the foreign concession to the Chinese city to meet with the two rebel commanders on December 4. The commanders were as friendly as they had been in the field and said "that it was their wish to live on terms of friendship and amity with all foreigners." The foreigners stated that they expected to have the same privileges of trade and residence as under the imperial government, and no Europeans or Americans should be harmed during the occupation. The rebel commanders agreed enthusiastically and offered to execute anyone who caused trouble with a foreign citizen. Then the consuls went back over to the foreign concession and closed down the imperial customs house in recognition of the fact that Ningbo was no longer under the control of the emperor and therefore they didn't owe him any more duties.

From the standpoint of the rebels, the occupation of Ningbo was a great success. It had been gained with minimal violence, and there had been no harm to foreign property. Moreover, there had been no clash at all between their forces and the European powers, which showed them that Parkes and Hope had been truthful when they had told the Taiping kings at Nanjing back in March that they wouldn't stand in the way of the rebels taking treaty ports other than Shanghai. It was grounds for renewed hope that the Taiping and the foreigners could coexist. By early January 1862, all was quiet in Ningbo city, and the members of the small European community had begun to invite Taiping officers to their dinner parties.[40] The rebels had shown the Europeans not only that the imperial forces could do nothing to slow their irresistible momentum but also that they were not—as the imperial propaganda from Shanghai had depicted them—a force of destruction bent on driving foreign trade from China.

However, Britain's ranking official on the ground, Consul Harvey, didn't think it was a success at all. On January 3, he wrote to London that although "tranquility prevails" in Ningbo, there was still no trade and the city was still empty of merchants (most of whom had moved to the large island of Zhoushan just offshore, which was as yet untouched by the civil war). It was now abundantly clear to him that the British didn't need to worry about coming to actual harm at the hands of the Taiping, but Harvey's job was to supervise trade, and already, just a few weeks after the capture of the city, he worried that commerce would never come back. There wasn't "the least symptom shown of the return of respectable Chinese merchants," he wrote.⁴¹ (His judgment, however, appears to have been premature: the official *China Trade Report* eight weeks later would report that "the people . . . are returning in numbers. The trade of the port is reviving, and there seems a fair probability of its entirely recovering itself.")⁴²

Harvey did allow that the Taiping had done their best to maintain peace and kept all their promises. They put up placards calling for the people to return to their occupations. They were planning to open a customs house of their own, with the same tariff rates the Qing had charged, and they were even granting a three-month duty-free period to celebrate their peaceful capture of the treaty port. He reported that they took pains to show "that they are not the scourge so often depicted" and demonstrated "a strong desire . . . to cultivate a good understanding with us." Nevertheless, beneath it all, Consul Harvey sensed only lies and deceit. Their cultivation of friendship, he was certain, was "based on fear and the want of money." They weren't to be trusted.⁴³

———

I n the dawn of the year 1862, China stood at the edge of the unknown. The upper ranks of government in Beijing and Nanjing were both in a state of metamorphosis, re-forming themselves for the next stage in a war whose end none could divine. Zeng Guofan's personal base of power was growing with the success of his army, and he continued the war, building a new headquarters in Anqing—now his own impregnable fortress—and planning with his commanders to begin the campaign downriver into the central realm of the rebels. His power in Anhui and the central kingdom behind it was now unchallenged, and as long as he remained loyal to the new government, the dynasty too would be unchallenged there. But, panning back, the dynasty had lost control of its territories almost everywhere that Zeng Guofan's army was not. Shi Dakai's rebel army coursed independently through Sichuan province west of Hunan. The Muslim territories in the southwest were in open rebellion against the Qing. The horseback armies of the Nian continued to scourge the northern plains. Informal militias, bandit gangs, and local strongmen filled the spaces between. There was no hope; there was no direction.

After the capture of Hangzhou, the Loyal King—his youth as a poor charcoal maker in southern China now all but lost to memory—commanded armies that totaled more than a million souls. Despite the terrible loss at

Anqing, which had cut the rebels off from the central kingdom and rent open the flank of their capital, there were still the vast riches of the east. And there, the empire's forces might as well not have existed at all. Li Xiucheng now had almost total control of Jiangsu and Zhejiang provinces, which together provided fully a quarter of the empire's yearly income in times of peace and were famed as "a territory in every respect unequalled for its resources by any other equivalent space in the whole world."[44] The next step in his own campaign, after Hangzhou and Ningbo, was the only logical one: Shanghai. It was the final piece of the puzzle. He needed its financial stores, its command of the coastline, its future revenue from foreign trade. He needed unbroken control of Jiangsu and Zhejiang without an imperial stronghold in their midst. And the events of the past two years had taught him how unlikely it was that the Taiping's British "brothers" would ever show them proper recognition or respect. And so, in January 1862, as the Heavenly King's promise expired, Li Xiucheng began to prepare his armies for a return to Shanghai—and not, this time, as lightly armed supplicants. Of course, Li Xiucheng had never really believed the Taiping could win the friendship of the foreigners anyhow, though Hong Rengan had always held him back from playing his full hand against them. But now, demoted from his position in charge of foreign relations, Hong Rengan no longer had the final say.

The British government had renewed its promise to stay out of the conflict and Parliament was dead set on neutrality, but to the foreign population on the ground, the will of Admiral Hope to intervene was almost physically palpable. Frederick Bruce tried to keep an open mind, but he still wanted to see an acceptance of the Taiping by native Chinese merchants at Ningbo before he could endorse their recognition by the British. Such "national recognition," he wrote on January 18, "should precede any more intimate relations between us and them."[45] He would wait and see. Meanwhile, Consul Harvey's bleak reports on the lifeless state of Ningbo under the rebels were starting on their way back to England. A letter from Hope to the Admiralty joined them, reporting on the fall of Hangzhou. If he knew anything of it, Hope said nothing of Li Xiucheng's offer to let the Manchus in Hangzhou go free, nor of his funeral preparations for the imperial governor. Neither did he note any contrast to Zeng Guofan's slaughter at Anqing (which was well known in Shanghai, thanks to reports from the passengers on two river steamers that had gotten tangled up in the mass of corpses floating down from the city). Hope simply reported, laconically, that in their conquest of Hangzhou, the rebels "are stated to have committed their usual atrocities."[46]

These alarming reports followed the secondhand intimations of Taiping destruction that Bruce had been forwarding to the Foreign Office for months. In their totality, Bruce hoped they would convince Lord Russell that no matter what the high-minded liberals of Parliament might want in China, the policy of nonintervention would mean the death of British trade there. And in light of the threat to its economy from the civil war in the United States, Britain could not forgo that trade lightly.

Copied, folded, and pasted into envelopes, the reports were stuffed into fat leather pouches of official correspondence for their two-month journey to England. They sailed first by packet to Shanghai, where they joined the rest of the mail to be packed in large wooden chests that were carried down to the Bund on the shoulders of Chinese porters who shuffled a quickstep, single file, dodging through the crowded and dirty streets down to the docks piled high with bales of cotton and wooden chests of opium, then finally up the planks of a long black mail steamer bobbing at its mooring. Those chests were the last freight loaded onto a vessel already heavy with passengers, its deck crowded with men and women gaily waving handkerchiefs to their well-wishers as they tried to mask their relief—relief to escape the filth and the disease, the alienation and dread, and to sail for home at last.[47]

The reports did not travel alone, however, for one of the passengers on the mail steamer that cast off from its dock and slipped into the current of the Huangpu River on January 15, 1862, was Harry Parkes, who had finally been granted leave to return home to England. The years of angry negotiation, travel, and torture had left him in a "nervous, shattered condition," and he was desperate for a calm respite from his contentious life in China.[48] He would return to England a war hero, acclaimed for his bravery in the face of Manchu captivity in Beijing. After all, it had been for his sake, primarily, that the Summer Palace had been burned. His suffering was Britain's lone point of moral clarity in that war, and Britain clung to it dearly. Thus he would return home a celebrity, toasted by London society, cheered by the public, created by the Queen a Knight Commander of the Order of the Bath at age thirty-four, one of the youngest men ever to receive the honor.

As convincing as Bruce thought the forwarded reports and letters might be, they couldn't begin to compare with soon-to-be-Sir Harry Parkes, who was a living voice, one the British public were eager to hear. And his view was now even darker than that of Bruce. The very last thing Parkes had done in China—for which even his longed-for leave had been delayed—was to try to renegotiate with the Taiping leaders in Nanjing for an extension of their promise to stay away from Shanghai. They had refused. The negotiations had broken down, ending in such bitter recrimination that one of Hope's commanders threatened that if the rebels came anywhere near Shanghai the Allies would not only drive them back as before but punish them with "such further consequences as your folly will deserve."[49] Parkes now knew, better than any of his countrymen, that the rebels had come to the end of their patience with British demands. And so he also returned home to England as a prophet, bearing witness to the storm that was coming.

"These are dark days in China," wrote a *New York Times* correspondent from Ningbo on January 17, "and we know not what will be on the morrow."[50]

PART THREE

The Great Peace

CHAPTER 12

THE POINT OF NO RETURN

Zeng Guofan needed a larger army. His tightly knit Hunan forces had prevailed in capturing the city of Anqing, but once that foothold was gained, a vast territory of rebel control with tens of millions of subjects spread out to their east. The Taiping still held several important towns in northern Anhui, where Chen Yucheng the Brave King now bristled in retreat, and both sides of the river downstream toward Nanjing were firmly in rebel hands as well. And of course, beyond Nanjing there was the entire eastern coast—which was a hopeless cause. His men were exhausted after their yearlong campaign for Anqing, and many wanted to go home; he worried that lethargy was setting in.[1] They could hold this one city quite securely, though, so while he mulled over his next steps, Zeng focused on reconstruction. He took over the government offices in Anqing. He petitioned Beijing to keep the city as the provincial capital despite its years outside imperial control. Under his direction, an army of laborers began rebuilding the city's Confucian academy and examination hall (the most tangible symbols of imperial civilization). They repaired the city wall. The new governor-general finally had a proper base of command in one of his three provinces.

The relatively small territory under Zeng Guofan's immediate control—mainly the southern half of Anhui province—was in a ghastly state. South of the river, through the mountainous counties around Qimen and Xiuning, the year and a half of fighting for Anqing had completely broken the agricultural cycle. The rice fields in the valleys were choked with weeds, the tea bushes on the hillsides unpruned and growing wild. The peasants who had survived the fighting by fleeing into the hills had run out of food and were starving. His own funds were short, so there was only so much he could do for them (it was those peasants who, by growing rice and tea, were supposed to support his army, not the other way around). Under Zeng's direction, the Anhui civil government set up relief stations in the mountainous southern part of the province to hand out porridge to the famine-stricken population. There were seven stations, each capable of feeding three thousand people, and he hoped they might do some good, though he admitted in a letter to his family in Hunan that things had gotten so bad in southern Anhui that he was starting to hear rumors of peasants eating their dead.[2]

The entire imperial war against the Taiping was now in Zeng Guofan's hands, and as his perspective shifted to account for a new field of combat that was far larger than his focused campaign for Anqing, he began reshaping his army to compensate. In November 1861, two months after the conquest of Anqing, he sent his brother Guoquan back to Hunan to recruit 6,000 more Hunanese soldiers for the coming push toward Nanjing. Politically, it was a risky move; he didn't yet know of the coup d'état in Beijing that had removed Sushun from power, and to continue to amass personal forces—recruited by his own brother in his own home province—was a provocation to critics in Beijing, who saw him as a growing threat to the central government's authority. But he was unaware of the change in government when he sent off his memorial to Beijing on November 16 explaining his decision to call up new forces from Hunan. "We can take advantage of the fear we have struck into the rebels and drive straight in at their nest in Nanjing," he promised—but only if his army had sufficient troop strength. "Nothing would be better than for Zeng Guoquan's forces to drive deep into the belly of the rebel territory," he wrote. "What a shame it would be to sit by and allow this opportunity to pass!" The new Hunan recruits, he explained, could garrison the cities and towns his army had already conquered, which would free up the veterans to go on campaign with his brother downriver toward the rebel capital.[3]

But even if his brother's recruitment efforts were successful, those extra forces wouldn't be enough. As he had maintained from the start, the only way to destroy the enemy's "nest" was to surround it completely and cut off all avenues of supply and reinforcement, so the field of war encompassed more than just the two hundred miles of riverine flatlands lying between Anqing and the rebel capital. Even if he could somehow push his brother's army straight through to Nanjing, and even if he could keep that army supplied along the river, the capital would still be open on all other sides. To cut Nanjing off completely, he would have to gain control of northern Anhui, where the Brave King's army still loomed. He would have to establish firm control of southern Anhui below the river, a territory to which he had barely managed to cling during the Anqing campaign. He would also need to control the southern approaches from Zhejiang province and its capital, Hangzhou. He especially needed the cities downstream to the east of Nanjing that the Taiping had so deftly conquered in 1860—Wuxi, Changzhou, and above all the garden city of Suzhou, where Li Xiucheng had made his base.

A strategy began to take shape in his mind. He envisioned three separate armies, one of which would depart from Anqing and march eastward downriver toward Nanjing. Another, under Zuo Zongtang, would enter the southern part of Zhejiang province from Jiangxi, then cut northward to come at the provincial capital of Hangzhou from below. The third—which posed the greatest challenge logistically—would begin in Jiangsu province and fight its way back inward toward Suzhou and Nanjing from the east. To realize this vision, he somehow had to find a way to position a loyal army clear on the opposite side of the rebel kingdom, but there was no safe circuit that could get them there, and sending thousands of soldiers right through the enemy's midsection posed more danger than he cared to consider. But the question was, in a sense, moot, because before he could come to any decision as to how to plant a force on the opposite side of Nanjing, such a force had to exist in the first place. And even as he sent his brother back to Hunan to recruit more soldiers, he worried that they were tapping their home province too deeply and the well of strong young Hunanese men would soon run dry.[4]

And so, in a major departure from earlier practice, he cast his net more widely and authorized a willowy thirty-eight-year-old scholar from Anhui named Li Hongzhang to return to his home in central Anhui in order to muster an entirely new provincial militia that could supplement Zeng's own forces from Hunan. Li Hongzhang was, like Zeng Guofan, a Hanlin scholar, part of the infinitesimal elite at the top of the examination system. He was eleven years younger than Zeng Guofan, and his father had passed the *jinshi* examination in Beijing in 1838 in the same small group with Zeng Guofan, which had bonded the two elder men together for life. When Li Hongzhang had first arrived in Beijing in 1844 after passing his provincial examination, Zeng Guofan had agreed to serve as his teacher while Li prepared to take the *jinshi*, which he passed with distinction in 1847.[5] Li Hongzhang was therefore tied to Zeng Guofan both through the friendship between Zeng and his father, which made Zeng something like an uncle to him, and, even more important, by having taken Zeng Guofan as his teacher. In Confucian parlance, a student and his teacher were like a son and his father.

Nevertheless, it had actually taken some time for Zeng Guofan to come to a point where he would trust Li Hongzhang with responsibility for an army. The brilliant young Li had lofty ambitions of his own, of which Zeng Guofan, as his teacher, was well aware. Despite their years of familiarity and even though Li Hongzhang's older brother already served on Zeng Guofan's staff, Zeng did not welcome his student when Li Hongzhang first came to the Hunan Army's headquarters looking for employment in 1858. In fact, he ignored Li completely for the first month he was there. Frustrated, Li Hongzhang finally pressed an aide to ask the general why he wouldn't see him or speak to him. Zeng Guofan replied to the aide with only slightly feigned sarcasm, suggesting that perhaps the Hunan Army was "too shallow a beach in which to harbor so large a ship as Li."[6]

Over the following years, the general worked to break the younger man of his arrogance (having him dragged roughly from bed by guards when he overslept, for example), and Li worked to convince the general of his loyalty and humility. They had their disagreements, and Li even abandoned him for a time at Qimen, but by early 1862 their relationship was solid and Zeng Guofan decided that he was the man to entrust with a personal command second in size only to his own. Zeng Guofan had commanders who were more loyal and who were more experienced and skilled in warfare than Li Hongzhang, but none of them had achieved the high rank in the examination system that the Hanlin scholar Li Hongzhang had attained. When it came to generals, Zeng Guofan placed a great premium on their scholarship.

Starting in early 1862, Li Hongzhang began to mobilize a regional militia nearly identical to the one from Hunan. He used the same recruitment methods Zeng had pioneered in Hunan: personal recruitment in the home district, forming companies of soldiers from the same homes to serve under officers already known to them. By these means he pulled together several thousand Anhui peasants whom he brought to Anqing in February 1862 to be trained by veteran units of Zeng Guofan's Hunan Army. The Anhui Army would follow the same lines of organization, the same methods of indoctrination, the same rules of camp and combat that Zeng Guofan had laid out for his Hunan troops. Li Hongzhang's command was thus a nearly perfect mirror image of the military force Zeng Guofan had built around himself, with the same inner logic of personal relationships—only from a different part of the empire (though even that line was blurred by the absorption into Li's force of some of the Hunan battalions that trained them). Otherwise it was a replica to scale, with the only significant difference being that it was subordinate; Li Hongzhang took orders from Zeng Guofan, while Zeng Guofan—despite the ritual of requesting permissions from Beijing—didn't really take orders from anyone.

The empress dowager and Prince Gong ultimately decided to keep Zeng Guofan in their service after the execution of Sushun and the purge of his followers. They had no particular reason to trust this Chinese general over a loyal ethnic Manchu, but they also knew they had no hope of containing the Taiping without his army's support (nor, given the delinquency of the traditional imperial forces, any possibility of reining him in should he defy their authority). And so, in late November 1861, two weeks after the execution of Sushun, they issued a series of edicts in the name of the child emperor, which reconfirmed the lofty civil and military appointments Xianfeng had originally granted to Zeng Guofan at Sushun's urging: Zeng would remain the governor-general of the three provinces of Anhui, Jiangxi, and Jiangsu, and he would simultaneously be imperial military commissioner for those same three provinces.[7] But the new regime did not stop there, and in a sign of their desperation to gain and hold on to Zeng Guofan's loyalty, Prince Gong and the empress dowager even increased the honors, giving him military control of Zhejiang province as well. The governors of all four provinces—the richest and most densely populated in the empire—would fall under his direct command. No other Chinese official in the Qing dynasty had ever held such power.

The news of his further promotion arrived in Zeng Guofan's headquarters before the news of the coup did, and it both stunned and mystified him. He received the edicts of reappointment and promotion on December 15, 1861, learning of his new responsibility for Zhejiang province just as it was crumbling under the rebel onslaught; Ningbo had fallen six days earlier, and the provincial capital, Hangzhou, was drowning in the siege that would break it in two weeks. It reawakened his old fears of inadequacy and failure. "This power is too great," he wrote in his diary. "My stature will be too high, and my undeserved reputation has outgrown itself. This terrifies me to the extreme." He had once been told that it was better to live a long life than a life of wealth and power, and only now did he finally understand what that meant. Awake in the middle of night, he sat at his desk and brooded over the fates of others in history whose reputations had grown so far beyond their actual merit. His conclusion was that they seldom came to a good end.[8]

Once he finally learned about the coup and the execution of the regents, however, the new surfeit of honors began to make more sense. On December 23, a letter from a friend in Beijing informed him that the imperial government had fallen into the hands of the unknown empress dowager, who now ruled "from behind a screen." Three days later, a shipment of priceless gifts arrived in Anqing for Zeng Guofan: rare ceremonial robes, furs, silks, an imperial jade ring, carpets, and other treasures sent by the empress dowager.[9] The message was clear. He was embarrassed by the new government's overreaching, desperate attempts to secure his loyalty and wrote repeatedly to decline the four-province military commission.[10] When in February 1862 he learned that they had named him an imperial grand secretary as well, he sent a memorial to the throne asking the government to please refrain from giving his family any more honors until they had actually managed to reconquer Nanjing.[11]

Despite his protestations, however, once it was clear that the empress dowager would do almost anything to ensure Zeng Guofan's continued loyalty, he began to make use of his new power. With complicity from Beijing, the early months of 1862 saw what was, essentially, a complete takeover of the civil administration of eastern China by Zeng Guofan and his protégés. While he held on to the top position as governor-general of Anhui, Jiangxi, and Jiangsu, he put his own trusted lieutenants into the individual governorships just below him. His loyal student Li Hongzhang became expectant governor of Jiangsu, the province that contained Shanghai, Suzhou, and Nanjing. His Hunanese neighbor Zuo Zongtang, the commander who had held open Qimen's supply lines during the Anqing campaign, was named governor of Zhejiang province, with the important cities of Ningbo and Hangzhou. Two of his other protégés became the governors of Jiangxi and Anhui. The entire imperial government in the theater of war, including parts of its upstream hinterland, was now commanded by men, primarily from Hunan, whose strongest bonds of personal loyalty were to Zeng Guofan and no one else.[12]

Regarding these appointments, if a province was under relatively stable imperial control, as Jiangxi was, a handpicked governor meant that Zeng Guofan could redirect much of its tax revenue (drastically reduced from peacetime levels but still meaningful in the aggregate) to support the salaries and materials needed by his troops in the provinces where the heaviest fighting was taking place. But in provinces such as Jiangsu and Zhejiang that were under rebel control, the governorships functioned more like prizes dangled before a given general's eyes; if he could reconquer his designated province from the rebels then he could take his seat of power in its capital and enjoy the life of power and prestige that would follow.

Of course, the imperial government was using exactly the same principle to impel Zeng Guofan himself. His powerful appointments and honors were the strongest incentive (really the only incentive) the central government could give him to sacrifice his life in a war to uphold the dynasty against the rebels. And Nanjing was the greatest prize of all. It was not just the rebel capital but the traditional seat of power of the towering governor-generalship of Jiangsu, Anhui, and Jiangxi. If the Taiping could be defeated, it could be his. As his brother Guoquan was recruiting new troops from Hunan to prepare for the campaign against Nanjing, and as his student Li Hongzhang was assembling the new Anhui Army, Zeng Guofan's farthest gaze was fixed on the recovery of the Taiping capital and the eternal personal glory—for himself, for his dear brothers, and for the entire Zeng family and its descendants—that awaited them there. Above any other factor, this was what guaranteed Zeng Guofan's continued loyalty to the Qing. For if the dynasty should fall, there would be no glory; there would be no power, no immortal inheritance for his sons. The government had led him into a position where the two goals—to recover the rebel capital for the dynasty and to gain the city of Nanjing for his family—were simultaneous and inseparable. And so, for the sake of his brothers and sons, he lashed himself anew to the Manchus even as their dynasty sputtered at the edge of collapse.

Things did not go well for Hong Rengan that winter. From the outset, his career in Nanjing had been riven by tensions. His unswerving loyalty to his cousin the Heavenly King pulled him in one direction, while the foreigners he tried to win over to the Taiping's side pulled him in another. The missionaries demanded that he "correct" the rebel doctrines, while his own people expected him to gain the foreigners' support in their war against the Manchus. Both, in their way, were proving impossible. The tensions had worsened rapidly during his absence for the Anqing campaign, and as Josiah Cox had seen, by the autumn of 1861, after his return, he was already close to the breaking point. The foreign missionaries were bringing him little but empty promises in Nanjing, while their countries' diplomats treated the Taiping kings rudely and high-handedly, making outrageous demands that Hong Rengan had to answer for. They took advantage of the rebels' constant appeals for friendship and gave nothing in return.

Hong Rengan had staked his reputation with his cousin on those appeals for friendship, and the many kings and commanders of the Taiping field armies continued to plead their affection for their British and American "brothers" because the Shield King had told them to. But as the appeals continued to fall on deaf ears, he came under attack in the capital. He was the target of whisper campaigns, embarrassed by charges that his cherished foreign missionaries were subverting the Heavenly King's authority and that by protecting and encouraging them, he might even be a danger to the Taiping cause himself. By the time Cox visited him, Hong Rengan was trying to remove himself from the world of the foreigners; when he got too close to them, as with Cox, it was his worried brother who stepped in to try to protect him. By the winter of 1862, the only missionary left in Nanjing was Issachar Roberts.

And then even Roberts left him.

As the American preacher told it, he had to leave Nanjing because on January 13, 1862, Hong Rengan finally lost his mind altogether. On that day, said Roberts, the Shield King broke into his upstairs suite of rooms with a long sword in hand, "without a moment's warning or just cause," and murdered Roberts's Chinese servant right where he stood. And then, "after having slain my poor harmless, helpless boy," Hong Rengan turned on Roberts himself, trying to provoke the white-bearded missionary into raising his hand so he could finish him with the very same sword. Hong Rengan leaped "most fiend-like" onto the corpse of the servant, stomping his silk-clad foot on its lifeless head. Then he rushed at Roberts, shoving the bench on which he was sitting. When Roberts didn't respond, Hong Rengan picked up a cup of tea and flung it into the preacher's face. Then he grabbed the old man, shook him, and struck an open-handed blow across the right side of his head. Roberts turned, and Hong Rengan struck him again, on the left, hard enough to make his ears ring. The preacher took the blows without resistance until Hong Rengan finally let him drop and shouted at him "like a dog, to be gone out of his presence."[13]

Roberts escaped on a passing British gunboat a week later, leaving behind all of his books and clothing in the rush. He turned up in Shanghai on January 30, wild-eyed and breathless, making his first appearance in the foreign settlement since his departure to join the rebels sixteen months earlier. He told anyone who would listen to him that Hong Rengan had gone insane. He published his account soon after arriving, with a long list of accusations: that Hong Rengan had murdered his servant, that he had tried to kill Roberts himself, that he had even stolen all of Roberts's books and clothing. "I have hitherto been a friend to [this] revolutionary movement," he wrote for all to read, but "am now as much opposed to them . . . as I ever was in favour of them." The rebels' chief foreign apologist would now be their shrillest critic.

It wouldn't come out until later, but the American preacher's story was mostly a product of his own eccentric imagination. Just as he had exaggerated freely to sing the praises of the rebels, so did he now do the same to excoriate them. The "slain" servant seems to have shown up later in Shanghai, quite alive. The books and clothing that Roberts accused Hong Rengan of stealing also arrived in Shanghai and were retrieved by the old missionary. And his story changed with retelling. In the original version, he said that Hong Rengan's "coolie elder brother" had goaded him on as he murdered the servant, but over the coming weeks the brother would take on a larger and larger role in the incident. In June, a pamphlet published in Hong Kong stated that Roberts had finally admitted that Hong Rengan himself actually hadn't attacked the servant; it was his brother who had beaten the poor man. Neither had the beating been entirely unprovoked; the servant had been found guilty of an indeterminate crime (one source said he had defecated in the king's path), and Roberts had been trying to shield him from punishment. That was precisely the kind of favoritism that had already opened Hong Rengan to attacks from within the palace and from which his brother was likely to take a hand to protect him. There was no evidence to corroborate any assault on Roberts himself.[14] It would appear that it was the Tennessee preacher who snapped that day, not the Shield King.

For his own part, Hong Rengan described the falling-out with Issachar Roberts as a minor incident, though he may have downplayed its importance to conceal his disappointment. All he said of it was that due to "some slight misunderstanding one day," Roberts "made a precipitate flight from the city and every effort failed to win him back."[15] But no matter what actually took place between the Shield King and Issachar Roberts on that cold January day in Nanjing, from that point on, Hong Rengan's side—and therefore the side of sympathy for the rebels on religious grounds—was no longer to be heard in Shanghai. The damage to Taiping foreign relations was serious. As one of their contemporaries put it with regret, the American preacher's abandonment of Nanjing meant that "the principal link which has connected our Protestant missionaries with the Taeping movement is now broken."[16] There was no longer any direct line of communication—be it accurate, exaggerated, fanciful, critical, or otherwise—to connect the rebels to the world outside their realm.

The timing could hardly have been worse, coming just as the foreigners in Shanghai were bracing for the approach of Li Xiucheng's armies. In such uncertain times, this was news to silence any voice that might speak in the rebels' defense. Because for the time being, at least, it appeared that the Taiping's most enlightened king—the gentle, round-faced darling of the foreign missionaries, the figurehead of a new regime to steer China into the global currents of the nineteenth century—had all along been nothing more than an illusion. And as the Shield King's outer semblance dissolved into the ether, the dark being that stepped from the wings to assume its place was a monster, just like all of the others.

While Zeng Guofan patiently expanded and trained his forces in Anqing through the winter of 1861–1862, the gentry and local officials downriver in isolated Shanghai were left to fend for themselves. They had sent a small delegation up to Anqing by steamship back in November to beg General Zeng, with ostentatious tears in their eyes, to send his Hunan forces down to their coastal entrepôt and protect them. They promised that if he could defend Shanghai, between the customs revenue and the contributions from local businessmen, they could provide him with hundreds of thousands of taels of silver a month. But Zeng initially demurred; he was well aware of the wealth that existed in Shanghai, but strategically his focus was on Nanjing, and Shanghai was just too far on the other side of it. From the inland perspective of a Hunanese farmer, Shanghai was the end of the world. He told them to be patient and said that perhaps when Li Hongzhang was finished drilling his army in the spring he could find some way to help them. But that wouldn't be for several months at least, and the delegation returned to Shanghai empty-handed.

Facing the near certainty of a Taiping attack during the winter months and with no assurance of protection from the British and French, the wealthy Chinese of Shanghai had nothing to fall back on but their expensive (and scarcely effective) foreign mercenary force under Frederick Townsend Ward. Driven by the continued promise of high pay and unrestrained plundering, the Salem-born filibuster had managed to continue his work despite the British government's attempts to shut him down. After escaping from Admiral Hope's flagship the previous summer, Ward had stolen back to his muddy base at Songjiang and reconvened the remnants of his tattered militia. There were only sixty-eight foreign mercenaries left after the earlier defeats and the British raids, but they still had their Napoleon field guns, and they still had the promise of riches if they could finally storm the gates of Qingpu, ten miles to the northwest.

Ward's soldiers had already failed to take that city from the Taiping in at least four attempts over the previous year, and when they tried again that summer, they fared no better. They used the same spearhead strategy as before—their small foreign force would blast the gates with their artillery and storm the walls, and then a large imperial force would follow after them to invade the city and drive out the rebel defenders. But once again, the imperial reinforcements failed to materialize on time. The defeat was brutal, with Ward losing nearly a third of his already shredded force. Not that it gained him any sympathy from the Shanghai foreign community; Ward's filibustering was a source of such maddening embarrassment there that the news of the small massacre at Qingpu was greeted with relief. Many hoped that this meant his ignominious career was finally over, and Shanghai's *North-China Herald* declared that the fresh defeat at Qingpu, following on the heels of the earlier arrests, had finally brought the foreign militia's "dishonourable career to a close." Frederick Bruce reported to Lord Russell on July 3 his "satisfaction that the Foreign Legion has been disbanded."[17]

But the last hadn't been heard from Ward. As the troubles in the United States began to bleed over into the international community, he surfaced again. In late August 1861, a rumor spread in Shanghai that a local clipper named the *Neva* had been purchased by a group of Californians ("rather hard characters" as one resident described them) who had flashed an envelope with a Montgomery postmark, which they said was a letter of marque from Jefferson Davis, the president of the Confederacy. The *China Daily Press* and *China Mail* in Hong Kong both reported that the leader of this gang of Confederate privateers was Ward. According to the reports, his group was going to outfit the *Neva* with guns taken from the U.S. munitions store in Shanghai (the master of which was a southerner) and then start sinking Union merchant ships off the China coast. [18]

The United States had only one naval vessel in China at the time, the little USS *Saginaw,* which sailed full speed from Hong Kong to Shanghai to hunt down the *Neva*—but only after two of its officers with southern sympathies resigned when they learned their mission. In the end, the *Neva* turned out to carry not cannons but whiskey, though the earlier reports made enough of a splash back in the United States that Ward became suddenly famous as America's man of adventure in China, or as *The New York Times* now called him, "the celebrated fillibuster."[19] On November 9, the *New York Herald* tried to dispel persistent rumors that he was serving the Confederates by publishing an editorial claiming Frederick Townsend Ward for the Union's side. It said that Ward was in fact dead set against secession and quoted as proof a letter he had written to a friend in New York (one of the few surviving letters from his hand, in fact, since his descendants, ashamed of his sordid career, later burned most of his correspondence). "I trust that by this time the government have shortened some of the seceding rascals by a head or two, and retaken Sumter, or, at least, laid siege to it," Ward wrote to his friend. "I only wish I could be with you to take a hand in the affair."[20]

No matter which side he was on, the outlaw Ward was by far the most conspicuous of his countrymen in China at a time when the pressures of the U.S. Civil War were beginning to wear heavily on the community of the treaty ports. There were ten times as many British as Americans in Shanghai ("and a most disagreeable snobbish set they are," wrote one Yankee), and though most of the Americans in China were northerners, their English neighbors were overwhelmingly pro-South. Nearly all Union naval power had been recalled to North America to blockade the southern ports—leaving only the *Saginaw,* which rotted out in December 1861 and left nothing at all. The American merchants in China were forced to depend on Her Majesty's warships to protect their business interests, and they deeply resented the dependence. Fights broke out at dinner parties when Englishmen made cracks about their war.[21]

The bad blood between the British and Americans in Shanghai came to the boiling point in early 1862 over the so-called *Trent* incident. Near Cuba, in November 1861, a U.S. captain had chased down and boarded the British mail steamer *Trent* to arrest two Confederate diplomats who were among its passengers. Britain, outraged at the American boarding of a ship under its flag, came to the brink of declaring war on the United States. As British forces sailed for Canada in preparation to invade from the north, Admiral Hope readied his forces in Shanghai to seize the homes, ships, and assets of their American neighbors.[22] (Though a hopeful rumor spread among the Americans that if that happened, Ward was going to launch his own preemptive attack on Hope's ships, steal them, and turn their cannons on the British settlement.)[23] The tension was eventually defused, but through the winter of 1862 every gun that sounded to announce the arrival of a steamer from North America saw a drove of anxious American patriots rushing down to the dock to ply the crew for news, desperate to know whether their country was at war with Britain. "In the event of a war," one of them predicted, "business will be entirely broken up and nearly all the Americans in this place will make tracks for San Francisco."[24]

Meanwhile, the Taiping were coming. The alarms first sounded on January 11, when the smoke of distant fires began to darken the horizon north of Shanghai. A new wave of refugees began arriving outside the city the next day, old women and children carrying their few possessions.[25] The fires came closer. Bells were rung, cannons cleaned, and the foreign consuls held a secret meeting to plan a defense for the city. The local volunteers mustered deep into the night, watching from the lookouts with apprehension as the nearing glow lit up the landscape to their north. Americans dusted themselves off and joined ranks with the British and French. "[I]f opportunity occurs," wrote one to his mother, "we will show the Englishmen that the clay we're made of is not inferior to their own."[26]

Their worry was real. Despite the easy repulse of the Taiping from Shanghai in 1860, there were scattered reports indicating that the rebels were now better armed and disciplined than the Allies expected. A British sailor named Goverston claimed on January 18 that he'd been captured and released a few miles outside Shanghai by a force of 15,000 rebels, who had plied him with drink and interrogated him about the city's defenses. He reported that they had been carrying British and German muskets and that an Arab in their ranks had told him that there was another unit on the way armed with Enfield rifles, as well as a secretive detachment of European soldiers. By his account, the rebel troops were "very fine-looking men" who seemed well fed. (Then again, by his own admission Goverston had gotten so drunk in Shanghai that he'd overstayed his shore leave, so he might have concocted the whole account to avoid punishment.) Harder evidence to back up Goverston's account came a few days later when a force of two or three thousand musket-toting rebels overran the town of Wusong ten miles to the north of Shanghai, capturing the outlet from the Huangpu River to the Yangtze Delta. A Royal Navy captain who witnessed the fighting reported that he was "quite astonished" at how well organized and equipped they were—compared not just to the paltry defenders of Wusong but to the elite imperial troops he remembered from the Peiho.[27]

Li Xiucheng had no desire to destroy Shanghai in the process of capturing it from the imperials, so he followed a strategy of wide encirclement, testing the resolution of the foreigners to resist his advance. In January, five main armies—some numbering in the thousands, some in the tens of thousands—occupied the towns surrounding Shanghai at a distance of several miles on each side. His supporters began pumping propaganda into Songjiang and Shanghai, large broadsheets promising safety and protection to all who came over to their side. In the broadsheets, Li Xiucheng pointed to the record of his army during its journey through Jiangxi and Hubei over the past year and its recent conquest of Zhejiang. "In all the places I have passed through," read one, "I have given comfort and peace to the people who have pledged their allegiance, and rank and salary to the [officers of the militia] who have surrendered."[28] "You are advised," it continued, " . . . to follow their example promptly, make up your minds like the sun and the moon, and come to us like running water." As for the foreigners, he reminded them to stay out of the conflict and warned that any who gave aid to the resistors "will be like a flying moth dashing into the fire, seeking his own extirpation."[29]

With the visible menace of massed troops in the distance and the threatened decline of trade as Shanghai's lines of communication to the interior were slowly and forcibly cut off, Li Xiucheng hoped to get the imperial authorities in Shanghai to surrender without any need for a direct assault on the city itself. Dread settled over the city. Admiral Hope sent to Hong Kong for British reinforcements, and the consul in Canton relayed to London the news of Shanghai's precarious position. "Our protective force is small," he said, "with a wide space to cover, crammed to overflowing with a refugee Chinese population, among whom, doubtless, is a large proportion of rebel element, ready, in the event of an attack in front, to create a panic behind."[30]

As new waves of refugees stumbled into the already overcrowded

Shanghai foreign settlement for protection, reports came that 80,000 Taiping troops were on the march from Suzhou, planning to take boats downriver from Qingpu to Shanghai and arrive on or about January 25.[31] The main body of British and French troops set themselves up to defend the walled Chinese city, while the broad foreign settlement with its masses of refugees was left to two hundred volunteers, some policemen with rifles and bayonets, and a contingent of Punjabi infantry at the farthest margin. On January 24, the day before the rumors said the Taiping would arrive, British and French authorities plastered the walls with their own broadsides in Chinese, announcing that Shanghai and its immediate area were under the protection of the Allies. Then they braced themselves for the coming attack.

But the Taiping didn't arrive on January 25. And the next day, with still no sign of the coming army, Heaven—or Providence, as *The North-China Herald* called it—intervened.[32] Shanghai lay in a subtropical zone that reached broiling temperatures in the summer and rarely went below freezing in the winter, but on January 26, 1862, as the city's defense forces watched out over the horizon for the approaching enemy, snow began to fall. It would fall for three days, over rebels and merchants, over refugees and missionaries, burying the houses and walls and fields in pristine white. The rivers froze over with treacherous sheets of ice, and the narrow horse paths threading through the complex of paddies in the countryside were obliterated, so that movement became nearly impossible. It reached two feet in Shanghai and a foot in Ningbo, paralyzing the lower Yangtze region completely. By January 30, the eastern seaboard was encased in ice and frost on what should have been auspicious as the first day of the Chinese New Year (year 1 of the new Qing emperor's reign, year 12 of the rebels). A Ningbo missionary in his solid home, fire blazing, still measured an indoor temperature of only thirteen degrees above zero at night, while out in the field, for mile upon mile, rebel soldiers hovered near death in their thin tents, shivering.[33]

The weather broke in early February, and as the snow and ice started to thaw, the weakened and dispirited Taiping forces stirred themselves back into motion. But now they found their problems of weather compounded by an unexpected resistance at Songjiang, the stepping-stone to Shanghai. It turned out that for the past several months, Frederick Townsend Ward—separately from his flirtations with his own country's war—had been training a new militia there. This one was different from the one that had collapsed back in June, primarily because he had finally given up on trying to recruit deserters from the European ships and started training local Chinese troops from Songjiang instead. He kept a minimal staff of experienced Americans and Europeans from his earlier militia to do the training and serve as officers but otherwise relied on Chinese soldiers—and as a Chinese soldier cost only a tenth the salary of a foreign mercenary, it was a much larger force as well.

Most of Ward's foreign officers had been with him since nearly the beginning, and his two lieutenants (who got to become colonels once he gathered enough troops to start calling himself a general) were both Americans like him. One was a whaler from Maine named Edward Forester, who'd been stranded by mutiny in Japan and later made his way to China.[34] The other was a flamboyant southerner from North Carolina named Henry Andrea Burgevine, the son of a French officer who'd served in the Napoleonic Wars and wound up his career as a French instructor in Chapel Hill. Burgevine himself had served two years as a volunteer in the French Army in the Crimea, but otherwise his prior career, which would hardly seem to have destined him to be a mercenary, included stints as a newspaper editor, as a postal clerk, and, from age nine to seventeen, as a page in the U.S. Senate.[35]

Ward taught his Chinese troops to respond to English-language commands and to follow standard bugle calls. He outfitted them in European-style uniforms that by all accounts were quite smart, with matching knickerbockers and jackets in blue (for artillery) or green (for infantry), and green turbans all around. In the heat of summer they all wore white knickerbockers and jackets with red facings.[36] Ward worked to train his men to fight and move in quick formation: to come into line, to form an infantry square, to fire only on command.[37] It was an echo of the "Canton Coolie Corps" that had so pleased the British during their invasion of Beijing, except that these men would carry guns rather than supplies.

He equipped his men with cutting-edge weapons from the arms dealers of Shanghai: Enfield rifles from England, the same that were being sold by the boatload to both armies in the United States,[38] along with smooth-bore British muskets and some Prussian rifles. With steady drill, they reportedly became good marksmen. Through the agency of his brother Henry Gamaliel Ward, who had followed him to China to get in on the action, Ward also began casting about for heavier artillery, even gunboats if they could be had. The money was there; his patron, Yang Fang, and his counterparts were flush with cash from their share of the foreign trade in Shanghai, and they were willing to pony up for the sake of their own protection. Despite the widely perceived immorality (and questionable legality) of making large-scale arms purchases for a Chinese force, Ward's brother even made so bold as to try to buy the USS *Saginaw* from the American minister (who refused).[39] When that failed, he tried to purchase a fleet of light gunships from the United States via his father, who set up shop in New York as a ship's merchant in the hope of building up a family fortune in cooperation with his sons in China.

Ward was hardly alone in equipping Chinese troops with Western arms, for at least since the fall of Ningbo there had been a steady commerce of weapons sold to the rebels by foreigners. The arms weren't the best of quality, but they easily outclassed the seventeenth-century matchlocks that had started the war, and they came in substantial quantities. The accounts of the secretive trade are hard to come by, but the records of captured shipments tell the tale well enough. In one instance, in 1862, the British firm Davidson and Company was caught running a ship via Singapore that turned out to carry three hundred cannons, a hundred cases of small arms, and fifty tons of ammunition for the rebels.[40] In another, the account book from a captured American ship revealed that its firm had just supplied the rebels at Wusong with nearly three thousand muskets, eight hundred pieces of artillery, eighteen thousand cartridges, and more than three million percussion caps.[41] The lower Yangtze region was a powder keg.

Ward's revamped militia fought its first pitched battle on February 3, 1862, while the ground still lay under its frozen cover, and they managed to hold their own at Songjiang against an army of 20,000 Taiping soldiers.[42] They laid out an ambush of hidden artillery batteries just outside the town and surprised the weakened rebel attackers who approached through the snow, mowing down more than two thousand of them before their commander called the retreat. Ward's men captured more than seven hundred of the escaping rebels alive and sent them in chains to Shanghai to be executed by the *daotai*.[43] Two days later, his militia went on the offensive, attacking a small hill halfway between Songjiang and Qingpu and forcing the Taiping commander to pull back from his positions there.

For the first time, the Shanghai gentry's private army was showing signs of life. The acting Jiangsu governor, Xue Huan (the same official who had produced Ward's false citizenship papers the previous summer), suggested changing the name of the force from the uninspired yet descriptive "Foreign Arms Corps" that they had been using to the more grandiose "Ever-Victorious Army."[44] The flowery title (wishful, as they had few actual victories) would be treated by some of Ward's later biographers as a sign of the Chinese worship of their foreign military leader,[45] though actually the new name, in replacing "Foreign Arms Corps," was little more than an attempt to entice more Chinese, who generally disliked foreigners, to enlist in the force—and to make it more palatable to Beijing, so the new government, to which it was now finally unveiled, wouldn't dwell on its loyalty to a non-Chinese commander.

In terms of that loyalty, though foreigners would always refer to the militia as "Ward's force" or "Ward's disciplined Chinese," it was in fact a part of the local military structure and Ward took his commands from the Shanghai officials and bankers who paid him. His immediate orders came from the Shanghai *daotai,* Wu Xu, who, from a handful of surviving instructions, appears to have been quite respectful of him, addressing Ward as *huixia,* an honorific term for "general," and elevating his name above the rest of the text whenever it appeared. But at the same time, his ingratiating respect was more than likely motivated by fear, for Wu Xu clearly did not trust Ward and his militia to act with any kind of restraint. In particular, he apparently worried about uncontrolled looting by Ward's men. In one order sending Ward to attack Qingpu, Wu Xu pleaded with him to leave as soon as the fighting was over. "Do not allow the Ever-Victorious Army to enter the city," he wrote. "That is the clean way to do things, to avoid trouble." He then repeated himself again, to emphasize the point: "As soon as you break into the city, give it to [your imperial counterpart] and go back to Songjiang. Don't let the Ever-Victorious Army enter the city."[46]

Despite the dangerous elements of the force under Ward's command, he was the best hope of the Shanghai gentry and they did what they could to maintain his loyalty. Yang Fang, the wealthy banker who had raised the funds to supply the force, even made so bold as to give his daughter Changmei in marriage to Ward in March 1862. It was an odd arrangement, for in Chinese terms she was damaged goods: her previous betrothed had died before their wedding, which made her all but unmarriageable to another Chinese husband while not even giving her the status of a widow.[47] There is no record of what happened to the Chinese woman to whom Ward had been engaged the previous summer, when Hope had arrested him, but Changmei most certainly was not her. Primarily, their marriage functioned as a business arrangement. For the banker Yang Fang, it kept Ward close at hand and helped ensure his loyalty (and short of marrying her to the foreigner, his unlucky daughter had no value at all by the calculations of the Shanghai business community). For Ward, it was a means of ensuring that Yang Fang came through with his promises of funding for the militia. In the middle was Changmei herself, an enigma whose only lasting legacy is a bit of jewelry that now resides in a museum in Salem, Massachusetts.

In Shanghai, the aftermath of the snowstorm found the British and French scrambling to improve their own defenses. Admiral Hope and his French counterpart, Rear Admiral Auguste Léopold Protet (a fellow veteran of the embarrassing Peiho repulse), met on February 13 to sign a joint agreement to defend Shanghai from the Taiping advance, and they began sketching plans to clear out Hope's long-cherished thirty-mile radius by organizing a land force that could take to the field against the rebels. Lord Russell had made it clear to Admiral Hope that Britain would not permit any intervention in the civil war save to prevent the torture and death of British subjects, but Hope, as was his wont, disregarded the standing orders and acted on the exigencies of the moment.

The forces at their disposal were scant; they had their gunships but only 1,550 regular troops, 650 of them British and the rest French, with a smattering of seamen in reserve.[48] There were an additional 200 civilian volunteers, including the Americans. The Qing imperial forces in and around Shanghai, which formally numbered about 10,000, were universally considered useless. Such a meager Allied force might be sufficient to hold the fortified walls of Shanghai's Chinese city against a Taiping attack, but it had no hope of beating the rebels in the field. Admiral Hope needed some way to increase his force, or else he would have to remain bottled up within the walls of Shanghai. And that was why, in one of the stranger twists of circumstance, Admiral Hope decided to take a new look at the renegade American filibuster whose militia he had previously been trying so hard to shut down.

As Ward appeared no longer to be trying to entice European sailors to desert their ships, and, more important, since his new Chinese force had actually managed to hold off a Taiping attack on Songjiang, Admiral Hope decided to put his hostility toward the American mercenary aside and try an alliance instead. Ward had no particular interest in protecting Shanghai, but support from Allied gunships would make his conquest of Taiping towns easier, so he agreed they should work together. By the end of February, Admiral Hope was already speaking of Frederick Townsend Ward in glowing new terms—no longer as a renegade or a filibuster but as a respectable expert "upon whose experience of the Chinese I am disposed to place very considerable reliance."[49]

Frederick Bruce gave tentative approval to Hope's plans to raise a land force, remarking in a letter of March 19 that "it requires but little experience in China to be assured that the effect of remaining on a strict defensive within the walls is to convince our assailants that we fear them, and are unable to meet them in the field."[50] But even though he approved Hope's intention to drive the rebels away from the immediate region around Shanghai, he insisted that the Allies could hold on to only Shanghai itself and it was up to the Qing forces to garrison any towns that might be taken back from the rebels. As far as Hope's proposal to cooperate with Ward, Bruce approved heartily. Following Hope's lead, Bruce felt that the American filibuster's hybrid force of foreign officers and Chinese soldiers was a model that might enable the Qing government to win the war. "I see no hopes of rescuing this country from universal anarchy and brigandage," Bruce told Hope in the same letter, "except in the organization of a military force on improved principles; and I agree that Colonel Ward's force affords a nucleus . . . which should be encouraged and augmented."

Zeng Guofan, however, was extremely wary of letting foreigners fight the dynasty's war. For one thing, he didn't think they would be particularly effective. At Qimen, he had known that there were foreigners in Li Xiucheng's campaign army but had dismissed them as "insignificant demons who have to be hired with money."[51] Loyalty, to him, was a far more effective motivator than greed. He did, however, recognize that foreigners might be a practical necessity in Shanghai. On February 20, soon after Ward's first victories near Songjiang, Zeng Guofan conceded in a memorial to the throne that it might be in the dynasty's interest to let the foreign mercenaries help defend Shanghai—and even Ningbo, where, he reasoned, they already lived and where they therefore might be expected to help with local defense for their own sakes. But he strongly advised the government against letting any of them campaign inland, especially to Suzhou or Nanjing. Since there were no foreign communities in those places, the Europeans would be acting on a purely mercenary basis, and this would open up serious dangers. "If they lose, we'll be a laughing-stock," he wrote. "But if they *win*, who knows what future dangers will ensue." It was anyone's best guess what they would demand afterward in return for their services. So he repeated that foreigners should be allowed only to protect Shanghai.[52]

Nevertheless, facing an insurmountable shortage of funds in Anqing, he finally came to the conclusion that Shanghai shouldn't be left *entirely* to the foreigners to defend, because he needed it for himself. That is, as long as the international city operated independently, under the *daotai*, Wu Xu, and the governor, Xue Huan, the gentry of Shanghai could fund their own mercenary force and pay their taxes to the central government, but there was nothing in it to be gained for Zeng Guofan's army—which risked mutinies if it didn't start paying its troops more than the fraction of their wages they had been getting. "There are ten million people and ten billion riches in the single county of Shanghai," he wrote to his brother on February 1, showing a change of heart, "and all the southeastern provinces put together can't compare to its wealth and population. We have to find some way to preserve it."⁵³ Ten days later he wrote, "I hear that at Shanghai we can take in five hundred thousand taels a month; I can't bear to sit by and watch it fall into enemy hands."⁵⁴

So Zeng Guofan and the Shanghai gentry finally found common ground. The gentry wanted Zeng's army to come downriver to protect their homes and personal livelihoods, while Zeng Guofan, for his part, saw Shanghai as a means of funding his campaign for Nanjing and as a possible base for launching an attack on Suzhou. Both sides were self-interested, but their immediate goals were the same, and in contrast to the brush-off he had given to the delegation from Shanghai back in November, by the spring of 1862 Zeng Guofan had decided he would try to send an army to Shanghai to break the Taiping siege. If successful, that army could be the third front in his strategy for cutting off Nanjing. The only problem that remained was how to get it there.

The Shanghai *daotai*, Wu Xu, solved the problem for him. In a quiet realization of the scheme that had been so firmly denied to Hong Rengan, Wu Xu managed to contract with a British firm, Mackenzie, Richardson & Company, to transport 9,000 soldiers and support personnel from Anqing down to Shanghai on British steamships. Both the imperials and the British authorities assumed (quite correctly) that the rebel shore batteries wouldn't dare fire on a ship under the Union Jack. And in stark contrast to Harry Parkes's curt lecture to the Taiping kings in Nanjing on the "rights and duties of neutrality" when he had told them the British couldn't possibly transport supplies to their starving garrison at Anqing, Admiral Hope in this case readily approved the use of British steamships to move Li Hongzhang's army, because it "would facilitate his plans for freeing Shanghae from the disagreeable proximity of the Tae-pings."⁵⁵

With three round trips in less than a month, by the end of April, Li

Hongzhang's army of 6,500 Anhui troops and their support personnel found themselves, with relative suddenness, encamped at Shanghai and ready to begin fighting their way inward toward Nanjing from the east. Li Hongzhang assumed power as the governor of the province, replacing Xue Huan and taking a position above the Shanghai *daotai*, Wu Xu, and in doing so he also took charge of the local imperial military forces—which meant that the Ever-Victorious Army was now his to command.

Zeng Guofan was delighted by the speed and safety with which Li Hongzhang's army had been moved, and he now had his loyal force on the other side of the rebel kingdom. But the expense of the move was an outrage: 180,000 taels of silver, representing roughly a third of the monthly Shanghai customs revenue, or the monthly salary of more than forty thousand of his soldiers. It was "shocking and pitiful!" he wrote in a letter home.[56] It confirmed his opinions about accepting foreign aid, and he took it as evidence that China would have to build its own steamships so the foreigners couldn't continue to take advantage of them. But worse than any issue of national pride, it cut to the bone of his civil responsibilities—for he was not just a military general but also the governor-general in charge of the welfare of the people who lived under his jurisdiction, and those 180,000 taels of silver represented an extravagant outlay of money from private donations, poured into the hands of greedy foreigners, at a time when the imperial coffers were bankrupt and he could barely supply his army in Anhui province, let alone provide for the general population under his control. And as he observed in the same letter home, as short as his army's rations might have been at the time, in Anhui it was only the soldiers who had anything to eat at all.[57]

The government in Beijing had actually ordered Zeng Guofan to send his brother Guoquan to Shanghai, rather than Li Hongzhang. But Guoquan coveted the glory of recovering Nanjing even more than Zeng Guofan himself did, and he refused outright to take his forces anywhere except to the rebel capital—to the point of delaying his return from Hunan with the new recruits until it was clear that Zeng Guofan would send Li Hongzhang down to Shanghai rather than himself. So, once again, Zeng Guofan ignored the wishes of the central government, and with the promise that he would fight in the central theater, Guoquan finally returned to Anqing in March. The green recruits were assigned to garrison duty, while the veterans rallied to go on campaign with him once again.

Li Hongzhang's Anhui troops were still getting ready for their passage to Shanghai when, on March 24, against a backdrop of misery and starvation in Anhui, Zeng Guofan saw his brother off from Anqing at the head of a concentrated force of 20,000 Hunanese soldiers on land and water, joined by 5,000 more under their younger brother Guobao. Eastward they went along the north bank of the Yangtze River as it faded into the distance. Ahead of them lay the heart of the Taiping Heavenly Kingdom and, deep within it, the citadel of Nanjing.[58]

<hr>

As the Taiping approach stalled, Shanghai found itself under a slow and distant siege. The price of rice went up 50 percent. The price of flour doubled. The price of firewood more than doubled, thanks in part to the cold weather.[59] But the feared assault by the Taiping hordes did not come. Instead, the encirclement of Shanghai wore on, and all waited to see what would come of it. The British authorities on the ground never questioned that neutrality allowed them to defend Shanghai from immediate threats, which clearly included the rebel armies that surrounded them. And in this they had full public support from their local constituents; the *North China and Japan Market Report* speculated that the entire Shanghai foreign community, save those members who were getting rich running guns to the Taiping, was now ready to see the Allies "test the neutrality clauses of the Treaties with shot and shell."[60]

Joint operations between Ward and the British and French forces began on a small scale on February 21, 1862, with an assault on the village of High Bridge, about eight miles from Shanghai. Ward had 600 men under his command, and Hope and Protet brought naval forces numbering 500 total, which they landed on shore with a 6-pounder rocket tube. The battle was over quickly, with only one Frenchman killed before the rebel garrison abandoned the village.[61] Pleased with the taste of success, they continued.

The reactions from the foreign population to the initial skirmishing were mixed. Some in Shanghai were delighted to see Hope taking an active hand against the rebels, none more so than the missionaries, whose giddy hopes for the advent of a Christian China under the Taiping had been dashed by the recent news of Hong Rengan's madness. Their disillusionment had left them bitter, and some now resented the rebels with a venom proportional to the loftiness of their former hopes. In a private letter on March 17, the Anglican bishop of Shanghai expressed full approval for Admiral Hope's operations and said he even wished Hope would go beyond the immediate defense of Shanghai. "It is said the authorities are only wanting to hear from Mr. Bruce, to knock [the rebels] out of all the walled towns in this Province," he wrote to the American missionary Samuel Wells Williams. "Indeed I hope they will not stop short of Nanking. It is time the country should be rid of these monsters."[62] But others charged that the British were unleashing chaos by provoking Taiping reprisals in the countryside and driving refugees into the city. "[A] great part of the miseries that the people around Shanghai are suffering," wrote another missionary to the *New-York Evangelist,* "must be laid to the policy that foreigners have pursued towards them."[63]

Ironically, some of the strongest voices of condemnation for Hope's newfound aggression came from the very Shanghai business community for whose sake, above all, he had taken up his fight. The merchants were hardly unanimous in their support for his actions, and many worried that this newly belligerent course of action against the Taiping would be self-destructive. The leading British trading firm, Jardine, Matheson and Company, wrote in its company circular on February 27, 1862, that "the policy the Allied Commanders are adopting will, it is feared, lead to disastrous consequences." It recounted the circumstances of the joint attack on High Bridge by Hope and Ward and stated that such actions could only serve to "exasperate a foe by no means to be despised." Given that "the whole country" beyond Shanghai was "in the hands of the Taepings," it warned that "should this suicidal policy be persisted in," it would "in the end materially interfere with, if not ruin, all trade."[64]

Though some missionaries might wish for it, and some businessmen might fear it, Admiral Hope still had no approval from London to mount a war against the rebels. The British government's policy was strict neutrality, so the fighting around Shanghai had to remain tightly restricted, responding only to the immediate threat to the city from the Taiping siege forces. Despite the blood that was shed in the small battles, both sides were still sounding each other out. "Fighting Jimmy" Hope had not, technically, gone on the offensive, and he hadn't engaged in any fighting beyond the immediate vicinity of Shanghai. But how he wished he could.

The tipping point finally came, as it almost inevitably had to, by way of an accident. On April 23, the Taiping in Ningbo had a celebration.[65] One of their commanders, by the name of Fan, had just returned from the provincial capital, Hangzhou, where he had been promoted. Things had been quiet in Ningbo for the past several months in spite of the spo-radic fighting to the north around Shanghai, and trade between Chinese and foreign merchants was on the rise. The Hong Kong correspondent of the London *Times* had reported a week earlier that the Taiping at Ningbo "maintain the same peaceful attitude towards foreigners" as before and the region's Chinese traders had "come to an understanding with the chiefs of the rebel garrison," so they were returning to their businesses. The pri-mary article of import was grain to feed the surrounding countryside, and Ningbo had begun to export Britain's most desperately needed commod-ity, cotton.[66] Indeed, cotton aside, the insatiable need of Zhejiang province for rice in wartime—and the ability of British and French ships to supply it cheaply from a bumper crop in Siam—meant that, notwithstanding a drop in silk and tea exports, the overall balance sheet for Ningbo foreign trade in the year ending June 30, 1862, would in fact show an increase of 82 percent over the previous year, when the city was still under imperial control.[67] It was scarcely the devastation that Consul Harvey had predicted. As an alternative to the scattered hostilities near Shanghai across the bay to the north, the *Times'* correspondent suggested hopefully that Ningbo "shows that there are other than warlike means of dealing with" the rebels.

Harvey himself, however, had steered even further to the extremes of prophetic doom. A letter he wrote to Frederick Bruce on March 20, which would be published in *The Times* a few months later, removed any quali-fications he had ever put on his intense hatred of the rebels—and in it he admitted that he had cherished and nurtured that hatred since long before anything that had ever happened at Ningbo. "I now . . . take the liberty of declaring," he wrote to Bruce, "once and for all (and for ten years I have firmly adhered to and been consistent in this opinion), that the Taeping rebellion is the greatest delusion as a political or popular movement, and the Taeping doctrines the most gigantic and blasphemous imposition as a creed, or ethics, that the world has ever witnessed." On and on it went, until it reached its most damning conclusion: "Your Excellency may rest assured that we shall only arrive at a correct appreciation of this movement, and do it thorough justice, when it is treated by us as land piracy on an extensive scale—piracy odious in the eyes of all men—and, as such, to be swept off the face of the earth by every means within the power of the Christian and civilized nations trading with this vast empire."[68]

In the course of the Taiping celebrations on April 23, at a little after ten in the morning, a salute was fired in General Fan's honor at the eastern gate of Ningbo, which faced the river that divided the Chinese city from the foreign settlement. The guns were not well aimed, and a handful of projectiles sailed across the river, whistling through the rigging of the French gunship *L'Étoile* as they passed and landing in the foreign settlement, where they struck and killed two or three Chinese residents (the number was never clear).[69] The commander of HMS *Ringdove,* which had also experienced uncomfortably close musket fire in recent days, wrote to the Taiping generals to complain. He received profuse apologies the very same day. General Huang, the second of the two Taiping generals in Ningbo, promised that he would find out which soldiers had been responsible and "punish them very severely."[70]

In Shanghai, Admiral Hope acted as soon as he heard that shots had been fired in Ningbo but before he learned about the apologies. He and the French admiral Protet dispatched a joint force under Captain Roderick Dew in the *Encounter* to ensure "proper reparation for this outrage."[71] On his arrival at Ningbo, however, Captain Dew learned about the apologies of the Taiping commanders and found them fully acceptable. In Dew's opinion the situation had already been defused, so he wrote a friendly letter to Generals Huang and Fan on April 27 to accept their apologies. Their messages, he wrote, were "so satisfactory, and tend so much to impress on us your wish to maintain friendly relations with the English and French," that he would not demand any further reparation other than removal of the specific guns that were aimed toward the foreign settlement, lest such an accident repeat itself. He reassured them that the British were neutral and that the rebels at Ningbo, as long as they remained friendly, "may rest assured that no breach of friendly relations shall emanate from our side."[72]

But then, strangely, on the following day, Dew sent another letter to the Taiping commanders. This time he was no longer content with the apologies he had accepted the day before, and accused them of allowing "grave insults" to the British that were "a breach of the amicable relations which we have wished to maintain with your people." He had been sent from Shanghai "with a considerable force," he wrote, "to demand . . . an ample apology for these insults." And now, on April 28, he demanded not just that they remove the guns from the gate where the salute had been fired, but that they remove *all* guns facing eastward in the direction of the foreign settlement, including a major new battery along the riverbank that was still under construction. They had twenty-four hours to begin dismantling the battery, he warned, or the British would do it themselves; and if they should be fired upon while doing so, "I shall look on it as an act of hostility, shall remove all foreign ships from the river, and our people from the settlement, and probably the capture of the city of Ningpo may follow."[73]

The sudden reversal of Dew's tone from friendly to hostile and the sudden retraction of his previous acceptance of the apology appear to have had two causes. The first was that he apparently figured out for the first time that there had been two incidents, not one: the shots fired earlier at the *Ringdove* and the salute that had killed residents of the settlement had been on different days. He decided that this constituted a pattern of aggression. The other reason was that new orders had just been received from London, and those orders were Lord Russell's response, at long last, to the reports that had been sent to him back in January. As it turned out, the combination of Consul Harvey's ominous predictions of the destruction of Ningbo, Admiral Hope's intimations of Taiping atrocities at Hangzhou, and Harry Parkes's testimony that a war with the Taiping rebels was fast approaching had secured exactly the response for which they all had been hoping.

As Lord Russell explained to the Admiralty after he read the reports, "The fall of Ningpo, if it has not been accompanied by all the atrocities which have been witnessed in the case of the capture of other cities, has [nevertheless] paralyzed all trade and industry, and has driven away the whole, or a greater part, of the peaceable population, and has scattered ruin and devastation far and wide." Influenced by Harvey's judgments, Russell decided that sharing a port with the Taiping was not an experience the British should allow to repeat itself. "The interests of humanity and commerce alike," he concluded, "demand that the city and port of Shanghae . . . should be preserved from a similar fate."[74]

But Russell did not draw the line at Shanghai. Similar protection, he decided, "should, as far as possible, be accorded to the other Treaty ports"—meaning that Ningbo would now fall under the umbrella of British military defense as well. Russell concluded by telling the Admiralty to inform James Hope that "the British flag is to be protected on the Yangtze by a naval force, and generally that British commerce is to have the aid of Her Majesty's ships of war."[75] Admiral Hope was given free rein to engage the Taiping forces in Shanghai, in the treaty ports, and practically anywhere else in China where he deemed them a direct threat to British trade interests. Those orders reached Shanghai just before Captain Dew left for Ningbo, and judging from his change of heart on April 28, it would appear that he had decided, upon reflection, to take them as license to find cause for war.[76]

The Taiping generals wrote back to Dew's second, threatening letter with a message as mollifying as the ones before. They apologized profusely, again. But they refused to remove the east-facing guns—which, they pointed out, were necessary to defend their city from the river. They said that their own people had suffered equally serious crimes and insults on the foreign side of the river, but they had never demanded apologies or reparations like this. This episode, they said, was simply an unfortunate and relatively minor accident. Nevertheless, they offered to remove all powder and shot from the guns at issue, stop up their embrasures, and open them again only if the city should come under attack. "We are inordinarily desirous of remaining on good terms with you," they insisted.[77] But they maintained that they had to be able to defend themselves.

Captain Dew cherished their refusal of his demands. A week later, on May 5, Consul Harvey brought the news that the deposed Ningbo *daotai* (the one who had lost the city in December) had just returned from his nearby exile with a ragtag fleet of 150 small, armed boats under an erstwhile coastal pirate named Apak, along with a mob of peasants, men and women alike, armed with "pitch-forks, bamboos with spikes, hoes, and some even with bludgeons."[78] This "strange army," as Dew described it to Hope, had come up the river with the intention of attacking Ningbo, and according to Harvey they were asking for British and French support. Furthermore, they planned to attack at exactly the point in the wall where Dew had just demanded that the Taiping remove all of their defensive guns; obviously, news of the friction at Ningbo had spread, and rather quickly at that. Captain Dew gave them his full approval, telling the *daotai* that "in consequence of the rebels refusing certain demands we had made, I should have no objection to their passing up" past the foreign settlement on their way to assault Ningbo.[79] So up they came and made camp on the foreign side of the river with Dew's blessing.

Dew then wrote once more to the Taiping commanders—first to reiterate Britain's noncombative position ("we maintain a perfect neutrality," he chirped)—and then to give them a perfectly impossible ultimatum: because they had refused to remove the battery of guns facing the foreign settlement, if they should now use those guns to fire on their attackers (who were going to attack from precisely that direction, for precisely that reason), he would deem it an act of war against Great Britain. "[I]f you fire the guns or muskets from the battery or walls opposite the Settlement, on the advancing Imperialists, thereby endangering the lives of our men and people in the foreign Settlement," he warned them, "we shall then feel it our duty to return the fire, and bombard the city."[80] He offered them a single option: abandon Ningbo immediately.

Later, it would seem obvious to the skeptics that the whole bloody denouement had been planned in advance.[81] Indeed, even Harvey himself underscored the utter improbability of the timing when he wrote to Frederick Bruce on May 9 that this motley force of imperial loyalists had materialized "just at the point when our correspondence with the Chiefs had become as angry as it could well be without our actually coming to blows" and that it therefore presented an "extraordinary, but fortunate, coincidence . . . by far too good an opportunity to be thrown aside and lost."[82]

The bombardment began early the next morning.

CHAPTER 13

VAMPIRES

Compared to the nearly bloodless capture of Ningbo by the rebels in 1861, the recovery of the city in May 1862 was an abattoir. At first, the motley imperial forces held back and let the Europeans do the dangerous work. The British and French shelled the city with the combined artillery of six gunships (with a break at two o'clock so Captain Dew could enjoy his dinner), and then they sent an Allied storming party over the wall to open the gates from inside. The mob of bludgeon-wielding peasants and their pirate counterparts had to be goaded into crossing the river and entering after them, but once inside, they warmed to their task.[1] According to an eyewitness account published two weeks later in Hong Kong's *China Mail*, the pirate army "in a few hours did more damage than the rebels did in the whole of the five months that they had possession," while the *daotai*, newly restored to power in his city, spent the entire day after the Allied attack "chopping off the heads of the unlucky rebels that he caught."[2]

Even more disturbing to the readers of that account than its descriptions of severed heads and entrails were the fears it fanned that the British were turning into mercenaries for the Manchu regime. For it alleged that "one of the principal murderers and torturers" at Ningbo was Consul Harvey's personal servant (known to the foreigners as "Harvey's boy"), a young man named Zheng Afu, who "was dressed up in silks, and who, stuck upon a pony, paraded the city with attendants, ordering them to execute unfortunates." More to the point, it claimed that in the free-for-all following the invasion of the city, Harvey's servant had been "issuing orders . . . to the English soldiers" and that those soldiers had actually been obeying him. The servant's central role was corroborated by an unrelated account from a Chinese official in Zhejiang, who identified the same Zheng Afu as being the liaison between the British forces and the *daotai*'s pirate army and said that "Harvey's boy" had, in collusion with Apak, lit the fuse on the morning of May 10 by secretly firing on the *Encounter* from the Taiping side of the river, killing two crewmen and giving Dew justification to launch a full-scale artillery barrage against the rebels in response.[3] The question of who was serving whom was entirely unclear.

It was a shocking end to Britain's promises of nonintervention, coming especially as many were pointing to Ningbo as evidence that the Taiping were genuinely friendly to foreigners and welcomed trade. The English-language papers in China (save the now very prointervention *North-China Herald*) printed livid complaints. "So much mystery and double-dealing has been practised by the allies to wrest this port from the Taipings," read one article in the *Overland Trade Report,* "and so little regard for veracity pervades the official dispatches regarding their doings, that the truth is most difficult to arrive at, and has certainly never yet been published. . . . The mode of accomplishing this design reflects indelible disgrace on British prestige." And from the Hong Kong *Daily Press:* "There never was a falser, more unprovoked, or more unjustifiable act than the taking of Ningpo by the allies from the Taipings. It should, in fairness, be recorded to the eternal disgrace of Captain Roderic [*sic*] Dew, of H.M.S. *Encounter.*"[4]

Half a world away, *The New York Times* published a report from its correspondent in Shanghai declaring the assault on Ningbo to be the end of Britain's mere defense of the treaty ports and the new dawn of her colonial expansion in China. "There is a deep significance in these events," he wrote. From where he stood, it seemed obvious that the Qing dynasty couldn't survive without the sustained military support of England and France—and now those countries had shown that they were willing to provide it. "But will they do it for nothing?" he asked his American readers. "No. They will ere long become the virtual rulers of the empire."[5] His concern that the British (and secondarily the French) were setting up to take over China as they had done to India was widespread in the aftermath of the Ningbo invasion. However, this journalist dwelled less on the morality of the Allied breach of neutrality than on his own country's lack of a role. "Should not the United States have something to say, too, in the control of these questions, in which they have such tremendous interests at stake?" he asked. (Or, as the same pages later put it, "if in this instance we hold back, we shall ere long find China ruled by England and France, to our disadvantage.")[6] The question of America's position in China was, however, one that would have to wait until her own civil war was ended, until the time when the United States could resume its place in the competitions of the world. Until then, the correspondent could only lament the parallel he now saw at work between his own country and China, both nations weakened and laid open to foreign manipulation thanks to (as he saw it) the internal destructions of the Confederacy and the Taiping. "May our great rebellion and that of the Chinese," he concluded, "soon be found hiding in holes and caves, and disturb our peace no more."

If in the rawest sense Consul Harvey, Captain Dew, and Admiral Hope had unleashed their intervention for the sake of improving British trade, their efforts brought little advantage in the near term. After the city had been back under imperial control for a month, a pair of European merchants reported to the *Daily Press* in Hong Kong that the *daotai* had raised taxes to the point of being "almost a prohibition of trade" and the pirate fleet under Apak was "blockading the river, and preventing any produce being brought to this place." As evidence to counter rumors that the Taiping had laid waste to Zhejiang province in the months before the recapture of Ningbo, they circulated the diary of a silk trader from their own firm who had traveled through the districts inland from the city while it was still under rebel control. He had found the region lively and fertile, with "crops in a flourishing condition" and the people generally "quite happy." He said he had been "treated respectfully" by "friendly" people wherever he went and that things had been "quiet" (repeated twenty-one times in the course of the short diary). The rebels were indeed plundering villages, he observed, but they gave ample warning and "did not wish to interfere with any foreigners trading." Even after the outbreak of hostilities, he wrote, "the rebels very friendly to foreigners; they treated us well."[7]

The moral outrage surfacing in Shanghai and Hong Kong was at first scarcely to be heard in England itself, where public opinion was swinging hard against the Chinese rebels. Harry Parkes had made it clear in interviews and public appearances that the Taiping were a legion of monsters. Consul Harvey's grim reports on the ostensible destruction of Ningbo, as if it had been wiped off the map, gained wide publication with little to dispute them.

By the summer of 1862, even Karl Marx wrote off the Taiping after reading Harvey's dispatches. Marx's final article on the global significance of the civil war in China was published in the Viennese paper *Die Presse* in July, and he spent most of it quoting from one of Harvey's letters to Frederick Bruce. In the passages Marx quoted, Harvey declared that the truth of the Taiping "does not agree with the illusions of English missionaries who tell fairy tales about 'the salvation of China.' . . . After ten years of noisy quasi-activity, they have destroyed everything and produced nothing." The Chinese rebellion was a movement of violence and beheadings, Harvey wrote (and Marx quoted), of "hooligans, vagabonds and evil characters," of "infamy on the women and girls, without any limit whatsoever," of "terrorization" and "horror scenes." In its sum, it represented an "enormous mass of nothingness."

From Harvey's testimony, Marx concluded that the Taiping were "devils" who were "not conscious of any task, except the change of dynasty." "They are an even greater scourge to the population than the old rulers," he wrote. "It seems that their vocation is nothing else than to set against the conservative disintegration [of China], its destruction, in grotesque horrifying form, without any seeds for a renaissance." And in his disgust, he wrote off not just the rebels but the entire Chinese Empire—as had Lord Elgin—for being hopelessly lost to antiquity and therefore irrelevant to the rapidly changing world beyond its borders. "But only in China was such a sort of devil possible," Marx concluded. "It is the consequence of a fossil form of social life."[8]

The editors of the London *Times* wanted war. A year after calling Hong Xiuquan a "*de facto* Sovereign" with whom Britain should build trade relations, in May 1862 they declared the Taiping instead to be "the Thug of China, the desolator of cities, the provider of human carrion to the wild dogs, the pitiless exterminator, the useless butcher." They denounced the British defenders of the neutral policy in newly scathing terms, singling out especially Thomas Taylor Meadows, the consul whose February 1861 letter in favor of the Taiping government had now finally become available in England. They called him a "Sinologue hugging his theory at home" and accused him of denying the "sounds of massacre and the glare of flame [that] are monopolizing the attention of every inhabitant of the place." There was no question, they declared, that "it is time to attack these robbers."[9]

What had changed in the intervening year, of course, was that Harvey, Parkes, and Hope had taught them that the Taiping were a force of mere anarchy. What had *not* changed, however, was *The Times'* belief that China, together with India, would be Britain's salvation from the U.S. Civil War. "If it be fated that America must pass away from us as a profitable customer," its editors wrote a few weeks later, " ... then China and India together promise to rise up in its place, and to help us to pass, although painfully, through our difficulty." Britain could now break free of its dependence on the United States ("with her prohibitory tariffs, her smoking mounds of burning cotton, her impoverished people, and her inevitably approaching bankruptcy") by turning instead to Asia, where the real potential for the future lay. And although Britain was suffering from "the evil effects of having relied too confidently" on the United States, thankfully, they wrote, "the good seed we sowed, and harrowed, and watered in the Far East is springing up and bearing fruit."[10]

In light of Harvey's reports, *The Times* now declared that the only route to Great Britain's economic survival lay down the path of the Taiping's annihilation. The rebels had become a "dragon who interferes between us and our golden apples." It was a simple humanitarian issue, as the editors now explained to their readers: if the tea market in Shanghai and Ningbo should be ruined by the Taiping, the British government would have to raise the tax rate on tea in order to preserve its much-needed revenue from the trade. That would bring great hardship to the tea-drinking lower classes of English society, including those who were already starving from the collapse of the textile industry in Lancashire. Politicians advocating neutrality who spoke in high-minded and abstract terms about the morals of foreign policy, they charged, ignore "all consideration for hardships to be suffered by the people." England's "pursuit of a perfect neutrality" cared not a whit "for the tea-consumers of England or the tea-producers of China, any more than we have for the cotton-spinners of Lancashire." So intervention was a matter of humanitarian relief, not just for the peasants of China but also for England's own poor. And even putting aside the matter of the suffering of the common people, they insisted that the fundamental economics alone, "as a matter of pounds, shillings, and pence," dictated "that this dragon who interferes between us and our golden apples should be killed by somebody."[11]

But the editors of the London *Times* were just as removed from the violence in China as those whose moral principles they ridiculed, and the elegance of their view in the summer of 1862 that the Taiping were a humanitarian menace—and that it would therefore be to England's honor to help the Qing government restore order to its empire—quickly withered in the face of the dark news coming back from Asia. For the floodgates were now open, and, with the blanket permission of Her Majesty's government as his shield, Admiral Hope was launching Britain into a war against the Chinese rebels whose moral complications were nearly unfathomable.

In league with the Ever-Victorious Army under Ward, and with ready approval from Li Hongzhang, the Allies embarked on an ambitious campaign against the Taiping strongholds around Shanghai in the late spring of 1862. They initially met with success, thanks largely to a ridiculous mismatch of equipment. On May 13, three days after the assault on Ningbo, a combined force out of Shanghai and Songjiang accomplished what Ward's militia had never been able to do on its own: it captured Qingpu from the Taiping, after bombarding it for two straight hours with forty pieces of heavy artillery including a 68-pounder and four enormous 110-pound naval Armstrong guns. After the British and French artillery blasted the south gate of Qingpu to splinters, 3,500 of Ward's Chinese troops stormed the breach, scaring the shell-shocked defenders into retreat as the military band played "God Save the Queen." There were scarcely any casualties on the Allied side.[12]

But the rebels soon showed they could fight back, and the Europeans found themselves drawn inexorably deeper into the war. Four days after the capture of Qingpu, Hope's French counterpart, Admiral Protet, led an assault on the village of South Bridge below Songjiang. Early in the fighting, a rebel sniper shot the French admiral through the chest, puncturing a main artery of his heart, and he died that night after a massive loss of blood. Protet's enraged French troops managed to capture the nearby fortified village of Zhelin from the rebels shortly afterward and took retribution for the death of their beloved admiral by massacring three thousand people there, including the women and children, before burning the entire settlement to the ground.[13]

Even the initial Allied victories against the Taiping were short-lived,

however, for it was one thing to storm a walled city, another to hold it—
and the Allies simply didn't have the manpower for the latter. Right after the
capture of Qingpu, news came that Li Xiucheng was bringing a large rebel
army down from Suzhou to descend on Songjiang in the Ever-Victorious
Army's absence.[14] Ward turned back to Songjiang with 2,000 of his men to
help hold the walls against the rebel attack, leaving his lieutenant Edward
Forester with only 1,500 to garrison Qingpu—which soon fell under siege
as well. Admiral Hope had taken his gunships back to Shanghai as soon as
the initial fighting for Qingpu ended, so Forester's troops were alone. They
managed to hold out for nearly a month, supplying themselves at one
point by ambushing a passing French smuggling ship loaded with arms
and ammunition for the rebels. But Forester's European officers nearly
mutinied after he turned down a Taiping offer to buy them out with gold,
and he had to lock some of them up for insubordination. Then came a
botched rescue attempt by Ward and Hope on June 10—which got hung
up on Hope's insistence that they torch the entire city to avoid having to
garrison it any longer. It ended with the hasty retreat of Hope and Ward,
the slaughter of all of Forester's men (starting with his imprisoned European officers, whose heads were impaled on spear points by the rebel vanguard), and the capture of Forester himself by the Taiping, who stripped
him naked and kept him prisoner for two months, until Li Hongzhang
paid his ransom.[15]

From there, things only got worse. In the summer, a graphic account
from a British soldier began to make the rounds of the world's newspapers,
describing what had happened to a group of rebel prisoners the British and
French had handed over to the Qing authorities at Shanghai. According to
his account, the imperial forces had butchered the prisoners as British soldiers stood idly by. That much alone wasn't enough to provoke a crisis, but
he also reported that this time their butchery had extended even to infants
and unborn children. His account read in part:

> A young female, apparently about eight months pregnant, who
> never uttered a groan or sigh at all the previous cruelties she had
> endured from the surrounding mob, had her infant cut out of her
> womb, and held up in her sight by one of its little hands, bleed-
> ing and quivering; when, at the sight, she gave one heartrending,
> piercing screech that would have awakened pity in a tiger, and
> after it had been in that state dashed on her breast, she, with a
> last superhuman effort, released her arms from those holding her

down, and clasped her infant to her bleeding heart, and died holding it there with such force that they could not be separated, and
were thus thrown together on the pile of other carcasses.

Another young woman among the prisoners awaiting her turn
to be disembowelled, with a fine boy of ten months old crowing
and jumping in her arms, had him snatched suddenly away from
her, and flung to the executioner, who plunged the ruthless knife
into his tender breast before his mother's eyes. Infants but recently
born were torn from their mother's breasts, and disembowelled
before their faces. Young strong men were disembowelled, mutilated, and the parts cut off thrust into their own mouths, or flung
among the admiring and laughing crowd of Chinamen.

The author of the account begged forgiveness for his complicity. "But no
more: I can write no more of these scenes," he said toward the end of the
letter. "I can now only regret for ever that I looked on the dreadful sight.
I am no longer fit to be a soldier." But it was his country which bore the
greatest moral burden for the events that day. "May God forgive England,"
he wrote, "for the part she is taking in this war."[16]

The shocking story swamped the media of the English-speaking world,
appearing in papers from Glasgow to Newfoundland and from Louisville
to San Francisco. It had first appeared in an English-language paper in
India, and its author was anonymous. Admiral Hope declared it to be "a
pure fabrication," though hardly anyone reported that. Even if it were,
Hope's rebuttal managed to stretch the bounds of credence even further
than the original account had. His main evidence to contradict it was the
word of Wu Xu, the Shanghai *daotai* who was Frederick Townsend Ward's
commander (and, typically, the executor of his prisoners). Without the
faintest whiff of cynicism, Hope reported that Wu Xu had assured him that
"the prisoners of all descriptions . . . have been treated with kindness and
humanity," and, as if they were merely a group of unruly children, that "far
from treating them harshly it was his intention to take care of them till they
could return to their friends."[17]

At any rate, the gruesome account was immediately believable to a
British public whose government had been painting the Manchus as a
barbaric horde of murderers ever since the kidnapping of the European
envoys in 1860. British opponents of intervention ran headlong with the
story. "I argue not whether the rebels are idolaters, Buddhists, Confucians,
Mahomedans, or pretended Christians," wrote Colonel Sykes to the Lon-

don *Daily News*, "they are human beings; they ask for our friendship, and the blood we shed in slaughtering them is reeking up to heaven in judgment against us."[18] *The Economist* declared that "the true policy would have been to avoid all but the most necessary intervention . . . and to have discouraged strongly and steadily all English meddling in Imperial affairs."[19] Its editors now worried that Great Britain had been dragged so deeply into the Chinese war that there was no way to salvage her honor *except* by colonizing the country.

And though the account may have sparked anger and shame in Britain, in the United States it sparked a vindictive fury. Anti-British sentiment in the northern states was running high in the summer of 1862, thanks to the obvious preference for the Confederacy on the part of Palmerston, Russell, and other leading members of the British government. Absent the as-yet-unissued Emancipation Proclamation, British sympathizers could frame the American war as being one of national liberation, rather than a war over slavery (which both sides still allowed). Many liberals in Britain celebrated the resistance of the South against northern tyranny, perhaps none quite so blatantly as William Gladstone, the chancellor of the Exchequer, who would all but throw in his lot with the Confederates the following October by telling a cheering audience in Newcastle, "There is no doubt that Jefferson Davis and the other leaders of the South have made an army; they are making, it appears, a navy; and they have made what is more than either—they have made a nation."[20]

In contrast to the British government's clear sympathy for the southern rebels in the United States—who at that point held the upper hand in their war—northern journalists used the bloody news from China to flog Britain ("John Bull") for being perfectly willing to hire itself out to a brutal, barbaric regime in order to put down a movement far more innocent than the slaveholding Confederacy. From the August 30 issue of *Vanity Fair:*

Our excellent friend, BULL, has just now an army in China.
An army in China! For what?
Why, to put down the Chinese rebels, to be sure, who are trying to depose their august, sublime, high, and mighty monarch.
And what has JOHN to do with that quarrel?
Nothing!

Their playfulness gave way to a screed against Britain's duplicity in the two civil wars: "O JOHN BULL! JOHN BULL! . . . You great beer-swilling

Hogshead of Hypocrisies! Now you pray, and then you plunder—now you pity and then you pillage—now you mourn and then you massacre—now you blubber the Black Man, and then you disembowel the Yellow Man . . ."[21]

The Saturday Evening Post carried it further, asking how the British could even dare to pass judgment on America's civil war after this revelation. "It appears," they wrote, "that the English Government, which seems to regard the rebellion in the United States as a very praiseworthy thing, holds a different view of the Chinese rebellion." It then printed a passage from the account of atrocities and concluded from it that "it does not become Englishmen to affect any great degree of horror at the necessarily distressing incidents of the present American rebellion, when their own history—from the first to the last—is such a constant record of blood, blood, blood!"[22]

Into this maelstrom of anger, hypocrisy, and reprisal, James Legge reinserted himself. Hong Rengan's old teacher and mentor in the London Missionary Society was still one of the most respected members of Hong Kong society, and with his translations of Confucius (with which Hong Rengan had helped him) he was also on his way to establishing himself as Britain's leading expert on China—in time, he would become the first professor of Chinese at Oxford.[23] Up to this point, however, he had mostly held back from making any public statements on the course of the rebellion or the career of his former assistant. But now, in reaction to the British intervention, he came out in public to add a voice of measured reason to the international debate over the war in China. In the fall of 1862, the leading missionary journals in Great Britain published a letter from Legge stating that he was bitterly opposed to the intervention and "much grieved to hear that our own government has approved . . . of Admiral Hope's proceedings." The British public had no idea what was really happening in China, he said, for the reports of the British papers had all along been twisted and one-sided, "intended to justify the most violent and vigorous proceedings" against the Taiping rebels.

But he was not writing to defend the Taiping themselves. Indeed, Legge had never held the rebel movement in much esteem, not since the days when he had tried to discourage Hong Rengan from going to Nanjing to rejoin his cousin. So strong had been his opinion then that Hong Rengan had waited until Legge was away on home leave before making his final departure. The bond of affection between the two men had not waned in the following years, though, and Legge took a keener interest in the move-

ment once he learned that his favorite Chinese person had become the
Shield King and chief minister of Hong Xiuquan. He took care of Hong
Rengan's brother and nephew until they were ready to go to Nanjing. And
he kept up an occasional correspondence with Hong Rengan over the years,
warning him more recently by letter that the tide was shifting and terrible
things were being said about the Taiping in the West.

In his public letter, Legge admitted that Hong Rengan had never managed to win him over to the movement. Despite some early optimism, he
had remained obstinate in his disregard for the religious aspects of the
rebellion, and he was particularly dismayed by the news that Hong Rengan had taken multiple wives. As if writing a eulogy for his lost friend, he
lamented that Hong Rengan had not proven to be up to the enormous
task before him. Surely, he wrote (in reference to Issachar Roberts), Hong
Rengan was not guilty of the charges that had been leveled against him. But
nevertheless, "he has made shipwreck of faith and of a good conscience,"
and Legge did not believe that the Chinese rebels would ever reach true
Christianity, even with Hong Rengan to guide them.

But—and this was the salient point of his letter—neither did that mean
that Britain should be free to commit violence against them. The Taiping's
friendliness to the Western nations was genuine, Legge maintained, and
"Had we been willing to enter into negotiations with them in 1860, or even
last year, we should have found that their calling us 'foreign brethren' had a
real, good, substantial meaning in it." But now, with Admiral Hope's blind
launching of hostilities, that great opportunity had been lost. The imperials were every bit as cruel as the rebels, if not more so, and the foreign
intervention would serve only to encourage and perpetuate that cruelty.
"We shall kill our thousands on the battle-field," Legge warned, "and the
governors of provinces will kill their tens of thousands in the execution
areas. . . . Our high officers will be the ministers to so many butchers of
human beings."

The time of the Manchus in China had passed, said Legge, like that of
the Stuarts in England or the Bourbons in France. Their reign could not
be prolonged. The only moral course available to England in China was to
withdraw herself and return to neutrality. No matter what terrible things
might come, it was China's war, and England had no part in it. "But let not
us call those rebels whom it calls rebels," Legge concluded plaintively. "Let
not us lend our armies and fleets to do for it what it cannot do for itself. If
we only did what was right, China would, by-and-by, in God's providence,

come to a better state than it is in at present. Whatever betide, a nation is no more justifiable than an individual, in doing evil that good may come."

As it turned out, without even need of the public outcry from abroad to hasten its end, Admiral Hope's campaign to clear the thirty-mile radius around Shanghai proved completely untenable on military grounds and quickly collapsed. Absent a major commitment of additional troops from back home that was not forthcoming, the combined forces of the British and French in Shanghai were simply too weak to hold a garrison against the rebels, even when they coordinated with Ward. And so, after the death of Protet and the gruesome debacle at Qingpu, Hope was forced to admit defeat. He pulled his ships back to Shanghai, abandoning the Allies' sites of victory to Li Xiucheng, and gave up on any objective beyond the immediate defense of the city.[24] But then again, that had been his basic charge all along. Of Hope's tendency to exceed his instructions, *The Spectator,* back in London, observed ruefully that "The chronic Indian disease, disobedience of English orders, has extended to China."[25] By October, Hope would be removed from service in China altogether, replaced by the far more moderate and diplomatic Rear Admiral Augustus Leopold Kuper (whose appointment followed rumors in England that there wasn't a single flag officer willing to take over the troubled China command).[26] Captain Dew of the *Encounter* was formally reprimanded by the Admiralty for having exceeded his orders at Ningbo. The Royal Navy would no longer take a direct role in fighting the rebels.[27] Frederick Townsend Ward, beholden to no foreign government, was left to keep fighting on his own, but he didn't mind that, since the British and French troops, for all the usefulness of their heavy artillery, had tended to get in the way of the looting.[28]

―――――――

Never in the entire war did things go as well for Zeng Guofan as they did that spring. First of all, for reasons having nothing to do with the foreign intervention at Shanghai and Ningbo, Duolonga's cavalry made great progress in their harassment of the Brave King, Chen Yucheng, in northern Anhui. After losing Anqing in September, Chen had retreated to the city of Luzhou, ninety miles to the north, which had been under rebel control since 1858. From that base, he began calling up Taiping forces and allies from the Nian bandit armies for a planned four-pronged campaign to the north into Henan and Shaanxi provinces, with a likely final goal of driving on to Beijing to take advantage of the weakness of the new government there.[29] Three of the armies marched north as planned in the early months of 1862, but the Brave King found himself holed up in Luzhou, under siege by Duolonga and other Hunan Army forces. They cut off his communications completely, so he had no news from the other campaign armies that would let him know where they had met with success or where he should take his own army if they escaped the siege.

On May 13, with supplies in Luzhou dwindling, the young Brave King took an army of 4,000 and broke through the Hunan siege camps on the north side of Luzhou. Duolonga's forces fell on the abandoned city behind him as the Brave King led his men on a forced march northward, through night and day, to rejoin the closest of their companion armies—which, according to the plan, had been sent to attack the city of Shouzhou, seventy miles to the northwest. That army was under the command of an imperial defector named Miao Peilin, a militia chief from northern Anhui who had come over to the Taiping during the Brave King's initial march through the region, when he had tried to break the siege of Anqing in the fall of 1860.[30] Miao Peilin's army had played a major role in supporting the Brave King during the failed Anqing campaign, and his was one of the four columns for the new push northward. When Chen Yucheng reached the gates of Shouzhou, he was relieved to see that Miao's army was there to meet him, and they controlled the city. Oddly, however, Miao himself was nowhere to be seen.

In the absence of communications, Chen Yucheng did not know that Miao Peilin had been soundly defeated at Shouzhou and on April 25 his entire army had surrendered to the imperials. Miao had gone back over to the dynasty's side, his life spared in exchange for promising to deliver the rebel general. And so, when Chen entered through the gate of Shouzhou to rejoin his companions, they immediately took him prisoner. In June, he was executed. In his one statement of confession, the Brave King showed no remorse, only sadness for his men. "It is Heaven's will that has brought me here," he told his captors, "and there is nothing that can be said of my past. I have long enjoyed the reputation of a victorious commander, but now I would prefer to look to the future. For the Taiping Heavenly Kingdom to lose me, one single man, it will be as if the mountains and the rivers of the kingdom have been reduced by half. I bear a great debt of gratitude to my Heavenly Dynasty and will not surrender. The general of a defeated army cannot beg for his life. But as for the four thousand men I command, they are veterans of a hundred battles, and I do not know whether they are still alive. You can cut me to pieces for the crimes I have committed, but this has nothing to do with them."[31]

While this was happening in northern Anhui, the Allied campaign outside Shanghai all but rolled out a carpet for Zeng Guofan's brother Guoquan in his march on Nanjing. In response to the joint campaign of Ward and the Allies, Li Xiucheng was forced to transfer his forces to the east, and he led his main army from Suzhou down to Songjiang to take command of the less skilled forces that were ranged around Shanghai. That shift—which was nearly simultaneous with the destruction of the Brave King's army in northern Anhui—left the Taiping garrisons along the Yangtze River between Anqing and Nanjing without any hope of reinforcement from the north or the east, just at the time that Zeng Guofan's brother was starting to fight his way through them toward the rebel capital.

A few months earlier, nobody could have predicted such hostility near Shanghai, let alone the presence of effective forces there opposed to the Taiping, and so the sudden drawing off of Taiping strength to the east came as a surprise to all involved. As the rebel garrisons on the Yangtze fell back from Zeng Guoquan's advance, abandoning their forts and setting fire to their stockades, he was bewildered by their lack of resistance and wondered what they were preparing for him down the road.[32] What he didn't realize was that they were preparing nothing, because the bulk of the Taiping armies had moved out of range. The outmatched garrison forces were falling back to Nanjing for their own safety, and for that he had Admiral Hope to thank.

It was a disaster for the Taiping. The rebel kings had known all along that Zeng Guofan's forces at Anqing would pose a threat from upstream, but they had never imagined that an attack would come so soon. Not Hong Rengan, who admitted later that "The Imps were upon us before we were nearly ready. They caught us unprepared."[33] And most of all not Li Xiucheng, who took the safety of the capital and the sovereign as his personal responsibility. In the Loyal King's own rueful words, the Hunan Army's unchecked progress down the Yangtze River from Anqing in the spring of 1862, through a succession of unready garrisons right up to the doorstep of the capital itself, was as smooth and as swift as the splitting of bamboo.[34]

By late May, Zeng Guoquan's forces were on the outskirts of Nanjing. Avoiding the heavy shore batteries along the city's northwest side, his naval support secured positions on opposite sides of the river just southwest (upstream) of the city. On the south bank they also captured an important junction that gave them control of the city's moat. Guoquan took his men overland, down below the city, and came at it from the south under the protection of the naval forces, which screened them from above.[35] On May 30, 1862, with Li Xiucheng still fighting Ward and Forester for control of Songjiang and Qingpu two hundred miles away to the east, Zeng Guoquan's forces pushed all the way to the base of a small hill just outside the south gate of Nanjing.[36]

The hill they targeted, which was guarded by a stone fort at its top, was known as Yuhuatai, or the "Terrace of Flowering Rain." It was a name bestowed in happier times, when a monk who preached on the wooded hill was said to have pleased Heaven so immensely that petals of flowers fell from the sky and swirled around him like a bright shower of rain. Now the trees had all been cut down to build stockades and watchtowers. There were no flowers. And the only rain was the damp gray drizzle that turned the brown earth below them into mud as the Hunan soldiers staked out their positions and began digging trenches at its base.

The impassive gray facade of the Nanjing city wall spoke of sheer invincibility to any soldier standing on the ground sixty feet below its battlements. But it had its vulnerabilities, and Yuhuatai was one of them. The sharp little hill, just over three hundred feet high and half a mile across, sat directly across from the Nanjing wall's south gate. That gate had been the primary point of landward defense for the city under the Ming, who had built it in grand fashion: a multistory granite edifice with nested courtyards and barracks for several thousand troops, horse ramps running up to it from behind, and enough width atop the rampart to race two horses abreast without fear of disturbing the gunners at their embrasures.

But with an insufficient garrison, which now numbered a fraction of what the Ming planners had built it for, the gate was less a site for the projection of power than a point of relative softness along an otherwise unbroken wall of granite. And from the base of Yuhuatai to the massive reinforced wooden doors of the south gate lay a perfectly flat stretch of only half a mile. A man on foot could cover it easily in eight or nine minutes; a galloping horse, in one. From a watchtower on the side of the hill, an observer could see right over the top of the Nanjing wall into the vast city that spread out behind it—the tiled roofs of the palaces, the ruins of the old Manchu city, even the back of the wall as it wrapped around the city's northern side in the far distance.[37] With naked eye he could track movement atop the south gate, and with a spyglass he could count the heads of the defending soldiers on the parapet. The long gray slab of the wall stretched away on both sides for what on the ground was miles, but from there, it was as if you could embrace the whole capital in your arms.

Yuhuatai was the base Zeng Guoquan wanted for his siege of Nanjing. The hill's defenders in their stone fort were as yet untouchable, but he planted his army right at its foot. He had fewer than 20,000 men under his command, including the naval support that kept open a corridor from the river for supplies, but they dug themselves in deep with an interconnected series of ten heavily barricaded camps between high earthen walls at the edge of the city. Once fully entrenched—though outsized and outnumbered—they were immovable, like a small, hard parasite fixed to the back of some gigantic mammal.

———————

Considering the difference between the matchlocks and swords of the Hunan Army and the modern arms sold by foreign weapons dealers, Zeng Guofan was remarkably unimpressed by what the foreigners had on offer. He had seen a few Western guns and found them finicky and complicated, prone to breaking down. You had to be careful when using them, he believed, and after twenty or thirty shots they had to be repaired.[38] But his primary objection to them was philosophical; he dismissed outright the notion that weapons of any kind could make a difference in the war. "The way to achieve victory is to be found in men, not in arms," he wrote to Guoquan when his brother asked to get some foreign guns for the Nanjing camp. Take Bao Chao, he said, who "has no foreign guns and no foreign powder, yet he repeatedly achieves great victories." Meanwhile, He Chun and Zhang Guoliang, the generals of the Green Standard's siege of Nanjing, had had some foreign cannons in the spring of 1860, "which did nothing to prevent their defeat." Military strength was a matter of talent, said Zeng Guofan, not tools. "A true beauty doesn't fuss over pearls and jade, and a great writer needs no more than brush and ink. If a general is truly skilled at war, why should he go grasping for foreign weapons?"[39] He did eventually cave in to his brother's persistent requests and sent agents to Canton and Shanghai in 1862 to purchase some foreign rifles and gunpowder for the camp at Nanjing. But those purchases were small, and he continued to insist, adamantly, that the traditional weapons of war—gingals and bird guns, swords, spears, Chinese cannons—had to remain the foundation of his army.[40]

As skeptical as Zeng Guofan may have been about imported small arms, he was well aware of the terror that the larger foreign equipment could strike into Chinese who had never seen such things before. This was true for the British guns such as the Armstrong, with its five-mile range, and it was especially true for the steamships that pushed upstream with such swiftness and agility through waters in which Chinese boats couldn't even make headway (there was a vast employment of river-dwelling men along the Yangtze to pull boats physically, by ropes, against the heavy current; their heavily planted footsteps over the centuries had worn deep, smooth grooves into the rocks along the shore).

Initially Zeng Guofan saw no use for steamships in his campaign against the rebels, except perhaps to carry the mail up and down the Yangtze.[41] In the summer of 1861, he wrote to the Xianfeng emperor that the Hunan Army already had a solid advantage over the rebels on water and its only weakness was on land, where no steamship could help them.[42] But by the spring of 1862, the transportation of Li Hongzhang's army by steamship to Shanghai had convinced him that there were genuine military uses for the vessels as well and the Chinese shouldn't be beholden to foreigners, who could charge whatever they wanted for rental.

Independently of whether he could use them himself, he believed that the very strangeness of the foreign ships and cannons constituted their primary advantage, and that was an advantage that should be deflated. As the Shanghai merchants knew when they hired their foreign mercenary corps, and as the Chinese commander near Canton knew when he dressed up his men like Europeans, ever since Britain's victory in the Opium War the coastal population of China had held an almost mystical belief in the superiority of foreign armies and their ships and guns—which in Zeng Guofan's opinion was due only to smoke and mirrors. China, he thought, should cut through the illusion. "The British and French can take exaggerated pride in the speed of their steamships and the long range of their foreign cannons, because they alone possess them," he wrote to Prince Gong, "and the Chinese tremble with fear because they've rarely seen such things before." So he encouraged the Qing government to buy some, if only to diminish their power to strike terror into the Chinese. "If we can buy them and make them our own," he wrote, "the Chinese will become accustomed to seeing them and they won't be afraid of them anymore. Then, the British and French will lose their edge."[43]

He started the process himself at his headquarters in Anqing. In February 1862, he purchased a small steamship from Shanghai and invited a handful of Chinese scientists and engineers to set up shop in Anqing to figure out how it was made. The ship soon broke down, and they could not repair it.[44] But by that summer, one of his engineers managed to build a working prototype of a steam engine. After inspecting it carefully and watching how the steam was used to move the wheel, Zeng Guofan wrote in his diary, "I am delighted that we Chinese can now use these cunning foreign techniques. Now they can't treat us so arrogantly on account of our ignorance."[45] A year later, their efforts at Anqing would result in a little steamer all of twenty-eight feet long that could make decent headway against the Yangtze currents.

The experiments of Zeng Guofan's engineers at Anqing had no immediate military value, but in the summer of 1862, while they were still developing their first small engine, his hope that Prince Gong might be able to purchase a few full-sized steamships from abroad became a real possibility. After Admiral Hope's failed attempt to intervene directly in the war, Frederick Bruce had been looking for some way to help the Qing government bring order back to its empire without exposing England to further embarrassment. So he supported a suggestion of British personnel at the Shanghai imperial maritime customs that the Qing government be allowed, through Prince Gong at the Office of Foreign Affairs, to purchase a few steamships from Great Britain. No such permission had been granted by the home government in London itself, but Bruce hoped they might agree that this was the best way to enable the imperial government of China to defend itself and protect the treaty ports without the need of relying on British forces to do it for them.

The man tasked with commissioning the steamers in England was Horatio Nelson Lay, a high-strung British linguist named (apparently in vain) after the illustrious admiral Horatio Nelson, who was no relation. He had learned to speak and read Chinese as a diplomatic translator and starting in 1859 had been employed at Shanghai by the Qing government to oversee the collection of customs duties. In the summer of 1862, he was home in England for a visit and received a letter from his successor at the imperial customs service authorizing him to purchase some steamships on behalf of the Chinese government.[46] It was an informal arrangement, and Lay had no contract, just an assurance that the Office of Foreign Affairs would come through with funds when the time came. From that rather basic assignment, however, Lay concocted what was, in the words of one of his contemporaries, "a magnificent scheme for regenerating China and exalting himself."[47] He decided, in short, to commission an entire fleet of advanced warships for the Qing government, with a full crew of European sailors and marines to man them.

Lay was quite sensitive to the mercenary issue and bristled at the suggestion that he was somehow a servant of the Qing government. He worked "*for* them," as he liked to put it, "not *under* them." His views on the relative status of Chinese and Europeans were among the more chauvinistic to be found at the time; as he put it in an open letter to Lord Russell: "the notion of a gentleman acting under an Asiatic barbarian is preposterous."[48] Lest his point somehow be misconstrued, he went on in that letter to clarify that "there is no such thing, at present, as equality between the European and the Asiatic. . . . The Chinese are, when compared with ourselves, but children; fractious, vicious children they often are, but it is as children and not as grown-up men that they should be treated."[49] Such views, another of his contemporaries later suggested, "quite unfitted him for working with the Chinese, either *under* or *for* them,"[50] but for the time being he considered himself to be the Qing emperor's agent in England, and he demanded to be treated as such.

In pitching his scheme to the British government, Lay said little about the Taiping or the confounding issue of neutrality in the civil war. Instead, he emphasized the ways in which a flotilla of gunships might serve Britain's long-term interests in China—by ensuring security for commerce on the Yangtze, for one thing, and by suppressing piracy on the coast. Eventually, he also thought, they might somehow open up the interior of China to British exploration, though the connection there was unclear (especially as the ships were to be under imperial control). He also pledged that the fleet would introduce steam power and telegraphs to China "under Chinese auspices" and that it would therefore "insure wholesome reforms in the administration of the Government throughout the Empire."[51] (He sidestepped the fact that it was only Hong Rengan, the prime minister of the Taiping, who had ever expressed any interest in such things.) Finally, he emphasized repeatedly and passionately that this would be not a mercenary force but rather a British fleet, with British commanders and sailors, which would work for (but not under) the emperor of China.

The Qing government might be paying the costs of the fleet, but Lay personally chose its commander, a decorated Royal Navy captain named Sherard Osborn who had been captain of the *Furious* during Elgin's first mission to China. According to the four-year contract Lay drew up, Osborn would take his orders only from the emperor and no other authority in China. Those orders from the emperor, moreover, would be transmitted exclusively by Lay, who would reside in the capital as a sort of naval chief of staff. Reflecting either Lay's opinion that all Chinese were children, or only that the emperor himself was a literal six-year-old, he stipulated that he would personally judge all of the emperor's orders and decline to transmit to Osborn any that lacked "reasonableness."[52]

And here is where it became so important that Alexander Dunlop had withdrawn his motion in May 1861 to recognize the Taiping as belligerents (which, it may be recalled, he did only after repeated assurances from Palmerston and Russell that England was, and would always remain, neutral in China). Without belligerent status, the Chinese rebels were not protected by Britain's Foreign Enlistment Act, which explicitly prohibited British firms from selling gunships to any party at war with a power with whom Britain was at peace. As the Qing were the only recognized power in China, British firms were perfectly free to sell them gunships to use against the Taiping rebels. By way of contrast, at precisely the same moment that Horatio Nelson Lay was in London trying to commission a war fleet for the Qing emperor, the chief naval agent of the Confederate States of America, James Bulloch, was in the same city with exactly the same purpose, and Lay succeeded where his American counterpart would fail. There were two recognized belligerent parties in the United States—both of which were technically at peace with England—and therefore Britain's shipmakers were legally restricted from selling gunships to either of them.[53]

The only way in which the Foreign Enlistment Act posed any kind of obstacle to Lay's Chinese scheme was in its application to Sherard Osborn and his crew. In its most basic form, the act forbade British subjects to enlist in the national militaries of foreign states, and Osborn's commission as commander of a Qing naval fleet would therefore require special permission from the Crown. Parliament still intended Britain to remain neutral in China, but Palmerston and Russell managed an end run around the expected objections of the lawmakers by suspending the act through two orders in council issued after Parliament went into recess in the summer of 1862, which guaranteed that they couldn't come up for discussion until Parliament reconvened the following February.

The first order in council, issued in August 1862, suspended the Foreign Enlistment Act specifically so that Horatio Nelson Lay and Sherard Osborn (as named) could serve the emperor of China. It granted them permission to equip the emperor with armed ships and also gave them exclusive authority to recruit a British crew for the ships. Such crew members could enlist only under Lay and Osborn, nobody else. Four months later, Palmerston's government issued a second order that dramatically broadened the original permissions to make it lawful for *any* British officer to enlist in the service of the Qing emperor, authorizing them "to serve the said Emperor in any military, warlike, or other operations, and for that purpose to go to any place or places beyond the seas, and to accept any commission, warrant, or other appointment from or under the said Emperor, and to accept any money, pay, or reward for their services."

However, there was one twist to the recruitment process. Though the British government could grant Osborn and Lay the right to enlist British subjects for the Qing navy, it could not grant them Chinese commissions—which were entirely in the power of the Qing emperor and for which they would have to wait until they had arrived in China. But before they could leave England, they would have to resign or take leave from their Royal Navy commissions in order to enlist with Osborn. So in the interim, Osborn would sail to China with a crew of sailors and marines who effectively held no national commissions whatsoever and who would therefore be every bit as unregulated and unaccountable in their behavior as the mercenaries they were intended not to be.

The reaction in the papers came first. Russell and Palmerston's turnaround in policy in China seemed almost perverse: overnight, Britain had gone from being the enemy of the Manchus to being their national arms dealers and would-be saviors. *Punch* magazine put it best: "our gallant friend Sherard Osborn . . . is to be sent off to smash, pound, and annihilate any Taepings who come near our Treaty Ports. We are sure he will cover himself with honours—not so sure that we can cover Lord Russell's propositions with a shield of logic."[54] Colonel Sykes, the former East India Company chairman, wrote to the London *Daily News* in bafflement, "Mr. Bruce and Consuls Medhurst and Harvey have repeatedly, in official documents, stated that the Imperial Government is the most corrupt and impotent on the face of the earth; and facts, in the torture and murder of our officers, and the murder of their captives in war, and the treatment of their prisoners in gaol, show them to be bloody and pitiless; and yet the object of our policy is to restore to efficient action a Government with such characteristics."[55]

By the time Parliament reconvened the following February, the authorization of the fleet was a fait accompli, but it still came under harsh criticism. On the first day of the new session, February 5, 1863, the Conservative leader, Benjamin Disraeli—hardly a sentimental moralist—took Palmerston to task for his sudden reversal of policy in China. "[T]he noble Lord who made war against the Tartar dynasty is now supporting the Tartar dynasty," he declared, "and making war against these rebellious subjects of the Emperor of China. We have completely changed our position. We are making war against the Taeping insurrection." In the same speech he chided Palmerston for failing to intervene on behalf of the South in the U.S. Civil War (which he termed "a great revolution"),[56] yet, he went on, the case of China showed that Palmerston was perfectly willing to get involved in the civil war of a country far less intimate with England than the United States. Nobody in the government seemed to have any clear idea who the Chinese rebels really were, he lamented, or what they really represented. "Who are the Taepings? What are the Taepings?" he asked. "Sir, I maintain that we have nothing to do with the Taepings. Whether they are patriots, or whether they are brigands, is nothing to the people of England. The status of the Taepings is a question for China, not for England."[57]

From the Liberal side, Colonel Sykes brandished a copy of the Taiping Bible in Chinese and defied anyone to call the Taiping blasphemers, while declaring that the "Tartar boy Emperor" to whom England was giving its military support actually had almost no influence "beyond the walls of Pekin."[58] Three days later, he asked in the House of Commons if equivalent permission had been granted to British officers to enlist under the Taiping, and Austen Layard, the undersecretary of state for foreign affairs, replied that it hadn't, adding snidely that "the Government had not the honour of being acquainted" with the "Taeping Emperor."[59]

But the dominant view of the fleet in England was optimistic. In a polite debate at the Royal Geographic Society in December 1862 attended by "every one interested in Chinese matters," Harry Parkes, Horatio Nelson Lay, and Sherard Osborn discussed the fleet and the future of China with William Gladstone, the chancellor of the Exchequer. Lay waxed poetic on the flotilla's potential to defuse the civil war in China and bring about the expansion of trade. Osborn told the audience that he was going to China "to spread peace, and not to shed blood" and he hoped in due time "to report that Nankin has been taken without the loss of one Taeping life after the assault was over." The icing on the cake was Lay's proposal, in one of his loftier flights of fancy, that the Taiping might be convinced to abandon China altogether and be transported as colonists to the islands of the eastern archipelago, "where there is waste land, and food, and labour, and a congenial climate." Gladstone, showing a change of heart since his eloquent and strenuous opposition to Palmerston's China war in 1857, gave Osborn and Lay his full and heartfelt approval, telling them to go forth "to carry to the Chinese the blessings, and not the curses, of civilization."[60]

The Times too gave Osborn's expedition its blessing, observing that although the British might feel a stronger affinity for the Americans than for the Chinese, nevertheless "We have almost as much material interest at stake in the battles between the Taepings and the Imperialists in China as we have in the contests between the Unionists and Secessionists in America." And with the coming departure of Osborn's fleet, the end of the Chinese war seemed the one closer at hand. "[T]here are a great many markets opening or closing in China as victory vibrates," said *The Times*, "and the tall chimneys in Lancashire may even yet feel the good effects of Imperial victories before they are allowed to experience any results from the vicissitudes of the next American campaign."[61]

Britain's shipmakers were delighted to have the Qing dynasty's business, and they put their best work on display. Though the first three vessels were bought secondhand and were therefore ready almost immediately (the *Mohawk, Africa,* and *Jasper,* now renamed *Pekin, China,* and *Amoy*), the rest had to be commissioned from scratch, and their construction would take a year. Lay decided to wait for all the ships to be finished and the legal paperwork to be complete before sending the squadron to China.[62] Once complete, there would be eight ships, including seven gunships and a store vessel. The gunships ranged in size from large oceangoing men-of-war to smaller paddle steamers with shallow draft that could skim China's muddy rivers (those had to be shipped in crates to Asia and assembled there). They would carry forty modern guns and a crew of four hundred, which Lay insisted would be exclusively "European officers and seamen, of the very best character." The Qing Empire had never needed a naval ensign before, so Lay invented one for it, in green and yellow with a little dragon in the middle.

By the time the ships were ready to sail to China in the summer of 1863, it turned out to have been worth the wait. They may have lacked the latest iron armor (unneeded, at any rate, against the largely feeble artillery of the Taiping), but otherwise they were the very state of the art. When the fleet's 241-foot flagship, *Kiang-Soo,* was first tested in Stokes Bay near Portsmouth in May 1863, it hit a peak speed of nineteen knots on the measured mile and averaged seventeen over four runs in one of the best performances ever recorded. It was rumored to be the fastest naval ship on the planet.[63]

In England, polite names were given to this powerful squadron of warships. It was known generally as the Anglo-Chinese Flotilla and its mission the Anglo-Chinese Expedition, emphasizing the gentlemanly cooperation it represented (or so its advocates claimed) between Great Britain and the imperial government in China, to protect their common trade interests and combat piracy along the coast. Later historians would call it the Lay-Osborn Flotilla, after the two Britons behind its inception. But in Shanghai at the time, where it was obvious that the fleet's sole purpose was to put down the Taiping Rebellion and where the foreign population reeled at Britain's newfound willingness to play mercenary for China's discredited imperial government, there was another name for it: the Vampire Fleet.

CHAPTER 14

FLOWERING RAIN

Death in those days came not just from the rain of the cannons and muskets, the explosions, or the hatchets and spears. It came not just from the
infections and the butchery or from the suicides. It came not just from the
aching famine in the war zone, where the threadbare remains of the farming population struggled to feed themselves and pay taxes to whichever
body claimed control over them. There was no place to escape. From the
once densely populated provinces of Jiangsu and Zhejiang, many people
continued to make their way into Shanghai or other treaty ports, where
the presence of foreign arms promised relative safety. Frederick Bruce was
deeply alarmed by reports of the number of refugees who were now crowding into the foreign settlements, and he insisted that he did not want to see
Britain become the protector of the Chinese people (though others back
home said this was a sign that if Britain just said the word, the people of
China would flock to its standard and welcome it as the new ruler of their
empire).

In Shanghai alone, by 1862 there were one and a half million people
crammed into the Chinese city and the foreign settlement in hopes of finding protection from the war outside.[1] The wealthiest of the refugees dwelled
in houses, but most were poor and lived in huts of woven reed mats or on

small boats that clogged up the waterways. Still others, who didn't even have mats to shelter them, packed the open spaces. With the coming of spring, the narrow rivers that skirted the settlement ran brown with the seasonal runoff, thick with mud and feces carried in from the rice paddies along the outlying watershed. Here and there, half-rotten carcasses—some animal, some human—floated along on the rank currents.[2] The rivers were the primary water supply for the Shanghai refugee population, and though by custom the water for drinking was always boiled, the water used for washing and for preparing food was not.

The first cases of cholera appeared in May 1862. They started with cramps, absent other symptoms. Then came vomiting. But the worst by far was the explosive, violent diarrhea that came later, pale and milky, that tore its victims inside out. Death often came in a matter of hours, though the onset of the disease could be hard to pinpoint since most of the Shanghai population already suffered from diarrhea. By June, it was a full-blown epidemic, ripping through the miserable hordes of refugees on their boats, in their hovels of straw matting, crowded into the buildings and streets. In the small foreign community, it killed ten or fifteen Europeans a day of the two thousand or so who lived in Shanghai and wreaked havoc on the crews of the military ships.[3] But it was the crowded, destitute Chinese population that suffered the worst. By June, there were hundreds of people dying every day and by July, thousands. At its peak, the cholera killed as many as three thousand a day in the foreign settlement. The streets of Shanghai lay thick with the unburied dead, some in makeshift boxes of thin boards, others just covered loosely with straw and left to rot in the midsummer heat.[4]

Some Chinese called it *fan sha:* the foreign infection.[5] From its origin in the treaty port, the disease spread outward. To the north, it followed a ghostly path up the coast that traced the old route of Elgin's invasion, now plied by the mail-carrying packet steamers. It reached the Taku forts by the middle of June and then slipped up the Peiho to Tianjin, where it killed twenty thousand people in the space of a few short, horrifying weeks. From there, it moved on into Beijing and unleashed itself on the defense-less imperial capital.[6]

The south, for some reason, was spared, but even as the disease crept up the coast toward Beijing, it also followed the Yangtze and its tributar-ies into the interior. The boats plying the river carried it up from Shang-hai into Anhui that summer—in their water stores, in the bowels of their passengers. From Zeng Guofan's headquarters it spread out through his army's supply lines, and by late summer the Hunan troops in their camps were falling in droves.[7] He listed the damage in memorials to the throne in August and September. Ten thousand of the men under his brother at the base of Yuhuatai—fully half of the Hunan Army's siege force—were sick and dying. Ten thousand more had been struck down in Bao Chao's army in southern Anhui, and even Bao Chao himself was sick (which drove Zeng Guofan nearly mad with worry, though fortunately for him the prized commander survived). The infection rate in Zuo Zongtang's army in Zhejiang province reached 50 percent, and for others it stood even higher, blighting 60 to 70 percent of the Hunanese soldiers in southern Anhui.[8] So many of the soldiers were sick and dying, he reported, that his army could no longer go on the offensive.[9]

Neither civilization had an answer. The British military in Shanghai distributed so-called cholera belts, wide cummerbunds of flannel that could be wrapped around the torso to keep it warm, on the theory that the disease was invited by a sweaty chill to the bowels. The chief British medical officer, based in Beijing, discounted sanitation as a factor after learning how many of the refugees living on boats in Shanghai had died (for to his mind, those were among the cleaner habitations in the city). Groping for a scientific explanation, he suspected "the operation of certain electrochemical changes in the atmosphere on certain constitutions."[10] Meanwhile, in Anqing, Zeng Guofan instructed his commanders to distribute Korean ginseng to the sick troops in the hope of at least giving them some relief from the symptoms.[11] But for the root cause of the epidemic, he blamed only himself. Unaware of how widespread it had become, he was certain that the disease that afflicted his army was a divine judgment on his own leadership and Heaven was punishing him for having amassed too much power. He went so far as to write to Beijing, asking the government to send another imperial commissioner who could divide and share his responsibilities—to reduce his power by half and thereby (hopefully) appease Heaven's anger and end the scourge.[12] The reply from the court assured him that the epidemic was not his fault alone. Nor, they told him, was it a sign that the dynasty itself had angered Heaven. He wept with relief when he read the letter.[13]

There is little indication of the effects of the epidemic in Nanjing or farther afield in the Taiping domain, but the diffusion of the rural population under the rebels (versus the urban crowding around Shanghai and Tianjin) and their relative isolation from the treaty ports may have worked to their advantage as the disease coursed through the international trading networks and along the imperial supply lines. The Taiping-held towns closest to Shanghai, however, were connected to the city by a steady stream of peddlers and smugglers (not to mention roving militias), and those towns appear to have been just as badly ravaged as Shanghai itself.[14] The epidemic finally spent itself in China proper by winter, moving northeast out of the empire through Manchuria and then across the water to an unsuspecting Japan. The Qing government was too distracted to collect any kind of comprehensive data, but the British tried. Their data were limited to the narrow range of the foreign intelligence networks, but in the region immediately surrounding Shanghai for about forty miles—which at that point contained several million inhabitants—they gauged in September, with the help of a Roman Catholic missionary, that the cholera had wiped out about one-eighth of the population.[15]

The Hunan Army's position at Yuhuatai had been a precarious one even before the epidemic struck. Zeng Guofan was deeply alarmed by his younger brother's reckless decision to pitch camp so close to the wall of Nanjing, and when he first reported the army's arrival to Beijing, he warned the ministers of the central government not to have high expectations. He pointed out that the generals of the Green Standard had laid siege to the Taiping capital for eight years with 70,000 troops at their disposal, yet nothing had come of their efforts. His brother, by contrast, had only 20,000.[16]

Then came the cholera, and by the autumn of 1862 Guoquan's forces were down to half their original fighting strength.[17] Zeng Guofan sent in sizable reinforcement armies, but even after committing everything he possibly could to the Nanjing siege, the Hunan Army's replenished forces still numbered fewer than 30,000 able-bodied troops, with no reserves left upon which to draw.[18] Yet the troops continued to deepen their trenches and buttress their fortifications. And they held their own against the Nanjing garrison's occasional sorties from the south gate, as well as attacks from the stone fort at Yuhuatai's peak. Those, at least, were fights in which the numbers on both sides were comparable.

But the same epidemic that decimated the Hunan Army's numbers gave Li Xiucheng an opening to lay off his campaign in the east and return to Nanjing. As the fighting slowed near Shanghai while the eastern armies tended to their sick and dead, he took advantage of the lull to respond to the Heavenly King's increasingly anxious calls for his return. In late summer, he withdrew to Suzhou, where he gathered three separate armies for a relief expedition to the capital—one to attack Bao Chao in southern Anhui, one to attack the naval forces on the river to break the Hunan Army's supply line, and the third—which he led personally—to destroy Zeng Guoquan's camp at Yuhuatai.[19] By late September they were under way, approaching from the south of Nanjing. Li Xiucheng had 120,000 men under his immediate command, though the rumors that swept the landscape in advance of their arrival put the number far higher—300,000, said some; 600,000, said others—and his coming was ushered in by a terror that all but darkened the sky.[20]

As soon as Zeng Guofan got wind of the rebels' preparations to relieve Nanjing, he began shipping rice, salt, powder, and shot to his brother at Yuhuatai—as much as the camp could hold. But he couldn't send any more reinforcements, at least not in the numbers that would be needed. Bao Chao was bogged down in southern Anhui, where the rebels were already making a fierce effort to regain lost ground (by December they would even retake Zeng Guofan's old headquarters in Qimen). And Zeng Guofan was also in the process of losing control over Duolonga and his cavalry force.

After chasing the Brave King north, Duolonga had begun to ignore Zeng Guofan's commands. When Zeng told him to come to Nanjing and hold the north bank of the river to give protection to his brother at Yuhuatai, Duolonga made excuses not to come. At the root was personal jealousy; Duolonga's army of 20,000 cavalry had played a critical role in blocking the Brave King's repeated attempts to rescue Anqing the previous year, but Zeng Guoquan was Zeng Guofan's brother, and he was the one who had gotten the lion's share of credit for recovering the city.[21] The proud Manchu commander had grown disaffected with his supporting role and lost interest in helping Zeng Guofan's family gain glory at his own expense. And so, rather than taking his cavalry east to Nanjing to support Zeng Guoquan, he instead gained an appointment to go in the opposite direction, northwest into dry Shaanxi province, to suppress a growing ethnic rebellion there.[22] An army of Muslims from neighboring Sichuan province had invaded Shaanxi in response to an outbreak of violence between Muslims and Chinese, and tens of thousands were said to have been killed.[23] Zeng Guofan was dismayed by the appointment of Duolonga to fight the Muslims, which to him was "like sending a stallion to capture a mouse."[24] But he underestimated the Muslims, and Duolonga would die in battle against them two years later, outside the walled town of Zhouzhi, forty miles west of the ancient capital Xi'an, without ever having returned to Zeng Guofan's campaign.

The assault on Yuhuatai began on October 13, though Zeng Guofan wouldn't know that until seven days later, when the first message from his brother arrived by courier, telling him that Li Xiucheng had just arrived outside his camp at the head of an enormous force. The updates from his brother kept arriving daily, but from his distant headquarters in Anqing there was little Zeng Guofan could do other than agonize. He transferred what meager reinforcements he could to Nanjing, but they amounted to only a few hundred men here and there. He consulted divinations in hopes of learning whether Heaven meant for the rebel armies to stay or disperse.[25]

Writing to his besieged brother from the safety of Anqing, Zeng Guofan tried to offer encouragement. If the Loyal King (the "False Loyal King," Zeng called him) had more than a hundred thousand soldiers, Zeng estimated that his army would need supplies on the order of sixty tons of rice per day. If Li Xiucheng couldn't get large barges of supplies to his camp—which would be the case as long as the Hunan naval forces could hold on to the junction of the river and moat—how could he possibly hold out for long? Zeng Guofan knew from his recent experience in southern Anhui how difficult it was to move supplies overland. Even if the rebels tried to supply Li Xiucheng's army from their stores inside the city, they would face the problem of exposure when moving large amounts of grain several miles around the wall from the open gates, and in any case the army's need for nearly two thousand tons per month would quickly use up the capital's reserves.[26]

Despite the outward optimism of his letters to his brother, however, in private Zeng Guofan was falling to pieces. A typical October diary entry was a chronicle of misery:

> Last night, I thought about my brother Guoquan, facing danger in ten thousand forms. Anxiety burned my heart. I repaired to my inner chamber and tried laying out scenarios on a Go board [to distract myself]. Then I paced back and forth, circling the room. At eleven o'clock I went to bed but could not fall asleep. Sometime after three in the morning I finally slept, and had nightmares.[27]

He all but stopped sleeping and began to refuse visitors out of exhausted distraction. Each day's letter from his brother brought increasingly dire news. In the one that reached him on October 24, Guoquan reported that they had been under constant attack for seven days and nights. He said they were holding firm ("a small comfort," commented Zeng in his diary). But the Taiping forces were trying out new weapons purchased from the foreign arms dealers. They were firing explosive shells into the camps—*luodi kaihua pao*, they called them in Chinese: the shells that bloom like flowers when they fall to Earth.[28]

Two days later, Zeng Guofan learned that another army of at least 100,000 rebels under Li Xiucheng's cousin the Attending King had left Zhejiang province to join the attack on the Hunan Army at Yuhuatai. But the news was delayed, and by the time Zeng found out about the enemy army's decampment, it had already been on the march for three weeks—which was more than enough time for it to have reached Nanjing.[29]

The next day, there was no letter from his brother at all.

Zeng Guofan stayed up all night waiting for a courier, consumed by the fear that Guoquan had met with disaster. *Has he been injured?* he wondered. *Or has the entire army been destroyed?*[30] It was, in fact, an injury—Zeng Guoquan had been struck in the face by shrapnel from one of the explosive shells. But though the wound was bloody, it turned out not to be life-threatening, and the grim parade of daily reports finally resumed. But Zeng Guofan's relief to know that his brother was still alive couldn't relieve his dread that Guoquan was never going to come back from Yuhuatai. He desperately sought reinforcements from Li Hongzhang in Shanghai. Li said he couldn't spare the Hunanese battalions that had come with his Anhui troops downriver, but he did offer to send the Ever-Victorious Army up to Nanjing. In a sign of the true depth of Zeng Guofan's desperation, against all of his own warnings that foreign mercenaries shouldn't be allowed inland, he reluctantly accepted the offer.[31]

But the force wasn't ready to come, and it would be weeks before it might be able to get to Nanjing (in fact, it never would, but Zeng didn't know that yet). So in November he sounded the retreat. Zeng Guofan wrote to his brother that if there should be any letup in the attacks, he should abandon Yuhuatai and the siege and retreat with his sick and wounded men back through the naval corridor to safety. It simply wasn't possible to hold out any longer, he warned.[32] Once they were safe, they could go to Bao Chao's aid. By that time, Zeng Guoquan's men had been holding out in their trenches for nearly a month under constant attack by a well-armed force many times larger than their own.

But Guoquan refused to leave. Against Zeng Guofan's pleading that he retreat to safety, he stubbornly held his position. In fact, despite the vast numerical advantage of the Taiping, in the fortified camp he was still the "host" of the battle and they were the "guest," and his men had been keeping up a murderous fire on the exposed attackers while being largely shielded by their own heavy walls and trenches. In a single furious day of battle in November, Zeng Guoquan estimated, his men had managed to kill several thousand rebels outside their camp, while suffering fewer than a hundred dead on their own side, with perhaps two hundred wounded.[33] But Li Xiucheng's soldiers were mining patiently under the outer walls and planting underground explosives to blast them open. The defense of the camps was a constant, desperate attempt to maintain the outer walls, feed the big guns, and keep up a constant matchlock fire on the attackers. The soldiers tried to spot the enemy's tunnels if possible, so they could breach them before the sappers reached the walls, but in case one were to get past them, they also worked to build new fortifications and trenches inside the safe zone of the camp to fall back on if and when the outer walls should explode.[34]

Zeng Guofan continued to suffer, wishing for his brother to retreat, wishing for an end to the constant anxiety and worry that were eating at him from within. He wrote to his oldest son, Jize, back in Hunan, asking him to leave home for a time and come join him at his Anqing headquarters. He was lonely and needed his family's company, and he told his son that if he came it would benefit both of them. He could help Jize with his studies as he prepared for the examinations, immersing himself again in the scholarship that gave him his only sense of peace. As for what his son could do for him, he told Jize that his presence "might help calm my heart palpitations."[35]

Miraculously, however, Guoquan survived. His men managed to breach most of the enemy's tunnels before they could do any damage, and when the earthwork defenses did give way, their backup fortifications held.[36] His tight Hunan forces endured a staggering total of forty-five days under attack before Li Xiucheng finally called off the operation on November 26.[37] Zeng Guofan, it turned out, had been correct in his initial assessment—without an effective waterborne supply route, Li Xiucheng had had to use the stores from the city, which had endangered the survival of the capital. The army he sent against the Hunan naval forces had failed to break their hold on the junction of the river and moat, so the Hunanese supply lines had stayed open while his own were blocked. Thus in the end it was the Loyal King's army, right at the edge of its own capital, and not Zeng Guoquan's invasion force, that had to give up the battle for want of provisions. Moreover, winter was coming and Li Xiucheng's men didn't have the clothing or equipment to fight through it; he had learned his lesson from the terrible snowstorm of the previous year.[38] Allowing subdivisions of his large force to return to Jiangsu and Zhejiang to address the troubles that were emerging there in his absence, the Loyal King himself took refuge inside the walls of the capital for the winter and licked his wounds, wondering how next to try to dislodge the enemy outside.

The Hunan Army had gained no new ground at Nanjing, and even the stone fort on Yuhuatai was still in rebel hands (Li Xiucheng directed much of the fighting from there, in fact). But the mere survival of the exhausted Hunan force after a month and a half under attack—under the very walls of the enemy's capital—was the stuff of legend. Nevertheless, Zeng Guofan still tried to persuade his brother to abandon the position at Yuhuatai and retreat to safety. Strategically, he insisted that preserving the army was more important than preserving any position.[39] But Guoquan stayed in place. Zeng Guofan felt no joy at the victory and feared that Li Xiucheng's withdrawal into Nanjing was just a temporary lull before the attacks would resume again.

The ongoing sleeplessness and fear took a physical toll on Zeng Guofan. He developed a severe ache in his teeth, so excruciating that sometimes he couldn't work at all. He felt old, exhausted. In a letter on December 5, he told his son Jize, "If I can just die soon, without being cursed by future generations, it would be a blessing."[40] Ten days later, he confided in another letter to his son that there was a darkness gripping his heart, which reminded him of when he had been back home in 1858 or in Qimen in the spring of 1861. The first instance was when he had resigned in depression after the death of his father and refused to continue fighting for the better part of a year. The second was when he had been trapped in southern Anhui with no supplies, facing what he was certain would be the end of his life. The darkness now, he told his son, was even worse than before. He asked him not to show the letter to his mother.[41]

But the worst was yet to come. That same afternoon, shortly after he finished writing to his son, a courier arrived with a letter from Guoquan at the Nanjing camp.[42] In all the time he had been worrying about Guoquan's safety, Zeng Guofan had given little thought to their other brother, Guobao, younger and less experienced than Guoquan, who had gone along to give support at the siege of Nanjing with command of 5,000 men. At thirty-four years old, Guobao was seventeen years Zeng Guofan's junior and the youngest of the general's three remaining male siblings. He was the one who had sworn vengeance when the rebels had killed their other brother at Three Rivers in 1858. Now, Guoquan was telling him that Guobao had fallen ill. The two elder brothers stayed in close contact over the following days, and although Guobao appeared at first to recover, and for a few days they rejoiced that the worst was over, in the end his fever came roaring back. It was typhoid, and just after dawn on the morning of January 11, Zeng Guofan opened the letter that told him his little brother was dead.[43]

CHAPTER 15

BLOOD AND HONOR

Frederick Townsend Ward took a bullet to the stomach on September 21, 1862, and died that night at Ningbo "in great agony."[1] In conjunction with Li Hongzhang's Anhui troops, Ward's militia had taken advantage of the absence of the Loyal King's armies to clear several towns near Shanghai in the late summer and early fall of 1862, and in September he took some of his force down to Zhejiang province at the behest of a new French-Chinese unit, modeled after his own, that aimed to drive the rebels out of the region surrounding Ningbo. The fighting there did not go well. Ward's dying words, fittingly enough, were a demand for money. He declared that Wu Xu and Yang Fang—the Shanghai *daotai* and his ostensible father-in-law—together owed him 140,000 taels in back pay (worth about $200,000 at the time; an enormous claim that his family back home would press with the Chinese government all the way into the twentieth century). In a bizarre final ignominy, the captain of the steamer tasked with carrying Ward's body back to Songjiang for burial turned out to be a passive-aggressive Confederate with a loathing for the late general, and he refused to transport the corpse. Under pressure from Ward's lieutenants he finally did accept the job but left port without reloading his coal stores. The ship bearing Frederick Townsend Ward's body to its resting place stalled out in open water somewhere in the bay between Ningbo and Shanghai and drifted aimlessly with the tide. After locking up the captain, Ward's lieutenants were able to get it moving again only by tearing down the wooden upper works of the ship and feeding them into the furnace. When the wood ran out, they dumped fifty barrels of pork from the hold into the boiler as well, and thereby managed to cook up enough steam to cajole it the rest of the way across.[2]

Things went downhill from there for the Ever-Victorious Army. After Ward's death, Li Hongzhang offered its command to Edward Forester, but Forester was so emotionally and physically shattered from his period of imprisonment by the rebels that he had to decline.[3] Moving down the list, the command fell to the North Carolinian Henry Burgevine, who enjoyed enthusiastic support from Hope—and especially from Frederick Bruce, who was keen to have an American in charge of the force since it blunted suspicions that Britain was aiming to take over China.[4] Burgevine was palatable to his countrymen because he was neutral vis-à-vis his own country's war (unlike his brother, who was adjutant general for the state of Arkansas),[5] and in character he was the very model of a southerner, gallant and charming—more so than the scowling Ward, to be sure—and everyone had high hopes when he took charge of the Chinese-foreign militia.[6] He did prove a highly capable commander, though the flip side of his outsized personality was a terrific temper and a propensity for the bottle.

Through the fall of 1862, under Burgevine's command the Ever-Victorious Army built on its successes under Ward and managed to drive the Taiping out of several more towns near Shanghai, continuing to take advantage of the absence of all the rebel armies that had decamped with Li Xiucheng back to Nanjing to break the Hunan Army's siege. By winter, the thirty-mile radius was all but cleared, but Burgevine was running into problems of his own. First Yang Fang fell several months behind on the payroll. Then Li Hongzhang ordered him to take the force up to Nanjing to help Zeng Guofan's brother—which looked to him and the other foreign officers like a suicide mission. Burgevine refused the orders to go to Nanjing, where the chances of death were far higher than the chances of loot. But Yang Fang refused to make up any of the soldiers' back pay until he did. Finally Burgevine's temper gave way. Frederick Townsend Ward had tried to ensure steady funding from Yang Fang by marrying his daughter, but Burgevine took a different, and perhaps more direct, tack. On January 4, 1863, he showed up at Yang Fang's home with a handful of his bodyguard troops and assaulted the banker, punching Yang Fang in the face and rob-bing him of 40,000 silver dollars, which he hauled back to Songjiang and used to pay off his men. Li Hongzhang declared Burgevine fired and put a bounty of 50,000 taels on his head.[7]

They ran out of Americans after that. Once Burgevine was out of the picture, it became clear that he (and Ward before him) had squandered their funds, run up large debts, and all but taken over the civil government of Songjiang from its Chinese officials. Frederick Bruce was mortified and insisted that the command of the Ever-Victorious Army had to be taken "out of the hands of adventurers" and put instead "under officers whose position in the military service of their own country is a guarantee both for their military knowledge and for their economical organization of the force."[8] Instead of filibusters and mercenaries, he wanted to see the Ever-Victorious Army led by honorable foreign military officers with proper commissions and reputations to preserve, who would be accountable to their home countries.

Obviously no such individuals would be forthcoming from the United States, since they were all needed back home, so Bruce reluctantly approved putting an Englishman in charge of the Ever-Victorious Army. As with his encouragement for Osborn's fleet, he was testing a new approach to British intervention in China—namely, to minimize direct British involvement and instead use certain units of the Qing military as Britain's proxy. His goal was simple: to find some way to restore order in China and expand trade, while still maintaining Britain's formal position of neutrality. The key to that strategy was to sell the Qing weapons and loan them a few gentleman officers of high reputation who could be relied upon *not* to engage in the kinds of atrocities and privateering that had marked the earlier campaigns and had brought such embarrassment to his country. As the second of Palmerston's two orders in council, which followed the news of Ward's death, had made it lawful for all British officers to enlist in the military of the Qing dynasty, there was no legal obstacle to Frederick Bruce's new attempt to find a hedge between neutrality and intervention.[9] Nevertheless, he would maintain to the end that Britain had no intention of fighting the Qing dynasty's war for it. "It is not our business to put down the Taeping insurrection, or to make war on the Taepings," he would write the following October. "Our exclusive business at Shanghae is to protect the port and the thirty-mile radius round it; and this we do, not from affection for the Chinese Government but because we are afraid of great prejudice to our interests were the disorderly Taeping hordes to seize Shanghae."[10] Others would see it differently.

A British officer, Captain Holland, was the first to try his hand at commanding the Ever-Victorious Army, and he promptly led it into its worst defeat ever. He was relieved of duty. The army's pay fell into further arrears, and the soldiers began looting shops in their home base of Song-jiang. Finally, a more promising replacement was found in the person of a young British officer of the Royal Engineers named Charles Gordon, who, for his service in this war, would be forever after known to his countrymen as "Chinese" Gordon and would enter the pantheon of British imperial heroes alongside Lawrence of Arabia. For his later service in Sudan, where he died, he would also be remembered to the readers of youth biographies as the man who "saved the British Empire."[11]

Gordon had classic English good looks, with a straight nose and high forehead, a serious mustache, and limpid blue-gray eyes. He was a graduate of the Royal Military Academy at Woolwich (which he entered two years after Frederick Townsend Ward was turned down by West Point), and he hailed from a long line of military officers who had married into wealth; his maternal grandfather's ships had been the ones ransacked in the Boston Tea Party.[12] He was an experienced cartographer and a visual thinker who made brilliant use of maps and sketches in his campaigns. He was also religiously asexual, never married, and had as early as age fourteen expressed a wish that he were a eunuch. He also happened to speak with a pronounced lisp.[13]

Gordon's appointment did nothing to stem suspicions that Britain was planning to make a play for power in China. "As well might you enchain the fibres of a vigorous oak with packthread as bind the expansion of British civilization in this province," wrote the editors of The North-China Herald when Gordon assumed his command; soon, they predicted, "the keys of every stronghold in this province will hang from the girdle of Britannia, who will then become the great arbitress of home as well as foreign affairs in this rich province of China."[14] Nevertheless, the future payoff of such intervention seemed rather murky to those back home. "China would undoubtedly benefit by a century of British rule," mused the London Spectator, but "Is it without an object that we are to bombard flourishing cities, without a policy that we suffer our subjects to assume the dominion over three hundred millions of Chinese?"[15] Gordon's appointment did, at least, help to appease the less stringent opponents of intervention—that is, those who were merely wary—because they could take comfort in knowing that it would be Gordon and Osborn, gentlemen both, and honorable, upstanding Christian servants of the queen, who would be leading the

Qing dynasty's imperial forces on land and water, rather than some group of dirty filibusters and deserters. Aid could be thus given, it was hoped, while still preserving neutrality (after a fashion, at least) and—more important—preserving Britain's national dignity.

By the time Charles Gordon inherited command of the demoralized and by then ironically named Ever-Victorious Army in March 1863, it carried a roster of 3,000 Chinese soldiers (though many had deserted), along with two shallow-draft paddle steamers and thirty pieces of field artillery left over from Ward's time.[16] There had been several larger guns as well, but Holland had managed to lose them. After its succession of inept commanders and the breach of faith with Yang Fang, the force's unpaid soldiers were sullen and obstreperous. When Gordon arrived at Songjiang to take up his new command, he ordered them to march in parade so he could view their state of discipline, and even that they refused. He blew up at them ("Damned nonthenth!" he reportedly shouted),[17] and then—depending on which version of events one reads—he either brought their pay up to date or else had one of the more insolent soldiers dragged out and shot, and thereby won back their loyalty.[18]

What gains Ward and Burgevine had managed were thanks primarily to the absence of Li Xiucheng's best forces while he tried to uproot the Hunan Army from its camp outside Nanjing. They had achieved little in the face of concentrated resistance from the rebels. But Gordon would pose a real threat to the Taiping in Jiangsu province because, unlike the filibusters who had preceded him—who were only out for themselves—he was willing to work closely with Li Hongzhang. Specifically, he campaigned in concert with Li Hongzhang's best tactical commander, a defector from the Taiping named Cheng Xueqi, while Li Hongzhang (following Zeng Guofan's example) coordinated from behind the scenes. Gordon never would come to have much respect for the soldiers and foreign officers of his own force, which he described as an out-of-control gang of murderers given to "indiscriminate looting and massacre."[19] But as an officer on loan from the queen with a reputation to preserve, he tried to serve the Qing emperor dutifully while maintaining British honor and therefore accepted his place in the local military hierarchy in a way that the soldiers of fortune before him had often resisted. At the same time, in contrast to Admiral Hope when he was still commanding the British naval forces in Shanghai, Gordon was for now serving under a Qing commission, on temporary leave at half pay from the Royal Engineers, and he was therefore perfectly free to take his fight outside the thirty-mile radius.

As soon as he got his men into shape, Gordon joined Cheng Xueqi in launching a joint campaign to take back Jiangsu province from the rebels. As a result of their cooperation, the spearhead strategy began to work. Gordon's small force could move swiftly through the narrow waterways on its shallow-draft steamers and open breaches in the walls of surprised Taiping towns with its artillery, while Cheng Xueqi's army—far better disciplined than its imperial counterparts, which had coordinated so poorly with Ward—showed up when expected, in force, and fought with absolute ruthlessness. Together, their combined forces drove the rebels completely out of the vicinity of Shanghai, and by the summer of 1863 they had cleared a path far enough inland to threaten Suzhou, the most important stepping-stone toward Nanjing from the east.

All looked well for the joint forces of Charles Gordon and Li Hongzhang, except that Henry Burgevine still had some life in him and wanted back in. After being ejected from the command of the Ever-Victorious Army, he had evaded capture and made his way up to Beijing, where he took refuge in the home of the U.S. minister, Anson Burlingame, in hopes of getting himself reappointed to the lucrative command (his salary alone was said to be 4,000 pounds a year).[20] By way of wooing the minister, Burgevine showered him with gifts—six cases of California wine, an atlas and a globe for Burlingame himself, two sedan chairs and some artworks for his wife, and an ornate box of French candy for his seven-year-old daughter.[21]

Burgevine chose his allies well, for Anson Burlingame was a true friend to the American filibusters. As Abraham Lincoln's minister to China, he had arrived in early 1862 with instructions that consisted of little more than an admonishment to avoid antagonizing the British or French, because there was no naval power to back him up if problems should arise. A scrappy and exceedingly well-spoken Massachusetts congressman and former Boston lawyer, the muttonchopped Burlingame had taken an immediate liking to his fellow New Englander Frederick Townsend Ward when he had first arrived. Notwithstanding the filibuster's claim to have become a Chinese subject, Burlingame saw Ward as a loyal American. "Neither self-exile, nor foreign service, nor the incidents of a stormy life," he wrote of Ward to the U.S. secretary of state, "could extinguish from the breast of this wandering child of the republic the fires of a truly loyal heart."[22] As Burlingame saw it, during a time when the United States could project no power in Asia thanks to its civil war at home, Ward's mercenary efforts outside Shanghai had been a means of building good favor with the Chinese government for Americans at large and ensuring that they would have influence in the country once the war was finally over.

Being Lincoln's emissary, Burlingame naturally brooked no sympathy for rebellion, and he never felt anything better than disgust for the Taiping. Prince Gong picked up on the analogy between their countries—the Qing as the Union, the Taiping as the Confederacy—and used it himself to encourage Burlingame's support for the dynasty. When at one point Burlingame sent Prince Gong a petition asking him to close China's ports to the Confederate raider CSS *Alabama*—which had been sailing the oceans destroying Union merchant vessels—Prince Gong readily assented, explaining to Burlingame that this was a problem their two countries had in common. "It appears from this," wrote Prince Gong to Burlingame, "that by the rebellion of the southern parts of the United States against their government, your country is placed very much in the same position that China is, whose seditious subjects are now in revolt against her."[23] To hear the comparison made by a Chinese statesman tickled Burlingame's wife beyond description. "They said, 'We see you are *just like us*,'" she wrote to her father, "'You have got a rebellion, and we have got one, too—so, *we can* appreciate your case.' I wonder what the 'Southern chivalry' will say to being put on a par with the 'Taepings!'"[24]

Just as he had admired Ward, so did Burlingame take a shine to Ward's successor. And so, when Burgevine showed up in Beijing and moved into the U.S. Legation in the spring of 1863, Burlingame promptly started lobbying the Office of Foreign Affairs to have him pardoned and reinstated.[25] Li Hongzhang wanted nothing to do with the man who had assaulted Yang Fang and who had refused orders to go to Nanjing, but the American minister pressed Burgevine's case directly with Prince Gong (joined in his efforts by Frederick Bruce, who in his Beijing loneliness had taken a fancy to his talkative American counterpart and still preferred to see the force led by someone who wasn't British). The prince finally relented, and Burgevine made his way back down to Shanghai in the company of an imperial commissioner carrying what he thought were orders from the Office of Foreign Affairs, instructing Li Hongzhang to put him back in charge of the Ever-Victorious Army.

But the letter from Prince Gong was in fact less a set of orders than a suggestion. Either way, Li Hongzhang flatly refused to honor it. Burgevine appealed directly to Charles Gordon, who, respectful of his chain of command, told Burgevine he would step down only if Li Hongzhang ordered him to. They then went on with their campaign for Suzhou without him. Frustrated, Burgevine returned to Beijing one more time, but now the Office of Foreign Affairs said there was nothing it could do to make Li Hongzhang reinstate his commission. Burgevine's temper kicked in again—this time more methodically. He made his way back down to Shanghai and rounded up seventy foreign mercenaries, including several discharged officers from his days with Frederick Townsend Ward. Then he stole one of the Ever-Victorious Army's gunboats, steamed up to Suzhou, and joined the rebels.[26]

From the standpoint of the foreign community in Shanghai and abroad—who believed foreigners to be the primary, if not sole, determinant of the course of the war in China—Burgevine's defection to the rebels along with the bulk of Ward's foreign officer corps looked certain to turn the tide of the war in Jiangsu. And sure enough, soon after he took up residence in Suzhou and began drilling Taiping troops to fight against Gordon, the battles started going in the rebels' favor. *The New York Times* greeted this news with a prediction that "if the rebels are wise enough to let him follow the bent of his genius it is apprehended that not only will the Taepings under his leadership recover the places that have been taken from them, but that even Shanghai itself will be in danger."[27] The headline in the *New York Herald* went even further, shouting "Yankee Chances of Succession to The Empire," as if this American might now capture the Qing throne for himself.[28] Even the London *Times* allowed that "thrones were once founded in India by men of less ability than those now engaged in China."[29]

From his new base in Suzhou, Burgevine started venturing out by night to the enemy lines, where Gordon's force was preparing an attack on the city, in order to meet secretly with his British counterpart and try to convince him to throw off his imperial commission. Gordon had, in fact, already come to the verge of quitting. The funding problems of his force were proving to be intractable, and he had difficulty controlling his men. Also, his sense of honor was offended by Cheng Xueqi's penchant for beheading prisoners. But he had decided to stay on after Burgevine went over, since he felt that his duty to England demanded the preservation of Shanghai from rebel capture.[30] But the *Herald*'s wild headline hadn't been so far off the mark, and Burgevine's ambitions were far greater than Shanghai: he proposed that he and Gordon should join their forces together, march north to the Manchu capital in Beijing, and bring down the dynasty for themselves.

The rumors of Burgevine's plan reached Frederick Bruce in Beijing, who feared that this would be the end of the Qing dynasty. He wrote to Lord Russell that it seemed likely that the Nian rebels in north China would support Burgevine if he led his Taiping forces north, "and success at Pekin would certainly overthrow the present dynasty, whether it led to the establishment of the Taepings or not."[31] But even if those events should not come to pass, Burgevine was only the most immediate of the threats facing the government in Beijing. Equally troubling to Bruce were the events that had led up to Burgevine's defection: namely, that Prince Gong and the Office of Foreign Affairs had proven powerless to exert their will over Li Hongzhang. To Bruce, that seemed clear enough evidence that no matter what might happen in the war against the Taiping, the dynasty's central government in Beijing—which was the party he was trying to preserve from collapse by loaning it British military officers and selling it munitions and ships—might not, in fact, be the real locus of authority in the empire anymore. Specifically, as he put it to Lord Russell around the same time Burgevine left for Suzhou, he worried that Zeng Guofan was shaping up to be "a formidable competitor for power in the centre of China."[32]

Zeng Guofan himself was rather amused by the news of Burgevine's disgraceful exit, which neatly confirmed his opinion of foreign mercenaries.[33] He was, however, livid that the Ever-Victorious Army's Chinese commander—the plump Wu Xu, whom Li Hongzhang had relieved as *daotai* in order to put him in charge of the expedition to Nanjing[34]—had never sent it to help his brother as promised. In Zeng Guofan's mind the Ever-Victorious Army was still a Chinese force, if a disreputable one; he had told his brother to make sure that its soldiers, who were not from Hunan, were kept separate from his own men after they arrived at Nanjing, in their own camp, where they couldn't cause trouble. And to Li Hongzhang he confided that his primary worry was that if they should live up to their promise and help conquer the rebel capital, the soldiers in the foreign-led force would try to steal most of the loot.[35] But those potential problems were nothing compared to a complete failure to show up. While he was still worrying about his brother's vulnerability at Yuhuatai, he wrote two scathing letters to Wu Xu, denouncing him as an unreliable lollygagger ("has there ever been procrastination like this that could be called 'reinforce-ment'?") and showering him with disgust. "I don't care whether you're a Chinese or a foreigner, someone from ancient times or today, a big official or a little one, a man with talent or a buffoon," he told Wu Xu. "If, in the midst of a crisis, you don't stand by your word, you're not worth a cent!"[36]

After the Ever-Victorious Army failed to help his brother, Zeng Guofan showed no further interest in mercenaries. What use Li Hongzhang might make of them in Jiangsu was up to his own initiative as provincial com-mander, but as far as the central headquarters in Anqing was concerned, although Zeng Guofan was increasingly interested in foreign technology, he wanted nothing to do with the foreigners themselves. When the new commander of British troops in China, Brigadier General Charles Staveley, traveled up to Anqing to pay Zeng Guofan a visit in April 1863, just after Gordon took charge of the Ever-Victorious Army, Zeng Guofan's reaction to his visit was something very much like boredom. He was on an inspec-tion tour down the Yangtze at the time and registered minor annoyance that Staveley, who found him absent from Anqing, had decided to follow him. He gave the British commander a single hour of his time, during which Staveley proposed that Zeng Guofan employ British officers to lead his own troops in suppressing the rebels. Staveley was pushing for some-thing much larger than the Ever-Victorious Army: 10,200 Chinese soldiers in seventeen battalions, each battalion with twenty-one officers. Staveley said he could provide the foreign officers at a rate of a little over 58,000 taels (roughly $80,000) a month and promised that they would be able to conquer Nanjing. Still sore from the exorbitant cost of shipping Li Hong-zhang's army to Shanghai, Zeng Guofan brushed him off. He told Staveley to take it up with the Office of Foreign Affairs in Beijing and then went back to his own business.[37]

Again, it wasn't that Zeng Guofan didn't want foreign aid at all, he just didn't want it to come with ties to foreigners themselves. He disdained their cultures. They were uncivilized and unruly, and they didn't understand the Confucian concepts of loyalty and trust. They were ignorant of the classics that would make a man a gentleman. Their countries were by and large greedy, and Britain and France especially took advantage of China when-ever they could. So he relied exclusively on ethnic Chinese who happened to be familiar with the foreigners and who could bring new knowledge and technology to him at Anqing without the need of employing Europeans or Americans. A number of bright young Chinese physicists and mathemati-cians, most of whom had learned their math and science from Protestant missionaries in the treaty ports (while keeping a safe distance from the religion they were teaching), joined him at Anqing. Zeng Guofan invited them to come to his headquarters and join his "tent government," as it was known, and employed them in various advisory positions on his staff.

One of the young men who would heed his call was Yung Wing, the Yale graduate, who had made little use of his Taiping passport since his visit to Hong Rengan in the autumn of 1860. He had in fact used it in 1861 to set up a shipping business in the Yangtze town of Wuhu, far from the treaty ports, and over the course of six months had managed to move nearly two thousand tons of tea down to Shanghai from rebel-controlled districts of southern Anhui.[38] But the profits weren't what he had hoped, and he came down with an illness that left him bedridden for two months, so he decided that the risks of disease, war, and robbery just weren't worth it and resigned himself to staying in Shanghai from then on.[39]

In the late autumn of 1863, three years after his visit to Nanjing, Yung Wing closed out his business in Shanghai and traveled up to the Hunan Army headquarters in Anqing for an interview with Zeng Guofan. His introduction came by way of two mutual acquaintances, a Chinese engineer and a mathematician, both of whom had already joined Zeng Guofan's staff and were helping with his steamship experiments. Yung Wing's arrogant demeanor toward his old acquaintance Hong Rengan back in 1860—his insistence that it was up to the rebels to earn his support by meeting his list of conditions—was no longer in evidence when he got to Anqing. Rather, he practically groveled before the Hunanese general, whose power seemed to him "almost regal," "almost unlimited." In Yung Wing's starstruck eyes, Zeng Guofan was, by this time, "literally and practically the supreme power in China."[40]

Zeng Guofan sized up Yung Wing slowly and patiently at their first meeting, with a little smile on his lips, taking in the aspect of this young man who had spent so much time with foreigners. His stare made Yung Wing feel "uneasy," but the impression he gained was apparently a good one. He said he could tell from his eyes that Yung Wing would make a fine commander. He asked if he was married. Yung Wing found it impossible to gauge the machinations inside the head of the general across from him, whose lingering gaze seemed to penetrate to his very soul.[41]

The interviews continued over the following two weeks, during which time Yung Wing lived in Anqing and marveled at the hum of activity that surrounded Zeng Guofan—a hundred secretaries, hundreds of advisers from all over the empire, all drawn to this city in Anhui province by "the magnetic force of his character and great name."[42] But Yung Wing had no idea of the uncertainty that dwelled behind the general's impenetrable facade—especially his private fears that his reputation was undeserved, his power illusory. As Zeng Guofan confided to Li Hongzhang not long after Yung Wing's visit, "On the thousand miles of the Yangtze there isn't a single boat that doesn't fly my colors, and for that reason both Chinese and foreigners imagine I wield great power. But they don't know that in reality my resources are insufficient and my soldiers are too few."[43] None of this was apparent to Yung Wing.

At the end of the two weeks, Zeng Guofan gave Yung Wing a mission. Or rather, he asked Yung Wing to tell him what his mission should be, what he could do for the Hunanese general. In dinner parties during his stay at Anqing, it had been made abundantly clear to the returned student what Zeng Guofan desired: machinery and weapons. Wanting to give the correct answer that would ingratiate him to this "great man of China,"[44] Yung Wing said nothing about making educational reforms, introducing the Bible to the schools, or establishing a modern banking system—which had been his absolute preconditions for joining the Taiping. Instead, he offered on the spot to go back to the United States and use his contacts there to purchase for Zeng Guofan all of the equipment he would need to build a modern industrial factory that could produce Western guns, cartridges, and cannons for the Hunan Army.[45]

Zeng Guofan approved the mission, and Yung Wing made his way back to the United States, where in 1864 he would manage (surprisingly, in light of the ongoing U.S. Civil War) to commission an entire factory's worth of steam-powered industrial machinery from the Putnam Machine Company in Fitchburg, Massachusetts, and arrange for it to be shipped to Shanghai. The timing and location being convenient, he even managed to drop down to New Haven for his tenth Yale reunion during the same trip. As his old classmates discussed the vagaries of the U.S. Civil War under the leafy elms of their quiet brick college, Yung Wing was inspired to try to enlist for half a year in the Union Army—now that he had done his part to seal the doom of his own country's rebellion.[46]

If Henry Burgevine's defection to the rebels gave them a new advantage in Jiangsu province, a separate power materialized on the imperial side only four weeks after his departure from Shanghai that seemed certain to neutralize it: on September 1, 1863, Captain Sherard Osborn finally arrived in Shanghai to assume command of his war fleet. Osborn had become something of a public intellectual back in England, publishing a pair of articles on "Progress in China" in *Blackwood's Edinburgh Magazine,* the second of which carried the audacious title "The Taepings and Their Remedy." There, he spelled out his grand expectations for his mission. "The Government and people of China both ask us to aid them in their hour of trouble," he wrote, "and in return they will assuredly grant us that access and commercial freedom for which we have so long laboured and so often fought." He promised that his "*European* Chinese force, crewed by Europeans in China" would introduce steam power, electricity, and railways to China and "open the country, throughout its length and breadth, to Christianity and commerce."[47]

When he actually got to China, however, Osborn learned that Horatio Nelson Lay's entire plan had been a hallucination. The Qing administrators had never intended to employ a European paranaval force. Not only that, they hadn't even been sure whether the handful of ships they had agreed to purchase would be part of an imperial navy or a provincial one. The internal correspondence pertaining to the fleet showed stark disagreement between what Prince Gong proposed to do with it and what Zeng Guofan wanted instead. An edict in November 1862 said that the fleet would be an imperial asset, to be first used against the Taiping rebels and then taken to sea to patrol China's coast (and, implicitly, to hold off future foreign aggressors). The ships, according to Prince Gong, would have multiethnic crews: the sailors would be men from Shandong province on the northeast coast, the gunners would be from Hunan in the central kingdom, and the marines would be Manchus.

But Zeng Guofan saw things differently. Specifically, he thought the fleet would make a useful addition to his own navy. It might be nice to use an assortment of peoples according to their talents, he wrote on January 30, 1863, in response to the imperial edict, but he pointed out that such mixing could also lead to disunity. In the plan he offered instead, the entire crew—captain, gunners, sailors alike—would be from Hunan. And since the Hunanese weren't a seagoing people, he scrapped the idea of patrolling the coast and said that the fleet should be used only on the inland rivers and lakes. He recommended that only a very limited number of foreigners be retained, perhaps three or four per ship, to operate the rudders and maintain the engines. All of the rest of the ships' crews could be drawn from the ranks of the Hunan Army, and once his men could master all of the jobs, they could take over from the foreigners completely. "At first we will use foreigners to teach Chinese how to operate the ships," he explained, "and then we will use Chinese to teach Chinese."[48] After the training and operation were fully under control of his Hunan Army, he wrote, "all of the navy on the Yangtze River will be from the same family, and can unite as one spirit." The squadron of steam-powered gunships would be absorbed into his naval fleet along with the long dragons, the fast crabs, and the brass-gunned sampans, and Zeng Guofan would control the whole of the Yangtze.

In yet another sign of the true balance of power in the empire, the general's wishes trumped those of the central government. So, when Sherard Osborn arrived in Shanghai on September 1, he found an official letter waiting for him from Prince Gong, informing him that a Hunan Army admiral would henceforth be serving as the war fleet's commander in chief. Osborn was demoted to assistant commander, with authority over only the foreign members of the ships' crews (who would, by Zeng Guofan's plan, be small in number and quickly phased out altogether). Furthermore, the letter stated, all orders directing the actions of the fleet would originate not from the Qing emperor, as Lay had promised, but from Zeng Guofan and Li Hongzhang.[49]

Osborn traveled to Beijing to protest, but Prince Gong refused outright to sanction the contract he had signed with Lay—especially the clauses pertaining to the chain of command, which would have given Osborn license to ignore everyone except the emperor. Horatio Nelson Lay had come back to China before Osborn in the late spring, expecting adulation, but now he was desperate, and he spent three weeks of October trying to convince the unlistening Office of Foreign Affairs in Beijing to go along with his plan and approve Osborn's contract. Prince Gong stopped showing up for meetings. A rumor spread in Shanghai that Zeng Guofan had threatened the prince that if he did not put Osborn's fleet under his command, he would "shut off all the supplies to the Imperial Government."[50]

Prince Gong's decision was final, and by late October, Sherard Osborn declared that he was resigning his Qing commission and would return to England. His grand visions—to be the commander in chief of the emperor's navy, to restore order to the empire, to conquer Nanjing "without the loss of one Taeping life," to awaken the ancient kingdom to the wonders of modern technology and ensure a welcome for British commerce—crumbled under the humiliation of being ordered to serve as a mere assistant in Zeng Guofan's personal military force. "I came here to serve the Emperor, and under him the Regent," complained Osborn, "not to be the servant of mere provincial authorities."[51]

Yet Osborn was the only one in his naval force with a commission to resign. During the time that he was making his anger known in Beijing, the four hundred uncommissioned crew members of his heavily armed fleet were waiting expectantly, without a mission, in a northern port to which he'd moved them after they'd started deserting in Shanghai to join the rebels.[52] Osborn refused to surrender control of his war fleet to Prince Gong when he resigned, which raised the looming threat that the entire flotilla of battleships might wind up in the hands of the Taiping—or even the U.S. Confederates, for whom the fleet conjured up visions of smashing the southern blockade or destroying the Union's global shipping lanes. Both parties had agents on the ground in Shanghai trying to buy them.[53]

The American minister, Anson Burlingame, had the greatest vested interest in keeping the ships out of the hands of the Confederacy, so he was the one who stepped in to mediate the dissolution of the fleet, which was eventually sold at a loss and sent back to India and England. After all the publicity and promises back home, the affair became a source of grinding embarrassment to the British. But more than that, it was a warning sign that the polite collaboration Bruce and Lay had imagined between their empire and that of the Manchus—on which they had managed to sell even the prime minister and the chancellor of the Exchequer—actually had no basis in reality. The new government of the Qing dynasty was turning out to be not at all the compliant and enlightened central authority Frederick Bruce had imagined it to be when he had convinced Russell and Palmerston that they should take its side against the rebels.

Fortunately for the dynasty, Charles Gordon did not take Henry Burgevine's bait. Sticking to his principles, Gordon declined to join the American's mission to unseat the Qing emperor and instead tried to convince Burgevine to come back to the imperial side, promising him immunity if he left the Taiping. To this end, it helped that the temperamental Burgevine was beginning to find it just as difficult to get along with his new employers as his old ones. He chafed at taking commands from the rebel generals, insisting that they should support him in leading an independent force.[54] His frequent visits to the enemy lines to meet with Gordon began to arouse suspicion. His stolen gunship blew up accidentally. An old injury was acting up, and he spent more and more of his time drunk. When on one occasion the Taiping commander at Suzhou sent him down to Shanghai with substantial funds to pay for a consignment of ammunition and guns, he returned instead with a cargo of brandy.[55] On another occasion, his best friend woke him up—at noon—to tell him that some of the officers were talking about his drinking problem, and Burgevine shot him through the cheek with a revolver for refusing to name names.[56] That was pretty much the end of it for Burgevine's defection. On October 15, 1863, in the midst of an attack on Suzhou by Gordon's force, several of his followers crossed back over to the imperial lines and surrendered. Burgevine himself joined them a few days later.[57]

Thanks to Gordon's personal promise of immunity (and another intervention by the now very active Anson Burlingame), Burgevine would escape execution by the Qing authorities for treason. But the condition of his release was that he had to leave China and could never come back. His story would end in 1865, when he broke the terms of the pardon and sneaked back into the country one last time to raise a new militia. He was captured by imperial forces and soon afterward turned up drowned in a Chinese river, in chains. The local authorities said the boat on which he was being transported had met with an accident and capsized. But nobody believed that.[58]

With the dissolution of the Vampire Fleet, Britain's proxy intervention reverted to the original collaboration between the land forces of Charles Gordon and Li Hongzhang in Jiangsu. With Burgevine's surrender from his rebel service in October, a major obstacle to their campaign for Suzhou had been removed. But even without Burgevine's help, the city's defenses were formidable. By November 1863, Gordon's Ever-Victorious Army, in concert with the Anhui forces under Li Hongzhang's turncoat commander, Cheng Xueqi, had managed to fight their way to a stalemate at Suzhou. The city was contained under a relatively effective siege, but after a series of bitter repulses in late November it looked unlikely that they could carry the gates by storm.

There was, however, dissent inside the city. The senior Taiping commander in Suzhou was a man named Tan Shaoguang, also known as the Esteemed King. He was prepared to defend his city to the death. But below him were six kings of subordinate status, who feared greatly for their men and their families and weren't so certain that the imperial forces could be held off. On November 28, Cheng Xueqi reported to Gordon that one of those lesser kings had secretly come to see him, promising to deliver the city peacefully if they could somehow remove the Esteemed King and his loyalists from power inside. By December 1, they were in serious negotiations with Cheng Xueqi and Charles Gordon to open the gates of the city to the imperial forces. The leader of this group, Gao Yongkuan the Receiving King, was as Gordon described him, "a man of medium height, dark complexion, and about thirty years of age, with a very intelligent and pleasing countenance."[59] He seemed afraid and asked for Gordon's help.

Gordon said he would approve any plan that could capture the city of Suzhou with minimal bloodshed, and he left it to Cheng Xueqi to arrange the terms under which the lesser kings might somehow defy the Esteemed King and deliver Suzhou to the imperialists. As a former rebel himself, Cheng Xueqi swore an oath of allegiance with those kings (he had already known the Receiving King from his earlier incarnation as a Taiping commander) and promised them safety. In his official report, Gordon stated that he had visited with Li Hongzhang in his offices soon afterward and made it clear to him that the surrendering kings must be treated with mercy. Li Hongzhang had agreed.[60]

At eleven in the morning on December 4, the Esteemed King held a banquet at his palace for the Receiving King and the others. After a luxurious dinner and a period of prayer, they repaired to a ceremonial hall, where they all put on their silk robes and crowns and took seats at a long table upon the stage. The Esteemed King began to give a speech, which turned tense when he began to talk about how the only rebels who really could be trusted were the ones from the south, who had joined in the beginning. Most of his guests were from Hunan and Hubei in the central kingdom. At that, one of the lesser kings stood up and took off his robe as a provocation. A scuffle ensued. Someone stabbed the Esteemed King with a dagger, and he fell over the table. Then they all fell on him, dragging him from the stage to the floor below and holding him down while an underling sawed off his head. Then they rallied their troops in preparation to open the city and sent a messenger to ride out to the imperial lines to find Cheng Xueqi and present him with the Esteemed King's severed head.[61]

Gordon ventured into Suzhou the following day, before the imperial forces entered, and confirmed that everything was peaceful inside. The six kings "appeared quite at ease" and seemed eager to hand over the city to Li

Hongzhang and be done with their part in the fighting. He asked them if they were content with what they had done, and they said yes. He visited them again the next morning at the home of the Receiving King, where he found them with their heads freshly shaved in preparation for the planned surrender later that day.[62] As before, they were in fine spirits. Gordon chatted with the Receiving King a little about the future. He was grateful to Gordon for having arranged a peaceful handover and said he would like to see him again soon.

When Li Hongzhang arrived by boat with his bodyguard forces to take control of the city later that day, however, events took a darker turn. The sound of musketry went up in the previously quiet city, and Gordon saw crowds rushing about. He heard the shout of soldiers as they ran through the streets of Suzhou. He found his counterpart, Cheng Xueqi, outside the wall and asked him what was going on, but Cheng was evasive and "looked disturbed." Finally, Cheng told Gordon that the kings had never shown up for the surrender. Worried, Gordon rode back into the city to find the Receiving King and make sure he was safe. The streets were now thronged with people, and he rode past lines of surrendered rebels and roving packs of imperial soldiers looting the shops and houses. When he finally got to the home of the Receiving King, he found it empty and ransacked.

Certain that the kings must have gone to meet Li Hongzhang as planned, Gordon began to suspect that Cheng Xueqi had been lied to and that Li had in fact taken the rebel kings prisoner when they surrendered. At the crack of dawn the next day, he set off on a hunt for Li Hongzhang, hoping to force him to set the Receiving King and the others free. After a few hours of searching he still couldn't find Li Hongzhang, but he did meet up again with Cheng Xueqi, who assured him that he had no idea what was happening. That wasn't true, however. According to a foreign officer who stayed behind when Gordon left to continue the hunt, Cheng Xueqi—the former Taiping—sat down on the ground and began to weep. He asked the foreign officer to take a message to Gordon. It was an apology, the gist of which was that he had only been following Li Hongzhang's orders. Gordon finally found the remains of the surrendered kings later that morning. The first thing he recognized was the Receiving King's head as it lay in the dirt. Then he sorted out some pieces of the others. "The hands and bodies were gashed in a frightful way and cut down the middle," he reported. The Receiving King's "body was partially buried."[63] Li Hongzhang's men had executed and dismembered them all.

Gordon exploded. His promises of faith to the Receiving King and the others had been broken; he had assured them they would be safe, and for Li Hongzhang to execute them so brutally, after they had betrayed their leader in order to give the city over to the imperialists, was to him an unthinkable crime against honor. He renounced his service under Li Hongzhang, declaring that he would never serve him again. "Bloodthirsty as it looks," he later wrote to his mother, "I am anxious for his trial and execution."[64] Gordon's righteous fury spread through the foreign community like a fire. On December 16, the Shanghai-based consular officers of ten countries unanimously approved a statement condemning Li Hongzhang for "acts of extreme treachery abhorrent to human nature, calculated to withdraw from the Imperial cause the sympathies of Western nations, and the aid of the gallant officers who have hitherto assisted them."[65]

The report of Gordon's outrage expanded through transmission and retelling, and by the time it reached the pages of the London *Times* it was an extravaganza of fury and vengeance, with Gordon and his English officers blasting their guns wildly at Li Hongzhang's men, trying in vain to stop the massacre. "They all fired and loaded and fired again on every mandarin and imperial soldier they met," said the report in *The Times,* and "Gordon is said to have shot thirty-five [imperials] himself." It said they had driven in as far as Li Hongzhang's quarters but hadn't been able to force their way in. "Everyone is disgusted to no ordinary extent," it concluded, "and the feeling of regret is universal that Gordon did not succeed in capturing [Li Hongzhang] and hanging him."[66]

It was a watershed moment that put an end to the British public's support for their country's part in the Chinese war. The bloody incident at Suzhou was so repulsive and so shocking to them less because of any vicarious anger they felt on Charles Gordon's behalf for the insult to his personal honor (although they did feel some of that) than—more importantly—because of what it revealed in the larger picture. It was so shocking precisely because it showed, once and for all, that this was Li Hongzhang and Zeng Guofan's war, not Charles Gordon's. It showed that the British supporters of his mission had been wrong—indeed, painfully naive—to imagine that "Chinese" Gordon was actually in charge of *anything* in the campaign against the Chinese rebels. They were wrong to congratulate themselves that Britain was showing the Qing government how to fight its own kind of war, to imagine that their gentleman officers were some kind of beacon to the imperial military, setting a model for them to follow. What the events at Suzhou finally made clear, in short, was that for all of their many protestations to the contrary, the proud British agents in China in fact were, and had been all along, nothing more than mercenaries.

The explosive rupture between Gordon and Li Hongzhang spelled the end of direct military cooperation between Britain and the Qing dynasty, and once again opened the prospect that Britain might now have to send in the forces needed to take control of the ruins of China as it had done in India. To many in Shanghai and abroad, this now seemed inevitable. As Hope had written in frustration when the imperial commander at Ningbo had first failed to avail himself of Dew's aid, that "the cowardice and imbecility of the mandarins" made collaboration with them impossible, the wreckage of Osborn's and Gordon's careers put the lie to Frederick Bruce's hopeful plan that Britain could use the Qing dynasty as its proxy in restoring order and commerce to China—or at least that it could do so with its honor intact. If the British really wanted peace in China, went the darkest line of reasoning, they would now have to make it themselves. "Only by pouring a strong military force into it," said *The New York Times,* "can either of the European Powers succeed in accomplishing the pacification of the Empire—which result, accomplished this way, would almost certainly be followed by the permanent subjugation of the Chinese Empire to European power."[67]

The colonization of China, or at least the southern half of it, was the path Frederick Bruce dreaded the most, and the papers back home in England inveighed loudly against it ("our business in China is to trade and not to rule," said *The Economist*).[68] But to those in the consular service with the highest ambitions, it was a result that could not come soon enough. Edward Bowra, a Briton in the Shanghai imperial customs who was gunning for Horatio Nelson Lay's old position of inspector general, gave perhaps the most honest assessment at the time. In December 1863, he found himself "delighted with the turn affairs are taking here." It was just after Gordon's angry resignation, and it looked to him as though the English officer might now decide to conquer Jiangsu province for Queen Victoria, rather than for Li Hongzhang and Zeng Guofan. "Daily some thing new turns up which effectually helps us on our way to territorial acquisition, or at all events to British occupation of southern China," wrote Bowra in his private diary. "And yet the government at home seems desirous of avoiding any such result."[69]

In his heart Bowra knew—just as Lord Elgin had before him—that the conquest of China was what his countrymen really wanted; they just couldn't stomach the truth of their own dark will. The home government were like "fools or children," he wrote, who would issue grand orders and then "grumble at the bill." They "habitually share the plunder, assist the encroachments, and protect and honor the adventurer, and yet in the same breath, pity the victim, denounce the expedition, and condemn the policy." If England was going to demand the continued expansion of commerce in China, he thought, it had damn well better not pretend horror at the bloodshed and territorial conquests that were the certain price of its desires.

But Bowra's aggressive hopes were not to be realized. The British government responded to the thunderous anger that welled up in Parliament after news of the resignations of *both* Osborn and Gordon reached home—after the public awakened to the barbarity of the imperial forces, the butchery to which their countrymen had been party—and in the end it proved stronger, in its way, than a child or a fool. After news of the beheadings in Suzhou reached England, amid a rapid crumbling of public approval, Palmerston's government immediately revoked the orders in council that had allowed British officers to serve in the Qing military. Separate instructions were dispatched to the British authorities in Shanghai "to withdraw explicitly from Major Gordon all leave and license to serve under the Emperor of China."[70]

So remarkably swift was Palmerston's renunciation of the intervention that by the time he could come under attack in the House of Commons, the debates were already moot; the policy his opponents assailed had, for all intents and purposes, already been terminated, and their discussions served mainly as a public flogging. Nevertheless, flog him they did. William Baxter, for one, "rejoiced" in the "failure" of Sherard Osborn's mission, "because it opened to us an escape from a situation of great embarrassment and difficulty."[71] Supporting a symbolic resolution that "further interference on the part of this Country in the Civil War in China is impolitic and unnecessary," William Ferrand, representing Devonport, declared that Palmerston's policy in China "had been condemned, not only by honorable Members on both sides of the House, but it was disapproved of by the country generally."[72] (Whether most lawmakers thought that disapproval worth acting upon with purely symbolic measures, though, was another question; the resolution against interference came as the last item on a Friday agenda with no other motions, and by the time the debate finished, there weren't even enough members left in the chamber to bring it to a vote.)

Richard Cobden, MP for Rochdale, injected new energy into the debates with a heavily contested resolution on May 31, 1864, to require the same policy of nonintervention in China that Britain maintained in the United States, remarking specifically on Frederick Bruce's "state of despair, because the policy recommended by him, or carried out there with his acquiescence, seems to have failed and broken down."[73] Colonel Sykes decried Britain's policy "of direct intervention on behalf of the Imperialists, and slaughtering the Taepings" and quoted a private letter from Charles Gordon to a missionary that "if half the pains had been expended upon the rebels which had been wasted upon the Imperialists the country would have been at peace long ago."[74]

In the end, the prime minister had to bow to the opposition and return to the policy of nonintervention—still allowing for the protection of Shanghai against direct attacks but no longer to take any part in the war beyond the treaty ports.[75] In defending himself against Cobden's resolution, Prime Minister Palmerston absolved his own good intentions and those of others who had supported the Chinese service of Sherard Osborn and Charles Gordon, but he acknowledged that his efforts to prop up the Qing government had not worked. "Those measures have failed," he admitted in a rare moment of contrition. "I am sorry for it."[76]

But there was a gloating aspect to his defeat as well, for he had gotten what he wanted. From the standpoint of the summer of 1864, when those debates were taking place in the House of Commons—three years into the U.S. Civil War, two years into the Lancashire cotton famine—Palmerston and the other proponents of intervention against the rebellion in China could point to a major expansion of trade in China that had resulted, as they saw it, from Britain's efforts to suppress the Taiping. Total revenues from the China trade had in fact tripled in the years since Britain started taking an active hand in putting down the rebels.[77] Palmerston and his supporters could argue, in other words, that their despised policy had in fact been a brilliant success, and no matter the moral questions or inconsistencies, their adventure in China had helped shelter England's economy from the ravages of the U.S. Civil War. "It was long felt that trade with China would open a vast field of commercial enterprise to us," said Palmerston proudly in the House of Commons on May 20, "and there can be no doubt that, among other things, the great expansion of commerce with that empire has contributed to enable us to meet without disaster the unfortunate obstructions to our commerce and manufactures occasioned by events still going on in America."[78] In other words, when one door had closed, another had been opened.

But even as the stewards and servants of the British government struggled over their national conscience, and even as that struggle played itself out through their chaotic and contradictory policies halfway around the world—now forward in China, now back, now mercenary, now principled, now elevating the Manchu dynasty, now reviling it—Zeng Guofan and his army had been holding with relentless focus to their one stubborn and singular purpose. And so, by the time the British finally withdrew back into the cloak of neutrality at Shanghai, their intervention in the Chinese civil war collapsing upon itself in an avalanche of moral anguish, their assistance was no longer needed.

CHAPTER 16

CROSSING THE MOUNTAIN

After Issachar Roberts left him in the winter of 1862, Hong Rengan had little contact with anyone else from the outside world. A stray German missionary named Wilhelm Lobscheid finally came through Nanjing a year and a half later, in the summer of 1863, while Gordon and the Anhui Army were making inroads in Jiangsu province. He found the Shield King bitter and defensive. "Have we ever broken faith with foreigners?" Hong Rengan asked him. "Have we ever retaliated [against] the enmity of England and France?" If the foreigners wanted to be the Taiping's enemies, they had better beware, he said. "We are fighting in our own country, and to rid ourselves of a foreign power, and woe to the stranger who falls into our hands after the first shot has been fired against Nanking." Lobscheid was dismayed by the sting of betrayal he heard in Hong Rengan's voice and wished for a new beginning between the rebels and the foreign powers. "Sir Frederick Bruce will one day be recalled to give an account of the ruinous course of policy he has advised his Government to adopt," he wrote to a Hong Kong paper after his return from Nanjing, "and foreign influence will at last prevail in the council of the rebels. But whether that will be upon the ruins of the silk and tea plantations, or upon the graveyards of thousands of British subjects, we shall soon have an opportunity of witnessing."[1]

Though Hong Rengan no longer managed foreign affairs, he was still the top-ranking official in the rebel court, and all of the capital's business still passed through his hands.[2] For the most part, the other kings still had to go through him to get access to his reclusive cousin the Heavenly King. And once the anger about the doings of missionaries had faded, his cousin gave him new responsibilities that in some ways were more personal, and therefore more trusting, than the ones he had given him before. In 1863, he asked Hong Rengan to take charge of his teenage son, the Young Monarch, and to ensure his safety no matter what happened to Hong Xiuquan himself. As the guardian of the heir apparent, Hong Rengan feared he might fall short "of the great trust reposed in me," and he was "filled with anxiety and gave way to tears."[3]

The immediate pressures of the war forced Hong Rengan to put aside his plans for a new government and a new diplomacy for China. The military campaigns and the supply lines simply had to come first, and as the problems on those fronts intensified, the dawn of his imagined state receded into the distance. His cherished reforms—the railroads, the law courts, the trading entrepôts, the newspapers, mines, banks, and industries—would all have to wait. It was all he could do to hold the leadership in the capital together. Hong Xiuquan's madness was growing as the military setbacks mounted, and intimations of doom drove his visionary mind toward its longed-for apocalypse. He refused to countenance a retreat, trusting only to the Heavenly Father, and began granting rewards and honors to his followers with careless abandon, creating so many new kings—more than a hundred of them—that his son the Young Monarch couldn't even keep all of their names straight.[4] The bickering of the officials in the capital was increasing and becoming more bitter, just at the time when it shouldn't.

Meanwhile, the famine in the countryside deepened. Despite the relief stations Zeng Guofan had set up in southern Anhui, conditions in that mountainous part of the province had deteriorated far beyond even the horror that had existed when he first took control of Anqing. "Everywhere in southern Anhui they are eating people," he wrote in his diary on June 8, 1863, a remark whose very banality signified the degree to which the unthinkable had become commonplace. It was one of several notations on cannibalism in his diary, though in this instance the concern that drove him to mention it wasn't so much that human meat was being consumed per se—for that was old news—but that it was becoming so expensive: the price per ounce had risen fourfold since the previous year, meaning that even this most dismal of sustenances was becoming unaffordable. There was cannibalism in Jiangsu province as well, he noted, east and south of Nanjing, though the price of human flesh there was reported to be lower. Charles Gordon saw its gruesome footprint for himself while on campaign, though he didn't think his brethren back in Shanghai could possibly understand the true horror of it. "[T]o read that there are human beings eating human flesh," he wrote to his mother, "produces less effect than if they saw the corpses from which that flesh is cut."[5]

Northern Anhui was a wasteland. Bao Chao tried to scout out a supply line through the province to support an army on the northern bank of the Yangtze across from Nanjing, but he gave up hope. In normal times, the flat midsection of Anhui was an unbroken plane of jade in the spring, with rice shoots glowing in the open sun that dazzled in reflection off the threadlike irrigation canals. But Bao Chao reported that in a journey of more than a hundred miles through the region in the spring of 1863, he hadn't seen so much as a blade of grass. There was no wood to be burned for cooking fires. There was nothing to support human life at all.[6] Similar dark reports came from Jiangsu, where the fighting had all but emptied the countryside for a hundred miles around Shanghai. Wild pigs scavenged in abandoned villages, feeding on the dried corpses of the dead. As governor-general, *this* was the region of Zeng Guofan's jurisdiction and lofty authority. "To hold such great responsibility in such terrible times," he brooded in his diary, "surely this is the most accursed existence of all."[7]

Yet the desolation had its silver lining. Whether or not Zeng Guofan actively supported a scorched-earth policy, he clearly saw in the devastation of the landscape the same benefits for counterinsurgent warfare that others, at other times in the world's history, would find as well. In a memorial to the throne on April 14, 1863, he described the ruin of southern Anhui. "Everything is yellow straw and white bones," he wrote. "You can travel an entire day without meeting a single other person." The most worrisome aspect of this desolation, as he saw it, was that the rebels, denied any access to food, might try to break out and head southwest into Jiangxi province.[8]

At the same time, he explained, there was much to find pleasing in the situation. The rebels depended on the support and acceptance of the peasants among whom they lived, and the famine conditions would create conflict. People would leave the regions surrounding the Taiping's area of control and "disappear like smoke," leaving them without supporters. If the farmers had no seeds, they would have to abandon their fields, leaving the rebels with nothing to eat. "Campaigning in a region with no people, the rebels will be like fish out of water," he wrote. "In a countryside devoid of cultivation, they will be like birds on a mountain with no trees."[9] The devastation, he expected, would eventually reach the point where the rebels could no longer survive.

———————

Zeng Guoquan finally captured the stone fort on Yuhuatai on June 13, 1863, in a sudden nighttime attack following months of quiet preparation. He took the position with little loss of life, though Zeng Guofan (who sought to gain as much credit for his brother as possible) reported to Beijing that six thousand rebel defenders had been killed in the battle.[10] With control of the hill, Zeng Guoquan now effectively shut down the south gate. From Zeng Guoquan's new vantage point atop Yuhuatai, the rebel capital spread out below like a giant Chinese chessboard. The game of encirclement was begun for real now, and his elder brother, back in his chambers in Anqing, playing his obsessive rounds of Go, laid his pieces carefully, plotting out the pattern of moves that would surround the city, cut off all points of escape, and bring the contest to its conclusion.

The western and northernmost gates of Nanjing opened onto the Yangtze River, which ran past the city in a northeasterly direction. On the bank of the river opposite the city lay gigantic Taiping forts that protected the mile-wide Yangtze corridor as it skirted the capital. On June 30, the Hunan river forces launched a furious attack on these forts. Taking advantage of a strong crosswind, the Hunanese sent in wave after wave of sampans, which rode in close-hauled on the downstream current, tacking sharply against the headwind, then fired their guns and came about, sails spread wide, to run before the wind that pulled them back upstream out of range in a grand whirl of coordinated motion. The Taiping shore batteries blasted away at the circulating sampans, wounding and killing more than two thousand Hunanese sailors, but in the end the forts were taken and all of the defenders slaughtered. The Hunan Army took full control of the Yangtze River where it met the northwest corner of Nanjing, and the rebels could no longer make crossings to the north of the city. The western gates of the city were now useless to them.[11]

The last Taiping general to cross the river before the forts were captured was Li Xiucheng, who returned on June 20 from an expedition to the north. He had left Nanjing with an army in February 1863, three months after he had failed to dislodge Zeng Guoquan from his camp at Yuhuatai, to try to break through the Hunan Army forces in northern Anhui and open a new supply line for the capital. His search through the wasteland of Anhui was as fruitless as Bao Chao's, and his troops were ravaged horribly by starvation in the course of their journey. Reduced to eating grass, they still repeatedly found the cities they attacked occupied by well-provisioned Hunan Army garrisons that drove them off with heavy casualties. The news that Zeng Guoquan had captured the fort on Yuhuatai in his absence was the final straw, and Li Xiucheng returned straight to the capital when he heard. The army with which he returned to Nanjing on June 20, crossing the river in stages ten days before the forts on the north bank fell, was by his own estimate smaller by a hundred thousand men than the one with which he had left in February. But no sooner did he return to the side of his besieged sovereign than he had to leave again, because his help was needed in Suzhou, which was threatened by Li Hongzhang, and Hangzhou, under attack by Zuo Zongtang's army. There were too many fronts, too few commanders, too few resources.[12]

Control of the river gave the Hunan forces dominance over the western gates of the city, and with the southernmost gate shut down by his brother's position on Yuhuatai, Zeng Guofan turned his attention to the northern and eastern faces of the city. Immediately after the river forts were captured, he sent Bao Chao to cross over to the city and lay siege to the Shence Gate, the primary inland gate on the city's north side. In that alone he was unsuccessful; disease broke out in Bao Chao's camp, and a call for help came from southern Anhui and Jiangxi, where the Hunan Army garrisons were contending with the flight of Taiping armies headed westward from Zhejiang. So Zeng Guofan had to remove Bao Chao from Nanjing and send him back to Anhui, leaving that gate open.

Through the summer and autumn of 1863, Zeng Guoquan's forces continued to spread out, conquering a succession of ten heavily defended bridges and mountain passes that gave them mastery of the roads southeast of the city.[13] In November, he sent a detachment northeast to the site of the Ming imperial tombs in the hills just east of the city, where he had his men build a three-mile wall linking to his southeastern positions, thereby blocking off the eastern approach almost completely. On the eastern side of Nanjing, the only gate that still remained open was the Taiping Gate, which opened outward a couple of miles to the west of the Hunan Army's blockade at the Ming tombs. Two powerful rebel forts watched over it from the side of a precipitous mountain that edged up against the city outside the wall at that point. The city-facing slope of the mountain was known as the Dragon's Shoulder, and the castle at its top was the Fortress of Heaven, while the one at its bottom was the Fortress of Earth. By December 1863, the Taiping Gate, with its two guardian fortresses, along with the Shence Gate on the north side of the city that Bao Chao had abandoned, were the only points of rebel control left on the city's entire twenty-three-mile circumference.

Quiet terror reigned inside Nanjing. With only the two gates still open and therefore only two roads leading away from the city, food supplies were limited and there was almost no traffic in or out. There were about thirty thousand people inside the walls, a third of them soldiers.[14] After Suzhou fell to Li Hongzhang in December, Li Xiucheng returned again to Nanjing and pleaded with the Heavenly King that they had to leave; they had to abandon the capital and lead an exodus down into Jiangxi province. But the Heavenly King refused, angrily accusing him of lacking faith.[15] The sovereign's intransigence was maddening, but Li Xiucheng was unwilling to defy his orders to stay put, so he began preparing the population inside for a prolonged siege. There was one advantage, though, in there being so few people in such a vast city. Under his direction they began opening up land in the northern part of the city for cultivation. With hard work, they could grow enough food to sustain themselves for a long time—perhaps even forever, if the walls held. But the entrapped society was not at peace. Hong Xiuquan's paranoia was mounting, and even his cousin couldn't temper the excesses of his mad cruelty. The people lived in fear of his grotesque and capricious punishments. For the crime of communicating with any-one outside the walls, people were now being pounded to death between stones or flayed alive in public.[16]

More might have fled the city and begged to be allowed to shave their heads and return to the side of the dynasty, except that they knew what had happened to the civilians in Anqing. By late December, they also knew what had happened to the kings who had surrendered at Suzhou.[17] Their judgment was wise. Several groups of women were sent out from Nanjing over the following months, and though they were not killed out-right, in a fate more uncertain they were "given" to the rural population as wives.[18] But even that indulgence would end. In the late spring of 1864, Zeng Guofan would advise his brother not to let any more women or chil-dren escape the city. Forcing the rebels to support the whole population inside, he explained, would accelerate their starvation. And he didn't want his brother to inadvertently let any of the rebels' family members survive.[19]

With the Brave King dead and the Loyal King torn between multiple fronts, Hong Rengan once again found himself thrust into military command. As the exits from the city were cut off one by one, his cousin told him to go out of the capital to rally troops from the nearby territories and bring them back to relieve Nanjing. But even the military novice Hong Rengan could sense that the tide had shifted. The death of the brilliant and charismatic Brave King had left a vacuum in Anhui to the north and west of Nanjing, and without him there it was now impossible to defend the capital from northern approaches, impossible to reopen the river crossing and the northern road through Pukou that had been their all-important outlet during the previous siege of Nanjing. (Li Xiucheng's attack on Hangzhou, which had broken that earlier siege, had started on the very crossing they were now unable to control.) There was no commander who could replace the Brave King, and despite the great numbers of troops who had followed him gladly while he lived, now that he was dead, his armies had dissolved, returning to their homes, heading north to join the Nian, or surrendering to the imperial side. "With the fall of the Brave King, the prestige of the troops was gone," wrote Hong Rengan in reflection, "and as a matter of course they dispersed."[20] To make matters worse, the news came that even Shi Dakai the Wing King had surrendered with his renegade army in Sichuan during the summer, and there was no longer any hope of his coming to the aid of Nanjing either.

Hong Rengan set out from the capital on the day after Christmas 1863, leaving his brother and his wives and children behind in Nanjing.[21] He journeyed first to Danyang, fifty miles to the east, where the Green Standard generals had met their end in 1860. The uncle of the Brave King commanded the garrison there, but he said there were no soldiers to spare for Hong Rengan to take back to Nanjing. So he prepared to continue onward, toward Changzhou, thirty miles farther east along the Grand Canal. But then the news came that Changzhou had fallen to Li Hongzhang's army, and he had to stay in Danyang through the winter. When spring broke, he traveled south into Zhejiang province, where the city of Huzhou, fifty miles north of the capital, Hangzhou, was still holding out.[22]

When Hong Rengan had gone out to raise an army back in 1861, the process of recruitment had been almost effortless—simply a matter of planting his standard, writing his poems, and then waiting as the multitudes came to him to lead them into battle. But not anymore. In both Danyang and Huzhou he found only vulnerability, not strength. The commanders were worried about attacks from the imperial forces who had just conquered Suzhou and Changzhou. The soldiers were afraid of food shortages and refused to leave the relative safety of their garrisons to follow him back to the capital.[23] In compromise, he made a home for the summer in Huzhou, promising the commanders that he would wait there with them until September, when the new harvest of grain in Nanjing would be ready to feed them all and they could march together back to the capital.[24]

Meanwhile, new recruitment was swelling the Hunan Army to an unprecedented size. By January 1864, there were 50,000 Hunan soldiers at Nanjing.[25] In total, Zeng Guofan commanded some 120,000 troops, about 100,000 of them on land and the rest in the river navy. Along with the 50,000 under his brother at Nanjing, there were 20,000 garrisoned in southern Anhui, 10,000 in northern Anhui, 13,000 roving with Bao Chao, and 10,000 stationed between Anhui and Suzhou.[26] And that wasn't even counting Li Hongzhang's Anhui Army, which followed up its conquest of Suzhou with a march toward Nanjing from the east, smashing through the walled cities of Wuxi and Changzhou in rapid succession. Nor did it count the army under Zuo Zongtang in Zhejiang province, fighting its way toward Hangzhou in preparation to come at Nanjing from the south. All of the forces were converging.

As the armies expanded, the battles continued to go their way. In February 1864, Zeng Guoquan's forces managed to capture the castle at the peak of the Dragon's Shoulder, the Fortress of Heaven. The rebels still held the Fortress of Earth at its base, which guarded the point where the mountain ridge met the city wall.[27] But with the control of the upper fort, the imperials dominated the field, and they were able to set up stockade camps at the Shence Gate and the Taiping Gate against little resistance. Once those final two gates were invested, the city was closed off completely.[28] Soon afterward, on March 31, the Zhejiang capital, Hangzhou, fell to Zuo Zongtang with support from the French-Chinese force out of Ningbo. The defenders who escaped the fallen city fled to Huzhou, fifty miles to the north, where they found refuge with Hong Rengan through the summer. The other rebel armies that were scattered throughout Zhejiang began abandoning the province, moving in a disorganized retreat westward into Jiangxi. With the loss of both Hangzhou and Suzhou, the Taiping no longer held any of the major eastern cities. There were no more avenues of rescue for the capital. All there was left was the siege.

———————

Zeng Guoquan had a dream. He dreamed that he was climbing up a high mountain peak, all the way to the summit. When he got to the top, however, he couldn't find any path to continue forward, so he turned around. But when he did, he saw that there was no longer any path behind him either. He told his secretary about this dream on a grim, rainy day at the end of March. "I fear it is not auspicious," he said sadly. His army's supplies were nearly exhausted—for, as it was turning out, the devastation of the countryside bode even worse for the Hunan Army siege forces than for their enemies. Even though their supply line along the Yangtze remained open and uncontested, by the spring of 1864 there was no longer much food that could come to them from it. The soldiers were surviving on rice gruel, nothing more. He worried that his battalion commanders, ashamed of being unable to provide better for their men, were no longer keeping discipline in the camps. "Our food is about to run out, and there's nowhere around to gather more," Zeng Guoquan confided to his secretary. "If we don't break this city in a month, our whole army is going to crumble to pieces." [29]

Inside the city, it was a different world. By April, broad expanses of land at the northern end of Nanjing sprouted green as the seedlings of the garrison's first crop of wheat broke through the surface of the newly cultivated soil. In contrast to the landscape for hundreds of miles all around them, theirs was an oasis of fertility and cultivation. The results of their labor were viewed with envy and bitterness by one of Zeng Guofan's admirals, peering through a glass from a distance. Even as the rebels inside the city looked forward to a bountiful harvest, his own men faced the prospect of starvation if they didn't bring the siege to a conclusion soon. [30]

Zeng Guoquan's forces managed to hold on into the early summer, but pressure was beginning to mount from Beijing, where the government was running out of patience. It demanded that Nanjing be conquered without further delay. But Guoquan wanted full credit for recapturing the city, so he resisted suggestions that Li Hongzhang's Anhui Army be brought up to Nanjing to supplement his Hunan forces. As commander in chief, Zeng Guofan was torn between the anticipation of victory, and concern that his brother's army at Nanjing would collapse from lack of supplies while he continued to stubbornly refuse help. He berated his brother's vanity. "Why must you have sole credit for conquering Nanjing?" he wrote to Guoquan on June 19. "Why should one person be the most famous under heaven?"[31] Zeng Guofan knew Beijing court politics better than his younger brother, who had no such experience, so he finally invited Li Hongzhang to join in the assault on Nanjing—knowing that a failure to do so would invite charges that his family put their personal ambitions above the good of the empire. Li Hongzhang, out of respect for his teacher's predicament, politely made an excuse not to come and allowed the Zeng family to continue as the sole force against Nanjing while blunting the criticisms from the court.[32]

By this time, Zeng Guoquan's siege works at Nanjing had expanded to a breadth of scale that was stunning by any standard. The Hunan Army had built a three-mile road for supplies through a bog, connecting the river to hard ground within two miles of Zeng Guoquan's headquarters on Yuhuatai. Charles Gordon visited him there as a private citizen after the Ever-Victorious Army was disbanded, and from the lookout atop the hill, gazing over the silent rooftops of Nanjing, he could see that there would be little resistance if and when the wall was finally breached. "For miles the wall is deserted entirely," he noted, "only here and there is a single man seen, miles from any support." All was quiet, and "a deathlike stillness" hung over the vast city.[33]

The lines of vallation encircled the rebel capital as far as the eye could see: mile after mile of continuous wooden breastworks punctuated by mud forts—more than a hundred of them—each with a few hundred men inside. In some places they ran dangerously close to the wall, just a hundred yards or so, but nobody was shooting at them from above. Indeed, a sense of quiet and repose (some would say boredom) permeated the muddy camps. Makeshift shops had sprung up, where enterprising locals sold goods to the soldiers. There were no visible sentinels. It wasn't that the Hunan troops were lazy, just that there wasn't anything they could do for the time being other than wait and pass the time. The real work was being done underground and out of sight.

In the absence of any guns that could penetrate the wall, the Hunan Army relied on a more ancient method of defeating a walled city: they dug under it. Zeng Guoquan's miners sank a series of pits around the city wall. Where the moat was interrupted or ran widely enough from the wall that they could begin their digging inside its reach, they dug down fifteen feet or so before starting inward horizontally toward the city. But where the moat protected the wall, they had to angle downward as deep as ninety feet underground to skirt safely below it.[34] To screen their efforts from the spotters who made occasional appearance on the wall, they threw up stockades in front of the digging—but as each tunnel lengthened, the rubble hauled out by the miners piled up higher and higher until it finally rose above its concealing stockade. There was also the problem that as the shallower mines lengthened, the grass on the surface above them turned brown, leaving a telltale path for which the spotters were specifically looking.[35]

The tunnels were about four feet wide and seven high, propped up internally with frames of wood and tree branches. If there was no water above them, the miners punched vertical holes through the surface for ventilation—which prevented suffocation but again risked attracting the attention of the spotters. Meanwhile, from inside the city, the Taiping were slowly digging their own countermines outward, guided by those same spotters. And when they managed to puncture the wall of an incoming mine, they used bellows to blast it full of noxious smoke or flushed it with boiling water or sewage to drown the miners and render the tunnel useless.[36] In the one instance where the Hunan Army's mine did get close enough to the wall for them to detonate a charge, it didn't generate enough explosive force and failed to make enough of a breach to allow the Hunan troops inside. In that case, the rebels simply built a new wall behind the existing one, to block off the point of damage.

By June, the Hunan Army had sunk mines at more than thirty sites around the city wall with nothing to show for their efforts except four thousand dead miners.[37] But on July 3, they finally captured the Fortress of Earth at the base of the Dragon's Shoulder on the eastern side of the city. Like the stone fort on Yuhuatai to the south, the Fortress of Earth looked right over into the city, but it did so from an even higher vantage point and from an even closer position that practically touched the side of the wall. With the fort in hand, Zeng Guoquan's forces set up a battery of more than a hundred cannons on the slope of the Dragon's Shoulder and began pounding a constant barrage over the wall, night and day, the guns bellowing over the ramparts and blasting the buildings and ground surface on the other side, sending the spotters and miners scurrying for safety. They began filling in the gap between the fort and the wall with rubble, earth, and bales of straw, hoping to level the surface to the point where they could simply walk over it into the city. And below the covering fire of their cannons, under the ground at the foot of the Dragon's Shoulder, Zeng Guoquan's most ambitious tunnel yet grew longer and longer.

The tunnel started about seventy yards out, its main artery carving straight for the wall, groping forward at a rate of fifteen feet a day through earth and stone. As it neared the base of the nearly fifty-foot-thick city wall, it divided into several branches, each worming its way separately underneath, sapping hollow chambers at intervals under the mammoth structure above. The defenders knew it was there, but the incessant ground-shaking cannon fire from the battery on the Dragon's Shoulder made it impossible to countertunnel against it. On July 15, Li Xiucheng led a blistering midnight sortie out of the Taiping Gate with a few hundred cavalry, trying to storm the stockade at the tunnel's opening, but the Hunan forces drove them back into the city. Three days later the tunnel was almost complete, and Zeng Guoquan gave the order to load the chambers under the wall with explosives. This time, desperate for a success after so many failures and fearing that the court had lost its patience, he erred on the side of abundance. His men packed six thousand cloth sacks under the wall, containing a total charge of twenty tons of gunpowder.[38]

They sprang the mine at noon on July 19. A battalion of four hundred handpicked veterans crouched low to the ground just before the wall, swords tightly gripped, steeling themselves to launch through the breach into close-quarters combat. At a distance behind them on the slope of the Dragon's Shoulder, a thousand more were ready to follow. The lit fuse simmered and worked its way slowly down into the pit, then disappeared into the dark mouth of the tunnel. As time stretched out anxiously above ground—first five minutes passed, then ten, then twenty, thirty—the fuse continued invisibly on its slow path below, sparking along the rough floor of the mine and finally splitting off like spider legs at the end to trace the last distance to its multiple targets. Then, with a terrific shuddering of the earth, the massive wall went up—and up—blasting outward and skyward in a thunderous convulsion of smoke and stone that first obliterated the sky and then rained back down with a hailstorm of granite rubble so deadly it crushed every man in the vanguard of four hundred who crouched below. But when the black smoke cleared over their mangled and broken bodies, it revealed a breach nearly two hundred feet wide, right through the wall.[39]

As the rumbling of the explosion echoed off into the distance, the Hunan Army forces arrayed on the Dragon's Shoulder gave up a shout and started running down the hill, storming the breach with swords aloft, clambering over the rubble and the bodies of their dead comrades to meet the Taiping defenders head-on. The first troops to force their way through the ranks of defenders made a beeline through the wide streets of the city, maps in hand, straight for the palace of the Heavenly King. But Li Xiucheng had beaten them there and spirited away Hong Xiucheng's son the Young Monarch before they could catch him. When the first Hunan troops arrived at the palace, they found it eerily empty and quiet—for the Heavenly King was already dead. He had perished more than six weeks before they broke through the wall, most likely of disease, and was already securely buried in his robes of state when they got there (Zeng Guofan would later have his body exhumed to make sure it really was he).[40] Confused, they reported to Zeng Guoquan that the Young Monarch had committed suicide. Other units raced around the inside shell of the wall to attack the gates from behind, driving out the rebel defenders and opening the massive doors or raising ladders as the other Hunan forces poured into the city from all directions.

In the chaos of occupation that evening, Li Xiucheng bid a tearful good-bye to his family and led the Young Monarch with a small party on horseback through the streets of Nanjing disguised as Hunan soldiers. With the luminous glow of a setting sun directly behind them, they charged the breach in the wall, broke through the line of surprised sentries, and vanished into the gloaming.[41]

When the Hunan troops couldn't find Li Xiucheng, Zeng Guoquan panicked. He wrongly believed that the Young Monarch was dead like his father, but if Li Xiucheng had gone free, he knew he could re-form his army elsewhere and continue his resistance. The long-fought conquest of Nanjing would be for naught. The war would never end. But in the end they did catch him. After charging the breach in the wall and evading the cavalry who chased them into the night, Li Xiucheng gave the Young Monarch his best horse to help him escape and was left with a broken nag that soon wore itself out and refused to run any farther. He sent the child king ahead with the others, keeping only a couple of horsemen in his own party, and took refuge in an abandoned temple on a hillside twelve miles to the south of Nanjing.

The small rebel band had no supplies and no plan. A group of local peasants eventually discovered them there, and when they realized who Li Xiucheng was, they wept and knelt on the ground before him. They begged him to shave his head so he wouldn't be caught and tried to find a place to hide him. But there were others in their community who figured out who this strange visitor was and saw riches to be had for turning him in. Two of them ("scoundrels," he called them) captured him and turned him over to Zeng Guoquan's forces on July 22, just three days after his escape.[42]

The whereabouts of the Young Monarch were unknown, but Zeng Guoquan finally had the Loyal King in hand. He was the most coveted prisoner of all, the last great military commander of the rebels. Without his leadership, bands of Taiping soldiers might continue to fight and survive and even carve out small kingdoms for themselves in remote corners of the empire, but they could never conjure the momentum they had enjoyed under his leadership. With his capture, the war was effectively finished.

The vaunted discipline of the Hunan Army broke down completely when Nanjing fell. The militia soldiers were unpaid and barely fed, and with this total victory in their final objective—after years of bitter campaign away from their families and their homes—they broke ranks and laid waste to the rebel capital in an orgy of uncontrolled looting. Zeng Guoquan issued proclamations forbidding his troops to murder civilians or kidnap women, but the commanders paid no attention (and in some cases even helped) as their soldiers ran amok. The rebels who stood against them were butchered in the streets, while younger women were dragged off and the remaining able-bodied men were forced into service as porters to carry away huge loads of loot from the city—gold, silver, silks, furs, jade. Even some of Zeng Guoquan's own aides who entered the city to investigate the looting were robbed and beaten by roving gangs of Hunan soldiers.[43] First the soldiers set fire to the palaces; then they burned the homes. And then it was as if the whole city had gone up in flames. A purplish red pall hung over the broken capital for days, until a heavy rainstorm came pouring down on the after-noon of July 25 and finally washed the city clean.[44]

Zeng Guoquan's secretary entered the city on July 26 and was over-whelmed by what he found inside. All of the rebel males who were still alive appeared to be carrying loads for the Hunan Army soldiers or helping them dig up stashes of buried treasure. It looked to him as though they were being set free afterward or at least escaping the city. But not the oth-ers. The elderly had been slaughtered with abandon. So had the sick and the infirm, who couldn't serve as forced labor. Most of the dead bodies he saw lying along the streets were those of old people, but there were count-less children as well. "Children and toddlers," he wrote in his diary, "some not even two years old, had been hacked up or run through just for sport."

As far as he could tell, there wasn't a single woman left in the city under forty years old. The living prostrated themselves on the ground. They showed signs of mutilation by soldiers who had tortured them to reveal the locations of hidden loot. "Sometimes they had ten or twelve cuts on them," he wrote, "sometimes several times that. The sound of their weeping and moaning carried into the distance all around."[45]

There was no question in his mind that all of this was the work of his own army. He listed in his diary the names of several of Zeng Guoquan's commanders he knew had taken part in the massacre and looting, writing in fury, "How can they face their general? How can they face the emperor? How can they face Heaven and Earth? How can they face *themselves*?" An unbreathable stench filled the air from the bodies that rotted in the streets, and Zeng Guoquan issued feeble orders that the battalions should at least drag corpses to the side of the road and cover them with rubble, so there would still be an open path for travel through the city.[46]

Little is known of what happened to the thousands of young women who were taken from Nanjing, but one, at least, managed to leave a record of what happened to her after the city fell. Her name was Huang Shuhua, and she was sixteen years old. The soldiers came, she said, and "They killed my two older brothers in the courtyard, then they went searching through the rooms of the house. One of the strong ones captured me and carried me out. My little brother tugged on his clothing, my mother threw herself down before him, weeping. He shouted angrily, 'All rebel followers will be killed, no pardons—those are the general's orders!' Then he murdered my mother and my little brother. My eldest brother's wife came out, and he killed her too. Then he dragged me away, so I don't know what became of my other elder brother's wife. I was grief-stricken, sobbing and cursing at him, begging him to kill me quickly. But he only laughed at me. 'You, I love,' he said. 'You, I will not kill.'"[47]

The soldier tied her up and put her on a boat to take her back home with him to Hunan. He was from Zeng Guofan's home county of Xiangxiang, the very place where Zeng's army—indeed, his whole campaign to bring order back to the empire—had originated. And now, after all those years, the forces Zeng Guofan had conjured were finally coming home with their legacy. At the soldier's village, the young woman would face the horror of spending the rest of her life as the wife of the man who had murdered her entire family. She wrote down her story on two slips of paper one evening while they were still traveling, as they stopped at an inn for the night. One slip of paper she hid on her body; the other she pasted to the wall of the inn. Then she somehow found the wherewithal to kill him, before she hanged herself.

Zeng Guofan finally took possession of Nanjing when he arrived from Anqing on July 28, nine days after his brother's forces breached the wall. Despite the loss of control over their troops, for the upper echelons of his army it was still a time for celebrations and the savoring of victory. Officers under his brother took him around the perimeter of the wall in a sedan chair, telling him tales of battles fought and won and showing him scenes of destruction that still leached their smoldering vapors into the air. The evenings were reserved for poetry and plays, for wine and song, for the sublime intermarriage of remembrance and forgetting. Operas were performed before grand banquets of more than a hundred tables, crammed with officers, secretaries, and advisers. And soon the honors would pour forth from the dynastic government, once the news of Zeng Guofan's victory reached them in Beijing, and the imperial capital went silent, and the empress dowager wept.[48]

But the empress dowager was far away; within Nanjing, it was the end of *his* war, not the dynasty's. Zeng Guofan seeded his reports on the fall of Nanjing with fabrications, claiming that a hundred thousand rebel soldiers had been killed in the fighting, inflating the glory of his family and his army, masking their looting and atrocities against civilians. He kept careful control over what the court would know. To that end, from the day he arrived in Nanjing he took over the interrogation of Li Xiucheng for himself. The Hunan Army commanders had already secured a long confession from Li Xiucheng in the week since he had been captured—pages upon pages detailing his origins and the history of the war and explaining the tactical decisions he had made, many of which they still did not understand. The honor of beginning the questioning had fallen to Guoquan, who had taken to the job with undisguised relish; his primary tools were an awl and a knife, and he managed to cut a piece out of Li Xiucheng's arm before the others made him slow down.[49]

When Zeng Guofan took over the interrogations on July 28, at last the two hoary, weatherbeaten commanders in chief of the civil war faced each other in person for the first time: square-shouldered Zeng Guofan on the one side, the weary-eyed scholar, his long beard turning gray; wiry, bespectacled Li Xiucheng on the other, the charcoal maker who had risen to command the armies of a nation. It would be no Appomattox moment, however. There was no wistful air of regret and respect between equals. For the defeated, it was no prelude to reconciliation, to twilight years on a rolling plantation. This war ended not in surrender but in annihilation. Zeng Guofan would spend long hours of the following evenings editing his counterpart's fifty-thousand-word confession, striking out passages that didn't paint his own army in a good light and having it copied and bound with thread for submission to the imperial government, before casually ordering Li Xiucheng's execution—in spite of orders he knew were coming from Beijing, that the rebel general be sent to the Qing capital alive.[50]

The last any foreigner saw of Hong Rengan was in Huzhou just before the fall of Nanjing. A mercenary named Patrick Nellis was there, a crew member from Sherard Osborn's fleet who had been crimped into the rebel service and was helping to defend the city. It was early in July, and the kingdom was collapsing all around, though the walls of Huzhou still held for the moment. Hong Rengan and another king spoke from a platform to an assembly in one of the courtyards. The lectures seemed to go on for hours. Nellis didn't speak any Chinese, so he couldn't understand much, just the names of a few places he recognized: *Suzhou. Hangzhou.* They were losing. *Jiangxi.* They were going to escape. After the speeches were over, Hong Rengan descended from the platform and came over to him.

He spoke to Nellis in English, but his diction was slow and halting from lack of use. The old fluency was gone. It had, after all, been a long time since any of the missionaries had come to visit him at his palace. And it had been a long time since he had entertained his foreign friends with dinners of steak and wine, serenading them with hymns sung in English. It had been a long time since he had reminisced with them about glad days past in the emerald beauty of Hong Kong, or enchanted them with his brilliant hopes for the future of the kingdom. That world was gone now. His hopes had all withered on the vine.

He asked Nellis what his nationality was.

"An Englishman," Nellis replied.

"I have never met a good foreigner," said Hong Rengan.[51]

They finally caught up with him in early October. After Li Xiucheng's capture in July, Hong Rengan left Huzhou to take over the protection of the Young Monarch. Along with a ragtag escort of soldiers and horsemen, they

survived for nearly three months, making it all the way down to the southern part of Jiangxi province, more than four hundred miles southwest of
Nanjing and only a hundred and fifty miles from the Meiling Pass, over
which he had first come from the south. In their search for a place of safety
they were, by the time the imperials scouted out their trail, closer to Canton and Hong Kong than to the fallen capital they had left behind. Their
flight ended in a remote, mountainous country fifteen miles northeast of a
town known as Stone Wall. Hong Rengan was bringing up the rear of the
ragged procession. The horses and men were exhausted, so they stopped
to make camp for the night. Instinct told him to continue on through the
darkness along the narrow rural paths, but they had no local guide who
could show them the way. The attack came near midnight, without warning. A sentry must have fallen asleep at his post. The imperial soldiers were
upon them before they could put on their armor or mount up their horses.
Hong Rengan fled on foot into the night, alone, wildly running through
the trees and into the dark mountains. But he came in the end to a place
where the hills pressed together from both sides, and there was no passage
to go forward.[52] There was no longer a path behind him either.

EPILOGUE

When Zeng Guofan arrived to take control of Nanjing in July 1864, for the dynasty it was an occasion not just of triumph but of terror as well. For he was, at that moment, the most powerful man in all of China. The rebel capital was crushed. His army was transcendent. He exercised a de facto military dictatorship over eastern and central China. And he had never been fully under the dynasty's control. Though his Hunan Army fought to uphold the rule of the Beijing government, his command fell largely outside of its direct influence, and even as the dynasty had relied almost entirely on him to prosecute its war against the rebels to its end, there wasn't a moment when his actions weren't watched from Beijing with a strong measure of dread.[1] As it turned out, Frederick Bruce's worry that Zeng Guofan would prove "a formidable competitor for power in the centre of China" grasped only a fragment of the real picture. For generations after the fall of the Taiping, the story would be told that several of Zeng Guofan's top commanders—including his brother Zeng Guoquan—had counseled him that the time was nigh to abandon the faltering Qing dynasty to its fated end and take power in Nanjing for himself, as the new emperor of China.[2]

But he did not do that. In truth, even as his campaign for Nanjing began to enter its final stages, he was already preparing to disband his personal army and relinquish his military power. He would hold on to his grand position as governor-general of Jiangxi, Jiangsu, and Anhui after the war, supervising the reconstruction of eastern China from his offices in Nanjing—a palatial complex of offices he ordered built right on top of the ruins of the Heavenly King's own palace. But just at the point when watchers in China and abroad waited on tenterhooks to see whether the victorious general would now send his army northward to Beijing to overthrow the emperor of the Manchus and clean up the mess of the Qing Empire, he had already made up his mind to cede power, to send his soldiers home, and to live out the rest of his life as a mere civil official within the imperial bureaucracy—the most powerful of the civil officials, to be sure, but still just an official and still a loyal subject of the child emperor and his regent, the empress dowager.

Zeng Guofan's seemingly paradoxical combination of power and submissiveness, which baffled those who knew him as a ruthless military leader, was a result of the sharp division of his inward and outward selves. The outward man was indeed a brilliant and merciless general, who, by the end of the war, was possessed of almost unlimited power. He wielded a battle-hardened army, the most fearsome in China, formed of soldiers from his own home province, loyal only to himself, who viewed him very much like a god. He accepted the death of multitudes with a calm equanimity (the same equanimity, to be sure, with which he had viewed the prospect of his own death in the war). This was the man Yung Wing had seen as "literally and practically the supreme power in China," the man Frederick Bruce had worried would take over the central empire. This was the man the Qing government feared, because it could not control him and he followed their orders largely at his own pleasure.

But the inward Zeng Guofan, the man known only to his brothers, his sons, and a handful of close friends, was a man of deep reverence and quietude who was often wracked by uncertainty and depression. He was a general who had never asked to be one. He was never truly sure of his own command or certain of his power. He was a man who wanted most of all to go back to his books and lead a quiet life of moral scholarship. And for that man, a grasp for power at the end of the war was utterly unthinkable. Skeptical as he may have been of the corruption, greed, and incompetence of the government bureaucrats in Beijing, Zeng Guofan never questioned the legitimacy of the emperor himself. Zeng Guofan's was, after its fashion, a religious kind of loyalty—a faith that Heaven had chosen the ruler of the empire, and whatever the court's advisers and secretaries and counselors might say or do, Heaven's choice must be followed.

Furthermore, those who later wondered why he didn't take the throne for himself—and there would be many—assumed that the rulership of China was somehow a thing to be desired. But for Zeng Guofan, especially given the tumultuous era in which he lived, power was a fearful prospect. It conjured up the terror of failure, of falling short of the great responsibilities laid upon him—and, indeed, the nagging fear that as his power and influence grew beyond all precedent, it would bring down divine punishment to crush him for overstepping his bounds. He knew that a conscientious emperor lived his life in fear, with the full weight of the kingdom on his shoulders, and the keenly judgmental eye of Heaven fixed upon him for his entire existence from coronation until death. Zeng Guofan had gotten a taste of such responsibility on a smaller scale in Anhui during the final years of the war, and he had found it the most accursed existence he could imagine. The emperor of China was not a man to be envied; he was a man to be pitied.

The demobilization of Zeng Guofan's army began in August 1864, less than a month after the fall of Nanjing, though his preparations were under way even before the city was taken. In May, he had put in for a sick leave—which, he explained to his brother Guoquan, was really just an excuse to go into hiding after the war ended, to escape critics who were growing suspicious of his power. He recommended that Guoquan do the same. "If by good fortune Nanjing should fall, we brothers will have to retire, and this can be our way to prepare," he wrote.[3] But Guoquan resented his elder brother's advice, and Zeng Guofan sent him scathing letters, warning him to toe the line. He had already seen memorials from the Board of Revenue speculating that Guoquan was trying to expand his economic powers, and he admonished his younger brother not to invite the jealousies of others. "Military commanders who have usurped fiscal power have never brought anything but evil to the country and harm to their own families," he wrote. "Even if you, my brother, are a complete idiot, surely you cannot be ignorant that you have to distance yourself from power to avoid being slandered."[4]

In spite of his efforts to recede from view, the attacks from the court would begin soon enough—first, charges of looting and mismanagement leveled at Zeng Guofan's brother Guoquan and his subordinates, accusing them of corruption and usurpation, of failure to keep discipline among their troops.[5] Then the critics in Beijing would turn on Zeng Guofan himself, accusing him of bringing misery to the people of eastern China in order to embezzle an enormous personal fortune, carping that he had gained his high offices not by talent but by mere luck. They would tear him down for his presumption and arrogance now that he had fulfilled his service and was no longer needed. For the scant eight years that remained of his life, they would give him no rest, would approve no retirement or pause in his duties, as his beard turned white and his eyesight dimmed into blindness. His diary in the years after the war was suffused with expressions of regret. His dream of returning to his scholarship, his home, his life of contemplation was deferred, and deferred again, until he found himself once again looking forward wistfully to the release that would come with death. "I would be happier there," he wrote in a letter home in 1867, "than I am in this world."[6]

The most widely accepted estimates put the death toll of China's nineteenth-century civil war at somewhere between twenty million and thirty million people. The figure is necessarily impressionistic, for there are no reliable censuses to compare from the time, so it is typically based on demographic projections of what the Chinese population should otherwise have been in later generations. According to one American study published in 1969, by as late as 1913, nearly fifty years after the fall of Nanjing, China's population had yet to recover to its pre-1850 level.[7] A more recent study by a team of scholars in China, published in 1999, estimated that the five hardest-hit provinces—Jiangxi, Hubei, Anhui, Zhejiang, and Jiangsu—together suffered a population loss of some eighty-seven million people between 1851 and 1864: fifty-seven million of them dead from the war, and the rest never born due to depressed birthrates. Their projection for the full scale of the war in all provinces was seventy million dead, with a total population loss of more than one hundred million.[8] Those higher numbers have recently gained wider circulation, but they are controversial; critics argue that there is no way to know how many of the vanished people died—from the war, from disease, from starvation—and how many took up lives elsewhere.[9] Nevertheless, even the most subjective anecdotal reports from travelers on the lower Yangtze testified to the deep scars on China's cities and countryside, which were still far from being healed even decades after the Taiping war, and those figures begin to give a sense of the unprecedented scale of destruction and social dislocation that consumed China in what is believed to be the deadliest civil war in all of human history.

Given the shocking scale of the chaos and violence, perhaps the most amazing outcome of all is that the Qing dynasty managed to remain in power afterward—and not just for a few limping years beyond the end of the Taiping but for nearly five decades, into the twentieth century, until a Chinese nationalist revolution finally brought it down in 1911. It can hardly be said, however, that the Qing dynasty won the war against the Taiping. Rather, it was saved—by a combination of Zeng Guofan's provincial military, on the one hand, and the haphazard foreign intervention of the British, on the other. Those two independent forces—one internal and one external—were both deeply suspicious of the other, though their separate campaigns against the rebels appear strangely, in historical hindsight, to have played out as if they were somehow coordinated. Both fought to salvage the reign of the Qing because they believed, for very different reasons, that its endurance would bring the better outcome for their own futures: Zeng Guofan, by preserving the system of honors, recognitions, morals, and scholarship that had rewarded him so well before the war; and the British, because some of them—influential enough in aggregate—believed that the preservation of the Qing dynasty against collapse and the prevention of a Taiping regime in China were the only way to ensure the continued growth of their own trade and thereby make up for their heavy losses elsewhere in the world, particularly in the United States.

If the aftermath of the war was a disappointment for Zeng Guofan, the eventual payoff for the British was even more questionable. The predicted boom in commerce that was supposed to follow the suppression of the rebellion never materialized. On the contrary, the end of the war proved disastrous for Shanghai. Lord Palmerston, it turned out, had been quite correct to link Britain's rising profits in China to her intervention against the Taiping—but not for the reasons he thought. It wasn't the bringing of peace that helped British trade, but the continuance of war. By preventing the Taiping from capturing Shanghai and by prolonging the violence in the province surrounding it, the British intervention created a set of conditions under which Chinese traders, wealth, and goods all poured into the safe zone of Shanghai to escape the chaos the British themselves were helping to perpetuate. The wealthy who fled to Shanghai drove up land prices and flooded the foreign traders in Shanghai with goods for resale. Moreover, as long as the war raged along the Yangtze River, Chinese traders were willing to pay high premiums for the security of shipping their goods in foreign bottoms, under flags that would not draw fire. But once the Taiping were suppressed, those advantages evaporated. Foreign shippers lost much of their edge when the Yangtze became safe again, and departing refugees left the Shanghai real estate market to collapse behind them. The boom of the war years gave way to an extended slump in which two of the largest British firms went bankrupt. Ironically, what nobody—least of all Palmerston—had realized was that restoring peace to China had never actually been in Britain's interests.[10]

There was little for the British to celebrate on the diplomatic side, either. The intervention did not buy them the goodwill or favor of the Manchu government they had expected, nor did it gain them any kind of renewed openness to foreign trade. Frederick Bruce would soon be derided for his "Mandarin-worshipping policy,"[11] which had turned the British government, as many saw it, into the lapdog of the Qing rulers. But in coming to terms with its role in the Chinese war, England's pride depended on the constant repetition of Bruce's version of events—to the point of nearly unanimous agreement—that it was the Taiping who had caused all the destruction in the war, that they were nothing more than a force of anarchy, that they were the enemy of all that was civilized or well governed. In that light, there was no question that Britain's intervention in the war was humanitarian. Thanks to the canonization of this version of events, Charles Gordon and Frederick Townsend Ward would go down in history as the great foreign heroes of the China war, who saved the Chinese from destruction. Against the shame of the Opium War and the destruction of the Summer Palace, Gordon and Ward stood as hopeful (and even benevolent) symbols of cooperation between Chinese and foreigners. By the same logic, the war itself would be forever labeled in English not as a civil war but as the Taiping Rebellion—a name that takes the side of the Qing dynasty and renders the Taiping mere rebels against the proper and legitimate government, outlaws and sowers of disorder who bore sole responsibility for the chaos of the time.

Voices of dissent were few, but some who had questioned the basis of their country's intervention at the time still managed to voice their continued disapproval afterward, even as they knew that such dissent was no longer welcome. Robert Forrest, the British consul who had traveled overland through the Taiping territories and who had lived for several months on a boat outside Nanjing, put it most poignantly in an article he wrote for the *Journal of the North-China Branch of the Royal Asiatic Society* in 1867.

In the article, Forrest disputed the conventional belief in Britain that the destruction of the Taiping had finally set the Chinese Empire right again but lamented that "facts, no matter how recorded, never overthrow prejudice, ... and my experiences of Taiping rule, although the result of a long residence at the Capital, will never be favourably regarded, if in any way opposed to existing ideas."[12] Pointing to the slump in trade that had followed the suppression of the Taiping, he mused that for all of the hatred his people had shown to the rebels during the war, "if it went to the vote to-morrow how many foreigners would not wish them back again?"

Nevertheless, he knew that none of his countrymen wanted to hear the truth, as he had experienced it, which was that the Taiping had never really been the monsters or locusts they were made out to be. "But if I were to tell what order did really reign at Nanjing," he wrote,

> very much like the Warsaw article it is true, but still order—that there were some uncommonly clever generals among the Heavenly King's officers ... that in places not actually the seat of war the ground was well cultivated—that the conduct of the Taiping troops was not one bit worse than that of the Imperialists—and that the inhabitants of such towns as Shaoxing and Hangzhou have asserted that their lot under Taiping rule was infinitely better than their unhappy fate when those cities were recovered and fell for a time into the hands of barbarian officers;—if I stated these things, with every proof, I should be reviled as a rebel and a speaker of blasphemy against the brilliant political dawn now spreading over the empire.[13]

When the end finally came for the Qing dynasty in 1911, it would come at the hands of a new generation of anti-Manchu revolutionaries who were well aware of their predecessors. Some cut their queues and wore their hair long to look like stylized Taiping rebels. Others wrote propaganda tracts condemning Zeng Guofan as the greatest traitor to his race who had ever lived, who butchered untold numbers of his fellow Chinese in order to uphold the racially alien dynasty of the Manchus. The most prominent leader of this new generation was a Cantonese named Sun Yatsen, who had grown up hearing stories of Taiping heroes and whose friends nicknamed him Hong Xiuquan.[14]

China had continued to weaken in the decades following the fall of Nanjing, in spite of valiant efforts by Li Hongzhang, Zuo Zongtang, and other former generals and Chinese officials to introduce reforms that would revive the country. They achieved remarkable success internally, suppressing the Nian and Muslim rebellions after the Taiping were vanquished, and restoring domestic order to the once broken empire. But crushing indemnities from foreign wars bankrupted the treasury, and the ongoing corruption and conservatism of the Manchu court hampered their attempts to introduce broad-based reforms. And while there may have been peace within the country, externally China was simply left behind by the breathtaking rise of its smaller neighbor Japan. For once again the Japanese benefited from the negative example of China. As the Japanese government in the 1850s had avoided its own Opium War by signing foreign treaties without overt hostility, so did influential young samurai in the 1860s look to China at the end of its civil war as a warning of what their country might become without dramatic change. A revolution later that decade gave way to a rapid program of industrialization and social transformation that bore a remarkable similarity in spirit—if not in religion—to what Hong Rengan had envisioned for his own thwarted state. By the 1890s, Japan's modernized navy would decisively overpower the Qing fleet, and Japan would take the island of Taiwan from China as its first major colony. By the early twentieth century, Chinese reformers would be looking to Japan as the model of what their own country must become if it were to have any chance of surviving into the future.

But perhaps it didn't have to turn out that way. In an interview with a British reporter in 1909, Japan's elder statesman Ito Hirobumi—four-time prime minister and chief architect of the nineteenth-century reform movement—looked to the violence just beginning to unfold in China in the run-up to the 1911 Revolution and declared it long overdue. In his opinion, the new Chinese revolutionaries were merely finishing the work that the Taiping had started fifty years earlier, and in which he firmly believed they would have been successful if left to their own devices. "The greatest mistake which you Western people, and more especially you English people, made in all your dealings with China," he told the reporter, "was to help the Manchus in putting down the Taiping Rebellion."[15]

Ito echoed the many observers from the time of the war who had argued on behalf of neutrality, who had maintained—ultimately in vain—that Britain must stay out because the warfare in China was part of a natural process of dynastic change that had to follow through to its end.

"There can be very little doubt that the Manchu Dynasty had reached the end of its proper tether when the Taiping Rebellion occurred," he insisted, "and, by preventing its overthrow, Gordon and his 'Ever-Victorious Army' arrested a normal and healthy process of nature. Nothing that the Manchus have done since then affords the slightest evidence that they deserved to be saved. Rather the contrary. And when they fall, as fall they must and will before very long, the upheaval will be all the more violent and all the more protracted for having been so long and unduly postponed."

Speaking with the benefit of hindsight more than forty years after the fall of Nanjing, Ito helped to vindicate the opinions of those British at the time—in Shanghai, in Parliament, in the papers—who had argued so strenuously that a foreign military intervention in the Chinese civil war to bring order back to the country would not, in the long run, be a boon for China but instead consign the Chinese to continued oppression by a corrupt power whose era of greatness and fair rule was long past. And his observation, looking back on the dynasty's continued reign after the war, that "Nothing that the Manchus have done since then affords the slightest evidence that they deserved to be saved" was a statement with which a very large number of Chinese in his own time would have readily agreed.

From the standpoint of our own time, a hundred years later still, Ito Hirobumi's prediction that when the Manchus were finally overthrown, "the upheaval [would] be all the more violent and all the more protracted for having been so long and unduly postponed" was unfortunately borne out as well. The Manchus fell two years after the interview, to be replaced by a republic that broke down almost immediately into civil war. Wracked by decades of internal violence, weakened and nearly helpless in the face of continued foreign encroachments, China would spend the following century trying to claw its way back to the position of power and prominence in the world it had held for so much of its earlier history. But by 1912, when the delayed process of reinvention finally began in earnest, the country was already so far behind its competitors that the thought of catching up seemed—until recently—to be all but impossible.

————————

If there is any moral at all to be gleaned from the outcome of this war, which brought so little of lasting benefit to either its victors or the country in which it was waged, it is not likely to be of the encouraging sort. For in a certain sense, the blame for the war's outcome might be laid at the feet of our intrepid preacher's assistant, Hong Rengan. After a few years among the missionaries in Hong Kong, he believed that he knew the hearts of the British and could therefore be the one to build a bridge between his own country and theirs. This belief led him to advocate a policy of appeasement and openness toward foreigners that ultimately proved the ruin of his own people. By the same token, blame could also be laid with the shy British ambassador Frederick Bruce for imagining, after a short residence in Shanghai and Beijing, that the Qing dynasts were a force of civilized monarchy standing against a chaotic horde of rebels who had no king or governing vision—and, on that basis, persuading his home government that it was necessary to intervene on behalf of what he thought was the only viable power in China.

Hong Rengan and Frederick Bruce had in common that each thought himself uniquely blessed with insight into what was good and knowable in the other's civilization, and they also had in common that they were both grievously wrong. So in the end, perhaps the tale of the foreign intervention and the fall of the Taiping is a tale of trust misplaced. It is a tale of how sometimes the connections we perceive across cultures and distances—our hopes for an underlying unity of human virtue, our belief that underneath it all we are somehow the same—can turn out to be nothing more than the fictions of our own imagination. And when we congratulate ourselves on seeing through the darkened window that separates us from another civilization, heartened to discover the familiar forms that lie hidden among the shadows on the other side, sometimes we do so without ever realizing that we are only gazing at our own reflection.

"Sooner or later," Heng said, . . ."one has to take sides—if one is to remain human."

—Graham Greene, *The Quiet American*

ACKNOWLEDGMENTS

Every research project has its moment of transcendence, and in this case it came on a sultry late-spring afternoon in Qimen, where I had just arrived after a bus ride through the mountains from Anqing. Leaving the tile-and-glass facades of Qimen's modern main streets, I wandered down an alley into the old part of the city and soon found myself lost in its twisting cobblestoned lanes, quiet and cool, lined with Ming-dynasty houses of stone and weathered cedar. I didn't know what I might find back there, but when I struck up a conversation with Zhang Ziqiang and told him what I was looking for, he led me through the mazelike alleys into the heart of the city until our narrow path opened onto the grand edifice of the building that once housed Zeng Guofan's military headquarters in the Taiping war—still intact, cavernous and derelict, unmarked, its intricately carved lacquer beams now partially covered with plastic to keep out the rain. While I was exploring around the outside of the headquarters, Zhi Pintai found me and invited me back to his apartment around the side of the building. A former Red Guard and sanitation worker, Mr. Zhi has devoted his retirement to the study of local history, collecting sources and stories about the city where he has spent his life—much of which has been lived in a subdivided antechamber of Zeng Guofan's old headquarters. In his apartment, piled high with papers and books, I spent a happy afternoon drinking tea and learning about Qimen's history, with a fresh portrait of Chairman Mao gazing down on us from the wall. And it struck me how sometimes the layers of history in China can be fused together as if by a lightning bolt through time—the child of Mao's Cultural Revolution now, in a quiet moment of his older age, inhabiting a structure steeped in the aura of a much earlier time of disorder, sifting through the fragments around him to make sense, in his own way, of the deeper currents of endurance that run below China's constantly changing surface.

I would like to thank the National Committee on U.S.-China Relations for helping facilitate my work through its Public Intellectuals Program, of which

I was a fellow from 2008 to 2010. Jan Berris, Dan Murphy, and my co-fellows in the program were mainstays of encouragement and support while I was writing this book, and I thank them collectively—especially those who put up with my long-winded musings on the Hunan Army during a trip to Changsha in the summer of 2009. Audiences at Harvard's Fairbank Center for East Asian Studies and the Johns Hopkins History Department Faculty Seminar gave useful feedback when I presented earlier forms of this project to them. In particular, Henrietta Harrison, Ian Miller, Hue-tam Ho Tai, William Rowe, and Marta Hansen gave especially helpful comments and suggestions on those occasions. A summer stipend from the National Endowment for the Humanities helped launch the research for this project, and funding from the UMass Amherst College of Humanities and Fine Arts carried it through to the end.

I am indebted to Robert Bickers, Tobie Meyer-Fong, and Heather Cox Richardson for taking on the great labor of reading and commenting on my draft manuscript in its entirety. Their questions, corrections, and suggestions for new sources helped strengthen this book immensely. As I did not take all of their advice, I would emphasize that any errors that might remain, whether of fact or interpretation, are entirely my own. In addition to reading the manuscript, Tobie Meyer-Fong was also a constant supporter and sounding board. She quizzed me on my sources, shared ideas from her own forthcoming research on the Taiping era, and in general kept me from feeling as if I was alone in wandering through these byways of China's nineteenth century. Every scholar should have such a colleague.

A special thanks to Jonathan Spence for encouraging me to go after the bigger themes, and for setting the bar so high. Thanks as well to Dave Merrill for designing the maps; to Lei Duan and Li Xiaoying for diligent and capable research assistance; to Yeewan Koon, Julie Niemeyer, and Jeff Moser for help with procuring artwork; to Joel Wolfe for reading chapters; to Adam Desjardins for helping me sort out military uniforms; to Sharon Domier for library support; to Chuck Wooldridge for sharing his knowledge of Nanjing; and to Huang Yuanzhong, John Delury, Matthew Grohowski, Mary Rankin, John Schrecker, Mary Bullock, and Susan Naquin for advice, introductions, leads, and questions answered large and small. Thank you also to the staffs of the Yale University Library, the Harvard-Yenching Library, the Massachusetts Historical Society, the Library of Congress, the Peabody Essex Museum, the Military Museum of the Chinese People's Revolution in Beijing, and the Taiping museum in Nanjing. Much of this book was written at the Siren Café in Greenfield and the Lady Killigrew in Montague, and I thank the proprietors of both for providing space to think and write.

The history department at the University of Massachusetts made it possible to balance teaching and writing without sacrificing either, and my students—on whom I first tried out many of the ideas in this book—kept me on my toes. I especially thank those, like Michael Nicholls, who asked the simple and direct questions whose utter impossibility of being answered sent my thoughts on this project into new directions.

Yu Wei, Chen Fangfang, and Yi Li all gave me help in Nanjing. Cheng Zhiqiang gave me advice on traveling to his hometown of Anqing. The Yale-China teachers in Xiuning, especially Brendan Woo, provided welcome guidance and hospitality when I came through town for research, and took me on a memorable hike up Huangshan. During that same visit to Anhui province in the spring of 2010, Jonathan Lowet of the National Committee and Zoe Durner-Feiler of Yale-China joined me in a scramble up the side of the Sheep's Pen north of Yixian, along a steep, loosely graveled path through knotted pines and dense, green-leaved tea bushes, to catch a glimpse of the view that was denied to Zeng Guofan when he tried to look out for the approach of the enemy on a fateful, fogbound afternoon in the late autumn of 1860.

Brettne Bloom has been a source of unflagging faith and encouragement from the start, and I am extremely fortunate to have her as my agent. At Knopf, Andrew Miller was the kind of editor I'd been told doesn't exist anymore; he was with me from beginning to end, reading and commenting on drafts going all the way back to my first efforts, and his deft editorial touch brought out the best in the manuscript while, thankfully, eliminating the worst. Andrew Carlson saw the book through production with good humor and grace, and gave me an additional round of good edits. My sincere thanks as well to Brian Barth and Soonyoung Kwon for crafting the book with such care.

Above all, I am grateful for the support and companionship of my wife, Francie, and for the joy that our daughter, Lucy, has brought into our lives. They are my anchor, my stars, and my compass, and I dedicate this book to them with love.

NOTES

ZGFQJ   *Zeng Guofan quanji* (The complete works of Zeng Guofan), 16 vols. (Beijing: Zhongguo Zhigong Chubanshe, 2001).

TPTG   Luo Ergang and Wang Qingcheng, eds., *Taiping Tianguo* (The Taiping Heavenly Kingdom), 10 vols. (Guilin: Guangxi Normal University Press, 2004).

PROLOGUE: HEAVEN'S CHILDREN

1. Xianfeng was actually absent from the palace on the day Nanjing fell, performing rituals and holding audience in Beijing. He had moved his main residence to the Forbidden City (which he detested) as a desperate response to the Taiping, denying himself the pleasures of the Summer Palace as an act of self-punishment. It did no good, and by 1854 he would move back into the Summer Palace full-time and spend most of his remaining years refusing to leave it. His short-lived self-punishment is mentioned in Wong Young-tsu, *A Paradise Lost: The Imperial Garden Yuanming Yuan* (Honolulu: University of Hawaii Press, 2001), pp. 113–114, citing *Yuanmingyuan* (Shanghai: Guji Chubanshe, 1991), vol. 1, pp. 544–545; Xianfeng's ritual activities on March 19, 1853, which place him in Beijing, are given in the court diary, *Qingdai qijuzhu ce. Xianfeng chao* (Taipei: National Palace Museum, 1983), Xianfeng 3 (1853), vol. 11. In further sign of his panic, Xianfeng had recently been praying to his ancestors for protection, and he issued two edicts blaming himself for the rebellion. See Mao Haijian, *Kuming tianzi: Xianfeng huangdi Yixin* (Taipei: Lianjing, 2008), p. 88. The description of the fall of Nan-

jing is based on that of Thomas Taylor Meadows, as narrated to him by the rebels he spoke to in Nanjing a month after the fact (during the voyage of the *Hermes*). Meadows's account was first published in *The North-China Herald* of May 7, 1853; also see Jen Yu-wen (Jian Youwen), *The Taiping Revolutionary Movement* (New Haven, Conn.: Yale University Press, 1973), pp. 117–118; some accounts cite a higher population of Manchus; others give a greater measure of heroism to the Manchu defenders, though the genocidal outcome is not a matter of dispute.

CHAPTER 1: THE PREACHER'S ASSISTANT

1. James Legge, "The Colony of Hong Kong," *The China Review* 3 (1874): 165, 173–175.
2. The Rev. Theodore Hamberg, *The Visions of Hung-Siu-Tshuen, and Origin of the Kwang-si Insurrection* (Hong Kong: China Mail Office, 1854), pp. 61–62.
3. "China," *The Times*, June 21, 1853.
4. Jonathan Spence, *God's Chinese Son* (New York: Norton, 1996), p. 198.
5. The report on the *Hermes* visit in *The North-China Herald* of May 7, 1853, notes, "The history of the originators of this insurrection is still involved in obscurity, which we trust strenuous efforts will be made to clear up."
6. Quoted in Dona Torr, ed., *Marx on China: 1853–1860* (London, Lawrence & Wishart, 1968), p. 1, n. 3.
7. Karl Marx, "Revolution in China and Europe," *New-York Daily Tribune*, June 14, 1853; in Torr, *Marx on China*, p. 1.
8. Ibid., p. 4.
9. "The Revolution in China" (editorial), *Daily Picayune*, May 22, 1853.
10. "The Rebellion in China," *North China Mail*, reprinted in *The Times*, April 8, 1853.
11. *The Times*, August 30, 1853 (editorial beginning "The Chinese revolution is in all respects").
12. Carl T. Smith, "Notes on Friends and Relatives of Taiping Leaders," *Journal of the Hong Kong Branch of the Royal Asiatic Society* 16 (1976): 117–134, see p. 121.
13. "The Confession of Hung Jen-kan," trans. in Franz Michael, *The Taiping*

Rebellion: History and Documents (Seattle: University of Washington Press, 1966–1971), vol. 3, pp. 1511–1530, see p. 1511.

14. Except where otherwise noted, the following section is based on Theodore Hamberg's *The Visions of Hung-Siu-Tshuen,* with quotations from pp. 10, 13, 14, 24, and 29.

15. Hamberg, *The Visions of Hung-Siu-Tshuen,* p. 63.

16. Shen Weibin, *Hong Rengan* (Shanghai: Shanghai Renmin Chubanshe, 1982), p. 21.

17. Smith, "Notes on Friends and Relatives," p. 122.

18. "The Confession of Hung Jen-kan," pp. 1511–1512.

19. Lauren F. Pfister, *Striving for "The Whole Duty of Man": James Legge and the Scottish Protestant Encounter with China* (New York: Peter Lang, 2004), pp. 32–33.

20. Legge, "The Colony of Hong Kong," p. 172.

21. Helen Edith Legge, *James Legge: Missionary and Scholar* (London: The Religious Tract Society, 1905), p. 91.

22. Ralph Wardlaw Thompson, *Griffith John: The Story of Fifty Years in China* (London: The Religious Tract Society, 1906), p. 125.

23. Ibid.

24. Smith, "Notes on Friends and Relatives," p. 125.

25. "The Taiping Rebellion: Its Rise and Fall," *The Merchant's Magazine and Commercial Review,* January 1865, pp. 38–49, see p. 44.

26. Described in John Scarth, *Twelve Years in China* (Edinburgh: Thomas Constable & Co., 1860), pp. 106, 239; also George Wingrove Cooke, *China: Being "The Times" Special Correspondence from China in the Years 1857–58* (London: G. Routledge & Co., 1858), p. 50.

27. Thomas Taylor Meadows, *The Chinese and Their Rebellions* (Stanford, Calif.: Academic Reprints, 1953, orig. published 1856 by Smith, Elder & Co.), p. 454.

28. Scarth, *Twelve Years in China,* pp. 237–238.

29. Yung Wing, *My Life in China and America* (New York: Henry Holt & Co., 1909); see p. 41 for his educational plans, p. 52 on relearning Chinese, pp. 53–54 for quotations.

30. James Legge, "The Colony of Hong Kong," p. 171.

31. Xia Chuntao, *Hong Rengan* (Wuhan: Hubei Jiaoyu Chubanshe, 1999), p. 51.

32. Jen Yu-wen (Jian Youwen), *The Taiping Revolutionary Movement* (New Haven, Conn.: Yale University Press, 1973), p. 355.

33. Pfister, *Striving for "The Whole Duty of Man*," p. 43.

34. Adapted from translation in Michael, *The Taiping Rebellion*, vol. 3, p. 836.

CHAPTER 2: NEUTRALITY

1. Alfred Moges, *Recollections of Baron Gros's Embassy to China and Japan in 1857–58* (London: Griffin, Bohn, and Company, 1861), p. 203; p. 206 lists fifteen English gunboats and four French, plus the British and French flagships. Sailing distance of 1,800 miles given in Thomas Bowlby, *An Account of the Last Mission and Death of Thomas William Bowlby*, ed. C. C. Bowlby (printed for private circulation, 1906), p. 154.

2. D. J. MacGowan, "Contributions to the History of the Insurrection in China," a companion to the *Shanghai Almanac* for 1857 (Shanghai, 1857), p. 3.

3. Lewis Hertslet (comp.), *A Complete Collection of the Treaties and Conventions . . . Subsisting between Great Britain and Foreign Powers . . .* (London: Butterworth, 1859), vol. 10, pp. 61–62.

4. MacGowan, "Contributions to the History of the Insurrection," p. 3.

5. Teng Ssu-yu, *The Taiping Rebellion and the Western Powers: A Comprehensive Survey* (Oxford: Clarendon Press, 1971), p. 191.

6. Ibid., p. 189.

7. Douglas Hurd, *The Arrow War: An Anglo-Chinese Confusion, 1856–1860* (London: Collins, 1967), p. 98.

8. James Bruce, Earl of Elgin, *Letters and Journals of James, Eighth Earl of Elgin*, ed. Theodore Walrond (London: John Murray, 1872), p. 199.

9. Ibid.

10. Ibid., p. 185.

11. Phosphorescence described in Sherard Osborn, "Notes, Geographical and Commercial, Made During the Passage of HMS *Furious*, in 1858, from Shanghai to the Gulf of Pecheli and Back," *Proceedings of the Royal Geographical Society of London* 3, no. 2 (November 22, 1858): 55–87; see p. 66, where Osborn notes that the phosphorescence was "as brilliant as any ever witnessed in equatorial regions."

12. Moges, *Recollections*, p. 208.

13. Ibid., p. 206.

14. Laurence Oliphant, *Narrative of the Earl of Elgin's Mission to China and Japan in the Years 1857, '58, '59*, 2 vols. (London and Edinburgh: William Blackwood and Sons, 1859), vol. 1, p. 295.

15. Augustus F. Lindley (Lin-le), *Ti-Ping Tien-Kwoh; The History of the Ti-Ping Revolution* (London: Day & Son, 1866), p. 621.

16. Moges, *Recollections*, pp. 209–210.

17. Oliphant, *Narrative*, vol. 1, p. 299.

18. "China: History of the Allied Expedition," *The New York Times*, August 20, 1858.

19. Ibid.

20. Elgin, *Letters and Journals*, p. 248.

21. Oliphant, *Narrative*, vol. 1, p. 305.

22. Osborn, "Notes, Geographical and Commercial," pp. 71–72.

23. Oliphant, *Narrative*, vol. 1, p. 316.

24. Osborn, "Notes, Geographical and Commercial," p. 72.

25. Elgin, *Letters and Journals*, p. 250.

26. Oliphant, *Narrative*, vol. 1, pp. 316–317.

27. Moges, *Recollections*, pp. 216–217.

28. Ibid., p. 217; Osborn, "Notes, Geographical and Commercial," p. 73.

29. Osborn, "Notes, Geographical and Commercial," p. 73.

30. Oliphant, *Narrative*, vol. 1, p. 326.

31. Osborn, "Notes, Geographical and Commercial," p. 73.

32. Immanuel C. Y. Hsü, *China's Entrance into the Family of Nations: The Diplomatic Phase, 1858–1880* (Cambridge, Mass.: Harvard University Press, 1968), pp. 67–68.

33. Elgin, *Letters and Journals*, p. 209.

34. John Morley, *The Life of William Ewart Gladstone* (New York: Macmillan, 1911), p. 563; for the speech itself, see *Hansard's Parliamentary Debates* (London: T. C. Hansard), March 3, 1857, vol. 144, cc. 1787–1808.

35. Elgin, *Letters and Journals*, p. 279.

36. "The First News Dispatch Over the Atlantic Cable," *The New York Times*, August 27, 1858; this particular cable, though the first successfully laid over the Atlantic, would last only about a month.

37. "Our Relations with China," *The New York Times*, August 20, 1858.

38. "The Chinese Treaties," *The New York Times*, September 23, 1858.

39. "End of the China War," *The New York Times*, August 27, 1858.

40. Elgin noted in his journal, "the Consul had contrived to make a pretty good treaty with Japan, evidently under the influence of the *contrecoup* of our proceedings in China"; Elgin, *Letters and Journals*, p. 263.

41. Elgin, *Letters and Journals*, p. 261.

42. Ibid., p. 274.

43. Ibid., p. 272.

44. Elgin to Malmesbury, January 5, 1859, in Foreign Office, Great Britain, *Correspondence Relative to the Earl of Elgin's Special Missions to China and Japan, 1857–1859* (London: Harrison and Sons, 1859), p. 440.

45. Ibid., p. 443.

46. Oliphant, *Narrative,* vol. 2, p. 299.

47. Elgin to Malmesbury, Shanghai, January 5, 1859, in *Correspondence Relative to the Earl of Elgin's Special Missions,* p. 443.

48. Elgin, *Letters and Journals,* p. 285.

49. Franz Michael, *The Taiping Rebellion: History and Documents* (Seattle: University of Washington Press, 1966–1971), vol. 2, p. 713.

50. Ibid., vol. 2, p. 720.

51. Ibid., vol. 2, pp. 724–725.

52. "Sir Thomas F. Wade, K.C.B.," *The Far East,* new ser., vol. 1 (July–December 1876): 37–41.

53. Thomas Wade, "Report on the Town of Woo-hoo," in *Correspondence Relative to the Earl of Elgin's Special Missions,* p. 448, romanization modified.

54. Thomas Wade, "Report on the Town of Nganking [Anqing]," in *Correspondence Relative to the Earl of Elgin's Special Missions,* p. 449; quoted in Scarth, *Twelve Years in China,* to make a similar point, p. 270.

55. Thomas Wade, "Translation of a Paper Handed to Captain Barker, R.N., by an Insurgent at Woo-hoo," in *Correspondence Relative to the Earl of Elgin's Special Missions,* p. 450.

56. Lindesay Brine, *The Taeping Rebellion in China: A Narrative of Its Rise and Progress* (London: John Murray, 1862), p. 268.

57. Elgin to Malmesbury, Shanghai, January 5, 1859, in *Correspondence Relative to the Earl of Elgin's Special Missions,* p. 442.

58. Elgin, *Letters and Journals,* pp. 304–305.

59. "Address of the Shanghae Merchants to the Earl of Elgin," Shanghai, January 18, 1859, in *Correspondence Relative to the Earl of Elgin's Special Missions,* pp. 457–458.

60. Ibid., p. 458.

61. "Bruce, Sir Frederick William Adolphus Wright," *Oxford Dictionary of National Biography* (Oxford, England: Oxford University Press, 2004–2010).

62. Frederick Wells Williams, *The Life and Letters of Samuel Wells Williams, LL.D.* (New York: G. P. Putnam's Sons, 1889), p. 299.

63. Edgar Stanton Maclay, *Reminiscences of the Old Navy: From the Journals and Private Papers of Captain Edward Trenchard, and Rear-*

Admiral Stephen Decatur Trenchard (New York: G. P. Putnam's Sons, 1898), p. 91.

64. Zhang Gongchen, *Senggelinqin chuanqi* (Biography of Senggelinqin) (Beijing: Zhongguo Renmin Daxue Chubanshe, 2003), p. 96.

65. Guo Songtao, *Yuchi laoren zishu* (Memoir of the Old Man at Jade Pond), excerpted in *Dierci Yapian Zhanzheng* (The Second Opium War), 6 vols., ed. Qi Sihe et al. (Shanghai: Shanghai Renmin Chubanshe, 1978–1979), vol. 2, p. 277; he is specifically referring here to the Nian rebels in north China.

66. Ibid., p. 277.

67. Zhang, *Senggelinqin chuanqi*, p. 97.

68. George Battye Fisher, *Personal Narrative of Three Years' Service in China* (London: Richard Bentley, 1863), pp. 190–193.

69. Williams, *Life and Letters*, p. 309.

70. James D. Johnston, *China and Japan: Being a Narrative of the Cruise of the U.S. Steam-Frigate* Powhatan *in the Years 1857, '58, '59, and '60* (Philadelphia: Charles Desilver, 1860), p. 234.

71. Williams, *Life and Letters*, pp. 308–311.

72. Maclay, *Reminiscences of the Old Navy*, p. 83.

73. *The Times*, September 16, 1859 (editorial beginning "We fear that we cannot accuse the Mongols"); quoted in Leavenworth, *The Arrow War with China*, p. 138.

74. Williams, *Life and Letters*, p. 310.

75. "Blood Is Thicker than Water," in Wallace Rice and Clinton Scollard, *Ballads of Valor and Victory: Being Stories in Song from the Annals of America* (New York: Fleming H. Revell, 1903), p. 84.

76. T. F. Tsiang, "China after the Victory of Taku, June 25, 1859," *American Historical Review* 35, no. 1 (October 1929): 79–84, see p. 81.

77. Ibid., pp. 83–84.

78. Samuel Wells Williams, letter to William Frederick Williams, July 5, 1859, from USS Powhatan off Peiho. Samuel Wells Williams Family Papers, Sterling Memorial Library, Yale University, New Haven, Conn.

79. Williams, *Life and Letters*, p. 312.

CHAPTER 3: THE SHIELD KING

1. Hong Rengan's route is given in his third Nanchang confession, "Nanchang fu tixun niqiu gong," in *TPTG*, vol. 2, pp. 412–414; also his confes-

sion at the Jiangxi governor's yamen, "Benbuyuan tixun niqiu gong," in ibid., pp. 415–416; description of the route through the Meiling Pass based on contemporaneous account (of a journey in the opposite direction) in William Charles Milne, *Life in China* (London: G. Routledge & Co., 1857), pp. 356–364.

2. Luo Ergang, *Lüying bingzhi* (Chongqing: Shangwu Yinshuguan, 1945).

3. Shen Weibin, *Hong Rengan* (Shanghai: Shanghai Renmin Chubanshe, 1982), p. 25.

4. Archibald Little, *Gleanings from Fifty Years in China* (London: Sampson Low, Marston & Co., 1910), p. 113.

5. Hong Rengan, third Nanchang confession, in *TPTG*, vol. 2, p. 413.

6. Shen Weibin, *Hong Rengan*, p. 26.

7. Xia Chuntao, *Cong shushi, Jidutu dao wangye: Hong Rengan* (From scholar and Christian to king: Hong Rengan) (Wuhan: Hubei Jiaoyu Chubanshe, 1999), p. 64.

8. Mao Jiaqi, *Guo zhu "Taiping Tianguo shishi rizhi" jiaobu* (Emendations to Guo [Tingyi's] *Daily Calendar of Events in the Taiping Heavenly Kingdom*) (Taipei: Taiwan Shangwu Yinshuguan, 2001), p. 127.

9. Xia Chuntao, *Hong Rengan*, p. 64.

10. Hong Rengan, third Nanchang confession, in *TPTG*, vol. 2, p. 413.

11. John Lovelle Withers, "The Heavenly Capital: Nanjing Under the Taiping, 1853–1864," Ph.D. diss., Yale University, 1983, pp. 159 ff.

12. Franz Michael, *The Taiping Rebellion: History and Documents* (Seattle: University of Washington Press, 1966–1971), vol. 2, pp. 15–16.

13. C. A. Curwen, *Taiping Rebel: The Deposition of Li Hsiu-Ch'eng* (Cambridge, England: Cambridge University Press, 1977), p. 200.

14. Ibid., p. 148.

15. Ibid., p. 83.

16. Ibid.

17. Hong Rengan, third Nanchang confession, in *TPTG*, vol. 2, p. 413.

18. Philip Kuhn, "The Taiping Rebellion," in *The Cambridge History of China* (Cambridge, England: Cambridge University Press, 1978), vol. 10, part 1, pp. 264–317.

19. William C. Wooldridge, "Transformations of Ritual and State in Nineteenth-Century Nanjing," Ph.D. diss., Princeton University, 2007, pp. 160–179.

20. Michael, *The Taiping Rebellion*, vol. 3, p. 735.

21. This was also the sentiment expressed by the Richmond *Daily Dispatch*,

which pronounced that "The warlike Tartars are certainly a nobler race than the sordid Chinese" ("Honorable War Not to Be Deplored," *The Daily Dispatch*, May 18, 1861).

22. D. J. MacGowan, "Contributions to the History of the Insurrection in China," a companion to the *Shanghai Almanac* for 1857 (Shanghai, 1857), p. 6.

23. W. A. P. Martin, "The Recognition of the Nanking Government," *The North-China Herald*, June 20, 1857.

24. Hong Rengan, *Zizheng xinbian* (A new work for the aid of government), translated in Franz Michael, *The Taiping Rebellion: History and Documents* (Seattle: University of Washington Press, 1966–1971), vol. 3, pp. 751–776, quotation on p. 758.

25. Ibid., pp. 758–759, 765.

26. Ibid., p. 759.

27. Ibid., p. 761.

28. "The Chinese Insurgents, and Our Policy with Respect to Them," *The London Review* 16, no. 31 (April 1861): 222–246, quotation on p. 229.

29. Hong Rengan, "A new work," p. 763.

30. Ibid., p. 771.

31. Hong Rengan, second confession at Xi Baotian's military camp, in *TPTG*, vol. 2, pp. 401–405; plan is given on p. 402.

32. Arthur W. Hummel, ed., *Eminent Chinese of the Ch'ing Period (1644–1912)* (Taipei: Chengwen, reprint, 1967), p. 294.

33. Curwen, *Taiping Rebel*, p. 188, n. 66.

34. Jen Yu-wen (Jian Youwen), *The Taiping Revolutionary Movement* (New Haven, Conn.: Yale University Press, 1973), p. 370.

35. Hong Rengan, second confession at Xi Baotian's military camp, *TPTG*, vol. 2, p. 403.

36. Ibid.

37. Ibid.

38. Ibid., p. 404.

39. Pamela Crossley, *Orphan Warriors: Three Manchu Generations and the End of the Qing World* (Princeton, N.J.: Princeton University Press, 1990), pp. 128–130.

40. Janet Theiss, "Managing Martyrdom: Female Suicide and Statecraft in Mid-Qing China," in *Passionate Women: Female Suicide in Late Imperial China*, ed. Paul S. Ropp, Paola Zamperini, and Harriet T. Zurndorfer (Boston: E. J. Brill, 2001): 47–76; see "Epilogue" on p. 74.

41. Crossley, *Orphan Warriors,* p. 129; Jen Yu-wen, *The Taiping Revolutionary Movement,* p. 372.

42. Based on Jen, *The Taiping Revolutionary Movement,* pp. 371–372.

43. Augustus F. Lindley (Lin-le), *Ti-Ping Tien-Kwoh; The History of the Ti-ping Revolution* (London: Day & Son, Ltd., 1866), p. 269.

44. Jen, *The Taiping Revolutionary Movement,* p. 380.

CHAPTER 4: SOUNDINGS

1. Xue Fengjiu, *Nanqing zaji* (Miscellaneous records of difficult circumstances), in *TPTG,* vol. 5, p. 273.

2. Ibid., p. 274.

3. C. A. Montalto de Jesus, *Historic Shanghai* (Shanghai: The Shanghai Mercury, Ltd., 1909), p. 41.

4. William Minns Tileston, letter to his mother, October 18, 1860, Massachusetts Historical Society, Boston, Mass.

5. Lindesay Brine, *The Taeping Rebellion in China: A Narrative of Its Rise and Progress* (London: John Murray, 1862), map after p. 254; "queer flat lonely" from Edward Bowra, diary, at School of Oriental and African Studies (PPMS 69, Bowra, Box 1, Folder 6), accessed via Adam Matthew Digital, "China: Trade, Politics and Culture, 1793–1980," entry for October 15, 1863.

6. Bowra diary, May 3, 1863, on his arrival in Shanghai.

7. Bowra diary, October 15, 1863, five months after arrival.

8. Ralph Wardlaw Thompson, *Griffith John: The Story of Fifty Years in China* (London: The Religious Tract Society, 1906), p. 47.

9. William C. Milne, quoted in Montalto de Jesus, *Historic Shanghai,* p. 43.

10. Bruce to Russell, June 10, 1860, in *Correspondence Respecting Affairs in China, 1859–1860* (London: Harrison and Sons, 1861), p. 66.

11. Loch, Henry Brougham, *Personal Narrative of Occurrences During Lord Elgin's Second Embassy to China in 1860* (London: John Murray, 1900), pp. 11–12.

12. Bruce to Russell, June 10, 1860, in *Correspondence Respecting Affairs in China, 1859–1860,* p. 66.

13. Bruce to Russell, May 30, 1860, in ibid., p. 60, romanization modified.

14. Bruce to Russell, June 10, 1860, in ibid., p. 67.

15. William Minns Tileston, letter to his mother, March 3, 1863, Massachusetts Historical Society, Boston, Mass.

16. Hallett Abend, *The God from the West* (Garden City, N.Y.: Doubleday, 1947), p. 73.

17. Ibid., p. 14.

18. Ibid., p. 15.

19. Holger Cahill, *A Yankee Adventurer: The Story of Ward and the Taiping Rebellion* (New York: Macaulay, 1930), p. 40.

20. Edward Forester, "Personal Recollections of the Tai-ping Rebellion," in *Cosmopolitan* 21, no. 6 (October 1896): 628.

21. D. J. MacGowan, "Contributions to the History of the Insurrection in China," a companion to the *Shanghai Almanac* for 1857 (Shanghai, 1857), p. 3.

22. Abend, *God from the West*, p. 74.

23. On stinkpots, see Joseph Needham, *Science and Civilisation in China* (Cambridge, England: Cambridge University Press, 1986), vol. 3, part 7, sect. 30 (continued), pp. 191–192.

24. Forester, "Personal Recollections," pp. 627–629.

25. Demetrius Boulger, *The History of China*, 2 vols. (London: W. Thacker & Co., 1898), vol. 2, p. 364.

26. "Visit of Missionaries to Soo-chow; Conferences with Hung-Jin," *The Missionary Magazine and Chronicle*, no. 294 (November 1860): 299–302, quotation on p. 300. (Hung-Jin is Hong Rengan.)

27. "Mission of Hung-Jin to Tae-Ping-Wang, Chief of the Chinese Insurgents at Nanking," *The Missionary Magazine and Chronicle*, no. 293 (October 1860), p. 277.

28. Joseph Edkins, "City of Su-Chow," *The Missionary Magazine and Chronicle*, no. 292 (September 1860), pp. 253–254.

29. "Visit of Messrs. Edkins, John, MacGowan, and Hall, to the Chinese Insurgents," *The Missionary Magazine and Chronicle*, no. 293 (October 1860), pp. 270–277.

30. Ibid., p. 273, with romanization modified.

31. "The Rebellion in China," *The New York Times*, September 1, 1860.

32. "The Chinese Insurgents, and Our Policy with Respect to Them," *The London Review* 16, no. 31 (April 1861): 222–246, quotation on p. 246.

33. "Visit of Messrs. Edkins, John, MacGowan, and Hall," p. 272. The authorship of this narrative is attributed to Joseph Edkins by Griffith John's biographer Richard Thompson. See Thompson, *Griffith John: The Story of Fifty Years in China*, p. 128.

34. Augustus F. Lindley (Lin-le), *Ti-Ping Tien-Kwoh; The History of the Ti-ping Revolution* (London: Day & Son, Ltd., 1866), pp. 71–72.

35. "Visit of Messrs. Edkins, John, MacGowan, and Hall," p. 276.

36. Ibid.

37. Ibid., p. 274.

38. Ibid., p. 275.

39. Ibid., pp. 276, 277.

40. Jane Edkins, letter to her mother-in-law, July 1860, in Jane R. Edkins, *Chinese Scenes and People: With Notices of Christian Missions and Missionary Life in a Series of Letters from Various Parts of China* (London: James Nisbet and Co., 1863), p. 129.

41. Jane Edkins, letter to her father, August 1860, in *Chinese Scenes and People,* p. 143.

42. Jane Edkins, letter to her mother-in-law, July 31, 1860, in *Chinese Scenes and People,* pp. 134–135.

43. Thompson, *Griffith John,* p. 138.

44. "Visit of Missionaries to Soo-chow; Conferences with Hung-Jin," *The Missionary Magazine and Chronicle,* no. 294 (November 1860), p. 301.

45. "Mission of Hung-Jin to Tae-Ping-Wang, Chief of the Chinese Insurgents at Nanking," *The Missionary Magazine and Chronicle,* no. 293 (October 1860), p. 277.

46. "Sketch of the Early History of Hung-Jin," *The Missionary Magazine and Chronicle,* no. 294 (November 1860), p. 296.

47. "Mission of Hung-Jin to Tae-Ping-Wang," p. 278

48. Cited in J. S. Gregory, *Great Britain and the Taipings* (London: Frederick A. Praeger, 1969), p. 135.

49. "The Chinese Revolution—Its Principles—British Duty and Policy," *Tait's Edinburgh Magazine,* November 1860, pp. 562–563, "Kwang-si" changed to "Taiping" for clarity.

50. "The Chinese Insurgents, and Our Policy with Respect to Them," *The London Review* 16, no. 31 (April 1861): 222–246, quotation on p. 225.

51. Ibid., p. 226.

52. Ibid., p. 223, romanization modified.

CHAPTER 5: AN APPOINTMENT IN THE NORTH

1. *Hansard's Parliamentary Debates* (London: T. C. Hansard), January 24, 1860, vol. 156, c. 21.

2. Ibid., c. 25.

3. Immanuel C. Y. Hsü, *The Rise of Modern China*, 3rd ed. (New York: Oxford University Press, 1983), p. 215; George Armand Furse, *Military Transport* (London, 1882), pp. 40–41 on commissariat; Robert Swinhoe, *Narrative of the North China Campaign of 1860* (London: Smith, Elder & Co., 1861), pp. 44–45 on numbers of cavalry horses; Michael Mann, *China, 1860* (Salisbury, Wiltshire: M. Russell, 1989), pp. 5–6 have a chart of overall numbers.

4. As quoted in R. K. I. Quested, *The Expansion of Russia in East Asia, 1857–1860* (Kuala Lumpur: University of Malaya Press, 1968), p. 261.

5. Nikolaĭ Pavlovich Ignat'ev, *The Russo-Chinese Crisis: N. P. Ignatiev's Mission to Peking, 1859–1860*, ed. and tr. John Evans. (Newtonville, Mass.: Oriental Research Partners, 1987), p. 100, romanization modified.

6. Bruce to Russell, Shanghai, December 5, 1859, in *Further Correspondence with Mr. Bruce, Her Majesty's Envoy Extraordinary and Minister Plenipotentiary in China* (London: Harrison and Sons, 1860), p. 1.

7. "The British Expedition to China (from our Special Correspondent)," *The Times*, August 29, 1860, reprinted in Thomas Bowlby, *An Account of the Last Mission and Death of Thomas William Bowlby*, ed. C. C. Bowlby (printed for private circulation, 1906), pp. 154–175, see especially pp. 158, 160.

8. Frederick Bruce to Joseph Edkins, Shanghai, July 28, 1860, in *Correspondence Respecting Affairs in China, 1859–1860* (London: Harrison and Sons, 1861), p. 92.

9. Bruce to Russell, Shanghai, August 1, 1860, in *Correspondence Respecting Affairs in China, 1859–1860*, p. 91.

10. On Meadows, see John King Fairbank, "Meadows on China: A Centennial Review," *The Far Eastern Quarterly* 14, no. 3 (May 1955): 365–371; for another positive assessment of Meadows's sources and insight, see pp. 152–153 of Pierre-Étienne Will, "Views of the Realm in Crisis: Testimonies on Imperial Audiences in the Nineteenth Century," *Late Imperial China* 29, no. 1 suppl. (June 2008): 125–159.

11. Thomas Taylor Meadows, *The Chinese and Their Rebellions* (Stanford, Calif.: Academic Reprints, 1953, orig. published by Smith, Elder & Co., London, 1856), p. 464; also quoted in Fairbank, "Meadows on China," p. 370.

12. Meadows, *The Chinese and Their Rebellions*, p. 465.

13. Meadows to Bruce, July 27, 1860, in *Correspondence Respecting Affairs in China, 1859–1860*, p. 93, romanization modified.

14. Bruce to Meadows, July 31, 1860, in ibid., romanization modified.

15. The letter is in Franz Michael, *The Taiping Rebellion: History and Documents,* 3 vols. (Seattle: University of Washington Press, 1966–1971), vol. 3, p. 1119.

16. Account in *The North-China Herald,* August 25, 1860, quoted in Augustus Lindley (Lin-le), *Ti-Ping Tien-Kwoh; The History of the Ti-Ping Revolution* (London: Day & Son, 1866), p. 297; C. A. Montalto de Jesus, *Historic Shanghai* (Shanghai: The Shanghai Mercury, Ltd., 1909), pp. 107–111.

17. Letter from Jane Edkins to her brother, Shanghai, September 4, 1860, in Edkins, *Chinese Scenes and People: With Notices of Christian Missions and Missionary Life in a Series of Letters from Various Parts of China* (London: James Nisbet and Co., 1863), pp. 147–151.

18. "The Advance of the Tai-ping Insurgents on Shanghai," *The North-China Herald,* August 25, 1860.

19. Ibid.

20. Account in *The North-China Herald,* reprinted in the *Nonconformist,* November 14, 1860; quoted in Lindley, *Ti-Ping Tien-Kwoh,* p. 297.

21. Earl Cranston, "Shanghai in the Taiping Period," *Pacific Historical Review* 5, vol. 2 (June 1936): 147–160, see p. 158.

22. "The Chinese Rebellion and the Allies," *The New York Times,* October 1, 1860.

23. Ibid.

24. "The Chinese Insurgents, and Our Policy with Respect to Them," *The London Review* 16, no. 31 (April 1861): 222–246, quotation on p. 246.

25. "The Visit of the Rebel Forces to Shanghai: No Attack Made by Them," *The New York Times,* November 17, 1860.

26. "The Chinese Revolution," *Tait's Edinburgh Magazine,* November 1860, p. 581.

27. Descriptions from Michael Mann, *China, 1860* (Salisbury, Wiltshire: M. Russell, 1989), p. 9; Bowlby, *An Account of the Last Mission,* pp. 38, 204; David Field Rennie, *The British Arms in North China and Japan: Peking 1860; Kagosima 1862* (London: John Murray, 1864), pp. 19, 43.

28. George Armand Furse, *Military Transport* (London, 1882), p. 41; rations on p. 72.

29. Rennie, *The British Arms in North China,* p. 98.

30. Mark S. Bell, *China: Being a Military Report on the North-Eastern Portions on the Provinces of Chih-li and Shan-tung; Nanking and Its*

Approaches; Canton and Its Approaches . . . and a Narrative of the Wars Between Great Britain and China (Calcutta, India: Office of the Superintendent of Government Printing, 1884), vol. 2, p. 423.

31. James Bruce, Earl of Elgin, *Letters and Journals of James, Eighth Earl of Elgin*, ed. Theodore Walrond (London: John Murray, 1872), pp. 376–377.

32. Robert Swinhoe, *Narrative of the North China Campaign of 1860* (London: Smith, Elder & Co., 1861), pp. 191–193.

33. Bowlby, *An Account of the Last Mission*, p. 165.

34. Swinhoe, *Narrative of the North China Campaign*, p. 195.

35. Rennie, *The British Arms in North China*, p. 112.

36. Laurence Oliphant, *Narrative of the Earl of Elgin's Mission to China and Japan in the Years 1857, '58, '59*, 2 vols. (London and Edinburgh: William Blackwood and Sons, 1859), pp. 362–363.

37. Bowlby, *An Account of the Last Mission*, p. 62.

38. Ibid., p. 63.

39. Harry Parkes's observation on the moon, from letter of August 6, 1860, in Stanley Lane-Poole, *The Life of Sir Harry Parkes*, 2 vols. (London: Macmillan and Co., 1894), vol. 1, p. 354; Parkes says ten to twelve boats, though Elgin gave the number as eight (*Letters and Journals*, p. 341).

40. George Allgood, *China War 1860: Letters and Journal* (London: Longmans, Green and Co., 1901), p. 41.

41. Bowlby claimed it was just the French, but Harry Parkes's letter of August 6 (see Lane-Poole, *The Life of Sir Harry Parkes*, vol. 1, p. 358) admits that both sides took part, the only difference being that the British tried to punish their own offenders while the French did not.

42. "Gengshen beilüe," (An account of what happened in the North in 1860), in *Dierci Yapian Zhanzheng* (The Second Opium War), 6 vols., ed. Qi Sihe et al. (Shanghai: Shanghai Renmin Chubanshe, 1978–1979), vol. 2, pp. 28–33, see p. 28.

43. Bowlby, *An Account of the Last Mission*, pp. 63–64.

44. Parkes, letter of August 6, 1860, in Lane-Poole, *The Life of Sir Harry Parkes*, vol. 1, p. 355.

45. Thomas Bowlby, diary entry for August 9, 1860, in Bowlby, *An Account of the Last Mission*, p. 73.

46. Bowlby, *An Account of the Last Mission*, p. 245.

47. Ibid., p. 285.

48. The Rev. R. J. L. M'Ghee, *How We Got to Pekin: A Narrative of the Campaign in China of 1860* (London: Bentley, 1862), p. 114.

49. Mann, *China, 1860*, p. 58.

50. Rennie, *The British Arms in North China*, p. 88 ("it was the first war-shot from an Armstrong gun").

51. Mann, *China, 1860*, p. 59, quoting James Hope Grant; Rennie, *The British Arms in North China*, pp. 91–92.

52. Allgood, *China War 1860*, pp. 75–76.

53. Ibid., p. 46.

54. Thomas Bowlby, diary entry for August 23, 1860, in Bowlby, *An Account of the Last Mission*, p. 83.

55. Parkes, letter of August 26, 1860, in Lane-Poole, *The Life of Sir Harry Parkes*, vol. 1, p. 364.

56. Mann, *China, 1860*, p. 91.

57. "The Capture of the Taku Forts (from our Special Correspondent)," *The Times*, November 3, 1860; reprinted in Bowlby, *An Account of the Last Mission*, p. 281.

58. "Parkes, Sir Harry Smith," *Oxford Dictionary of National Biography* (Oxford, England: Oxford University Press, 2004–2010). "Parkes had possessed a short, lean frame, with a large head, thinning fair hair descending to full sideburns, and bright blue eyes. His quick gait and alert features were tokens of a brusque and irritable temperament. He was a zealot for official work and could barely endure passive recreation."

59. See J. Y. Wong, "Harry Parkes and the 'Arrow' War in China," *Modern Asian Studies* 9, no. 3 (1975): 303–320.

60. Thomas Bowlby, diary entry for September 1, 1860, in Bowlby, *An Account of the Last Mission*, p. 90.

61. Parkes, letter of August 26, 1860, in Lane-Poole, *The Life of Sir Harry Parkes*, vol. 1, p. 368.

62. Bowlby, *An Account of the Last Mission*, pp. 37, 93.

63. Swinhoe, *Narrative of the North China Campaign*, p. 197; Lane-Poole, *The Life of Sir Harry Parkes*, vol. 1, p. 369.

64. Elgin, journal, September 8, 1860, in *Letters and Journals*, p. 350.

65. Bowlby, *An Account of the Last Mission*, pp. 289, 292.

66. Bowlby, diary, September 3, 1860, in ibid., p. 93.

67. "Gengshen beilüe," XF10/7/1–2 (August 17–18, 1860), in *Dierci Yapian Zhanzheng*, vol. 2, pp. 28–29.

68. Weng Tonghe, *Weng wengong gong riji*, diary entries for XF10/7/10 and XF10/7/23 (August 26 and September 8, 1860), in *Dierci Yapian Zhanzheng*, vol. 2, pp. 88–89.

69. Allgood, *China War 1860*, p. 80.

70. Rennie, *The British Arms in North China*, pp. 161–162; Elgin, *Letters and Journals*, p. 355.

71. The secret order is mentioned in Weng Tonghe's diary entry for XF10/7/24 (September 9, 1860), in *Dierci Yapian Zhanzheng*, vol. 2, p. 89; Henry Loch witnessed the secret preparations—see Henry Brougham Loch, *Personal Narrative of Occurrences During Lord Elgin's Second Embassy to China in 1860* (London: John Murray, 1900), pp. 88–90.

72. "Gengshen ducheng jieyan shiji," (A record of affairs under martial law in the capital in 1860), in *Dierci Yapian Zhanzheng*, vol. 2, p. 34.

73. "Gengshen beilüe," XF10/8/3 (September 17, 1860), in *Dierci Yapian Zhanzheng*, vol. 2, pp. 29–30.

74. Elgin, *Letters and Journals*, pp. 356–357.

75. Swinhoe, *Narrative of the North China Campaign*, pp. 253–254.

76. Viscount Garnet Wolseley, *Narrative of the War with China in 1860, to Which Is Added the Account of a Short Residence with the Tai-ping Rebels at Nankin* . . . (London: Longman, Green, Longman and Roberts, 1862), p. 189.

77. Wu Kedu, "Wang ji bian," (Extreme transgressions), in *Dierci Yapian Zhanzheng*, vol. 2, pp. 66–69; see p. 67.

78. Wenxiang, diary, *Wen wenzhong gong shilüe* (Taipei: Wenhai Chubanshe, reprint of 1882 edition), *juan* 2, pp. 32a–33b; Zhao Liewen, diary entry for XF10/9/24 (November 6, 1860), in *TPTG*, vol. 7, pp. 70–71; Wu Kedu, "Wang ji bian," in *Dierci Yapian Zhanzheng*, vol. 2, p. 66.

79. "Gengshen beilüe," XF10/8/8–19 (September 22–October 3, 1860), *Dierci Yapian Zhanzheng*, vol. 2, pp. 30–31.

80. Ibid., XF10/8/22 (October 6, 1860), *Dierci Yapian Zhanzheng*, vol. 2, p. 31.

81. Allgood, *China War 1860*, p. 84.

82. Alexander Bruce Tulloch, *Recollections of Forty Years' Service* (London: William Blackwood and Sons, 1903), pp. 117–118.

83. Ibid., p. 119.

84. Elgin, *Letters and Journals*, pp. 361–362.

85. Loch, *Personal Narrative*, pp. 102–103.

86. "Deposition of Bughel Sing, sowar, 1st troop Fane's Horse; and also of sowar Khan Sing, of the same regiment," quoted in Loch, *Personal Narrative*, p. 165.

87. Tulloch, *Recollections of Forty Years' Service*, p. 117.

88. Rennie, *The British Arms in North China*, pp. 166–167; James Hevia, *English Lessons: The Pedagogy of Imperialism in Nineteenth-Century China* (Durham, N.C.: Duke University Press, 2003), p. 90.

89. Sarah A. Southall Tooley, *The Personal Life of Queen Victoria* (London: Hodder and Stoughton, 1897), p. 256; Hevia, *English Lessons,* pp. 86–88.

90. Account quoted in Rennie, *The British Arms in North China,* pp. 165–166; also Swinhoe, *Narrative of the North China Campaign,* p. 331.

91. Swinhoe, *Narrative of the North China Campaign,* p. 330.

92. Ibid., pp. 330–331.

CHAPTER 6: A RELUCTANT GENERAL

1. Zeng Guofan, diary entries for XF10/9/2, XF10/9/3 and XF10/9/4 (October 15–17, 1860), in *ZGFQJ,* vol. 10, p. 3591.

2. Andrew C. K. Hsieh, "Tseng Kuo-fan, A Nineteenth Century Confucian General," Ph.D. diss., Yale University, 1975, pp. 9–13.

3. A. L. Y. Chung, "The Hanlin Academy in the Early Ch'ing Period," *Journal of the Hong Kong Branch of the Royal Asiatic Society,* vol. 6 (1966): 100–119; p. 101 puts number at one hundred through the eighteenth century.

4. Jen Yu-wen makes a similar observation in *The Taiping Revolutionary Movement* (New Haven, Conn.: Yale University Press, 1973), p. 218.

5. Hsieh, "Tseng Kuo-fan, A Nineteenth Century Confucian General," p. 17.

6. Zeng Guofan, family letter of DG22/12/20 (January 20, 1843), in *ZGFQJ,* vol. 6, p. 2012.

7. Hsieh, "Tseng Kuo-fan, A Nineteenth Century Confucian General," p. 22, and many other places.

8. Zhu Dong'an, *Zeng Guofan zhuan* (Biography of Zeng Guofan) (Tianjin: Baihua Wenshu Chubanshe, 2000), p. 51.

9. Joanna Waley-Cohen, "Militarization of Culture in Eighteenth-Century China," in *Military Culture in Imperial China,* ed. Nicola di Cosmo (Cambridge, Mass.: Harvard University Press, 2009), pp. 278–295.

10. Hsieh, "Tseng Kuo-fan, A Nineteenth Century Confucian General," p. 64; see also p. 209, n. 29, for original reference to Tang Jian's biography.

11. Zhu Dong'an, *Zeng Guofan zhuan,* p. 55.

12. Hsieh, "Tseng Kuo-fan, A Nineteenth Century Confucian General," p. 78.

13. William James Hail, *Tseng Kuo-fan and the Taiping Rebellion, with a Short Sketch of His Later Career* (New Haven, Conn.: Yale University

Press, 1927), p. 148, citing letters from XF2/12/16 to XF2/12/22 (January 24–30, 1853); specifically, he expected two parts success to eight parts effort.

14. *Zeng Guofan nianpu* (Chronological biography of Zeng Guofan), in *ZGFQJ*, vol. 1, p. 158, entry for XF2/12/13 (January 21, 1853).

15. Thomas Wade, "The Army of the Chinese Empire," in *Chinese Repository*, vol. 20 (January–December 1851), pp. 250–280, 300–340, and 363–421; see p. 421.

16. Dai Yingcong, "Military Finance of the High Qing Period," in *Military Culture in Imperial China*, ed. Nicola di Cosmo (Cambridge, Mass.: Harvard University Press, 2009), pp. 296–316.

17. Ralph Powell, *The Rise of Chinese Military Power, 1895–1912* (Princeton, N.J.: Princeton University Press, 1955), pp. 13–16.

18. Zeng Guofan, memorial dated XF1/3/9 (April 10, 1851), in *ZGFQJ*, vol. 2, p. 385.

19. Zeng Guofan, letter to Kui Yinting, in *ZGFQJ*, vol. 13, p. 4747.

20. Zeng Guofan, memorial dated XF2/12/22 (January 30, 1853), in *ZGFQJ*, vol. 2, pp. 401–402.

21. Ibid.

22. Zeng Guofan, memorial dated XF5/4/1 (May 16, 1855), in *ZGFQJ*, vol. 2, pp. 561–562.

23. Luo Ergang, *Xiangjun xin zhi* (A new history of the Hunan Army) (Taipei: Liming Wenhua Shiye Gongsi, 1988), pp. 201–210.

24. Zeng Guofan, instructions from the Jiangxi Field Headquarters, in *ZGFQJ*, vol. 5 (pidu), p. 1678.

25. Zeng Guofan, "She" (Forgiveness), in *ZGFQJ*, vol. 16 (wenji), pp. 5968–5969.

26. Quoted in Li Zhiming, *Xiangjun: chengjiu shusheng xunye de "minbing"* (The Hunan Army: accomplished "people's militia" of elite scholars) (Shanghai: Guji Chubanshe, 2007), p. 52.

27. Maochun Yu, "The Taiping Rebellion: A Military Assessment of Revolution and Counterrevolution," in *A Military History of China*, ed. David Graff and Robin Higham (Boulder: Westview, 2002), pp. 135–152, see p. 148.

28. Luo Ergang, *Xiangjun xin zhi*, pp. 201–202.

29. Jen, *The Taiping Revolutionary Movement*, p. 227.

30. Green Standard pay scale given in Wade, "The Army of the Chinese Empire," *Chinese Repository*, vol. 20 (1851), p. 414: 4.2 taels per month in the Hunan Army versus 1.5 taels per month in the Green Standard.

31. Zeng Guofan, "Xiaoyu xinmu xiangyong" (Instructions to new recruits), in *ZGFQJ*, vol. 15 (wenji), pp. 5953–5955; prizes listed on p. 5955.

32. Ibid., p. 5953.

33. Ibid., p. 5955.

34. Zeng Guofan, "Ying gui" (Rules of camp), section on "Zhaomu zhi gui" (Rules for recruitment), in *ZGFQJ*, vol. 15 (wenji), p. 5999.

35. Hail, *Tseng Kuo-fan and the Taiping Rebellion*, p. 201, n. 34.

36. Hsieh, "Tseng Kuo-fan, A Nineteenth Century Confucian General," pp. 98–99.

37. Zeng Guofan, "Tao yuefei xi," (A call to arms against the Guangxi bandits) in *ZGFQJ*, vol. 15 (wenji), p. 5768.

38. As described in "Gengshen (jia) binan riji" (A diary of avoiding calamity in 1860–1861), entry for XF11/2/19 (March 29, 1861), in *TPTG*, vol. 6, p. 214.

39. Jen, *The Taiping Revolutionary Movement*, p. 100.

40. Wang Kaiyun, *Xiangjun zhi* (Annals of the Hunan Army) (Changsha: Yuelu Shushe, 1983), p. 159; see also Luo Ergang, *Xiangjun bingzhi*, p. 93; Zeng Guofan, "Ying gui" (Rules of camp), in *ZGFQJ*, vol. 16 (wenji), pp. 5996–5999; Luo Ergang dates this version of the *ying gui* to 1860 in Qimen and notes that it wasn't changed afterward (Luo Ergang, *Xiangjun bingzhi*, p. 92).

41. Luo Ergang, *Xiangjun bingzhi*, pp. 94–95.

42. William Minns Tileston, letter to his mother, February 12, 1863, Massachusetts Historical Society, Boston, Mass.

43. Specifically, 40 fast crabs, 50 long dragons, and 150 armed sampans.

44. Zhu Dong'an, *Zeng Guofan zhuan*, p. 102.

45. Ibid., p. 103; Jen, *The Taiping Revolutionary Movement*, p. 236.

46. Jen, *The Taiping Revolutionary Movement*, p. 242, quoting from Xue Fucheng, *Yong'an biji*.

47. Zhu Dong'an, *Zeng Guofan zhuan*, p. 144 on Duolonga; Wang Kaiyun, *Xiangjun zhi*, p. 62.

48. Zeng Guofan, "Ai min ge" (Song of loving the people), in *ZGFQJ*, vol. 16 (wenji), pp. 5966–5967.

49. Zeng Guofan, instructions from Jiangxi Field Headquarters, in *ZGFQJ*, vol. 5 (pidu), p. 1671.

50. *Zeng Guofan nianpu*, entry for XF4/12/25 (February 11, 1855), in *ZGFQJ*, vol. 1, p. 189.

51. Jen, *The Taiping Revolutionary Movement*, pp. 328–336.

52. Zeng Guofan, family letter of XF10/4/24 (June 13, 1860), in *ZGFQJ*, vol. 7, p. 2389.

53. Zeng Guofan, instructions from Jiangxi Field Headquarters, in *ZGFQJ*, vol. 5 (pidu), p. 1674.

54. Zeng Guofan, memorial dated XF9/6/22 (August 8, 1859), in *ZGFQJ*, vol. 3, p. 814.

55. Zeng Guofan, memorial dated XF9/6/18 (August 4, 1859), in ibid., pp. 809–811.

56. Jen, *The Taiping Revolutionary Movement*, p. 341; Zeng Guofan, letter to Zuo Zongtang, in *ZGFQJ*, vol. 13 (letters), p. 4959.

57. Zhao Liewen, *Neng jingju riji*, entry for TZ3/4/8 (May 13, 1864), in *TPTG*, vol. 7, p. 249; Zhu Dong'an, *Zeng Guofan zhuan*, p. 147.

58. He almost immediately (in June) made the provincial treasurer of Jiangxi serve as director of supplies for his army. See David Pong, "The Income and Military Expenditure of Kiangsi Province in the Last Years (1860–1864) of the Taiping Rebellion," *The Journal of Asian Studies* 26, no. 1 (November 1966): 49–65, p. 57.

59. Zeng Guofan, memorial dated XF9/10/17 (November 11, 1859), in *ZGFQJ*, vol. 3, pp. 820–822.

60. Zhu Dong'an, *Zeng Guofan zhuan*, p. 152.

61. Formations given in Zhang Dejian, *Zeiqing huizuan* (Intelligence reports on the Taiping rebels) (Taipei: Wenhai Chubanshe, 1968, reprint of 1855 original), pp. 366–378.

62. Zeng Guofan, "Bing" (The Military), in *ZGFQJ*, vol. 16 (wenji), pp. 5992–5993.

63. Zeng Guofan, letter to Li Xuyi (Li Xi'an) in *ZGFQJ*, vol. 14 (letters), p. 5092.

64. Zeng Guofan, family letters of XF10/8/4 and XF10/8/5 (September 18 and 19, 1860), in *ZGFQJ*, vol. 7, pp. 2407–2408.

65. Zeng Guofan, family letter of XF10/9/14 (October 27, 1860), in ibid., p. 2419; Zhu Dong'an makes a related argument on pp. 156–161 of *Zeng Guofan zhuan*.

66. Zeng Guofan, family letter of XF10/9/17 (October 30, 1860), in *ZGFQJ*, vol. 7, p. 2420.

67. Zeng Guofan, diary entries for middle of XF10/9 (late October 1860), in *ZGFQJ*, vol. 10, pp. 3594–3595.

68. Zeng Guofan, family letter of XF10/9/4 (October 17, 1860), in *ZGFQJ*, vol. 7, p. 2416.

69. Zeng Guofan, family letter of XF10/9/1 (October 14, 1860), in ibid., pp. 2414–2415.

70. Zeng Guofan, diary entry for XF10/9/24 (November 6, 1860), in *ZGFQJ*, vol. 10, p. 3596.

CHAPTER 7: THE FORCE OF DOCTRINE

1. Augustus F. Lindley (Lin-le), *Ti-Ping Tien-Kwoh; The History of the Ti-ping Revolution* (London: Day & Son, Ltd., 1866), p. 281.

2. Hong Rengan, third Nanchang confession, in *TPTG*, vol. 2, p. 414.

3. Hong Rengan, second confession at Xi Baotian's military camp, in *TPTG*, vol. 2, p. 404.

4. Hong Rengan, confession at the Jiangxi governor's *yamen*, in ibid., vol. 2, p. 416.

5. A rubbing of the tablet was preserved by the British and Foreign Bible Society and is reproduced in Thomas Jenner's pamphlet "The Nanking Monument of the Beatitudes" (London: William Clowes and Sons, 1911); it is also described in Joseph Edkins, "Narrative of a Visit to Nanking," in Jane R. Edkins, *Chinese Scenes and People: With Notices of Christian Missions and Missionary Life in a Series of Letters from Various Parts of China* (London: James Nisbet and Co., 1863), pp. 241–307, see p. 264; Edkins translates *fu* incorrectly as "happiness."

6. From the account of J. S. Burdon in Prescott Clarke and J. S. Gregory, *Western Reports on the Taiping: A Selection of Documents* (Honolulu: University Press of Hawaii, 1982), p. 240; description of tablet from Catharina Van Rensselaer Bonney, *A Legacy of Historical Gleanings* (Albany, N.Y.: J. Munsell, 1875), p. 341.

7. Thomas W. Blakiston, *Five Months on the Yang-tsze* (London: John Murray, 1862), pp. 49–51; Josiah Cox, "A Missionary Visit to Nanking and the 'Shield King,'" in *The Wesleyan Missionary Notices*, 3rd ser., vol. 10 (April 1862): 61–66, see esp. p. 62.

8. Edmund F. Merriam, *A History of American Baptist Missions* (Philadelphia: American Baptist Publication Society, 1900), p. 59.

9. George Blackburn Pruden, Jr., "Issachar Jacox Roberts and American Diplomacy in China During the Taiping Rebellion," Ph.D. diss., The American University, 1977, pp. 34–35.

10. Merriam, *A History of American Baptist Missions*, p. 59.

11. Pruden, "Issachar Jacox Roberts and American Diplomacy in China," pp. 164–166.

12. Ibid., pp. 193–195.

13. Ibid., p. 215.

14. Notice in the *Vermont Chronicle,* February 6, 1855, p. 22. "Wang" changed to "King" for clarity.

15. W. A. P. Martin, *A Cycle of Cathay* (New York: F. H. Revell Co., 1896), p. 29.

16. Edkins, "Narrative of a Visit to Nanking," p. 275.

17. Viscount Garnet Wolseley, *Narrative of the War with China in 1860, to Which Is Added the Account of a Short Residence with the Tai-ping Rebels at Nankin* . . . (London: Longman, Green, Longman and Roberts, 1862), p. 338.

18. Masataka Banno, *China and the West, 1858–1861: The Origins of the Tsungli Yamen* (Cambridge, Mass: Harvard University Press, 1964), p. 71.

19. Clarke and Gregory, *Western Reports on the Taiping,* pp. 253–254.

20. Jane Edkins, letter to her mother-in-law, Chefoo, December 12, 1860, in Edkins, *Chinese Scenes and People,* p. 192.

21. Ralph Wardlaw Thompson, *Griffith John: The Story of Fifty Years in China* (London: The Religious Tract Society, 1906), p. 143.

22. Jane Edkins, letter to her brother Simon, Chefoo, December 11, 1860, in Edkins, *Chinese Scenes and People,* p. 189.

23. Thompson, *Griffith John,* pp. 147–148.

24. Clarke and Gregory, *Western Reports on the Taiping,* p. 278.

25. Thompson, *Griffith John,* p. 150.

26. William Robson, *Griffith John: Founder of the Hankow Mission Central China* (London: S. W. Partridge & Co., n.d. [1901?]), p. 51.

27. Yung Wing, *My Life in China and America* (New York: Henry Holt & Co., 1909), p. 96 (he erroneously gives the date as 1859).

28. Ibid., pp. 100–101.

29. Ibid., p. 110.

30. Ibid., p. 109.

31. Ibid., p. 134.

32. Weng Tonghe, *Weng wengong gong riji,* diary entry for XF10/7/25 (September 10, 1860), in *Dierci Yapian Zhanzheng,* 6 vols., ed. Qi Sihe et al. (Shanghai: Shanghai Renmin Chubanshe, 1978–1979), vol. 2, p. 89.

33. Jerome Ch'ên, "The Hsien-fêng Inflation," *Bulletin of the School of Oriental and African Studies, University of London,* 21, no. 1–3 (1958): 578–586.

34. After a two-month delay, both reports reached him on November 2. See

Leone Levi, ed., *Annals of British Legation* (London: Smith, Elder, & Co., 1862), vol. 10, p. 313.

35. *The Times*, November 16, 1860 (editorial beginning "The Empire of China, as most readers know, has two capitals").

36. A. A. Hayes, "An American Soldier in China," *The Atlantic Monthly*, February 1886, 193–199, quotation on p. 194.

37. "The Chinese Rebellion," *The New York Times*, September 1, 1860.

38. Quoted in Lindley, *Ti-Ping Tien-Kwoh*, p. 296.

39. "Pinghu biji," (Pinghu diary), in *TPTG*, vol. 5, p. 29.

40. J. S. Gregory, *Great Britain and the Taipings* (London: Frederick A. Praeger, 1969), pp. 88–89.

41. Zhao Liewen, *Neng jingju riji*, entry for XF10/7/5 (August 21, 1860), in *TPTG*, vol. 7, p. 67.

42. James Bruce, Earl of Elgin, *Letters and Journals of James, Eighth Earl of Elgin*, ed. Theodore Walrond (London: John Murray, 1872), p. 376.

43. Quoted in Gregory, *Great Britain and the Taipings*, pp. 89–90.

44. Quoted in ibid., pp. 95–96; a similar exchange between Elgin and Bruce is mentioned in Thomas Bowlby's diary entry for September 1, 1860, while Elgin was in Tianjin and Bruce in Shanghai. See James Bowlby, ed. C. C. Bowlby (printed for private circulation, 1906), *An Account of the Last Mission and Death of Thomas William Bowlby*, p. 91.

45. Zhao Liewen, *Neng jingju riji*, entry for XF10/7/23 (September 8, 1860), in *TPTG*, vol. 7, p. 68.

46. Ibid. In translating this, I have assumed that there is an error in the transcription of the diary in *TPTG*, which reads, "The emperor of the Qing is *not* the emperor of a lost country" (emphasis added).

47. Zhao Liewen, *Neng jingju riji*, entry for XF10/9/4 (October 17, 1860), in *TPTG*, vol. 7, p. 69.

48. "Gengshen (jia) binan riji" (A diary of avoiding calamity in 1860–1861), entry for XF10/8/27 (October 11, 1860), in *TPTG*, vol. 6, p. 206.

49. Wang Shihui, *Xianfeng Xiangshan yue fen jishi* (A record of actual events under the rebels in Xiangshan during the Xianfeng reign), in *TPTG*, vol. 5, p. 219.

50. Wang Yishou, *Yuenan zhi* (A chronicle spanning hardships), in ibid., p. 143.

51. "Lu zai muzhong" (Firsthand account of Taiping military organization), in ibid., p. 436.

52. Zhang Xiaoqiu, *Yuefei jilüe* (Brief records of the Guangxi bandits), in *TPTG*, vol. 4, p. 56.

53. Wang Yishou, *Yuenan zhi,* in *TPTG,* vol. 5, p. 144.

54. Kathryn Bernhardt, "Elite and Peasant During the Taiping Occupation of the Jiangnan, 1860–1864," *Modern China* 13, no. 4 (October 1987): 379–410; Xiaowei Zheng, "Loyalty, Anxiety, and Opportunism: Local Elite Activism during the Taiping Rebellion in Eastern Zhejiang, 1851–1864," *Late Imperial China* 30, no. 2 (December 2009): 39–83.

55. Bernhardt, "Elite and Peasant," pp. 384–388.

56. Ibid., pp. 383–384.

57. See, for example, "Gengshen (jia) binan riji" (A diary of avoiding calamity in 1860–1861), in *TPTG,* vol. 6, p. 200, on "true longhairs" (*zhen changmao*) being only a minority.

58. Blakiston, *Five Months on the Yang-tsze,* pp. 48–49.

59. Wang Yishou, *Yuenan zhi,* in *TPTG,* vol. 5, p. 157.

60. Mr. Tang (no given name), "Qiuwen riji" (Qiuwen diary), entry for XF11/3/2 (April 11, 1861), in *TPTG,* vol. 6, pp. 346–347; "Gengshen (jia) binan riji" (A diary of avoiding calamity in 1860–1861), entry for XF11/2/27 (April 6, 1861), in *TPTG,* vol. 6, pp. 214–215.

61. The prompt from the *Analects* is recorded in "Gengshen (jia) binan riji" (A diary of avoiding calamity in 1860–1861), entry for XF11/3/8 (April 17, 1861), in *TPTG,* vol. 6, p. 215; also in Mr. Tang (no given name), "Qiuwen riji" (Qiuwen diary), entry for XF11/3/2 (April 11, 1861), in *TPTG,* vol. 6, p. 346.

62. Edkins, "Narrative of a Visit to Nanking," pp. 280–281.

63. Ibid., p. 301.

64. Hong Rengan, *Yingjie guizhen* (A hero's return to the truth), trans. in Franz Michael, *The Taiping Rebellion: History and Documents* (Seattle: University of Washington Press, 1966–1971), vol. 3, pp. 799–831, quotations on pp. 804, 806, 807.

65. Ibid., p. 817.

66. Hong Rengan, third Nanchang confession, in *TPTG,* vol. 2, p. 414.

67. C. A. Curwen, *Taiping Rebel: The Deposition of Li Hsiu-Ch'eng* (Cambridge, England: Cambridge University Press, 1977), pp. 121–122.

68. Curwen, *Taiping Rebel,* p. 122 (from folio 72).

69. Date given by William Muirhead, who wrote on February 12, 1861, that Hong Rengan had left the previous Sabbath, which would have been Sunday, February 10, the first day of that lunar year.

70. W. Muirhead, "Visit of the Rev. W. Muirhead to the City of Nanking," *The Missionary Magazine and Chronicle,* vol. 25 (July 1861): 197–209; see p. 206. Muirhead's article is dated February 1861.

CHAPTER 8: THE PERILS OF CIVILIZATION

1. Reported in *The Economist*, February 9, 1861, p. 146.

2. *The Times*, December 25, 1860 (editorial beginning "The news which arrived just as the bells were ringing their first Christmas chime").

3. "Capture of Pekin," *The Illustrated News of the World*, December 15, 1860.

4. The full text of the letter is in Hugo's collected works, *Oeuvres Complètes: Pendant l'Exil: 1852–1870* (Paris, 1883), pp. 267–270.

5. This is from the 1861 letter, though he also repeated the same theme in 1870: *"S'associer à l'Angleterre pour donner à la Chine le spectacle de l'Europe vandale, stupéfier de notre barbarie les barbares, détruire le palais d'Été de compte à demi avec le fils de lord Elgin qui a mutilé le Parthénon,"* in *Oeuvres Complètes: Pendant l'Exil: 1852–1870*, p. 530.

6. *Hansard's Parliamentary Debates* (London: T. C. Hansard), February 14, 1861, vol. 161, c. 392.

7. Ibid., c. 410.

8. James Bruce, Earl of Elgin, *Letters and Journals of James, Eighth Earl of Elgin*, ed. Theodore Walrond (London: John Murray, 1872), pp. 391–392.

9. Ibid., p. 393.

10. Arthur W. Hummel, ed., *Eminent Chinese of the Ch'ing Period (1644–1912)* (Taipei: Chengwen reprint, 1967), p. 666.

11. Lolan Wang Grady, "The Career of I-Hsin, Prince Kung, 1858–1880: A Case Study of the Limits of Reform in the Late Ch'ing," Ph.D. diss., University of Toronto, 1980, pp. 23–24.

12. Grady's translation, from ibid. pp. 94–95.

13. Ibid., p. 100.

14. Ibid., pp. 100–101.

15. Jennifer Rudolph, *Negotiated Power in Late Imperial China: The Zongli Yamen and the Politics of Reform* (Ithaca, N.Y.: Cornell University East Asia Program, 2008), pp. 184–185.

16. R. K. I. Quested, *Sino-Russian Relations: A Short History* (Boston: George Allen & Unwin, 1984), pp. 71–77; Quested, *The Expansion of Russia in East Asia, 1857–1860* (Kuala Lumpur: University of Malaya Press, 1968), pp. 64–153.

17. Quested, *Sino-Russian Relations*, pp. 75–77.

18. Mao Jiaqi, *Guo zhu "Taiping Tianguo shishi rizhi" jiaobu* (Emendations to Guo [Tingyi's] *Daily Calendar of Events in the Taiping Heavenly Kingdom*) (Taipei: Taiwan Shangwu Yinshuguan, 2001), p. 151. The super-

intendent of trade was Xue Huan, who was also governor of Jiangsu province, though he later relinquished that post to focus on trade in the southern treaty ports. See Rudolph, *Negotiated Power,* p. 113.

19. Mao Jiaqi, *Guo zhu,* pp. 149–150.

20. Zeng Guofan, memorial dated XF10/11/8 (December 19, 1860), in *ZGFQJ,* vol. 3, pp. 879–882.

21. Masataka Banno, *China and the West, 1858–1861: The Origins of the Tsungli Yamen* (Cambridge, Mass.: Harvard University Press, 1964), p. 209 and p. 332, n. 26.

22. Quoted in Mao Jiaqi, *Guo zhu,* p. 154: "if we send the foreign ships there, not only will there be no possibility of a joint attack, but furthermore I fear . . . that [the unescorted Russians] might decide to collaborate with the rebels and give rise to new problems."

23. Earl Grey's speech, quoted here and in following paragraphs, is in *Hansard,* February 19, 1861, vol. 161, cc. 546–569.

24. Ibid., c. 580.

25. Meadows to Russell, February 19, 1861 (received April 12, 1861), in *Papers Relating to the Rebellion in China, and Trade in the Yang-tze-kiang River* (London: Harrison and Sons, 1862), p. 3.

26. J. S. Gregory, "Stephen Uhalley, Jr. and Westerners in China: A Further Comment," *The Journal of Asian Studies* 35, no. 2 (February 1976): 364–365.

27. Among other locations, Holmes's letter is published in the *Church Missionary Intelligencer* of December 1, 1860.

28. "The Chinese Insurgents, and Our Policy with Respect to Them," *The London Review* 16, no. 31 (April 1861): 222–246; quotations, including from *Overland Register,* on pp. 232, 235, and 242.

29. John Scarth, *British Policy in China: Is Our War with the Tartars or the Chinese?* (London: Smith, Elder and Co., 1860), front cover.

30. Ibid., pp. 23, 31, and 32.

31. *The Economist,* May 11, 1861, p. 513.

32. "China," *Dublin University Magazine,* May 1861, p. 569.

33. *Dictionary of National Biography* (New York: Macmillan, 1909), vol. 19, p. 258.

34. Sykes's speech quoted here and in following paragraphs is in *Hansard,* March 12, 1861, vol. 161, cc. 1841–1856.

35. Ibid., cc. 1858–1859.

36. *Hansard,* April 12, 1861, vol. 162, c. 522.

37. Description of rain from Thomas W. Blakiston, *Five Months on the Yang-tsze* (London: John Murray, 1862), pp. 1–2.

38. "Fighting Jimmy": Robert S. Rantoul, "Frederick Townsend Ward," *Historical Collections of the Essex Institute* 44, no. 1 (January 1908): 1–64, p. 31; according to Alexander Michie, *The Englishman in China During the Victorian Era* (Edinburgh: William Blackwood and Sons, 1900), p. 349, Hope was "a tall, noble-looking man, with a prepossessing and most gentlemanlike appearance."

39. Stanley Lane-Poole, *The Life of Sir Harry Parkes,* 2 vols. (London: Macmillan and Co., 1894), vol. 1, pp. 265–266.

40. Harry Parkes, "Report of an Interview with Rebel Authorities at Nanking, March 1, 1861," in *Papers Relating to the Rebellion in China, and Trade in the Yang-tze-kiang River,* pp. 35–37.

41. Lane-Poole, *The Life of Sir Harry Parkes,* vol. 1, p. 263.

42. Ibid., p. 264.

43. Parkes to Hammond, June 12, 1861, in *Papers Relating to the Rebellion in China, and Trade in the Yang-tze-kiang River,* p. 45.

44. Lane-Poole, *The Life of Sir Harry Parkes,* vol. 1, p. 265.

45. "Report by Mr. Parkes of Visit to Woo-Hoo and Tae-Ping," March 28, 1861, in *Papers Relating to the Rebellion in China, and Trade in the Yang-tze-kiang River,* p. 31.

46. Hope to Admiralty, April 6, 1861, in *Correspondence Respecting the Opening of the Yang-tze-kiang River to Foreign Trade* (London: Harrison and Sons, 1861), p. 10.

47. Michie, *The Englishman in China,* p. 376.

48. There was some controversy over whether the promise to stay thirty miles from Shanghai was just for the year or in perpetuity. Parkes's original report said nothing about a year, but Bruce later referred to the Taipings having promised to stay out of Shanghai "for a twelvemonth," and Parkes returned almost a year later to ask for an extension (which was refused). Also, in his instructions for his successor Kuper on October 15, 1862, Hope referred to the agreement as having been "but limited to the year." See Bruce to Hope, Beijing, June 16, 1861, in *Papers Relating to the Rebellion in China, and Trade in the Yang-tze-kiang River,* p. 56; and "Extract from a Memorandum dated October 15, 1862, addressed to Rear-Admiral Kuper by Vice-Admiral Sir J. Hope, on resigning the Command of the Station," in *Further Papers Relating to the Rebellion in China* (London: Harrison and Sons, 1863), p. 111.

49. "Report by Mr. Forrest of Journey from Shanghae to Nanking," in *Correspondence Respecting the Opening of the Yang-tze-kiang River to Foreign Trade,* pp. 27–30.

50. As per the captain of the *Centaur,* who described the banks of the Grand Canal as "literally white with human bones." Aplin to Hope, March 21, 1861, in ibid., p. 21.

51. "Report by Mr. Forrest of Journey from Shanghae to Nanking," in ibid., p. 29.

52. A battalion commander in Zeng Guofan's army received 50 taels per month. Sixty taels per month was a little over $1,000 per year; William Mills Tileston, a young American working at a firm in Shanghai, was paid $900 per year.

53. Forrest to Bruce, April 20 and May 1, 1861, in *Papers Relating to the Rebellion in China, and Trade in the Yang-tze-kiang River,* pp. 41–42.

54. Medhurst to Bruce, May 6, 1861, enclosing "Deposition" of John Hinton, in ibid., pp. 42–43.

55. The letter is in the Frederick Townsend Ward Papers, Manuscripts and Archives, Sterling Memorial Library, Yale University, New Haven, Conn.

56. Teng Ssu-yu, *The Taiping Rebellion and the Western Powers: A Comprehensive Survey* (Oxford, England: Clarendon Press, 1971), p. 305.

57. Caleb Carr, *The Devil Soldier: The American Soldier of Fortune Who Became a God in China* (New York: Random House, 1992), pp. 150–151.

58. Edward Forester, "Personal Recollections of the Tai-ping Rebellion," *Cosmopolitan* 21, no. 6 (October 1896): 629; Carr, *Devil Soldier,* pp. 153–154.

CHAPTER 9: ENDURANCE

1. Descriptions based in part on Thomas W. Blakiston, *Five Months on the Yang-tsze* (London: John Murray, 1862), p. 61; Viscount Garnet Wolseley, *Narrative of the War with China in 1860, to Which Is Added the Account of a Short Residence with the Tai-ping Rebels at Nankin* . . . (London: Longman, Green, Longman and Roberts, 1862), pp. 369–372.

2. As described by Laurence Oliphant in *Narrative of the Earl of Elgin's Mission to China and Japan in the Years 1857, '58, '59,* 2 vols. (London and Edinburgh: William Blackwood and Sons, 1859), vol. 2, pp. 363–364.

3. Augustus F. Lindley (Lin-le), *Ti-Ping Tien-Kwoh; The History of the Ti-ping Revolution* (London: Day & Son, Ltd., 1866), p. 345; Wolseley, *Narrative of the War with China in 1860,* p. 371.

4. Zhang Dejian, *Zeiqing huizuan* (Intelligence reports on the Taiping rebels) (Taipei: Wenhai Chubanshe, 1968, reprint of 1855 original), p. 173.

5. Lindesay Brine, *The Taeping Rebellion in China: A Narrative of Its Rise and Progress* (London: John Murray, 1862), p. 307.

6. Zhu Hongzhang, *Cong rong jilüe* (Zhu Hongzhang's account of the campaign against the rebels) (Taipei: Wenhai Chubanshe reprint, 1968), p. 68.

7. "Report by Mr. Parkes of Visit to Ngan-king [Anqing], March 24, 1861," in *Correspondence Respecting the Opening of the Yang-tze-kiang River to Foreign Trade* (London: Harrison and Sons, 1861), pp. 25–27, see p. 26.

8. Jen Yu-wen (Jian Youwen), *The Taiping Revolutionary Movement* (New Haven, Conn.: Yale University Press, 1973), p. 412.

9. This reflects the reality of what they tried to accomplish, which differs somewhat from the description of their strategy that Li Xiucheng provided in his confession.

10. From Guan Wen memorial, quoted in Mao Jiaqi, *Guo zhu "Taiping Tianguo shishi rizhi" jiaobu* (Emendations to Guo (Tingyi's) *Daily Calendar of Events in the Taiping Heavenly Kingdom*) (Taipei: Taiwan Shangwu Yinshuguan, 2001), p. 157.

11. Parkes, "Report of Mr. Parkes of his Visit to the Ying Wang at Hwang-chow, March 22, 1861," in *Papers Relating to the Rebellion in China, and Trade in the Yang-tze-kiang River* (London: Harrison and Sons, 1862): 53–56, see p. 55.

12. Zeng Guofan, family letter of XF10/7/3 (August 19, 1860), in *ZGFQJ*, vol. 7, p. 2400.

13. Zeng Guofan, diary entry for XF10/10/11 (November 23, 1860), in *ZGFQJ*, vol. 10, p. 3600.

14. Zeng Guofan, diary entries for XF10/10/11 and XF10/10/19 (November 23 and December 1, 1860), ibid., pp. 3600, 3602.

15. Zhu Dong'an, *Zeng Guofan zhuan* (Biography of Zeng Guofan) (Tianjin: Baihua Wenshu Chubanshe, 2000), p. 162.

16. Chen Chang, *Tingjun jilüe* (History of Bao Chao's army) (Shanghai: Shanghai Shenbao Guan, 1882), *juan* 3, p. 26b.

17. Zeng Guofan, family letter of XF10/10/20 (December 2, 1860), in *ZGFQJ*, vol. 7, p. 2430.

18. C. A. Curwen, *Taiping Rebel: The Deposition of Li Hsiu-Ch'eng* (Cambridge, England: Cambridge University Press, 1977), pp. 122–123.

19. Chen Chang, *Tingjun jilüe, juan* 3, p. 27a.

20. Zeng Guofan, family letter of XF10/11/14 (December 25, 1860), in *ZGFQJ*, vol. 7, pp. 2436–2437. (N.B.: there is a typographical error in *Zeng Guo-*

fan quanji, where this letter is listed as XF10/11/4 rather than XF10/11/14.)

21. Zeng Guofan, letter to Hu Linyi of XF10/11/16 (December 27, 1860), quoted in Mao Jiaqi, *Guo zhu*, p. 150.

22. Zeng Guofan, family letters of XF10/11/18, XF10/11/22, and XF10/11/24 (December 29, 1860, and January 2 and 4, 1861), in *ZGFQJ*, vol. 7, pp. 2437, 2438–2439.

23. Zeng Guofan, memorial dated XF10/11/28 (January 8, 1861), in *ZGFQJ*, vol. 3, pp. 887–888.

24. Jen Yu-wen (Jian Youwen), *The Taiping Revolutionary Movement*, p. 415; Zhu Dong'an, *Zeng Guofan zhuan*, p. 163.

25. Zeng Guofan, diary entry for XF11/3/5 (April 14, 1861), in *ZGFQJ*, vol. 10, p. 3641; also quoted in Zhu Dong'an, *Zeng Guofan zhuan*, p. 164.

26. Zeng Guofan, diary entry for XF11/3/13 (April 22, 1861), in ibid., p. 3644.

27. Zeng Guofan, family letter of XF11/3/13 (April 22, 1861), in *ZGFQJ*, vol. 7, pp. 2475–2476.

28. Ibid., p. 2476.

29. "Report of Mr. Parkes of His Visit to the Ying Wang at Hwang-chow, March 22, 1861," in *Papers Relating to the Rebellion in China, and Trade in the Yang-tze-kiang River*, pp. 53–56, quotation on p. 54.

30. Ibid., p. 54.

31. Lindley, *Ti-Ping Tien-Kwoh*, p. 350.

32. "Report by Mr. Parkes of Visit to Ngan-king [Anqing], March 24, 1861," in *Correspondence Respecting the Opening of the Yang-tze-kiang River to Foreign Trade*, pp. 25–27.

33. "Report by Mr. Parkes on Communications with the Insurgents at Nanking, March 29 to April 2, 1861," in *Papers Relating to the Rebellion in China, and Trade in the Yang-tze-kiang River*, pp. 10–15, see p. 12.

34. As reported by Garnet Wolseley, who passed by in the spring of 1861; Wolseley, *Narrative of the War with China in 1860*, p. 370.

35. "Report by Mr. Parkes of Visit to Ngan-king [Anqing], March 24, 1861," p. 27.

36. Curwen, *Taiping Rebel*, p. 123.

37. Ibid.

38. Ibid., pp. 124–125.

39. "Li Hsiu-ch'eng's letter to Lai Wen-kuang Seeking Military Information," trans. in Franz Michael, *The Taiping Rebellion: History and Documents*, 3 vols. (Seattle: University of Washington Press, 1966–1971), vol. 3, pp. 1043–1044; the letter wound up in the British Museum.

40. Jen, *The Taiping Revolutionary Movement*, pp. 421–422.

41. Xia Chuntao, *Hong Rengan* (Wuhan: Hubei Jiaoyu Chubanshe, 1999), p. 257.

42. Zeng Guofan, family letter of XF11/4/24 (June 2, 1861), in *ZGFQJ*, vol. 7, p. 2506.

43. Hong Rengan, "Ti yuci jinbi," (On receiving the golden brush), in *Hong Rengan xuanji* (The selected works of Hong Rengan), ed. Yangzhou Shifan Xueyuan Zhongwen Xi (Beijing: Zhonghua Shuju, 1978), p. 62; translation based on Michael, *The Taiping Rebellion*, vol. 3, p. 835.

44. Hong Rengan, "Zhi ge" (The end of fighting), in *Hong Rengan xuanji*, p. 67.

45. Xia Chuntao, *Hong Rengan*, p. 261.

46. Ibid., p. 248; Jen, *The Taiping Revolutionary Movement*, p. 423.

47. Zeng Guofan, family letter of XF11/5/4 (June 11, 1861), in *ZGFQJ*, vol. 7, p. 2514; also letter of XF11/5/14 (June 21, 1861), in *ZGFQJ*, vol. 7, p. 2522.

48. Wang Kaiyun, *Xiangjun zhi* (1879 edition), *juan* 5, p. 8a.

49. Zeng Guofan got the news on July 9; see his family letter of XF11/6/2 (July 9, 1861), in *ZGFQJ*, vol. 7, p. 2527.

50. Zhu Hongzhang, *Cong rong jilüe*, pp. 73–74; Zhu says 10,000, but Zeng Guoquan reported to Zeng Guofan that the number was 8,000 (which matches with the weapons count). See Zeng Guofan, family letter of XF11/6/4 (July 11, 1861), in *ZGFQJ*, vol. 7, p. 2528.

51. Zeng Guofan, family letter of XF11/6/4 (July 11, 1861), in *ZGFQJ*, vol. 7, p. 2528.

52. Zeng Guofan, family letter of XF11/6/5 (July 12, 1861), in ibid.

53. Zeng Guofan, family letter of XF11/6/12 (July 19, 1861), in ibid., p. 2530.

54. Zeng Guofan, family letter of XF11/4/24 (June 2, 1861), in ibid., p. 2506.

55. Zeng Guofan, family letter of XF11/4/26 (June 4, 1861), in ibid., pp. 2508–2509.

56. Zeng Guofan, family letter of XF11/5/6 (June 13, 1861), in ibid., p. 2516; the ship unloaded 3,000 *dan*, one *dan* being equal to 2.75 bushels, or 124 pounds of rice. At a later date, Zeng Guofan estimated one *dan* of rice per day as being the amount necessary to sustain 100 soldiers. At that rate, the 3,000 *dan* would last 30,000 people ten days at normal rations; see Zeng Guofan, family letter of TZ1/9/2 (October 24, 1861), in ibid., p. 2624.

57. Zeng Guofan, family letter of XF11/5/6 (June 13, 1861), in ibid., p. 2516.

58. "The Prince of Kung to Mr. Bruce," July 18, 1861, in *Papers Relating to the Rebellion in China, and Trade in the Yang-tze-kiang River*, pp. 67–68; Bruce to Medhurst, Beijing, July 23, 1861, in ibid., p. 68; quotation is

from Bruce to Russell, Beijing, July 30, 1861, ibid., pp. 64–65; Jen Yu-wen, on p. 426 of *The Taiping Revolutionary Movement*, claims the British actually set up a naval blockade alongside Zeng's navy, but he gives no source for the claim.

59. William James Hail, *Tseng Kuo-fan and the Taiping Rebellion, with a Short Sketch of His Later Career* (New Haven, Conn.: Yale University Press, 1927), p. 233, citing unnamed memorial.

60. Zeng Guofan, family letter of XF11/3/24, in *ZGFQJ*, vol. 7, pp. 2483–2484, quotation on p. 2484.

61. Hail, *Tseng Kuo-fan*, p. 234.

62. Jen, *The Taiping Revolutionary Movement*, p. 422; see also Zeng Guofan, family letter of XF11/5/30 (June 30, 1861), in *ZGFQJ*, vol. 7, p. 2526.

63. Based on descriptions in Zhu Hongzhang, *Cong rong jilüe*, pp. 76–77; also Zhao Liewen, *Neng jingju riji*, entry for XF11/8/13 (September 17, 1861), in *TPTG*, vol. 7, p. 107; Long Shengyun, *Xiangjun shigao*, p. 262; the entry on Chen Yucheng (the Brave King) in Arthur W. Hummel, ed., *Eminent Chinese of the Ch'ing Period (1644–1912)* (Taipei: Cheng-wen reprint, 1967), p. 106 says six days and nights of fighting and gives the starting date of August 21, but according to Zhu Hongzhang, the fighting began in earnest on August 27 (7/22 on the lunar calendar) and ended the night of September 3 (7/29).

64. Long Shengyun, *Xiangjun shigao*, p. 262, n. 2; Augustus Lindley, Zhu Hongzhang, and Wang Kaiyun all said the garrison had left the city (by agreement, according to Lindley; by tunnel, according to Zhu Hong-zhang), contradicting Zeng Guofan's report that they defeated the city by blowing up the wall. Zhao Liewen says the Hunan Army dug a tun-nel but it wasn't complete until early September (the end of the sev-enth lunar month), and the army used it to enter the city only after the fighting was already done. He describes the chained gunners and says there was no resistance when the Hunan Army entered. See *Neng jingju riji* (Zhao Liewen's diary), entry for XF11/8/13 (September 17, 1861), in *TPTG*, vol. 7, p. 108.

65. Zhao Liewen, *Neng jingju riji*, entry for XF11/8/13 (September 17, 1861), in *TPTG*, vol. 7, pp. 107–108.

66. Zeng Guofan, family letter of XF11/5/18 (June 25, 1861), *ZGFQJ*, vol. 7, p. 2523.

67. Jian Youwen, *Taiping Tianguo quanshi* (Hong Kong: Mengjin Shuwu, 1962), vol. 3, p. 1893, concludes that everyone inside was killed, regard-less of age or gender; Long Shengyun says the women were carried

off and all of the men and boys slaughtered (*Xiangjun shigao,* p. 262); Zhao Liewen says the children were spared and more than ten thousand women were carried off by the soldiers, while several dozen committed suicide (*Neng jingju riji,* XF11/8/13, in *TPTG,* vol. 7, p. 108).

CHAPTER 10: HEAVEN AND EARTH

1. David Field Rennie, *Peking and the Pekingese: During the First Year of the British Embassy at Peking,* 2 vols. (London: John Murray, 1865), vol. 1, pp. 267–269; for further rumors of the emperor's death in Beijing that August, see ibid., pp. 317, 335.
2. "Pinghu biji," (Pinghu diary), in *TPTG,* vol. 5, p. 31.
3. Zhao Liewen, *Neng jingju riji,* entry for XF11/8/1 (September 5, 1861), in *TPTG,* vol. 7, p. 96.
4. Zeng Guofan, diary entry for XF11/7/30 (September 4, 1861), in *ZGFQJ,* vol. 10, pp. 3684–3685.
5. Zeng Guofan, diary entry for XF11/8/10 (September 14, 1861), in ibid., p. 3687.
6. Zeng Guofan, diary entry for XF11/8/10 (September 14, 1861), in ibid., pp. 3687–3688.
7. Evelyn S. Rawski, *The Last Emperors: A Social History of Qing Imperial Institutions* (Berkeley: University of California Press, 1998), pp. 140–141; three-quarters of his consorts never conceived at all.
8. Hong Rengan, "Proclamations on the Extermination of Demons," trans. in Franz Michael, *The Taiping Rebellion: History and Documents* (Seattle: University of Washington Press, 1966–1971), vol. 3, pp. 859–869, quotation on p. 863, romanization and capitalization modified.
9. Rennie, *Peking and the Pekingese,* vol. 1, p. 173.
10. Ibid., pp. 173–174.
11. Parkes to Bruce, Beijing, May 10, 1861, in *Papers Relating to the Rebellion in China, and Trade in the Yang-tze-kiang River* (London: Harrison and Sons, 1862), pp. 23–35; quotations on p. 32.
12. Hong Rengan, letter to Li Xiucheng, in *Hong Rengan xuanji,* ed. Yangzhou Shifan Xueyuan Zhongwen Xi (Beijing: Zhonghua Shuju, 1978), p. 56.
13. Michael, *The Taiping Rebellion,* vol. 3, p. 1526.
14. Xu Chuanyi, *Taiping Tianguo Anhui sheng shigao* (Draft history of Anhui province during the Taiping Rebellion) (Hefei: Anhui Renmin Chubanshe, 1991), p. 283.

15. Michael, *The Taiping Rebellion,* vol. 3, p. 969.

16. Ibid., vol. 1, pp. 159–160.

17. Thomas W. Blakiston, *Five Months on the Yang-tsze* (London: John Murray, 1862), p. 49.

18. Ibid., p. 52.

19. Ibid., p. 54.

20. Ibid., pp. 52–54.

21. Jane R. Edkins, *Chinese Scenes and People, With Notices of Christian Missions and Missionary Life* . . . (London, James Nisbet & Co., 1863), pp. 201–206, for quotations in this paragraph and following.

22. Ibid., pp. 29–33.

23. Griffith John, letter to the Rev. Dr. Tidman, Hankow, November 5, 1861, reprinted in *The Missionary Magazine and Chronicle,* no. 309, new ser., no. 26 (February 1862): 36–37.

24. Parkes to Bruce, Beijing, May 10, 1861, in *Papers Relating to the Rebellion in China, and Trade in the Yang-tze-kiang River,* quotation on p. 35.

25. Roberts, letter to *The North-China Herald,* March 30, 1861; quoted in Prescott Clarke and J. S. Gregory, *Western Reports on the Taiping: A Selection of Documents* (Honolulu: University Press of Hawaii, 1992), p. 263.

26. "Our editorial of last week . . . ," *The North-China Herald,* September 14, 1861.

27. Introduction to letter from I. J. Roberts, *China Mail,* no. 856 (July 11, 1861).

28. "The Taeping Rebels," *The Louisville Daily Journal,* May 8, 1862, for example, says that "it has been considered strange that the Christian nations of the Western world have not shown them more practical sympathy. This feeling has largely prevailed in our own country, in consequence of the well-known fact that the missionary, Mr. Roberts, who was the instructor of the 'Heavenly Ruler,' is an American."

29. Letter from I. J. Roberts, *China Mail,* no. 856 (July 11, 1861).

30. Rawski, *The Last Emperors,* p. 103.

31. Ibid., p. 127.

32. Arthur W. Hummel, ed., *Eminent Chinese of the Ch'ing Period (1644–1912)* (Taipei: Chengwen reprint, 1967), p. 668; Rawski, *The Last Emperors,* p.103.

33. Rennie, *Peking and the Pekingese,* vol. 2, pp. 141, 125.

34. Lolan Wang Grady, "The Career of I-Hsin, Prince Kung, 1858–1880: A Case Study of the Limits of Reform in the Late Ch'ing," Ph.D. diss., University of Toronto, 1980, p. 101.

35. Rennie, *Peking and the Pekingese*, vol. 2, pp. 128–129.

36. Ibid., vol. 2, p. 160.

37. Hummel, *Eminent Chinese*, p. 668; William Robson, *Griffith John: Founder of the Hankow Mission Central China* (London: S. W. Partridge & Co., n.d. [1901?]), p. 60, citing eyewitness account of Lockart; see also Rennie, *Peking and the Pekingese*, vol. 2, pp. 125–166.

38. Rennie, *Peking and the Pekingese*, vol. 2, p. 134.

39. William Minns Tileston, letter to his mother, Shanghai, October 18, 1860, Massachusetts Historical Society, Boston, Mass.

40. Edward Bowra, diary, at School of Oriental and African Studies (PPMS 69, Bowra, Box 1, Folder 6), accessed via Adam Matthew Digital, "China: Trade, Politics and Culture, 1793–1980," entry for June 1, 1863 (manuscript pp. 35–36).

41. Josiah Cox, "A Missionary Visit to Nanking and the 'Shield King,'" in *The Wesleyan Missionary Notices*, no. 100, 3rd ser. (April 1862): 61–66, quotation on p. 62.

42. "Extract from the Journal of the Rev. Josiah Cox," in *The Wesleyan Missionary Notices*, no. 101, 3rd ser. (May 1862): 69–76, quotation on p. 70.

43. Cox, "A Missionary Visit to Nanking and the 'Shield King,'" p. 62.

44. Ibid., p. 65; Since J. S. Gregory's 1956 dissertation, Western historians have consistently misattributed this quotation to Hong Rengan himself—it was a sign of his family's protective concern, not of his own shift in policy.

45. Ibid., p. 62, emphasis added.

CHAPTER 11: CROSSINGS

1. "The New War in China," *The London Review*, July 12, 1862, p. 27.

2. Eugene A. Brady, "A Reconsideration of the Lancashire 'Cotton Famine,'" *Agricultural History* 37, no. 3 (July 1963): 156–162, see p. 159.

3. "A History of the External Trade of China, 1834–81," in *Decennial Reports on the Trade, Navigation, Industries, etc., of the Ports Open to Foreign Commerce, and on Conditions and Development of the Treaty Port Provinces*, 5th issue (1922–1931) (Shanghai: Statistical Department of the Inspectorate of Customs, 1933), vol. 1, pp. 1–144; see p. 56; also see chart in Brady, "A Reconsideration," p. 159.

4. Brady, "A Reconsideration,'" pp. 156–158.

5. "A History of the External Trade of China, 1834–81," pp. 61 and 77.

6. David McLean, letter of January 10, 1863, from Shanghai. In letter book held at School of Oriental and African Studies, University of London (MS380401/11), p. 26. Accessed via Adam Matthew Digital, "China: Trade, Politics and Culture, 1793–1980."

7. Quoted in James McPherson, *Battle Cry of Freedom: The Civil War Era* (New York: Oxford University Press, 1988), p. 388.

8. *The Times*, May 13, 1861 (editorial beginning "Every successive mail brings proof of the soundness of our latest policy towards China").

9. *Hansard's Parliamentary Debates* (London: T. C. Hansard), May 31, 1861, vol. 163, cc. 379–381.

10. Ibid., cc. 381–383.

11. Ibid., c. 391.

12. Ibid., cc. 383–385.

13. Ibid., c. 386.

14. Ibid., c. 388.

15. Ibid., c. 401.

16. *The Times*, June 3, 1861 (editorial beginning "Our House of Commons, which claims to unite all power and all dexterity").

17. C. A. Curwen, *Taiping Rebel: The Deposition of Li Hsiu-Ch'eng* (Cambridge, England: Cambridge University Press, 1977), p. 258, n. 14.

18. Mao Jiaqi, *Guo zhu "Taiping Tianguo shishi rizhi" jiaobu* (Emendations to Guo [Tingyi's] *Daily Calendar of Events in the Taiping Heavenly Kingdom*) (Taipei: Taiwan Shangwu Yinshuguan, 2001), p. 168.

19. Curwen, *Taiping Rebel*, p. 128.

20. Shen Zi, *Bikou riji* (A diary of avoiding the bandits), entry for XF11/12/7 (January 7, 1862), in *TPTG*, vol. 8, p. 77.

21. Shen Zi, *Bikou riji*, entry for XF11/12/6 (January 5, 1862), in *TPTG*, vol. 8, p. 77.

22. Curwen, *Taiping Rebel*, p. 129.

23. Ibid., p. 260, n. 26, quoting Xu Yaoguang.

24. Bruce to Consul Sinclair, Tianjin, December 21, 1860, in *Papers Relating to the Rebellion in China, and Trade in the Yang-tze-kiang River* (London: Harrison and Sons, 1862), p. 2.

25. Bruce to Hope, Tianjin, December 23, 1860, in ibid.

26. Hope, "Orders Addressed to Captain Dew," Nagasaki, May 8, 1861, in ibid., p. 16.

27. Russell to Bruce, July 24, 1861 and August 8, 1861, in ibid., pp. 23 and 46.

28. Bruce to Hope, Beijing, June 16, 1861, in ibid., pp. 56–59.

29. Mao Jiaqi, *Guo zhu*, p. 167.

30. Hope to Bruce, Hong Kong, July 11, 1861, in *Papers Relating to the Rebellion in China, and Trade in the Yang-tze-kiang River,* p. 60.

31. "Memorandum by Mr. Alabaster, on the condition of the Tae-ping Insurgents at Cha-poo," in ibid., pp. 61–62.

32. Harvey to Bruce, Ningbo, June 18, 1861, in ibid., p. 66; specifically: "Captain Dew informed the Taoutae that he had been instructed by the Admiral to examine and concert measures for the defence of Ningpo against any rebel attacks; and that though not actually in possession of orders to resist an onslaught on the city, he had no doubt that he would find those orders at Shanghae on his return."

33. Hope to Admiralty, Shanghai, December 22, 1861, in ibid., pp. 90–91.

34. Harvey to Bruce, Ningbo, November 12, 1861, in ibid., p. 83.

35. The Ven. Archdeacon Moule, *Personal Recollections of the T'ai-p'ing Rebellion, 1861–1863* (Shanghai: Shanghai Mercury Office, 1898), pp. 8–9.

36. "Memorandum by Mr. Parkes on the Capture of Ningpo by the Rebels," in *Papers Relating to the Rebellion in China, and Trade in the Yang-tze-kiang River,* pp. 92–96, see esp. p. 94.

37. Moule, *Personal Recollections,* p. 11.

38. Harvey to Hammond, Ningbo, December 18, 1861, in *Papers Relating to the Rebellion in China, and Trade in the Yang-tze-kiang River,* p. 89.

39. Moule, *Personal Recollections,* p. 9.

40. W. H. (William Henry) Sykes, *The Taeping Rebellion in China: Its Origin, Progress, and Present Condition* (London: Warren Hall & Co., 1863), p. 34.

41. Harvey to Hammond, Ningbo, January 3, 1862, in *Papers Relating to the Rebellion in China, and Trade in the Yang-tze-kiang River,* p. 106.

42. Quoted in Stephen Uhalley, Jr., "The Taipings at Ningpo: The Significance of a Forgotten Event," *The Journal of the Hong Kong Branch of the Royal Asiatic Society,* vol. 11 (1971): 17–32, p. 20; also in Sykes, *The Taeping Rebellion in China,* p. 19.

43. Harvey to Bruce, Ningbo, December 31, 1861, in *Papers Relating to the Rebellion in China, and Trade in the Yang-tze-kiang River,* pp. 107–108.

44. Lindesay Brine, *The Taeping Rebellion in China: A Narrative of its Rise and Progress* (London: John Murray, 1862), p. 333.

45. Bruce to Russell, Beijing, January 18, 1862, in *Papers Relating to the Rebellion in China, and Trade in the Yang-tze-kiang River,* p. 143.

46. Vice Admiral Sir J. Hope to the Secretary to the Admiralty, Shanghai, January 9, 1862, in ibid., p. 106.

47. Mail steamer description based on Edward Bowra's diary entry for October 11, 1863.

48. Stanley Lane-Poole, *The Life of Sir Harry Parkes*, 2 vols. (London: Macmillan and Co., 1894), vol. 1, p. 465.

49. "Commander Bingham to the Tae-ping Authorities at Nanking," January 1, 1862, in *Papers Relating to the Rebellion in China, and Trade in the Yang-tze-kiang River*, p. 104.

50. "Our China Correspondence," *The New York Times*, March 29, 1862 (dateline January 17).

CHAPTER 12: THE POINT OF NO RETURN

1. Zhu Dong'an, *Zeng Guofan zhuan* (Biography of Zeng Guofan) (Tianjin: Baihua Wenshu Chubanshe, 2000), p. 188; citing family letters of TZ1/10/16–17 (December 7–8, 1862).

2. Zeng Guofan, family letter of TZ1/3/4 (April 2, 1862), in *ZGFQJ*, vol. 7, p. 2588.

3. Zeng Guofan, memorial dated XF11/10/14 (November 16, 1861), in *ZGFQJ*, vol. 3, p. 962.

4. Zhu Dong'an, *Zeng Guofan zhuan*, p. 187.

5. Arthur W. Hummel, ed., *Eminent Chinese of the Ch'ing Period (1644–1912)* (Taipei: Chengwen reprint, 1967), p. 464.

6. Stanley Spector, *Li Hung-chang and the Huai Army: A Study in Nineteenth-Century Chinese Regionalism* (Seattle: University of Washington Press, 1964), pp. 18–19.

7. Lolan Wang Grady, "The Career of I-Hsin, Prince Kung, 1858–1880: A Case Study of the Limits of Reform in the Late Ch'ing," Ph.D. diss., University of Toronto, 1980, pp. 118–119.

8. Zeng Guofan, diary entry for XF11/11/14 (December 15, 1861), in *ZGFQJ*, vol. 10, p. 3717.

9. Zeng Guofan, diary entry for XF11/11/25 (December 26, 1861), in ibid., pp. 3720–3721.

10. See, for example, Zeng Guofan's memorial dated TZ1/1/10 (February 8, 1862), in *ZGFQJ*, vol. 3, pp. 981–982.

11. Zeng Guofan, memorial dated TZ1/1/22 (February 20, 1862), in ibid., pp. 986–987.

12. For appointments, see Zhu Dong'an, *Zeng Guofan zhuan*, p. 185.

13. "Letter from Rev. I. J. Roberts," January 22, 1862, in *Papers Relating to the Rebellion in China, and Trade in the Yang-tze-kiang River* (London: Harrison and Sons, 1862), pp. 142–143, for this paragraph and following.

14. John A. Rapp, "Clashing Dilemmas: Hong Rengan, Issachar Roberts, and a Taiping 'Murder' Mystery," *Journal of Historical Biography* 4 (Autumn 2008): 27–58; Lindesay Brine, *The Taeping Rebellion in China: A Narrative of Its Rise and Progress* (London: John Murray, 1862), p. 299.

15. "The Confession of Hung Jen-kan," trans. in Franz Michael, *The Taiping Rebellion: History and Documents* (Seattle: University of Washington Press, 1966–1971), vol. 3, pp. 1511–1530, quotation on p. 1527.

16. Brine, *The Taeping Rebellion in China*, p. 299.

17. "The Chinese Foreign Legion," *The North-China Herald*, June 8, 1861; Bruce to Russell, July 3, 1861, in *Papers Relating to the Rebellion in China, and Trade in the Yang-tze-kiang River* (London: Harrison and Sons, 1862), p. 61.

18. "Colonel Ward and the Supposed Privateer Neva," *New York Herald*, November 9, 1861.

19. Whiskey: William Minns Tileston, letter to his mother, Shanghai, September 2, 1861, Massachusetts Historical Society, Boston, Mass.; celebrated fillibuster: "The Rebels at Work in Chinese Waters," *The New York Times*, November 3, 1861; seceding rascals: "Colonel Ward and the Supposed Privateer Neva," *New York Herald*, November 9, 1861.

20. William Minns Tileston, letter, October 5, 1862, Massachusetts Historical Society, Boston, Mass.

21. "From Hong Kong: The End of Our Squadron in the China Seas," *The New York Times*, February 23, 1862.

22. Hallett Abend, *The God from the West* (Garden City, N.Y.: Doubleday, 1947), p. 139; Augustus Allen Hayes, "Another Unwritten Chapter in the Late War," *The International Review*, vol. 11 (1881): pp. 519ff.

23. Holger Cahill, *A Yankee Adventurer: The Story of Ward and the Taiping Rebellion* (New York: Macaulay, 1930), p. 152.

24. William Minns Tileston, letter to his mother, Shanghai, March 5, 1862, Massachusetts Historical Society, Boston, Mass.

25. Extract from "Shanghai Shipping News," January 13, 1862, in *Papers Relating to the Rebellion in China, and Trade in the Yang-tze-kiang River*, pp. 130–131.

26. William Minns Tileston, letter to his mother, Shanghai, June 2, 1862, Massachusetts Historical Society, Boston, Mass.

27. Capt. Willes to Vice-Admiral Sir J. Hope, Wusong, January 20, 1862, in

Papers Relating to the Rebellion in China, and Trade in the Yang-tze-kiang River, p. 139 ("having had an opportunity of seeing the Imperialist troops in the Peiho expedition, I was quite astonished at their apparent equipment and organisation").

28. "A Proclamation Urging the People and Soldiers at Shanghai and Sung-chiang to Surrender," in Michael, *The Taiping Rebellion*, vol. 3, pp. 996–998, quotation on p. 997.

29. Ibid., p. 998.

30. Robertson to Hammond, Canton, January 29, 1862 in *Papers Relating to the Rebellion in China, and Trade in the Yang-tze-kiang River*, p. 129.

31. Extract from *Daily Shipping and Commercial News*, in ibid., pp. 129–130.

32. *The North-China Herald*, February 1, 1862.

33. Jonathan Spence, *God's Chinese Son* (New York: W. W. Norton, 1996), p. 302; The Ven. Archdeacon Moule, *Personal Recollections of the T'ai-p'ing Rebellion, 1861–1863* (Shanghai: Shanghai Mercury Office, 1898), p. 15.

34. "A Remarkable Career: Col. Forrester, Once Commander in a Chinese Army," *The Sarnia Observer*, November 21, 1890; that article says he was from Maine, though another, in the Baltimore *Sun*, says he was from Jefferson County, New York ("Remarkable Romance in Real Life: A New York Sailor Ruling a Chinese City," *The Sun*, August 6, 1862).

35. D. J. MacGowan, "Memoir of Generals Ward and Burgevine, and of the Ever Conquering Legion," *The Far East*, new ser., vol. 2 (January–June 1877): 104; Robert Harry Detrick, "Henry Andrea Burgevine in China: A Biography," Ph.D. diss., Indiana University, 1968, pp. 11–12.

36. Cahill, *A Yankee Adventurer*, pp. 148–149.

37. Caleb Carr, *The Devil Soldier: The American Soldier of Fortune Who Became a God in China* (New York: Random House, 1992), pp. 162–165.

38. John Keegan, *The American Civil War: A Military History* (New York: Knopf, 2009), pp. 7, 44.

39. Richard J. Smith, *Mercenaries and Mandarins: The Ever-Victorious Army in Nineteenth-Century China* (Millwood, N.Y.: KTO Press, 1978), p. 90.

40. "China: Important Defeat of the Rebels," *Otago Witness*, July 26, 1862.

41. "List of Articles Abstracted from a Pocket-Book Found on Board a Vessel with Arms &c., for Sale to the Rebels," in *Further Papers Relating to the Rebellion in China* (London: Harrison and Sons, 1863), p. 103.

42. Mao Jiaqi, *Guo zhu "Taiping Tianguo shishi rizhi" jiaobu* (Emendations to Guo [Tingyi's] *Daily Calendar of Events in the Taiping Heavenly Kingdom*) (Taipei: Taiwan Shangwu Yinshuguan, 2001), p. 172.

43. Report from *Daily Shipping and Commercial News,* February 10, 1862, in *Papers Relating to the Rebellion in China, and Trade in the Yang-tze-kiang River,* p. 155.

44. Mao Jiaqi, *Guo zhu "Taiping Tianguo shishi rizhi" jiaobu,* p. 173.

45. See, e.g., Carr, *Devil Soldier,* pp. 214–215.

46. From the Frederick Townsend Ward Papers, Sterling Memorial Library, Manuscripts and Archives, Yale University, New Haven, Conn.

47. Carr, *Devil Soldier,* pp. 83, 211–212.

48. "Minute of Conference between the Military and Naval Authorities, at Shanghae, February 13, 1862," in *Papers Relating to the Rebellion in China, and Trade in the Yang-tze-kiang River,* p. 149.

49. Hope to Bruce, Shanghai, February 22, 1862, in *Further Papers Relating to the Rebellion in China,* p. 10.

50. Bruce to Hope, Beijing, March 19, 1862, in ibid., pp. 10–11.

51. Zeng Guofan, family letter of XF11/5/1 (June 18, 1861), in *ZGFQJ,* vol. 7, p. 2511.

52. Zeng Guofan, memorial dated TZ1/1/22 (February 20, 1862), in *ZGFQJ,* vol. 3, pp. 987–988.

53. Zeng Guofan, family letter of XF11/12/14 (January 13, 1862), in *ZGFQJ,* vol. 7, p. 2580.

54. Zeng Guofan, family letter of XF11/12/14 (January 13, 1862), in ibid., p. 2581.

55. Medhurst to Bruce, Shanghai, March 21, 1862 (relaying Admiral Hope's words), in *Further Papers Relating to the Rebellion in China (In Continuation of Papers Presented to Parliament, May 2, 1862)* (London: Harrison and Sons, 1862), p. 9.

56. Zeng Guofan, family letter of TZ1/3/4 (April 2, 1862), in *ZGFQJ,* vol. 7, p. 2588.

57. Ibid.

58. Guo Tingyi, *Taiping Tianguo shishi rizhi* (Taipei: Taiwan Shangwu Yinshuguan, 1976), p. 873; on Zeng Guoquan's arrival from Hunan and subsequent departure, see Zeng Guofan's diary entries for TZ1/2/15 and TZ1/2/24 (March 15 and 24, 1862), in *ZGFQJ,* vol. 10, pp. 3745, 3747.

59. Medhurst to Hope, Shanghai, February 19, 1862, in *Papers Relating to the Rebellion in China, and Trade in the Yang-tze-kiang River,* pp. 152–153.

60. Extract from the *North China and Japan Market Report,* February 21, 1862, in *Papers Relating to the Rebellion in China, and Trade in the Yang-tze-kiang River,* p. 154.

61. Sir William Laird Clowes, *The Royal Navy: A History from the Earliest*

Times to the Death of Queen Victoria, 7 vols. (London: Sampson Low, Marston and Company, 1903), vol. 7, p. 165.

62. William J. Boone to Samuel Wells Williams, March 17, 1862. Samuel Wells Williams Family Papers, Sterling Memorial Library, Manuscripts and Archives, Yale University, New Haven, Conn.

63. "Present State of the Rebellion in China," *New-York Evangelist,* July 3, 1862.

64. Quoted in Augustus F. Lindley, *Ti-Ping Tien-Kwoh; The History of the Ti-ping Revolution* (London: Day & Son, Ltd., 1866), p. 454.

65. Harvey to Bruce, Ningbo, May 9, 1862, in *Further Papers Relating to the Rebellion in China,* p. 37; Moule, *Personal Recollections,* p. 17.

66. "China (from Our Own Correspondent)," *The Times,* May 26, 1862 (dateline April 15, 1862).

67. *Reports on the Trade at the Ports in China Open by Treaty to Foreign Trade, for the Year 1865* (Shanghai: Imperial Maritime Customs' Press, 1866). The historical chart on p. 10 shows the total trade revenue from Ningbo increasing from 145,264 taels in 1861 to 263,862 taels in 1862.

68. "The Rebellion in China," *The Times,* June 17, 1862.

69. Moule, *Personal Recollections,* p. 17, says three were killed.

70. "Hwang, General Commanding in Ningpo, to Commander Craigie," in W. H. Sykes, *The Taeping Rebellion in China: Its Origin, Progress, and Present Condition* (London: Warren Hall & Co., 1863), p. 37; also in *Further Papers Relating to the Rebellion in China,* p. 44.

71. James Hope, "Orders Issued to Captain Dew," April 25, 1862, in *Further Papers Relating to the Rebellion in China,* pp. 44–45.

72. "Captain Dew to Generals Hwang and Fau," Ningbo, April 27, 1862, in ibid., p. 48.

73. "Captain Dew to the Officer in Command of Tae-ping Troops, Ningpo," Ningbo, April 28, 1861, in ibid., p. 46.

74. Russell to Admiralty, March 11, 1862, in *Papers Relating to the Rebellion in China, and Trade in the Yang-tze-kiang River,* p. 111.

75. Ibid., romanization modified.

76. The Hong Kong correspondent of *The Times* reported on April 27 that news of the new orders had come in "the mail just received," which would have been a few days previous, meaning the orders would have reached Hope shortly before Dew left for Ningbo. See "China," *The Times,* June 12, 1862.

77. "Generals Hwang and Fau to Captain Dew," in *Further Papers Relating to the Rebellion in China,* p. 49.

78.   78. Dew to Hope, Ningbo, May 7, 1862, in *Further Papers Relating to the Rebellion in China*, p. 50.

79.   Ibid.

80.   "Captain Dew and Lieutenant Kenney to the Tae-ping Chiefs," in *Further Papers Relating to the Rebellion in China*, p. 51.

81.   Sykes, *The Taeping Rebellion in China*, p. 43. See also Lord Naas's speech in the House of Commons, July 6, 1863, referring to Capt. Dew and Apak: "it appeared rather a curious thing that a British captain should enter into communication with one whom, in the pursuit of his well-known calling if he was caught outside the bar at Shanghai, he would have felt bound to hang." *Hansard's Parliamentary Debates* (London: T. C. Hansard), July 6, 1863, vol. 172, cc. 279–280.

82.   Harvey to Bruce, Ningbo, May 9, 1862, in *Further Papers Relating to the Rebellion in China*, pp. 37–39, quotation on p. 38.

CHAPTER 13: VAMPIRES

1.   The Ven. Archdeacon Moule, *Personal Recollections of the T'ai-p'ing Rebellion, 1861–1863* (Shanghai: Shanghai Mercury Office, 1898), pp. 19–20.

2.   *The China Mail*, May 22, 1862; quoted in Augustus F. Lindley, *Ti-Ping Tien-Kwoh; The History of the Ti-ping Revolution* (London: Day & Son, Ltd., 1866), p. 536.

3.   Stephen Uhalley, Jr., "The Taipings at Ningpo: The Significance of a Forgotten Event," *Journal of the Hong Kong Branch of the Royal Asiatic Society* 11 (1971): 17–32, see pp. 27–28.

4.   Quoted in Lindley, *Ti-Ping Tien-Kwoh*, pp. 537–538.

5.   "Events in China," *The New York Times*, July 29, 1862.

6.   "The Rebellion in China," *The New York Times*, August 14, 1862.

7.   "Travels in China from Ningpo Through the Silk Country into the Fai Chow Tea District and on to Shanghai," originally published in the Hong Kong *Daily Press*, July 10, 1862; reprinted in W. H. Sykes, *The Taeping Rebellion in China: Its Origin, Progress, and Present Condition* (London: Warren Hall & Co., 1863), pp. 49–53.

8.   Karl Marx, "Chinese Affairs," *Die Presse*, July 7, 1862; reprinted in Schlomo Avineri, ed., *Karl Marx on Colonialism and Modernization* (New York: Anchor, 1969), pp. 442–444.

9.   *The Times*, May 16, 1862 (editorial beginning "Nature has been so indul-

gent as to create for even the most noxious and ferocious of her off-spring some humble friend").

10. *The Times,* June 14, 1862 (editorial beginning "What is going on in China?").

11. Ibid.

12. "Operations in China," *The Times,* July 16, 1862; Edward Forester, "Personal Recollections of the Tai-ping Rebellion," second of three installments, *Cosmopolitan* 22, no. 1 (November 1896): 34–38, p. 35 on size of Ward's force present.

13. Sir William Laird Clowes, *The Royal Navy: A History from the Earliest Times to the Death of Queen Victoria* (London: Sampson Low, Marston, and Company, 1903), vol. 7, p. 166.

14. Forester, "Personal Recollections of the Tai-ping Rebellion," pp. 35–36.

15. Ibid., pp. 36–37.

16. Sykes, *The Taeping Rebellion in China,* pp. 84–85.

17. Vice Admiral Sir J. Hope to the Secretary to the Admiralty, Shanghai, October 20, 1862, in *Further Papers Relating to the Rebellion in China* (London: Harrison and Sons, 1863), pp. 112–114.

18. W. H. Sykes, letter to the editor of the London *Daily News,* September 10, 1862; reprinted in Sykes, *The Taeping Rebellion in China,* pp. 46–47.

19. "The True Danger in China," *The Economist,* August 2, 1862.

20. "The Crisis of the American War," *Blackwood's Edinburgh Magazine* 92, no. 565 (November 1862), p. 636; James McPherson, *Battle Cry of Freedom* (New York: Oxford University Press, 1988), pp. 552–553.

21. "Bull in China," *Vanity Fair,* August 30, 1862, p. 107.

22. "English Consistency," *The Saturday Evening Post,* August 9, 1862, p. 2.

23. As to Legge's reputation back home at this time, on July 6, 1863, Lord Naas referred to him in the House of Commons as "a man who knows China better almost than any other Englishman, and who is a perfectly unbiassed witness." *Hansard's Parliamentary Debates* (London: T. C. Hansard), July 6, 1863, vol. 172, c. 294.

24. Holger Cahill, *A Yankee Adventurer: The Story of Ward and the Taiping Rebellion* (New York: Macaulay, 1930), pp. 193–194; Hallett Abend, *The God from the West* (Garden City, N.Y.: Doubleday, 1947), p. 180; Robert Harry Detrick, "Henry Andrea Burgevine in China: A Biography," Ph.D. diss., Indiana University, 1968, pp. 71–72.

25. *The Spectator* of June 21, 1862, quoted in W. H. Sykes, letter of October 17, 1862, to the editor of the London *Daily News,* in Sykes, *The Taeping Rebellion in China,* p. 62.

26. The entry for James Hope in the *Oxford Dictionary of National Biography* refers to "reservations about his diplomatic skills" after his China service; as to the undesirability of replacing him, see John Pakington's speech in the House of Commons on February 24, 1863: "Let me ask, is it true, or is it not true, that the gallant admiral who was appointed to succeed Sir James Hope in China has declined the command? There are current rumours that the Board of Admiralty have already applied to some four or five flag officers to succeed the gallant officer, and that no one can he found to undertake it." (*Hansard*, vol. 169, c. 781.)

27. Sir William Laird Clowes, *The Royal Navy: A History from the Earliest Times to the Death of Queen Victoria*, 7 vols. (London: Sampson Low, Marston and Company, 1903), vol. 7, pp. 172–174.

28. Cahill, *A Yankee Adventurer*, p. 194.

29. Jen Yu-wen (Jian Youwen), *The Taiping Revolutionary Movement* (New Haven, Conn.: Yale University Press, 1973), pp. 463–466; "Ying Wang Chen Yucheng koushu" (The Brave King Chen Yucheng's confession), in *TPTG*, vol. 3, p. 267.

30. Jen, *The Taiping Revolutionary Movement*, pp. 410–411.

31. "Ying Wang Chen Yucheng koushu" (The Brave King Chen Yucheng's confession), in *TPTG*, vol. 3, p. 267.

32. Zhu Hongzhang, *Cong rong jilüe* (Zhu Hongzhang's account of the campaign against the rebels) (Taipei: Wenhai Chubanshe, 1968, reprint of 1890 original), p. 78.

33. "The Confession of Hung Jen-kan," trans. in Franz Michael, *The Taiping Rebellion: History and Documents* (Seattle: University of Washington Press, 1966–1971), vol. 3, pp. 1511–1530, quotation on p. 1528.

34. C. A. Curwen, *Taiping Rebel: The Deposition of Li Hsiu-Ch'eng* (Cambridge, England: Cambridge University Press, 1977), p. 136.

35. Zeng Guofan, memorial dated TZ1/5/17 (June 13, 1862), in *ZGFQJ*, vol. 3, p. 1036.

36. Wang Kaiyun, *Xiangjun zhi* (Annals of the Hunan Army) (Yuelu Shushe edition, 1983), p. 63; Guo Tingyi, *Taiping Tianguo shishi rizhi* (Daily calendar of events in the Taiping Heavenly Kingdom) (Taipei: Taiwan Shangwu Yinshuguan, 1976), pp. 902–903.

37. Based on personal observation and also a description by Charles Gordon in Curwen, *Taiping Rebel*, p. 298.

38. Zeng Guofan, letters to brothers of TZ1/5/20 and TZ1/6/2 (June 16 and 28, 1862), in *ZGFQJ*, vol. 7, pp. 2603, 2606.

39. Zeng Guofan, family letter of TZ1/9/11 (November 2, 1862), in ibid., pp. 2628–2629.

40. Zeng Guofan, letter to his brother of TZ1/9/29 (November 20, 1862), in ibid., p. 2638.

41. Zeng Guofan, memorial dated XF11/7/18 (August 23, 1861), in *ZGFQJ*, vol. 3, p. 950.

42. Zeng Guofan, memorial dated XF11/7/18 (August 23, 1861), in ibid., p. 948.

43. Ibid.

44. Gideon Chen, *Tseng Kuo-fan: Pioneer Promoter of the Steamship in China* (Beijing: Yenching University Economics Department, 1935), pp. 37–38.

45. Zeng Guofan, diary entry for TZ1/7/4 (July 30, 1862), in *ZGFQJ*, vol. 10, p. 3786; Chen, *Tseng Kuo-fan*, p. 41.

46. Hosea Ballou Morse, *The International Relations of the Chinese Empire*, vol. 2: *The Period of Submission, 1861–1893* (London: Longmans, Green, and Co., 1918), p. 35.

47. Andrew Wilson, *The "Ever-Victorious Army": A History of the Chinese Campaign under Lt.-Col. C. G. Gordon . . .* (Edinburgh: William Blackwood and Sons, 1868), p. 260.

48. Horatio Nelson Lay, *Our Interests in China: A Letter to the Right Hon. Earl Russell* (London: Robert Hardwicke, 1864), p. 19.

49. Ibid., p. 20.

50. Samuel Wells Williams, *The Middle Kingdom* (New York: Charles Scribner's Sons, 1883), vol. 2, p. 694.

51. "Memorandum," enclosure in doc. 151, in Ian Nish, ed., *British Documents on Foreign Affairs: Reports and Papers from the Foreign Office Confidential Print* (Frederick, Md.: University Publications of America, 1994), Part I, Series E (Asia, 1860–1914), vol. 19, p. 207.

52. The text of the agreement is reprinted in Morse, *The International Relations of the Chinese Empire*, vol. 2, p. 37.

53. Frank J. Merli, *The Alabama, British Neutrality, and the American Civil War* (Bloomington: Indiana University Press, 2004); see chap. 7, "The Confederacy's Chinese Fleet, 1861–1867," on Bulloch and Lay.

54. "Punch's Essence of Parliament," *Punch*, August 9, 1862, p. 52.

55. "Events at Ningpo," a letter to the editor of the London *Daily News*, dated August 29, 1862; reprinted in Sykes, *The Taeping Rebellion in China*, pp. 35–46, quotation on p. 45.

56. *Hansard's Parliamentary Debates* (London: T. C. Hansard), February 5, 1863, vol. 169, c. 81.

57. Ibid., c. 86.

58. Ibid., c. 99.

59. *Hansard,* February 9, 1863, vol. 169, c. 187.

60. *The Times,* December 12, 1862 (editorial beginning "The Royal Geographical Society").

61. Ibid.

62. Horatio Nelson Lay, *Our Interests in China,* p. 15; Sherard Osborn, "Progress in China, Part II: The Taepings and Their Remedy," *Blackwood's Edinburgh Magazine* 93, no. 568 (February 1863): 133–148, see p. 147.

63. "The Anglo-Chinese Expedition," *The Times,* May 8, 1863; *The Times* reported that the ship "was unanimously pronounced by all the naval and scientific authorities present to be one of the fastest vessels afloat." Anson Burlingame wrote to Secretary of State Seward that "One of the vessels, I am told, is the fastest war vessel in the world"; see Burlingame to Seward, November 7, 1863, in *Papers Relating to Foreign Affairs, Accompanying the Annual Message of the President to the Second Session, Thirty-Eighth Congress,* Part III (Washington, D.C.: Government Printing Office, 1865), p. 345.

CHAPTER 14: FLOWERING RAIN

1. Yu Xingmin, *Shanghai, 1862 nian* (Shanghai, 1862) (Shanghai: Renmin Chubanshe, 1991), p. 14; Earl Cranston, "Shanghai in the Taiping Period," *Pacific Historical Review* 5, no. 2 (June 1936): 147–160, see p. 155.

2. "Medical Statistical Returns of the East Indian and China Station," in *A Copy of the Statistical Report of the Health of the Navy, for the Year 1862* (Return to an Order of the Honourable The House of Commons, June 26, 1865), pp. 204–248, see pp. 232–233; Kerrie L. MacPherson, *A Wilderness of Marshes: The Origins of Public Health in Shanghai, 1843–1893* (New York: Oxford University Press, 1987), p. 81.

3. Edward Bowra, diary entry for July 29, 1862 (manuscript p. 72), School of Oriental and African Studies, accessed via Adam Matthew Digital, "China: Trade, Politics and Culture, 1793–1980."

4. James Henderson, *Memorials of James Henderson, MD, . . . Medical Missionary to China* (London: James Nisbet and Co., 1867), p. 147; unburied bodies, boxes and straw: "Medical Statistical Returns of the East Indian and China Station," p. 229; three thousand per day: MacPherson, *A Wilderness of Marshes,* p. 30, citing report of Robert Alexander Jamieson.

5. MacPherson, *A Wilderness of Marshes*, p. 280, n. 50.

6. David Field Rennie, *The British Arms in North China and Japan: Peking 1860; Kagosima 1862* (London: John Murray, 1864), p. 316.

7. Wang Kaiyun, *Xiangjun zhi* (Annals of the Hunan Army) (Changsha: Yuelu Shushe, 1983), p. 64 on the epidemic moving through the Hunan Army in August.

8. Zeng Guofan, memorial dated TZ1/8/29 (September 22, 1862), in *ZGFQJ*, vol. 3, pp. 1065–1066.

9. Zeng Guofan, memorial dated TZ1/7/21 (August 22, 1862), in ibid., p. 1053.

10. Rennie, *The British Arms in North America*, p. 317.

11. Zeng Guofan, instructions from the Anqing Headquarters, in *ZGFQJ*, vol. 5 (pidu), p. 1699.

12. Wang Kaiyun, *Xiangjun zhi*, p. 64.

13. Zeng Guofan, diary entry for TZ1/9/1 (October 23, 1862), in *ZGFQJ*, vol. 10, p. 3814.

14. "Medical Statistical Returns of the East Indian and China Station," p. 226: "This disease, it would appear, had been prevailing to a large extent for some time amongst the Chinese rebels."

15. *Correspondence between Military Authorities at Shanghai and War Office Respecting the Insalubrity of Shanghai as a Station for European Troops* (Parliamentary Papers, 1863 [466]), p. 17; *The British Medical Journal*, vol. 2 for 1864 (July–December), issue of September 24, 1864, p. 378: "It is estimated that between Shanghai and Scon-Kiang, distant some 40 miles, about an eighth of the Chinese population died from cholera in 1862."

16. Zeng Guofan, memorial dated TZ1/5/17 (June 13, 1862), in *ZGFQJ*, vol. 3, p. 1037.

17. Jen Yu-wen (Jian Youwen), *The Taiping Revolutionary Movement* (New Haven, Conn.: Yale University Press, 1973), p. 519.

18. Wang Dun, *Xiangjun shi* (A history of the Hunan Army) (Changsha: Hunan Daxue Chubanshe, 2007), p. 553.

19. Long Shengyun, *Xiangjun shigao* (Draft history of the Hunan Army) (Chengdu: Sichuan Renmin Chubanshe, 1990), p. 412.

20. Wang Dun, *Xiangjun shi*, p. 553.

21. Zhu Dong'an, *Zeng Guofan zhuan* (Biography of Zeng Guofan) (Tianjin: Baihua Wenshu Chubanshe, 2000), p. 193.

22. Wang Kaiyun, *Xiangjun zhi*, pp. 62–63.

23. Zhao Liewen, *Neng jing ju riji*, entry for TZ1/6/20 (July 16, 1862), in *TPTG*, vol. 7, p. 153.

24. Wang Kaiyun, *Xiangjun zhi*, p. 63.

25. Zeng Guofan, diary entry for TZ1/8/27 (October 20, 1862), in *ZGFQJ*, vol. 10, pp. 3812–3813.

26. Zeng Guofan, family letter of TZ1/9/2 (October 24, 1862), in *ZGFQJ*, vol. 7, p. 2624; he writes that they will need 1,000 *dan* per day to supply 100,000 soldiers. One *dan* is equivalent to 2.75 bushels, or about 124 pounds of rice.

27. Zeng Guofan, diary entry for TZ1/9/7 (October 29, 1862), in *ZGFQJ*, vol. 10, p. 3816.

28. Zeng Guofan, diary entry for TZ1/9/2 (October 24, 1862), in ibid., p. 3814, mentions bombs and explosive shells; Zeng Guofan, family letter of TZ1/9/4 (October 26, 1862), mentions that they were purchased from foreigners and uses the term *luodi kaihua pao*. *ZGFQJ*, vol. 7, p. 2625.

29. Zeng Guofan, diary entry for TZ1/9/4 (October 26, 1862), in *ZGFQJ*, vol. 10, p. 3815.

30. Zeng Guofan, diary entry for TZ1/9/5 (October 27, 1862), in ibid., p. 3815.

31. Zeng Guofan, diary entry for TZ1/9/17 (November 8, 1862), in ibid., p. 3820; Zeng Guofan, letter to Li Hongzhang TZ1/9/20 (November 11, 1862), in Yuelu Shushe edition of *Zeng Guofan quanji* (Changsha: Yuelu Shushe, 1992), vol. 5, pp. 3176–3177.

32. Zeng Guofan, family letter of TZ1/9/21 (November 12, 1862), in *ZGFQJ*, vol. 7, p. 2634.

33. Long Shengyun, *Xiangjun shigao*, p. 414.

34. Zhu Dong'an, *Zeng Guofan zhuan*, p. 200.

35. Zeng Guofan, letter to Zeng Jize of TZ1/10/4 (November 25, 1862), in *ZGFQJ*, vol. 7, p. 2640.

36. Zhu Hongzhang, *Cong rong jilüe* (Zhu Hongzhang's account of the campaign against the rebels) (Taipei: Wenhai Chubanshe reprint, 1968), p. 89.

37. Zeng Guofan, diary entry for TZ1/10/11 (December 2, 1862), in *ZGFQJ*, vol. 10, p. 3831 (the message got to him on his fifty-second birthday by the lunar calendar).

38. Curwen, *Taiping Rebel: The Deposition of Li Hsiu-Ch'eng* (Cambridge, England: Cambridge University Press, 1977), p. 138.

39. Zeng Guofan, letter to Guoquan of TZ1/10/15 (December 6, 1862), in *ZGFQJ*, vol. 7, p. 2645.

40. Zeng Guofan, family letter of TZ1/10/14 (December 5, 1862), in ibid., p. 2644.

41. Zeng Guofan, letter to Jize of TZ1/10/24 (December 15, 1862), in ibid., p. 2648; quoted in Zhu Dong'an, *Zeng Guofan zhuan,* p. 199; the letter actually says Qimen in the spring of 1860 (Xianfeng 10), which must be an error because he didn't arrive in Qimen until the summer of 1860, and it was the following spring when everything went wrong for him there.

42. Zeng Guofan, diary entry for TZ1/10/24 (December 15, 1862), in *ZGFQJ,* vol. 10, p. 3834.

43. Zeng Guofan, diary entries for TZ1/10/24 to TZ1/11/22 (December 15, 1862–January 11, 1863), in ibid., pp. 3834–3843; Zeng Guofan, letter to Guoquan, TZ1/11/22 (January 11, 1863), in *ZGFQJ,* vol. 7, p. 2655.

CHAPTER 15: BLOOD AND HONOR

1. Edward Forester, "Personal Recollections of the Tai-ping Rebellion," part 3, in *Cosmopolitan* 22, no. 2 (December 1896): 209–216, see p. 216.

2. Ibid.

3. Hosea Ballou Morse, *The International Relations of the Chinese Empire,* vol. 2: *The Period of Submission, 1861–1893* (London: Longmans, Green, and Co., 1918), p. 83.

4. Burlingame to Seward, Beijing, June 20, 1863, in *Papers Relating to Foreign Affairs, Accompanying the Annual Message of the President to the First Session, Thirty-Eighth Congress,* part II (Washington, D.C.: Government Printing Office, 1864), pp. 859–863; on p. 861: "To show me that he did not wish to have an English officer at the head of the Ward force, [Bruce] showed me that he himself had urged the appointment of General Burgevine, an American—a fact I did not know when I wrote my despatch."

5. Thomas Lyster, *With Gordon in China: Letters from Thomas Lyster, Lieutenant Royal Engineers* (London: T. Fisher Unwin, 1891), p. 113; Robert Harry Detrick, "Henry Andrea Burgevine in China: A Biography," Ph.D. diss., Indiana University, 1968, p. 7.

6. Jane Burlingame, letters to her father, April 10, 1863 ("He is a nice man, very different from Ward."), and to her sister, May 22, 1863 ("He is a fine young man, and a general favorite here."), Burlingame Papers, Box 3, Library of Congress, Washington, D.C.

7. Holger Cahill, *A Yankee Adventurer: The Story of Ward and the Taiping Rebellion* (New York: Macauley, 1930), p. 249; Detrick, "Henry Andrea Burgevine in China: A Biography," p. 114.

8. Bruce to Russell, Beijing, March 14, 1863, in *Papers Relating to the Affairs of China (In Continuation of Papers Presented to Parliament in March, 1863)* (London: Harrison and Sons, 1864), p. 67.

9. Jack J. Gerson, *Horatio Nelson Lay and Sino-British Relations, 1854–1864* (Cambridge, Mass.: Harvard East Asian Monographs, 1972), pp. 180–181.

10. Bruce to Major-General Brown, Beijing, October 6, 1863, in *Papers Relating to the Affairs of China (In Continuation of Papers Presented to Parliament in March, 1863)*, p. 163.

11. Per jacket flap copy for Arthur Orrmont, *Chinese Gordon: Hero of Khartoum* (New York: G. P. Putnam's Sons, 1966).

12. Archibald Forbes, *Chinese Gordon: A Succinct Record of His Life* (New York: Funk and Wagnalls, 1885), p. 9.

13. Richard Davenport-Hines, "Gordon, Charles George," *Oxford Dictionary of National Biography* (Oxford, England: Oxford University Press, 2004–2010); lisp: Cahill, *A Yankee Adventurer,* p. 255.

14. The *North-China Herald* editorial is quoted in "British Ambition: New Developments," *The New York Times,* June 15, 1863 (dateline Shanghai, March 15, 1863).

15. "The Conquest of Southern Asia," *The Spectator,* October 31, 1863; reprinted in *The Living Age,* no. 1018 (December 5, 1863): 457–459, quotation on p. 459.

16. 3,000 soldiers: Richard J. Smith, *Mercenaries and Mandarins: The Ever-Victorious Army in Nineteenth-Century China* (Millwood, N.Y.: KTO Press, 1978), p. 118; Jen Yu-wen puts the figure at 5,000 in *The Taiping Revolutionary Movement* (New Haven, Conn.: Yale University Press, 1973), p. 495; William Hail puts it at 2,250 in *Tseng Kuo-fan and the Taiping Rebellion, with a Short Sketch of His Later Career* (New Haven, Conn.: Yale University Press, 1927), p. 264; A. Egmont Hake describes one of the shallow-draft steamers in *Events in the Taeping Rebellion, Being Reprints of Mss. Copied by General Gordon, C.B. in His Own Handwriting . . .* (London: W. H. Allen and Co., 1891), p. 256.

17. Cahill, *A Yankee Adventurer,* p. 256.

18. Had one shot as an example: Hake, *Events in the Taeping Rebellion,* p. 12; paid their arrears: Cahill, *A Yankee Adventurer,* p. 256.

19. "Memorandum Embodying the Substance of Major Gordon's Reports on Affairs at Soochow, Between the 28th of November and 7th December, 1863 (translation of which was forwarded by Sir F. Bruce to the Foreign Board at Peking)," in *Correspondence Relative to Lieut.-Colonel*

Gordon's Position in the Chinese Service (London: Harrison and Sons, 1864), pp. 7–11, quotation on p. 8.

20. Lyster, *With Gordon in China*, p. 110.

21. Jane Burlingame, letter to her sister, Beijing, May 11, 1863, Burlingame Papers, Library of Congress, Washington, D.C.

22. Burlingame to Seward, Beijing, October 27, 1861, reprinted in appendix to Robert S. Rantoul, "Frederick Townsend Ward," in *Historical Collections of the Essex Institute* 44, no. 1 (January 1908): 55–56.

23. Prince Kung to Anson Burlingame, March 16, 1864, in *Papers Relating to Foreign Affairs, Accompanying the Annual Message of the President to the Second Session, Thirty-Eighth Congress,* part III (Washington, D.C.: Government Printing Office, 1865), p. 377.

24. Jane Burlingame, letter to her father, March 28, 1864, Burlingame Papers, Library of Congress.

25. Jane Burlingame, letter to her sister, May 11, 1863, Burlingame Papers, Library of Congress.

26. Demetrius C. Boulger, *The Life of Gordon,* 2 vols. (London: T. Fisher Unwin, 1896), vol. 1, pp. 57–58 on Burgevine's character and temper, p. 90 on leaving for Taiping; also Bruce to Russell, Beijing, September 9, 1863, quoted in Hake, *Events in the Taeping Rebellion,* pp. 298–299.

27. "The Chinese Civil War," *The New York Times,* November 1, 1863.

28. "Important from China," *New York Herald,* November 4, 1863.

29. Quoted in "The War in China," *Chicago Tribune,* November 11, 1863.

30. William James Hail, *Tseng Kuo-fan and the Taiping Rebellion, with a Short Sketch of His Later Career* (New Haven, Conn.: Yale University Press, 1927), pp. 265–266; "Colonel Gordon's Chinese Force," *Blackwood's Edinburgh Magazine* 101, no. 616 (February 1867): 165–191, see p. 189.

31. Bruce to Russell, Beijing, September 9, 1863, in *Papers Relating to the Affairs of China (in Continuation of Papers Presented to Parliament in March, 1863),* pp. 155–156.

32. Quoted in Teng Ssu-yu, *The Taiping Rebellion and the Western Powers: A Comprehensive Survey* (Oxford, England: Clarendon Press, 1971), p. 315.

33. Stanley Spector, *Li Hung-chang and the Huai Army: A Study in Nineteenth-Century Chinese Regionalism* (Seattle: University of Washington Press, 1964), p. 60.

34. Detrick, "Henry Andrea Burgevine in China," p. 109, n. 90 (citing *The North-China Herald* for November 29, 1862).

35. Zeng Guofan, letter to Li Hongzhang of TZ1/9/20 (November 11, 1862), in Yuelu Shuyuan edition of *Zeng Guofan quanji* (Changsha: Yuelu Shuyuan, 1992), vol. 5, pp. 3176–3177.

36. Zeng Guofan, letter to Wu Xu, *ZGFQJ*, vol. 5 (pidu), pp. 1706–1707.

37. Zeng Guofan, diary entry for TZ2/2/20 (April 7, 1863), in *ZGFQJ*, vol. 10, p. 3868.

38. Yung Wing, *My Life in China and America* (New York: Henry Holt & Co., 1909), p. 127ff.; he shipped 65,000 chests at 60 pounds per chest.

39. Ibid., pp. 113–136.

40. Ibid., p. 142.

41. Jonathan Spence, *The Search for Modern China* (New York: W. W. Norton, 1999), p. 196; Yung Wing, *My Life in China and America*, p. 144.

42. Yung Wing, *My Life in China and America*, p. 148.

43. Zhao Liewen, *Neng jingju riji*, entry for TZ3/4/8 (May 13, 1864), in *TPTG*, vol. 10, p. 249.

44. Yung Wing, *My Life in China and America*, p. 144.

45. Ibid., p. 152.

46. Spence, *The Search for Modern China*, p. 196. His offer to join the Union Army was declined, on the grounds that China needed him.

47. Sherard Osborn, "Progress in China, Part 2: The Taepings and Their Remedy," *Blackwood's Edinburgh Magazine* 93, no. 568 (February 1863): 133–148, quotation on p. 148.

48. Zeng Guofan, memorial dated TZ1/12/12 (January 30, 1863), in *ZGFQJ*, vol. 3, p. 1108.

49. Morse, *International Relations of the Chinese Empire*, vol. 2, pp. 38–40.

50. Edward Bowra, diary, at School of Oriental and African Studies (PPMS 69, Bowra, Box 1, Folder 6), accessed via Adam Matthew Digital, "China: Trade, Politics and Culture, 1793–1980," entry for November 5, 1863.

51. "Captain Osborn's Remarks upon Prince Kung's Letter of Instructions," Beijing, September 28, 1863, in *Correspondence Respecting the Fitting Out, Dispatching to China, and Ultimate Withdrawal, of the Anglo-Chinese Fleet under the Command of Captain Sherard Osborn* (London: Harrison and Sons, 1864), pp. 10–12, quotation on p. 11.

52. Hake, *Events in the Taeping Rebellion*, p. 307; Morse, *International Relations of the Chinese Empire*, vol. 2, p. 41; see also Augustus F. Lindley, *Ti-Ping Tien-Kwoh; The History of the Ti-ping Revolution* (London: Day & Son, Ltd., 1866), pp. 577, 579–582, for a scathing (and extremely partisan) description of their behavior in Shanghai.

53. Burlingame to Seward, November 7, 1863, in *Papers Relating to Foreign*

Affairs, Accompanying the Annual Message of the President to the Second Session, Thirty-Eighth Congress, part III (Washington, D.C.: Government Printing Office, 1865), p. 344; also Frank J. Merli, *The Alabama, British Neutrality, and the American Civil War* (Bloomington: Indiana University Press, 2004), pp. 174–175; Morse, *International Relations of the Chinese Empire,* vol. 2, p. 42.

54. "Statement of C. F. Jones, Lately Commanding the Steamer 'Kajow,'" in *Papers Relating to the Affairs of China (in Continuation of Papers Presented to Parliament in March, 1863),* pp. 172–175.

55. Jen, *The Taiping Revolutionary Movement,* p. 501; Lindley, *Ti-Ping Tien-Kwoh,* p. 642.

56. "Statement of C. F. Jones, Lately Commanding the Steamer 'Kajow,'" p. 174.

57. Hake, *Events in the Taeping Rebellion,* p. 332.

58. Morse, *The International Relations of the Chinese Empire,* vol. 2, pp. 88–89; Boulger, *Life of Gordon,* p. 93.

59. Gordon, "Memorandum on the Events Occurring Between the 28th November and 6th December, 1863, inclusive," in *Papers Relating to the Affairs of China (in Continuation of Papers Presented to Parliament in March 1863),* pp. 195–198.

60. Hake, *Events in the Taeping Rebellion,* pp. 375 and 196.

61. Ibid., p. 196.

62. Ibid., p. 490.

63. Ibid., p. 198.

64. Charles Gordon to his mother, December 24, 1863, quoted in Smith, *Mercenaries and Mandarins,* p. 146.

65. "Minutes of a Meeting held at the British Consulate, Shanghae, December 16, 1863," in *Papers Relating to the Affairs of China (in Continuation of Papers Presented to Parliament in March 1863),* pp. 192–193.

66. "The Civil War in China," *The Times,* January 29, 1864 (quoting letter dateline Hong Kong, December 15, 1863).

67. "The Chinese Civil War," *The New York Times,* December 20, 1863.

68. *The Economist,* January 9, 1864.

69. Edward Bowra, diary entry for December 13, 1863 (typescript pp. 78–79).

70. Layard to Lugard, Foreign Office, April 25, 1864, in *Correspondence Relative to Lieut.-Colonel Gordon's Position in the Chinese Service,* p. 17.

71. *Hansard,* May 20, 1864, vol. 175, c. 530.

72. *Hansard,* April 22, 1864, vol. 174, c. 1547.

73. *Hansard,* May 31, 1864, vol. 175, c. 916.

74. Ibid., cc. 965–966.

75. "The Future of China," *The New York Times* editorial, June 26, 1864.

76. *Hansard*, May 31, 1864, vol. 175, c. 968.

77. *Reports on the Trade at the Ports in China Open by Treaty to Foreign Trade, for the Year 1865* (Shanghai: Imperial Maritime Customs' Press, 1866), p. 11, for total trade statistics showing a rise from 2,531,763 taels in FY1861 to 7,728,747 taels in FY1864, an increase of 205 percent.

78. *Hansard*, May 20, 1864, vol. 175, c. 533.

CHAPTER 16: CROSSING THE MOUNTAIN

1. Wilhelm Lobscheid, "The Taipings: A Visit to Nanking, and an Interview with the Kan-Wong," letter to the Hong Kong *Daily Press*, dated June 10, 1863; quoted in Augustus Lindley (Lin-le), *Ti-Ping Tien-Kwoh; The History of the Ti-ping Revolution* (London: Day & Son, Ltd., 1866), pp. 600–601.

2. Hong Renzheng's second confession, in *TPTG*, vol. 2, p. 437; Huang Wenying's confession, trans. in Franz Michael, *The Taiping Rebellion: History and Documents* (Seattle: University of Washington Press, 1966–1971), vol. 3, p. 1534.

3. "The Confession of Hung Jen-kan," trans. in Michael, *The Taiping Rebellion*, vol. 3, pp. 1507–1530, quotation on p. 1513.

4. "Hong Tianguifu qinshu Taiping Tianguo zhuwang mingdan," (The Young Monarch's listing of the names of the Taiping kings) in *TPTG*, vol. 2, pp. 426–427.

5. Zeng Guofan diary entry for TZ2/4/22 (June 8, 1863), in *ZGFQJ*, vol. 10, p. 3890; it went from 30 cash per catty to 120; Charles Gordon, letter to his mother, quoted in Demetrius Boulger, *The Life of Gordon*, 2 vols. (London: T. Fisher Unwin, 1896), vol. 1, p. 118.

6. Zeng Guofan, family letter of TZ2/4/10 (May 27, 1863), in *ZGFQJ*, vol. 7, p. 2702.

7. Zeng Guofan diary entry for TZ2/4/22 (June 8, 1863), in *ZGFQJ*, vol. 10, p. 3890.

8. Zeng Guofan, memorial dated TZ2/2/27 (April 14, 1863), in *ZGFQJ*, vol. 3, p. 1131; also cited and translated in C. A. Curwen, *Taiping Rebel: The Deposition of Li Hsiu-Ch'eng* (Cambridge, England: Cambridge University Press, 1977), p. 275, with a similar remark on scorched-earth tactics.

9. Zeng Guofan, memorial dated TZ2/2/27 (April 14, 1863), in *ZGFQJ*, vol. 3, p. 1131.

10. Long Shengyun, *Xiangjun shigao* (Draft history of the Hunan Army) (Chengdu: Sichuan Renmin Chubanshe, 1990), p. 418.

11. Ibid., p. 419; Lindley, *Ti-Ping Tien-Kwoh*, pp. 621–622; Guo Tingyi, *Taiping Tianguo shishi rizhi* (Daily calendar of events in the Taiping Heavenly Kingdom) (Taipei: Taiwan Shangwu Yinshuguan, 1976), p. 999, gives a date of June 30 and says that 20,000 defenders were annihilated.

12. Long Shengyun, *Xiangjun shigao*, p. 419; Curwen, *Taiping Rebel*, pp. 138–140.

13. Listed in Long Shengyun, *Xiangjun shigao*, p. 419.

14. John Lovelle Withers, "The Heavenly Capital: Nanjing Under the Taiping, 1853–1864," Ph.D. diss., Yale University, 1983, p. 233; according to Withers, there were probably only about 10,000 soldiers in the garrison of Nanjing.

15. Curwen, *Taiping Rebel*, p. 140; Li Xiucheng gives his arrival in Nanjing as early December and blames Li Hongzhang's successful capture of Suzhou on the fact that he was absent from that city. But according to Hong Rengan's fourth confession at Nanchang, it was only after the loss of Suzhou that Li Xiucheng returned to Nanjing. See Hong Rengan, fourth Nanchang confession, in *TPTG*, vol. 2, p. 414.

16. Curwen, *Taiping Rebel*, p. 151.

17. William James Hail, *Tseng Kuo-fan and the Taiping Rebellion, with a Short Sketch of His Later Career* (New Haven, Conn.: Yale University Press, 1927), p. 283.

18. Ibid., p. 285.

19. Zeng Guofan, family letter of TZ3/3/24 (April 29, 1864), in *ZGFQJ*, vol. 8, p. 2800.

20. "The Confession of Hung Jen-kan," trans. in Michael, *The Taiping Rebellion*, vol. 3, p. 1527.

21. Hong Rengan, second Nanchang confession, in *TPTG*, vol. 2, p. 412.

22. Hong Rengan, fourth Nanchang confession, in ibid., p. 414.

23. "The Confession of Hung Jen-kan," trans. in Michael, *The Taiping Rebellion*, vol. 3, p. 1513.

24. Hong Rengan, second confession at Xi Baotian's military camp, in *TPTG*, vol. 2, pp. 401–405, see p. 405.

25. Wang Kaiyun, *Xiangjun zhi* (Annals of the Hunan Army) (Changsha: Yuelu Shushe, 1983), p. 68.

26. Wang Dun, *Xiangjun shi* (A history of the Hunan Army) (Changsha: Hunan Daxue Chubanshe, 2007), p. 175.

27. Wang Kaiyun, *Xiangjun zhi*, p. 68.

28. Long Shengyun, *Xiangjun shigao*, p. 420.

29. Zhao Liewen, *Neng jingju riji*, entry for TZ3/2/23 (March 30, 1864), in *TPTG*, vol. 7, pp. 227–228; Zeng Guofan made an almost identical statement about the necessity of breaking Nanjing before the Hunan Army's supplies ran out in a memorial dated TZ3/4/12 (May 17, 1862). See Wang Dun, *Xiangjun shi*, p. 176.

30. Long Shengyun, *Xiangjun shigao*, p. 420, quoting letter from Peng Yulin; Charles Gordon didn't note any cultivation when he visited in June 1864, but he was at the south end of the city, and as Peng Yulin did see the cultivation (which is confirmed by Hong Rengan's confessions), it must have been going on at the city's northern end near the Yangtze. Gordon's account is reprinted in Curwen, *Taiping Rebel*, pp. 297–299, n. 42.

31. Zeng Guofan, family letter of TZ3/5/16 (June 19, 1864), in *ZGFQJ*, vol. 8, p. 2818.

32. Hail, *Tseng Kuo-fan and the Taiping Rebellion*, p. 288.

33. Observations of Charles Gordon, who visited Yuhuatai as a private observer after disbanding the Ever-Victorious Army; quoted in Curwen, *Taiping Rebel*, pp. 297–299, n. 42.

34. Zhao Liewen gives the depth of 7 to 8 *zhang* (a *zhang* being 11.75 feet at the time) for the tunnel under the moat by Yuhuatai in *Neng jingju riji*, entry for TZ2/12/2 (January 10, 1864), in *TPTG*, vol. 7, p. 212.

35. Wang Dun, *Xiangjun shi*, p. 176; Jonathan Spence, *God's Chinese Son* (New York: W. W. Norton, 1996), p. 324 (for this paragraph and the following).

36. Wang Dun, *Xiangjun shi*, p. 176.

37. Long Shengyun, *Xiangjun shigao*, pp. 420–421.

38. Zhu Hongzhang, *Cong rong jilüe* (Zhu Hongzhang's account of the campaign against the rebels) (Taipei: Wenhai Chubanshe reprint, 1968), p. 120, says 6,000 cloth sacks of gunpowder; Wang Dun, *Xiangjun shi*, p. 177 gives the figure of 30,000 *jin* of powder (40,000 pounds); as for the total reserves, in Zeng Guofan's letter to Zeng Guoquan on TZ3/5/5 (June 6, 1864) he says he has just shipped 40,000 *jin* of gunpowder, to be added to a previous shipment of 50,000 *jin* and another 90,000 *jin* coming from Shanghai (for a total of 120 tons). The letter is in *ZGFQJ*, vol. 8, p. 2813.

39. Zhu Hongzhang, *Cong rong jilüe*, pp. 121–123; Wang Dun, *Xiangjun shi*, p. 177; Curwen, *Taiping Rebel*, p. 299.

40. Zeng Guofan, family letter of TZ3/6/29 (August 1, 1864), in *ZGFQJ*, vol. 8, p. 2831.

41. Curwen, *Taiping Rebel*, pp. 154–155.

42. Ibid., pp. 155–156.

43. Jonathan Porter, *Tseng Kuo-fan's Private Bureaucracy* (Berkeley: Center for Chinese Studies, University of California, 1972), p. 69, n. 107.

44. Purplish red clouds: Zhao Liewen, *Neng jingju riji*, entry for TZ3/6/17 (July 20, 1864), in *TPTG*, vol. 7, p. 270; Zhao believed that 70 percent of the fires were set by the Hunan Army; rain: ibid., entry for TZ3/6/22 (July 25, 1864), in ibid., p. 274.

45. Zhao Liewen, *Neng jingju riji*, entry for TZ3/6/23 (July 26, 1864), in *TPTG*, vol. 7, p. 274.

46. Zhao Liewen, *Neng jingju riji*, entry for TZ3/6/21 (July 24, 1864), in ibid., p. 274.

47. *Xiangxiang xianzhi* (Gazetteer of Xiangxiang county) (1874), final *juan*, p. 26; quoted in Zhu Dong'an, *Zeng Guofan zhuan* (Tianjin: Baihua Wenshu Chubanshe, 2000), p. 225.

48. Andrew C. K. Hsieh, "Tseng Kuo-fan, A Nineteenth Century Confucian General," Ph.D. diss., Yale University, 1975, pp. 166–167.

49. Zhao Liewen, *Neng jingju riji*, entry for TZ3/6/20 (July 23, 1864), in *TPTG*, vol. 7, p. 272.

50. 50,000 characters: Zeng Guofan, letter to Zeng Jize on TZ3/7/7 (August 8, 1864), in *ZGFQJ*, vol. 8, p. 2833; according to his diary on the same day, he edited it down to about 28,000 characters (130 pages, 216 characters per page). See *ZGFQJ*, vol. 11, p. 4025.

51. "Statement of Patrick Nellis," in Prescott Clarke and J. S. Gregory, *Western Reports on the Taiping: A Selection of Documents* (Honolulu: University Press of Hawaii, 1982), pp. 412–416; quotations, in paraphrase form, on p. 415; Spence, *God's Chinese Son*, p. 329.

52. Hong Rengan's fourth Nanchang confession, in *TPTG*, vol. 2, p. 415.

EPILOGUE

1. Luo Ergang's observation, from *Xiangjun xin zhi* (A new history of the Hunan Army) (Taipei: Liming Wenhua Shiye Gongsi, 1988), p. 285.

2. See, e.g., Xiao Yishan, "Zeng Guofan buzuo huangdi" (Zeng Guofan

does not become emperor), in *Qingdai tongshi* (Comprehensive history of the Qing dynasty) (Taipei: Shangwu Yinshuguan, 1962–1963), vol. 3, pp. 778–781.

3. Zeng Guofan, letter to brother of TZ3/3/26 (May 1, 1864), in *ZGFQJ*, vol. 8, pp. 2800–2801.

4. Quoted in Zhu Dong'an, *Zeng Guofan zhuan* (Biography of Zeng Guofan) (Tianjin: Baihua Wenshu Chubanshe, 2000), p. 236.

5. Andrew C. K. Hsieh, "Tseng Kuo-fan, A Nineteenth Century Confucian General," Ph.D. diss., Yale University, 1975, p. 168.

6. Zeng Guofan, family letter of TZ6/6/6 (July 6, 1867), in *ZGFQJ*, vol. 8, p. 2975; translation modified from Andrew Hsieh's in "Tseng Kuo-fan, A Nineteenth Century Confucian General," Ph.D. diss., Yale University, 1975, p. 171; on Zeng's depression in his later years, see ibid., pp. 170–172.

7. Hua Qiang and Cai Hongjun, "Taiping Tianguo shiqi Zhongguo renkou sunshi wenti" (The question of China's population loss in the Taiping Rebellion), in *Wan Qing guojia yu shehui* (State and society in the late Qing) (Beijing: Chinese Academy of Social Sciences, 2007), here citing Dwight Heald Perkins, *Agricultural Development in China, 1368–1968* (Chicago: Aldine Publishing Co., 1969), pp. 274–283.

8. Ge Jianxiong, Hou Yangfang, and Zhang Genfu, *Renkou yu Zhongguo de xiandaihua: 1850 nian yilai* (Population and China's modernization: 1850 to the present) (Shanghai: Xuelin Chubanshe, 1999), p. 109; cited in Hua and Cai, "Taiping Tianguo shiqi," pp. 69–70.

9. See Hua and Cai, "Taiping Tianguo shiqi," pp. 70–75.

10. On the postwar depression in Shanghai, see Robert Bickers, *The Scramble for China: Foreign Devils in the Qing Empire, 1832–1914* (London: Allen Lane, 2011), p. 182.

11. "Asia: Important from China and Japan; Foreign Relations with China Out of Joint," *New York Herald,* December 28, 1865.

12. Robert James Forrest, "The Christianity of Hung Tsiu Tsuen," *Journal of the North-China Branch of the Royal Asiatic Society,* new ser., no. 4 (December 1867): 187–208, quotation on p. 188; reprinted in part in Prescott Clarke and J. S. Gregory, *Western Reports on the Taiping: A Selection of Documents* (Honolulu: University Press of Hawaii, 1982), p. 427, romanization modified.

13. Forrest, "The Christianity of Hung Tsiu Tsuen," p. 188, romanization modified, "T'ien-wang" changed to "Heavenly King," "Ch'ang-mao" to "Taiping."

14. Sun's nickname: Marie-Claire Bergère, *Sun Yat-sen,* trans. Janet Lloyd (Stanford, Calif.: Stanford University Press, 1998), p. 33; Harold Schiffrin, *Sun Yat-sen and the Origins of the Chinese Revolution* (Berkeley: University of California Press, 1968), pp. 5, 23.

15. Valentine Chirol, "The Chinese Revolution," *The Quarterly Review* 216, no. 431 (April 1912): 536–553, quotations on pp. 538–539.

SELECTED BIBLIOGRAPHY

Abend, Hallett. *The God from the West.* Garden City, N.Y.: Doubleday, 1947.

Adams, Ephraim Douglass. *Great Britain and the American Civil War.* New York: Russell & Russell, 1958.

Allgood, George. *China War 1860: Letters and Journal.* London: Longmans, Green and Co., 1901.

Banno, Masataka. *China and the West, 1858–1861: The Origins of the Tsungli Yamen.* Cambridge, Mass.: Harvard University Press, 1964.

Bernhardt, Kathryn. "Elite and Peasant During the Taiping Occupation of the Jiangnan, 1860–1864." *Modern China* 13, no. 4 (October 1987): 379–410.

Bickers, Robert. *The Scramble for China: Foreign Devils in the Qing Empire, 1832–1914.* London: Allen Lane, 2011.

Blakiston, Thomas W. *Five Months on the Yang-tsze.* London: John Murray, 1862.

Bonney, Catharina Van Rensselaer. *A Legacy of Historical Gleanings.* Albany, N.Y.: J. Munsell, 1875.

Boulger, Demetrius C. *The Life of Gordon.* 2 vols. London: T. Fisher Unwin, 1896.

Bowlby, Thomas. *An Account of the Last Mission and Death of Thomas William Bowlby.* Ed. C. C. Bowlby. Printed for private circulation, 1906.

Brine, Lindesay. *The Taeping Rebellion in China: A Narrative of Its Rise and Progress.* London: John Murray, 1862.

Burlingame, Anson. Anson Burlingame Papers, Manuscripts Division, Library of Congress, Washington, D.C.

Cahill, Holger. *A Yankee Adventurer: The Story of Ward and the Taiping Rebellion.* New York: Macaulay, 1930.

Callery, Joseph-Marie. *History of the Insurrection in China: With Notices of the Christianity, Creed, and Proclamations of the Insurgents.* New York: Paragon Book Reprint Co., 1969, orig. published London, 1853.

Carr, Caleb. *The Devil Soldier: The American Soldier of Fortune Who Became a God in China.* New York: Random House, 1992.

Cheang, Sarah. "Women, Pets, and Imperialism: The British Pekingese Dog and Nostalgia for Old China." *Journal of British Studies* 45 (April 2006): 359–387.

Chen Chang. *Tingjun jilüe* (History of Bao Chao's army). Shanghai: Shanghai Shenbao Guan, 1882.

Chen, Gideon. *Tseng Kuo-fan: Pioneer Promoter of the Steamship in China.* Beijing: Yenching University Economics Department, 1935.

Ch'ên, Jerome. "The Hsien-fêng Inflation." *Bulletin of the School of Oriental and African Studies, University of London* 21, no. 1–3 (1958): 578–586.

Chen Qitian. *Zeng Guofan pingluan yaozhi* (The essential principles of Zeng Guofan's suppression of disorder). Taipei: Taiwan Shangwu Yinshuguan, 1967.

Chung, A. L. Y. "The Hanlin Academy in the Early Ch'ing Period." *Journal of the Hong Kong Branch of the Royal Asiatic Society* 6 (1966): 100–119.

Clarke, Prescott, and J. S. Gregory. *Western Reports on the Taiping: A Selection of Documents.* Honolulu: University Press of Hawaii, 1982.

Clowes, Sir William Laird. *The Royal Navy: A History from the Earliest Times to the Death of Queen Victoria.* 7 vols. London: Sampson Low, Marston and Company, 1903.

Cooke, George Wingrove. *China: Being "The Times" Special Correspondence from China in the Years 1857–58.* Wilmington, Del.: Scholarly Resources, Inc., 1972, orig. published London by G. Routledge & Co., 1858.

Cox, Josiah. "A Missionary Visit to Nanking and the 'Shield King.'" *The Wesleyan Missionary Notices,* 3rd ser., vol. 10 (April 1862): 61–66.

Cranston, Earl. "Shanghai in the Taiping Period." *Pacific Historical Review* 5, no. 2 (June 1936): 147–160.

Crossley, Pamela. *The Manchus.* Cambridge, Mass.: Blackwell, 1997.

—————. *Orphan Warriors: Three Manchu Generations and the End of the Qing World.* Princeton, N.J.: Princeton University Press, 1990.

Cui Zhiqing. *Hong Xiuquan pingzhuan, fu <Hong Rengan pingzhuan>* (Biography of Hong Xiuquan, including a biography of Hong Rengan). Nanjing: Nanjing Daxue Chubanshe, 1994.

Curwen, C. A. *Taiping Rebel: The Deposition of Li Hsiu-Ch'eng.* Cambridge, England: Cambridge University Press, 1977.

Dai Yingcong. "Military Finance of the High Qing Period." In *Military Culture in Imperial China,* ed. Nicola di Cosmo. Cambridge, Mass.: Harvard University Press, 2009.

Davis, John Francis. "A View of the Great Valley of the Yang-tse-keang Before and Since Its Occupation by the Rebels." *Proceedings of the Royal Geographic Society* 3 (1859): 164–171.

Deng Yuanzhong. *Americans and the Taiping Rebellion: A Study of American-Chinese Relationship, 1847–1864.* Taipei: China Academy in Hwa Kang, 1982.

Detrick, Robert Harry. "Henry Andrea Burgevine in China: A Biography." Ph.D. diss., Indiana University, 1968.

Di Cosmo, Nicola. Ed. *Military Culture in Imperial China.* Cambridge, Mass: Harvard University Press, 2009.

Dong Xun. *Huanduwo shushi laoren shouding nianpu* (Chronological auto-biography of Dong Xun). Taipei: Wenhai Chubanshe reprint, 1968, orig. published 1892.

Du Wenlan. *Jiangnanbei daying jishi benmo* (History of the great encampments South and North of the river). Taipei: Tailian Guofeng Chubanshe reprint, 1969, orig. published 1869.

———. *Pingding yuefei jilüe* (A record of the suppression of the Guangxi bandits). Qunyuzhai, 1870.

Edkins, Jane R. *Chinese Scenes and People: With Notices of Christian Missions and Missionary Life in a Series of Letters from Various Parts of China.* London: James Nisbet and Co., 1863.

Edkins, Joseph. "Narrative of a Visit to Nanking." In Jane R. Edkins, *Chinese Scenes and People.* London: James Nisbet and Co., 1863, pp. 241–307.

Elgin, James Bruce, Earl of. *Letters and Journals of James, Eighth Earl of Elgin.* Ed. Theodore Walrond. London: John Murray, 1872.

Elliott, Mark C. *The Manchu Way: The Eight Banners and Ethnic Identity in Late Imperial China.* Stanford, Calif.: Stanford University Press, 2001.

Extracts from "The Taepings as They Are, by One of Them." London: Harrison and Sons, 1864.

Fairbank, John King. "Meadows on China: A Centennial Review." *The Far Eastern Quarterly* 14, no. 3 (May 1955): 365–371.

Fang Zongcheng. *Botang shiyou yanxing ji* (An account of the words and deeds of Fang Zongcheng's friends and teachers). Taipei: Wenhai Chubanshe, reprint, 1968.

Fisher, George Battye. *Personal Narrative of Three Years' Service in China.* London: Richard Bentley, 1863.

Forbes, Archibald. *Chinese Gordon: A Succinct Record of His Life.* New York: Funk and Wagnalls, 1885.

Foreign Office, Great Britain. *Correspondence Relative to the Earl of Elgin's Special Missions to China and Japan, 1857–1859.* London: Harrison and Sons, 1859.

Forester, Edward. "Personal Recollections of the Tai-ping Rebellion." *Cosmopolitan* 21, no. 6 (October 1896): 625–629; continued in 22, no. 1 (November 1896): 34–38; continued in 22, no. 2 (December 1896): 209–216.

Furse, George Armand. *Military Transport.* London, 1882.

"Gengshen beilüe," (An account of what happened in the North in 1860). In *Dierci Yapian Zhanzheng,* ed. Qi Sihe et al. 6 vols. Shanghai: Shanghai Renmin Chubanshe, 1978–1979, vol. 2, pp. 28–33.

"Gengshen (jia) binan riji," (A diary of avoiding calamity in 1860–1861). In *Taiping Tianguo* (The Taiping Heavenly Kingdom), ed. Luo Ergang and Wang Qingcheng. 10 vols. Guilin: Guangxi Normal University Press, 2004, vol. 6, pp. 198–290.

Gerson, Jack J. *Horatio Nelson Lay and Sino-British Relations, 1854–1864.* Cambridge, Mass.: Harvard East Asian Monographs, 1972.

Giquel, Prosper. *A Journal of the Chinese Civil War, 1864.* Ed. Steven A. Leibo. Honolulu: University of Hawaii Press, 1985.

Gordon, Charles George. *General Gordon's Private Diary of His Exploits in China; Amplified by Samuel Mossman.* London: S. Low, Marston, Searle, and Rivington, 1885.

Gordon, Henry William. *Events in the Life of Charles George Gordon, from Its Beginning to Its End.* London: Kegan Paul, Trench, & Co., 1886.

Grady, Lolan Wang. "The Career of I-Hsin, Prince Kung, 1858–1880: A Case Study of the Limits of Reform in the Late Ch'ing." Ph.D. diss., University of Toronto, 1980.

Graff, David, and Robin Higham, eds. *A Military History of China.* Boulder, Colo.: Westview, 2002.

Gregory, J. S. "British Intervention Against the Taiping Rebellion." *The Journal of Asian Studies* 19, no. 1 (November 1959): 11–24.

———. *Great Britain and the Taipings.* London: Frederick A. Praeger, 1969.

———. "Stephen Uhalley, Jr. and Westerners in China: A Further Comment." *The Journal of Asian Studies* 35, no. 2 (February 1976): 364–365.

Guo Tingyi. *Taiping Tianguo shishi rizhi* (Daily calendar of events in the Taiping Heavenly Kingdom). Taipei: Taiwan Shangwu Yinshuguan, 1976.

Guo Yisheng, ed. *Taiping Tianguo lishi ditu ji* (Historical maps of the Taiping Heavenly Kingdom). Beijing: Zhongguo Ditu Chubanshe, 1989.

Hail, William James. *Tseng Kuo-fan and the Taiping Rebellion, with a Short Sketch of His Later Career.* New Haven, Conn.: Yale University Press, 1927.

Hake, A. Egmont. *Events in the Taeping Rebellion, Being Reprints of Mss. Copied by General Gordon, C.B. in His Own Handwriting . . .* London: W. H. Allen and Co., 1891.

Hamberg, The Rev. Theodore. *The Visions of Hung-Siu-Tshuen and Origin of the Kwang-si Insurrection.* Hong Kong: China Mail Office, 1854.

Hansard's Parliamentary Debates (Third Series). London: T. C. Hansard, 1853–1864.

Harris, David. *Of Battle and Beauty: Felice Beato's Photographs of China.* Santa Barbara, Calif.: Santa Barbara Museum of Art, 1999.

Hayes, A. A. "An American Soldier in China." *The Atlantic Monthly* (February 1886): 193–199.

Henderson, James. *Memorials of James Henderson, MD, . . . Medical Missionary to China.* London: James Nisbet and Co., 1867.

Hevia, James. *English Lessons: The Pedagogy of Imperialism in Nineteenth-Century China.* Durham, N.C.: Duke University Press, 2003.

Hong Rengan. *Hong Rengan xuanji* (The selected works of Hong Rengan). Ed. Yangzhou Shifan Xueyuan Zhongwen Xi. Beijing: Zhonghua Shuju, 1978.

———. *Hong Rengan zishu* (The confession of Hong Rengan). In *Taiping Tianguo wenxian huibian* (Collected documents on the Taiping Heavenly Kingdom), ed. Yang Jialuo. Taipei: Dingwen Shuju, 1973, pp. 846–855.

———. *Taiping tianri* (Narrative of the early years of the Taiping). In *Xuxiu siku quanshu, shi bu, zashi lei* (A continuation of the Four Treasuries). Shanghai: Commercial Press Reprint, 1948, pp. 359–377.

Horowitz, Richard Steven. "Central Power and State Making: The Zongli Yamen and Self-Strengthening in China, 1860–1880." Ph.D. diss., Harvard University, 1998.

Hsieh, Andrew C. K. "Tseng Kuo-fan, A Nineteenth Century Confucian General." Ph.D. diss., Yale University, 1975.

Hsü, Immanuel C. Y. *China's Entrance into the Family of Nations: The Diplomatic Phase, 1858–1880.* Cambridge, Mass.: Harvard University Press, 1968.

———. *The Rise of Modern China,* 3rd ed. New York: Oxford University Press, 1983.

Hummel, Arthur W., ed. *Eminent Chinese of the Ch'ing Period (1644–1912).* Taipei: Chengwen, reprint, 1967.

Hurd, Douglas. *The Arrow War: An Anglo-Chinese Confusion, 1856–1860.* London: Collins, 1967.

Ignat'ev, Nikolaï Pavlovich. *The Russo-Chinese Crisis: N.P. Ignatiev's Mission to Peking, 1859–1860.* Ed. John Evans. Newtonville, Mass.: Oriental Research Partners, 1987.

Jansen, Marius. *China in the Tokugawa World.* Cambridge, Mass: Harvard University Press, 1992.

Jen Yu-wen (Jian Youwen). *The Taiping Revolutionary Movement.* New Haven, Conn.: Yale University Press, 1973.

Johnston, James D. *China and Japan: Being a Narrative of the Cruise of the U.S. Steam-Frigate* Powhatan *in the Years 1857, '58, '59, and '60*. Philadelphia: Charles Desilver, 1860.

Kuhn, Philip. *Rebellion and Its Enemies in Late Imperial China: Militarization and Social Structure, 1796–1864*. Cambridge, Mass.: Harvard University Press, 1970.

Lane-Poole, Stanley. *The Life of Sir Harry Parkes*. 2 vols. London: Macmillan and Co., 1894.

Lao Bolin. *Sanhe zhi yi* (The battle of Three Rivers). Changsha: Yuelu Shushe, 1988.

Lay, Horatio Nelson. *Our Interests in China: A Letter to the Right Hon. Earl Russell*. London: Robert Hardwicke, 1864.

Leavenworth, Charles S. *The Arrow War with China*. London: Sampson Low, Marston and Co., 1901.

Legge, Helen Edith. *James Legge: Missionary and Scholar*. London: The Religious Tract Society, 1905.

Legge, James. "The Colony of Hong Kong." *The China Review* 3 (1874): 165, 173–175.

Li Chun. *Hong Rengan*. Shanghai: Shanghai Renmin Chubanshe, 1957.

Li Xiucheng. *The Autobiography of the Chung-Wang*. Trans. W. T. Lay. Shanghai: Presbyterian Mission Press, 1865.

Lindley, Augustus F. *The Log of the Fortuna: A Cruise on Chinese Waters*. London: Cassell, Petter & Galpin, 1870.

——— (Lin-le). *Ti-Ping Tien-Kwoh; The History of the Ti-ping Revolution*. London: Day & Son, Ltd., 1866.

Little, Archibald. *Gleanings from Fifty Years in China*. London: Sampson Low, Marston & Co., 1910.

Liu Tieming. *Xiangjun yu Xiangxiang* (The Hunan Army and Xiangxiang). Changsha: Yuelu Shushe, 2006.

Loch, Henry Brougham. *Personal Narrative of Occurrences During Lord Elgin's Second Embassy to China in 1860*. London: John Murray, 1900.

Long Shengyun. *Xiangjun shigao* (Draft history of the Hunan Army). Chengdu: Sichuan Renmin Chubanshe, 1990.

Luo Ergang. *Li Xiucheng zishu yuangao zhu* (Commentary on the original draft of Li Xiucheng's confessional statement). Beijing: Zhonghua Shuju, 1982.

———. *Lüying bingzhi* (Military organization of the Green Standard Army). Chongqing: Shangwu Yinshuguan, 1945.

————. *Xiangjun bingzhi* (Military organization of the Hunan Army). Beijing: Zhonghua Shuju, 1984.

————. *Xiangjun xin zhi* (A new history of the Hunan Army). Taipei: Liming Wenhua Shiye Gongsi, 1988.

————, ed. *Taiping Tianguo wenwu* (Relics of the Taiping Heavenly Kingdom). 2 vols. Nanjing: Jiangsu Renmin Chubanshe, 1992.

————, ed. *Taiping Tianguo wenxuan* (Documents on the Taiping Heavenly Kingdom). Hong Kong: Nanguo Chubanshe, 1969.

———— and Wang Qingcheng, eds. *Taiping Tianguo* (The Taiping Heavenly Kingdom). 10 vols. Guilin: Guangxi Normal University Press, 2004.

Lyster, Thomas. *With Gordon in China: Letters from Thomas Lyster, Lieutenant Royal Engineers.* London: T. Fisher Unwin, 1891.

MacGowan, D. J. "Contributions to the History of the Insurrection in China," a companion to the *Shanghai Almanac* for 1857. Shanghai, 1857.

————. "Memoir of Generals Ward and Burgevine, and of the Ever Conquering Legion." *The Far East*, new ser., vol. 2 (January–June 1877): 102–108, 119–124; vol. 4 (July–December 1877): 22–26, 44–50, 58–66, 75–83, 103–110.

Maclay, Edgar Stanton. *A History of the United States Navy from 1775 to 1894.* 2 vols. New York: D. Appleton and Co., 1895.

————. *Reminiscences of the Old Navy: From the Journals and Private Papers of Captain Edward Trenchard, and Rear-Admiral Stephen Decatur Trenchard.* New York: G. P. Putnam's Sons, 1898.

Mann, Michael. *China, 1860.* Salisbury, Wiltshire: M. Russell, 1989.

Mao Haijian. *Kuming tianzi: Xianfeng huangdi Yixin* (The unfortunate Son of Heaven: Yixin, the Xianfeng emperor). Taipei: Lianjing, 2008.

Mao Jiaqi. *Guo zhu "Taiping Tianguo shishi rizhi" jiaobu* (Emendations to Guo [Tingyi's] *Daily Calendar of Events in the Taiping Heavenly Kingdom*). Taipei: Taiwan Shangwu Yinshuguan, 2001.

————. *Taiping Tianguo yu lieqiang* (The Taiping Heavenly Kingdom and the foreign powers). Nanning: Guangxi Renmin Chubanshe, 1992.

Martin, W. A. P. *A Cycle of Cathay.* New York: F. H. Revell Co., 1896.

Meadows, Thomas Taylor. *The Chinese and Their Rebellions.* Stanford, Calif.: Academic Reprints, 1953, orig. published 1856 by Smith, Elder & Co., London.

————. "Description of an Execution Ground at Canton." *Journal of the Royal Asiatic Society* 16 (1856): 54–58.

Medhurst, W. H. *China: Its State and Prospects, with Especial Reference to the Spread of the Gospel.* London: John Snow, 1838.

Mei Yingjie et al., eds. *Xiangjun renwu nianpu* (Chronological biography of major figures in the Hunan Army). Changsha: Yuelu Shushe, 1987.

Merli, Frank J. *The* Alabama, *British Neutrality, and the American Civil War.* Bloomington: Indiana University Press, 2004.

Merriam, Edmund F. *A History of American Baptist Missions.* Philadelphia: American Baptist Publication Society, 1900.

M'Ghee, The Rev. R. J. L. *How We Got to Pekin: A Narrative of the Campaign in China of 1860.* London: Bentley, 1862.

Michael, Franz with Chung-li Chang. *The Taiping Rebellion: History and Documents.* 3 vols. Seattle: University of Washington Press, 1966–1971.

Michie, Alexander. *The Englishman in China During the Victorian Era.* Edinburgh: William Blackwood and Sons, 1900.

Moges, Alfred, Marquis de. *Recollections of Baron Gros's Embassy to China and Japan in 1857–58* (authorized translation of *Souvenirs d'une ambassade*). London and Glasgow: R. Griffin, Bohn, and Co., 1861.

Montalto de Jesus, C. A. *Historic Shanghai.* Shanghai: The Shanghai Mercury, Ltd., 1909.

Morse, Hosea Ballou. *The International Relations of the Chinese Empire.* Vol. 2: *The Period of Submission, 1861–1893.* London: Longmans, Green, and Co., 1918.

Moule, The Ven. Archdeacon. *Personal Recollections of the T'ai-p'ing Rebellion, 1861–1863.* Shanghai: Shanghai Mercury Office, 1898.

Ng, Kam-yuen. "The Interaction between Hong Kong and Mainland China: The Tai Ping Tian Guo Movement as a Case Study." Ph.D. diss., Chinese University of Hong Kong, 2003.

Oliphant, Laurence. *Narrative of the Earl of Elgin's Mission to China and Japan in the Years 1857, '58, '59.* 2 vols. London and Edinburgh: William Blackwood and Sons, 1859.

Osborn, Sherard. "Notes, Geographical and Commercial, Made During the Passage of HMS *Furious,* in 1858, from Shanghai to the Gulf of Pecheli and Back." *Proceedings of the Royal Geographical Society of London* 3, no. 2 (November 22, 1858): 55–87.

————. "Progress in China, Part II: The Taepings and Their Remedy." *Blackwood's Edinburgh Magazine* 93, no. 568 (February 1863): 133–148.

Pfister, Lauren F. *Striving for "The Whole Duty of Man": James Legge and the Scottish Protestant Encounter with China.* New York: Peter Lang, 2004.

Pi Mingyong. *Xiang Jun* (The Hunan Army). Taiyuan: Shanxi Renmin Chubanshe, 1999.

Pong, David. "The Income and Military Expenditure of Kiangsi Province in the Last Years (1860–1864) of the Taiping Rebellion." *The Journal of Asian Studies* 26, no. 1 (November 1966): 49–65.

Porter, Jonathan. *Tseng Kuo-fan's Private Bureaucracy.* Berkeley: Center for Chinese Studies, University of California, 1972.

Powell, Ralph. *The Rise of Chinese Military Power: 1895–1912.* Princeton, N.J.: Princeton University Press, 1955.

Pruden, George Blackburn, Jr. "Issachar Jacox Roberts and American Diplomacy in China During the Taiping Rebellion." Ph.D. diss., The American University, 1977.

Pu Yinghua. *Zeng Guofan bingfa* (Zeng Guofan's art of war). Taipei: Zhaowen She, 1996.

Qi Sihe et al., eds. *Dierci Yapian Zhanzheng* (The Second Opium War). 6 vols. Shanghai: Shanghai Renmin Chubanshe, 1978–1979.

Qingdai qijuzhu ce. Xianfeng chao (Qing court diary: Xianfeng reign). Taipei: National Palace Museum, 1983.

Quested, R. K. I. *The Expansion of Russia in East Asia, 1857–1860.* Kuala Lumpur: University of Malaya Press, 1968.

————. "Further Light on the Expansion of Russia in East Asia: 1792–1860." *The Journal of Asian Studies* 29, no. 2 (February 1970): 327–345.

————. *Sino-Russian Relations: A Short History.* Boston: George Allen & Unwin, 1984.

Rantoul, Robert S. "Frederick Townsend Ward." *Historical Collections of the Essex Institute* 44, no. 1 (January 1908): 1–64.

Rapp, John A. "Clashing Dilemmas: Hong Rengan, Issachar Roberts, and a Taiping 'Murder' Mystery." *Journal of Historical Biography* 4 (Autumn 2008): 27–58.

Rawski, Evelyn S. *The Last Emperors: A Social History of Qing Imperial Institutions.* Berkeley: University of California Press, 1998.

Reilly, Thomas H. *The Taiping Heavenly Kingdom: Rebellion and the Blasphemy of Empire.* Seattle: University of Washington Press, 2004.

Rennie, David Field. *The British Arms in North China and Japan: Peking 1860; Kagosima 1862.* London: John Murray, 1864.

————. *Peking and the Pekingese: During the First Year of the British Embassy at Peking.* 2 vols. London: John Murray, 1865.

Roberts, I. J. "Tae Ping Wang: The Chinese Revolutionist." *Putnam's Monthly Magazine* 8, no. 46 (October 1856): 380–383.

Robson, William. *Griffith John: Founder of the Hankow Mission Central China.* London: S. W. Partridge & Co., n.d. (1901?).

Rudolph, Jennifer. *Negotiated Power in Late Imperial China: The Zongli Yamen and the Politics of Reform.* Ithaca, N.Y.: Cornell University East Asia Program, 2008.

Scarth, John. *British Policy in China: Is Our War with the Tartars or the Chinese?* London: Smith, Elder and Co., 1860.

————. *Twelve Years in China: The People, the Rebels, and the Mandarins.* Wilmington, Del.: Scholarly Resources, Inc., 1972, orig. published 1860 by Thomas Constable & Co., Edinburgh.

Shanghai Xinbao zhong de Taiping Tianguo shiliao (Historical materials on the Taiping in the Shanghai *Xinbao*). Shanghai: Shanghai Tushuguan, 1964.

Shen Weibin. *Hong Rengan.* Shanghai: Shanghai Renmin Chubanshe, 1982.

Shen Zi. *Bikou riji* (A diary of evading the bandits). In *Taiping Tianguo* (The Taiping Heavenly Kingdom), ed. Luo Ergang and Wang Qingcheng. 10 vols. Guilin: Guangxi Normal University Press, 2004, vol. 8, pp. 1–264.

Shih, Vincent Y. C. *The Taiping Ideology: Its Sources, Interpretations, and Influences.* Seattle: University of Washington Press, 1967.

"Sir Thomas F. Wade, K.C.B." *The Far East,* new ser., vol. 1 (July–December 1876): 37–41.

Smith, Carl T. "Notes on Friends and Relatives of Taiping Leaders." *Journal of the Hong Kong Branch of the Royal Asiatic Society* 16 (1976): 117–134.

Smith, Richard J. *Mercenaries and Mandarins: The Ever-Victorious Army in Nineteenth-Century China.* Millwood, N.Y.: KTO Press, 1978.

So Kwan-wai, Eugene P. Boardman, and Ch'iu P'ing. "Hung Jen-kan, Taiping Prime Minister, 1859–1864." *Harvard Journal of Asiatic Studies* 20, no. 1–2 (June 1957): 262–294.

Spector, Stanley. *Li Hung-chang and the Huai Army: A Study in Nineteenth-Century Chinese Regionalism.* Seattle: University of Washington Press, 1964.

Spence, Jonathan. *God's Chinese Son.* New York: W. W. Norton, 1996.

————. *The Search for Modern China.* New York: W. W. Norton, 1999.

Suppression of the Taiping Rebellion in the Departments Around Shanghai. Shanghai: Kelly & Co., 1871.

Swinhoe, Robert. *Narrative of the North China Campaign of 1860.* London: Smith, Elder & Co., 1861.

Sykes, W. H. (William Henry). *The Taeping Rebellion in China: Its Origin, Progress, and Present Condition.* London: Warren Hall & Co., 1863.

Tang Haoming. *Tang Haoming pingdian Zeng Guofan jiashu* (Zeng Guofan's family letters, annotated by Tang Haoming). 2 vols. Changsha: Yuelu Shushe, 2002.

Taylor, Charles. *Five Years in China: With Some Account of the Great Rebellion . . .* New York: Derby & Jackson, 1860.

Teng, S. Y. "Hung Jen-kan, Prime Minister of the Taiping Kingdom and his Modernization Plans." *United College Journal* (Hong Kong) 8 (1970–1971): 87–95.

Teng, Ssu-yu. *The Taiping Rebellion and the Western Powers: A Comprehensive Survey.* Oxford, England: Clarendon Press, 1971.

Teng, Yuan Chung. "The Failure of Hung Jen-k'an's Foreign Policy." *The Journal of Asian Studies* 28, no. 1 (November 1968): 125–138.

————. "Note on a Lost Taiping Book." *The Journal of Asian Studies* 23, no. 3 (May 1964): 447–448.

————. "Reverend Issachar Jacox Roberts and the Taiping Rebellion." *The Journal of Asian Studies* 23, no. 1 (November 1963): 55–67.

Theiss, Janet. "Managing Martyrdom: Female Suicide and Statecraft in Mid-Qing China." In *Passionate Women: Female Suicide in Late Imperial China,* ed. Paul S. Ropp, Paola Zamperini, and Harriet T. Zurndorfer. Boston: E. J. Brill, 2001, pp. 47–76.

Thompson, Ralph Wardlaw. *Griffith John: The Story of Fifty Years in China.* London: The Religious Tract Society, 1906.

Tileston, William Minns. William Minns Tileston Letters, Massachusetts Historical Society, Boston, Massachusetts.

Torr, Dona, ed. *Marx on China: Articles from the* New York Daily Tribune, *1853–1860.* London: Lawrence & Wishart, 1968.

Tsiang, T. F. "China after the Victory of Taku, June 25, 1859." *American Historical Review* 35, no. 1 (October 1929): 79–84.

Tulloch, Alexander Bruce. *Recollections of Forty Years' Service.* London: William Blackwood and Sons, 1903.

Uhalley, Stephen, Jr. "The Foreign Relations of the Taiping Revolution." Ph.D. diss., UC Berkeley, 1967.

————. "The Taipings at Ningpo: The Significance of a Forgotten Event." *Journal of the Hong Kong Branch of the Royal Asiatic Society* 11 (1971): 17–32.

Wade, Thomas F. "The Army of the Chinese Empire . . ." *The Chinese Repository* 20, no. 5 (May 1851): 250–280; continued in 20, no. 6 (June 1851): 300–339; continued in 20, no. 7 (July 1851): 363–471.

Wagner, Rudolf G. *Reenacting the Heavenly Vision: The Role of Religion in the Taiping Rebellion.* Berkeley: Institute of East Asian Studies, University of California, 1982.

Waley-Cohen, Joanna. "Militarization of Culture in Eighteenth-Century

China." In *Military Culture in Imperial China,* ed. Nicola di Cosmo. Cambridge, Mass.: Harvard University Press, 2009, pp. 278–295.

Wang Ding'an. *Xiangjun ji* (A record of the Hunan Army). Changsha: Yuelu Shushe, 1983, orig. text dated 1889.

Wang Dun. *Xiangjun shi* (A history of the Hunan Army). Changsha: Hunan Daxue Chubanshe, 2007.

Wang Ermin. *Huaijun zhi* (Annals of the Anhui Army). Beijing: Zhonghua Shuju, 1987.

Wang Kaiyun. *Xiangjun zhi* (Annals of the Hunan Army), published in a single volume with Guo Zhenyong, *Xiangjun zhi pingyi* (An appraisal of *Annals of the Hunan Army*) and Zhu Deshang, *Xu xiangjun zhi* (Continued *Annals of the Hunan Army*). Changsha: Yuelu Shushe, 1983.

Wang Shihui. *Xianfeng Xiangshan yuefen jishi* (A record of actual events under the rebels in Xiangshan during the Xianfeng reign). In *Taiping Tianguo* (The Taiping Heavenly Kingdom), ed. Luo Ergang and Wang Qingcheng. 10 vols. Guilin: Guangxi Normal University Press, 2004, vol. 5, pp. 207–219.

Wang Yeh-chien. "The Impact of the Taiping Rebellion on Population in Southern Kiangsu." *Harvard Papers on China* 19 (1965).

Wang Yishou. *Yuenan zhi* (A chronicle spanning hardships). In *Taiping Tianguo* (The Taiping Heavenly Kingdom), ed. Luo Ergang and Wang Qingcheng. 10 vols. Guilin: Guangxi Normal University Press, 2004, vol. 5, pp. 139–163.

Ward, Frederick Townsend. Frederick Townsend Ward Papers, Manuscripts and Archives, Sterling Memorial Library, Yale University, New Haven, Conn.

Weng Tonghe. *Weng wengong gong riji* (Diary of Weng Tonghe). Excerpted in Qi Sihe et al., eds. *Dierci Yapian Zhanzheng* (The Second Opium War). 6 vols. Shanghai: Shanghai Renmin Chubanshe, 1978–1979, vol. 2.

Wenxiang, *Wen wenzhong gong shilüe* (Events in the life of Wenxiang). Taipei: Wenhai Chubanshe, 1968, reprint of 1882 original.

Will, Pierre-Étienne. "Views of the Realm in Crisis: Testimonies on Imperial Audiences in the Nineteenth Century." *Late Imperial China* 29, no. 1 suppl. (June 2008): 125–159.

Williams, Frederick Wells. *Anson Burlingame and the First Chinese Mission to Foreign Powers.* New York: Charles Scribner's Sons, 1912.

————. *The Life and Letters of Samuel Wells Williams, LL.D.: Missionary, Diplomatist, Sinologue.* New York and London: G. P. Putnam's Sons, 1889.

Williams, Samuel Wells. *The Middle Kingdom.* New York: Charles Scribner's Sons, 1883.

————. Samuel Wells Williams Family Papers, Manuscripts and Archives, Sterling Memorial Library, Yale University, New Haven, Conn.

Wilson, Andrew. *The "Ever-Victorious Army": A History of the Chinese Campaign under Lt.-Col. C. G. Gordon* . . . Edinburgh: William Blackwood and Sons, 1868.

Withers, John Lovelle. "The Heavenly Capital: Nanjing Under the Taiping, 1853–1864." Ph.D. diss., Yale University, 1983.

Wolseley, Garnet Wolseley, Viscount. *Narrative of the War with China in 1860, to Which Is Added the Account of a Short Residence with the Tai-ping Rebels at Nankin* . . . London: Longman, Green, Longman and Roberts, 1862.

Wong, J. W. *Deadly Dreams: Opium, Imperialism, and the Arrow War (1856–1860) in China.* Cambridge, England: Cambridge University Press, 1998.

Wong, J. Y. "Harry Parkes and the 'Arrow' War in China." *Modern Asian Studies* 9, no. 3 (1975): 303–320.

Wong Young-tsu. *A Paradise Lost: The Imperial Garden Yuanming Yuan.* Honolulu: University of Hawaii Press, 2001.

Wooldridge, William C. "Transformations of Ritual and State in Nineteenth-Century Nanjing." Ph.D. diss., Princeton University, 2007.

Wright, Mary Clabaugh. *The Last Stand of Chinese Conservatism: The T'ung-Chih Restoration, 1862–1874.* Stanford, Calif.: Stanford University Press, 1967.

Wu, James T. K. "The Impact of the Taiping Rebellion upon the Manchu Fiscal System." *Pacific Historical Review* 19, no. 3 (1950): 265–275.

Xia Chuntao. *Cong shushi, Jidutu dao wangye: Hong Rengan* (From scholar and Christian to King: Hong Rengan). Wuhan: Hubei Jiaoyu Chubanshe, 1999.

Xiangxiang xianzhi (Gazetteer of Xiangxiang county, Hunan). 1874.

Xiao Yishan. *Qingdai tongshi* (Comprehensive history of the Qing dynasty). Taipei: Shangwu Yinshuguan, 1962–1963.

Xu Chuanyi. *Taiping Tianguo Anhui sheng shigao* (Draft history of Anhui province during the Taiping Rebellion). Hefei: Anhui Renmin Chubanshe, 1991.

Xu Liting. *Xianfeng, Tongzhi di* (Emperors Xianfeng and Tongzhi). Changchun: Jilin Wenshi Chubanshe, 1993.

Xue Fengjiu. *Nanqing zaji* (Miscellaneous records of difficult circumstances). In *Taiping Tianguo* (The Taiping Heavenly Kingdom), ed. Luo Ergang and Wang Qingcheng. 10 vols. Guilin: Guangxi Normal University Press, 2004, vol. 5, pp. 271–288.

Yang Yiqing. *Hunan difang zhi zhong de Taiping Tianguo shiliao* (Materials on the Taiping Heavenly Kingdom from Hunan gazetteers). Changsha: Yuelu Shushe, 1983.

Yu Bingkun et al., eds. *Qing zhengfu zhenya Taiping Tianguo dang'an shiliao* (Archival materials on the Qing government's suppression of the Taiping). 26 vols. Beijing: Guangming Ribao Chubanshe, 1990–.

Yu, Maochun. "The Taiping Rebellion: A Military Assessment of Revolution and Counterrevolution." In *A Military History of China*, ed. David Graff and Robin Higham. Boulder, Colo.: Westview, 2002.

Yu Xingmin. *Shanghai, 1862 nian* (Shanghai, 1862). Shanghai: Renmin Chubanshe, 1991.

Yung Wing. *My Life in China and America*. New York: Henry Holt & Co., 1909.

Zeng Guofan. *Zeng Guofan jiaxun* (Zeng Guofan's family instructions). Ed. Cheng Xiaojun and Tang Zhaomei. Shenyang: Liaoning Guji Chubanshe, 1997.

————. *Zeng Guofan quanji* (The complete works of Zeng Guofan). 16 vols. Beijing: Zhongguo Zhigong Chubanshe, 2001.

————. *Zeng Guofan weikan wanglai hangao* (Unpublished correspondence of Zeng Guofan). Changsha: Yuelu Shushe, 1986.

Zhang Dejian. *Zeiqing huizuan* (Intelligence reports on the Taiping rebels). Taipei: Wenhai Chubanshe, 1968, reprint of 1855 original.

Zhang Gongchen. *Senggelinqin chuanqi* (Biography of Senggelinqin). Beijing: Zhongguo Renmin Daxue Chubanshe, 2003.

Zhang Hongxing. "Wu Youru's 'The Victory Over the Taiping': Painting and Censorship in 1886 China." Ph.D. diss., School of Oriental and African Studies, University of London, 1999.

Zhang Xiaoqiu, *Yuefei jilüe* (Brief records of the Guangxi bandits). In *Taiping Tianguo* (The Taiping Heavenly Kingdom), ed. Luo Ergang and Wang Qingcheng. 10 vols. Guilin: Guangxi Normal University Press, 2004, vol. 4, pp. 46–60.

Zhang Yun. *Zeng Guofan yu Xiangjun* (Zeng Guofan and the Hunan Army). Shenyang: Liaoning Renmin Chubanshe, 2008.

Zhao Liewen. *Neng jingju riji* (Diary of Zhao Liewen). In *Taiping Tianguo* (The Taiping Heavenly Kingdom), ed. Luo Ergang and Wang Qingcheng. 10 vols. Guilin: Guangxi Normal University Press, 2004, vol. 7, pp. 42–366.

Zheng Xiaowei. "Loyalty, Anxiety, and Opportunism: Local Elite Activism during the Taiping Rebellion in Eastern Zhejiang, 1851–1864." *Late Imperial China* 30, no. 2 (December 2009): 39–83.

Zhongyang Yanjiuyuan Jindaishi Yanjiusuo, ed. *Jindai Zhongguo dui Xifang ji lieqiang renshi ziliao huibian* (Collection of materials on the understanding of the West in modern China). Nankang: Academia Sinica Institute of Modern History, 1972.

Zhu Dong'an. *Zeng Guofan zhuan* (Biography of Zeng Guofan). Tianjin: Baihua Wenshu Chubanshe, 2000.

Zhu Hongzhang. *Cong rong jilüe* (Zhu Hongzhang's account of the campaign against the rebels). Taipei: Wenhai Chubanshe, 1968, reprint of 1890 original.

INDEX

Page numbers in *italics* refer to maps.

Blackwood's Edinburgh Magazine, 326

Blakiston, Thomas, 220–1

blasphemy, 81–2, 146–7, 175–6, 228, 275, 301

blockades, naval, 137, 143, 204, 213

Blue Books, 29, 176–7, 186

Bouncer, 201

Bowlby, Thomas, 97, 100, 102, 103, 104, 105, 108–9, 164–5, 394*n*

Bowra, Edward, 333–4

Brave King, *see* Chen Yucheng

Brown Bess muskets, 92

Bruce, Frederick, 43–4, 72–4, 89–94, 95, 140–2, 145, 150, 151, 152, 169–70, 175–89, 212–13, 230–48, 261, 270, 274, 275, 279, 282–3, 295, 297, 300, 303, 304, 315, 316, 320, 322, 328, 333, 335, 337, 355, 356, 360, 364, 421*n*

Buchanan, James, 36

Buchanan, Walter, 236

Buddhism, 16, 53, 59–60, 62, 80, 156

Bull Run, First Battle of, 232

Burgevine, Henry Andrea, 266, 315–16, 318, 319–21, 325–6, 328–9, 421*n*

Burlingame, Anson, 319–20, 328, 418*n*

cannibalism, 215, 252, 338–9

Canton (Guangzhou), 8, 13, 14, 20, 21–2, 28, 29, 41, 42, 50, 77, 96, 102, 103, 127, 147, 150–1, 170–1, 173, 231, 295, 354

Canton Coolie Corps (CCC), 96, 266

Catholic Church, 9, 59, 73, 80

cavalry, 87, 96, 101, 104, 105, 107, 209–10

Centaur, 188

Changsha, 116, 127–8

Changzhou, 69, 154, 253, 343, 344

Cheng Hao, 160–1

Cheng Xueqi, 318, 319, 320–1, 329–31

Cheng Yi, 160–1

Chen Yucheng (Brave King), 64, 65, 191–203, 207–12, 219, 239, 251, 291–3, 343

Chiang Kai-shek, 170

children, 62, 93–4, 155, 186, 191, 285, 286–7, 342–3, 350–2

child soldiers, 155, 186

China

    agriculture in, 7, 9, 17, 27, 34, 42, 51–2, 55, 56, 155–6, 186–8, 219–20, 252, 338–40, 345–6

    bandit gangs in, 9, 35, 50, 56, 63, 119, 121, 122, 124, 131, 135, 150, 291–2

    civilization of, 35, 48–9, 58, 90, 159, 164–7, 236, 237

    as closed society, xxiii, 10–11, 90

    coastal areas of, 45–9, 219–20, 251, 326

    disease in, 7–8, 17, 19–20, 99, 187, 211, 213, 304–7, 313

    domestic market of, 11, 28, 232

    dynasties of, 3–4, 54, 58, 63, 90–1, 120, 124, 142, 158, 160, 161, 180, 211, 294, 341; *see also* Qing empire

    economic conditions in, 10–11, 25–6, 35, 71–2

    education in, 3–4, 13–14, 20, 22, 114–16, 251, 253–4

    ethnic Chinese in, xxv, xxvii, 3–4, 11–12, 28–9, 30, 63, 118, 129, 157, 160, 161, 177–9, 255, 323

ILLUSTRATION CREDITS

Brave King: photo by the author.

Zeng Guofan: Hosea Ballou Morse, *The International Relations of the Chinese Empire,* vol. 2 (New York: Longmans, Green, & Co., 1910–1918). Courtesy of the Yale University Library.

Zeng Guoquan: Peng Hongnian, *Ziguangge gongchen xiaoxiang bing Xiangjun pingding Yuefei zhantu* (Shanghai: Dianshizhai, 1900).

Duolonga: Peng Hongnian, *Ziguangge gongchen xiaoxiang bing Xiangjun pingding Yuefei zhantu* (Shanghai: Dianshizhai, 1900).

Bao Chao: Peng Hongnian, *Ziguangge gongchen xiaoxiang bing Xiangjun pingding Yuefei zhantu* (Shanghai: Dianshizhai, 1900).

Li Hongzhang: Library of Congress.

Lord Elgin and Prince Gong: George Allgood, *China War 1860: Letters and Journal* (London: Longmans, Green and Co. 1901). Courtesy of the Yale University Library.

Taku Forts 1: George Allgood, *China War 1860: Letters and Journal* (London: Longmans, Green and Co., 1901). Courtesy of the Yale University Library.

Taku Forts 2: George Allgood, *China War 1860: Letters and Journal* (London: Longmans, Green and Co., 1901). Courtesy of the Yale University Library.

Beijing Wall: George Allgood, *China War 1860: Letters and Journal* (London: Longmans, Green and Co., 1901). Courtesy of the Yale University Library.

Harry Parkes: Stanley Lane-Poole, *The Life of Sir Harry Parkes,* vol. 1 (New York: Macmillan, 1894). Courtesy of the Yale University Library.

James Hope: W. Laird Clowes, *The Royal Navy: A History from the Earliest Times to the Present,* vol. 7 (Boston: Little, Brown & Co., 1897–1903). Courtesy of the Yale University Library.

Frederick Bruce: Alexander Michie, *The Englishman in China During the Victorian Era,* vol. 1 (Edinburgh: W. Blackwood and sons, 1900). Courtesy of the Yale University Library.

Anson Burlingame: Library of Congress.

Ward and Burgevine on *Harper's Weekly* front page: Library of Congress.

Charles "Chinese" Gordon: A. Egmont Hake, *Events in the Taeping Rebellion* (London: W. H. Allen and Co., 1891). Courtesy of the Yale University Library.

Shanghai Bund: John Thomson, *Illustrations of China and its People* (London: S. Low, Marston, Low, and Searle, 1873–74). Courtesy of the Beinecke Library, Yale University.

Stephen R. Platt received his Ph.D. in Chinese history from Yale University, where his dissertation was awarded the Theron Rockwell Field Prize. He is an associate professor at the University of Massachusetts, Amherst, and is also the author of *Provincial Patriots: The Hunanese and Modern China*. An undergraduate English major, he spent two years after college as a Yale-China teacher in Hunan province. His research has been supported by the Fulbright program, the National Endowment for the Humanities, and the Chiang Ching-Kuo Foundation. He lives in Greenfield, Massachusetts, with his wife and daughter.

A NOTE ON THE TYPE

This book was set in Minion, a typeface produced by the Adobe Corporation specifically for the Macintosh personal computer, and released in 1990. Designed by Robert Slimbach, Minion combines the classic characteristics of old-style faces with the full complement of weights required for modern typesetting.

Composed by North Market Street Graphics,
Lancaster, Pennsylvania

Printed and bound by Berryville Graphics,
Berryville, Virginia

Designed by Soonyoung Kwon